W9-DEU-766

THE INFORMED READING TEACHER

Research-Based Practice

Bill Harp

University of Massachusetts—Lowell

Jo Ann Brewer

University of Massachusetts—Lowell

Upper Saddle River, New Jersey
Columbus, Ohio

Library of Congress Cataloging in Publication Data
Harp, Bill.
The informed reading teacher: research-based practice / by Bill Harp and Jo Ann Brewer.
p. cm.
Includes bibliographical references and index.
ISBN 0-13-088338-7
1. Reading teachers—United States. 2. Reading—United States. I. Brewer, Jo Ann. II. Title.

LB2844.1.R4H37 2005
372.41—dc22

2003066034

Vice President and Executive Publisher: Jeffery W. Johnston
Editor: Linda Ashe Montgomery
Editorial Assistant: Laura Weaver
Development Editor: Hope Madden
Production Editor: Mary M. Irvin
Design Coordinator: Diane C. Lorenzo
Cover Designer: Thomas Borah
Cover Images: Index Stock
Photo Coordinator: Valerie Schultz
Production Manager: Pamela D. Bennett
Director of Marketing: Ann Castel Davis
Marketing Manager: Darcy Betts Prybella
Marketing Coordinator: Tyra Poole

This book was set in Times by Carlisle Communications, Ltd. It was printed and bound by Courier Kendallville, Inc. The cover was printed by Coral Graphic Services, Inc.

Photo Credits: Marc P. Anderson/PH College: 2. Todd Yarrington/Merrill: 9, 420. Anthony Magnacca/Merrill: 27, 102, 133, 191, 210, 217, 292, 297, 300, 319, 342, 391, 464, 479. Shirley Zeiberg/PH College: 32. Anne Vega/Merrill: 49, 74, 116, 150, 177, 277, 310, 350, 358, 434, 446. Cynthia Cassidy/Merrill: 56. Pearson Learning: 68. Tom Watson/Merrill: 108. Scott Cunningham/Merrill: 161, 230, 335, 395, 402, 470. Barbara Schwartz/Merrill: 184, 415. Larry Fleming/ PH College: 201. Linda Peterson/Merrill: 252. KS Studios/Merrill: 257. Laima Druskis/PH College: 374. Robert Vega/Merrill: 459.

Pearson Education Ltd.
Pearson Education Singapore Pte. Ltd.
Pearson Education Canada, Ltd.
Pearson Education—Japan
Pearson Education Australia Pty. Limited
Pearson Education North Asia Ltd.
Pearson Educación de Mexico, S.A. de C.V.
Pearson Education Malaysia Pte. Ltd.

10 9 8 7 6 5 4 3 2 1
ISBN: 0-13-088338-7

To Cassi, Hillary, and Nathan, who have learned to love reading and writing, and who have taught us much about both.

PREFACE

The Informed Reading Teacher: Research-Based Practice models the idea that the best literacy teacher is the informed literacy teacher. We want you to be able to make very wise, informed instructional decisions when you are teaching by developing the knowledge base necessary to know what to do for effective literacy teaching, and to know why you are doing what you are doing.

Because theory and teaching methods are the foundation for good literacy instruction, a clear and concise presentation of these elements is the building block for our text. Thorough and applied coverage of literacy skills and strategies instruction, and a view of these elements as they play themselves out in the classroom, work together in this text to present a complete picture of quality literacy instruction.

Certainly, we have our own favored materials and approaches. We embrace the use of quality children's literature in teaching reading. We subscribe to balance in a literacy program—balance between skills and strategies, between reading rich text with the focus on meaning making and breaking the process apart to focus on small elements such as sound/symbol relationships. What we have tried to do with this text is not promote our favorites to the exclusion of other possibilities, but to offer you a rich array of approaches and materials so that you can make your own informed decisions.

HOW DOES A TEACHER BECOME INFORMED?

Through Research

The key to becoming and staying informed is reading and understanding the research constantly being done on learning in general, and literacy learning in particular. Our chapters are, of course, founded on the most important and most up-to-date research in the area of education and literacy.

- Accessible and engaging writing makes the research clear and manageable.
- *Looking at the Research* features throughout every chapter distill key concepts from pinnacle research and link them to classroom teaching.
- The Companion Website offers alternate views on research pieces, allowing users to weigh each study and engage in global discussions on what the research says about literacy teaching.

This concrete approach to research will help you not only ground your teaching in research, but also weigh the research to form your own conclusions about literacy teaching.

Through Assessment and Evaluation

We believe that, in order to be an informed teacher, you need to have as many ways of knowing your learners as possible.

- Chapter 3, *Assessing and Evaluating Children's Literacy Growth,* focuses entirely on assessment and evaluation, demonstrating the importance of weaving assessment and evaluation through all literacy teaching.
- *Assessment and Evaluation* features beginning in Chapter 4 highlight an array of assessment and evaluation tools, identifying specific strategies and the most appropriate contexts for their use.
- Chapter sections throughout Part 3 model assessment and evaluation in K–2, 3–5, and 6–8 classrooms.

Through Experience

Chapters in Part 2 will build on the theoretical underpinnings covered in Part 1 to help you see good literacy teaching in action. Part 3 takes that a step further, detailing the methods in practice in elementary classrooms. These elements come together to help prepare you for your own classroom experiences. We continue to emphasize the importance of classroom experiences in two special features throughout the chapters.

- *Real Teachers, Real Practice* features in most chapters introduce you to teachers who invite you into their classroom to share their day-to-day literacy experiences, illustrating chapter content as they do.
- *Thinking as a Teacher* features end each chapter, challenging you to think through issues typical of those teachers face daily.

Becoming an informed teacher of reading is not easy. Our hope is that this text will help you develop deep understandings of the nature of reading and writing, become familiar with a wide variety of materials and approaches, and develop the ability to look at the individual child's needs to select from this knowledge the best instructional approach. You will be an INFORMED teacher of reading.

We encourage you to approach the studying of this text with a powerful professional commitment to becoming the best teacher of reading you can become. And to that end, we wish you and your students the greatest success.

SUPPLEMENTS LIST

- *Instructor's Manual:* This companion piece, free to adopting professors, is a rich resource of supplemental materials, including a chapter-by-chapter test bank, chapter outlines, and suggested readings.
- *Videos:* A library of literacy videos is available free to adopting professors. Titles cover such important literacy topics as guided reading, higher-order thinking skills, reciprocal teaching, the inquiry method, story retellings, word problems, and upper and lower case letters.
- *Companion Website:* This online environment, integrated into text through margin notes as well as research features, provides self-assessments, chapter-by-chapter web links, a global discussion forum, immediate access to state and national standards, as well as valuable resources for the professor, including chapter-by-chapter PowerPoint presentations.

For the Student

- *Chapter Objectives*—outline key concepts from the text
- *Interactive self-quizzes*—these multiple choice and essay self assessments, complete with hints and automatic grading that provide immediate feedback for students, help users gauge their own understanding of chapter concepts.
- *Web Destinations*—links to www sites that relate to chapter content
- *Standards links*—takes you directly to NCTE/IRA standards, as well as each state's standards, to help prospective teachers get a firm grasp on the precise expectations they will face in the classroom.
- *Message Board*—this virtual bulletin board allows users to post—or respond to—questions or comments to/from a national audience concerning the research being done on literacy.

For the Professor

Every Companion Website integrates **Syllabus Manager™**, an online syllabus creation and management utility.

- *Syllabus Manager™* provides you, the instructor, with an easy, step-by-step process to create and revise syllabi, with direct links into Companion Website and other online content without having to learn HTML.
- Students may log on to your syllabus during any study session. All they need to know is the web address for the Companion Website and the password you've assigned to your syllabus.
- After you have created a syllabus using **Syllabus Manager™**, students may enter the syllabus for their course section from any point in the Companion Website.
- Clicking on a date, the student is shown the list of activities for the assignment. The activities for each assignment are linked directly to actual content, saving time for students.
- Adding assignments consists of clicking on the desired due date, then filling in the details of the assignment—name of the assignment, instructions, and whether or not it is a one-time or repeating assignment.
- In addition, links to other activities can be created easily. If the activity is online, a URL can be entered in the space provided, and it will be linked automatically in the final syllabus.
- Your completed syllabus is hosted on our servers, allowing convenient updates from any computer on the Internet. Changes you make to your syllabus are immediately available to your students at their next log on.

ACKNOWLEDGMENTS

We are honored that your instructor has chosen this text for your study. Our hope is that the hours of work we have put into writing this text will result in improved literacy instruction for children. We are greatly indebted to the contributions of our reviewers. The book is more comprehensive and more finely crafted because of their helpful suggestions. To each of them we sincerely say, "Thank you." The reviewers were:

Helen R. Abadiano, Central Connecticut State University; Peggy Albers, Georgia State University; Anthony Applegate, Holy Family College; Denise M. Bartelo, Plymouth State College; Thomas Bean, University of Nevada, Las Vegas; Carol Bond, The University of Memphis; Carol Christy, University of Idaho; Debra K. East, Indiana University; Zhihui Fang, University of Florida; Patricia P. Fritchie, Troy State University Dothan; Carol J. Fuhler, Iowa State University; Lara Justice, University of Virginia; and Susan Blair-Larsen, The College of New Jersey.

Bill Harp
The Graduate School of Education
University of Massachusetts Lowell
William_Harp@uml.edu

Jo Ann Brewer
The Graduate School of Education
University of Massachusetts Lowell
JoAnn_Brewer@uml.edu

EDUCATOR LEARNING CENTER: AN INVALUABLE ONLINE RESOURCE

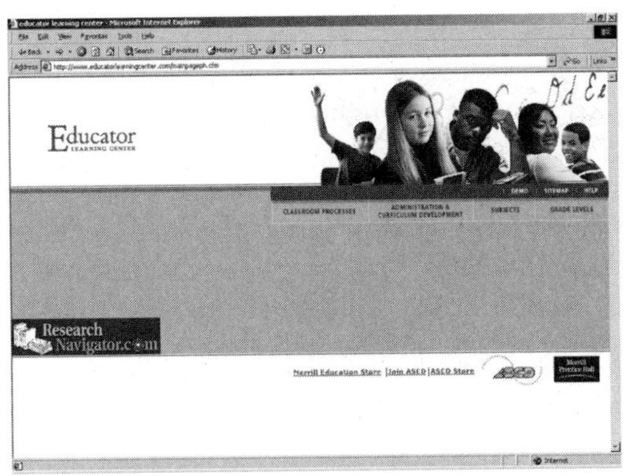

Merrill Education and the Association for Supervision and Curriculum Development (ASCD) invite you to take advantage of a new online resource, one that provides access to the top research and proven strategies associated with ASCD and Merrill—the Educator Learning Center. At www.EducatorLearningCenter.com you will find resources that will enhance your students' understanding of course topics and of current educational issues, in addition to being invaluable for further research.

HOW THE EDUCATOR LEARNING CENTER WILL HELP YOUR STUDENTS BECOME BETTER TEACHERS

With the combined resources of Merrill Education and ASCD, you and your students will find a wealth of tools and materials to better prepare them for the classroom.

Research

- More than 600 articles from the ASCD journal *Educational Leadership* discuss everyday issues faced by practicing teachers.
- A direct link on the site to Research Navigator™ gives students access to many of the leading education journals, as well as extensive content detailing the research process.
- Excerpts from Merrill Education texts give your students insights on important topics of instructional methods, diverse populations, assessment, classroom management, technology, and refining classroom practice.

Classroom Practice

- Hundreds of lesson plans and teaching strategies are categorized by content area and age range.
- Case studies and classroom video footage provide virtual field experience for student reflection.
- Computer simulations and other electronic tools keep your students abreast of today's classrooms and current technologies.

LOOK INTO THE VALUE OF EDUCATOR LEARNING CENTER YOURSELF

A four-month subscription to Educator Learning Center is $25 but is FREE when used in conjunction with this text. To obtain free pass codes for your students, simply contact your Merrill/Prentice Hall sales representative, and your representative will give you a special ISBN to give to your bookstore when ordering your textbooks. To preview the value of this website to you and your students, please go to www.EducatorLearningCenter.com and click on "Demo."

ABOUT THE AUTHORS

Bill Harp, Ed.D.

Bill Harp is professor of Language Arts and Literacy in The Graduate School of Education, University of Massachusetts—Lowell where he works with masters and doctoral students. He is the editor of *The Bill Harp Professional Teachers' Library,* an imprint of The Christopher-Gordon publishing company. Dr. Harp is currently working on the third edition of *Handbook of Literacy Assessment and Evaluation,* also published by Christopher-Gordon. Bill's teaching experience ranges from Head Start through sixth grade. He has been an elementary school principal and director of programs for the gifted.

Jo Ann Brewer, Ed. D.

Jo Ann Brewer is professor of Language Arts and Literacy in the Graduate School of Education, University of Massachusetts—Lowell, where she works with masters and doctoral students. The fifth edition of her textbook *Introduction to Early Childhood Education: Preschool through Primary Grades* was released in the summer of 2003. Her classroom teaching experiences include many years in kindergarten and primary grade classrooms in Texas. As an administrator, she has had experience in classrooms in California. As a faculty member she has worked in elementary schools in Oregon, Arizona, and Massachusetts. Currently she is working with a group of preschool directors who are interested in increasing the literacy opportunities for the children in their programs. *The Informed Reading Teacher: Research-Based Practice* is one of several books authored by Dr. Brewer.

CONTENTS

PART 1 FOUNDATIONS OF READING INSTRUCTION 1

1 BECOMING LITERATE: LANGUAGE, READING, AND WRITING AS DEVELOPMENTAL PROCESSES 3

What Do Teachers Need to Know About Typical Language Development? 5

Definition of Language 5 • Characteristics of Language 5 • Learning Language 6 • Language Delays 6 • Supports for Learning Language 8 • Learning About Language 10 • Learning Through Language 12 • Language and Reading and Writing 13

What Do Teachers Need to Know About the Typical Sequence of Learning to Read? 14

Definitions of Reading 15 • Reading Process 16 • The Continuum of Reading Development 17

What Do Teachers Need to Know About the Typical Sequence of Learning to Write? 19

Stages in the Development of Writing 20 • Stages in the Development of Spelling 20

What Are the Connections Between Language, Reading, and Writing? 26

Why Is It Important for All Classroom Teachers to Understand the Developmental Nature of Reading, Writing, and Language Skills? 28

Classroom Environment 28 • Instructional Experiences 28 • Thinking as a Teacher 30 • Field-Based Activities 30 • References 30

2 APPROACHES TO READING INSTRUCTION 33

What Are the Most Common Approaches to Reading Instruction? 36

Two Competing Views of Reading 36 • Phonics-Based Approaches 38 • Sight-Based Approaches to the Teaching of Reading 43 • Integrated Anthology Approach 44 • The Language Experience Approach (LEA) 48 • Literature-Based Approach 52 • Whole Language 54 • A Balanced Approach to Literacy Instruction 56

How Do I Decide Which Approach to Use? 59

History of Approaches 60 • Developing Your Philosophy 60 • Becoming an Increasingly Skilled Kidwatcher 64 • Becoming Increasingly More Informed as a Reading Teacher 64 • Thinking as a Teacher 65 • Field-Based Activities 65 • References 65

3 ASSESSING AND EVALUATING CHILDREN'S LITERACY GROWTH 69

What Is Meant by the Terms Assessment and Evaluation? 71

Distinguishing Assessment from Evaluation 71 • Principles of Assessment and Evaluation 72

How Do I Assess and Evaluate Children's Understandings of the Reading and Writing Processes? 73

Interviewing Children About Their Perceptions of Reading 73 • Published Tools to Evaluate Children's Perceptions of Reading 75 • Assessing and Evaluating Children's Perceptions as Writers 76

How Do I Assess and Evaluate Reading Performance Through Oral Reading? 77

Informal Reading Inventories 77 • Running Records 82 • Influence of the Reading First Grants 88

How Do I Assess and Evaluate Readers' and Writers' Growth Over Time? 89

Anecdotal Records 89 • Developmental Checklists for Reading 90 • Using Rubrics to Mark Progress Over Time 90

What Do I Need to Know About Standardized Tests? 94

Criterion-Referenced and Norm-Referenced Tests 94 • Becoming an Informed Norm-Referenced Test Consumer 96

What Do I Need to Know About Standards, Accountability, and High-Stakes Testing? 99

Understanding Standards 99 • An Opposing Viewpoint 99

How Do I Organize to Make the Best Use of the Assessment and Evaluation Tools I Have? 101

Thinking as a Teacher 105 • Field-Based Activities 105 • References 105

4 ACHIEVEMENT FOR ALL STUDENTS: MEETING SPECIAL NEEDS 109

What Is My Role as a Classroom Teacher Regarding Children with Special Needs? 111

Be a Mindful Kidwatcher 112 • Understanding Education as Collaboration 113

How Can Children with Special Needs in My Classroom Get Services? 114

Understanding IDEA 114 • Referring a Child for Special Education Consideration 116 • Sources of Support for IDEA 118 • Understanding Section 504 120

What Kinds of Accommodations May I Make for Children with Special Needs? 125

Learning Disabilities 125 • Speech or Language Impairments 131 • Mental Retardation 134 • Attention Deficit/Hyperactivity Disorder 137 • Gifted and Talented 138 • Students for Whom English Is a Second Language 142 • Thinking as a Teacher 145 • Field-Based Activities 145 • References 146

PART 2 PRACTICAL IMPLICATIONS OF READING AND WRITING RESEARCH 149

5 GUIDING THE DEVELOPMENT OF DECODING SKILLS 151

What Are Decoding Skills? 154

Cueing Systems 154 • Sight Vocabulary Development 157 • Using Decoding Skills 158

How Do Children Best Learn to Use Decoding Skills? 159

Instruction Is Guided by Carefully Considered Principles 159 • Children Develop Sight Vocabularies 160 • Children Have Visual Discrimination, Auditory Discrimination, and Phonemic Awareness 164 • Children Learn the Graphophonic Cueing System—Phonics 166 • Children Learn to Use Syntactic Cues 173 • Children Learn the Use of Semantic Cues 174 • The Components of Skills Lessons 175

How Do I Create an Environment in Which My Students Learn Decoding Skills? 177

Systematic Assessment of Pupil Progress 178 • A Collaborative Model for the Delivery of Reading Instruction 178 • Build Strong Links to Parents 179 • Foster High Pupil Engagement 179 • Be Well Prepared for Small Group Instruction 179 • Provide Explicit Phonics Instruction 180 • Provide Time for Independent Reading 180 • Thinking as a Teacher 180 • Field-Based Activities 181 • References 181

GUIDING THE DEVELOPMENT OF READING STRATEGIES 185

What Are Reading Strategies? 187

The Reading Process 187 • Strategic Reading 188

How Do Children Best Learn to Use Reading Strategies? 190

High Quality Strategy Instruction 190 • Techniques for Teaching Reading Strategies 190

How Do I Create a Learning Environment That Supports the Teaching and Learning of Reading Strategies? 199

Visual Reminders 200 • Demonstrations 202 • Children Learn the Language of Miscue Analysis 202 • Children Learn Collaborative Strategic Reading 202 • Thinking as a Teacher 206 • Field-Based Activities 206 • References 207

7 GUIDING THE DEVELOPMENT OF VOCABULARY 211

How Complex Is the Task of Vocabulary Learning? 213

Word Learning Is Incremental 213 • Word Learning Requires Understanding Multiple Meanings 213 • Word Learning Is Multidimensional 214 • Word Meanings Are Related 215 • The Relationship Between Learning a Word and the Kind of Word Being Learned 215

How Do I Guide the Development of Word Consciousness in My Students? 217

Word Play 217 • Modeling Enthusiasm for Words in Your Own Speech and Language 221 • Celebrating Children's Discovery and Use of Language 221

What Other Components Shall I Include in My Vocabulary Curriculum? 223

Wide Reading 224 • Teaching Individual Words 224 • Teaching Strategies for Learning Words Independently 233

How Will I Know a Good Vocabulary Program When I See One? 241

Thinking as a Teacher 241 • Field-Based Activities 243 • References 243 • Appendix: Greek and Latin Affixes and Roots 245

8 GUIDING THE DEVELOPMENT OF COMPREHENSION 253

What Is Meant by the Term Reading Comprehension? 255

How Do I Help Children Develop Reading Comprehension Abilities? 256

Planning for Guided Reading Instruction 257 • Experience-Text-Relationship (ETR) Approach 262

How Do I Guide the Development of Comprehension Ability Before Reading a Text? 262

Activating Background Knowledge 263 • Exploring the Reasons for Reading a Text 266 • Exploring Text Structures 266 • Prediction Making 270

How Do I Guide the Development of Comprehension Ability During the Reading of a Text? 272

Cooperative Learning—Cooperative Support 272 • Comprehension Monitoring 274 • Graphic and Semantic Organizers 277 • Question Answering 278 • Question Generating 281

How Do I Guide the Development of Comprehension Ability After Reading the Text? 285

Aesthetic Stance to Text 285 • Efferent Response to Text 286 • Thinking as a Teacher 289 • Field-Based Activities 289 • References 289

9 GUIDING THE DEVELOPMENT OF READING FLUENCY 293

What Is Reading Fluency? 295

What Are Effective Classroom Strategies for Helping Children Achieve Fluency in Reading? 295

Development of Sight Vocabulary 295 • Repeated Readings of Text 296 • Concern for Prosody 299 • Previewing Text 299 • Reader's Theater and Choral Reading 300 • Activities Using Songs 302

Do I Need to Be Concerned About Reading Rate with My Learners? 304

Thinking as a Teacher 307 • Field-Based Activities 308 • References 308

10 WRITING IN THE READING PROGRAM 311

Why Is There a Chapter on Writing in a Book Devoted to Teaching Reading? 313

Contributions of Writing to Learning to Read 314 • Other Studies of the Effect of Writing on Learning to Read 314

What Is the Writing Process? 315

A Recursive Model of the Writing Process 315

What Are the Components of Quality Writing Instruction? 318

Teacher Modeling 319 • Time to Write 320 • Authentic Writing Experiences 320 • Classroom Environment 320 • Access to the Tools of Writing 321 • Clear Writing Goals 321 • Appropriate Assessment 322 • Comprehensive Reading 325

What Is Writer's Workshop? 325

Organizing and Planning Focus Lessons 326 • Selecting Topics for Writing 327 • Status of the Class 329 • Writing Conferences 329 • Advising Writers About Revisions 333 • Sharing Time 333

How Do I Help Young Writers Learn to Write? 334

Journal Writing 334 • Drawing in the Writing Program 336 • Interactive Writing 336 • Demonstrating Writing 337 • Guided Writing 337 • Thinking as a Teacher 338 • Field-Based Activities 338 • References 338

PART 3 PLANNING FOR BALANCED LITERACY PROGRAMS 341

11 SUPPORTING LITERACY WITH LITERATURE IN THE CLASSROOM 343

How Do I Select Good Literature for the Classroom? 346

Selecting Fiction for Classroom Study 346 • Selecting Poetry for Study in the Classroom 348 • Selecting Biography for Study in the Classroom 348 • Selecting Information Books for Study in the Classroom 348 • Selecting Alphabet Books for Study in the Classroom 349 • Selecting Books for Independent Reading 349 • Selecting Multicultural Literature 351 • Illustration in Children's Books 351 • Book Selection Aids 353

How Can I Organize Instruction in Literature? 353

Organizing for Reading Aloud in the Literature Program 354 • Selecting Books for Read-Alouds 356 • Preparing for a Read-Aloud 357 • Organizing for Reading Instruction Using Genre Studies 359 • Organizing for Reading Instruction Using Literature Study Groups 362 • Organizing for Reading Instruction Using Author/Illustrator Studies 364 • Organizing for Reading Instruction Using Core Book Experiences 366 • Combining Organizational Patterns 366

How Does Using Literature Encourage Growth in Literacy? 367

Literature in the Reading Program 367 • Literature in the Writing Program 368 • Literature in Independent Reading 369 • Thinking as a Teacher 370 • Field-Based Activities 370 • References 371

12 BUILDING A K–2 READING PROGRAM 375

How Do I Create a Classroom Environment That Will Help Me Be an Effective Teacher? 376

Room Arrangement 376 • Learning Centers 378 • Daily Schedule 378 • Evaluating the Environment 381 • Materials for Instruction 382

What Assessments Will I Use to Get Started in the Instructional Program? 382

Kindergarten Assessment 382 • First- and Second-Grade Assessment 383 • Technological Aids in Assessment and Record Keeping 383

What Are the Essential Elements of a Quality Instructional Program? 384

Inquiry in the Literacy Program 385 • An Inquiry Study in Action 386 • Learning Language 388 • Learning Through Language 389 • Learning About Language 391 • Centers in the Literacy Program 393 • Possibilities for Literacy Centers 394

How Do I Handle Management and Record Keeping? 396

Getting Started 396 • Efficient Organization 397 • Monitoring Learning 397

How Do I Capitalize on Diversity in the Classroom? 397

Learning About Your Students 397 • Helping Children Learn in English 398 • Involve the Family and Their Culture 398 • Conclusion 399 • Thinking as a Teacher 399 • Field-Based Activities 399 • References 400

13 BUILDING A LITERACY PROGRAM GRADES 3–5 403

What Is the Nature of Third, Fourth, and Fifth Graders? 404

How Do I Challenge Unmotivated Readers at This Level? 404

How Do I Create a Classroom Environment That Will Help Me to Be an Effective Teacher? 405

Classroom Arrangement 405 • Daily Schedule 408 • Managing the Work Areas 408 • Instructional Materials 409

What Assessments Will I Use to Get Started in the Instructional Program? 410

Assessing Reading 410 • Assessing Writing 410 • Assessing English Language Learners 411

How Do I Plan Instruction for Grades 3–5? 412

Topics for Inquiry 412 • Inquiry: Folk Literature 413 • Learning Research Skills 413 • Learn Language 419 • Learn Through Language 422 • Learn About Language 427 • Guided Reading 428 • Strategy Lessons 429

How Do I Handle Management and Record Keeping? 430

Thinking as a Teacher 431 • Field-Based Activities 432 • References 432

14 BUILDING A LITERACY PROGRAM GRADES 6–8 435

How Do I Create a Classroom Environment That Will Help Me to Be an Effective Teacher? 436

Classroom Arrangement 436 • Schedule 436 • Instructional Materials 437

What Assessments Will I Use to Get Started in the Instructional Program? 438

Informal Assessment 438 • Interest Inventory 438 • Self-Evaluation 438 • Formal Assessments 438

How Will I Plan Instruction for the Middle School Classroom? 440

Planning Inquiry 441 • Learn Language 442 • Learn Through Language 445 • Learn About Language 448

How Will I Modify Instruction for Struggling Readers? 453

Selection of Texts 453 • Responses to Reading 453 • Instruction of Struggling Readers 457 • What Supports Will I Need to Offer My English Language Learners? 457 • What the Law Requires for English Language Learners 458 • Structured English Immersion and Sheltered English Instruction 458 • Thinking as a Teacher 460 • Field-Based Activities 460 • References 460

PART 4 ONGOING PROFESSIONAL GROWTH 463

15 BECOMING AN EVEN MORE INFORMED READING TEACHER 465

How Do I Become an Even More Informed Reading Teacher? 467

Self-Study of Your Own Practice 467 • Studying the Knowledge Base 468

What Should I Know About Professional Organizations That Support the Teaching and Learning of Reading? 475

International Reading Association (IRA) 475 • National Council of Teachers of English (NCTE) 477 • Other Professional Organizations with Links to Literacy 478

What Should I Know About Professional Conferences? 478

Conferences on Many Levels 479

What Internet Resources Are Available to Help Me Stay Informed? 480

American School Directory 480 • Topica 481 • International Federation of Library Associations and Institutions 481 • Kathy Schrock's Guide for Educators 481 • Thinking as a Teacher 481 • Field-Based Activities 482 • References 482

APPENDIX A: ***Motivation to Read Profile* 483**

APPENDIX B: ***The Reader Self-Perception Scale* 491**

APPENDIX C: ***Forty-Five Phonic Generalizations* 495**

APPENDIX D: ***The Yopp-Singer Test of Phoneme Segmentation* 499**

APPENDIX E: ***Metacomprehension Strategy Index* 501**

APPENDIX F: ***Literature Circle Individual Evaluation* 505**

INDEX **507**

Note: Every effort has been made to provide accurate and current Internet information in this book. However, the Internet and information posted on it are constantly changing, so it is inevitable that some of the Internet addresses listed in this text book will change.

SPECIAL FEATURES

REAL TEACHERS, REAL PRACTICE

Kelly King, first grade 4
Joanne Morrissey, first grade 34
Nichole Duffy, second grade 70
Amy Gaddes, middle school science 110
Stephanie Anders, K–first grade 153
Kate McLaughlin, second grade 186
Leah Alvarado, fifth grade 212
Judy Snetsky, first grade 254
Susie Gummere, first grade 294
Susan Smith, eighth grade 312
John Clark, middle school 344
Julie Taylor, fifth grade 466

ISSUES IN LITERACY

Instruction in Language 14
School Board's Influence Over Publishers 41
Using the Required Basal 48
Basalization of Children's Literature 53
Placing Second Language Learners in Literacy 145
Phonics Research Controversy 166
How Much Is Enough Writing? 328
Comics in the Classroom 350
Children's Books: Censorship 353

LOOKING AT THE RESEARCH

What the Research Says About Learning the Concept That Print Has Meaning 15
What the Research Says About the Development of Writing 19
What the Research Says About the Connection Between Reading and Writing 24
What the Research Says About the Connections Between Reading and Writing 26
What Place Does Phonics Have in the Total Reading Program? 39
What the Research Says About Balanced Instruction 59
What the Research Says About Early Literacy Assessment and Evaluation Tools 88
What the Research Says About Teachers' and Administrator's View of Assessment Tools 100

What the Research Says About Accommodations 128
What the Research Says About Comprehension Instruction for Children with Learning Disabilities 130
What the Research Says About Phonemic Segmentation and Onset-Rime Segmentation 168
What the Research Says About Helping Children Make Explicit Connections Between Sound Segments and Letters 171
What the Research Says About Best Practices 178
What the Research Says About Teacher Behavior and Children's Learning of Reading Strategies 199
What the Research Says About How Effective Teachers Use Instructional Time 205
What the Research Says About Types of Words and Learning Them 216
What the Research Says About Encounters with Words 222
What the Research Says About Learning Words 228
What the Research Says About Using Computers to Teach Vocabulary 240
What the Research Says About Your Role in Guiding the Reading of Children 256
What the Research Says About Explicit Instruction of Text Comprehension 262
What the Research Says About Story Mapping Before Reading 271
What the Research Says About Sight Vocabulary 295
What the Research Says About the Music/Reading Connection 302
What the Research Says About the Connection Between Reading Rate and Fluency 305
What the Research Says About the Importance of Writing in a Reading Program 313
What the Research Says About Children Learning to Write 318
What the Research Says About Managing Writing Instruction 326
What the Research Says About Revision 333
What the Research Says About Drawing the Reading Program 335
What the Research Says About Books in the Curriculum 346
What the Research Says About Literature-Based Programs 354
What the Research Says About Reading Aloud 354
What the Research Says About the Influence of Reading Material on Writing 368
What the Research Says About Time Spent in Reading 369
What the Research Says About Excellent Reading Teachers 476

ASSESSMENT AND EVALUATION TOOLBOX

Gray Oral Reading Test, Fourth Edition (GORT-4) 118
Stanford Diagnostic Reading Test—Fourth Edition (SDRT—4) 127
Test of Reading Comprehension, Third Edition (TORC—3) 135
Test of Phonological Awareness (Torgensen & Bryant, 1994) 165
Yopp-Singer Test of Phoneme Segmentation 165
Ekwall/Shanker Reading Inventory 166
An Observation Survey of Early Literacy Achievement 173

K-W-L Chart 191
Venn Diagram 196
Metacomprehension Strategy Index 206
The Peabody Picture Vocabulary Test–III 215
First Steps Oral Language Developmental Continuum 223
Comprehensive Receptive and Expressive Vocabulary Test (CREVT) 233
The Lexile Framework for Reading (LFR) 260
Expository Retelling Checklist 270
Retellings 280
Cloze Procedure 284
Comprehension Strategy Checklist 288
Dynamic Indicators of Basic Early Literacy Skills (DIBELS) 306
Gray Oral Reading Tests (GORT) 307
The Test of Written Language–3 315
Analyzing Student Writing 318
Writing Rubric 321
Planning Forms for Before-Writing Conferences Before Our Writing Conference 331
A Reading Conference Planning Form 360
Literature Circle Individual Evaluation 362
Literature Circle Self-Evaluation 363
Assessing the Difficulty of Text (Goldilocks Strategy) 365

PART

1

FOUNDATIONS OF READING INSTRUCTION

I am going to be an effective teacher of reading because I not only know what to do, but I know why I do it.

The statement at the top of this page is our guiding goal throughout this book. Becoming an informed reading teacher means that you will be effective because you not only know what to do as a teacher, but you know why you are doing it. You are designing and choosing best practices because you know what the research says—you are an *informed* reading teacher. Everything we do in this text is intended to help you meet this goal—to be able to confidently make the statement at the top of this page.

The first part of the text lays the groundwork for your understanding of the reading process and the creation of a literacy-rich classroom environment. In Part One we will explore learning to read and write as developmental processes, look at approaches to reading instruction, explore the issues in assessment and evaluation, and lay the groundwork for working with children who have special needs.

We hope you will use the following set of reading process questions to examine your developing knowledge. It is early in the book for you to have answers to these questions, but we offer them here as a starting point so you can consider them frequently as you move through the text. We will present them again from time to time.

READING PROCESS QUESTIONS

- How do I understand the reading process?
- How do I get children to understand the reading process?
- How do I teach children to monitor their use of the reading process?
- How do I discern that children are monitoring their use of the reading process?

Chapter 1

Becoming Literate: Language, Reading, and Writing as Developmental Processes

LOOKING AT THE RESEARCH

Language learning is linked with motivation as well as strategies in learning to read. From this viewpoint, classroom activities should be designed to motivate students for reading and writing and to provide them with opportunities to use oral language for meaningful communication purposes (Guthrie, 1999; Guthrie et al., 1996).

Focus Questions

- What do teachers need to know about typical language development?
- What do teachers need to know about the typical sequence of learning to read?
- What do teachers need to know about the typical sequence of learning to write?
- What are the connections between language, reading, and writing?
- Why is it important for all classroom teachers to understand the developmental nature of reading, writing, and language skills?

REAL TEACHERS, REAL PRACTICE

Meet Kelly King, *a first-grade teacher*

One of the greatest achievements of early childhood is mastering spoken language. As a teacher of young children, one of my many tasks is to assist students with fine-tuning the more subtle aspects of language. And when you take the time to foster oral language development, the transition to teaching students how to read and write becomes easier. In my own classroom, I approach this task in three parts: by thinking carefully about how I set up the classroom, by forging relationships with students' families, and by planning activities every day that are rich in opportunities to practice the art of speaking.

At the beginning of each school year I put a lot of effort into creating a classroom environment that invites students to listen and speak the English language. Daily routines consistently include sing-alongs, sharing time, and shared readings of familiar books. An inviting listening center is created to give children the opportunity to hear stories many times. Students are also given daily access to felt boards, housekeeping, or puppet areas where dramatic play scenarios give children time to practice and experiment with the language that they hear at home and at school.

The home/school connection is another integral part of aiding students in mastering oral language. Parents have a wealth of information to offer teachers regarding what their children can do and have experienced. I reach out to families even before the school year begins with a letter introducing myself and asking for information that will help me understand their children better. I spend the early part of the school year inviting parents into my classroom and assigning homework activities that allow families to share part of themselves with me and the rest of the classroom. The connections one makes with families is essential, especially with children who may be struggling with language.

Second language learners, in particular, will make specific errors in language that teachers need to consider as they evaluate their students. For example, suppose a child whose first language is Spanish struggles with use of prepositions such as on, in, *and* at. *Conferring with the student's family may help a teacher to discover that in Spanish there is one word for all three English words and that the child does not have trouble with prepositions in her native language. In all languages there are differences that young children learning two languages will need time to differentiate. Just as irregular verbs are often overgeneralized by almost all young English language learners, second language learners also make specific overgeneralizations. Investigating this issue with families will help a teacher to understand what a young child is currently working out and constructing in his or her language development.*

Once routines and relationships are firmly established, exposing students to activities that will aid children as they develop an understanding of the language used around them becomes the next step. This includes linking school experiences to students' prior knowledge, using photos and factual picture books to support new vocabulary, using rich and accurate language when participating in group discussions, and pointing out and encouraging the use of "sophisticated" words, such as tremendous *instead of* great.

A rich vocabulary and solid command of oral language is a key indicator of a child's readiness and likely success as a young reader. What families and teachers do to facilitate language sets the stage for reading and writing development. It is an important part of the curriculum in early grades that deserves as much thought and planning as any other subject an educator is charged with teaching.

WHAT DO TEACHERS NEED TO KNOW ABOUT TYPICAL LANGUAGE DEVELOPMENT?

Learning to use language is an almost universal accomplishment and is mastered without formal instruction (Pinker, 1994). If a child is in an environment where language is used, then the child will learn to use language unless there are severe problems. How do children master the complexities of using language in what seems to be an effortless process? If much of the language learning has taken place before a child begins school, then what do teachers need to know about language development?

Definition of Language

Language can be defined rather narrowly to include only spoken or sign language or much more broadly to include any system of communication used by a social community. For our purposes, **language** is defined as a system of communication used by human beings that is produced either orally or by signs. Speech is the oral or manual expression of language. Before we discuss learning language, we should clarify some of the characteristics of language.

Characteristics of Language

Certain defining characteristics are universal to all languages. Even though casual observers would listen to various languages and be struck by how different they are, they actually have much in common. These universal characteristics are that language is rule-governed, arbitrary, and dynamic.

Rule-governed. Language is rule-governed. For example, all languages have rules that determine how words are ordered in sentences. Native speakers of the language learn these rules intuitively, and only those speakers who make a scientific study of the language are likely to be able to verbalize the rules. To illustrate such rules, hold up four new yellow pencils and ask a group to describe what you have in your hand. If they say "pencils," ask for more detail. They might say "long pencils." If asked again, they might say "long yellow pencils." Finally, they would say "four long yellow pencils." The placement of number words in a series of modifiers is governed by a rule. Native English speakers would never say "yellow four pencils."

Arbitrary. A second universal characteristic of language is that it is arbitrary. There are no logical connections between the sounds we use to label a certain object and the object itself. It is merely by common social agreement that we use a particular combination of sounds to represent that object. For example, nothing in the sounds of the word *table* is connected to the object. Only a very few words, such as *buzz* and *hiss,* have any concrete connection with their referents, or the objects or ideas they represent.

Dynamic. Third, language is dynamic, always changing. New words are constantly entering our lexicon and others are being discarded. Think how recently *e-mail, e-commerce, Internet* and *stem cell* have entered our lexicon. Meanings are also changing. With a little thought, you can probably list 30 or 40 words that have new or changed meanings within the last 5 to 10 years. *Program, virus,* and *pot* are terms that communicate meanings today that are different than their former meanings. These universal characteristics of language are interesting, but they do not explain how children learn to use language.

Learning Language

Halliday (1982), a respected researcher in language development, has noted that children engage simultaneously in learning language, learning about language, and learning through language. He and other researchers have described the typical sequence of learning language. This sequence is commonly considered invariable, but the rate of development is certainly variable. Not all children will achieve the same milestones as are typical for any given age, but they will continue to make progress in ways that are predictable.

Almost everyone uses language so effortlessly that it is easy to forget what a complicated phenomenon it is. If you have learned or are in the process of learning a second language, you have a better idea about the difficulty of learning language. Most children move from differentiated crying (crying that varies in sound, depending on the stimulus—hunger, wetness, tiredness, and so on) through cooing, babbling, and one-word sentences. Soon they will deliver longer utterances and learn to produce negatives and questions. At the same time, children's comprehension of spoken language is developing rapidly. By the time they begin school, most children will have mastered the basic forms in their native language (Berk, 2003). This means that they can comprehend and produce statements and questions, change a statement to a question, embed clauses, understand implied subjects, and so on.

Berk's (2003) summary of the accomplishments in language development that are typical for various ages are displayed in Figure 1.1. This summary includes what children typically master in each of the systems of language: phonology, morphology, semantics, syntax, and pragmatics. As you read about each of these systems, you will want to refer to this summary again.

Language Delays

Some children will have delayed language development and will not reach the milestones listed in the Berk summary at the ages she has assigned as typical. There are many reasons for language delays, and you may need help from your speech pathologist and school nurse to determine what these reasons are for a specific child. One of the common reasons for speech problems is hearing loss. Children with repeated ear infections are often delayed in their speech because of their hearing problems. Other conditions that interfere with language development are autism, brain injury, and mental retardation. For children who have no observable physical or mental problems, their environment may not have supported their language learning or they may be lacking in experiences that promote language learning.

Figure 1.1
Summary of Language Development

AGE	PHONOLOGY	SEMANTICS
Birth–1 year	Has categorical speech perception. Organizes speech sounds into phonemic categories of native language. Babbles using intonation and sound patterns resembling those of native language.	Prefers sound pattern of native language. Detects words in speech stream. Uses preverbal gestures.
1–2 years	Uses systematic strategies to simplify word pronunciation.	Says first words. Vocabulary grows to several hundred words.
3–5 years	Shows great improvement in pronunciation.	Coins words to fill in for words not yet mastered. Understands metaphors based on concrete, sensory comparisons.
6–10 years	Masters syllable stress patterns signaling subtle differences in meaning.	At school entry, has vocabulary of about 10,000 words. Grasps meanings of words on the basis of definitions. Appreciates multiple meanings of words, which enhances understanding of metaphors and humor.
11 years–adulthood	Masters syllable stress patterns of abstract words.	Has vocabulary of over 40,000 words that includes many abstract terms. Understands subtle, nonliteral word meanings, as in irony and sarcasm.

(Continued)

Source: From Laura E. Berk, *Child development,* 6e (pp. 386–387). Published by Allyn and Bacon, Boston, MA. Copyright © 2003 by Pearson Education. Reprinted by permission of publisher.

Figure 1.1
Summary of Language Development *Continued*

GRAMMAR	PRAGMATICS	METALINGUISTIC AWARENESS
Begins to develop sensitivity to natural phrase units.	Establishes joint attention. Engages in vocal exchanges and turn-taking games.	
Combines two words in telegraphic speech. As 3-word sentences appear, gradually adds grammatical morphemes.	Engages in conversational turn-taking and topic maintenance.	
Forms sentences that reflect adult grammatical categories. Continues to add grammatical morphemes in a regular order. Masters many complex grammatical structures.	Masters additional conversational strategies, such as the turnabout. Begins to grasp illocutionary intent. Adjusts speech in accord with social expectations.	Shows the beginnings of metalinguistic awareness. "Nose your touch!" "That's backwards!"
Refines complex grammatical structures, such as the passive voice and infinitive phrases.	Uses advanced conversational strategies, such as shading. Continues to refine understanding of illocutionary intent. Engages in effective referential communication in highly demanding contexts.	Displays rapid development of metalinguistic awareness.
Continues to refine complex grammatical structures.	Referential communication continues to improve.	Continues to refine metalinguistic awareness.

Go to the Weblinks in Chapter 1 on our Companion Website at www.prenhall.com/harp to find links related to the development of language.

Supports for Learning Language

As children are faced with the task of developing language, environmental conditions can foster or impede language growth.

An Environment for Learning Language. Development of language is fostered by an environment that offers models (examples of mature language forms), engages the child in experiences involving language, has expectations for the child's success, accepts the child's approximations of mature language, and responds to the child's efforts to communicate. Babies are born into a language community that provides the models they need to learn to communicate. Babies hear adults talking to them and to each other and begin very early to recognize the tones and sounds of the language around them. Parents and caretakers of in-

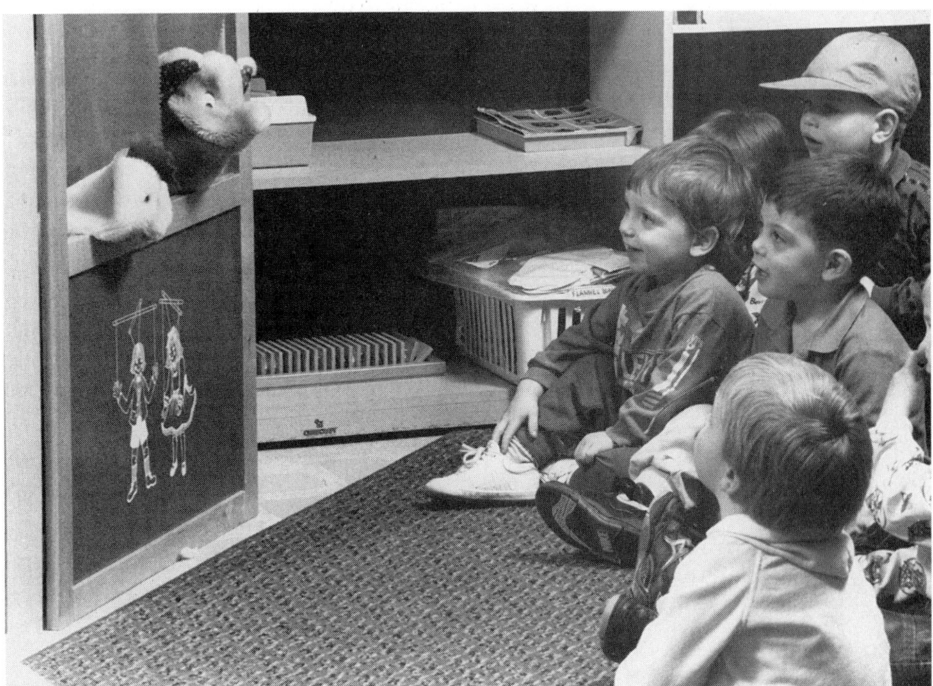

Using puppets is one way of practicing language.

fants and toddlers spend time talking to them, smiling at them, and generally engaging them in language by imitating the sounds babies produce and smiling at their gurgles. Most parents and caretakers use language that linguists call **motherese** to talk to infants. Motherese includes speaking slowly, stretching out the vowel sounds slightly, and naming whatever the child is offered or seems to be looking at. It is common to hear adults saying, "Oh, do you see the _____?" as they follow the infant's gaze.

Caregiver Support for Learning Language. Parents and caregivers continue to support the child's language growth by adjusting their expectations as the child gains language skill. For example, as the child is able to sit up and clap his hands, parents often begin teaching the pat-a-cake rhyme. When they think the child can control his arm and hand movements to allow him to touch his face as desired, then they may teach the child to name his nose, eyes, ears, and so on. These rituals are repeated over and over to the enjoyment of both. Adults also begin to raise the standards for what is acceptable speech from the child. An infant is not expected to even try to produce words, but by the time the child is about a year old, parents are urging her to say *mama* and *daddy.* In a few more months, they are urging closer and closer approximations to common words such as bottle and water and whatever else the child wants. The next step is an expectation that the child produce words that are close to the mature models and add the word *please* when she wants something.

Another caretaker characteristic is response to the child's attempts to communicate. This does not necessarily mean praise or reward for producing language, but it does mean continued interaction and reactions to the child's utterances. For example, a two-year-old may say "Daddy sock?" with the rising intonation to indicate that this is a question. The adult would answer and probably extend the child's words by saying, "Yes, that is Daddy's sock. Can you take Daddy's sock to him?" Response can also be simply doing what the child has requested such as handing her a cookie when she asks for one.

Learning About Language

As children are learning language, they are also learning about language. For example, a child who is learning that the rule in English requires that "ed" be added to a verb to indicate past tense applies that rule to all verbs for a period of time. Applying this rule results in productions such as "goed" or "holded." Learning about language also includes learning when to use certain kinds of language and to whom to speak about what. For example, a toddler wanting a cookie would not ask a younger sibling for a cookie, but would ask someone who might be able to provide the cookie such as an adult or older sibling.

Learning about language means mastering the phonological system, the morphological system, the semantic system, the syntactical system, and the pragmatic system of language. All human languages contain these systems and each system has rules that determine how they operate in both oral and written language.

Phonology. The **phonological** system, the sounds that can be used in a language, is usually mastered in the initial stages of learning language. Any human child can produce the sounds that are used in any human language, but children begin to recognize the sounds and tones used in their native language early and use those sounds in their babbling. Most linguists place the number of sounds used in English at or about 44.

In addition to sounds, phonology also includes rules for combining sounds and patterns of stress and intonation. Different languages use different sounds and allow different combinations of sounds in words. Some languages, for example, make use of clicks produced with the tongue that are totally absent in English. Some languages allow the *ng* sound at the beginning of words, but it is not a possible beginning of an English word. In some languages, such as Chinese, differences in pitch indicate different meanings for the same combination of sounds. In her book *The Bonesetter's Daughter,* Amy Tan's character creates an entire sentence using only one syllable, *gu,* repeatedly spoken with different pitches. When the sentence is translated to English it reads: "The blind bone doctor from the gorge repaired the thigh of the old grain merchant" (p. 349). The task of the child is to learn to distinguish differences in **phonemes**—the smallest units of sound in a language—and intonational patterns that signal different meanings.

Morphology. **Morphemes** are the smallest units of meaning in any language. An example of a morpheme is the /s/ on the end of *cows* that denotes the plural form of *cow.* Some words are morphemes and some are combinations of morphemes. *Cow* is an example of a word that is a morpheme. *Cows* is a combination of the free morpheme *cow* and the bound morpheme /s/. The /s/ is "bound" because it signals meaning but has no meaning if it is used alone. Other morphemes signal changes of tense, person, or number rather than changing the meaning of the word such as the /ed/ in *walked* or the /ing/ of *singing.* Mastering English morphology includes learning how to form possessives, plurals, and verb tenses.

Syntax. The **syntactical** system of a language contains the rules for combining words into phrases and sentences and for transforming sentences into other sentences. The syntactical system provides us with information about word meanings because of their place in a sentence. For example, if you heard "The cribbit zooked the lattle" you would know that the event took place in the past and that zooked was something done to the lattle. Different languages have different syntactical rules. For example, in English we usually place the adjective before the noun (yellow house); in Spanish the adjective usually follows the noun (casa amarilla). The appropriate placement of clauses and modifiers is also governed by the rules of syntax. For example, in English, it is not acceptable to split an infinitive such as saying, "He wants to fully [sic] understand the adjectives in the book" (although we see it commonly in the writing of students and do it ourselves sometimes!).

Children mastering the syntactical system learn how to construct negatives, questions, compound sentences, passives, imperatives, and eventually complex sentences that employ embedded forms. Children in school may still be confused by such sentence patterns as "Before you sharpen your pencil, please put your books on your desk." Young children will often embed a clause but not in the mature form. They might say, "The chair, what I sitting on, is yellow."

Chomsky (1965) would argue that syntax is not learned, at least not in the typical use of the word *learned.* He bases this argument on the observation that speakers rarely make syntactical errors in their native language and that young children use correct syntax from the time they begin to use utterances of more than one word. Cook's work (1988) supports Chomsky when he reports that first and second language acquirers acquire rules of grammar that have never been taught. For example, a child would say "more milk" when his cup was empty, but not "milk more." Speakers often make errors that teachers feel they must correct, but they tend to be errors in acceptable social usage, not errors in syntax.

Semantics. The **semantic** system governs meaning at the word, sentence, and text level. Learning semantics means acquiring vocabulary and meanings associated with words. Children commonly use words that are part of adult language but assign their own meanings. A very young child may use a word such as *horsie* to stand for all large four-legged animals. As the semantic system is refined, *horsie* is replaced by *cow, mule, elk, moose,* and so on. There is not a one-to-one correspondence between a word and its referent. For example, when readers encounter the word *cat* in print, each may picture a different cat according to individual experience, but they also share enough meaning to understand the author's use of the term.

In thinking about semantics, think about some words that are learned by association, by having the word and the object presented together such as *bottle, ball,* and *blanket.* Other words are learned as children develop ideas to fit words presented to them by adults. For example, love is a complex concept; it cannot be learned by association with an object. So when a 3-year-old says, "I love you," it may represent a beginning concept of the abstract love, but it is certainly not a mature understanding of the meaning.

A complication in semantics is the multiple meanings represented by such common words as *run* and *play.* Most dictionaries list a hundred or so meanings for these words. Language learners have to determine which meaning is indicated by the context—the speaker, the occasion, and what is happening at the time. Sentences by themselves can have ambiguous meanings and can only be comprehended through inferring the meaning from other sentences around them or from other clues in the context. An example is "The turkey was too old to eat." Does it mean a live turkey had grown too old and is now unable to eat on its own, or that the turkey has grown so old that it would not be edible if it were killed and dressed, or does it mean that the turkey meat in the refrigerator is likely spoiled and no longer safe to eat? At the word level, the meanings of words are influenced by the surrounding words. We could never comprehend many common words without a context.

At the text level, think about the differences in the meanings of *cat* in the nursery rhyme about the gingham dog and the calico cat, in a newspaper report about a cat burglar, in a veterinarian's report on diseases in cats, or in Tennessee Williams' play *Cat on a Hot Tin Roof.* Without a context and experience, much of what we read and hear would be incomprehensible.

Vocabulary learning is an important component of continued language development at any age. For example, the words we have been using to describe language are a specialized vocabulary used by linguists and teachers. Few people outside these professions know or use these terms. In helping children learn language, a focus on vocabulary is much more useful than drilling on syntactical forms.

Pragmatics. The broadest of the language systems is **pragmatics,** the use of language to express intentions and to get things done. Social uses of language include the rules of politeness and the degree of formality appropriate to any given speech situation. For example, some cultures have rules that forbid younger people initiating conversations with older people. Pragmatics governs the use of the formal *usted* and informal *tu* in Spanish. Pragmatics determines what language is acceptable when we speak to our parents and what language we use with our friends. A speaker of any language would not be considered competent in that language before mastering the basic rules for language use in various social contexts.

The most dramatic changes in language development in the school years are in pragmatics, the social uses of language. Children come to school able to produce virtually all basic language forms, but conversational skills are still underdeveloped. As children move through school years and into adulthood, they master conversational competence (Hulit & Howard, 2002).

It is pragmatics when teachers try to help children understand the differences in "outside and inside voices" or the changes in language that are necessary when speaking to a visiting adult as opposed to a friend on the playground. It is also pragmatics when we try to help children learn how to stay on topic in a discussion and the appropriate language for disagreeing. Pragmatics, more than any other system of language, takes years to learn. Mastering the pragmatic rules of a language determines whether we are considered to be competent users of our language.

Learning Through Language

As children are learning language and learning about language, they are also learning through language. Think about how children learn about something like elephants or tigers. For typical American children, these creatures are not part of their experience unless they have visited a zoo. Teachers and caregivers teach children about these animals through descriptions of their size, color, habitat, and so on. Even though these lessons might be accompanied by photographs, videos, and models, it is still primarily through language that children develop concepts of these animals. The academic language of the various content disciplines challenges learners of all ages, and children must master this language to succeed in school. Learning through language means that children must use language to learn new information as they listen, read, or talk with others. As you have noticed from reading the new vocabulary words that describe language, learning through language can be a challenge even for students with many years of experience in school.

Limitations of Learning Through Language. For young children, learning through language has its limits. A teacher may explain geometric shapes, but without experience with the geometric shapes themselves, the language may be meaningless. Children learning about most concepts need both experience (the hands-on kind) and the language labels to express their understandings. For example, a teacher may plan an experience to learn about the life cycle of butterflies. First, the children are encouraged to observe the eggs, then the larvae, then the chrysalis, and finally the adult butterfly. At each stage of the butterfly life cycle, the teacher provides the language to describe what the children are observing. Children may be encouraged to keep their own records of the experience and to label their drawings with the correct words for the process. All this learning takes place in a context of learning through language.

Older children face the same challenges in learning the academic language of the content disciplines. For example, think about what the student must know in order to answer the question, "What were the factors that led to the Civil War?" If the student knows the facts about the Civil War, he must still know what the word factor means in this question and how to answer such a question appropriately. In science, mathematics, and social studies, specialized vocabulary may be a challenge to learners. Without knowledge of the vocabulary of each discipline, learning is typically delayed.

Language and Reading and Writing

Language development is critical to children's success as learners of reading and writing. In fact, oral language provides the foundation for reading and writing long before formal instruction in reading or writing is appropriate (Glazer, 1989; Sulzby, 1996), and it is through oral language that we know if children understand what they have read or heard read. Figure 1.2

Figure 1.2
Goals for Oral Language Preschool Through Third Grade

Preschool	Kindergarten	First Grade	Second and Third Grades
• Understands the overall sequence of events in stories • Understands and follows oral directions • Connects information and events to life experiences when being read a story • Knows that it is the print that is read in stories • Pays attention to separable and repeating sounds in language (e.g., Peter, Peter, Pumpkin Eater) • Uses new vocabulary and grammatical construction in own speech • Demonstrates understanding of literal meaning of stories by asking questions and making comments	• Begins to track print when listening to a familiar text being read or when re-reading own writing • Makes appropriate switches from oral to written language situations • Connects information and events in text to life and life experiences to text • Retells, re-enacts, or dramatizes stories or parts of stories	• Makes transition from emergent reading to "real" reading • Shows evidence of expanding language repertory, including increasing use of standard, formal language registers • Discusses features of stories and main ideas and prior knowledge of topics in informational texts	• Reads and comprehends stories and informational text appropriate for grade level • Participates in creative responses to texts such as discussions, dramatizations, and plays

Source: Reprinted by permission from E. H. Hiebert et al., *Every Child a Reader: Applying Reading Research in the Classroom* (Topic I). Copyright © 1998 by the Center for the Improvement of Early Reading Achievement.

outlines the goals for oral language accomplishments from preschool through third grade. These goals reflect the connections between oral language and written language. Notice that the goals at all levels include both oral language and print language goals.

ISSUES IN LITERACY

INSTRUCTION IN LANGUAGE

What is the responsibility of the classroom teacher when children come to school without typical language development? Many children come to school speaking dialects that are nonstandard and many come whose first language is not English. How can a teacher help all children develop language abilities?

Visit the Issues module in Chapter 1 of our Companion Website to research more thoroughly and record your thoughts about this topic.

Clearly, language development is essentially about learning to communicate with others. The development of oral language competence lays the groundwork for the development of reading and writing, which are also systems of language. Experts agree that children need a foundation in oral or sign language before they can be expected to learn to read or to benefit from formal reading instruction. For example, if you are reading an article and come across the word *empennage,* you could probably sound it out. The dictionary marks it as \am·p ·′nazh\ or \em-\. Now that you have produced these sounds and blended them together, can you understand the word? If this word is part of your personal lexicon, the answer is yes, but if you do not know this word, sounding it out is not a useful strategy. In order to help you understand the article you are reading, your teacher might have helped you learn the meaning of the word before you read it or might have chosen to let you try to understand it from the context first and then discussed it with you. But without language, you would not be able to read at all.

It is clear that children learning to read must have language, but there is no clear guideline that they must have a vocabulary of a given number of words, that they can use a given number of patterns, or that they know other elements of language. As a teacher, you must assess children's language development and ask yourself before every lesson if the children have the language skills to be successful in that specific activity. If not, then starting with learning the language is critical to their success as readers and writers.

As we think in the next section about the development of reading and how children become readers, you will notice similarities and differences in learning oral language and reading and writing printed language.

WHAT DO TEACHERS NEED TO KNOW ABOUT THE TYPICAL SEQUENCE OF LEARNING TO READ?

Reading is an interactive process involving the ideas and language of the author and the ideas and language of the reader. We once thought of the reader as a blank slate on which the ideas of the author were to be written, an empty vessel into which the thoughts of the author could be poured. Today, however, experts believe that meaning is created—or recreated—through

LOOKING AT THE RESEARCH

What the research says about learning the concept that print has meaning

In the midst of gaining facility with the symbol systems of language and toys, children acquire through interactions with others the insights that specific kinds of marks—print—also can represent meanings (IRA/NAEYC statement, 1998). The print we use with children makes a difference in their understandings. Just labeling everything in a classroom will not be useful unless the children are involved in the labeling and engaged in deciding what to label and what the labels should say.

What questions might you ask or directions might you give children that would involve them in this labeling process?

Go to our Companion Website at www.prenhall.com/harp to read what others have said in response to this question and to add your comments to the global discussion on the Threaded Message Board.

the interaction between the ideas and language of the author and the ideas and language of the reader (Rosenblatt, 1978). The meaning produced by this interaction may be unique to the reader and may not match exactly the meaning created by other readers. Each reader has different sets of experiences and different knowledge to bring to the reading experience; therefore you would expect their meanings to vary somewhat. Take the example of reading the well-known children's book, *Charlotte's Web* (White, 1952). Second graders reading this book may read it as a simple tale of a spider and pig and interpret it as a story of friendship. Adults reading the same book may see much deeper themes, such as the place of death in the cycle of life. Each reader has read the same story, but adults read much more into the book than children because they have many different life experiences and reading experiences to bring to the reading of this book.

Definitions of Reading

Several experts have offered definitions of reading in an attempt to come to a workable definition of the complex behavior of reading. Clay (1991) recognizes that what the reader brings to the text is critical. Of her definition of reading she says,

> I define reading as a message-getting, problem-solving activity which increases in power and flexibility the more it is practiced. My definition states that within the directional constraints of the printer's code, language and visual perception responses are purposefully directed by the reader in some integrated way to the problem of extracting meaning from cues in a text, in sequence, so that the reader brings a maximum of understanding to the author's message. (p.6)

More simply stated, Clay views the reading process as a problem-solving activity in which the problem is one of getting the author's message by using the cues on the printed page and the reader's background knowledge.

The notion that the reader creates meaning was further explained by Rosenblatt (1978):

> The reader brings to the text his past experience and present personality. Under the magnetism of the ordered symbols of the text, he marshals his resources and crystallizes out from the stuff of memory, thought and feeling a new order, a new experience, which he sees as the poem. This becomes part of the ongoing stream of his life experience, to be reflected on from any angle important to him as a human being. (p. 12)

Rosenblatt so clearly recognized that the reader transacts with the text to create new meaning; she named the "product" of that transaction "the poem." Her definitions of the reader, the text, and the poem are interesting.

The reader is the person seeking to make meaning by transacting with (actively reading) a text of whatever kind. The text is the collection of word symbols and patterns on the page, the physical object you hold in your hand as you read (or the screen of a computer or the billboard beside the road). The poem is the literary work created as the reader transacts with the text.

One of the greatest advances in our thinking about reading from the thinking of Rosenblatt is that the meaning is not solely in the text itself. Meaning is created through the transaction between the reader and the text. Reading is a process resulting in meaning created by the blending of the author's ideas and the background knowledge of the reader. The ability of the reader continues to develop as the reader engages in more meaningful reading experiences; subsequently skill is achieved as the reader moves through observable stages. Without making meaning, one cannot be said to be reading. If a child says all the words on a page but has no meaning for them, that is not reading.

Reading Process

Reading is a complex mental activity in which a reader uses symbols to create meaning. It is complex because it requires employing knowledge of print and other symbols, knowledge of possible meanings of these symbols, and knowledge of the world—all to be coordinated in the process of gaining meaning from text. Trying to condense the complexity of reading in a model or schematic is difficult, but the model developed by Goodman, Watson, and Burke (1996) illustrated in Figure 1.3 comes closest to capturing what happens when a reader reads than any other model. On the left they have represented the text as a creation between what the writer intended to say and what the reader perceives to be the meaning. Keep in mind as you examine this model that all these steps take place almost simultaneously and mostly unconsciously.

As readers look at the text, they make informed predictions about what it is going to say, sample the text to confirm their predictions (look at the letters and words as much as they need to in order to get meaning from them). If they believe that they have made meaning, they may check again to confirm that the print says what they thought it did by either rereading or rethinking. If they confirm the meaning they have created, then that meaning is integrated with what they know and feeds back into the cycle of predicting, inferring, and sampling. If, on the other hand, the reader cannot confirm the meaning, then he must go back to the text to reread in order to get more samples or rethink the original predictions and inferences or do both.

According to Goodman, Watson, and Burke (1996), the reader takes from the print only the amount of information needed to create meaning. Beginning readers who have little experience in reading focus almost entirely on the print. As readers gain more experience, more of their attention is devoted to the context of the print and how it fits their expectations. If, however, their expectations prove faulty, then they must focus more carefully on the print itself.

Figure 1.3
Model of the Reading Process
Source: Goodman, Y. M., Watson, D. J., and Burke, C. L. (1996). *Reading strategies: Focus on comprehension.* Katonah, NY: Richard C. Owen Publishers, Inc. Reprinted with permission.

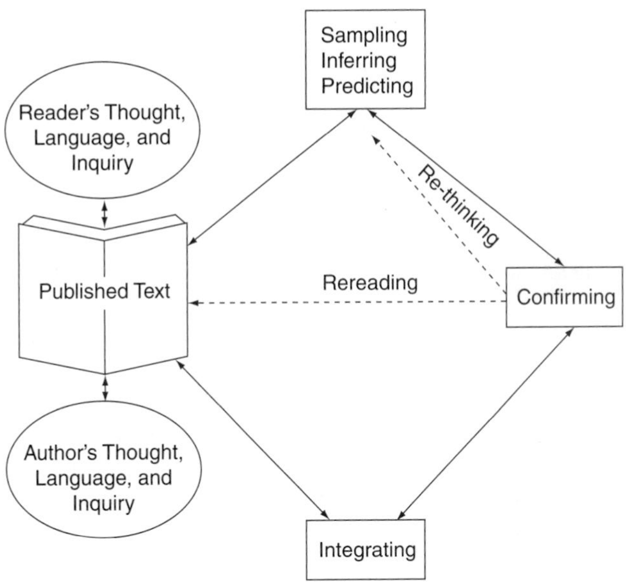

This process, as noted previously, is mostly unconscious and is consciously available to the reader only occasionally. For example, you might glance at a headline in the newspaper and think it says something, then realize that simply could not be possible. Then you examine the print more carefully to see where you made your error. The thinking that what you thought it said was not possible is based on your knowledge of newspaper headlines, the restrictions on writing headlines, and or on topics that could not be addressed in a newspaper (at least not a reputable family newspaper).

The Continuum of Reading Development

There is not a time in a child's life where one can say that literacy is beginning. Rather, children are continually in the process of becoming literate (Teale & Sulzby, 1986). As children begin to read, they develop skills in manipulating the sounds in words, gain a larger sight vocabulary, and use phonics and other strategies for decoding new words. As beginners, it is difficult for them to read silently, and they read word for word. These behaviors often result in losing the meaning because these early readers focus entirely on the print. However, they enjoy being able to read a text independently and delight in finding familiar words in books and in their environment.

As readers gain more skill in applying reading strategies, they develop more independence in reading. They are able to rely on phonics and also learn what to do if sounding out the letters fails to help them decode a word. They also become more skillful in monitoring their comprehension and knowing what to do if they are not comprehending the text. Independent readers exhibit much more fluency when they read orally, and they are beginning to read without vocalizing. Some children at this stage develop strong preferences for reading one kind of material over another such as reading books in one interest area like horses, mysteries, or books by the same author.

At a higher level of development, skilled readers can read a wide variety of genres and use a wide array of strategies to meet their reading needs. These readers are flexible in their reading. For example, they can adjust their reading speed to fit the purpose of their reading and the material they are reading. Skilled readers can respond to the texts they read in a variety of ways—both privately and publicly. There is no point at which one can say that there is nothing more to be learned about reading; all of us can become more skilled as readers as we tackle new genres or select new authors to read or read highly specialized professional material. In later chapters we will discuss in detail the development of strategies that influence how readers make decisions when they engage in the act of reading.

As readers, children use what they know about oral language to help them create meaning from printed language. They must use their knowledge of the phonemes used in the language in order to make sense of letter-sound relationships. They also use what they know about semantics to gain meaning from print. The effectiveness of sounding out a word depends on knowing what the word means once it is sounded out. Readers also make use of their knowledge of syntax to verify that a word they have decoded could actually be used in an English sentence. For example, if the child had determined that the word in the blank in this sentence, "The _____ kicked the ball" was "bad," the sentence would not sound like an English sentence. Children also make use of their knowledge of morphological structures to understand plurals, prefixes, and suffixes and how they change the meaning of the words. Readers also employ their knowledge of pragmatics and their schema about the world to interpret meanings in print. For example, a child is reading about a turtle, and the text says that the turtle moves very fast. A reader with any experience knows that either words have been decoded incorrectly or that there is an error in the text.

This continuum of reading development does not have a clear beginning point unless we say that birth is the beginning of learning to use language and therefore the beginning of reading. It also has no end point as we encourage readers to become lifelong learners. Our job as teachers is to help each child move along the continuum with confidence and to help children become skilled readers so that they continue to read and grow as learners long past their formal schooling experiences.

According to Chall (1996), children move through stages of development in reading. The performance of children as readers at different stages is qualitatively different from their performance at other stages, and children move from one stage to the next as a result of interactions in their environment. She viewed the reading behavior of children at each stage as problem-solving behavior and reminds us that "at all stages of development, reading depends upon full engagement with the text—its content, ideas, and values. Thus, motivation, energy, daring, and courage are aspects to be considered in the full development of reading" (p. 12).

Chall's stages include:

Stage 0: Prereading, Birth to Age 6

Stage 1: Initial Reading, or Decoding, Stage: Grades 1–2, Ages 6–7

Stage 2: Confirmation, Fluency, Ungluing from Print: Grades 2–3, Ages 7–8.

Stage 3: Reading for Learning the New: A First Step

Stage 4: Multiple Viewpoints, High School, Ages 14–18

Stage 5: Construction and Reconstruction—A World View: College, Age 18, and Above. (Chall, 1996, p. 13–23)

Chall's stages are most useful in thinking about how readers change in a predictable way over time. The prereading stage, as we now think of it, is a very important stage in learning to read. Chall described it as the time when children learned about letters, words, and books. She noted that it is often marked by pretend reading. In today's world, we know that many children receive reading instruction very early and most have reading instruction in kindergarten. This instruction may blur the lines between the prereading stage and the initial reading stage for many children.

Chall describes the primary task of the initial reading period as learning letter sound correspondences. She believed that the focus of readers in this stage was the print and that they could not focus on meaning as more mature readers were able to do.

Stage 3, as Chall describes it, is the time when readers begin learning as much from reading as they previously could only learn from listening and watching. Many teachers of young readers would feel that their learners are learning from print from the beginning of reading as they read nonfiction or information books at the beginning of their reading experiences.

Stages 4 and 5 are descriptions of readers beyond the scope of this book, but, as a teacher, it is useful to think of the continuing growth of readers and that their experience with becoming better readers does not end at grade 8.

Written language is related to oral language as readers learn to make sense of what they see in print and as they learn to create the print for themselves and others to read. How children learn to write is important knowledge for teachers.

WHAT DO TEACHERS NEED TO KNOW ABOUT THE TYPICAL SEQUENCE OF LEARNING TO WRITE?

Learning to write, like learning language and learning to read, is a developmental process that can be observed. This learning is highly responsive to environment so that children with no experience with written language and no opportunities to participate in writing will reflect that inexperience in their writing attempts. It is difficult to imagine a child in this country not being exposed to print since it is around us everywhere—on buildings, on street signs, in stores, on our clothing, and just about everywhere else. It is possible that children have not attended to the print in their environment and have had limited opportunities to write themselves.

LOOKING AT THE RESEARCH

What the research says about the development of writing

In a study that examined the reading and writing instruction and outcomes in six classrooms, three using a basal program and three using a process approach based on trade books, the researchers found that in both groups children's writing was influenced by their reading achievement. Reading and writing skills grew in tandem, and the sophistication of children's writing more often was related to their reading level than to the type of instruction they experienced in writing (Stahl & Pagnucco, 1996). Materials selected for reading should therefore have something to offer the child as a writer. If a teacher helps a child understand an expository text that is organized around questions and answers, that child can then use a question/answer format in her own writing.

Select one of your favorite picture books and examine it in terms of what it might offer readers as a model for writing. Go to our Companion Website at www.prenhall.com/harp and add the title of the book you selected and your thoughts about how it models writing to the global discussion on the Threaded Message Board.

Stages in the Development of Writing

Children's initial, and mostly unconventional, attempts at writing are executed with a plan in mind (Clay, 1975). Children do not learn all about language on any one level of organization before they begin to manipulate units at higher levels. For example, when they know a few letters, they produce several words before they know all the letters of the alphabet. Children construct their understanding of written language in a developmental sequence that is distinguishable and similar for every child. As soon as children begin to make marks with writing instruments, they are beginning to learn about written language and how it works. Clay (1975) describes the stages in developing writing as follows:

> 1. He has a concept of signs (uses letters, invents letters, uses punctuation).
> 2. He has a concept that a message is conveyed (i.e., he tells you a message but what he has written is not that message).
> 3. A message is copied, and he knows more or less what that message says.
> 4. Repetitive, independent use of sentence patterns like 'here is a . . . ').
> 5. Attempts to record own ideas, mostly independently.
> 6. Successful composition. (p. 66)

As young children work at writing, they often make marks on the page and call them letters. Clay defined a concept of letters as the time when children know letters are used in writing, even though some of the letters used by the child are pseudo-letters. With experience, the child learns that writing is used to convey messages and can provide an oral translation of what he has written on the page. In the third stage, the child begins to pay attention to print in the environment and often copies either whole messages or parts of messages and usually knows what they say, at least generally if not word for word. In the next stage, a child masters a form such as a pattern sentence. Many first graders write such patterns in their journals as "I like Joey. I like Tad. I like Sol." With a little more experience, the writer records his own ideas or experiences with little help. Clay defines a successful composition as one in which the writer is able to convey the message of her choice in a way that communicates with a reader.

Of course, children are learning about other parts of the system of written language as they are learning about what it means to communicate through writing. One of the systems of written language that must be mastered in order to communicate clearly is the spelling of words.

Stages in the Development of Spelling

The stages in the development of spelling knowledge recognized by many researchers (Clay, 1975; Ferreiro & Teberosky, 1982; Temple et al., 1993) are identified as scribbling, linear repetitive writing, random letter writing, early phonemic writing, transitional writing, conventional writing, and proficient writing. The authors of *First Steps* (Dewsbury, 1997) have described the development of spelling as preliminary spelling, semi-phonetic spelling, phonetic spelling, transitional spelling, and independent spelling. Bear, Invernizzi, Templeton, and Johnston (1996) and his colleagues have described spelling development as preliterate, early letter name, middle and late letter name, within word pattern, syllable juncture, and derivational constancy. Each of these researchers observed children's spelling behavior over time and developed schemes for describing what they observed. All of them observed the same kind of developmental patterns, and the important message is the same from all of them. That message is that learning to spell is an observ-

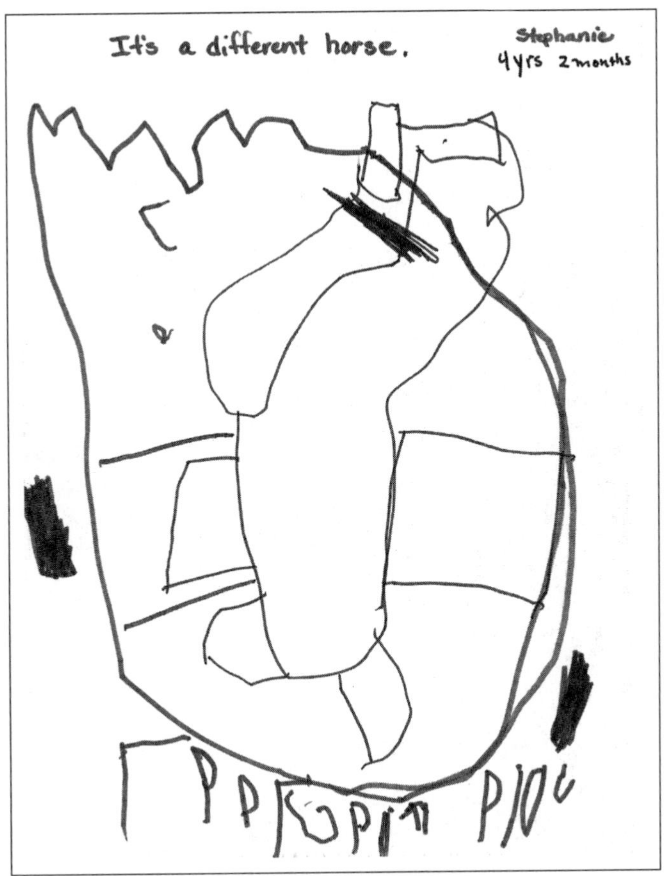

Figure 1.4
Scribbling Stage

able, developmental process and that teachers must be able to assess a child's development in spelling to plan appropriate instruction for that child.

Scribbling Stage. The first stage in the development of writing is scribbling (Figure 1.4). Just as children babble before they use words, they scribble all kinds of forms before they learn which of those forms are letters and which are not. Scribbling is a way of gaining control of the writing instrument and of the various lines and circles needed to form letters. It is interesting to note that children have been "writing" on the walls and tables of their homes for as long as writing "tools" (crayons and markers) have existed. We failed to recognize the importance of this early writing until recently. Now we know that scribbling is the first stage in the long process of learning to write. The scribble in Figure 1.4 says "It's a different horse," so the child has an idea that the scribble conveys a message.

Linear Repetitive Stage. The second stage is linear repetitive writing in which children have discovered that writing in English is usually horizontal and moves in a string across the page (Figure 1.5). At this stage children look for a concrete connection between words and their referents. They will create a word referring to something larger with a longer string of forms than a word referring to something smaller. Another characteristic of this stage is that the scribbling begins to take on the characteristics of the language seen in the environment. For example, some languages have curls, sweeping lines, and dots that are represented in the scribbles of the child. In Figure 1.5, this writing says, "I love you."

Figure 1.5
Linear Repetitive Stage

Random Letter Stage. In this stage children learn which forms are acceptable as letters and use them in some random order to record words or sentences. They may produce a string of letters that have no relation to the sounds of the words they are attempting to record. They may also include some forms that are not recognizable as letters because their repertoire of letters is so limited. Children in this stage often write their own names over and over, but assign meanings to these words other than their name. Figure 1.6 is an example of random letter writing. This piece is a poem that reads: "A poem/Trees light/so bright/Up in the sky." At the beginning of this figure is a good example of the child moving from random letter to phonemic writing. This piece reads, "Brandon, I love you." Note that the name Brandon is almost correct, and you can clearly read *love* and a *u.* The rest seem to be random letters.

Phonemic Stage. In this stage children begin to make the connection between letters and sounds. The beginning of this stage is often described as "letter name" writing because children write the letters whose name and sound are the same. This is when they are likely to write the word *you* with the letter *U,* as in Figure 1.6. Children in this stage know that words cannot be written with strings of repeated letters. Figure 1.7 is an example of early phonemic writing. This piece is an interview. The first question reads, "What is your favorite kind of ice cream?" The second question reads, "Are your parents nice when they are angry?"

Figure 1.6
Random Letter Stage

Figure 1.7
Phonemic Stage

R') intrvow

Wot is your fafrot cind
of iscrem. No yes choclot
are youn parins nise
won thau une agre
yes NO

LOOKING AT THE RESEARCH

What the research says about the connections between reading and writing

Writing supports the learning of reading because children engaged in writing acquire letter and word knowledge as they work to encode their oral language into print (Chomsky, 1970, 1979). When children can encode the sounds of the language, they understand the letter/sound relationships. Writing can be an excellent assessment of which letter/sound relationships the child knows and what instruction in letter/sound relationships would be useful.

Look at the writing sample in Figure 1.7. What letter/sound relationships does the child understand? What instruction would be appropriate for this writer?

Go to our Companion Website at www.prenhall.com/harp to share your answers to these questions on the Threaded Message Board.

Transitional Stage. As children gain more experience with the written language system, they begin to learn its conventions and to spell some words in conventional ways even though the spelling is not phonetic. A good example is the word *love.* Being exposed to this word so often, children begin early to spell it in its conventional form. In this stage children are moving from their phonetic spelling to standard or conventional spelling as illustrated in Figure 1.8. In this sample, written by a first grader, the child spells many words conventionally, but some are spelled phonetically (*know, see, creatures, of, turtle, took, three, used, traveling).* The more commonly used words such as *that, bird, years, die,* and *because* are spelled conventionally.

Conventional Stage. Conventional writing is characterized by the ability of the writer to choose text forms that are appropriate to the audience and purpose of the writing, to write in a wide range of genres, to demonstrate mastery of a variety of sentence patterns, and to create meaningful paragraphs. These writers are also beginning to use vocabulary that is appropriate for the specific audience and can punctuate most sentences correctly. Figure 1.9 is an example of conventional writing. This sample was written by a fourth grader and is an unedited draft. Note that most words are spelled conventionally. As you can probably determine, this is a reading response journal entry written after the author had read Chapter 4 in *Shiloh* (Naylor, 1991).

Proficient Stage. Although most children will be conventional writers at the end of their elementary school experience, some will be proficient. Proficient writing is characterized by good control of the elements of writing, including conventional spelling and punctuation. Proficient writers have control of an extensive vocabulary and use it to express specific meanings. They can edit and revise their writing at all stages of the writing process. These writers have mastered a wide range of genres and are skilled at selecting the most appropriate forms for the audience and purpose of their writing.

Figure 1.8
Transitional Stage

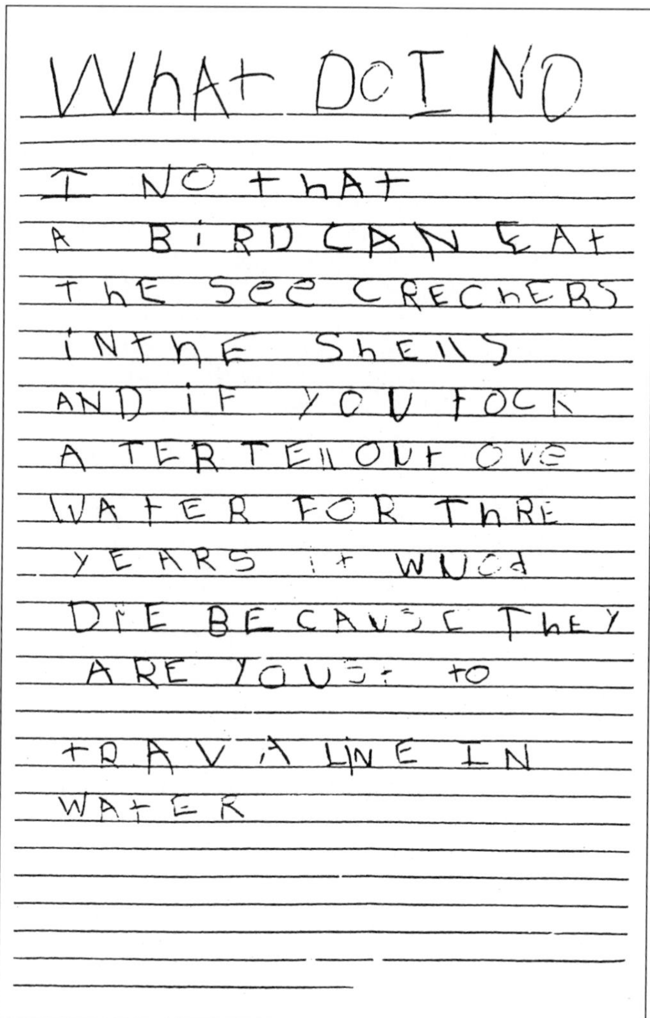

Just as children move slowly from babbling to adult speech, they need time to adopt the conventions of written language. Children put considerable time and effort into mastering adult speech. Support from sensitive adults aids them in their task. Our hope is that children will have effective and meaningful support as they proceed from scribbling to mature written language. In future chapters we will provide more explicit detail about supporting developing and skilled learners in the classroom and how teachers make the decisions about what kind and how much support to provide. As children gain skill as readers, they become better writers, and since both reading and writing are based on language, each system can support and enhance learning in the other systems.

One of the developmental checklists that can help teachers assess young children's language use, their reading abilities, and their understandings of written language is the *Teacher Rating of Oral Language and Literacy (TROLL): A Research-Based Tool* (Dickinson, McCabe, & Sprague, 2001). This scale is designed to help teachers record their observations of young children's literary learning and note children's strengths in each area.

Figure 1.9
Conventional Stage

1-4-94 Chapter 3

I think Marty's dad cares about how much Marty likes Shiloh because on page 34 and 35 he asks questions about the dogs like, "Dogs okay?" and "Got to keep them healthy, though, or you won't have 'em long." I think that Marty lives on a farm. I think that the people in Marty's community are nice when it said on page 33 that Mrs. Elison always leaves a little loaf of banana bread or cinamon roll for Marty's father. I think Marty will really be a vet when he gets older because he is so good to animals and cares for them and if somone wants to be something as much as Marty they probably will be that.

WHAT ARE THE CONNECTIONS BETWEEN LANGUAGE, READING, AND WRITING?

LOOKING AT THE RESEARCH

What the research says about the connections between reading and writing

Reading and writing are complementary processes and children should engage in them simultaneously (Clay, 1991). In fact, combining reading and writing instruction improves the learning of both reading and writing (McGinley & Tierney, 1989).

Some teachers schedule a block of time for reading instruction and another block of time for writing instruction. Even though the schedule may look as if reading and writing are separate, the instruction in each of the time blocks is about both reading and writing. How might teachers be accomplishing this?

Go to the Weblinks in Chapter 1 on our Companion Website at www.prenhall.com/harp to link to sites presenting research on the connections between reading and writing, then to the chapter's Threaded Message Board to add your comments to the global discussion.

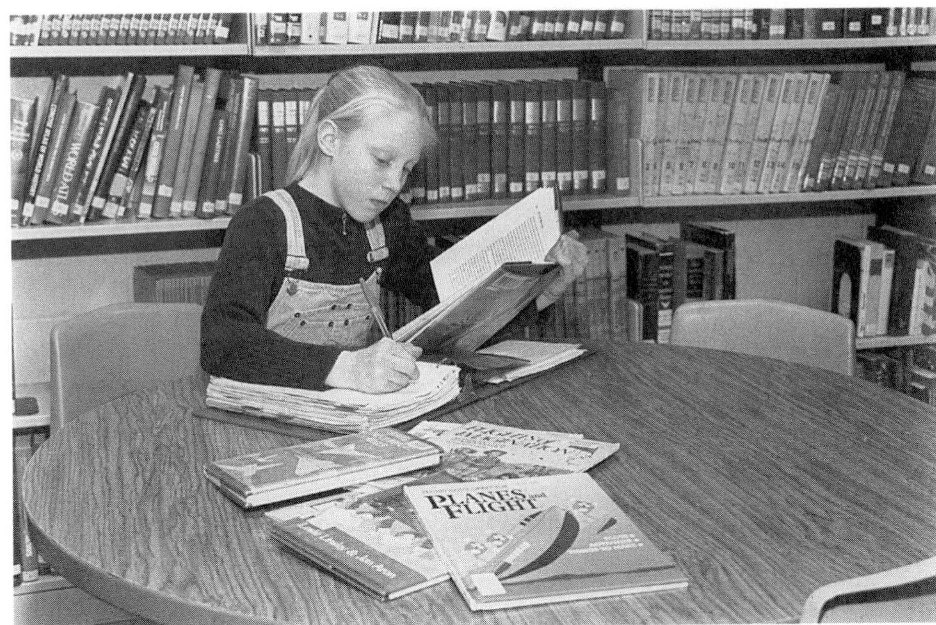

Children become better at both reading and writing when they do them together.

Remember that children learning to write are also learning to read and continuing to develop their oral language skills and abilities. Growth in any of the systems supports growth in each of the other systems (Harp & Brewer, 1996). For example, a child learning to write in English must analyze the word or words he wishes to write, begin at the left of the word, and place the letters sequentially from left to right in order to record a word. Of course, before a child writes a word, she must know that word and what it means. Children writing are children reading, and children doing either writing or reading are using language.

There is not a standard number of words that a child must know and use in oral language before learning to write. Some children are learning to scribble when they have only limited productive language vocabularies. These same children may also be learning to recognize their favorite books and notice that the octagonal red sign says "stop." As a child builds a vocabulary of words he can write, these words are automatically in his reading vocabulary. Once a child learns to read a set of words, then the reading influences what and how the child writes. Literacy is a continuum transcending oral and written mediums of communication, with different discourse styles overlapping both (Biber, 1988; Scott, 1988; Spiro & Taylor, 1987; Wallach, 1990). For example, think of a child reciting a familiar nursery rhyme as she looks at a book with illustrations. The picture of Humpty Dumpty triggers the recitation of the rhyme, and the words become part of the child's speaking vocabulary while at the same time she is observing that the print is not the same for Humpty Dumpty and other rhymes in the book.

Just as a child does not have to know all the possible words before learning to read, he does not have to know all about reading before learning to write. Not so many years ago, teachers believed that children needed to know how to read many words before they could learn to write. In 1970, Chomsky published an article called "Write Before Reading" that was significant in helping teachers think about how writing could support learning to read. Most teachers since the early 1970s have encouraged children's attempts at early, unconventional writing, knowing that as they learned to create messages, they were also learning how to get meaning from the messages of others. Most teachers now understand that struggling readers may need writing experiences to support their reading development.

WHY IS IT IMPORTANT FOR ALL CLASSROOM TEACHERS TO UNDERSTAND THE DEVELOPMENTAL NATURE OF READING, WRITING, AND LANGUAGE SKILLS?

Our purpose in this chapter has been to build foundational knowledge from which you can draw throughout the rest of this book. Clearly, language, reading, and writing are connected by our human desire and need to communicate. Brian Cambourne (1988), an Australian teacher and researcher, suggests that the conditions that facilitate language learning can be replicated in the classroom to foster learning to read and write. We think Cambourne's work makes sense, draws the ideas of this chapter together, and sets the stage for thinking about creating classroom environments that support literacy development.

Classroom Environment

> According to Cambourne (1988), newly-born members of any society have no foreknowledge of the language culture into which they're born. If they are to become full members of that culture they are faced with the task of working out how to make meaning using the same language conventions that the rest of the community uses. This is a daunting task but fortunately, over the millennia, a pedagogy has been developed which maximizes the probability that the task will be successfully completed by the overwhelming majority of the community. This pedagogy is one which perfectly matches the contours of the contexts in which the learning takes place, i.e. it fits in with the social, physical and emotional parameters of what could be called the 'family unit.' Although the family unit differs from culture to culture and has differed from age to age, there are certain core features which seem to be constant across time and cultures.
>
> For example, the young learners are always in proximity to proficient users of the language. Furthermore, among these proficient users (the 'experts') there is usually at least one with whom the learner forms a significant bond. Most probably there is a ring of 'experts' of different degrees of language proficiency with whom bonds can be formed. There is a community of 'user experts.' Within this framework there are certain conditions present which contribute to the learning processes which take place. (p. 32)

Figure 1.10 is a schematic of the conditions that Cambourne says are in place to facilitate language learning and that we can recreate in our classrooms to facilitate learning to read and write. As you examine this schematic, consider what evidence you would look for in a classroom in order to determine that each of the conditions (listed down the center of the chart) is in place.

Instructional Experiences

As a teacher, you will want to plan instructional experiences that help all learners move along the developmental continuums in reading, writing, speaking, and listening. You will want each child to learn with confidence and to feel that learning is something enjoyable and important. To be that kind of teacher, you will need basic knowledge of the development of communication systems to evaluate your classroom instruction and the experiences you plan for the children.

Let it suffice for now to say that the research on the reading/writing connection suggests that our goal is to create a print-rich classroom environment in which children are reading to learn to read better, reading to learn to write better, writing to learn to write

Figure 1.10
Cambourne's Conditions for Literacy Learning

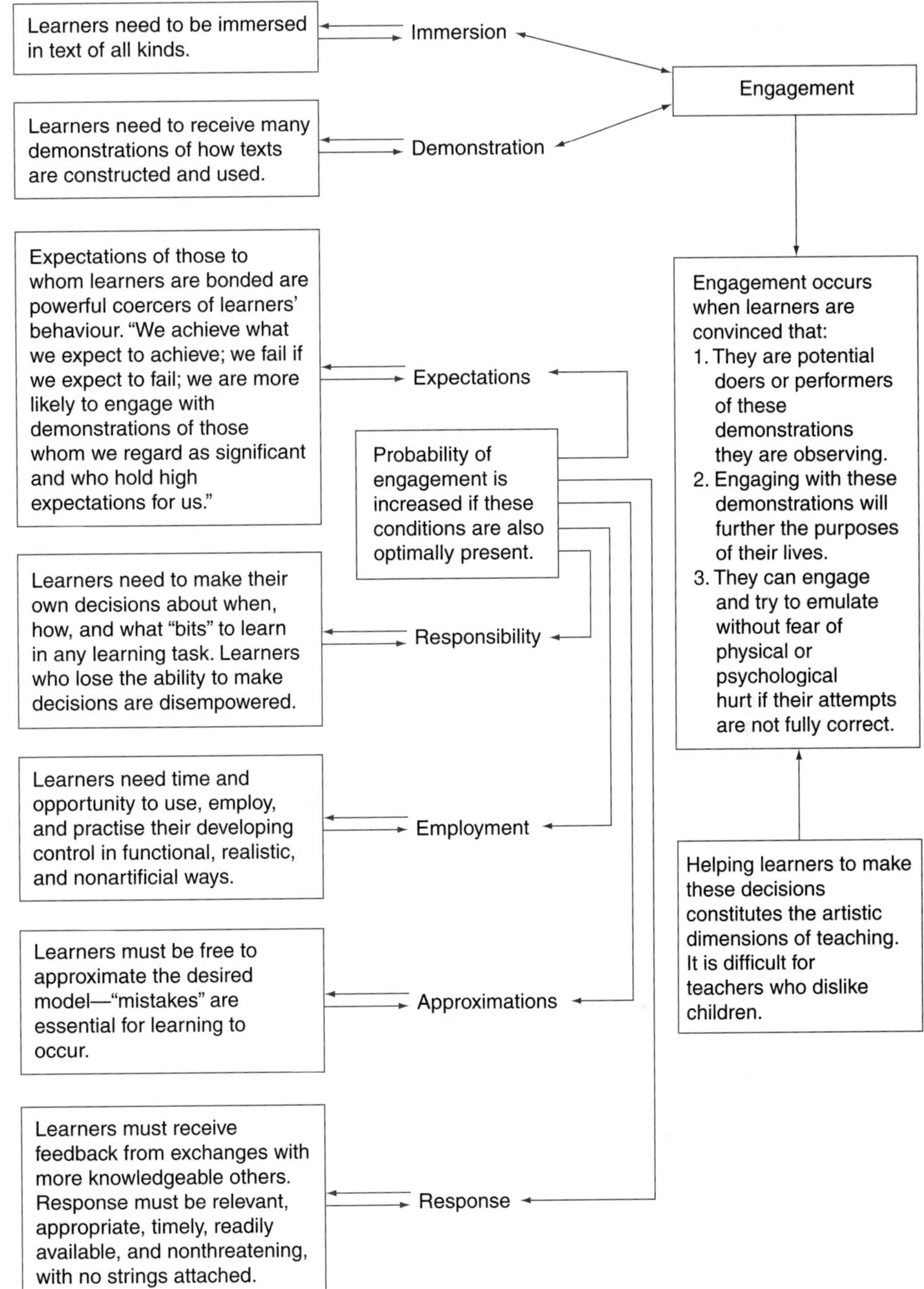

Learners need to be immersed in text of all kinds.
Immersion
Engagement
Learners need to receive many demonstrations of how texts are constructed and used.
Demonstration
Expectations of those to whom learners are bonded are powerful coercers of learners' behaviour. "We achieve what we expect to achieve; we fail if we expect to fail; we are more likely to engage with demonstrations of those whom we regard as significant and who hold high expectations for us."
Expectations
Probability of engagement is increased if these conditions are also optimally present.
Engagement occurs when learners are convinced that:
1. They are potential doers or performers of these demonstrations they are observing.
2. Engaging with these demonstrations will further the purposes of their lives.
3. They can engage and try to emulate without fear of physical or psychological hurt if their attempts are not fully correct.
Learners need to make their own decisions about when, how, and what "bits" to learn in any learning task. Learners who lose the ability to make decisions are disempowered.
Responsibility
Learners need time and opportunity to use, employ, and practise their developing control in functional, realistic, and nonartificial ways.
Employment
Helping learners to make these decisions constitutes the artistic dimensions of teaching. It is difficult for teachers who dislike children.
Learners must be free to approximate the desired model—"mistakes" are essential for learning to occur.
Approximations
Learners must receive feedback from exchanges with more knowledgeable others. Response must be relevant, appropriate, timely, readily available, and nonthreatening, with no strings attached.
Response

Source: From Brian Cambourne. (1995, November). "Toward an Educationally Relevant Theory of Literacy Learning: Twenty Years of Inquiry," *The Reading Teacher, 49*(3), 182–202. Reprinted with permission of Brian Cambourne and the International Reading Association.

better, and writing to learn to read better. Since both writing and reading have their foundation in oral language, they are continuing to become more skillful users of language in its oral form as well.

THINKING AS A TEACHER

1. Your principal asks if you want to purchase a kit to help children develop oral language skills. Most of the kits you have seen contain replicas of fruits, animals, and so on and photographs of various objects. Some come with a puppet or other props. What do you say and why?
2. A parent complains that her child talks all the time about the writing she is doing in reading class. The parent is concerned that her child is not learning to read. What responses could you make to the parent?
3. The father of a 5-year-old who wrote "wusr apon a time ther was a robot thet dint aint have a oonere" expresses concern at the open house that his son is not learning to spell properly. How will you explain the developmental nature of spelling ability, and what will you say to make the father feel better about his son's progress?

FIELD-BASED ACTIVITIES

1. Listen to your students talking. Record some examples of their speech in various situations (classroom discussion, playground, lunchroom, unstructured time with other children) and compare their language with that found in the reading textbooks or social studies and science textbooks. Are the topics, sentence lengths, constructions, and level of formality similar to children's speech? Different from children's speech? Should they be similar or different?
2. Record on videotape or audiotape a read-aloud session with children. What kinds of language patterns and interactions did you use? For example, you might note the number of questions you asked, the number of questions the children asked, the number repetitions you used, and perhaps the number of times you encouraged children to fill in words as they listened to you read.
3. Interview three children about reading and writing. Ask each of them the following questions: Are you a good reader/writer? What would you do to help someone learn to read/write? Think about their concepts of reading and writing and how these might influence your instruction.

REFERENCES

Bear, D. R., Invernizzi, M., Templeton, S., & Johnston, F. (1996). *Words their way: Word study for phonics, vocabulary, and spelling instruction.* Columbus, OH: Merrill.

Berk, L. (2003). *Child development* (4th ed.). Boston: Allyn and Bacon.

Biber, D. (1988). *Variation across speech and writing.* New York: Cambridge University Press.

Cambourne, B. (1988). *The whole story: Natural learning and the acquisition of literacy in the classroom.* New York: Scholastic.

Cambourne, B. (1995). Toward an educationally relevant theory of literacy learning: Twenty years of inquiry. *The Reading Teacher, 49*(3), 182–190.

Chall, J. S. (1996). *Stages of reading development.* Ft. Worth, TX: Harcourt Brace.

Chomsky, C. (1970). Reading, writing and phonology. *Harvard Educational Review, 40,* 287–309.

Chomsky, C. (1979). Approaching reading through invented spelling. In L. B. Resnick & P. A. Weaver (Eds.), *Theory and practice in early reading, Vol. 2.* Mahwah, NJ: Erlbaum.

Chomsky, N. (1965). *Aspects of the theory of syntax.* Cambridge, MA: MIT Press.

Clay, M. M. (1975). *What did I write?* Auckland, New Zealand: Heinemann.

Clay, M. M. (1991). *Becoming literate: The construction of inner control.* Auckland, New Zealand: Heinemann.

Cook, V. (1988). *Chomsky's universal grammar.* Oxford, England: Blackwell.

Dewsbury, A. (1997). *First steps: Spelling developmental continuum.* Portsmouth, NH: Heinemann.

Dickinson, D. K., McCabe, A., & Sprague, K. (2001). *Teacher rating of oral language and literacy (TROLL): A research-based tool.* CIERA Report #3-016. Ann Arbor, MI: Center for the Improvement of Early Reading.

Ferreiro, E., & Teberosky, A. (1982). *Literacy before schooling.* Portsmouth, NH: Heinemann.

Glazer, S. M. (1989). Oral language and literacy development. In D. S. Strickland & L. M. Morrow (Eds.), *Emerging literacy: Young children learn to read and write* (pp. 16–26). Newark, DE: International Reading Association.

Goodman, Y. M., Watson, D. J., & Burke, C. L. (1996). *Reading strategies: Focus on comprehension.* Katonah, NY: Richard C. Owen Publishers, Inc.

Guthrie, J., & Alverman, D. (Eds.). (1999). *Engaged reading: Processes, practices, and policy implications.* New York: Teachers College Press.

Guthrie, J., et al. (1996). Growth of literacy engagement: Changes in motivations and strategies during concept-oriented reading instruction. *Reading Research Quarterly, 31,* 306–325.

Halliday, M. A. K. (1982). Three aspects of children's language development: Learning language, learning through language, learning about language. In Y. Goodman, M. Haussler, & D. Strickland (Eds.), *Oral and written language development research: Impact on schools.* Urbana, IL: National Council of Teachers of English.

Harp, B., & Brewer, J. (1996). *Reading and writing: Teaching for the connections.* San Diego, CA: Harcourt.

Hulit, L. M., & Howard, M. R. (2002). *Born to talk: An introduction to speech and language development.* Boston: Allyn and Bacon.

International Reading Association & National Association for the Education of Young Children. (1998). Learning to read and write: Developmentally appropriate practices for young children. *The Reading Teacher, 52,* 193–216.

McGinley, W., & Tierney, R. J. (1989). Traversing the topical landscape: Reading and writing as ways of knowing. *Written Communication, 6,* 243–260.

Pinker, S. (1994). *The language instinct.* New York: William Morrow.

Rosenblatt, L. M. (1978). *The reader, the text, the poem: The transactional theory of the literary work.* Carbondale, IL: Southern Illinois University Press.

Scott, C. M. (1988). Spoken and written syntax. In M. Nippold (Ed.), *Later language development: Ages nine through nineteen* (pp. 49–95). Boston: College Hill.

Spiro, R. J., & Taylor, V. M. (1987). On investigating children's transitions from narrative to expository discourse: The multidimensional nature of psychological text classification. In P. Tierney, L. Anders, & J. N. Mitchell (Eds.), *Understanding readers understanding* (pp. 77–93). Hillsdale, NJ: Erlbaum.

Stahl, S., & Pagnucco, J. (1996). First graders reading and writing instruction in traditional and process-oriented classes. *Journal of Educational Research, 89,* 131–144.

Sulzby, E. (1996). Roles of oral and written language as children approach conventional literacy. In C. Pontecorvo, M. Orsolini, B. Burge, & L. Resnick (Eds.), *Children's early text construction* (pp. 25–46). Mahwah, NJ: Erlbaum.

Tan, A. (2001). *The bonesetter's daughter.* New York: Putnam.

Teale, W. J., & Sulzby, E. (1986). *Emergent literacy: Writing and reading.* Norwood, NJ: Ablex.

Temple, C. A., Nathan, R. G., Temple, F., & Burris., N.A. (1993). *The beginnings of writing.* Boston: Allyn and Bacon.

Wallach, G. (1990). Magic buries Celtics: Looking for broader interpretations of language learning and literacy. *Topics in Language Disorders, 10*(2), 63–80.

Children's Literature Cited

Naylor, P. R. (1991). *Shiloh.* New York: Atheneum.

White, E. B. (1952). *Charlotte's web.* (G. Williams, Illus.) New York: HarperCollins.

Chapter 2

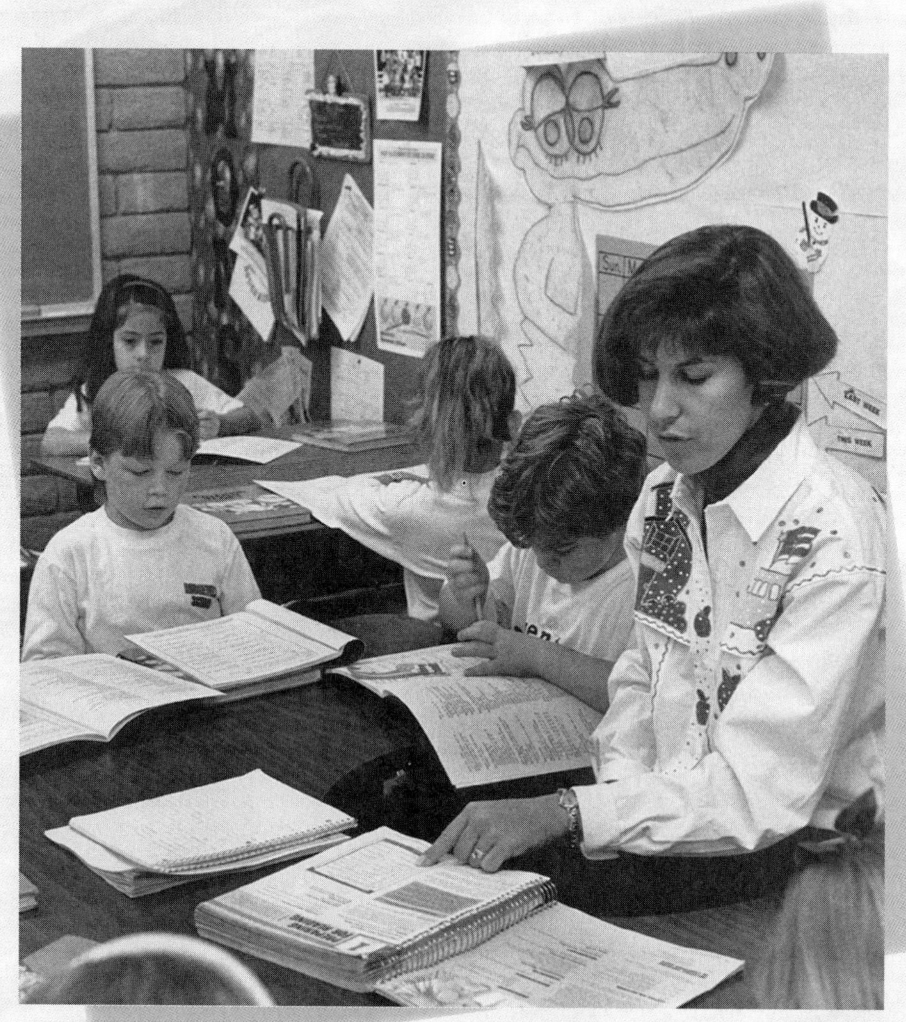

Approaches to Reading Instruction

LOOKING AT THE RESEARCH

Hoffman (1998), in reviewing years of research on innovation, offers the following principles and understandings:

- We strive for excellence in teaching. We envision that excellence (Haberman, 1994).
- We connect/"network" and explore our understandings within a community of learners (Fullan, 1996).
- We create working structures and relationships that encourage risk taking and diverse thinking rather than pressure toward conformity.
- We continuously observe, assess, and evaluate the world we live in (Joyce & Calhoun, 1995).
- We puzzle over the complexities of learning and teaching.
- We innovate to solve problems.
- We reflect on our experiences and we refocus (Schon, 1987).
- What looks like a healthy change environment for teachers looks in many ways like a healthy learning environment for kids. (p. 110)

The important message here is that the teacher, not the materials or approaches, is the most important variable in the teaching of reading. You will discover, as you study this chapter, that many approaches to the teaching of reading have been developed, tried, and abandoned in favor of newer approaches. The profession seems to be perpetually in search of the "silver bullet," the one best approach, the answer to all our instructional challenges. Research that sought, many years ago, to discover the best approach to beginning reading concluded that the most important variable in the teaching of reading is the teacher (Bond & Dykstra, 1967, 1997). We need to keep this discovery in mind as we are offered a wide array of published instructional materials—often each one touted as an improvement over previous ones.

In fact, the drive to find the "perfect" instructional material/method/solution has gone so far that many state legislatures across the United States pass laws that require teachers to use a single instructional method. This often pertains to a prescriptive phonics program (Duffy & Hoffman, 1999). Duffy and Hoffman point out detrimental effects of such legislation:

> Children are hurt because laws mandating one "perfect method" prevent teachers from using different methods with kids who need them.
>
> The professional nature of teaching is threatened because restrictive laws discourage the thoughtful innovation, risk taking, and creativity that is at the heart of professional life.
>
> Our professional community suffers because legislating a single answer silences those colleagues exploring alternative possibilities. (p. 10)

Again, the most important variable in the teaching of reading is an informed teacher. This is clearly illustrated in the "Real Teachers, Real Practice" essay by Joanne Morrissey.

Focus Questions

- What are the most common approaches to reading instruction?
- How do I decide which approach to use?

REAL TEACHERS, REAL PRACTICE

Meet Joanne Morrissey, *a first-grade teacher*

During my Reading and Language Arts block of 2 1/2 hours per day, I integrate spelling, handwriting, phonics, reading, and writing. The use of the anthology is an important tool to this process. We have The Treasures of Literature Anthology, *published by Harcourt Brace. The teacher's manual is like going to the mall. Just like at the mall I don't buy everything I see; I do not try to do all the activities suggested in the manual. I love to browse through each area picking out the important skills I can teach and the enrichment projects suggested for integrating literature into the curriculum.*

There are six anthology books with many stories in each, used in first grade. For the first several books it is intended that these stories are for read-

ing aloud and for shared reading because the reading levels are too difficult for first graders. The vocabulary taught for each story is in a controlled format, but the stories read are at a higher reading level. For example, the first anthology book introduced 21 readiness level vocabulary words. The stories in this book have a much higher reading level. These controlled vocabulary words are practiced in a duplicated Take Home Reader *that is at the appropriate reading level.*

Each week a new story from the anthology is presented in a whole group setting. My presentation begins with an introduction to the vocabulary that will be in the story. First I show a word and say the word, and the children repeat the word. Together we do a word study on the vocabulary words. "What do you notice about these words?" The children begin to tell me anything they notice about a word. For example, "The word see *has the double* e*." "The words* can *and* an *rhyme." "The words* you *and* yes *begin the same." "The word* did *begins like my name." All student responses are accepted. At first many are repeated. The word study helps the children make connections with the phonics they are learning, understand how words work, and apply their knowledge in solving new words. Word meaning, sentence fill-in, chart work, and various phonic skills are part of vocabulary practice through out the week.*

The story is first introduced by title, author, with some background, and a picture walk to make some predictions about the story. In the beginning of the school year much emphasis is placed on how to look at print. So many little details are discussed about the book to reinforce book handling, directionality of reading, one-to-one matching speech to print, locating known and unknown words, and the use of meaning, structure, and visual cues in the story. The story is read aloud to the whole group either with a tape and big book presentation or as a shared reading, each child having his/her own book to follow. Throughout the week this story and the run off Take Home *book for this story, with controlled vocabulary, are reread several times—whole group, small group, partner reading, choral reading, and reading to self in a low voice.*

The anthology manual and practice workbook present all the language arts skills needed for reading and writing. During the week several language arts skills are introduced or reinforced. This is either done in a whole group setting or during the guided reading time with small groups of four to six children. During the guided reading time the anthology book is not used as the reading instruction tool. Small books that are leveled and matched to the readers are used. During the guided reading time the children have different activities from a work board to complete while I am working with a small group. Stories from the anthology can be used for rereading, as an activity. Vocabulary pages from the practice book can be assigned. The anthology also has many writing projects that connect to the literature. There are open-ended questions at the end of each story. As part of their writing assignment from the work board, I will ask the children to answer one of the questions with an illustration. I will give specific criteria for their writing, depending on the assignment. For example, I might say, "Answer in three complete sentences. You need to have capital letters and correct punctuation."

The manual also suggests various art, drama, math, science, and social studies activities to integrate the literature into the curriculum. I use some of these activities for enrichment. I find it easy and enjoyable to have the real storybooks on hand for the children to use during their free time. Many children look for these books to take home from the school library.

The anthology is a motivator for reading great literature and a springboard for learning skills needed in reading. It is not the only tool for reading instruction, but it is an important part of a strong reading curriculum.

There is no one best approach to the teaching of reading. You, the teacher, are the most important variable in teaching reading. The informed reading teacher understands a variety of approaches and can select the approach that will be most beneficial to students at any point in time. When you are confronted with competing approaches, you will probably make your selection based upon research about the approach, your personal philosophy of literacy instruction, and your understanding of what your students need, just as Joanne Morrissey described.

WHAT ARE THE MOST COMMON APPROACHES TO READING INSTRUCTION?

Over the years a number of approaches to the teaching of reading have been in vogue. Each approach has had strong advocates and equally strong critics. An individual teacher may embrace one approach and reject another because of the model of reading instruction embraced by that teacher. Before we examine specific approaches, consider the four models of reading instruction defined by Garcia and Pearson (1991), presented in Figure 2.1. Stahl (1997) suggests that these models represent a continuum from highly teacher-directed, task-analytic approaches to more student-directed, holistic approaches. He also asserts that they range from a reliance on contrived materials designed for specific instructional purposes to the use of "natural" materials written primarily for an audience of young readers.

As you explore each of the approaches to reading instruction described in this section, consider which of the models in Figure 2.1 would be embraced by advocates of each of the approaches. You need to know which philosophy supports the approach, what research supports the approach, and how the approach looks in practice. Think about the approaches as tools in your toolbox. You will be able to select the tool or combination of tools to best serve your students.

Two Competing Views of Reading

For generations, education professionals have debated whether reading instruction should focus first on phonics or first on meaning making. Advocates of each viewpoint have amassed research results to support their views. Strongly held beliefs characterize each viewpoint. In fact, viewpoints are now so strongly held that some state legislatures are writing laws to dictate which view of the reading process is to be embraced and thus which approaches to reading instruction may be used. We can categorize these strongly opposing views as either a bottom up view of reading or a top-down view of reading.

Figure 2.1
Models of Reading Instruction

Direct Instruction

- This model begins with an analysis of the task to be learned, breaking it down to its smallest components.
- Focus is usually on teaching complex skills.
- Students are taught each component, both singly and in combination with other components.
- Teachers model the desired behavior, providing practice and feedback at each step.
- Teachers assess whether reteaching is necessary.
- Contemporary versions of this model include explanations of the importance of the strategy or skill; how, when, and where it is to be used; and when its use is inappropriate.

Explicit Explanation

- This approach is similar to direct instruction in that they both involve explicit definitions of strategies used in reading.
- Greater emphasis is placed on practicing the strategy in the context of reading text.
- A strategy may be introduced using specially constructed materials.
- Responsibility is gradually released to the student for execution of the strategy.
- In the beginning of instruction, use is demonstrated by the teacher; by the end the student executes the strategy independently.

Cognitive Apprenticeship

- These approaches set up a master-apprentice relationship between student and teacher.
- The teacher's role is to scaffold the learning, withdrawing support as students are able to proceed on their own.
- Initially the apprentice watches the teacher model the processes of comprehension.
- Gradually the teacher gives more and more responsibility to the student.
- Finally, the teacher watches the student perform comprehension tasks.
- Advocates of this model view reading as the orchestration of complex processes and believe that teaching reading skill by skill creates a distorted view of reading.

Whole Language

- This approach is not precisely defined, but clarified by a set of strongly held beliefs.
- Language (oral and written) is used for authentic purposes; under such circumstances children learn language best.
- Authentic reading and writing tasks use whole texts, not focusing on parts of language for their own sake.
- Advocates believe in child-centered learning, empowering children to direct their own learning. Instruction occurs in response to students' needs as they are attempting to use language for communication.
- Whole language is not a method or collection of activities, but rather a philosophy underlying all the teacher's instructional decisions.

Source: Adapted from Garcia, G. E., and Pearson, P. D. (1991), in Stahl, S. A. (1997). Instructional models in reading: An introduction. In S. A. Stahl & D. A. Hayes (Eds.), *Instructional models in reading*. Mahwah, NJ: Lawrence Erlbaum Associates, Inc. Reprinted with permission.

Bottom-up View of Reading. Educators who advocate beginning instruction in reading with sound/symbol relationships, building to words, building to sentences, and then building to stories are said to have a "bottom-up" view of the reading process. In this view, instruction is text-based and begins with the smallest pieces of language—the sounds (phonemes) and their written symbols (graphemes). Instruction then moves to blending sounds in words, to reading words, and then to reading sentences and longer pieces of text. The ultimate goal of instruction is comprehension, but beginning instruction lays heavy emphasis on decoding sound/symbol relationships.

Top-down View of Reading. Educators who oppose the bottom-up view of reading argue that instruction should begin with whole stories. As a part of reading whole stories, children's attention may be drawn to sentences, words in sentences, and sounds in words. This is known as a reader-based view of reading instruction. One of the approaches from which you may choose is the phonics-based approach.

Phonics-Based Approaches

Several web sites are devoted to issues related to phonics instruction. Go to the Weblinks in Chapter 2 on our Companion Website at www.prenhall.com/harp for links and/or addresses for those sites.

Phonics-based approaches are designed to teach children to unlock or decode the sound/symbol relationships in our language. Our language is alphabetic: Sounds are represented by letters. Phonics-based approaches are designed to begin reading instruction by teaching children to associate the graphemes (letters) with the phonemes (sounds) they represent.

Marilyn Adams (1990) asserts that the case for teaching phonics is best based on studies comparing the relative effectiveness of different approaches to teaching beginning reading. These studies "suggest, with impressive consistency, that programs including systematic instruction on letter-to-sound correspondences lead to higher achievement in both word recognition and spelling, at least in the early grades and especially for slower or economically disadvantaged students" (p. 30). Even with the research supporting phonics programs, there are clearly competing views about the nature of phonics instruction.

Competing Views About Phonics Instruction. There are two competing views about how children should be taught phonics and about the kind of phonics children should learn. One approach is known as *synthetic phonics,* and the other approach is known as *analytic phonics.* Understanding both approaches so that you can draw on both as the needs of your learners dictate will benefit your students. A much more detailed discussion of phonics instruction is offered in Chapter 5.

Synthetic Phonics. Synthetic phonics presents individual sound/symbol associations in isolation and then directs children to blend these individual sounds into words. For example, a child would be taught the /m/ sound, then the short /a/ sound, and then the /t/ sound. First he would practice these sounds in isolation and then be asked to blend them together faster and faster until the word *mat* is pronounced.

Analytic phonics. In the analytic approach, children are first taught to read a word and then to analyze the individual sounds within the word. They are taught to decode unfamiliar words by looking to see if they can find an analogous word. For example, if the child knows the sounds in *cake* and the sounds in *me,* she can sound out *make* by combining the /m/ sound from *me* and the /ake/ sound from *cake* to decode *make.* These competing views of phonics instruction are reminiscent of the two major views of reading instruction.

LOOKING AT THE RESEARCH

What place does phonics have in the total reading program?

Effective reading instruction includes teaching children to break apart and manipulate the sounds in words (phonemic awareness), teaching them that these sounds are represented by letters of the alphabet that can then be blended together to form words (phonics), having them practice what they've learned by reading aloud with guidance and feedback (guided oral reading), and applying reading comprehension strategies to guide and improve reading comprehension. These recommendations come from the *Report of the National Reading Panel: Teaching Children to Read* (National Institute of Child Health and Human Development, 2000).

How might you use this research to respond to advocates of a focus on phonics instruction in isolation? What is your best prediction about why reading comprehension is included in these results?

Go to the Weblinks in Chapter 2 on our Companion Website at www.prenhall.com/harp to link to sites presenting research on the role of phonics in the reading program; then go to the chapter's Threaded Message Board to add your comments to the global discussion.

The Philosophy of Phonics-Based Approaches. Advocates of phonics-based approaches to reading instruction hold a bottom up view of reading. Many educators, parents, and politicians take a "phonics first" stance, arguing that reading instruction should begin with phonics in isolation, that breaking the code is fundamental to learning to read. These advocates support synthetic approaches and see phonics instruction as something apart from the reading program. Often teachers who subscribe to this approach will spend 20 to 30 minutes each morning drilling students on sound/symbol relationships and then moving into whatever reading program has been selected.

Others take the position that phonics instruction is critical to learning to read, but argue that phonics should be taught systematically with children learning sound/symbol relationships, blending those sounds into words, and then reading those words in connected text. Such text has come to be known as "decodable text."

Decodable Text. The National Institute for Child Health and Human Development (NICHD) in reviewing 30 years of research on reading asserts that children need "extensive practice applying their knowledge of sound-spelling relationships to the task of reading as they are learning them. This integration of phonics and reading can only occur with the use of decodable text" (Grossen, 2002, p. 11). Decodable texts are composed of words that use sound/symbol relationships children have already learned to decode, plus a limited number of sight words that have been systematically taught. For example, after children have learned the sound/symbol relationships for *a, s, m, b, t, ee, f, g,* and *I,* they will be invited to read "Sam sees a big fist." This is the nature of decodable text. Consistent with the NICHD findings, many phonics-based approaches advocate the use of decodable text. There is, however, a more moderate stance regarding the use of decodable text.

Heidi Mesmer (1999) points out that even with a dearth of research on decodable text, publishers are producing it and lawmakers are advocating its widespread use. Mesmer suggests that decisions about reading materials are highly complex and are better made by considering which books will work for which readers at which developmental stages—under the guidance of a knowledgeable teacher.

Phonics-based approaches not only advocate the use of decodable text, they also call for highly systematic instruction.

Systematic Instruction. NICHD has identified seven key principles of effective reading instruction based on research done at its centers (Grossen, 2002). The seven key principles of systematic instruction are:

1. Begin teaching phonemic awareness directly at an early age (kindergarten).
2. Teach each sound-spelling correspondence explicitly.
3. Teach frequent, highly regular sound-spelling relationships systematically. There are 40 to 50 sound-spelling relationships necessary to read. Refer to Figure 2.2 for a display of the 48 most regular sound-letter relationships.
4. Show children exactly how to sound out words.
5. Use connected, decodable text for children to practice the sound-spelling relationships they learn.

Figure 2.2
The 48 Most Regular Sound-Letter Relationships

a as in fat	g as in goat	v
m	l	e
t	h	u-e as in use
s	u	p
i as in sit	c as in cat	w "woo" as in well
f	b	j
a-e as in cake	n	i-e as in pipe
d	k	y "yee" as in yuk
r	o-e as in pole	z
ch as in chip	ou as in cloud	kn as in know
ea beat	oy toy	oa boat
ee need	ph phone	oi boil
er fern	qu quick	ai maid
ay hay	sh shop	ar car
igh high	th thank	au haul
ew shrewd	ir first	aw lawn

Source: Grossen, B. (2002). *30 years of research: What we now know about how children learn to read* (p. 10). Washington, DC: National Institutes of Child Health and Human Development. Retrieved from *http://daisy.ym.edu.tw//sijrlee/30years. html*

6. Use interesting stories to develop language comprehension. Because highly controlled, decodable texts cannot provide coherent stories in the early stages of reading acquisition, teachers are urged to read stories to children.
7. Balance, but don't mix. The use of interesting stories to develop comprehension should be balanced with the decoding instruction described in the first five principles. However, while children are learning to decode, both kinds of instruction should be conducted separately from each other.

ISSUES IN LITERACY

SCHOOL BOARD'S INFLUENCE OVER PUBLISHERS

In November 1999 the Texas Board of Education adopted instructional materials for use in first-grade language arts and reading. Prior to this adoption the Commissioner of Education, in response to board members' concerns, offered publishers an opportunity to submit plans to increase the amount of decodable text in the first-grade materials. On November 5, 1999, the board approved the plans submitted by the publishers and adopted the instructional materials with the stipulation that the publishers implement the plans to increase the percentage of decodable text in their first-grade programs. The board required all first-grade reading textbooks designated by the publishers as decodable text for practice of letter-sound correspondences to meet a minimum average of 80% decodability (Nelson, 2000).

Since the states of Texas and California dominate the world of textbook publishing because of their large populations and statewide adoptions of texts, the influence of these boards is dramatic.

How much influence should Boards of Education have over publishers? Go to the Weblinks in Chapter 2 on our Companion Website at www.prenhall.com/harp for links to this report and to add your comments on this question to the Threaded Message Board.

Phonics-Based Approaches in Action. It would be inaccurate to assign a single methodology to all phonics-based approaches. There is considerable variation across published materials. Our purpose here is to give you a sense of the synthetic phonics approach in action. To do this we will draw examples from *The Wilson Reading System,* and ask that you keep in mind that this is just one example. *The Wilson System* was originally designed for use in one-on-one instruction with at-risk readers. However, it has become increasingly popular for use with whole classes of emergent readers.

The Wilson Reading System (2000) is described by its authors as a way to teach students directly and systematically how to decode fluently and accurately. Unlike some phonics programs, Wilson teaches "total word construction" so that students learn to encode (spell) sound/symbol relationships as they learn to decode them. The curriculum consists of 12 steps or sections, each step emphasizing a certain phonic element or generalization. For example, Step 1 focuses on closed syllables with three sounds. Selected initial and final consonant sounds are taught, then some vowel sounds, and then the blending of these sounds. Step 4 focuses on vowel-consonant-E syllables. Mastery must be achieved at each step before the students are moved on to the next step. Wilson lesson plans consist of 10 parts. Parts 1 through 5 place an emphasis on decoding:

1. *Sound Cards for Quick Drill*—students are shown cards with a letter or letter combinations on them. Students orally name the letter or letters and the corresponding sound(s). Key words are used with vowels and as needed with other sounds.
2. *Teach/Review Concepts for Reading*—students are taught to segment sounds using a finger tapping procedure. This part of the lesson stresses phoneme segmentation and blending followed by word structure.
3. *Word Cards*—the skills learned in part 2 of the lesson are applied to reading single words on flashcards.
4. *Wordlist Reading*—this part involves the application of skills to the reading of single words on a controlled wordlist in the Student Reader. Lists are controlled so that only those skills previously taught are applied.
5. *Sentence Reading*—students practice learned skills by reading sentences containing previously learned words.

Parts 6 through 8 of the Wilson lesson plan place an emphasis on encoding.

6. *Quick Drill*—letter formation is taught as needed and every lesson includes a phoneme drill when the teacher says a sound and the student identifies the corresponding letter(s) by locating the letter card, saying the letter name, sound, and key word.
7. *Teach/Review Concepts for Spelling*—here students apply the finger tapping procedure to segment sounds for spelling, and they assemble word cards to spell sound sequences, syllables, and word parts.
8. *Written Work*—here the teacher dictates sounds, words, and sentences; the student repeats the dictation and then writes. A procedure for proofreading is taught here as well.

Parts 9 and 10 of the Wilson lesson plan emphasizes reading comprehension.

9. *Passage Reading*—a student silently reads a short passage with a controlled vocabulary, retells the passage, and then reads the passage aloud.
10. *Listening Comprehension*—here the teacher reads a noncontrolled vocabulary text to the student. The student is asked to visualize the text and retell. The visualization and retelling are done to develop comprehension skills at a level higher than the student's current decoding level. The teacher selects trade books or other grade level texts, or the student chooses the material.

What Constitutes Sound Phonics Instruction? Stahl, Duffy-Hester, and Stahl (1998) reviewed years of research on phonics instruction and concluded that "research (and common sense) suggest the following principles of good phonics instruction" (p. 339). You may find these principles helpful as you wend your way through the controversial field of phonics instruction.

- Good phonics instruction should develop the alphabetic principle. Children must learn that letters can represent sounds.
- Good phonics instruction should develop phonological awareness. Phonological awareness is the awareness of sounds in spoken words.
- Good phonics instruction should provide a thorough grounding in the letters. Efficient word recognition is dependent on children's thorough familiarity with letters.
- Good phonics instruction should not teach rules, need not use worksheets, should not dominate instruction, and does not have to be boring.

- Good phonics instruction provides sufficient practice in reading words—in isolation, in stories, and in writing words.
- Good phonics instruction leads to automatic word recognition.
- Good phonics instruction is one part of reading instruction.

Sight-Based Approaches to the Teaching of Reading

Advocates of sight-based approaches subscribe to a top-down view of reading instruction. Sight-based approaches, also known as whole-word approaches, are designed to teach reading by systematically building an increasingly large body of words children can decode instantly. Sight words are words that are immediately recognized as a whole and do not require word analysis for identification. As an adult, almost all of the words you meet in reading material are sight words. You can decode them without having to stop and think about them.

The Philosophy of Sight-Based Approaches. Advocates of sight-based approaches maintain that there is far too much inconsistency in the sound/symbol patterns of our language for instruction in phonics to be effective and that readers need to develop a large sight vocabulary. No matter how much phonics children are taught, some words will have to be learned by sight because they cannot be sounded out. "The" is an example of such a word. They argue that we learn to read increasingly more difficult texts by learning an increasingly large body of sight words. In typical sight-based programs, phonics instruction, if included at all, is not introduced until students have learned a large body of sight words. Chall (1989) discovered that children who were taught using sight-based approaches demonstrated an early advantage in reading rate and comprehension of silent reading and to some extent in interest, fluency, and oral reading expression. However, as would be expected, these children did not develop word attack skills as did those children taught in phonics-based approaches.

Sight-Based Approaches in Action. The instructional goal in sight-based approaches is to build an increasingly large sight vocabulary. The idea is to give children texts that are composed of words in the children's sight vocabulary with only a few challenging words. The challenging words are then presented for study on flash cards placed in pocket charts, on the chalkboard, or on chart paper before the text is read, and then reinforced during the reading of the text. Typically the challenging words are revisited after the text is read.

Many teachers use predictable or patterned texts to teach and reinforce sight vocabulary. Bridge, Winograd, and Haley (1983) published a procedure for using predictable books to build sight vocabulary. The procedure, adapted here, consists of three lessons.

Lesson One: Select a text to read that has vocabulary you want to introduce. Perhaps you will use a big book (enlarged text version of the story) so the children can easily see to follow along with you. Read the book aloud to the group. Read the book aloud a second time, and invite the children to join with you when they can predict what comes next. The children might read the text chorally or take turns reading parts of the book. After the children have read the text several times, cover up the illustrations or copy the text onto chart paper so that they have to attend to the words.

Lesson Two: You and the students read the text from the chart or from the big book with the illustrations covered up. Give the students sentence strips with lines from the story. Have the children place the sentence strips under the corresponding line in the text. Give the children individual word cards they can then place under the corresponding words on the chart.

Lesson Three: Place individual word cards from sections of the story in random order at the bottom of the chart or big book with the illustrations covered. Have students read the whole story aloud together. Have the students match the word cards to the words in the text. Many basal readers were based on sight reading approaches, and others were more focused on phonics approaches. Modern basals usually have an eclectic mix of approaches.

Integrated Anthology Approach

Go to the Weblinks in Chapter 2 on our Companion Website at www.prenhall.com/harp for links to various publishers of basal readers.

Basal readers are sequentially graded sets of pupil texts, teacher's guides, workbooks, and supplementary materials. For many years basals have been the most popular approach to the teaching of reading. They have been in use in U.S. schools since McGuffey wrote the first one in 1836. Estimates at one time suggested that 95 percent of school children in the United States learned to read using basal readers (Langer, Applebee, Mullis, & Foertsch, 1990).

With the push to use more children's literature in the teaching of reading, the design and intent of basal readers has changed. For many years, basal readers were designed only for reading instruction, and many of the stories were written to introduce or reinforce selected words, skills, or moral values. In recent years two significant changes have occurred. The reading selections in the basals have been chosen from previously published children's literature, and the instructional focus has broadened to include reading, writing, spelling, grammar, and even handwriting. These new basals are now called *integrated anthologies* because they integrate the teaching of the language arts in the form of anthologies of children's literature.

McCarthey and Hoffman (1995) compared older basal materials with newer basal materials at the first-grade level. Many of the changes they found in the "newer" (1993) basals still hold true today. They found that the newer basals contained fewer words but substantially more unique words than the old. Vocabulary control has been reduced or abandoned in newer basals. Newer basals were more diverse in terms of format, organization, and genres of literature. New basals contained selections with more complex plots and more highly developed characters, and they required more interpretation on the part of the reader. Decoding demands placed on the reader by the new series were much greater than the older basals.

The Philosophy of Integrated Anthologies. Contemporary anthologies are designed differently from the more traditional basals. Figure 2.3 illustrates the significant differences between these two sets of instructional materials.

You can see how today's anthologies differ from the basal readers of the past. However, not all anthologies are alike. The authors of anthology series bring widely differing philosophies about literacy instruction to their task. Some reading series are written by persons holding a strong bottom-up view of reading, some are written by persons holding an equally strong top-down view, and yet others are written by persons who subscribe to a balance between these views. One publisher might offer an anthology with highly decodable text in the kindergarten and first-grade materials, where another publisher might offer original children's literature at these levels of instruction. In the teacher's guide to anthologies you will find a statement describing the philosophy of the authors of the series. You will want to apply your best critical reading skills to these selections to discern the orientation of the authors to reading instruction, and then you will want to examine the instructional activities carefully to see if the stated philosophy is reflected in the recommended instruction.

Figure 2.3
Comparison of Traditional Basal and Today's Anthology

Basal	Anthology
Material written for the beginning levels with a highly controlled vocabulary	Uses children's literature in largely unabridged formats
Focused primarily on teaching reading	Integrates the teaching of reading and other language arts
Offers pupil texts, teacher's guides, workbooks, assessment and evaluation tools	Offers pupil texts, teacher's guides, workbooks, assessment and evaluation tools, classroom libraries of multiple copies of titles, little books that can be photocopied for children to take home
Balances code emphasis and meaning emphasis with attention to skills	Balances code emphasis and meaning emphasis with attention to skills and strategies
Assumption was that teachers would place children in static ability groups	Assumption is that teachers place children in different groups at different levels chosen from approximately 20 levels ranging from kindergarten to eighth grade
Focus on a set of subskills that would lead to reading	Incorporates all of the language arts, viewing reading and writing as processes
Ancillary materials included word cards and pocket charts	Ancillary materials include word cards, pocket charts, videotapes, audiotapes, computer software, management system

Integrated Anthologies in Action. In exploring the nature of an integrated anthology designed for use in fourth grade, we will refer to the Multimedia Teacher's Edition for Grade 4, Volume One of Scott Foresman's *Reading: Seeing Is Believing.* Basal reading programs are usually referred to by the name of the publisher rather than the title of the text, so this would be referred to as "the Scott Foresman basal" or "the Scott Foresman anthology."

In the "Read Me First" section you would notice that the teacher's manual is organized around four classroom routines: Instructional Routines, Environment Routines, Student Routines, and School/Home Routines. The suggested activities in each routine are designed to help the teacher answer four questions:

1. How do I teach all the reading skills and strategies I am accountable for and for which I have the research to validate my instructional methods?
2. How do I create a learning environment that maximizes learning and minimizes interruption throughout each day?
3. How do I involve the other students with meaningful activities when I am working with a small group?
4. How do I involve the family to reinforce the skills and strategies I am teaching in my classroom?

Figure 2.4 presents the 5-Day Planner for the first week of an integrated theme, Focus on Family. Examine it carefully to see the kind of planning support offered to the teacher who uses this guide and to identify the curricular areas that are integrated throughout the week.

5-Day Planner

Part 1 Prepare and Read
Part 2 Guide Comprehension
Part 3 Practice, Apply & Extend

Customize your week with the Teacher's Resource Planner CD-ROM!

Daily Instruction	Day 1	Day 2
Reading **Comprehension** **Vocabulary**	**Reading, pp. 20–22b** ✓ **Comprehension:** Setting • Read "The Red Fox" Activate Prior Knowledge • Assess Prior Knowledge Introduce Vocabulary biscuits, rumpled, dough, teasing, prairie, wrinkled, raisins Build Vocabulary: Classify Words	**Reading, pp. 22–31** ✓ **Vocabulary:** Context Clues • Unfamiliar Words Reading Strategies • Preview and Predict • Set Purposes Read "A Visit with Grandpa" ✓ **Comprehension:** Setting Reading Strategies • Self-Question/Fix-Up • Predict
Word Study **Phonics** **Spelling**	**Word Study, p. 43h** **Spelling:** Vowel Sounds in *few, moon* • Pretest	**Word Study, pp. 27, 43h** **Phonics:** Vowel Digraphs **Spelling:** Vowel Sounds in *few, moon* • Think and Practice
Oral Language **Speaking** **Listening** **Viewing**	**Oral Language, pp. 21, 22a** Skill Lesson: Talk About It Activate Prior Knowledge • Build Background	
Writing **Grammar, Usage, and Mechanics**	**Writing/Grammar, pp. 22a, 43e** **Writing** • Build Background ✓ **Grammar:** Recognize and Write Statements	**Writing/Grammar, pp. 22, 23, 43e** **Writing** • Vocabulary: Write About It • Response Log ✓ **Grammar:** Recognize and Write Questions
Self-Selected Reading **Read Aloud**	**Self-Selected Reading and Read Aloud, p. 20b** Set up an Independent Reading Work Station. D.E.A.R. Drop Everything And Read	**Self-Selected Reading and Read Aloud, p. 26** Have children select books about taking responsibility for one's actions to read independently. D.E.A.R. Drop Everything And Read

Figure 2.4
Five-Day Planner
Source: Scott Foresman. *Seeing Is Believing,* Multimedia Teacher's Edition, Volume One, Grade Four. Copyright © 2000 by Pearson Education. Reprinted by permission of Pearson Education, Inc.

Target Skill of the Week:
Setting

Objectives of the Week:
Students will

- understand that setting is the time and place in which a story occurs
- use context clues to find meanings of unfamiliar words
- identify words with vowel digraphs
- write an e-mail message

Day 3

Reading, pp. 33–40
Read "A Visit with Grandpa"
Read About the Author: Mildred Pitts Walter
Comprehension:
✓ REVIEW • Sequence
Literary Devices: Jargon
✓ **Vocabulary:** Unfamiliar Words
Reading Strategies
- Self-Question/Fix-Up
- Check Predictions

Reader Response
- Comprehension Check

Word Study, p. 43h
Spelling: Vowel Sounds in *few, moon*
- Proofread and Write

Oral Language, p. 40
Reader Response
- Open for Discussion

Writing/Grammar, pp. 43c, 43e
Writing: E-mail Message
- Prewrite
- Prewriting Strategy: Determine Audience and Purpose
- Draft

✓ **Grammar:** Incomplete Statements and Questions

Self-Selected Reading and Read Aloud, p. 34
Choose a contemporary story about learning a lesson to read aloud.

Day 4

Reading, pp. 41–43
Selection Test (Practice Book, pp. 5–6)
Vocabulary: Content Area Words
herds Southwest
pasture cattle
Reading Strategies: Social Studies Textbook
- Preview and Predict
- Set Purposes

Read "Ranching and the Cowboys"
Critical Thinking: Reading Across Texts
- Connect Ideas and Themes

Word Study, pp. 43g–43h
Phonics
- Vowel Digraphs

REVIEW • CVCe and VCCV Patterns
Spelling: Vowel Sounds in *few, moon*
- Review

Oral Language, p. 40
Reader Response
- Picture It

Writing/Grammar, pp. 43c, 43f
Writing: E-mail Message
- Revise
- Edit

✓ **Grammar:** Teach Sentences

Self-Selected Reading and Read Aloud, p. 20b
Students select a story from the Independent Reading Work Station to practice reading aloud for fluency.

Day 5

Reading, pp. 43a–43b, 43d, 43i–43j
Comprehension
✓ • Setting
✓ REVIEW • Sequence
Improve Fluency: Read with Expression
Literary Devices: Jargon
✓ Research Skills: Textbook/Trade Book

Word Study, p. 43h
Spelling: Vowel Sounds in *few, moon*
- Posttest

Oral Language, p. 43d
Speaking: The Purpose of Speaking

Writing/Grammar, pp. 43c, 43f
Writing: E-mail Message
- Publish

✓ **Grammar:** Review Simple Sentences

Self-Selected Reading and Read Aloud, pp. 362–363
Students select a story from the Theme Bibliography.

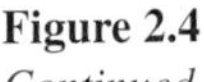

Figure 2.4
Continued

ISSUES IN LITERACY

USING THE REQUIRED BASAL

If you teach in some schools, you will be required to use a basal that has been selected by the school system. Some schools choose such a program because they believe it gives children who move from school to school familiar, consistent instruction. Others choose such a system because they believe it serves as guidance for inexperienced teachers. Others may feel such a system will guarantee that every child gets quality instruction. How can an informed teacher of reading make the best use of the basal prescribed? What kinds of instructional decisions will you have to make in order to use a basal effectively?

Visit the Companion Website to research this issue more thoroughly and record your thoughts about this topic on the threaded message board.

The Language Experience Approach (LEA)

Go to the Weblinks in Chapter 2 on our Companion Website at www.prenhall.com/harp for links to sites that focus on language experience as an approach to reading instruction.

The language experience approach was created in the 1960s in reaction to the traditional basal readers. Basals at that time had highly controlled vocabularies that sounded nothing like real language and communicated little meaning. The Dick and Jane series, for example, became famous for language like "See Spot. See Spot run. Look. Look. Look. See Spot." Supporters of the language experience approach, subscribing to a top-down view of reading, believed that the best materials for reading instruction were texts that children had composed themselves. Roach Van Allen (1976) was one of the best known proponents of LEA. Russell Stauffer organized a Special Interest Group in Language Experience as part of the International Reading Association, which continues to be an active group.

The Philosophy of the Language Experience Approach. Advocates of LEA believe that everything children read in beginning reading instruction should be as meaningful and relevant to the children as possible. They argue that the most meaningful language to a child is that child's own language. The language experience approach to reading brings together the child's experiences and the child's expressions about experiences through the processes of speaking, reading, and writing.

At the beginning stages children dictate their comments/reactions to a stimulus to the teacher or another scribe. They then learn to read this text. LEA advocates believe the connection between experience and language is the greatest advantage of using the language experience approach. The belief is that when children dictate and/or write their own reading material, the materials for reading instruction are always relevant, current, and meaningful. As children's abilities develop, they move from dictating ideas to the teacher to writing them themselves.

The core philosophy of LEA is rooted in the notion that

> learning is based on the background and experience of the learner and that his efforts to communicate that experience may take many forms. For communication it is the recognition that each student brings to school a unique language personality. Teachers strive to preserve this language personality at the same time that certain common understandings about how other people communicate effectively are habituated. (Allen, 1976, p. 3)

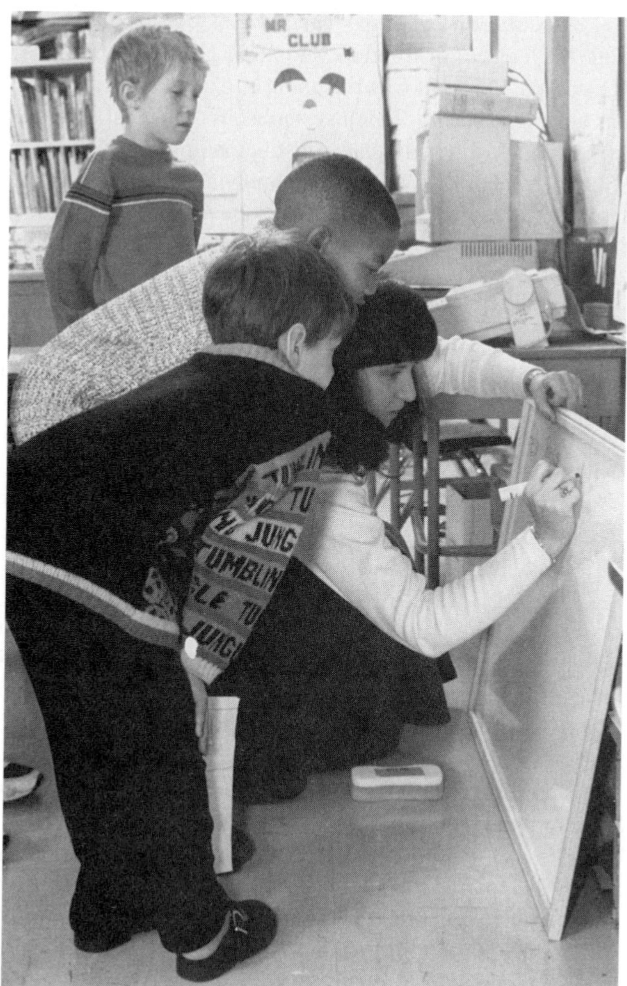

In the language experience approach, teachers often scribe children's stories for them.

Because each child has experiences and interests, and writing is often based on everyday classroom activities, language experience classrooms are very busy places.

The Language Experience Approach in Action. While the language experience approach to reading instruction is not highly prescribed, most advocates use some basic steps. Understanding these steps will help you visualize the approach in action. However, LEA is a child-centered approach. True language experience advocates would always let the needs of learners dictate instruction rather than adhering to a prescribed set of steps. LEA is about making professional decisions concerning reading instruction and being accountable for those decisions. These are the basic steps in language experience for young children:

1. selection of purpose for instruction
2. presentation of stimuli
3. discussion
4. dictation or writing
5. reading
6. skills instruction as needed
7. extension to the work of other authors

Selection of Purpose. The first step in language experience instruction is to determine the focus of instruction. Suppose a child has brought a frog to school, and the children are excited and want to write about it. You would consider the age, experience, and previous writing of the children in establishing the most important goals of this specific writing experience. If the children are just beginning to read and write, you might want to emphasize the /fr/ blend. If they are beginning independent readers, you might want to concentrate on the sight words they recognize. If they have a little more experience, you might focus on the different structures of reports about frogs and toads, narratives about frogs, and personal observations about frogs. The purpose for instruction serves as a guide in determining how the other steps are implemented.

Presentation of Stimuli. Finding something for children to dictate or to write about should not be a problem when you have created a classroom in which interesting things are happening. In a classroom where animals, visitors, and activities are evolving out of both your own and the children's interests, the stimuli for language experience are just daily activities. In response to the children's interest in frogs and toads, you might find books and poems about frogs. You might bring tadpoles into the classroom for the children to watch, talk about, write about, and read about. The tadpoles, frogs, and books about toads and frogs all become the stimuli for writing.

Discussion. After a common experience, you will want to engage the children in discussing it, so the group has a common direction. Usually the discussion is short, sometimes to help the children focus on the experience, sometimes to share ideas about format or audience for their writing, sometimes to explore pertinent words. If, in the class with the new frog, you wanted to focus on the structure of reports about frogs, the discussion would include reminders about the scope, content, and presentation of reports.

Dictation or Writing. The choice of taking dictation from the students or asking them to write independently depends on the goals of instruction and/or the age and ability of the students. Dictation would be preferred if the goal were to help younger children record their words quickly so instruction could focus on learning to recognize given words on sight. Dictation might also be the choice if you wanted to help the children create a group story or to assist a child whose motor disabilities made writing a struggle.

Taking dictation for a specific purpose does not mean children cannot do their own writing on the same topic. After you had taken dictation about the tadpoles and frogs, for example, the children could be encouraged to do their own writing related to their art experiences or to the experience of preparing the terrarium for the frog habitat. The main use of dictation should be to record group responses rather than individual responses.

When you take dictation, you have an obligation to record children's words as they are dictated. If the child's language forms are not standard English constructions, you may help the child (over a period of time) think about alternate ways of expressing a thought in more standard English. If the point of taking dictation is to help children see that thoughts can be recorded in print and that print can serve as a way of storing those thoughts for later reading, then the words must be exact. The words of a child who speaks a dialect should be spelled in conventional spelling. However, when the child reads the passage aloud, you must expect dialectal pronunciation. Making changes in the children's words gives children the message that their words are not good enough and they cannot communicate successfully. This is not to say that you should not help children move toward competence in standard English; but for a beginning reader, it is important to remember the purpose of taking dictation, which is to let children see their own ideas in print. Figure 2.5 is the language experience chart the teacher wrote when kindergarten children dictated their ideas about frogs.

Reading. In the language experience approach, both oral reading by you and choral reading with the children are important. Assume you have taken the dictation from a group

Figure 2.5
Language Experience Chart About Frogs

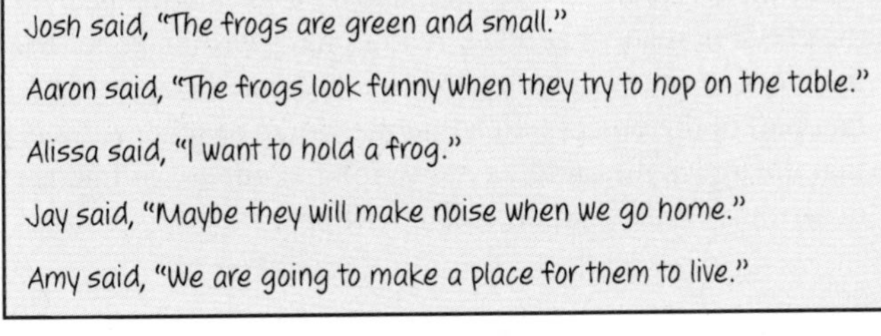
Josh said, "The frogs are green and small."

Aaron said, "The frogs look funny when they try to hop on the table."

Alissa said, "I want to hold a frog."

Jay said, "Maybe they will make noise when we go home."

Amy said, "We are going to make a place for them to live."

of emergent readers displayed in the language experience chart in Figure 2.5. Here are some typical reading activities you might do with the children using that chart.

- First you read the chart aloud to them.
- Then you ask the children to read aloud with you as you move your hand or a pointer under the words.
- Ask for volunteers to read parts of the chart aloud. The reason for including the children's names in the charts of beginning readers is to assist individual children in locating their contribution to the chart. They are more likely to be able to read their names than any other words.
- End the activity by inviting the group to read the whole chart aloud with you again.

The next day:

- Read the whole chart with the group.
- Invite children to volunteer to take sentence strips you made after school yesterday and match them to the lines of the chart.
- Ask for volunteers to match individual word cards to words on the chart.

The next day:

- Distribute photocopies of the text from the chart for children to read individually.
- When you are confident that words from the chart are in a child's sight vocabulary, write the words on individual cards to put in the child's own Word Bank. A Word Bank is a private collection of words that are in the child's sight vocabulary.

In addition to these illustrations of language experience reading, you would read aloud to your students frequently. Read-aloud sessions would include reading the children's work and reading narrative or information books related to the topic. Having the children listen to you read and reading aloud with you aids the development of fluent, efficient reading.

Skills Instruction as Necessary. Skills instruction in language experience is a natural outgrowth of the reading, not an overlay. You carefully observe the children as they work with the chart, and you carefully make decisions about which skills to teach and/or reinforce. Skills might be as simple as letter-sound relationships or directionality of print or as complex as examining the development of fictional characters or analyzing the language used to achieve a particular mood. In between these extremes, instruction can focus on phonics, sight words, clarity, coherence of text, and story structure. Instruction can also focus on the mechanics of writing, such as capitalization, punctuation, and paragraphing. Revisit the children's dictation in Figure 2.5 and consider the possibilities for skill instruction that are apparent in that chart. Remember, the key here is to take your lead from what you observe the children doing.

Extension to the Work of Other Authors. The final step in LEA is to extend the study of the topics the children are reading and writing about to the work of other authors.

After the children have written about frogs and toads, then you would read aloud or have the children read what other authors have written about frogs and toads. This extension to the work of other authors is often a neglected step in the LEA process, but it is an important part of the process. Reading the works of other authors provides the chance to observe that the topics the children are writing about are of interest to others and provides models of writing for use in their future writing.

Literature-Based Approach

Go to the Weblinks in Chapter 2 on our Companion Website at www.prenhall.com/harp for links to sites that focus on literature-based instruction.

The literature-based approach to reading instruction is defined as teaching children to read using pieces of literature, both fiction and nonfiction, which were written for purposes other than use as a text for reading instruction. If you walked into your local bookstore, almost all the books in the children's section would have been written to inform or entertain young readers. Authors of children's books would rarely consider writing a book that was a "second grade" book or a book that featured certain spelling patterns; they simply want to tell a good story as well as they can. Some recent publications are not written as simply good stories as publishers have found a lucrative market in publishing books that fit certain criteria of difficulty. Several well-known children's authors have contributed books that follow the guidelines for easy-to-read books. Generally speaking, most authors of children's literature do not consider guidelines for reading difficulty as they write a story. However, all effective writers consider their audience. When an author sits down to write a story, he may be thinking that it would be a story that very young children would probably like or a story that young adults would appreciate. His focus is on the interests of his audience and the development of the story, not on a grade level.

The Philosophy of the Literature-Based Approach. Advocates of the literature-based approach take a top-down view of reading instruction. Literature-based reading instruction is marked by the following characteristics and beliefs:

- Materials for instruction are whole pieces of real literature.
- Instruction in strategies and skills is provided in the context of real reading.
- Instruction in strategies and skills is provided on an as-needed basis.
- There are no comprehension worksheets or prereading vocabulary study exercises.
- Children are encouraged to discuss various interpretations of their reading with adults and peers.
- Children have choices in their reading material.
- The focus is on understanding what is read, or constructing meaning.
- Instruction includes literary elements and exploration of various genres.
- Readers and writers make connections with real life.
- The literature for reading includes material from a broad range of cultures and ethnic groups.
- Teachers believe that knowledge must be constructed by the learners.
- Assessment is an integral component of instruction and drives instruction.

The Literature-Based Approach in Action. Literature-based reading does not imply that the teacher simply arranges for books and time for reading them. It does mean that the teacher is responsible for instruction in literacy (Strickland & Morrow, 1989). A literature-based reading program requires knowledge of children's literature, organizational skills, assessment skills, and the ability to differentiate instruction to meet the needs of each of your learners. In other words, an effective teacher of a literature-based program must be highly skilled. Literature-based instruction typically includes the use of readers' workshop and

ISSUES IN LITERACY

BASALIZATION OF CHILDREN'S LITERATURE

Some teachers create or buy worksheets to accompany pieces of children's literature. They might include pre-reading and post-reading exercises such as vocabulary introduction activities and comprehension questions. Some have charged that this is the "basalization" of children's literature. Are such activities at odds with the philosophy of the literature-based approach?

Visit the Companion Website to research this issue more thoroughly and record your thoughts about this topic on the threaded message board.

writers' workshop. These are large blocks of instructional time focused on reading and writing. These workshop formats will be discussed in detail in later chapters.

There are many ways to engage children with literature. Some teachers use individualized reading, some use literature circles, and some study novels as a class. Here individualized reading is described as an example of literature based instruction in the section that follows. Literature circles and class novels will be described in later chapters, but all have the same basic philosophy. Jeanette Veatch (1954) argued for individualized reading as an approach to instruction:

> Free-choice reading (or, as we shall call it, individualized reading) can change children's attitudes toward reading; ease the problem of dealing with a great range of reading abilities in one classroom; take the drudgery out of the reading period; challenge the brilliant child without discouraging the slow child; increase the number of books read; and most of all, make school happier for everybody concerned. (p. 28)

Individualized Reading. Over the years teachers have supported individualized reading because they see it as the answer to problems with text difficulty, lack of interest, and inappropriate skill instruction that are frequently cited problems with other approaches to reading.

Individualized reading is defined as reading instruction that is organized so that each child is reading a book of his or her choice and all instruction is provided individually or in small groups.

Go to the Weblinks in Chapter 2 on our Companion Website at www.prenhall.com/harp for links to sites devoted to individualized reading instruction.

Individualized reading instruction does not mean that group activities are impossible, nor does it mean that group instruction never takes place. As individual children are reading, you will find that there are times when several children are facing the same needs for instruction. Specific instruction can be planned for this small group. At other times, you may want all readers to participate in some activity even though they are all reading different texts. For example, you might choose to have each child produce a book report that can be presented to the class on video or in a Power Point presentation. Another time you might require that each child present a book talk aimed at convincing his classmates to read a book.

Steps in Individualized Reading. A plan for individualized reading requires that each child chooses a book to read. Even choosing a book will require some instruction on how to choose a book and what a reader looks for to make a good selection. After a book is selected, the child reads it generally at his or her own pace, but children are usually required to spend a given amount of time reading each day. That might be 25-30 minutes for younger readers and 45 minutes for older readers. As the children are engaged in reading, you will arrange for conferences with each child. At about 5-10 minutes per conference, you can usually do six to eight conferences each day. That means that in a class of 28 children, each child would get an individual conference about twice a week. Individualizing instruction requires that you keep excellent records of the books the child is reading, the conferences, the instruction offered and reinforced, and the next reading goals for every child.

Skill or Strategy Instruction. Groups can be arranged for skill or strategy instruction, for those who are reading on similar topics, or for those who want to talk about their books with a friend. These groups are fluid and dynamic, not static. Children will be expected to keep a record of their own reading, usually in the form of a response journal about their reading, and to record their evaluation of their growth as a reader.

You and the children will plan together additional activities that will be meaningful to the children as readers. For example, two children are reading historical fiction about the American Revolution—one from the loyalist point of view and one from the patriot point of view. Several choices would be worthwhile as follow-ups to the reading. The two readers might choose to debate their stands on the issues of the war, or they might do additional research and read from original sources as much as possible about people who took a stand for one side or the other. They might read other works by the same authors. They might switch books and plan to discuss them on a regular basis, or they might choose another piece of historical fiction set in the same period to read and compare it to their original book. Or they could simply start on another topic.

Monitoring Individualized Reading. Teachers who monitor individualized reading programs must have some system for knowing where each child is working at the beginning of the reading period. First, if a child is finishing a book, she might need a conference before choosing what to do next. In addition, if a child is not making progress, then the teacher must know immediately. A child will not be allowed to "read" the same three chapters every day. Some teachers call this a status report and keep a simple chart on a clipboard where they can record quickly the status of each child at the beginning of every work period.

You will want your conference time with each child to be as productive as possible. Toward that end we offer two checklists to help children prepare for a conference with you and to guide your conference activities. They are displayed in Figure 2.6.

Individualized reading will be discussed in more detail as one of the options when organizing classroom literature instruction in Chapter 11.

Whole Language

Go to the Weblinks in Chapter 2 on our Companion Website at www.prenhall.com/harp for links to sites dealing with whole language.

Most whole language teachers use high quality children's literature as the primary instructional materials for reading. However, whole language is more than a literature-based approach to the teaching of reading. Whole language is a philosophy about teaching and learning that is child-centered and embraces using good children's literature. It emphasizes teaching skills in the context of real reading and writing activities, integrating curriculum and instruction, and teaching skills when children need them (Goodman, 1986; Smith, 1978). However, whole language came to be misunderstood or inappropriately applied by some teachers. An array of myths grew round the whole language movement. One such myth was that whole language teachers do not teach skills such as phonics. Another myth was that if you filled a room full of children and wonderful books, the children would learn to read—without the teacher teaching.

As the mythology surrounding whole language grew, the philosophy also became the scapegoat for some serious problems. For example, when the reading performance scores of California fourth graders plunged on the National Assessment of Educational Progress (NAEP), many people blamed whole language approaches. In fact, a literature-based approach, not whole language, had been dictated for use by California teachers without the

Figure 2.6
Reading Conference Checklists

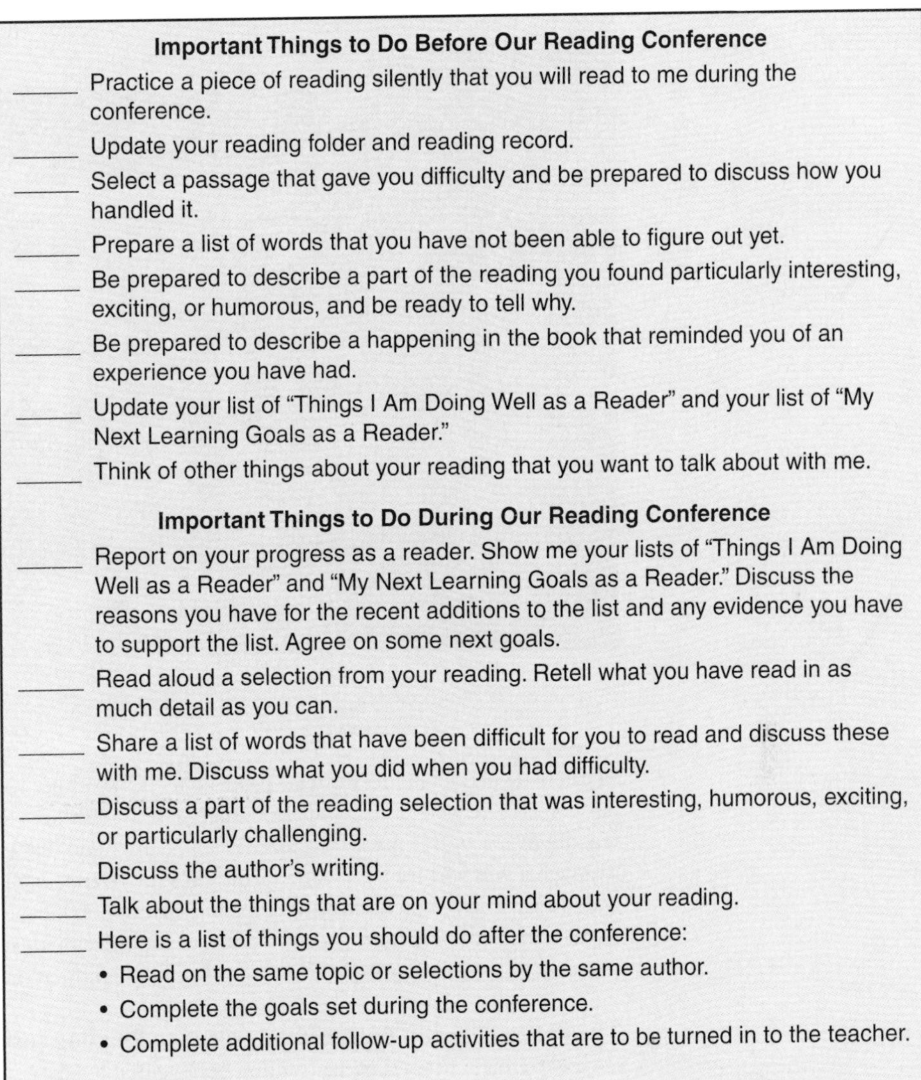

Important Things to Do Before Our Reading Conference

_____ Practice a piece of reading silently that you will read to me during the conference.
_____ Update your reading folder and reading record.
_____ Select a passage that gave you difficulty and be prepared to discuss how you handled it.
_____ Prepare a list of words that you have not been able to figure out yet.
_____ Be prepared to describe a part of the reading you found particularly interesting, exciting, or humorous, and be ready to tell why.
_____ Be prepared to describe a happening in the book that reminded you of an experience you have had.
_____ Update your list of "Things I Am Doing Well as a Reader" and your list of "My Next Learning Goals as a Reader."
_____ Think of other things about your reading that you want to talk about with me.

Important Things to Do During Our Reading Conference

_____ Report on your progress as a reader. Show me your lists of "Things I Am Doing Well as a Reader" and "My Next Learning Goals as a Reader." Discuss the reasons you have for the recent additions to the list and any evidence you have to support the list. Agree on some next goals.
_____ Read aloud a selection from your reading. Retell what you have read in as much detail as you can.
_____ Share a list of words that have been difficult for you to read and discuss these with me. Discuss what you did when you had difficulty.
_____ Discuss a part of the reading selection that was interesting, humorous, exciting, or particularly challenging.
_____ Discuss the author's writing.
_____ Talk about the things that are on your mind about your reading.
_____ Here is a list of things you should do after the conference:
- Read on the same topic or selections by the same author.
- Complete the goals set during the conference.
- Complete additional follow-up activities that are to be turned in to the teacher.

Source: Harp, B. (2000). *The Handbook of Literacy Assessment and Evaluation.* Reprinted with permission of Christopher-Gordon Publishers, Inc.

benefit of adequate training, combined with large class sizes and large numbers of children for whom English is not their first language.

Krashen (1995) and McQuillan (1998) found that among the best predictors of the NAEP performance was the number of books per student in the school library. California, at the time, was spending much less than the rest of the country on school libraries and had far too few librarians per pupil (Krashen, 1999). Many factors contributed to the low performance of California children, yet whole language was blamed.

Conservative segments of the nation's parent population took up the fight against whole language and in favor of "a return to the basics." Because of the myth that whole language teachers do not teach phonics, many parents and politicians began pushing for increased phonics instruction in schools. In California and other states, the legislators have mandated such instruction. The controversy surrounding whole language gave rise to a movement to bring balance into the nation's reading instruction.

Word study is part of a balanced approach to literacy.

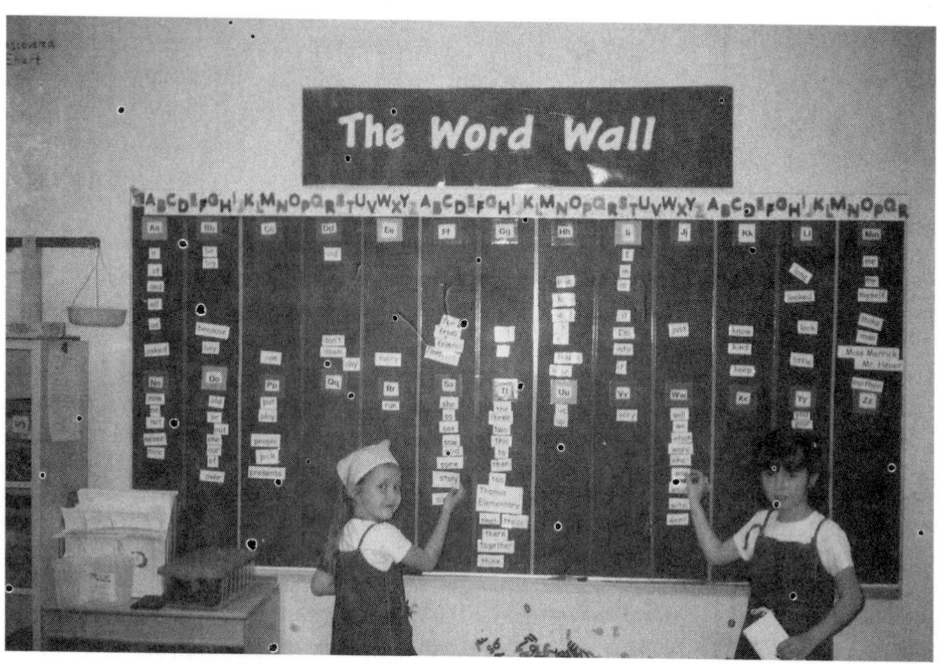

A Balanced Approach to Literacy Instruction

The debates about reading from the proponents of the different approaches have resulted in what has come to be known as a balanced approach. As teachers and parents began to realize that reading instruction is not a "one size fits all" matter and that teachers have always been trying to do what was best for their learners, the calls for balance in reading instruction became louder and louder. The notion of balance in reading instruction means that a reading program strikes a balance in instruction between word study, engaging with meaningful texts and literature study, instruction in reading skills and strategies, and thoughtful, communicative writing instruction.

The Philosophy of a Balanced Approach to Reading Instruction. Advocates of a balanced approach to reading instruction believe that teachers must engage in careful decision making to bring balance:

Go to the Weblinks in Chapter 2 on our Companion Website at www.prenhall.com/harp for links to sites that provide information about balanced literacy instruction.

- between phonics instruction and comprehension instruction
- between systematic skill instruction and systematic strategy instruction
- between taking the reading process apart to teach components and keeping the process whole to celebrate reading and literature
- between engaging children with texts to teach skills and strategies and engaging children with texts to develop appreciation and enthusiasm for reading
- between teacher-directed explicit instruction and child-centered discovery learning, and between whole to part and part to whole instruction that ends with engagement with meaningful whole texts
- between textual diets (some children want to read only nonfiction, while others want a steady diet of fiction)
- between curriculum goals that may be in conflict such as those dictating or legislating the use of certain instructional materials (isolated phonics instruction or decodable text, for example) with much more holistic goals such as experiencing a wide range of genres

Fitzgerald (1999) points out at least three common characteristics of balanced approaches to reading instruction. First is a focus on equal weighting of something (as described previously). Second, the focus is on the method of doing the classroom program, particularly on the teacher's work in planning, setting up, and conducting the program. Third, there is generally a shared perspective on what aspects of the reading process are most important—the kinds of reading knowledge children should attain from the methods the authors of the program advocate.

Advocates of a balanced approach also embrace integration of the language arts: reading, writing, speaking, listening, and viewing. They further embrace integration of subjects across the curriculum. For example, in a balanced approach you might be meeting objectives of the mathematics curriculum at the same time you are meeting objectives in the writing curriculum. In a balanced approach children are being exposed to great literature in a classroom that is well managed and well organized where individual learning needs of children are being met. Further, in a balanced approach you use assessment data and knowledge about the learners' culture, values, and strengths to design instruction. A balanced approach to reading instruction may best be defined by what it is that effective teachers do.

Pressley (2002) builds a case for understanding that when researchers observe the work of effective teachers in early literacy classrooms, there is a match between what these teachers do and what defines a balanced approach.

The Balanced Approach in Action. A balanced approach to reading requires a balance of whole language and skills instruction. Of this balance, Pressley (2002) says,

> This balance seems more defensible than instruction that is only immersion in reading and writing, on the one hand, or predominately skills driven, on the other. . . . Good reading involves the learning and use of word recognition and comprehension strategies, the effectiveness of strategies use depending, in part, on the reader's prior knowledge about the world, including knowledge built up through reading. (p. 333)

If you elect to take a balanced approach to reading instruction, you will find your days filled with the necessity of making decisions. Dixie Lee Spiegel (1999) has helped teachers understand the criteria to use in striking a balance in some of the critical decisions you must make in implementing a balanced approach. These decisions are teacher-directed explicit instruction versus learner-directed discovery, isolated skill emphases versus use only of whole texts, and standardized norm-referenced assessment versus authentic forms of assessment.

In finding the balance between teacher-directed explicit instruction and learner-directed discovery, consider the following.

Looking at the Learner. Move more toward teacher-directed instruction if:

- the child has tended to fall behind peers without teacher direction
- the child runs the risk of a cumulative deficit because he never quite learns what the others do
- the joy of self-directed discovery is tarnished by loss of confidence and interest because the child "never quite gets it" on her own

Move more toward learner-directed instruction if:

- the child has been able to induce learning strategies primarily through her own explorations of literacy
- the child will be held back by having to listen to suggestions for accomplishing a task he already knows how to do
- the child's interest will flag by having to listen to the "how" when the child wants to get on with the doing

Looking at the Task. Move more toward teacher-directed explicit instruction if:

- most readers need to know this strategy or concept
- the ability to use a particular strategy is needed now

Move more toward learner-directed instruction if:

- the concept or strategy is easily learned through exploration
- the concept does not provide a foundation for other concepts, and therefore doesn't need to be learned at a particular time
- children are not engaged in the curriculum
- children are not taking responsibility for their own learning

In Finding a Balance Between Isolated Skill Emphases and Use Only of Whole Texts. Move more toward a strategy focus if:

- the child cannot move around roadblocks met when interacting with the whole text
- the child has only one way of moving around a roadblock
- the child needs to focus on the strategy long enough to learn it

Move more toward a holistic focus if:

- the child is practicing the strategy only with artificial texts
- the child cannot transfer the strategy to authentic, whole texts
- the child cannot use the strategy spontaneously and simultaneously with other strategies when reading in authentic texts for her own purposes

In Finding the Balance Between Standardized Norm-Referenced Assessment and Authentic Forms of Assessment. Move more toward standardized, norm-referenced assessment if:

- you'll get fired if you don't administer these tests!
- you need a touchstone against which to compare your students' progress as a group
- other stakeholders (parents, administrators) cannot gain a meaningful sense of children's progress

Move more toward authentic assessment if:

- student progress or teacher competence is being judged solely on the students' performance on unfamiliar or invalid tests
- important decisions are being made about individual children based solely on standardized tests
- information about student progress and processes is needed rather than information about their comparative status (pp. 247–257)

You can see that a balanced approach to reading takes a middle ground rather than the extremes. The either-or dichotomy that characterizes some thinking about approaches is rejected in favor of striking a balance in favor of the needs of the learner.

Go to the Weblinks in Chapter 2 on our Companion Website at www.prenhall.com/harp for links to sites featuring Four Blocks.

Four Blocks Program. Several teachers have designed approaches to reading instruction that they say are balanced. One of the best known of these is the Four Blocks program designed by Patricia Cunningham and Dorothy Hall (Cunningham & Allington, 1999). Four Blocks encourages teachers to plan reading instruction that includes guided reading (a strategy we will discuss in detail in Chapter 8), self-selected reading, writing, and working with words.

Balanced instruction does not mean that each child is given an equal amount of instruction in phonics and some other approach to reading instruction. Balanced instruction is supposed to mean that you attend to what the child knows about how printed language works and provide her with instruction that will lead to growth in literacy skills.

LOOKING AT THE RESEARCH

What the research says about balanced instruction

A study by Baumann and Ivey (1997) explored what diverse second-grade students learned about reading, writing, and literature through a yearlong program of strategy instruction integrated within a rich, literature-based classroom. Students grew in overall instructional reading level and came to view reading as a natural component of the day; demonstrated high levels of engagement with books; developed skill in word identification, fluency, and comprehension; and grew in written composition abilities. The authors attributed this achievement to balance between the literature-rich environment and the contextualized strategy instruction as well as a balance between teacher-initiated instruction and instruction in response to students.

How can you use these findings to inform your instruction? What is meant by contextualized strategy instruction? What forms of balance do you see in the description of activities in this report?

Go to the Weblinks in Chapter 2 on our Companion Website at www.prenhall.com/harp to link to sites presenting research on the balanced approach to literacy instruction. Then go to the chapter's Threaded Message Board to add your comments to the global discussion.

To balance reading instruction properly, you must know about phonics, individualized reading, language experience, whole language, and sight word strategies. Then for any given child, you will not neglect any aspect of good reading instruction, nor will you choose only one approach and use it exclusively for every child.

HOW DO I DECIDE WHICH APPROACH TO USE?

You learned early in this chapter about a classic study in reading instruction that found the teacher was more important than any method in promoting excellence in reading (Bond & Dykstra, 1967, 1997). The most important variable in the effectiveness of reading instruction is the teacher. A knowledgeable teacher who can draw from an array of approaches—and believes in the approaches he or she is using—will be an effective reading teacher. The key is to be an informed teacher making mindful professional decisions. To make the most mindful professional decisions you will need to consider the nature and purpose of each approach described previously, the history of reading approaches, your own emerging philosophy of literacy instruction, and your growing abilities as a kidwatcher.

History of Approaches

Over the past 50 years approaches to reading instruction have come and gone, frequently to reappear later in a slightly modified form. Studying Figure 2.7, Milestones in Reading Instruction, will give you a sense of this history. The history begins with a brief look at reading instruction from the colonial period forward, with increased detail beginning in the 1940s.

Developing Your Philosophy

You may wish to visit our Companion Website at www.prenhall.com/harp and post your philosophy statement. You will find other postings there from students all over the country who are using this text and struggling to articulate their philosophy. You may find it informative to read other students' statements.

What you believe about reading instruction—how you view the reading process—will have a profound effect on the choices you make about approaches. Now is a good time for you to begin articulating your philosophy of reading instruction. You may want to begin writing your philosophy, revisiting it often, and amending your writing as your philosophy deepens and expands.

One of the first issues you may want to address as you formulate your philosophy is your position on top-down versus bottom-up approaches to reading. Answer these 10 questions, and consider your emerging philosophy.

1. Do you want young readers to believe that reading is constructing meaning or unlocking sounds?
2. Do you believe that children should first read their own language or first read a controlled vocabulary so that sound-symbol relationships are consistent?
3. Do you believe that before children read a selection, they should hear it well read by another, or should children usually decode a selection on their own?
4. Do you believe that children learn to read by reading and writing, or do you believe that they must master word identification skills before they can read?
5. Do you believe that the information children bring to the printed page affects their understanding, or do you believe that all the meaning resides in the words?
6. Do you believe that children understand an author's ideas without reading every word, or must they understand every word in order to comprehend a selection?
7. Do you believe that when children read aloud, they may substitute meaningful alternatives to the printed words, or must they read every word accurately?
8. Do you believe that when a child reads incorrectly you should say, "Here is what you read, does that make sense?" or should you simply correct the child's errors?
9. In reading, are the basic units of instruction sentences and paragraphs, or are the basic units of instruction sounds, letters, and words?
10. Do you believe that the structure of a sentence often determines the meanings of words, or are word meanings independently stable?

If you answered yes to the first part of each question you have an emerging philosophy that would be described as embracing top-down or whole-to-part instruction. If you agreed with the second half of each question you have an emerging bottom-up or part-to-whole philosophy. Most of you probably had some answers agreeing with the first half of the statements and some with the second half of the statements. As you learn more about teaching reading from your coursework and experience, your own beliefs will be solidified. Many of the decisions you make about which approach or approaches to use at any point in time will be informed by your philosophy. Your choices of approaches will also be guided by your skillful observation of your learners.

Figure 2.7
Milestones in Reading Instruction

1600s

- *The New England Primer.* The first reading text for the American colonies;has a strong religious emphasis.

1700s

- Noah Webster published the *Grammatical Institute.* Ultimately its three parts are printed separately, becoming the first set of consecutive readers in the history of American reading instruction.

1800s

- William H. McGuffey publishes the McGuffey readers, the first series of its kind.

A In *Adam's* Fall We Sinned all.
B Thy Life to Mend This *Book* Attend.
C The *Cat* doth play And after slay.
D A *Dog* will bite A Thief at night.
E An *Eagles* flight Is out of sight.
F The Idle *Fool* Is whipt at School.

1920s

- The first Newbery Award was awarded for *The Story of Mankind* by Hendik Willem Van Loon in 1922.

1930s

- The first Caldecott Award was awarded to Dorothy P. Lathrop for her illustrations in *Animals of the Bible, A Picture Book* in 1938.
- Scott Foresman and Company published the Dick and Jane basal series in 1930. This program continues to be published until 1965.

Reading Excellence

1940s

- Basal readers emphasize learning whole words and reading for meaning.
- World War II leads to the discovery of thousands of illiterate young men in the military.
- Size and number of teacher manuals with basals increases, as does emphasis on secondary school reading instruction.
- Basals incorporate Emmett Bett's design for directed reading.
- Basals emphasize reading readiness, a balanced approach, word recognition, comprehension, study activities, evaluation, and testing.
- Innovative use of informal assessment with basals begins with Bett's Informal Reading Inventory.

1950s

- Expanding knowledge and technology gives new importance to learning to read.
- Korean War renews emphasis on improved reading instruction for national strength.

(Continued)

Note: The authors are deeply indebted to the work of Nila Banton Smith, John Savage, Tom Devine, Jay Simmons, and Denise Marchionda. Without them, we could not have put this timeline together.

Figure 2.7
Milestones in Reading Instruction *Continued*

- Rudolf Flesh's *Why Johnny Can't Read* becomes a best seller, beginning public outcry about the status of reading instruction based on Flesh's assertions of adequately taught phonics.
- Russians launching Sputnik, giving new urgency to education and increasing criticism of contemporary reading instruction.
- Jeanette Veatch introduces Individualized Reading as an instructional approach using literature.
- William S. Gray is elected the first president of The International Reading Association in 1955.

1960s

- Russell Stauffer publishes a basal series using The Directed Reading-Thinking Activity.
- The Columbia-Carnegie Study reports basic readers from a graded series are used by approximately 90% of first through third grade teachers.
- Structural linguists Charles Fries and Leonard Bloomfield advocate looking at the regularity in English to teach reading.
- Linguistic Readers emphasizing word patterns rather than phonics are published as an alternative to traditional sounding out practices.
- Basal publishers greatly expand the size of teacher manuals, offer multiple texts, supplemental texts, simplified texts for slow readers, and paperbacks. Vocabulary is tightly controlled. Skill development and workbooks are provided at all grade levels.
- Basal publishers include supplemental materials such as word cards, big books, duplicating masters, and testing programs.
- Programmed Reading becomes popular with the use of teaching machines and "teacher proof" materials.

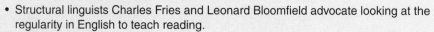

- The Johnson administration passes the Elementary and Secondary Education Act, which provides equality of education in poverty areas. Title One becomes standard in most school districts.
- Roach Van Allen and Russell Stauffer promote The Language Experience Approach to reading instruction.
- U.S. Office of Education First Grade Studies reports that the most important variable in the teaching of reading is the teacher.
- Jeanne Chall publishes *Learning to Read: The Great Debate,* revealing the superiority of code emphasis over meaning emphasis approaches, which increases interest in phonics.
- Kenneth Goodman publishes *Reading: A Psycholinguistic Guessing Game,* beginning a professional dialogue about the nature of the reading process.
- *Sesame Street* and *The Electric Company* come to television, increasing interest in early reading.

1970s

- Basals reduce whole word and reading for meaning emphases in favor of phonics instruction.

Figure 2.7
Continued

- Emphasis on a hierarchy of skills, skills mastery, and increased assessment and evaluation of skill attainment increases.
- Public pressure on accountability in school increases when lawsuits are brought against districts for failure to teach.
- Assessment and evaluation of oral reading behavior moves away from simply counting errors to engaging in miscue analysis.

1980s

- The Whole Language Movement gains momentum with emphasis on child-centered instruction, reading for meaning, and integrated instruction.
- Interest in early literacy increases with research on emergent literacy.
- Kenneth Goodman's *What's Whole in Whole* lends support to the whole language movement.
- Lucy Calkins, Nancy Atwell, and Jane Hansen's work on Readers' Workshop leads to renewed interest in independent reading.
- Most states require a state-wide achievement test.
- Basal publishers begin producing anthologies of children's literature, integrating the teaching of reading and the other language arts.
- Reading Recovery is introduced in the United States in 1984. The first-grade intervention program is developed in New Zealand by Marie Clay.

1990s

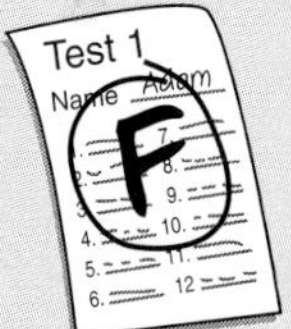

- Reading test scores in California decline, and whole language is blamed.
- A move toward developing state and even national performance standards leads to high-stakes testing in most states.
- National press and politicians call for a return to phonics instruction, which is mandated by legislation in some states.
- Marie Clay, Margaret Mooney, Irene Fountas, and Gay Su Pinnell recommend moving away from directed reading activities to guided reading activities.
- Research supported by the National Institute of Child Health and Human Development supports the value of phonemic awareness.
- The increased emphasis on decoding leads to a rebirth of materials that resemble the old linguistic texts of the 60's under the banner of decodable text.
- Richard Vacca, President of the International Reading Association, calls for balance in reading instruction.
- Balanced Reading Instruction becomes so popular that basal publishers advertise their programs as "balanced."
- The National Research Council publishes *Preventing Reading Difficulties in Young Children* which recommends instruction in both word recognition and comprehension.
- The National Reading Panel is commissioned by Congress to review research in reading and to make recommendations for national policy.

(Continued)

Figure 2.7
Milestones in Reading Instruction *Continued*

- The Reading Excellence Act is added to the renewal of the Elementary and Secondary Education Act to fund programs to improve reading performance in elementary schools.

2000s

- The reports of the subcommittees of the National Reading Panel are published in 2000, promoting phonics and phonemic awareness as important components of a reading program. These reports become the basis for promoting specific programs designed for reading instruction. Many reading professionals take issue with the methods and conclusions of the panel.
- The No Child Left Behind Legislation passes in 2002, requiring states to hold schools accountable for their progress in teaching children to read through extensive testing.

Reading Excellence Act

The authors are deeply indebted to the work of Nila Banton Smith, John Savage, Tom Devine, Jay Simmons and Denise Marchionda. Without them we could not have put this timeline together.

Becoming an Increasingly Skilled Kidwatcher

The concept of kidwatching is not new. It grew out of the child-study movement that reached a peak in the 1930s, and has been popularized in contemporary education by Yetta Goodman (1985):

> The term *kidwatching* has caught on among those who believe that children learn language best in an environment rich with opportunities to explore interesting objects and ideas. Through observing the reading, writing, speaking and listening of friendly, interactive peers, interested kidwatching teachers can understand and support child language development.
>
> The term *kidwatching* is used to reinstate and legitimatize the significance of professional observation in the classroom. Those who support such child study understand that the evaluation of pupils' growth and curriculum development are integrally related. (p.10)

You will come to be able to observe carefully each of your learners, coming to deeper and deeper understandings about what they know about language and how it works, reading and how it works, and writing and how it works. You will be able to observe their strengths and their struggles, and in so doing you will be able to identify their next learning steps. Then you will be able to use this valuable information to select the appropriate approach to instruction for individuals, small groups, and your whole class. You will learn a great deal more about assessing and evaluating learning in the next chapter. You will be able to make increasingly more informed choices about approaches as you become more knowledgeable about teaching reading.

Becoming Increasingly More Informed as a Reading Teacher

College students often take a course and then give the content of that course little thought after they take the final examination. The course you are taking on teaching reading is not like other courses you have taken. It is truly a foundation for a career-long learning effort on your part. Each day you teach, you will become a more informed reading teacher.

This will happen as you reflect on your teaching and on your professional discussions with colleagues. Each lesson you teach will prepare you to be a better teacher. Each time you help a child overcome frustration over reading, you will become a more informed teacher. Each accomplishment your learners master, each article you read in professional journals, each conference you attend, and each conversation you have with a colleague about an accomplishment or frustration will help you become a more reflective, informed teacher. This text and the course you are enrolled in are only the beginning! As you become more informed, you will be able to make more insightful decisions about which approaches to select to meet individual children's needs. Contemporary wisdom within our profession suggests that informed teachers focus on the needs of learners, select from an array of approaches and materials, and bring balance to their reading instruction.

THINKING AS A TEACHER

1. You are offered a position in a school system where the policy is that all teachers must use the adopted integrated anthology. What issues should you consider? What questions do you have to answer for yourself, and what questions will you ask the administrators in the school? How will you resolve this dilemma?
2. You are teaching in a primary (K–3) school that touts its balanced literacy program. Many of the parents you have spoken with think that "balanced" means giving every child every aspect of the program—equal amounts of each program component. Other parents obviously assume that "balanced" means child-centered, or giving each child exactly what he or she needs. Consider two important questions: (1) How will you resolve the different points of view in your own mind? (2) How will you help parents understand this difference of opinion?
3. The research seems to indicate that phonemic awareness and phonics are important parts of early reading instruction. Having children read real literature is another important aspect of early literacy instruction. How do you believe these two program components should be combined? What is your current thinking on the approach to reading instruction that you will embrace?

FIELD-BASED ACTIVITIES

1. Ask your instructor to identify some schools you could visit that use two of the approaches described in this chapter. Visit those schools, write a description of the approach used in each school, and then write a comparison/contrast of the two approaches.
2. Select an approach as described in this chapter and then interview a teacher who uses that approach. Prepare about five questions to ask in the interview that cover topics such as what he or she likes about the approach, the significant challenges in using that approach, and the ways in which children seem to respond to that approach.
3. Visit an elementary school and examine the materials used for reading instruction. Do these materials fit your philosophy of reading instruction? Why or why not?

REFERENCES

Adams, M. J. (1990). *Beginning to read: Thinking and learning about print.* Cambridge, MA: The MIT Press.

Allen, R. V. (1976). *Language experiences in communication.* Boston: Houghton Mifflin.

Barton, A., & Wilder, D. (1962). *Columbia-Carnegie study of reading research and its communication.* New York: Scholastic.

Baumann, J. F., & Ivey, G. (1997). Delicate balances: Striving for curricular and instructional equilibrium in a second-grade, literature/strategy-based classroom. *Reading Research Quarterly, 32,* 244–275.

Betts, E. A. (1946). *Foundation of reading instruction.* New York: American Book Co.

Bloomfield, L., & Barnhart, C. L. (1961). *Let's read.* Detroit, MI: Wayne State University Press.

Bond, G. L., & Dykstra, R. (1967, 1997). The cooperative research program in first-grade reading instruction. *Reading Research Quarterly, 2,* 5–142. (Reprinted in *Reading Research Quarterly, 32*(4): 348–427.)

Bridge, C. A., Winograd, P. N., & Haley, D. (1983). Using predictable materials vs. preprimers to teach beginning sight words. *The Reading Teacher, 36,* 884–891.

Chall, J. S. (1989). Learning to read: The great debate twenty years later. A response to "Debunking the great phonics myth." *Phi Delta Kappan, 71,* 521–538.

Cunningham, P. M., & Allington, R. L. (1999). *Classrooms that work: They can all read and write.* New York: Longman.

Duffy, G. G., & Hoffman, J. V. (1999). In pursuit of an illusion: The flawed search for a perfect method. *The Reading Teacher, 53,* 10–16.

Fitzgerald, J. (1999). What is this thing called "balance?" *The Reading Teacher, 53,* 100–107.

Flesch, R. (1955). *Why Johnny can't read.* New York: HarperCollins.

Fullan, M. (1996). "Turning systematic thinking on its head." *Phi Delta Kappan, 77,* 420–423.

Garcia, G. E., & Pearson, P. D. (1991). Modifying reading instruction to maximize its effectiveness for all students. In M. S. Knapp & P. M. Shields (Eds.), *Better schooling for the children of poverty* (pp. 30–31). Berkeley, CA: McCutcheon.

Goodman, K. S. (1967). Reading: A psycholinguistic guessing game. *Journal of the Reading Specialist, 6,* 126–135.

Goodman, K. S. (1986). *What's whole in whole language?* Portsmouth, NH: Heinemann.

Goodman, Y. (1985). Kidwatching: Observing children in the classroom. In A. Jaggar & M. T. Smith-Burke (Eds.), *Observing the language learner.* Urbana, IL & Newark, DE: National Council of Teachers of English & International Reading Association.

Grossen, B. (2002). 30 years of research: What we now know about how children learn to read. Washington, DC: National Institutes of Child Health and Human Development. Retrieved from *http://daisy.ym.edu.tw/~jrlee/30years.html*

Haberman, M. (1994). The top ten fantasies of school reformers. *Phi Delta Kappan, 75,* 689–692.

Hoffman, J. V. (1998). When bad things happen to good ideas in literacy education: Professional dilemmas, personal decisions, and political traps. *The Reading Teacher, 52,* 102–112.

Joyce, B., & Calhoun, E. (1995). School renewal: An inquiry, not a formula. *Educational Leadership, 52,* 51–55.

Krashen, S. (1995). School libraries, public libraries, and NAEP scores. *School Library Media Quarterly, 23,* 235–237.

Krashen, S. (1999). *Three arguments against whole language & why they are wrong.* Portsmouth, NH: Heinemann.

Langer, J. A., Applebee, A. M., Mullis, I. V. S., & Foertsch, M. A. (1990). *Learning to read in our nation's schools: Instruction and achievement in 1988 at grades 4, 8, and 12.* Princeton, NJ: Educational Testing Service.

McCarthey, S. J., & Hoffman, J. V. (1995). The new basals: How different are they? *The Reading Teacher, 49,* 72–75.

McQuillan, J. (1998). *The literacy crisis: False claims and real solutions.* Portsmouth, NH: Heinemann.

Mesmer, H. A. E. (1999). Scaffolding a crucial transition using text with some decodability. *The Reading Teacher, 53,* 130–142.

National Institute of Child Health and Human Development. (2000). *Report of the National Reading Panel: Teaching children to read.* Washington, DC: Author.

National Research Council. (1998). *Preventing reading difficulties in young children.* Washington, DC: National Academy Press.

Nelson, J. (2000). Report on percentage of decodable text in conforming first grade language arts-reading instructional materials. Retrieved from *http://www.tea.state.tx.us/sboe/schedule/2001/decodabletext.html*

Pressley, M. (2002). *Reading instruction that works: The case for balanced teaching.* New York: Guilford Press.

Schon, D. (1987). *Educating the reflective practitioner.* San Francisco: Jossey-Bass.

Smith, F. (1978). *Reading without nonsense.* New York: Holt, Rinehart and Winston.

Spiegel, D. L. (1999). Meeting each child's literacy needs. In L. Gambrell, L. Morrow, S. Neuman, & M. Pressley (Eds.), *Best practices for literacy instruction.* New York: Guilford Press.

Stahl, S. A. (1997). Instructional models in reading: An introduction. In S. A. Stahl & D. A. Hayes (Eds.), *Instructional models in reading.* Mahwah, N. J.: Lawrence Erlbaum Associates, Inc.

Stahl, S. A., Duffy-Hester, A. M., & Stahl, K. A. D. (1998). Everything you wanted to know about phonics (but were afraid to ask). *Reading Research Quarterly, 33,* 338–355.

Stauffer, R. G., & Burrows, A. T. (1960–1962). *The Winston basic readers, communication program.* Philadelphia, PA: John C. Winston.

Strickland, D. S., & Morrow, L. M. (1989). *Emerging literacy: Young children learn to read and write.* Newark, DE: International Reading Association.

Veatch, J. (1954). Individualized reading—for success in the classroom. *The Educational Trend.* Washington, DC: Croft.

Wilson, B. A. (2003). *Wilson reading system instructor's manual.* Millbury, MA: Wilson Language Training.

Chapter 3

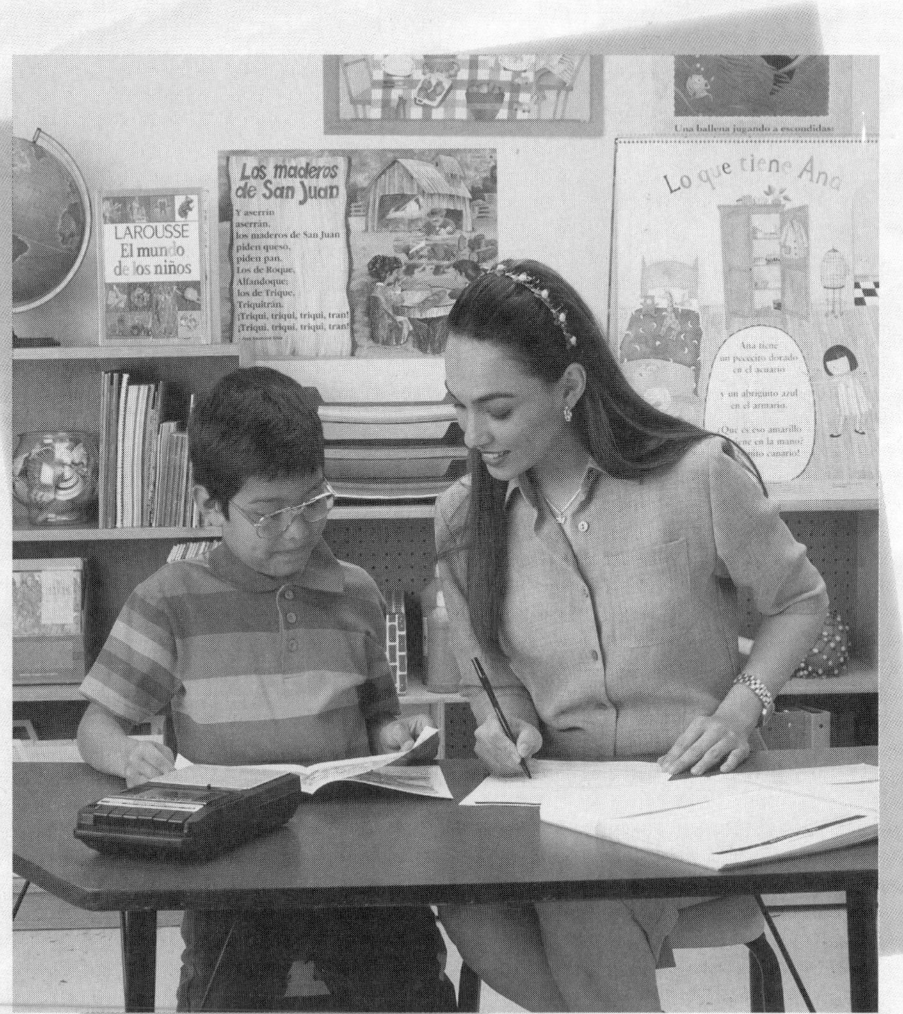
Una ballena jugando a escondidas:
Los maderos de San Juan
Y aserrín
aserrán,
los maderos de San Juan
piden queso,
piden pan.
Los de Roque,
Alfandoque;
los de Trique,
Triquitrán.
¡Triqui, triqui, triqui, tran!
¡Triqui, triqui, triqui, tran!
LAROUSSE
El mundo de los niños
Lo que tiene Ana
Ana tiene
un pececito dorado
en el acuario
y un abriguito azul
en el armario.

Assessing and Evaluating Children's Literacy Growth

LOOKING AT THE RESEARCH

Forty-nine children in grades one through four were asked to describe themselves as readers and writers. They were also asked how they go about reading and writing. None of the children had experience discussing their understanding of the reading and writing processes. Nor was it common for these children to assess their own abilities.

Guice and Johnston (1995) concluded that teachers must be concerned about the theories children hold about literacy and about themselves as literate learners. They further concluded that standardized assessment practices obscure rather than reveal the complexities of children's understandings of literacy concepts and do not support self-assessment.

Focus Questions

- What is meant by the terms *assessment* and *evaluation?*
- How do I assess and evaluate children's understandings of the reading and writing processes?
- How do I assess and evaluate reading performance through oral reading?
- How do I assess and evaluate readers' and writers' growth over time?
- What do I need to know about standardized tests?
- What do I need to know about standards, accountability, and high-stakes testing?
- How do I organize to make the best use of the assessment and evaluation tools I have?

REAL TEACHERS, REAL PRACTICE

Meet Nichole Duffy, *a second-grade teacher. Here are her thoughts on portfolio assessment*

The more accessible portfolios are to students, the more they use them and the more beneficial they become. I use an open-topped file crate with a hanging file for each child. The students' names appear on a plastic tab that projects above the file. When a child pulls on his or her tab, the whole file lifts ups; this helps avoid papers and folders being misfiled. Resting in the hanging file is the portfolio folder with two pockets and a three-pronged clasp.

One pocket holds a form for recording writing goals. During Writer's Workshop, the children keep their portfolio folders with them. The piece they are working on is kept in the folder, and when they are ready to conference with me, we record a goal for the next writing piece on the record form. As an increasing number of writing skills and techniques are introduced during the year, the children take a more active role in determining their goals for future writing efforts. Goals can range from "Use a capital letter at the beginning of each sentence" to "Incorporate a simile into the description." Published pieces are put in the class library for others to enjoy and "sloppy copies" (first drafts) are put in the hanging file to make room in the portfolio folder for the most current piece in progress.

The second pocket contains a reading log. Children are reminded to make note of selections they have finished at the end of independent reading times. Periodically, individual children and I conference about the types of books read in regard to text difficulty, content, author, and genre. Doing so helps the children reflect upon their reading interests and progress.

Also in the literacy folder is a collection of running records. I have made a form with the traditional running record template on the front and a self-evaluation form on the back. After the child has read the selection, he or she reflects on the aspects of reading done successfully and practices that would benefit reading next time. I tend to use the self-evaluation form after decoding skills and comprehension strategies have been modeled during instruction. These running records can be collected on the three prongs of the literacy folder.

The final reading component is a journal in which children respond to selections they have read. The writing prompts are generally questions at the critical or creative level. Responses are often shared in literature circles to generate discussion about the text. I can gain insight about the depth of their comprehension and connection to the text through their writing and sharing. While I consider these journals a part of the portfolio, I house them in a separate location to ease the flow of classroom traffic.

One of the most important steps in using portfolio assessment successfully is establishing time to meet with students. I listen to them read and conference with them about their progress during sustained silent reading time. Writing conferences are held during Writer's Workshop, which I conduct three times per week. The other children are finishing their pieces and those who have completed pieces are working on short-term, less structured writing projects. I manage to meet with about six children per week in reading and six in writing. With planning, practice, and a decrease in standard, whole-class assessment, the activities related to portfolio assessment could be increased. The use of portfolios is a valuable practice, certainly worthy of our precious educational time, because it individualizes instruction while also generating ideas for whole-class lessons. They also serve as an excellent tool for communicating with parents. Parents, students, and I can see the succession of literacy goals set and the evidence of progress toward them.

The opening research piece underscores the importance of helping children articulate their understandings of the reading and writing processes and to evaluate their use of the processes. The "Real Teachers, Real Practice" essay by Nichole Duffy demonstrates that teachers can create environments in which this important assessment and evaluation occur. The assessment and evaluation of children's literacy growth are driven by some critical questions.

WHAT IS MEANT BY THE TERMS ASSESSMENT AND EVALUATION?

The terms *assessment* and *evaluation* are like "paper and pencils," "white boards and markers," and *q* and *u:* They just go together. You need to learn never to think of one without the other. Assessment is useless without evaluation, and evaluation is impossible without assessment. **Assessment** means collecting data on our learners. **Evaluation** means using data to make informed instructional decisions about your learners (Harris & Hodges, 1995). In good teaching, they go hand in hand.

Distinguishing Assessment from Evaluation

Assessment can take many forms. Assessment can be as simple as looking at a sample of a child's work or as complex as giving a standardized test. One purpose of this chapter is to help you understand how frequent and regular assessment can inform instructional practice. Thus, it is important for you to realize that testing is only one form of assessment. Also valuable are other forms of assessment, such as student work samples, student-teacher conferencing, rubrics, oral reading checks, and checklists.

Assessment relates to the tools teachers use to collect data about students' learning. Evaluation is the interpretation of that data. Thus, the information you glean from evaluation drives instruction. Whenever you collect assessment data, challenge yourself to answer the questions: "What does this tell me about this child as a learner? What strengths do I see and where shall I take this child next?" Answering these questions is the purpose of assessment and evaluation.

At the heart of the word *evaluation* is the concept of value. Teachers, parents, and children should evaluate growth in literacy in terms of what they value in readers and writers. When teachers in workshops are asked to list the things they value most in readers and writers, the lists never begin with "correctly sounding out short vowel sounds" or "accurate spelling in rough drafts." High on the lists are more likely to be statements such as "enjoys reading, reads for recreation, writes creatively and thoughtfully." What we value in reading and writing can inform the design of assessment and evaluation activities.

Consider the weekly spelling test often given on Fridays in many classrooms. When carefully examined, this practice suggests that what we value most in spellers is correct spelling of words in isolation on a test one day a week. Is that really what we value in spellers? Probably not. What we really value in spellers is correct spelling daily in the context of edited and polished writing. Therefore, we should be evaluating spelling performance daily in the context of writing across the curriculum rather than only once a week on a spelling test. In deciding what to evaluate in literacy, it is imperative to determine first what we value in emergent, developing, and fluent readers and writers.

Principles of Assessment and Evaluation

It seems logical then that teachers and parents might come together and list what they value in readers and writers at each stage of development. Assessment tools could then be selected or designed to collect data on what is valued, thus leading to appropriate evaluation. If all this sounds complex, it is, but you will find sorting it out less challenging if your work in assessment and evaluation is guided by a set of principles.

Principle One: Assessment and Evaluation Are First and Foremost Helpful for the Individual Learner. A primary goal is the ongoing, daily collection of data on individual learners. These data will inform your instruction and are effectively used when you share them with your learners. For example, invite a child to join you in reviewing the data on a sample of his or her oral reading, analyze the results, and then together you can set the child's next learning goals.

Similarly, you might review a piece of writing with a child and collaboratively identify the strengths and next goals. The involvement of children in the assessment and evaluation process is critical if they are to take responsibility for their learning.

Principle Two: Reflecting on What You Know About the Reading Process Is Essential for Effective Teaching. You will want to assess and evaluate learners' understanding of the reading process, their ability to monitor their use of the process, their ability to take corrective action when the process falls apart, and their ability to apply skills and strategies.

Principle Three: Teacher Observation Is at the Center of Assessment and Evaluation. Your increasingly refined abilities to observe carefully children as readers will result in making informed instructional decisions. However, your observations should be supported by a deepening knowledge about learners, the reading process, and the interactions of the two. For example, an untrained observer will listen to a child read and hear only mistakes, whereas the experienced observer, who is knowledgeable about the reading process, will hear much more. This observer will hear prediction making, prediction confirmation, rereading when meaning is lost, and the growing ability of the reader to self-monitor the use of the reading process.

Principle Four: Literacy Is Continually Assessed in a Variety of Contexts. Assessment and evaluation instruments are varied, and testing is only one form of assessment and evaluation. In addition to appropriate tests, listening to children read orally, observing children in independent reading, guided reading, and buddy reading, and questioning them during reading conferences are all appropriate and important assessment tasks. Seeking such evidence that children are developmentally moving from emergent reading behaviors to developing reading behaviors to maturing reading behaviors is an important role for teachers. Recording ways children interact with print, listen to stories, use literacy acts in dramatic play, and make use of environmental print is also critical to your assessment and evaluation of their progress.

Principle Five: Assessment and Evaluation Strategies Are Developmentally and Culturally Appropriate. Like learning to speak, learning to read and write are developmental processes. Most children move through stages of development in predictable, describable ways. Learning activities should honor the developmental nature of literacy, focus on meaning, and give children many, many opportunities to practice literacy in ever-increasingly accurate approximations of adult reading and writing. Assessment tools in literacy must be consistent with these developmental perspectives. To the extent possible, assessment and evaluation of literacy for children for whom English is a second language should occur in the child's home language. As children become more proficient in English, assessment tools in English may be used. Assessment and evaluation strategies honor the cultural norms that may differ from those of majority children. For example, in some Native American cultures eye contact and competition are not acceptable. Teachers who do not understand this could draw inaccurate conclusions about such students' performance.

Principle Six: The Careful and Thoughtful Communication of Information from Assessment and Evaluation Is a Critical Part of the Process. The most important audience for your assessment and evaluation conclusions is your learners. You can accomplish thoughtful communication by providing constructive written feedback on assignments, by debriefing samples of oral reading behavior, through comments you make during lessons, and in conferences with your learners. Another critically important audience is parents and other caregivers. Plan to hold regular conferences with parents in which you share progress reports. Some teachers successfully engage children in part of the conference with parents. You may find it helpful to write monthly classroom newsletters to parents in which some assessment and evaluation data are reported such as new strategies that have been learned, growth on running records, or new goals for reading. You may find it essential to make frequent phone calls to parents to keep them informed of their children's progress. One of the things you will most carefully want to monitor is your students' deepening understandings of the reading and writing processes.

HOW DO I ASSESS AND EVALUATE CHILDREN'S UNDERSTANDINGS OF THE READING AND WRITING PROCESSES?

In summarizing years of research on reading comprehension, Flood, Lapp, and Fisher (2003) conclude that "good readers are strategic readers who actively construct meaning as they read; they are self-motivated and self-directed; they monitor their own comprehension by questioning, reviewing, revising, and rereading to enhance their overall comprehension" (p. 931). Informed teachers monitor the developing perceptions of readers about the reading process. They carefully observe to see that readers are becoming increasingly strategic. Assessment and evaluation of readers' perceptions of reading and the reading process may be done through interviews and the use of published tools.

Interviewing Children About Their Perceptions of Reading

You will want to make time at the beginning of the school year to interview each of your learners about their views of reading. Such interviews will also help you learn more about children who join your class during the year. Short interviews need consist of only a few critical questions. Longer interviews, if you can find time for them, will yield considerably more information.

Reading interviews are an important way to discover the child's perceptions of the reading process.

Short Reading Interviews. You can learn a good deal about a reader's perceptions by asking just three questions.

1. What is reading?
2. What do you do when you read?
3. If you were going to help someone become a better reader, how would you do it?

Consider the responses to these three questions made by two first graders presented in Figure 3.1.

What inferences can you draw about Walker's perceptions of reading? What inferences can you draw about Hillary's perceptions of reading? How do their responses to the same questions differ? What instructional implications do you see in their responses?

Longer Reading Interviews. If you have time to conduct more extensive reading interviews, you may wish to add the following questions. Some of these questions relate directly to a text the child or children have just read and are discussing with you.

- What are you doing well as a reader?
- What is something new you have learned to do as a reader?
- What would you like to be able to do better as a reader?
- When you have trouble with your reading, what do you do?
- What parts of this text were difficult for you?
- What made them difficult?
- What parts of this text were easy for you?
- What made them easy?
- When you have difficulty understanding your reading, what do you do?

Figure 3.1
Two First Graders' Responses to the Short Reading Interview

1. What is reading?

   Walker: "Reading is sounding out words. Like when you look at the letters in the words and make the sounds."

   Hillary: "Reading is like watching TV only you have to make the pictures yourself unless the author puts lots of pictures in the book."

2. What do you do when you read?

   Walker: "You find the words on the page and put your finger down. Then you say the sounds in the words and you make a word. You say all of the words or you just think them to yourself."

   Hillary: "You read the words and you think about what they say. You make a story when you put the words together."

3. If you were going to help someone become a better reader, how would you do it?

   Walker: "I would tell them lots of the sounds letters make so they could read more words."

   Hillary: "I would tell them to remember the words and to think about what is happening in the story. Like think about the beginning of the story and the end of the story."

Of course, you would need to simplify these questions for young readers. With emerging or struggling readers you might simply ask: What is reading? What do you do when you read? When you come to a word you do not know, what do you do? (Harp, 2000).

You can learn a great deal about children's perceptions of the reading process in their answers to "What do you do when you read?" For example, if a child answers, "I sound out words," this may suggest that he thinks of reading as decoding rather than making meaning. In this instance you may choose to probe the child's understandings with further questions. If the response is "I hear the story" or "I make pictures in my head," you can be reasonably certain the child views reading as a meaning making process. You may discover that, at least for some of your learners, you want more information than you can get from interviews alone. In this case you can use published tools to evaluate children's motivation to read and their self-perceptions as readers.

Published Tools to Evaluate Children's Perceptions of Reading

We recommend two published tools for evaluating children's motivation to read and their self-perceptions as readers. These tools are the *Motivation to Read Profile* and the *Reader Self-Perception Scale.* If these instruments yield low scores for some of your learners, this will alert you to work diligently to help these children see the value and joy in reading. You will accomplish this by sharing your enthusiasm and love for reading on a daily basis.

Motivation to Read Profile. The *Motivation to Read Profile (MTRP)* consists of a written survey and a conversational interview designed to assess second- through sixth-grade children's self-concepts as readers and the value they see in reading (Gambrell, Palmer, Codling, & Mazzoni, 1996).

The group administered survey consists of multiple choice questions such as:

My friends think I am _____
_____ a very good reader
_____ a good reader
_____ an OK reader
_____ a poor reader

I worry about what other kids think about my reading _____
_____ every day
_____ almost every day
_____ once in a while
_____ never

The one-on-one interview consists of questions such as:

Tell me about the most interesting story or book you have read this week (or even last week).
Tell me about your favorite author.

The profile yields a score for Self-Concept As A Reader, a score for Value of Reading, and a Full Survey score. The complete Survey can be found in Appendix A.

Reader Self-Perception Scale. *The Reader Self-Perception Scale* is designed to assess how children in grades four through six feel about themselves as readers. You may find this tool especially helpful with struggling readers (Henk & Melnick, 1995).

The scale is designed to tap into children's perceptions of their current level of progress in learning to read; their perceptions of their performance to compare with the performance of classmates; perceptions of feedback about their reading from teachers, classmates, and family members; and their internal feelings during reading (Harp, 2000). The complete scale can be found in Appendix B.

Assessing and Evaluating Children's Perceptions as Writers

You may find it useful to assess and evaluate children's perceptions of themselves as writers and of the writing process. As with reading, this can be done through interviews and the use of a published tool, the *Writer Self-Perception Scale.*

Short Writing Interviews. Three helpful questions you can ask learners about writing are:

- What is writing?
- What do you do when you write?
- If you were going to help someone become a better writer, how would you do it?

Longer Writing Interviews. If you have time for more in-depth writing interviews, you might want to ask:

- What are you doing well as a writer?
- What is something new you have learned to do as a writer?
- What would you like to be able to do better as a writer?
- When you have trouble with your writing, what do you do?

Writer Self-Perception Scale. The *Writer Self-Perception Scale* may be used with children in fourth through sixth grade to assess how they feel about themselves as writers (Bottomley, Henk, & Melnick, 1997). The scale measures writers' perceptions of their general performance; specific progress with explicit dimensions of writing such as focus, clarity, organization, style, and coherence; performance in comparison to peers; feedback from teachers, classmates, and family members; and internal feelings they experience during writing (Harp, 2000).

Once you have established your children's perceptions of reading and the reading process, it becomes necessary to observe their oral reading behavior. You have several useful tools from which to choose in assessing and evaluating children's reading performance through their oral reading.

HOW DO I ASSESS AND EVALUATE READING PERFORMANCE THROUGH ORAL READING?

The goal of teachers of reading is to help all children become fluent, strategic readers who comprehend well a variety of increasingly more challenging texts. One of the best ways to monitor children's progress is through frequent oral reading checks. In an oral reading check, we listen to the individual child read and then carefully analyze her oral reading behavior for insights into her understanding and use of the reading process. We analyze her mistakes, called *miscues,* to determine what we can about her use of the cueing systems, her ability to monitor her reading and take corrective action, and her comprehension. A form of oral reading check that has been widely used for many years is the informal reading inventory.

Informal Reading Inventories

Informal reading inventories (IRIs) usually consist of sequentially graded word lists, sequentially graded reading selections, directions for recording and analyzing miscues, and a scheme for measuring comprehension.

The graded word lists are used to determine which of the reading selections the child should read first. In this discussion, examples will be drawn from the *Analytical Reading Inventory* by Mary Lynn Woods and Alden J. Moe (2003). The *Analytical Reading Inventory* is a good example of a typical informal reading inventory. The sequence of activities involved in using the *Analytical Reading Inventory* consists of using the graded words lists, introducing the narrative passage, student's reading and teacher's coding, retelling, and scoring.

Using the Graded Words Lists. Twenty-word graded word lists ranging from primer (pre-first grade) through grade six are provided in the *Inventory.* Begin by having the child read the easiest list and continue through increasingly more difficult lists. The grade level of the most difficult list on which the child correctly reads all 20 words indicates the level at which the child should begin reading the narrative texts.

Introducing the Narrative Passage. Open the Student Booklet to the indicated passage, and explain that the student will be reading aloud while you write in your Teacher Record. Ask the student to read the title and make a prediction of what the story is about. Then ask the student to read the first one or two sentences silently, and then make another prediction about the content of the selection. Figure 3.2 illustrates the Teacher Record Data for a second-grade selection as read by a fourth-grader, Jenny Stone.

Figure 3.2
Teacher Record Data

FORM C, LEVEL 2	Reader's Passages page 34

Prior Knowledge/Prediction

☐ Read the title and predict what the story is about. *About a road, it's got a lot of cars.*
Q: What do you know about a busy road?
SR: We live near a road that has a lot of cars.

☐ Read the first two sentences and add more to your prediction.
The boy yells at his dog because he's going to get hit.
Q: What do you know about a dog getting hit on a road?
SR: I had a dog that got hit when she ran across the road.

Prior Knowledge
☑ a lot
☐ some
☐ none

	The Busy Road (*Buzzy SC*)	O	I	S	A	Rp	Rv
1	"Look out, you'll get hit!" I/yelled as my dog ran across/the						
2	busy road./*Thud* was the noise I heard, and then I saw my pup/ (*Thad SC*; *no SC* / *nose*)						
3	lying in the street. "Oh, no!" I shouted. I felt scared inside. "Rex is (*scar SC*)						
4	my best friend!" I wanted to cry out. I knew that he was hurt, but						
5	he'd be all right/if I could get help fast. I knew I had to be brave. (*ready*)			/			
6	"Mom! Dad!" I/yelled as I ran/straight home. I tried to fight (*str SC*; *hold*)			/			
7	back the tears. They/started rolling down my face/(anyway) as I (*The*; *st* / *street*)	/		//			
8	blasted through the door. "Rex has been hit, and he needs help/ (*to*)			/			

The text is continued on the next page.

Cueing Systems

LINE #	Miscue	Grapho-phonically Similar I M F (word level)	Syntactically Acceptable Unacceptable (sentence level)	Semantic Change in Meaning (CM) No Change in Meaning (NCM) (sentence level)
5	*ready*	I	A	CM
6	*hold*		A	NCM
7	*The*	IM	U	CM
7	*street*	I	U	CM
8	*to*	IF	A	CM

The cueing system grid is continued on the next page.

Source: *Analytical Reading Inventory: Comprehensive Assessment for All Students,* 7/e by Woods/Moe, © 2003. Reprinted by permission of Pearson Education, Inc., Upper Saddle River, NJ.

Figure 3.2
Continued

		O	I	S	A	Rp	Rv
9	now!" I cried out. "Please hurry so we can save him!"						
	TOTALS Number of miscues 6 Number of self-corrections 4	1		5			

Fluency: Does the reader . . .

- ☐ read smoothly?
- ☐ read word-by-word?
- ☑ read words in meaningful phrases?
- ☑ use pitch, stress, and intonation to convey the meaning of a text?
- ☐ repeat words and phrases because he or she is monitoring the meaning (self-correcting)?
- ☑ repeat words and phrases because he or she is just trying to sound out the words? *noise, straight*
- ☑ use punctuation to divide the text into units of meaning? *most times*
- ☐ ignore the punctuation?

Rating Scale

1 = clearly labored, disfluent reading/very slow pace
2 = slow and choppy reading/slow pace
3 = poor phrasing/intonation/reasonable pace
(4) = fairly fluent reading/good pace

Cueing Systems				
LINE #	Miscue	Grapho-phonically Similar I M F (word level)	Syntactically Acceptable Unacceptable (sentence level)	Semantic Change in Meaning (CM) No Change in Meaning (NCM) (sentence level)

Summary

- ☑ Most, ☐ few, ☐ no miscues were graphophonically similar to the word in the passage.
- ☑ Most, ☐ few, ☐ no miscues were syntactically matched.
- ☐ Most, ☑ few, ☐ no miscues maintained the author's meaning.
- ☑ The self-corrections demonstrate that the reader monitors the meaning.

Form C, Level 2

Student's Reading and Teacher's Coding. The instructions say to explain to Jenny before she begins to read that after each passage you will ask for a retelling and also ask some comprehension questions. Figure 3.2 illustrates the coding of Jenny's miscues on each line of the text. The coding of miscues is not standardized across informal reading inventories and other forms of oral reading checks. In the case of the *Analytical Reading Inventory,* omissions are indicated by circling the omitted word, insertions are indicated by writing the inserted word, and substitutions are coded by writing them above the text word. A line is drawn through words you pronounce for the student, repeated words are underlined, and reversals are coded with a curved line. All of these miscues are counted as errors in the *Analytical Reading Inventory.* Self-corrections, hesitations, ignored punctuation, and change or no change in meaning are noted but not counted as errors.

In the illustration in Figure 3.2 you will note that Jenny made six miscues. One was an omission, and the other five were substitutions. For example, look at the fifth line of the text. Here Jenny substituted *ready* for *right.* In the Cueing Systems analysis box in Figure 3.2, the teacher noted that this substitution was similar to the cue in the initial position in the word, that the substitution was semantically acceptable, and that it changed meaning. Examine the analysis for the other four substitutions.

Figure 3.2 also illustrates the examiner's comments on Jenny's oral reading of the passage. Note that Jenny's teacher observed that Jenny used pitch, stress, and intonation to convey meaning, that she repeated some words in an attempt to sound them out, and that most of the time she effectively used punctuation.

Retelling. After the passage has been read, you ask the reader to retell the story: "Retell everything that you can remember from the passage, and I will write down what you say." Examine Figure 3.3 to see the retelling recorded by Jenny's teacher and the probing and responses she noted.

Figure 3.3 also illustrates a rubric for scoring the inclusion of story elements in the retelling and a place for examiner's comments. As you can see, Jenny's retelling was thorough—so thorough, in fact, that the teacher did not need to ask some of the comprehension questions in the examiner's manual for this selection. Notice the six possible comprehension questions. They are identified by the reader, text relationship (RTR). RIF questions assess how the student "retells in fact" from the text. PIT questions focus on how a reader "puts information together" from the text. CAR questions emphasize "connections between author and reader"—from head to text. EAS questions concern how the student "evaluates and substantiates" from head to text. You will note that the teacher did not ask Jenny questions 1, 2, and 5 because Jenny shared these ideas in her retelling (the teacher gave her credit on the comprehension analysis). The teacher did ask Jenny the other questions and made note of her answers.

Scoring. When you use the scoring guide for a passage, you give a rating for the reader's performance in word recognition and comprehension. The word recognition score is derived from the number of errors, and the comprehension score is based on an evaluation of the retelling and answers to comprehension questions.

Functional Reading Levels. Both word recognition performance and comprehension performance are rated as: *independent,* which means that text at this level of difficulty is appropriate for reading independently; *instructional,* which means that text at this level is appropriate for instructional purposes; and *frustration,* which means that the text is inappropriate for this reader at this time. Note the Scoring Guide included in Figure 3.3. In Jenny's case, this second-grade selection would have to have been read with no more than one word recognition error to be considered at her independent level. Her six errors cause

Figure 3.3

Retelling Evaluation, Story Elements Rubric, and Comprehension Questions

Retelling *Well, this is a story about a dog and the boy yells at his dog, "Look out, you're gonna get hit!" The dog runs across the busy road, and he gets hit anyway. The boy feels real scared. He starts to cry. If he can get help fast, it will be okay. Then he runs home to tell his mom and dad. If they hurry up, they can save the dog.*

Retelling Summary: ☑ many details, logical order ☐ some details, some order ☐ few details, disorder

Note: Indicate any probing with a "P"

Story Elements	All	Some	None
Main Character(s)	✓		
Time and Place	✓		
Problem	✓		
Plot Details in Sequence	✓		
Turning Point	✓		
Resolution	✓		
Reader's Thumbnail Summary: *A dog gets hit on a busy road.*			

Comprehension Questions and Possible Answers

\+ (RIF) 1. Who is the main character in this story? (a child, boy or girl)

\+ (PIT) 2. What is the problem in the story? (the dog ran across a busy street and got hit)

\+ (PIT) 3. Do you think the dog is an old dog or a young one? (a young dog, the child calls the dog a pup) *He said that it's a pup.*

\+ (CAR) 4. What do you know about the phrase **fight back the tears?** (you try not to cry, you try to be brave, you try to keep the tears from rolling down your cheeks) *It's when you don't want to cry.* What does the phrase **fight back the tears** have to do with this story? (when the child ran home to get mom and dad, he/she tried to fight back the tears) *The boy held back his tears.*

\+ (PIT) 5. Why did the child run home? (to get help fast so he/she could save the dog)

\+ (EAS) 6. Do you think the dog will be all right? You think this because . . . (yes, the child is getting help fast; no, maybe they can't hurry fast enough) *because the story said that if he can get help fast, it will be okay.*

Reader Text Relationship (RTR) From the Text ☑ adequate ☐ not adequate From Head to Text ☑ adequate ☐ not adequate

Scoring Guide Summary

WORD RECOGNITION
- Independent ..... 1 *-6*
- Instructional 6
- Frustration ..... 12+

COMPREHENSION
- Independent ..... 0 *-0*
- Instructional 1-2
- Frustration ..... 3+

Emotional Status: *confident*

Form C, Level 2

Source: *Analytical Reading Inventory: Comprehensive Assessment for All Students,* 7/e by Woods/Moe, © 2003. Reprinted by permission of Pearson Education, Inc. Upper Saddle River, NJ.

her word recognition performance to be rated at the instructional level. However, because her retelling was so complete and her responses to comprehension questions were accurate, her comprehension is rated at the independent level. This means second-grade material is at Jenny's independent reading level. The comprehension score carries heavier weight in the overall rating of the selection than does the word recognition score.

Because Jenny's performance on this selection was rated at the independent level, you would have her read the next most difficult passage. You would continue having her read increasingly more difficult selections until you could determine her instructional reading level and her frustration level. The *Analytical Reading Inventory* recommends that once you determine the child's frustration level, you read passages to him or her until you reach the level at which the child can comprehend 75% of the material. This "listening level" is thought to be a measure of the student's reading potential.

To get a complete picture of Jenny's performance on this informal reading inventory, examine Figure 3.4. Here you will see her teacher's summary of her performance on the reading of three selections. Note that her independent reading level is second-grade material, her transitional instructional level is third-grade material, and her frustration level is fourth grade. Also carefully note the analysis of Jenny's reading strengths and weaknesses at the bottom of the form. The authors of the *Analytical Reading Inventory* describe four reading levels. These levels are illustrated in Figure 3.5. The goal is to provide children with text at their instructional level for instructional purposes and to provide independent level texts for practice reading.

Setting Instructional Goals. Once you have all of Jenny's data summarized on the Student Profile Summary, you can begin to determine instructional goals for Jenny. What instructional goals would you set for Jenny?

Your list of goals might consist of:

Several useful informal reading inventories are available. For a list of recommended inventories, please visit the Weblinks in Chapter 3 on our Companion Website at www.prenhall.com/harp.

1. increasing oral reading fluency and willingness to attempt challenging words
2. instruction on decoding vowel sounds, especially in the middle and ends of words
3. instruction in determining answers to comprehension questions that call for combining author and reader information and for evaluations

It is likely that, as Jenny's teacher, you would feel the use of the *Analytical Reading Inventory* had been a great help in identifying next learning steps for her. Another form of highly useful oral reading check is running records. Taking and analyzing running records helps teachers to look at children's reading behaviors in powerful ways they otherwise would be unable to do.

Running Records

Running records are a tool for recording all that we can observe about a child's behavior as he is reading aloud to us. This valuable tool is used extensively in New Zealand where Marie Clay (1993) invented it, and it is now popular in the United States. Teachers tell us that once they begin taking running records on children's oral reading, they never look at readers the same way again. They view children's reading behavior with much more informed and analytical eyes. To use running records, you need first to learn a set of conventions for marking oral reading behavior, then you need to learn how to analyze the behavior you recorded.

Running Record Conventions. Unlike the conventions used in informal reading inventories, the conventions used in running records are standardized. Clay has successfully made the case that all teachers should learn and use the standard set of conventions. This way you can share a running record you took with a reading specialist, a special educator,

Figure 3.4
Jenny's Student Profile Summary

STUDY SHEET 4 ● Overview of Components

STUDENT PROFILE SUMMARY

Student *Jenny Stone* Grade *4* Sex *F* Age *9-10* (yrs. + mos.)

School *Merrill Elementary* Administered by *M.L Woods* Date *9/25/2001*

Level	Word Lists	Narrative Passages		
FORM *C*	% correct	Word Recognition	Comprehension	Listening and/or Silent
Preprimer	-----------			
Primer	-----------			
Level 1	*95*			
Level 2	*100*	*- 6 definite instr.*	*- 0 independent*	
Level 3	*100*	*- 13 trans. instr.*	*- 3 1/2 trans. instr.*	
Level 4	*85*	*- 16 frustration*	*- 4 1/2 frustration*	*Silent - 7 frust.*
Level 5	*40 (only 10 words)*			*Lis. - 2 1/2 def. ins.*
Level 6	-----------			
Level 7	-----------			
Level 8	-----------			
Level 9	-----------			

Reading Levels

Narrative Passages, Form C

Independent *2*

Instructional *3 (transitional)*

Frustration *4*

Listening *5 (definite)*

Expository Passages

Science, Form S (at grade level)		Social Studies, Form SS (at grade level)	
WR.	Comp.	WR.	Comp.
Frust.	*Frust.*	*Frust.*	*Frust.*
Listening Passage ___		Listening Passage ___	
Comprehension ___		Comprehension ___	

OVERVIEW OF READING BEHAVIORS

1. Predictions
   - ☑ Reader most often made a logical prediction from the title.
   - ☑ Reader most often made a logical prediction from the first two sentences.

2. Reader had prior knowledge of
   - ☐ many passages
   - ☑ some passages
   - ☐ few passages

3. Types of Oral Reading Miscues
   - ☑ Omissions ☐ Insertions
   - ☑ Substitutions ☐ Aided words
   - ☑ Repetitions ☐ Reversals

   Reader Self-Corrects
   ☐ a lot ☑ sometimes ☐ seldom

4. Fluency Analysis
   1 = labored, disfluent reading/very slow pace
   2 = slow and choppy reading/slow pace
   3 = poor phrasing/ intonation/reasonable pace
   4 = fairly fluent reading/good pace

   4 independent
   3 instructional
   1 frustration

5. Cueing Systems: Miscue Analysis
   Graphophonic Similarities
   ☑ Initial ☐ Medial ☐ Final

   Syntactic: Most miscues were
   ☑ acceptable ☐ unacceptable

   Semantic: Most miscues caused
   ☑ change in meaning *at upper passages* ☑ no change in meaning *at lower passages*

6. Retelling Analysis: The reader most often retold
   - ☐ many details, logical order
   - ☑ some details, some order
   - ☐ few details, disorder

   Reader most often summarizes
   ☑ adequately ☐ not adequately

7. Comprehension Questions Analysis
   The examiner
   ☐ asked few ☑ asked many

   Reader's Strength(s)
   - ☑ Retells In Fact (RIF)
   - ☑ Puts Information Together (PIT)
   - ☐ Combines Author and Reader (CAR)
   - ☐ Evaluates and Substantiates (EAS)

   Reader Text Relationship (RTR)
   Reader responds adequately
   ☑ From the Text ☐ From Head to Text

8. Emotional Status at Various Reading Levels
   Reader was
   - ☐ relaxed/confident
   - ☐ slightly nervous
   - ☐ stressed/little confidence

   Independent Level *confident*
   Instructional Level *less confident*
   Frustration Level *stressed*
   Listening Level *relaxed, attentive*

an administrator, or another teacher at your grade level, and you would all be able to understand the child's reading behavior. The conventions used to mark a running record are displayed in Figure 3.6.

Taking the Running Record. To take a running record you need a text (a book or a few pages), a child to do the reading, a piece of paper on which to record the oral reading

Figure 3.5
Analytical Reading Inventory Four Reading Levels

Independent Level
Word Recognition = 99%; Comprehension = 90%

Definite Instructional Level
Word Recognition = 95–98%; Comprehension = 75–89%

Transitional Instructional Level
Word Recognition = 91–94%; Comprehension = 51–74%

Frustration Level
Word Recognition 90% or less; Comprehension = 50% or less

Source: *Analytical Reading Inventory: Comprehensive Assessment for All Students,* 7/e by Woods/Moe, © 2003. Reprinted by permission of Pearson Education, Inc. Upper Saddle River, NJ.

Figure 3.6
Running Record Conventions

Convention	Example
ACCURATE READING	✓ ✓ ✓ ✓
SUBSTITUTION (counted as an error)	boat / barge
OMISSION (counted as an error)	– / rat
INSERTION (counted as an error)	at / –
TTA "Try that again" (counted as one error, then score re-reading)	[little beet sail / small boat sailed] TTA
TOLD (counted as an error)	– / table | T
SELF-CORRECTION (not counted as an error)	his | SC / her |
REPETITION (R) (not counted as an error)	✓The horse ran away. or R4
APPEAL (the appeal is not counted, but the word told is counted)	– | App | / house | | T

Source: Adaptations for some conventions used for recording running records from: *An Observation Survey of Early Literacy Achievement,* © 2002, pp. 63–65. Reprinted by permission.

The authors recommend in addition, that further useful information may be gained by recording the following not included in Clay's research and analysis.

Convention	Example
SOUND OUT (not counted as an error)	c-a-t / cat
SOUND THROUGH (not counted as an error)	l-lit / little
PAUSE (not counted as an error)	//

behaviors, and a pencil. Avoid the temptation to make a photocopy of the text. One of the great values of learning to use running records is that you can take one when you have a snippet of time. It is quick and easy to assemble a reader, a text, and a paper and pencil. If you must run to the photocopy machine before you take a running record, you will have complicated the process too much.

Choose a text that the child has recently read. Try to select a text that is at the child's instructional or independent reading level, not at the frustration level.

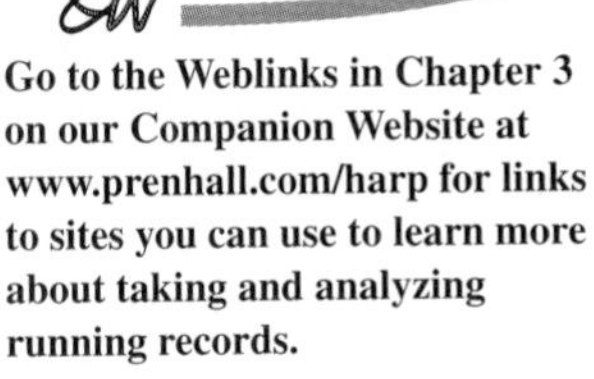

Go to the Weblinks in Chapter 3 on our Companion Website at www.prenhall.com/harp for links to sites you can use to learn more about taking and analyzing running records.

Figure 3.7 illustrates a text entitled *My Dog Got Away!,* the running record taken on Tyler's reading of that text, and the analysis of errors. Note that the oral reading behavior was recorded using the conventions, with items from the text recorded below a horizontal line and Tyler's oral reading behavior recorded above the line. After the complete running record was taken, Tyler was asked to retell all he could remember from the reading. His teacher made a notation about the quality of the retelling.

Analyzing the Running Record. First, examine each line of the running record and identify errors. Make a tally mark in the error count column for each error and a mark in the self-correction count column for each self-correction. Note that self-corrections are not counted as errors. Tyler's teacher tallied errors for when she told him the word *short,* for when he substituted *He is* for *He's,* for when he substituted *dogs* for *good* and *dad* for *bad,* for when he substituted *How* for *Oh,* and for when she told him *What.* This makes a total of six errors. Tyler had one self-correction, which the teacher tallied in the self-correction count column.

Figure 3.7
Text, Running Record, and Analysis

		COUNT E	COUNT SC	E MSV	SC MSV
My dog got away!	✓ ✓ ✓ ✓				
Have you seen my dog?	✓ ✓ ✓ ✓ ✓				
He's short, not tall.	✓ –/short | T ✓ ✓	1			
Have you seen my dog.	✓ ✓ ✓ ✓ ✓				
He's brown, not gray.	He is/He's ✓ ✓ ✓	1		(M)(S)(V)	
Have you seen my dog?	✓ ✓ ✓ ✓ ✓				
He's happy, not sad.	He/He's | SC ✓ ✓ ✓		1	(M)(S)(V)	M S (V)
Have you seen my dog?	✓ ✓ ✓ ✓ ✓				
He's fat, not thin.	✓ ✓ ✓ ✓				
Have you seen my dog?	✓ ✓ ✓ ✓ ✓				
He's good, not bad.	✓ dogs/good ✓ dad/bad	1 1		M S V M S (V)	
My dog got away!	✓ ✓ ✓ ✓				
Oh, there's my dog!	How/Oh ✓ ✓ ✓	1		M S V	
What a great day!	–/what | T ✓ ✓ ✓	1			
		6	1	M S V 2 2 3	V 1

Second, analyze each error and self-correction. We cannot analyze omissions and insertions or words that we tell the child. Therefore, no analysis is done on Tyler's first error. We move on down to this next error—the substitution of *He is* for *He's,* and write an *M, S,* and *V* in the error analysis column.

In considering whether or not to circle the *M,* we ask ourselves if we have evidence that the child is reading for meaning. Do we think the meaning of the text influenced the error? In this case, Tyler's teacher saw evidence that he was reading for meaning, and she circled the *M.*

In considering whether or not to circle the *S,* we ask ourselves if we have evidence that the child is using his knowledge of language structure (syntax) in making the error. Tyler's substitution of *He is* for *He's* was syntactically acceptable. Therefore, his teacher circled the *S.*

In considering whether or not to circle the *V,* we ask ourselves if we have evidence that the visual information in the print influenced the error in any way. The text and the error were highly similar visually. Tyler's teacher concluded that he was using visual information in making the error, and she circled the *V.*

A similar analysis continues for each error throughout the running record. After you have analyzed each error, you need to analyze each self-correction. Self-corrections are analyzed twice: once as an error (though not counted as an error) and once as a self-correction. Examine the self-correction Tyler made when he substituted *He* for *He's.* No tally is made in the error count column, but one tally is made in the self-correction count column. The self-correction is then analyzed as an error. In this case you would ask why Tyler made the error in the first place. It appears that he is reading for meaning since "He is" and "He's" mean the same thing. Similarly, it appears that Tyler was using his knowledge of syntax because the substitution is syntactically acceptable. It further appears that Tyler was attending to visual cues. So Tyler's teacher circled the *M, S,* and *V* in analyzing the self-correction as an error.

Next, the self-correction is analyzed as a self-correction. Here you ask why Tyler made the self-correction. It appears that his miscue did not look right to him and so he corrected it. Therefore, his teacher circled the *V,* indicating her opinion that Tyler self-corrected because of his more intense use of the visual cues.

When the analysis of all errors and self-corrections is complete, tally the number of errors, the number of self-corrections, and the number of times you circled *M, S,* and *V* in each of the error analysis columns. By tallying the number of times you circled *M, S,* and *V,* you gain a sense of whether or not the reader is reading for meaning, monitoring the process through self-corrections, and bringing balance to his use of the syntactic and visual cueing systems.

The next step is to calculate the error ratio, the accuracy rate and the self-correction ratio. Work through the following steps to do this (refer again to Figure 3.7):

1. Count the total number of running words in the text (61 in this case).
2. Count the total number of errors (6 in this case).
3. Calculate the error ratio. In this case that is 6/61, which reduces to 1:10. The error ratio is 1 in 10.
4. Calculate the accuracy rate. First subtract the number of errors from the number of running words. In this case that is $61 - 6 = 55$. Divide the answer by the number of running words. In this case that is $55/61 = .901$. Multiply the answer by 100. In this case that is $.901 \times 100 = 90.1$. Round off the answer. In this case that is 90. The accuracy rate is 90%.
5. Calculate the self-correction ratio by dividing the number of self-corrections by the sum of the errors plus the self-corrections. In this case that is $1/6+1$ or 1/7. Tyler's self-correction ratio is 1 in 7.

Figure 3.8
Tyler's Running Record Sheet

Name: Tyler   Date:

Text: My Dog Got Away

Seen   Unseen

Retelling: Tyler offered an accurate retelling with details. No prompting was required.

Scores: Running Words / Errors 61/6   Error Rate: 1:10   Accuracy: 90%
SC Rate: 1:7

Analysis of Errors: Tyler is reading for meaning. This text is at Tyler's instructional reading level. He should be encouraged to do more careful checking of visual detail, particularly at the beginnings of words. He needs encouragement to ask himself if his errors look right, sound right, and make sense. This will improve his self-correction ratio.

Figure 3.8 presents the complete running record on Tyler's reading of this selection. Note that his teacher has entered the calculations in the specified places and has written an evaluation of the retelling as well as an analysis of the errors. In writing the analysis of the errors, try always to identify one or two goals for future instruction. Stick to the facts. Avoid evaluative statements such as "good" or "best" reading.

One of the benefits of learning to take and analyze running records is that all you need is a child, a text, a piece of paper, and a pencil. Once you learn how, you can take them "on the run" as you find snippets of time through the day.

Go to the Weblinks in Chapter 3 on our Companion Website at www.prenhall.com/harp to link to the Wireless Generation web site.

Running Records on Your Handheld Computer. You may find it even easier to take and analyze running records using a handheld computer. The software designers at Wireless Generation have created the software for a handheld computer that allows you to take and analyze running records on your handheld. The system is known as mCLASS Reading. The developers have partnered with many publishers of leveled texts. You download the texts from the mCLASS web site, take the running record on individual children using your handheld, and upload the data to their secure web site. From there you can access the data analysis you would otherwise calculate by hand, plus a variety of other reports that track student progress by reading level and permit you to gain insight into each student's needs.

Some teachers prefer a more structured approach to the assessment and evaluation of oral reading. In this case, you may prefer to use Joetta Beaver's (1997) *Developmental Reading Assessment.*

Developmental Reading Assessment (DRA). The DRA is a set of leveled texts and forms useful in analyzing a child's oral reading behavior. At easier text levels you ask the child to read the text aloud as you take a running record. With higher level texts the child reads the first few paragraphs aloud, makes predictions about what will happen next, and reads the rest of the story silently. At most levels you ask the child to retell what she can remember from the story, and you take a running record on a section of oral reading. In short, the DRA is an organized set of materials designed to help you track children's progress as readers over time using literature, taking and analyzing running records, evaluating retellings, and plotting progress on a developmental continuum.

The information you gain from carefully observing children's oral reading behavior will be useful to you in marking a child's progress as a reader. With young readers, you will probably want to do an oral reading check on each child every three weeks. With children in third grade and above, you may take oral reading checks much less often. You will find oral reading checks useful at any grade level with struggling readers. Observing oral reading behavior is a way to take a focused look at a reader's growth. We also need to take a developmental perspective of our learners' growth as readers and writers over time, and these are useful tools to help us.

LOOKING AT THE RESEARCH

What the research says about early literacy assessment and evaluation tools

In a study sponsored by the Center for the Improvement of Early Literacy Instruction, Samuel Meisels and Ruth Piker (2001) reviewed 89 assessment and evaluation tools designed to measure performance on 133 skills in early literacy achievement. The most frequent student responses elicited by the measures were oral responses and writing. Identification, production, and recall were all included among the types of mental processing skills. Teacher observations were used prominently throughout the measures.

The researchers called for improvements in the measures. Recommendations included: more instruments that allow children to construct meaning with the teacher rather than producing discrete answers, more measures written in languages other than English, increased measures that call for written responses, measures that permit children to demonstrate what they know in multiple ways, and assessments that permit students to engage in cooperative group work in constructing products and answers.

Reflect on the reading tests you have taken or the ones you have observed children taking in classrooms. To what extent have the recommendations of these researchers been considered in the design of the tests you have seen?

Go to our Companion Website at www.prenhall.com/harp and then to the chapter's Threaded Message Board to add your comments to the global discussion about these questions.

Influence of the Reading First Grants

Reading First is a new national initiative for which Congress has allocated nearly $5 billion to be distributed among the 50 states, the District of Columbia, Puerto Rico, and outlying areas over the next several years. These grants will likely have a profound effect on the teaching and learning of reading. Successful grants will propose instructional programs based on scientifically proven research results. This essentially means the research accepted by the National Reading Panel, as discussed in Chapter 2. Instructional programs must focus on phonemic awareness, phonics, fluency, vocabulary, and comprehension—the categories endorsed by the National Reading Panel (U. S. Department of Education, n.d.).

Reading First grants focus on the primary grades and support professional development for teachers, the purchase or development of instructional materials, and the administration of assessments or diagnostic instruments. The validity and reliability of these instruments must be clearly established before they can be included in a grant. While the U.S. Department of Education does not have an approved list of such instruments, an "approved list" is emerging within the profession, based on the instruments that have been included in successfully funded grants.

This "approved list" includes, but is not limited to: DIBELS (see Chapter 9), *Comprehensive Test of Phonological Processing, Degrees of Reading Power, Gates-MacGinitie Reading Test, Gray Oral Reading Test, Peabody Picture Vocabulary Test,* and *Stanford Diagnostic Reading Test.* You will encounter discussions of many of these instruments in Assessment and Evaluation Toolboxes beginning in Chapter 4.

HOW DO I ASSESS AND EVALUATE READERS' AND WRITERS' GROWTH OVER TIME?

The most powerful assessment and evaluation tool you have at your disposal is your own observation of your learners. Of course, you will become better at making keen, insightful observations as you gain more experience, but even from the beginning your observational skills will be useful. Every encounter you have with children should, in a sense, be diagnostic. For example, you may observe that a child never chooses to go to the library corner, so you introduce the child to a new book. You note that a child usually writes short sentences, so you engage this child in some sentence expansion activities.

You need to search continually for signs that point to what the child knows and needs to learn next, how the child learns and feels, what challenges the child and what fails to capture the child's interest. Much of the time your observations will become the basis for your instructional decisions. To make your observations useful, you will need to write them down.

Anecdotal Records

Some teachers who respect their own observations and thoughts record them in notebooks. Called *anecdotal records,* these notes can then be referred to at a later time such as during planning or parent conferences. Making anecdotal records allows you to comment both on the products children produce (a written piece or oral reading) and on their use of processes such as the reading process or the writing process (Rhodes & Nathenson-Mejia, 1992). If you carry a supply of gummed blank labels in your pockets (or place stacks of them conveniently around your room), you can pull a label out and record your observations as you are moving about observing your students at work. Later you can transfer the label to the child's designated page in a loose-leaf binder. Figure 3.9 lists the anecdotal notes taken by a first-grade teacher over a short period of time.

Using Anectodal Records. Anectodal records can be immediately useful to you as a reminder of a goal you wish to set with a child later in the day or within the next few days. They also capture your perceptions of children's growth over time. To capitalize on this feature of anecdotal records, you may wish to create a schedule by which you will periodically review the running records you have taken on five of your children. Write a summary for each of the children highlighting the major observations in the reviewed records and setting learning goals for the next few weeks. Place the dated summaries in the binder with each set of records. After you have reviewed one set of five children, schedule a time when you will review the next set of five. Build a schedule so that within a nine-week grading period,

Figure 3.9
First-Grade Anecdotal Records

- Jim did not begin writing for 10 minutes after the writing workshop began. After I typed his story, he illustrated it. Jim scribbled on his desk and refused to wipe it off. I am wondering if he is apprehensive and afraid of writing—clearly an opinion on my part. I will watch Jim's writing behavior very carefully for the next few days.
- Christina's illustrations in her book about her brother are highly detailed. She used the word wall several times to confirm spellings as she was drafting her book today.
- Mack can read the menu and write it on the board for the kids to see. Mack has improved the writing in his journal. Now he asks me questions and draws little puzzles for me to figure out.
- For the first time today, Shelley miscued and noticed that what she read did not make sense. She reread and corrected her mistake. Hooray!

you have reviewed the records and set goals as many times as is practical. You may wish to draw on these summaries and goal statements in writing reports to parents.

Developmental checklists for reading and writing are another tool you can use to guide your observations.

Developmental Checklists for Reading

Developmental checklists in reading are observation guides that can add necessary structure to kidwatching (Goodman, 1996). With 25 or more learners in a classroom, it is difficult to make the kinds of careful observations teachers need to make without some well-organized system. Developmental checklists provide for these systematic observations.

The Reading Development Checklists illustrated in Figures 3.10 a,b, and c describe attitudes, understandings, and behaviors valued in emergent readers, developing readers, and fluent readers (Harp, 2000). They are offered here as examples to get you started using developmental checklists. You may wish to modify the checklists as you gain experience using them.

As you can see from looking through the checklists, the attitudes, understandings, and behaviors of readers change significantly as they move from the emergent stage through the developing stage and into fluency. A checklist like those included here—and modified to fit you and your learners—will be an important tool for you to use to make your observations richer and more helpful. Similar checklists for writing are illustrated in Chapter 10.

In addition to developmental checklists, the collection of rubrics will help you document growth over time. You may decide to keep selected rubrics in the binder where you store the checklists.

Using Rubrics to Mark Progress Over Time

Rubrics are defined by Rickards & Cheek (1999) as "scoring guides that use specific written criteria to distinguish among levels of student proficiency on a common task" (p. 9). A rubric must list what needs to be done (much like a checklist) and define levels of proficiency for each part of the task. For example, a writing checklist might list title, indentation, topic sentence, capitalization, and so on. It is easy to mark that a piece of writing has a title or does not. However, indentation could be used appropriately on some paragraphs and not others. How can it be marked? A rubric to evaluate performance on writing might list the same elements as a checklist, but it would then list de-

Figure 3.10a
Developmental Checklist for Emergent Readers

Name ______________________________

In the space to the left, record the date of your observation. Use the space under each item to write comments.

_______ Enjoys listening to stories, rhymes, songs, and poems

_______ Is eager to participate in group stories, rhymes, songs, and poems

_______ Approaches books with enthusiasm

_______ Revisits some books

_______ Knows that his/her language can be written and then read

_______ Understands how to handle books for reading

_______ Is able to make predictions and follow plot

_______ Knows some print conventions (period, question mark)

_______ Knows some book conventions (front cover, back cover, title page)

_______ Uses reading in play activities

_______ Uses pictures to help create meaning

_______ Is developing finger, print, voice match

_______ Identifies some words

_______ Is beginning to use graphophonic cues

_______ Is beginning to develop strategies to use when meaning fails

Figure 3.10b
Developmental Checklist for Developing Readers

Name ______________________________

In the space to the left, record the date of your observation. Use the space under each item to write comments.

_______ Is eager to attend to long books in reading and listening

_______ Shows an interest in meeting challenges of texts

_______ Displays confidence as a reader/Is willing to take risks and make predictions

_______ Is eager to share ideas with others

_______ Has increasing knowledge of book and print convention

_______ Understands how background knowledge contributes to meaning

_______ Appreciates the value of predicting, confirming, and integrating

_______ Has several strategies to invoke when meaning fails

_______ Increasingly makes more accurate predictions

_______ Reads increasingly more complicated texts across a range of genre

_______ Chooses to read independently

scriptors for various levels of performance. For example, indentation might be marked 4 (uses appropriate indentation throughout the piece), 3 (uses appropriate indentation throughout most of the piece), 2 (uses appropriate indentation occasionally), or 1 (does not use appropriate indentation).

Rubrics can be written for almost any task from cleaning a room to writing a sonata. They can address participating in literature discussions, making oral reports, or writing assignments. A rubric must list what is to be evaluated and describe the levels of proficiency for each performance level. Rubrics have the advantage of helping learners know exactly what is expected of them and knowing how to meet the criteria for success. Figure 3.11 is an example of a rubric for oral story retelling developed by Rickards and Cheek (1999).

You could use the story retelling rubric when you take a running record. You could store selected rubrics that document growth in comprehension and use them in parent conferences or in preparing your comments on reports to parents.

Figure 3.10c
Developmental Checklist for Fluent Readers

Name ____________________________________

In the space to the left, record the date of your observation. Use the space under each item to write comments.

_______ Expects books to offer a variety of meanings, some satisfying, some not

_______ Is confident as a reader

_______ Eagerly participates in book discussions, author studies, and other forms of response to literature

_______ Appreciates the power of reading

_______ Uses the cueing systems to best meet reading needs and demands of the text

_______ Understands the role of purpose in reading

_______ Knows how to use the library to get information and meet needs

_______ Knows how to use electronic media to get information and meet needs

_______ Demonstrates increasing sophistication in prediction, sampling, confirming, and integrating as a reader

_______ Is developing study skills and can use textbook features

_______ Is able to summarize, outline, and retell in detail

From: Harp, B. (2000). *Handbook of Literacy Assessment and Evaluation.* Norwood, MA: Christopher-Gordon Publishers, Inc.

Measures of children's perceptions of reading and the reading process, oral reading checks, anecdotal records, and rubrics will all be useful to you in documenting the effectiveness of your literacy instruction and your learners' growth as readers and writers. In fact, they may prove to be the most useful assessment and evaluation tools you use. However, they are likely not the only tools you will use.

School committee members and school administrators who are in decision-making positions typically want to know how children in your school district are performing in comparison to children elsewhere. To answer this question, they will turn to the use of standardized tests.

Figure 3.11
Rubric for Oral Story Retelling

Score Point 4

Without prompting, the student correctly tells the characters and setting and fully describes the story's problem and solution. Events are described thoroughly and sequenced accurately.

Score Point 3

With a minimum of prompting, the student correctly identifies the characters and setting and explains the story's problem and solution. Events are described and sequenced accurately.

Score Point 2

With prompting, the student identifies the characters, setting, problem, solution, and events, though the information is minimal and may contain slight inaccuracies.

Score Point 1

Even with prompting, the student does not identify the necessary story elements, and/or information contains significant inaccuracies.

Source: D. Rickards & E. Cheek (1999). *Designing Rubrics for K–6 Classroom Assessment.* Christopher-Gordon Publishers, Inc. Reprinted with permission.

WHAT DO I NEED TO KNOW ABOUT STANDARDIZED TESTS?

Standardized tests are designed so that the test items and the administration procedures are the same each time the test is administered. This standardization serves two purposes. It assures that the test and its administration remain consistent across administrations in a variety of locales, and it permits the comparison of the performance of one group of test takers with another. Standardized tests are typically used to compare the performance of one group of learners with another: classroom to classroom, school to school, district to district, or state to state. The purposes for giving a standardized test usually determine whether the test selected is criterion-referenced or norm-referenced.

Criterion-Referenced and Norm-Referenced Tests

To make comparisons of performance across groups and tests, we need test results in the form of scores. Standardized tests typically yield one of two kinds of scores: criterion-referenced scores or norm-referenced scores. When tests results are evaluated using criterion-referenced data, the individual student's performance is compared with a predetermined, arbitrarily set criterion. For example, a score of 70% might be considered minimal performance, a score of 80% might be considered satisfactory performance, and a score of 90% might be considered excellent performance. Scores on criterion-referenced tests permit comparisons only against this predetermined criterion, not against the performance of other students. When a standardized test is norm-referenced, performance on the test is compared to the performance of students who have taken the test in the past.

When a norm-referenced test is developed, it is administered to a group representative of the people for whom the test was designed, the norming sample. Why *sample?* Suppose the test were designed for use by fourth, fifth, and sixth graders. Ideally it would be given to all fourth, fifth, and sixth graders in the country, and their performance would become the norms for the tests. However, this is not practical. Test makers must instead select a sample of those students for whom the test is intended—the norming *sample.* The performance of

Figure 3.12
Knowledge Tested at Each Level of The *Gates-MacGinitie Reading Tests* (1998)

Test Level	Grade Level	Knowledge Tested
Level PR	Prereading	Literacy concepts, oral language concepts, phonemic awareness, letters and letter-sound correspondences, and story listening comprehension
Level R	Beginning reading skills	Initial consonants and consonant clusters, use of final consonants and consonant clusters, use of vowels, and recognition of story words
Levels 1 & 2	First and Second Grade	Word decoding, word knowledge, and comprehension
Levels 3–12	Grades 3 through 12	Vocabulary and comprehension

Source: W. H. MacGinitie & R. K. MacGinitie. (1998). Gate-MacGinities Reading Tests. Chicago, IL: Riverside Publishing.

the norming sample becomes the yardstick against which all future performance is judged. The statistics that describe the performance of the norming sample become the norms for the test. For example, if in the norming sample the average score of fourth graders was 87 correct responses, the norm becomes 87 as the average fourth-grade standard. When your fourth graders take the same test, they are then compared with the fourth graders (and others) in the norming sample. Your school district's announcement that its fourth graders are scoring "above the national average in reading comprehension" means its average fourth-grade scores were higher than the average fourth-grade scores in the norming sample.

In addition to being either criterion-referenced or norm-referenced, standardized tests are also typically either achievement tests or diagnostic tests. It is important for you to understand this distinction.

The Nature of Achievement Tests. Achievement tests are designed to measure how much students have learned in a particular curriculum area. In today's educational environment administrators are being held accountable for student achievement as never before. District administrators, school committees, and building principals seek norm-referenced achievement data so that comparisons can be made between children in the district and national norms. Achievement tests are thus given to measure performance across a wide range of school subjects, such as math computation, math reasoning, mechanics of language, spelling, decoding in reading, reading comprehension, science, and social studies.

Some achievement tests measure performance in only one area of the curriculum. For example, the *Gates-MacGinitie Reading Test* (1998) is designed to test achievement in reading from prereading abilities through adult reading. Figure 3.12 displays the abilities The Gates-MacGinitie tests at each level.

The Nature of Diagnostic Tests. Diagnostic tests sample a single curriculum or skill area in considerable depth. By using a diagnostic test, it is possible to determine a student's strengths and weaknesses for a particular skill. For example, a diagnostic test can be used to measure students' development in reading comprehension or word recognition. Typically, diagnostic tests are used by specialists in reading or learning disabilities rather than by classroom teachers. To develop a sense of how reading diagnostic tests differ

Figure 3.13
Knowledge Tested at Each Level of the *Stanford Diagnostic Reading Test* (1995)

Test Level	Grade Level	Knowledge Tested
Red Level	Second half of grade 1 and first half of grade 2	Phonic analysis of consonants (single, blends, digraphs) and vowels (short and long), vocabulary and comprehension
Orange Level	Second half of grade 2 and the first half of grade 3	Phonic analysis of consonants and vowels, listening vocabulary, reading vocabulary, comprehension
Green Level	Second half of grade 3 and first half of grade 4	Phonic analysis of consonants and vowels (long, short, and other), listening vocabulary, reading vocabulary, comprehension (initial understanding, interpretation, critical analysis, and reading strategies)
Purple, Brown, and Blue Levels	Middle of grade 4 through grade 12	Reading vocabulary—synonyms, classification, word parts, and content area words; comprehension—paragraphs with questions; type of text—recreational, textual, functional, and by mode of comprehension

Source: *Stanford Diagnostic Reading Test: Fourth Edition.* Copyright © 2002, 1995 by Harcourt Education Measurement, a Harcourt Assessment Company. Reproduced by permission.

from reading achievement tests, examine Figure 3.13, which presents the components of the *Stanford Diagnostic Reading Test, Fourth Edition,* 2002.

Comparing Achievement Tests with Diagnostic Tests. By comparing Figures 3.12 and 3.13, you will see that achievement tests measure several areas in limited depth, whereas diagnostic tests measure areas in considerably greater depth. As a classroom teacher you are likely to have much more involvement with achievement tests than diagnostic tests. You will probably be asked by your building principal to set aside time in the fall and again in the spring for achievement testing using a test that measures student progress. As an informed reading teacher, you are responsible for becoming a proficient test giver. In addition, you will want to become knowledgeable about interpreting the data each standardized test provides you about your students' annual progress. This may be critical to your perceived success as a teacher.

Becoming an Informed Norm-Referenced Test Consumer

You may have little or nothing to say about what norm-referenced tests are used in your school. These decisions are often made in the central office or by the school board. And yet, you are the person who will likely be asked to administer the test to your learners, and you are the person parents will first contact when they have questions or concerns about their children's performance on a norm-referenced test. For these reasons, you must be an informed test consumer. You will need to understand the various kinds of scores used to interpret test performance, and you must be able to carefully examine a test and its manual and make a decision about whether or not the test is appropriate for your learners. At minimum, you need to consider the test's validity and reliability and the nature of the norming sample.

Scores Used to Interpret Performance on Norm-Referenced Tests. Several different kinds of scores are used to interpret performance on a norm-referenced test. The raw score, the number of items scored correctly, is not informative. It does not explain how a student performed in comparison to the norming sample. Other scores used to interpret performance make such comparisons: percentile scores, stanine scores, grade equivalent scores, and normal curve equivalent scores (Harp, 2000).

Percentile Scores. Percentile scores range from 1 to 99 and indicate the percentage of students in the norming sample who earned raw scores the same as or lower than a given student's score.

Stanine Scores. Stanine scores distribute performance on a test over nine unequal categories. The middle, fifth segment brackets the mean of the distribution.

Grade Equivalent Scores. Grade equivalent scores are based on the grade at which an average person from a norming sample earns a given score. The International Reading Association has condemned the use of grade scores because they are so easily misunderstood (Harris & Hodges, 1995).

Normal Curve Equivalent Scores. Normal curve equivalent scores (NCE) range from 1 to 88 with a mean of 50. NCE scores can be averaged and are often used to report performance in reading programs.

Validity of the Test. The validity of a test is the degree to which the test actually tests what it claims to test. This requires examining the construct validity and the content validity of the test you are using.

Construct Validity. Construct validity is the degree to which the test measures the theoretical construct—in this case reading—that it claims to measure. In order to apply this test of validity, you must have a well-defined mental construct of reading. Suppose, for example, you were asked to give a test of reading comprehension. You examine the items on the test, and all of them ask students to select from four choices the best synonym for a target word. In your judgment would this test have construct validity as a test of reading comprehension? We hope your answer would be a resounding "NO!" Certainly, understanding synonyms is a part of reading comprehension, but it is a only small part. A true test of reading comprehension would include many more items, and certainly some would be based on the actual reading of text to determine if the reader can make sense of the text he is reading and make connections from it to his prior knowledge. In this case, the synonym test does not adequately test the theoretical construct of reading.

Content Validity. Establishing content validity means comparing the nature and breadth of the test items with the curriculum you teach. The test has content validity if it tests what you teach. Let us revisit the synonym example. Suppose you are using an integrated anthology to teach reading, and this program asks children to demonstrate knowledge of vocabulary by defining words and using them in sentences. The norm-referenced test you are asked to administer tests vocabulary knowledge by asking students to select the best synonym for a target word. Does this test have content validity for your learners? No, it does not. It does not ask for the same kind of vocabulary knowledge that you are developing using the anthology. Another example of the lack of content validity would be a test that measures children's ability to decode words by asking them to read a list of nonsense words when your reading program always involves them in reading real words in connected text.

When you are satisfied the test you are using has construct and content validity, you will need to examine the reliability of the test.

Reliability of the Test. A test is reliable if it yields the same results over time or across equivalent forms of the test. For example, if your students take Form A of a test of reading comprehension the first of the week and then take Form B of the test at the end of the week, their performance on the two forms should be about the same if the test is reliable. Or if you gave one-half of your students the even-numbered test items and the other half the odd-numbered test items, their performance should be about the same.

Reliability is usually described by a statistic called a *coefficient of correlation.* Correlation describes the degree to which two variables move together. A perfect correlation coefficient would be +1.0. This means that when a test is given twice (or two forms are used), the student who scores the highest on the first test also scores the highest on the second test. The student who scores second highest on the first test also scores second highest on the second test, and so on. Rarely do we find a perfect, +1.0 correlation. We could be comfortable about the test's reliability if the correlation coefficient is +0.85 or better.

Even if a norm-referenced test passes your requirements for validity and reliability, it will not be an appropriate test to use with your students unless they are fairly represented in the norming sample.

Nature of the Norming Sample. You need to determine whether children like your students in terms of race, ethnicity, geographical location, and socioeconomic status are included in the norming sample. To understand the importance of the nature of the norming sample, suppose your professor came into class and announced, "I have decided to stop using the quizzes I create in this class to measure your performance. Instead, I will use a new norm-referenced test on the teaching of reading and writing. After I created the test items, I used the doctoral students in reading as the norming sample." How would this announcement by your professor make you feel?

Probably you would feel worried. Such a norm-referenced test would not fairly assess your performance. It would not be fair because you and your classmates are not represented in the norming sample. The nature of the norming sample is an important question for you and your students. Your performance and that of your students will be judged by it.

Reviewing a Publisher's Description of Their Standardized Test. Reputable test publishers supply validity and reliability data in the examiner's manual or a technical supplement to the examiner's manual. They also supply detailed demographics on the norming sample. Critical test consumers carefully examine this information to assess the validity and appropriateness of the test for their students and the reliability of the test. If the test you use fails to satisfy any one of the conditions of validity, reliability, or nature of the norming sample, you should deem it inappropriate for your students. If after reviewing any test description, you believe it to be an inappropriate test for your student population, it is professionally sound practice to say so to your principal. You might also want to communicate your concerns in a letter to the district's testing coordinator or the official or committee that selects the tests. You may decide to point out these shortcomings to parents when discussing their children's performance. These actions are all part of being an informed reading teacher.

Many teachers do not like to stir up trouble. They just want to do the best job possible for their students—and to give that all of their energy. However, we are in an age of accountability. Building administrators are held accountable for performance of children in their schools. In turn, classroom teachers are held accountable today as never before. We have entered the age of standards, accountability, and high stakes testing.

WHAT DO I NEED TO KNOW ABOUT STANDARDS, ACCOUNTABILITY, AND HIGH-STAKES TESTING?

A national accountability movement has led to the creation of learning standards in most states. An informed teacher of reading understands standards and the controversy surrounding them.

Understanding Standards

Standards are being written by state departments of education, the U.S. Department of Education, school systems, and others groups associated with education. Schools are expected to develop curricula consistent with each of the standards, and the state then develops tests to measure performance on the standards. Elected and government officials view these tests as a means of forcing curricular change. The assumption that changing assessment will force changes in curricula was verified in a study of secondary schools. As high-stakes testing was put into place, curriculum and instructional practices changed to be consistent with the test (Barnes, Clarke, & Stephens, 2000).

In many states graduation from high school is contingent on passing these tests, thus the label *high-stakes testing*. High-stakes testing adds a degree of urgency to every teacher becoming an informed test consumer. Typically, general standards are broad statements outlining what students should know and be able to do in each curriculum area. The general standards are usually followed by performance standards, which further specify learning expectations in each curriculum area by grade level.

Selected general reading and literature standards are presented in Figure 3.14, followed by examples of grade level learning standards. These are taken from the *Massachusetts English Language Arts Curriculum Framework, 2001.* As you examine these illustrations notice how the grade level standards relate to the general standards.

You can tell by examining Figure 3.14 that learning standards can be stated specifically. Many teachers welcome this detail in curriculum and report that uniform curriculum goals from grade level to grade level are helpful. Some teachers have praised high-stakes testing because it has forced teachers to teach to the test. However, on this point there is considerable disagreement.

An Opposing Viewpoint

In his book, published by the Association for Supervision and Curriculum Development, James Popham (2001) clearly articulates an opposing point of view:

> . . . today's educators are increasingly caught up in a measurement-induced maelstrom focused on raising students' scores on high-stakes tests. The term "maelstrom" captures all too accurately the reality of this test-obsession: It's a hazardous whirlpool that can drag us down, even when we approach it cautiously.
>
> Because U.S. society currently accepts the idea that good test scores equal good education, everybody wants students to score well on high-stakes tests. The first negative effect of today's high-stakes testing programs is that such programs divert educators' attention from the genuinely important educational decisions they ought to be making. Thousands of American educators find themselves caught up in a score-boosting obsession that seriously detracts from their effectiveness in teaching children. The critical question of "How do we teach Tracy the things she needs to know?" is forced aside by this far less important one: "How do we improve Tracy's scores on the high-stakes test she will be taking?" (p.16)

Figure 3.14
Selected General Reading and Literature Standards with Excerpts from Accompanying Learning Standards

General Standard 7 Beginning Reading: Students will understand the nature of written English and the relationship of letters and spelling patterns to the sounds of speech.

Learning Standard Grades PreK–K: Demonstrate understanding of the forms and functions of written English: recognize that printed materials provide information or entertaining stories; know how to handle a book and turn the pages; identify the covers and title page of a book.

Learning Standard Grades 1–2: Demonstrate orally that phonemes exist: generate the sounds from all the letters and letter patterns, including consonant blends, long- and short-vowel patterns, and onsets and rimes, and combine these sounds into recognizable words; use knowledge of vowel digraphs, vowel diphthongs, and r-controlled letter-sound associations to read words.

General Standard 8, Understanding a Text: Students will identify the basic facts and main ideas in a text and use them as the basis for interpretation.

Learning Standard Grades 3–4, For imaginative/literary texts: Identify and show the relevance of foreshadowing clues. Identify sensory details and figurative language. For example, students read *The Cricket in Times Square,* by George Selden, noticing passages that contain figurative language and sensory details, such as: "*And the air was full of the roar of traffic and the hum of human beings. It was as if Times Square were a kind of shell with colors and noises breaking in great waves inside it.*" Then students discuss the effect of the images and draw an illustration that captures their interpretation of one image. Identify the speaker of a poem or story; make judgments about setting, characters, and events, and support them with evidence from the text.

Massachusetts English Language Arts Curriculum Framework, 2001

In reality, classroom teachers don't have a say in whether or not to use high-stakes tests. The goal of our profession is to prepare children as best we can for success in school, to maximize the use of information from high-stakes tests to improve instruction, and to select other assessment and evaluation measures that will help us know our learners better. Your job will then be to orchestrate the management of all of this assessment and evaluation data in ways that best serve your students.

LOOKING AT THE RESEARCH

What the research says about teachers' and administrators' view of assessment tools

In a study sponsored by the Center for the Improvement of Early Reading Achievement, researchers surveyed teachers in successful schools. Teachers revealed that they use many informal reading tasks to assess children's skills, knowledge, and fluency on a daily basis. They choose to use "internal" assessment under their control rather than "external," high-stakes assessments created by publishers or mandated by others. Paradoxically, teachers believe that administrators pay more attention to external, high-stakes assessments than to assessments of daily work that are linked to instruction (Paris, Paris, & Carpenter, 2001).

We will return to this question at the end of the chapter, but take a moment now to reflect on the purposes for using assessment and evaluation tools from a principal's point of view and that of a classroom teacher. How would their purposes for testing differ, and what differences can you imagine they would want in terms of the data they collect and analyze?

Go to our Companion Website at www.prenhall.com/harp and then to the Threaded Message Board to add your comments to the global discussion on this issue.

HOW DO I ORGANIZE TO MAKE THE BEST USE OF THE ASSESSMENT AND EVALUATION TOOLS I HAVE?

You have many options to collect information about your learners' strengths and identify their next learning steps. With a classroom of children this is both a challenge and a necessity. With so many demands on your time and attention as a teacher, it is important to be as well organized as possible to make the best use of those assessment and evaluation tools. The following is a set of suggestions—helpful hints, we hope—drawn from our own experiences as teachers and from our work in the classrooms of many teachers.

Identify Required Assessment and Evaluation Tools. Find out at the beginning of the school year which assessment and evaluation tools you are required by the school district to use at your grade level. Carefully consider the kinds of information you will get from each tool and for what purposes you will be able to use that information.

Identify Additional Assessment and Evaluation Tools. Carefully consider what additional assessment and evaluation tools you will want to add to the list of required tools, if there is one.

Create Your Assessment and Evaluation Plan. Recognizing that often assessment and evaluation is spontaneous and cannot always be planned in advance, nevertheless, make a calendar for each week of the school year. On this calendar note the assessment tools you plan to use each week. This way you will be sure to plan for the required assessments.

Establish a Place for Taking Running Records. Select a small table or desk and set up a place in your room to take running records. Stock the spot with running record forms and sharpened pencils. Or, put a stack of running record forms in several convenient spots around your classroom so that you can get them easily when you want to take a running record as you move from child to child.

Create a Monitoring Notebook. Get a three-ring binder and index dividers so that you can make a section in the binder for each student. Put several pieces of blank paper in each student's section. Get some gummed, blank name labels on which you can record anecdotal notes. When you have recorded an observation on a label, date it and put it in the appropriate child's section of the binder. You may put many other items in the monitoring notebook for each of your students: running record forms, developmental checklists, strategy checklists (see Chapter 6), and comprehension checklists (see Chapter 8).

Create Reading and Writing Portfolios. Get two file folders for each child. Create a reading portfolio in one and a writing portfolio in the other. Use vertical files or plastic file boxes to store the folders where you and the children can access them easily. Create forms that you can staple to the inside cover of the folders with the following

Monitoring notebooks are a way to organize large amounts of student data.

headings at the top of two columns: "Things I'm Doing Well as a Reader" and "My Goals as a Reader." The writing portfolio should have similar headings for writing. These forms may be used when you hold reading and writing conferences with your students. Lewis (1997) found that when teachers used portfolios, they spent more time discussing with students the criteria for high-quality work, they assigned more demanding work, and students did more writing across the curriculum.

Carefully plan the contents of the reading portfolios and writing portfolios. You might want to review Nichole Duffy's comments on her use of portfolios in the "Real Teachers, Real Practice" section at the beginning of this chapter. Potential contents of the reading portfolios include:

- Checklists of activities to do before, during, and after a conference, which were presented in Chapter 2.
- Running records as "work samples" of reading. The running records could include evaluation of progress by both you and the child.
- Reading developmental checklists. You may choose to keep these in the portfolio rather than the monitoring notebook. In either case, plan to mark each child's developmental checklist regularly. You may want to put this activity on the calendar so that you don't overlook anyone.
- Summaries of anecdotal notes that relate to reading. Once a month, review the anecdotal notes you have taken on a child about reading behavior. Create a dated summary of these to place in the portfolio.
- Records of books the child has read for practice during a grading period. You may also want to keep a list of the books a child has read for guided reading. Some schools produce computer printouts of the books a child has checked out of the media center. These might also be placed in the reading portfolio.

Potential contents of the writing portfolio include:

- Checklists of activities to do before, during, and after a conference, which were presented in Chapter 2.

- Writing samples with evaluations by you and the author attached.
- Writing developmental checklists updated regularly (unless you keep these in the monitoring notebook).
- Summaries of anecdotal notes that relate to writing.

Target Certain Children for Assessment and Evaluation Each Week. Each week make a list of the children you plan to make focused literacy observations of the following week. This way you won't feel as if you need to observe all children equally—an impossibility—and you won't overlook careful observation of some of your children. This plan won't be perfect, and it will likely be changed. You will have to respond to spontaneous opportunities for assessment and evaluation. However, this plan will help you systematically collect data on all your learners.

Take a closer look each time you see this magnifying glass for ways to use assessment to keep you informed.

Remember That Assessment and Evaluation Go Hand in Hand. Never assess (collect data) without evaluating (interpreting) that data to identify a child's strengths and next learning needs. *You will get better and better at this as you gain more experience.*

Become Familiar with Many Tools. Carefully examine the Assessment and Evaluation Toolboxes that appear throughout most of the remaining chapters in this text. They highlight assessment and evaluation tools that may be used in conjunction with each area of the literacy curriculum. No teacher would use all of the tools presented. They are here to help you broaden your knowledge base about assessment and evaluation.

It is important to realize that assessment and evaluation tools differ widely, and different tools yield different kinds of data that satisfy the needs of different audiences. Roger Farr (1993) illustrated this well in a classic article he wrote about solving the assessment puzzle. Examine Figure 3.15, which is reprinted from Farr's article. You will see the five typical, and varying, audiences listed down the left-hand side. The general public

Audiences	The information is needed to:	The information is related to:	Type of information:	When information is needed:
General public (and the press)	Judge if schools are accountable and effective	Groups of students	Related to broad goals; norm- & criterion-referenced	Annually
School administrators/ staff	Judge effectiveness of curriculum, materials, teachers	Groups of students & individuals	Related to broad goals; criterion- & norm-referenced	Annually or by term/semester
Parents	Monitor progress of child, effectiveness of school	Individual student	Usually related to broader goals; both criterion- & norm-referenced	Periodically; 5 or 6 times a year
Teachers	Plan instruction, strategies, activities	Individual student; small groups	Related to specific goals: criterion-referenced	Daily, or as often as possible
Students	Identify strengths, areas to emphasize	Individual (self)	Related to specific goals; criterion-referenced	Daily, or as often as possible

Figure 3.15
Assessment Audiences and Purposes
Source: Figure from Farr, Roger. (1992, September). Putting it all together: solving the reading assessment puzzle. *The Reading Teacher, 46*(1), 26–37.

Tool Name/Type	Grade Levels	Information Gained
Reading Interviews	PreK through high school	Attitudes toward reading and perceptions of the reading process
Motivation to Read Profile	Second through sixth grade	A child's self concept as a reader and the value he or she places on reading
Reader Self-Perception Scale	Fourth through sixth grade	How children feel about themselves as readers
Writing Interviews	PreK through high school	Attitudes toward writing and perceptions of the writing process
Writer Self-Perception Scale	Fourth through sixth grade	How children feel about themselves as writers
Informal Reading Inventories	Kindergarten through adult	Word recognition score, comprehension score, retellings, use of strategies, miscues analysis
Running Records	Kindergarten through adult	Word recognition accuracy, retelling, error ratio, self-correction rate, strategic reading, use of the cueing systems, miscue analysis
Developmental Reading Assessment	Kindergarten through third grade	Oral reading accuracy, phrasing and fluency, reading strategies, miscue analysis, comprehension, reading preferences
Anecdotal Records	Elementary grades	Critical observations, insights, questions, plans
Developmental Checklists for Reading	Kindergarten through eighth grade	Developmental markers from emergent reader to fluent reader behaviors, attitudes, and understandings
Rubrics	All grade levels	Specific criteria by which assignments and activities are to be evaluated
Achievement Tests	All grade levels	Performance across all aspects of the curriculum or performance across a wide range of sub-areas in one subject such as reading
Diagnostic Tests	All grade levels	In-depth analysis of performance in a single area of the curriculum or one aspect of a curriculum area such as reading

Figure 3.16
Assessment and Evaluation Tools Presented in Chapter 3

and press want and need different assessment and evaluation data than do school administrators. The information school administrators want and need is different from that desired by parents, and parents want and need very different information than do teachers and students. Carefully examine this figure to come to a deeper appreciation of the differences in the kinds of assessment and evaluation information sought and the purposes for collecting it.

Figure 3.16 presents a summary of the assessment and evaluation tools included in this chapter. Review it to test your understanding of what you have learned, and use it to guide your rereading of some sections.

THINKING AS A TEACHER

1. You have accepted a new position as a fourth-grade teacher and are thrilled to have a job at the school of your choice. However, you learn at lunch on the first day that several of the veteran teachers are quite concerned that the local newspaper publishes the scores on a norm-referenced achievement test. The paper not only publishes the scores for fourth, fifth, and sixth graders by grade level, but by room as well, including the teacher's name. What questions might you have of your colleagues? How do you feel about this practice? What do you see as the positive and negative aspects of this practice? What response(s) might you make to this situation?
2. Reconsider the scenario in #1. The local school board and superintendent condone this practice. Carefully consider three questions: What would be their motivation for condoning this practice? Why might they view this practice quite differently than classroom teachers do? What does this practice suggest about their views of the reading process?
3. You can imagine that it would be easy to be overwhelmed by assessment and evaluation data on your students. Review the suggestions made in this chapter for organizing data collected on your students. Decide on a plan you think you can put into place with your next class. Go to the Weblinks in Chapter 3 on our Companion Website at *www.prenhall.com/harp* and then to the chapter's Threaded Message Board to add your plan to the global discussion.

FIELD-BASED ACTIVITIES

1. Interview five classroom teachers about their opinions of norm-referenced tests. Ask them what use they have made of norm-referenced test data. Begin to formulate your own position regarding norm-referenced testing in the elementary school.
2. Take a running record on three children: a kindergartner, first grader, and second grader. Complete the analyses and share your findings with the classroom teacher or a classmate. Write an entry in your Online Journal or Learning Log about what you learned by doing these activities, what unanswered questions you have, and how you plan to get answers to them. Many students have told us that once they begin taking running records on children's oral text reading, they never view children as readers "quite the same way again." What do you suppose they mean by this statement, and what might be the implications for classroom practice?
3. Interview three classroom teachers, perhaps a first-grade teacher, a third-grade teacher, and a sixth-grade teacher. Find out how they organize their classroom and time to use assessment and evaluation information most effectively. Analyze how their answers compare to the helpful hints we offered in this chapter.
4. Interview a teacher and/or visit the web site of your state education agency to learn about testing requirements in your state. Then visit web sites of other states and make comparisons between the states.

REFERENCES

Barnes, M., Clarke, D., & Stephens, M. (2000). Assessment: the engine of systemic curricular reform? *Journal of Curriculum Studies, 32*(5): 623–651.

Beaver, J. (1997). *Developmental reading assessment.* Parsippany, NJ: Celebration Press.

Bottomley, D. M., Henk, W. A., & Melnick, S. A. (1997). Assessing children's views about themselves as writers using the Writer Self-Perception Scale. *The Reading Teacher, 51,* 286–296.

Clay, M. M. (1993). *An observation survey of early literacy achievement.* Portsmouth, NH: Heinemann.

Farr, R. (1993). Putting it all together: Solving the reading assessment puzzle. *The Reading Teacher, 46,* 26–37.

Flood, J., Lapp, D., & Fisher, D. (2003). Reading comprehension instruction. In J. Flood, D. Lapp, J. R. Squire, & J. M. Jensen (Eds.), *Handbook of research on teaching the English language arts.* Mahwah, NJ: Erlbaum.

Gambrell, L. B., Palmer, B. M., Codling, R. M., & Mazzoni, S. A. (1996). Assessing motivation to read. *The Reading Teacher, 49,* 518–533.

Goodman, Y. (1996). Kidwatching: An alternative to testing. In S. Wilde (Ed.), *Notes from a kidwatcher: Selected writings of Yetta M. Goodman.* Portsmouth, NH: Heinemann.

Guice, S., & Johnston, P. H. (1995). *Assessment, self-assessment, and children's literate constructs.* Report Series 3.11. Washington, DC: Office of Educational Research and Improvement.

Harp, B. (2000). *The handbook of literacy assessment and evaluation.* Norwood, MA: Christopher-Gordon Publishers.

Harris, T. L., & Hodges, R. E. (Eds.). (1995). *The literacy dictionary: The vocabulary of reading and writing.* Newark, DE: International Reading Association.

Henk, W. A., & Melnick, S. A. (1995). The reader self-perception scale (RSPS): A new tool for measuring how children feel about themselves as readers. *The Reading Teacher, 48,* 470–481.

Karlsen, B., & Gardner, E. F. (1995). *Stanford diagnostic reading test–4.* San Antonio, TX: Harcourt Brace.

Lewis, A. C. (1997). Changing assessment, changing curriculum. *Education Digest, 62,* 13–18.

MacGinitie, W. H., & MacGinitie, R. K. (1998). *Gates-MacGinities Reading Tests.* Chicago, IL: Riverside Publishing.

Massachusetts Department of Education. (2001). *Massachusetts English language arts curriculum framework.* Malden, MA: Author.

Meisels, S. J., & Piker, R. A. (2001). *An analysis of early literacy assessment used for instruction.* CIERA Report #2-013. University of Michigan, Ann Arbor, MI. Center for the Improvement of Early Reading Achievement.

Paris, S. G., Paris, A. H., & Carpenter, R. D. Effective Practices for Assessing Young Readers. CIERA report 3-013. University of Michigan, Ann Arbor, MI. Center for the Improvement of Early Reading Achievement.

Popham, W. J. (2001). *The truth about testing: An educator's call to action.* Alexandria, VA: Association for Supervision and Curriculum Development.

Rhodes, L. K., & Nathenson-Mejia, S. (1992). Anecdotal records: A powerful tool for ongoing literacy assessment. *The Reading Teacher, 45,* 502–509.

Rickards, D., & Cheek, E. (1999). *Designing rubrics for K–6 classroom assessment.* Norwood, MA: Christopher-Gordon.

Standford Diagnostic Reading. (2002). San Antonio, TX: Harcourt Education Measurement.

U. S. Department of Education. (n.d.). Frequently asked questions. Retrieved from *http://www.ed.gov/offices/OESE/readingfirst/faq.html*

Woods, M. L., & Moe, A. J. (2003). *Analytical reading inventory: Comprehensive assessment for all students including gifted and remedial.* Columbus, OH: Merrill.

Chapter 4

Achievement for All Students: Meeting Special Needs

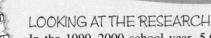

LOOKING AT THE RESEARCH

In the 1999–2000 school year, 5,666,415 students in the United States received special education services. The following table shows the distribution of students by disability.

Disability Category	Number	Percent of Total*
Specific Learning Disabilities	2,861,333	50.4
Speech or Language Impairments	1,086,849	19.1
Mental Retardation	613,207	10.8
Emotional Disturbance	469,407	8.2
Other Health Impairments	253,795	4.4
Multiple Disabilities	112,345	1.9
Hearing Impairments	71,539	1.2
Orthopedic Impairments	71,264	1.2
Autism	65,396	1.1
Visual Impairments	26,540	0.5
Developmental Delay	19,057	0.3
Traumatic Brain Injury	13,843	0.2
Deaf/Blindness	1,840	0.03

Source: U.S. Department of Education (2001). *Twenty-third annual report to Congress on the implementation of the Individuals with Disabilities Education Act.* (p. A-2–A-4). Washington, DC: Author.

* Does not total 100% because of rounding.

With this many students qualified to receive special education services, it seems highly likely that you will have one or more children in your classroom with disabilities.

Focus Questions

- What is my role as a classroom teacher regarding children with special needs?
- How can children with special needs in my classroom get services?
- What kinds of accommodations may I make for children with special needs?

REAL TEACHERS, REAL PRACTICE

Meet Amy Gaddes, ***a middle school science teacher***

Sharing the responsibility of teaching inclusion in my middle school science classroom has been both challenging and gratifying. My inclusion partner and I have vigilantly planned every lesson to ensure that not only our students with special needs but all *of our students receive instruction that matches their learning style. Observers have often told us that they cannot distinguish between our two populations. We have taken this as an ultimate compliment because we feel it captures the philosophy and goals of our coteaching model.*

In our lessons, we have focused on offering seeds of scientific inquiry to inspire the curiosity of our students. This inquiry takes many pathways, most of which require reading. Students are required to make meaning from labs, traditional textbooks, graphs and tables, as well as authentic scientific literature. The language of this science discourse is often elusive even to the most proficient reader. Scientific nomenclature, formulas, and abstract concepts make science reading demanding for most middle school students. As we collaborate, I come to the planning table with the hands-on labs, demonstrations, and samples of support literature. My inclusion partner comes equipped with a variety of strategies designed to reach each child on our inclusive roster. The results are often exciting.

We carefully planned our unit on plate tectonics and the theory of Pangea, the super-continent that drifted apart into the seven continents we know today. My partner devised an active reading activity that presented the foundation vocabulary needed for this lesson. The homogeneously grouped students rotated between three stations. Those students who we have found struggle with abstract science concepts began with the classroom aide where concrete definitions of the vocabulary/language of plate tectonics were provided. The second group, run by the special education teacher, started with a manipulative of a jigsaw puzzle simulating Pangea. The most abstract thinkers were able to start with me as I presented the theoretical framework of the scientific causes for continental drift. I demonstrated a 3-D model that required inferring and problem-solving skills. Although each student rotated through all three stations, they were able to start at a point that provided the necessary scaffolding for their reading and reason-

ing capacities. By providing an active reading activity at the beginning of the sequence, the struggling science students felt more secure approaching the intangible tasks. Prior to my involvement in this inclusion partnership, I believed I was addressing my students' needs with my basic instructional techniques. This joint venture has supported the enhancement of my repertoire as both a science teacher and a reading teacher.

The opening research piece suggests that you will have a diverse group of learners in your classroom. Amy's comments underscore the importance of collaboration between classroom teachers and special education teachers. These two important issues lead to some critical questions.

WHAT IS MY ROLE AS A CLASSROOM TEACHER REGARDING CHILDREN WITH SPECIAL NEEDS?

No one in the school, aside from parents, will know your students as well as you will. You will be the most critical link between the prescribed curriculum and your learners. Through your daily interactions, observations, and assessment and evaluation strategies, you will come to know your students well as readers and writers (as well as mathematicians, scientists, artists, musicians, and social scientists). You will be carefully monitoring your students' progress on a daily basis. Teachers want each of their learners to succeed and to meet or exceed all of their expectations. Unfortunately, not all children will make the progress you expect. In fact, in some schools many children will not make adequate progress. This is the reason for the No Child Left Behind Act (NCLB) of 2001.

Go to the Weblinks in Chapter 4 on our Companion Website at www.prenhall.com/harp to link to sites presenting information on the No Child Left Behind Act.

The *NCLB* redefines the federal role in K-12 education and is intended to help close the achievement gap between disadvantaged and minority students and their peers. The NCLB infused federal dollars into K-3 classrooms to improve the teaching and learning of reading through Reading First grants. The goal is that every child will be reading by grade three. The act also forces stronger accountability for results, expanded options for parents, and an emphasis on teaching methods that have been proven through research.

While the goals of NCLB are laudable, it may not be realistic to expect all children to reach the same level of achievement at nearly the same time. For some children with special needs, these expectations are unrealistic. Yet, it is the job of every classroom teacher to take each learner as far as he or she can go. The diversity in achievement, motivation, learning needs, and parental support is great in every classroom. Not all struggling readers qualify for special education services, but it is your responsibility to accommodate their needs within your classroom to the greatest extent possible.

Allington (2001) makes the case for intensive, expert instruction:

> Teachers need support in order to become more expert with every year of teaching. In my view it is an organizational responsibility to provide such support every single day of the school year. Similarly, teachers cannot be expected to adapt and differentiate their lessons if they are provided with lots of copies of a single text and almost no other books. Nor can teachers be expected to design school days so that much reading and writing is accomplished if they have few books and an instructional day that is effectively reduced in length by bad organizational plans, plans that nibble away, and sometimes gobble up, instructional time. Schools must be organized so teachers and students have every possible

> minute needed for instruction. None of this is rocket science. All of it is based in scientific studies of effective schools, classrooms, and teachers. (p. 119)

To achieve the goal of intensive, expert instruction for all your learners, you will need to become a very mindful kidwatcher.

Be a Mindful Kidwatcher

The systematic collection of data on your learners for your monitoring notebook (Chapter 3) will provide the framework for being a mindful kidwatcher. Each week you will want to spend time reflecting on the progress made by each of your students.

Consider Learning Goals. Consider the goals you have set for each child and the specific, observable data you have collected to assess and evaluate progress. Note which children are not meeting the goals, and plan to alter your materials, approaches, or methods with each child. Document your observations and plans in your monitoring notebook.

Plan Instructional Modifications. Modify your instructional approaches if a child is not making expected progress. For example, you may decide to move a child to a lower level of text for instruction. You may decide to try phonics instruction in the context of known words rather than by learning sounds in isolation and then blending those sounds. You may try to learn more about a child's cultural background to see if you can modify your approach. For example, some Native American cultures believe it is disrespectful to make eye contact with a teacher. If you have been insisting that a child look at you during instruction or when you are disciplining the child, you may be running counter to the child's cultural mores. You will want to learn as much as you can about the child so that you can make informed modifications in your instruction. Figure 4.1 illustrates this process.

Hopefully, your modifications will succeed, and the process ends. However, if it does not, you must not decide that you are a failure or that the child is a failure. Instead, explore avenues available within your school to collaborate with others to build success for the child.

Figure 4.1
Being a Mindful Kidwatcher

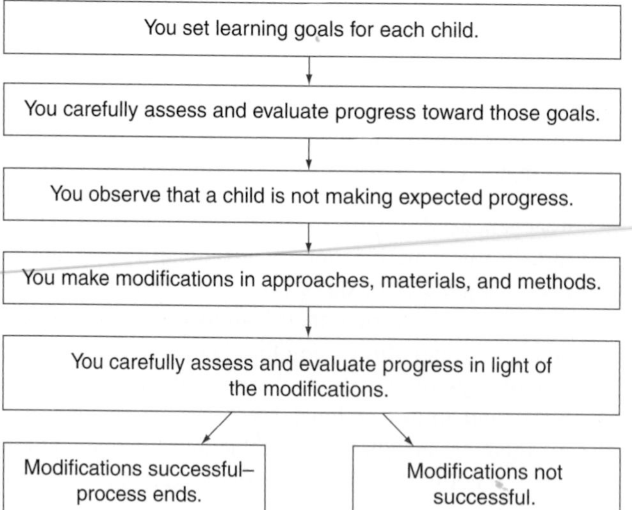
You set learning goals for each child.
You carefully assess and evaluate progress toward those goals.
You observe that a child is not making expected progress.
You make modifications in approaches, materials, and methods.
You carefully assess and evaluate progress in light of the modifications.
Modifications successful–process ends.
Modifications not successful.

Understanding Education as Collaboration

There is truth in the old adage that it takes a village to raise a child. Find out what plans are in place in your school to help children who are not succeeding. Your first task may be to discover the processes and procedures that are in place to meet the special needs of learners.

Learning Processes and Procedures. Talk with your principal to discover the processes and procedures already in place. Typically, the school policy manual spells out these activities. Find out whom to contact when you have concerns about a child's learning or behavior. Discover what steps you need to take and what forms you need to complete. You are a key person in getting help for children with special needs, but you are not alone. You also need to learn about available staff resources.

Learning About Staff Resources. Your school may offer the services of a counselor, a special education teacher, a speech pathologist, an occupational therapist, a physical therapist, and others who are dedicated to working with children with special needs. Find out who these resource people are and how you can take advantage of their services. School policy probably describes a formal process for referring children for special education consideration. However, there may be an informal process for engaging these resource persons as well. You should learn about both processes.

Increasingly in schools collaboration and teaming have become the model for getting services to children. *Interactive teaming* describes the process whereby a group of team members engage mutually to provide the best possible education for a student (Thomas, Correa, & Morsink, 1995). The intervention assistance team is an example of such teaming.

Making Referrals to the Intervention Assistance Team. When the modifications you have made for a child's learning are not working, the next step is to engage the parents or caregivers, consult with another teacher at your grade level, and try new modifications. This process is illustrated in Figure 4.2. If the modifications are successful, the process ends. If the modifications are not successful, it is time to make a referral to the Intervention Assistance Team (IAT), also known as a preferral team or student assistance team.

Figure 4.2
When Your Instructional Modifications Don't Succeed

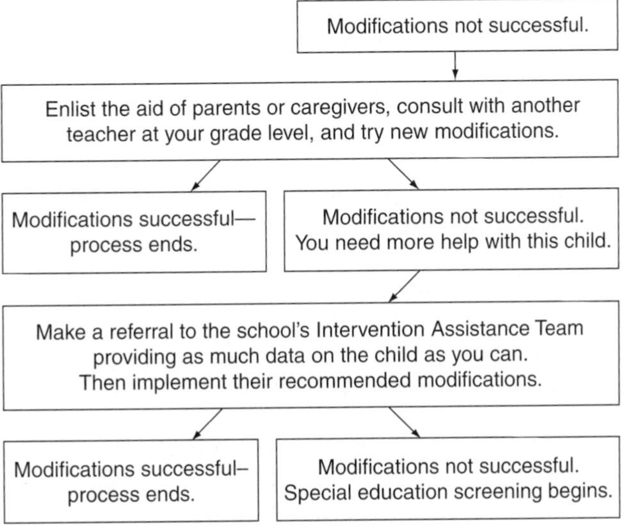

The IAT is composed of you, other teachers at your grade level, special education teachers, perhaps the principal, and other resource persons. The IAT's job is to consider all the data you provide about the child's learning. Here is another key role you play. Give the team details about the modifications you have tried and the child's performance in light of those modifications. The parent is notified, and the team brainstorms further modifications. The primary purposes of this team are to recommend instructional or behavioral management interventions you can implement immediately and to reduce the chances of erroneously identifying a child for special education (Salvia & Ysseldyke, 1995). You may have subsequent meetings with the team to share data on the child's progress and to further brainstorm modifications. If the modifications are successful, the process ends. If not, you move into a formal process to have the child screened for special education.

HOW CAN CHILDREN WITH SPECIAL NEEDS IN MY CLASSROOM GET SERVICES?

Two federal laws provide avenues through which you can get services for children with special needs in your classroom. These laws are The Individuals with Disabilities Act (IDEA) and Section 504 of the Rehabilitation Act of 1973. IDEA provides some federal funding to state and local education agencies to guarantee special education and related service for those students who meet the eligibility criteria. Section 504 does not provide additional funding, but requires that both public and private schools receiving federal financial assistance for educational purposes not discriminate against children with handicaps.

The process by which children are qualified for special education services is spelled out in IDEA, which was reauthorized by Congress in 1997 (U.S. Department of Education, 2001).

Understanding IDEA

The intent and spirit of this law is that schools will welcome all children and hold high expectations for all children's learning and progress. The law stipulates that children with disabilities will participate and progress in the general education curriculum, as appropriate, and that preschool children will participate in appropriate activities.

Free Appropriate Public Education. IDEA mandates a free, appropriate public education (FAPE) to begin at age 3 and extend to age 21. When an elementary school provides early childhood programs to nondisabled children, they also are required to provide early childhood special education. In the 1999–2000 school year 588,300 preschool children with disabilities were served, or about 5 percent of all preschoolers who lived in the United States and outlying areas. State-reported data for 1999–2000 indicate that 67 percent of preschoolers who received services under IDEA were white, 16 percent were black, 14 percent were Hispanic, 2 percent were Asian/Pacific Islander, and 1 percent were American Indian/Alaska Native (U.S. Department of Education, 2001).

Specific learning disabilities continued to be the most prevalent disability among this population in the 1999–2000 school year. Of the students ages 6 through 21 served outside the regular classroom for less than 21 percent of the school day, approximately 70 percent were white, 14 percent were black, 12 percent were Hispanic, 2 percent were Asian/Pacific Islander, and 1 percent were American Indian/Alaska Native (U.S. Department of Education, 2001).

Special Education as a System of Services. One of the most significant changes in the 1997 reauthorization of IDEA may be the clarification of special education as a service and not a place. Special education is defined as a system of specially designed instruction and services, not a place a child goes. The instruction and services must meet the unique needs of a child with a disability, including instruction in the regular classroom, in hospitals and institutions, in other settings, and in physical education. All services are provided at no cost to the parents (Brown, McIntire, Wood-Garnett, & Avoke, 2001). While it is important to get each child with special needs the services he or she deserves, some parents and teachers are uncomfortable that, in the process, the child is labeled as having a disability.

Parent and Child Participation in Shared Decision Making. The 1997 reauthorization also increased the emphasis on parent participation and shared decision making, including the child in decision making when appropriate. The act now specifies that the regular education teacher must be a member of the team that plans the child's instruction and that children with disabilities must be included in state- or district-wide testing programs.

Least Restrictive Environment. IDEA further requires that special education services must be provided in the least restrictive environment (LRE). This part of the law requires that to the maximum extent appropriate, children with disabilities will be educated with children who are not disabled. It further stipulates that special classes, separate schooling, or other removal of children with disabilities from the regular educational environment will occur only when the nature or severity of the disability is such that education in regular classrooms, even with supplementary aids and services, cannot be successful (20 U.S.C., Sec. 1412[a][5]). The notion of educating children with disabilities in the least restrictive environments has led to a continuum of educational services. This continuum is illustrated in Figure 4.3.

Figure 4.3
Continuum of Educational Services

Specialized Facilities—Nonpublic School
Student needs more protective or more intensive education setting than can be provided in public schools. (Day or residential program)

Special School
Student receives prescribed program under the direction of a specially trained staff in a specially designed facility within the public school system. (Day program)

Full-time Separate Classroom
Student receives prescribed program under the direction of a special class teacher.

Regular Classroom and Resource Room
Student receives prescribed program under the direction of the regular classroom teacher; in addition, he or she spends part time in a specially staffed and equipped resource room.

Regular Classroom with Supplementary Instruction and Services
Student receives prescribed program under the direction of the regular classroom teacher; in addition, he or she receives supplementary instruction or service from an itinerant or school-based specialist.

Regular Classroom with Consultation to Teacher
Student receives prescribed program under the direction of regular classroom teacher who is supported by ongoing consultation from specialists.

Regular Classroom
Student receives prescribed program under the direction of the regular teacher.

The IEP is a critical element in the IDEA process.

Continuum of Services. In examining Figure 4.3 you will note that, moving from the bottom to the top of the figure, the severity of disabilities increases. Moving from the top to the bottom, the number of children served in a setting increase. Thus, most of the children with disabilities experience their prescribed program in the regular classroom from their regular teacher—you. Children with slightly more severe disabilities are served in the regular classroom with the teacher in consultation with specialists. Children with more severe disabilities are served in the regular classroom with supplementary instruction from specialists. And so it continues through children spending part of the day in a resource room in their school, to a full-time separate classroom with a special education teacher, to a special school, and, ultimately, to a separate institution. What constitutes the least restrictive environment for a student will be determined as part of the process of certifying him or her for special education services.

Referring a Child for Special Education Consideration

As a classroom teacher you will play a key role in referring a child for special education consideration and in implementing the child's individual educational program (IEP) if he or she is qualified for services. Parents may also refer children for consideration.

The Process of Identifying a Child for Special Education. The process of identifying a child for special education is spelled out in IDEA. Following the work of the Intervention Assistance Team, you or the parent make the decision to refer the child for special education consideration. The process that begins at this point is illustrated in Figure 4.4. The sequence of steps must be followed as prescribed by IDEA.

Nondiscriminatory Multifactored Evaluation (MRE). The law states that parents' consent for testing and evaluation must be obtained. Without this no further evalua-

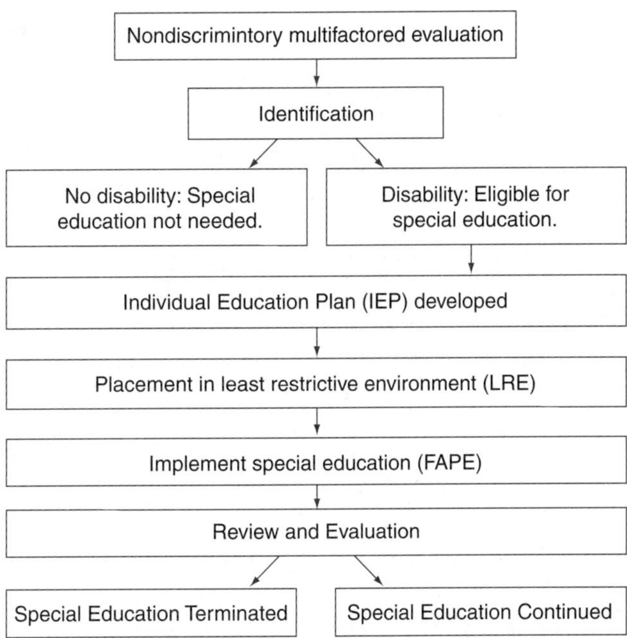

Figure 4.4
The Special Education Process

tion can be done, regardless of how severe you determine the child's needs to be. If the parents consent to an evaluation, it must not discriminate in any way on the basis of race, culture, language, or gender. A multifactored evaluation must address all areas related to the suspected disability (for example, vision, hearing, academic performance, general intelligence), and a variety of assessment tools and strategies must be used. The evaluation must yield data to determine whether or not the child has a disability, the kinds of services for which the child is qualified, and the extent to which the child can participate in the regular curriculum.

Identification. A team consisting of the regular classroom teacher, the parents, and persons whose speciality relates to the possible disability carefully review all data. Parents are equal partners in this process and must be involved in the review of the data and the decision regarding the eligibility of the child for special education services.

Individualized Education Program (IEP). The IEP is the centerpiece of the special education process (Heward, 2000). The IEP team must meet within 30 days of eligibility determination. With full participation by parents, the IEP is written to describe a program of special instruction specifically tailored to the needs of the student. In addition to prescribing instruction, the IEP is to specify related services, assistive technology, supplemental aids and services to meet the child's needs without regard to cost or availability in the school district. The nature of the IEP is carefully spelled out in IDEA. Figure 4.5 displays these requirements.

You can see by examining these requirements that the IEP must carefully describe the child's current levels of performance, the educational plan to be implemented, the timeline for implementation, the circumstances under which the plan is to be executed, and the plan for evaluating the child's progress in meeting the specified goals. IDEA requires that once the IEP is designed, it must be implemented in the least restrictive environment.

Placement in Least Restrictive Environment (LRE). Simply stated, the IEP must carefully detail the extent to which the child is, with the parents' permission, removed from the regular classroom.

ssessment and Evaluation Toolbox

GRAY ORAL READING TEST, FOURTH EDITION (GORT-4)

The GORT-4 is an individually administered, norm-referenced measure of oral reading and comprehension. Each of the two forms contains 14 reading passages of increasing difficulty which students are asked to read orally and then respond to five comprehension questions per passage. The authors state the purposes of the test as: (a) to help identify those students who are significantly below their peers in oral reading proficiency and who may profit from supplemental help; (b) to aid in determining the particular kinds of reading strengths and weaknesses individual students possess; (c) to document students' progress in reading as a consequence of special intervention programs; and (d) to serve as a measurement device in investigations where researchers are studying the abilities of school-age students (Wiederholt & Bryant, 2001, p. 4).

Implement Special Education. Services related to special education, assistive technology, program modifications, and other supports must be implemented as described in the IEP. All the while, the child is to participate in the school's general curriculum and extracurricular activities. Parents may request changes at any time.

Review and Evaluation. The IEP must specify what achievement is expected for the child and by when this achievement is due. Benchmarks and objectives are clearly stated, as are plans for assessing and evaluating progress. IDEA specifies that the IEP must be evaluated at least annually. At the time of the annual evaluation, special education services may be terminated, or the IEP may be modified and services continued.

Figure 4.6 illustrates aspects of an IEP written for Ricky (a pseudonym), who is eligible for special education services because he is diagnosed with autism. Autism presents severe impairments in social, emotional, and intellectual functioning (Kanner, 1943). Children with autism often have great difficulty interacting with and responding to other people. The figure represents some of the entries in each of the major sections of the IEP.

As you have come to deeper understandings about the process of special education, you have probably developed a greater appreciation for your role. It is a serious responsibility to do all you can to see that children in your classroom get the services they need. Some helpful sources of support are available for your efforts.

Sources of Support for IDEA

You should become familiar with five organizations. You may want to visit their web sites to learn more about how they might assist you in understanding and implementing IDEA (Brown, McIntire, Wood-Garnett, & Avoke, 2001).

IDEA Local Implementation by Local Administrators Partnership. ILIAD will answer your questions about the Individuals with Disabilities Education Act, keep you informed about ideas that work, and support your efforts to help all children learn. Contact ILIAD at: 1110 North Glebe Road, Suite 300, Arlington, VA 22201-5704; *www.ideapractices.org*

Figure 4.5
Individualized Education Program

IEP Team Membership must include:

1. The parents (or surrogate parent) of the child;
2. At least one regular education teacher of the child (if the child is, or may be, participating in the regular education environment).
3. At least one special education teacher, or if appropriate, at least one special education provider of the child.
4. A representative of the local education agency (LEA) who—
   i. Is qualified to provide, or supervise the provision of, specially designed instruction to meet the unique needs of children with disabilities;
   ii. Is knowledgeable about the general curriculum; and
   iii. Is knowledgeable about the availability of resources of the LEA;
5. An individual who can interpret the instructional implications of evaluation results, who may be a member of the team described above;
6. At the discretion of the parent or the school, other individuals who have knowledge or special expertise regarding the child, including related service personnel as appropriate; and
7. The student, if age 14 or older, must be invited. Younger students may attend if appropriate. (34CFR 300.344)

All IEPs must include the following seven components:

1. A statement of the child's present levels of educational performance, including
   i. How the child's disability affects the child's involvement and progress in the general curriculum; or
   ii. For preschool children, as appropriate, how the disability affects the child's participation in appropriate activities;
2. A statement of measurable annual goals, including benchmarks or short-term objectives, related to
   i. Meeting the child's needs that result from the child's disability to enable the child to be involved in and progress in the general curriculum; and
   ii. Meeting each of the child's other educational needs that result from the child's disability;
3. A statement of the special education and related services and supplementary aids and services to be provided to the child, or on behalf of the child, and a statement of the program modifications or support for school personnel that will be provided for the child
   i. To advance appropriately toward attaining the annual goals;
   ii. To be involved in and progress in the general curriculum and to participate in extracurricular and other nonacademic activities; and
   iii. To be educated and participate with other children with disabilities and nondisabled children in [such] activities;
4. An explanation of the extent, if any, to which the child will not participate with nondisabled children in the regular class and in the activities described in paragraph (3);
5. A statement of
   i. Any individual modifications in the administration of state- or district-wide assessments of student achievement that are needed in order for the child to participate in such assessment; and

(Continued)

Figure 4.5
Individualized Education Program *Continued*

ii. If the IEP team determines that the child will not participate in a particular state- or district-wide assessment of student achievement (or part of an assessment), a statement of
   (A) Why that assessment is not appropriate for the child; and
   (B) How the child will be assessed;

6. The projected date for the beginning of the services and modifications described in paragraph (3) and the anticipated frequency, location, and duration of those services and modifications; and
7. A statement of
   i. How the child's progress toward the annual goals described in paragraph (2) will be measured; and
   ii. How the child's parents will be regularly informed (through such means as periodic report cards), at least as often as parents are informed of their nondisabled children's progress of
      (A) Their child's progress toward the annual goals; and
      (B) The extent to which that progress is sufficient to enable the child to achieve the goals by the end of the year. (20U.S.C., Sec. 1414[d][1][A])

Families and Advocates Partnership for Education. The FAPE project is a strong partnership that aims to improve educational outcomes for children with disabilities. It links families, advocates, and self-advocates to communicate the new focus of IDEA. Contact FAPE at: 8161 Normandale Boulevard, Minneapolis, MN 55437-1044; *www.fape.org*

The Policymaker Partnership. The PMP at the National Association of State Directors of Special Education is education's policy connection to IDEA. It includes links to ILIAD, FAPE, and ASPIIRE. Contact the PMP at: 1800 Diagonal Road, Suite 320, Alexandria, VA 22314-2840; *www.ideapolicy.org*

Associations of Service Providers Implementing IDEA Reforms in Education Partnership. ASPIIRE is a leadership initiative of the Council for Exceptional Children. Contact the association at: 1110 North Glebe Road, Suite 300, Arlington, VA 22201-5704; *www.ideapractices.org*

The Council for Exceptional Children. The CEC is the largest special education professional organization in the world. Its membership includes teachers, specialists, administrators, and parents of children with disabilities and gifted and talented children. The EC publishes two journals: *Exceptional Children* and *Teaching Exceptional Children.* It also publishes a quarterly newsletter. Find out more at: *www.cec.sped.org*

You may well face the frustration of referring a child for a special education screening only to learn that he or she does not qualify. Yet you know the child has needs that you alone cannot meet in your classroom. Help may be available for this child under Section 504.

Understanding Section 504

Section 504 is a civil rights statute (Section 504 of the Rehabilitation Act of 1973). It requires that schools, public or private, that receive federal financial assistance for educational purposes not discriminate against children with "handicaps." In this case *handicaps* essentially means *disabilities.* To be eligible for services under Section 504, the student must have a physical or mental condition that substantially limits one or more major life

can be provided by a parent, friend, teacher, psychologist, doctor, or any appropriate person or agency (AAMR, 2002a, p. 4).

Supports for Students with Mental Retardation. According to the American Association on Mental Retardation, providing individualized supports can improve personal functioning, promote self-determination and societal inclusion, and improve the personal well-being of a person with mental retardation. Among the recommended supports are the following:

Teaching and Education Activities

- interacting with trainers and teachers and fellow trainees and students
- participating in making decisions on training and educational activities
- learning and using problem-solving strategies
- using technology for learning
- learning and using functional academics (reading signs, counting change, and so on)
- learning and using self-determination skills

Behavioral Activities

- learning specific skills or behaviors
- learning and making appropriate decisions
- accessing and obtaining mental health treatments
- incorporating personal preferences into daily activities
- maintaining socially appropriate behavior in public
- controlling anger and aggression (AAMR, 2002a, pp. 4–5)

AAMR suggests many other forms of support. The suggestions included here are typical of those you may find in a student's IEP.

Attention Deficit/Hyperactivity Disorder

Approximately 4% to 6% of the U.S. population has Attention Deficit/Hyperactivity Disorder (AD/HD). While AD/HD is not a category of disability listed in IDEA, it is included under the "Other Health Impairments" category. Children with AD/HD may qualify for services under IDEA when the disorder both limits their alertness to the educational environment and adversely affects their educational performance (Gregg, 1996-2003). It is likely that your classroom will have at least one or two children with AD/HD (Barkley, 2000).

Definitions of Attention Deficit/Hyperactivity Disorder. The American Psychiatric Association (APA, 1994) defines AD/HD as follows:

> The essential feature of Attention-Deficit/Hyperactivity Disorder is a persistent pattern of inattention and/or hyperactivity-impulsivity that is more frequent and severe than is typically observed in individuals at a comparable level of development.

The American Psychiatric Association (1994) identifies three subtypes of AD/HD, predominately inattentive type, predominately hyperactive-impulsive type, and combined type. Children with predominately inattentive type AD/HD have trouble paying attention in class, are forgetful and easily distracted. These children often appear to be daydreaming, confused, lost in thought, apathetic or unmotivated, sluggish, and slow moving (Barkley, 1990). Children with predominantly hyperactive-impulsive type AD/HD often fidget with their hands and feet, squirm in the seats, run about or climb excessively, feel restless, and often have difficulty playing or engaging in leisure activities quietly. These children have difficulty waiting their turn, blurt out answers before the question is fully asked, and interrupt or intrude on others (APA, 2000). Children with combined type of AD/HD have features of both inattention and hyperactivity/impulsivity.

Perhaps a way to deepen your understanding of AD/HD is to consider the description of AD/HD by Edward Hallowell, a medical doctor with the condition. Of AD/HD Hallowell (1992) writes:

Go to the Weblinks in Chapter 4 on our Companion Website at www.prenhall.com/harp to link to sites of professional associations working for persons with AD/HD such as the Attention Deficit Disorder Association (www.add.org) and Children and Adults with Attention-Deficit/Hyperactivity Disorder (www.chadd.org).

> . . . it's like being super-charged all the time. You get one idea and you have to act on it, and then, what do you know, but you've got another idea before you've finished up with the first one, and so you go for that one, but of course a third idea intercepts the second, and you just have to follow that one, and pretty soon people are calling you disorganized and impulsive and all sorts of impolite words that miss the point completely. Because you are trying really hard. It's just that you have all these invisible vectors pulling you this way and that which makes it really hard to stay on task. (p. 1)

To foster success of children with AD/HD in your classroom, you must work closely with their parents to get them the services and accommodations they need.

Accommodations for Children with AD/HD. A thorough evaluation determining the diagnosis of AD/HD should provide a basis for a comprehensive treatment program. In addition to medication, a comprehensive treatment program may include teacher training, parent training, family therapy, or individual counseling. Other considerations are creating a supportive environment; teaching the person organizational skills, study skills, memory skills, and time management skills; helping the child learn how he or she learns best; and identifying the kind of physical setting in which learning is best accomplished (Booth, 1998).

Figure 4.11 presents a list of possible accommodations for children with AD/HD. Note they are categorized by goal or activity. When you read some of these suggestions you may think, "But I can't let all of the children do this." Recall the discussion earlier in this chapter about the concept of fairness. It is giving each child what he or she needs, not giving all children the same thing. This may make some of these suggestions seem more workable.

Thus far, we have introduced definitions of and accommodations for children with learning disabilities, children with communication disorders, children with mental retardation, and children with attention deficit/hyperactivity disorder. Children with these special needs will appropriately have individual education plans written for them under IDEA. However, there are likely to be two other groups of children with special needs in your classroom who are not served under IDEA. They will not have IEPs written for them. These are children who are gifted and talented and those for whom English is a second language.

Gifted and Talented

The ways in which school systems deal with children who are gifted and talented vary tremendously. According to 1996 data, 37 states have state-mandated gifted and talented programs. States that do not have mandated programs provide discretionary state-supported programs. The ways in which giftedness and talent are defined vary greatly as does the percentage of enrolled children identified as gifted and talented. For example, Alabama identifies 2.4% of enrolled students as gifted and talented whereas Michigan identifies 14% (Council of State Directors of Programs for the Gifted, 1994). This discrepancy may, in part, be explained by the fact that no clear-cut definition of gifted and talented exists (Mathews, 1998). No federal

Figure 4.11
Accommodation Suggestions for Students with AD/HD

For Beginning Activities
- Give small amounts of work
- Provide signals to begin
- Use timers and encourage self-monitoring
- Use verbal and written directions
- Provide additional structure (e.g., large-lined paper)
- Highlight directions using larger fonts or colors

For Keeping on Task
- Increase frequency of positive reinforcement
- Use peer assistants
- Make tasks interesting
- Break tasks into smaller "manageable" units
- Allow breaks
- Use hands-on activities

For Listening
- Teach note taking and encourage use of notebook organizers
- Use positive reinforcement
- Allow doodling
- Allow standing

For Excessive Activity
- Use activity as rewards (errands, wash boards, move desks)
- Allow standing during class
- Encourage active participation
- Reward sitting

For Impulsive Behavior
- Provide acceptable alternatives
- Encourage trying to continue with another part of the assignment before interrupting the teacher
- Recommend note taking during lectures
- Recommend writing down questions and answers before blurting out
- Teach acceptable social behavior for conversations, for class behavior, and for interacting with peers
- Reward listening and appropriate behaviors

For Working Independently
- Ensure tasks match ability levels
- Provide brief directions
- Use brief tasks
- Use checklists for self-monitoring
- Use positive reinforcement

For Following Class Rules
- Keep rules simple
- Post and review class rules
- Model and role-play following rules
- Be consistent with enforcement of rules
- Provide students with copies of rules

Source: M. A. Mastropieri and T. E. Scruggs. (2000). *The inclusive classroom: Strategies for effective instruction* (p. 145). Upper Saddle River, NJ: Merrill. Reprinted with permission.

law mandates special education for children who are talented or gifted, so no source of a definition such as IDEA exists. However, the government has made attempts at definitions.

Definitions of Gifted and Talented. In 1988, the following definition of *gifted* was approved by the federal government:

> The term *gifted and talented students* means children and youth who give evidence of high performance capability in areas such as intelligence, creative, artistic, or leadership capacity, or in specific academic fields, and who require services or activities not ordinarily provided by the school in order to fully develop such capabilities. (PL 100-297, sec. 4103, definitions)

The United States Department of Education proposed a new definition in 1993:

> Children and youth with outstanding talent perform or show the potential for performing at remarkably high levels of accomplishment when compared with others their age, experience, or environment. These children and youth exhibit high performance capability in intellectual, creative, and/or artistic areas, possess an unusual leadership capacity, or excel in specific academic fields. They require services or activities not ordinarily provided in the schools. Outstanding talents are present in children and youth from all cultural groups, across all economic strata, and in all areas of human endeavor. (p. 3)

Go to the Weblinks in Chapter 4 on our Companion Website at www.prenhall.com/harp for links to the home pages of the National Association for Gifted Children (www.nagc.org), the World Council for Gifted and Talented Children (www.WorldGifted.org) and GT World (www.gttworld.org).

Note that the Department of Education definition highlights the notion that talent and giftedness occur in all cultural groups and in all economic strata. These are important ideas for you to keep in mind as you consider whether or not you have children in your classroom who are talented and/or gifted. Clark (1997) has created a set of questions you might find helpful in identifying students who may be gifted and/or talented. These questions are displayed in Figure 4.12. Notice that giftedness in the areas of cognitive ability, academic performance, leadership ability, and the visual or performing arts are all included in the questions.

Accommodations for Children Who Are Gifted and/or Talented. You will be challenged to provide learning accommodations for gifted and talented children in your classroom. Some models for meeting the needs of these children have them spend some of their school day or week in other settings such as resource classes or university classes. One way to facilitate planning for working with gifted and talented children in your classroom is to use the PASS variables described earlier in this chapter in the discussion on mental retardation. Other possibilities for accommodating the needs of these children include acceleration, enrichment, the adaptation of instructional materials, and the adaptation of instructional and evaluation procedures.

Acceleration. Acceleration refers to moving students through the curriculum at a faster pace than general education students. Acceleration can mean admitting a child to school early, skipping grades, providing level appropriate curriculum, or testing out of classes. Advancing students places them in grades that match their achievement levels. For example, a fourth grader who is working at sixth-grade level academically might be advanced to the sixth-grade class. Another example is maintaining students in the age-appropriate class, but providing them with the appropriate level curriculum (sixth-grade level, in this example). It might also mean advancing students several grade levels only in specific academic classes. Universities may allow students who are gifted and talented to enroll in classes when prerequisite criteria are met.

Enrichment. The common element across enrichment programs is the expansion of the curriculum. Students are allowed and encouraged to study topics in depth that extend beyond the scope of the general education curriculum. The goals behind enrichment activities are to allow opportunities for critical thinking and problem solving through in-depth analyses of specific content areas. This may be accomplished by having students work on independent projects within the general education classroom, or to have enrichment activities take place off campus such as in business or industry.

Adapting Instructional Materials. In the case of either acceleration or enrichment, it may be necessary for general educators to adapt curriculum materials to better meet the needs of students who are gifted or talented. Prioritize objectives for students and carefully complete pretesting of content to be covered. When students have demonstrated mastery of content, be prepared to move them ahead in the curriculum or design suitable enrichment

Figure 4.12
Questions About Classroom Behavior that Can Guide Your Identification of Gifted and Talented Students

In the classroom does the child
- ask a lot of questions?
- show a lot of interest in progress?
- have lots of information on many things?
- want to know why or how something is so?
- become unusually upset at injustices?
- seem interested and concerned about social or political problems?
- often have a better reason than you for not doing what you want done?
- refuse to drill on spelling, math facts, flash cards, or handwriting?
- criticize others for dumb ideas?
- become impatient if work is not perfect?
- seem to be a loner?
- seem bored and often have nothing to do?
- complete only part of an assignment or project and then take off in a new direction?
- stick to a subject long after the class has gone on to other things?
- seem restless, out of seat often?
- daydream?
- seem to understand easily?
- like solving puzzles and problems?
- have his or her own idea about how something should be done? and stay with it?
- talk a lot?
- love metaphors and abstract ideas?
- love debating issues?

This child may be showing giftedness cognitively.

Does the child
- show unusual ability in some area? maybe reading or math?
- show fascination with one field of interest? and manage to include this interest in all discussion topics?
- enjoy meeting or talking with experts in this field?
- get math answers correct, but find it difficult to tell you how?
- enjoy graphing everything? seem obsessed with probabilities?
- invent new obscure systems and codes?

This child may be showing giftedness academically.

Does the child
- try to do things in different, unusual, imaginative ways?
- have a zany sense of humor?
- enjoy new routines or spontaneous activities?
- love variety and novelty?
- create problems with no apparent solutions? and enjoy asking you to solve them?
- love controversial and unusual questions?
- have a vivid imagination?
- seem never to proceed sequentially?

This child may be showing giftedness creatively.

Does the child
- organize and lead group activities? sometimes take over?
- enjoy taking risks?
- seem cocky, self-assured?
- enjoy decision making? stay with that decision?
- synthesize ideas and information from a lot of different sources?

This child may be showing giftedness through leadership.

Does the child
- seem to pick up skills in the arts—music, dance, drama, painting—without instruction?
- invent new techniques? experiment?
- see minute detail in products or performances?
- have high sensory sensitivity?

This child may be showing giftedness through visual or performing arts ability.

Source: From *Growing up gifted 5/e* (p. 282) by Clark, Barbara (1997). © Reprinted by permission of Pearson Education, Inc. Upper Saddle River, NJ.

activities that enable them to study more in depth in that area. Seek assistance from teachers who work with students who are gifted or talented, from guidance counselors, and from the families of the students.

Adapting Instructional and Evaluation Procedures. Be prepared to adapt your instructional procedures for students who are gifted or talented. They may not require intensive or explicit instruction on new content. You may be able to meet with them independently and briefly explain new concepts and content, thus allowing more time for either acceleration or enrichment activities. Students who are gifted or talented may also be able to provide tutorial assistance to age peers if the teacher is careful that the gifted child gets excellent instruction. Be aware that some gifted and talented youth may also require explicit instruction in study and organizational skills when work demands increase for them. Finally, evaluation methods can be modified to allow for assessment of enrichment and acceleration activities. More performance-based measures may need to be devised to obtain true indicators of students' abilities on such tasks.

Source: These suggestions are adapted from M. A. Mastropieri and T. E. Scruggs. (2000). *The inclusive classroom: Strategies for effective instruction* (pp. 151–152). Upper Saddle River, NJ: Merrill. Reprinted with permission.

Students for Whom English Is a Second Language

The 2000 census reveals that about 18 percent of U. S. children between the ages of 5 and 17 live in households where languages other than English are spoken. Although many of these children speak English "very well" (self-reported), others do not speak English at all. Figure 4.13 summarizes the languages spoken in the United States of residents 5 and older. With such large numbers of children speaking languages other than English, it is probable that you will have second language learners in your classroom wherever you teach.

ESL, LEP, ELL. These designations are ways of describing children whose first language is not English. ESL means English as a Second Language and more often refers to a type of program than to the children in that program. LEP means limited English proficient and is a common way of designating children who are not native speakers of English. ELL means English language learners and is another way of describing nonnative English speakers. The children to whom these designations refer are all learning to speak English. Many children whose families speak a language other than English have gained enough skill with English that they are not in any of these groups. One of your assessment tasks each year will be to determine the English language abilities of your students.

Just knowing the language that your students speak is not enough. If, for example, you have five children who speak Spanish, you must know more than that before you can begin to plan for their instruction. You will need to know what kind of Spanish they speak; Mexican, Cuban, and Puerto Rican Spanish are all different. There are variations of Spanish, of course, in different parts of a given country just as the English spoken in Louisiana, New Mexico, and Massachusetts differs. Spanish speaking children born in the United States may also speak different Spanish. You will need to know or make some intelligent inferences about the degree of assimilation into the mainstream culture, the amount of English they hear at home, and the wishes of their parents about learning English and maintaining the native language or not maintaining it.

In many schools, children who are not strong speakers of English are enrolled in bilingual classes and are not mainstreamed into regular classes until they reach a level of proficiency that makes it possible for them to function successfully in a regular classroom. However, in many schools bilingual programs are not offered for all of the many languages represented in the school. Many districts may have children speaking 80 or more different languages; obviously there are not teachers and materials for bilingual education in all these languages. Often schools with many languages have teachers who are trained to teach children English as a second language, and these teachers can help you assess the

Figure 4.13
Languages Spoken by U.S. Residents Age 5 and Older

Language	Number of Speakers
English only	215,423,557
Spanish or Spanish Creole	28,101,062
French (Patois, Cajun)	1,643,838
French Creole	453,368
Italian	1,008,370
Portuguese or Portuguese Creole	564,630
German	1,383,442
Yiddish	178,946
Other West Germanic Languages	251,135
Scandinavian Languages	162,252
Greek	365,436
Russian	706,242
Polish	667,414
Serbo-Croatian	233,865
Other Slavic Languages	301,079
Armenian	202,708
Persian	312,085
Gujarathi	235,988
Hindi	317,057
Urdu	262,900
Other Indic Languages	439,289
Other Indo-European Languages	327,946
Chinese	2,022,149
Japanese	477,997
Korean	894,063
Mon-Khmer, Cambodian	181,889
Miao, Hmong	168,063
Thai	120,464
Laotian	149,303
Vietnamese	1,009,627
Other Asian Languages	398,434
Tagalog	1,224,241
Other Pacific Island Languages	313,841
Navajo	178,014
Other Native American Languages	203,466
Hungarian	117,973
Arabic	614,582
Hebrew	195,374
African Languages	418,505
Other Unspecified Languages	144,575

Source: U.S. Census Bureau (2000). Summary tables on language use and English ability. Washington, DC: Author.

level of English skill of your children. In most schools, ESL teachers pull children from their regular classrooms for English instruction.

Some states have determined that bilingual programs are to be replaced by "sheltered English" programs. These programs require that all teachers have some knowledge of how to help children learn English in the regular classroom. Sheltered English requires that teachers make accommodations for English learners while teaching the content that is usually taught in any given grade level. Sheltered English as described by most experts is suitable for intermediate or more advanced speakers of English. Advocates of sheltered English suggest that beginning speakers of English will need about 30% of their instruction in their native language for maximum learning (Baker, 1998).

Accommodations for ESL Students. Applying the principles of Sheltered English or Specially Designed Academic Instruction in English (California State Department of Education, 1994) means that children have "(1) access to the core curriculum, (2) English language development, and (3) opportunities for social integration into your multicultural classroom community" (Peregoy & Boyle, 2001, p. 65). Sheltered English requires that for content objectives, the learner has multiple opportunities to understand and process the material. To meet language objectives, you must identify both language learning opportunities and the language demands in the content lessons. Your planning must also include language related lesson modifications, and finally, you must think about how you will help students meet social objectives. Peregoy and Boyle have illustrated these principles in Figure 4.14.

An example of these principles in action might be a study of pond life in the spring. The students will view a video that explains the various animals living in a pond. As each animal is introduced, if the name is not shown on the video, the teacher will hold up a card with the name of the animal. The next activity will be a field trip to a pond where students will work in pairs and collect animals. They will be provided with containers appropriate for storing the collected animals. When they return to school, students will work in small groups to identify the animals they have collected. As each animal is identified, an explanatory card will be prepared that tells how the animal is classified, what it eats, what eats it, and any other information about the animal. As students finish their cards, they contribute their information to a class diagram of the food chain in a pond. When the study is completed, students will preserve this information to

Figure 4.14
Sheltered English Instruction

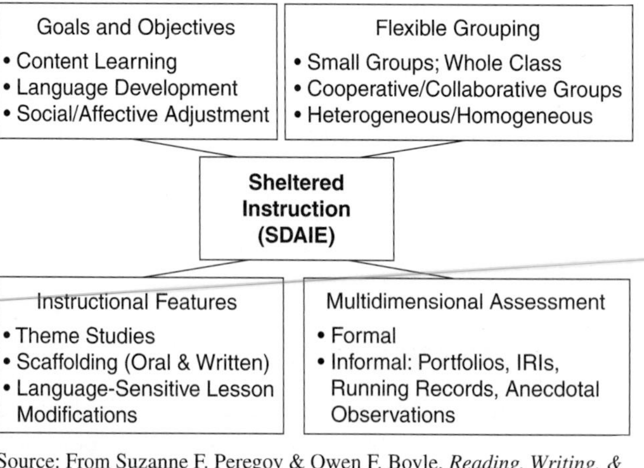

Source: From Suzanne F. Peregoy & Owen F. Boyle, *Reading, Writing, & Learning in ESL: A Resource Book for K–12 Teachers, 3/e.* Published by Allyn and Bacon, Boston, MA.

ISSUES IN LITERACY

PLACING SECOND LANGUAGE LEARNERS

Children are often placed in special education classes on the basis of their lack of skill in English. No child should be tested in English except to determine how much English they speak and understand. No placement or achievement test in English should determine a child's needs for services unless the child is a competent speaker of English. Lack of ability in speaking English is not a basis for placement in any program for children with special needs. How do you feel about this issue.

Visit the Companion Website to research this issue more thoroughly and record your thoughts about this topic on the threaded message board.

use in comparing the next habitat they explore. In addition to the content objectives of classifying pond life and understanding the food chain in a pond, language objectives would include learning the language of animal classification, habitat, and reporting.

The content is organized around a theme so that it is more comprehensible. The class would be grouped into pairs, small groups, and whole class (for some activities). These groups would be mixed in ability. The social/affective goals would include learning how to work with a partner, a small group, and the whole class in productive ways. Assessment would be informal, using portfolios and anecdotal observations.

Planning for the success of all children, regardless of their ability to speak English is critically important. We cannot afford to waste the minds of young children simply because they cannot speak English.

THINKING AS A TEACHER

1. You and your colleague in the classroom next door are both in your first year of teaching. In the spring of the year he admits to you that he hasn't made any special education referrals this year because he is afraid he will look like a failure. How will you respond?
2. You have a child whose writing ability is not developing to your expectations. In fact, you have seen no development at all. What are your understandings about the possibilities available in most schools to help you work with this problem? How might you approach the child's parents about your concerns?
3. Compare and contrast IDEA and Section 504. What are your understandings about the differences between these two laws? What are some specific examples of situations in which a student could be served under the IDEA? What are some specific examples of Section 504?

FIELD-BASED ACTIVITIES

1. Arrange an interview with a practicing classroom teacher. Learn the details of the ways in which his or her school implements the requirements of the IDEA. Find out what concerns this teacher has about IDEA and the IEP process.
2. Visit the web sites of the Council for Exceptional Children (*www.cec.sped.org*) and other sources of support for IDEA listed in this chapter. Write a reflection of your

impressions of each web site, focusing particularly on the specific ways in which you can imagine the information would be helpful to you.

3. Arrange to spend several days observing in a school. Arrange to observe in several inclusive classrooms. Begin your observation in each school without knowing which children have special needs. After you have observed for a day, ask the teacher to identify the children with special needs. See if you were able to identify them in any way yourself. Carefully note the accommodations made for their needs.

REFERENCES

Allington, R. L. (2002). *Big brother and the national reading curriculum: How ideology trumped evidence.* Portsmouth, NH: Heinemann.

Allington, R. L. (2001). *What really matters for struggling readers: Designing research-based programs.* New York: Addison Wesley Longman.

Allington, R. L., & McGill-Franzen, A. (1992). Unintended effects of educational reform in New York State. *Educational Policy, 6,* 396–413.

American Association on Mental Retardation. (2002a). *Mental retardation definition, classification, and systems of support* (10th ed.). Washington, DC: Author.

American Association on Mental Retardation. (2002b). *Definition of mental retardation.* Retrieved from *http://161.58.153.187/Policies/faq_mental_retardation.shtml*

American Psychiatric Association. (1994). *Diagnostic and statistical manual of mental disorders* (4th ed.). Washington, DC: Author.

American Psychiatric Association. (2000). *Diagnostic and statistical manual of mental disorders* (4th ed., text revision). Washington, DC: Author.

American Speech-Language-Hearing Association. (1993). Definitions of communication disorders and variations. *ASHA, 35* (Suppl. 10), pp. 40–41.

Baker, K. (1998). Structured English immersion: Breakthrough in teaching limited-English-proficient students. *Phi Delta Kappan, 79,* 199–204.

Barkley, R. A. (1990). *Attention deficit hyperactivity disorder.* New York: Guilford Press.

Barkley, R. A. (2000). *Taking charge of AD/HD: The complete, authoritative guide for parents* (Rev. ed.). New York: Guilford Press.

Berko Gleason, J. (2001). *The development of language.* Boston: Allyn and Bacon.

Booth, R. C. (1998). Basic information about attention deficit disorders. Highland Park, IL: Attention Deficit Disorder Association. Retrieved from *www.add.org/content/abc/basic.htm*

Brown, V. L., Hammill, D. D., & Wiederholt, J. L. (1995). *Test of reading comprehension, examiner's manual* (3rd ed.). Austin, TX: Pro-ed.

Brown, F., McIntire, J., Wood-Garnett, S., & Avoke, S. (2001). *Implementing IDEA: A guide for principals.* Arlington, VA: Council for Exceptional Children.

California State Department of Education. (1994). *Building bilingual instruction: Putting the pieces together.* Sacramento, CA: Bilingual Education Office.

Carlisle, J. F. (n.d.). Deciding on appropriate accommodations for students with learning disabilities. University of Michigan , Ann Arbor, MI. Center for the Improvement of Early Reading Achievement.

Clark, B. A. (1997). *Growing up gifted* (p. 282). Upper Saddle River, NJ: Merrill/Prentice Hall.

Council of State Directors of Programs for the Gifted. (1994). *The 1994 state of the states gifted and talented education report.* Washington, DC: Author.

deBettencourt, L. U. (2002). Understanding the differences between IDEA and Section 504. *TEACHING Exceptional Children, 34,* 16–23.

Deshler, D. (1998). Grounding interventions for students with learning disabilities in "powerful ideas." *Learning Disabilities Research and Practice, 13,* 29–34.

Federal Register. (1977, September 29). *Procedures for evaluating specific learning disabilities.* Washington, DC: Department of Health, Education, and Welfare.

Gersten, R., Fuchs, L. S., Williams, J. P., & Baker, S. (2001). Teaching reading comprehension strategies to students with learning disabilities: A review of research. *Review of Educational Research, 71,* 279–320.

Gregg, S. (1996–2003). IDEA, The final regulations, and children with AD/HD. Landover, MD: CHADD. Retrieved from *www.chadd.org/WEBPAGE.CFM?CAT_ID=5&SUBCAT_ID=21&SEC_ID=0*

Heward, W. L. (2000). *Exceptional children: An introduction to special education.* Upper Saddle River, NJ: Merrill.

Hollowell, E. M. (1992). What's it like to have ADD? Highland Park, IL: Attention Deficit Disorder Association. Retrieved from *www.add.org/content/abc/hallowell.htm*

Hughes, C. A., & Schumaker, J. B. (1991). Test-taking strategy instruction for adolescents with learning disabilities. *Exceptionality, 2,* 205–221.

International Reading Association. (2003). *The role of reading instruction in addressing the overrepresentation of minority children in special education.* Newark, DE: Author.

Kanner, L. (1943). Autistic disturbances of affective contact. *Nervous Child, 2,* 217–250.

Karlsen, B., & Gardner, E. F. (1995). *Stanford diagnostic reading test, direction for administering* (4th ed.). San Antonio, TX: Harcourt Brace Educational Measurement.

Kirk, S. A. (1962). *Educating exceptional children.* Boston: Houghton Mifflin.

Lavoie, R. D. (1989). *Understanding learning disabilities: How difficult can this be? The F.A.T. City Workshop videotape.* New York: PBS Video.

Lavoie, R. (2002). *Reflections on the state of the art.* [Online]. Retrieved from *http://www.ldonline.org/mminds/lavoie_paper.html*

Lenz, B. K., & Hughes, C. A. (1990). A word identification strategy for adolescents with learning disabilities. *Journal of Learning Disabilities, 23,* 149–158, 163.

Liberman, I. Y., & Shankweiler, D. (1991). Phonology and beginning reading: A tutorial. In L. Reiben & C.A. Perfetti (Eds.), *Learning to read: Basic research and its implications.* Hillsdale, NJ: Erlbaum.

Mastropieri, M. A., & Scruggs, T. E. (2000). *The inclusive classroom: Strategies for effective instruction.* Upper Saddle River, NJ: Merrill.

Mathews, J. (1998, June 7). Across area, "gifted" has no clear-cut definition: School guidelines mystify many parents. *The Washington Post,* A1, A16.

McLeskey, J., & Waldron, N. (1990). The identification and characteristics of students with learning disabilities in Indiana. *Learning Disabilities Research, 5,* 72–78.

National Center for Education Statistics. (1994). *U.S. Department of Education statistics.* Washington, DC: U.S. Department of Education.

Peregoy, S. F., & Boyle, O. F. (2001). *Reading, writing, & learning in ESL. A resource book for K-12 teachers.* New York: Addison Wesley Longman.

Potter, D. C., & Wall, M. E. (1992, April). *Higher standards for grade promotion and graduation: Unintended effects of reform.* Paper presented at the American Educational Research Association, San Francisco.

Proudfoot, L. (1997). *Richard Lavoie: Understanding the learning disabled child.* [Online]. Retrieved from *http://www.growing-up.com/lavoie.html*

Rosenfeld, S. J. (n.d.). Section 504 and IDEA: Basic similarities and differences. [Online]. Retrieved from *http://www.ldonline.org/ld_indepth/legal_legislative/edlaw504.html.*

Salvia, J., & Ysseldyke, J. E. (1995). *Assessment in special and remedial education* (6th ed.). Boston: Houghton Mifflin.

Schumaker, J. B., & Deshler, D. (1992). Validation of learning strategy interventions for students with LD: Results of a programmatic research effort. In B. Y. L. Wong (Ed.), *Contemporary intervention research in learning disabilities: An international perspective* (pp. 22–46). New York, NY: Springer.

Stuttering Foundation of America. (1997). *The child who stutters at school: Notes to the teacher.* Memphis, TN: Author.

Thomas, C. C., Correa, V. I., & Morsink, C. V. (1995). *Interactive teaming: Consultation and collaboration in special programs* (2nd ed.). Upper Saddle River, NJ: Merrill/Prentice Hall.

U.S. Department of Education (2001). *Twenty-third annual report to Congress on the implementation of the Individuals with Disabilities Education Act* (p. A-2–A-4). Washington, DC: Author.

Voltz, D. L., Elliott, R. N., & Harris, W. B. (1995). Promising practices in facilitating collaboration between resource room teachers and general education teachers. *Learning Disabilities Research and Practice, 10,* 129–136.

Wiederholt, L., & Bryant, B. (2001). *Examiner's manual: Gray Oral Reading Tests–4.* Austin, TX: Pro-Ed.

PART 2

PRACTICAL IMPLICATIONS OF READING AND WRITING RESEARCH

Part Two of this text draws heavily on research to inform your instruction in helping learners get from print to language (decoding skills), develop reading strategies, and develop vocabulary, comprehension, and fluency—all critical to becoming a successful reader. Chapter 10 focuses on the important role writing plays in the reading curriculum and underscores our conviction that reading instruction reinforces writing ability, that writing instruction reinforces reading ability. They go hand in hand. These chapters present many opportunities to engage with our Companion Website, to think about implications of research findings, and to discover new assessment and evaluation tools.

READING PROCESS QUESTIONS

You have much more information about the teaching of reading than you had when you first encountered these reading process questions. Answer them now and compare your current answers to those you gave when you encountered these questions at the opening of Part One.

- How do I understand the reading process?
- How do I get children to understand the reading process?
- How do I teach children to monitor their use of the reading process?
- How do I discern that children are monitoring their use of the reading process?

Chapter 5

Guiding the Development of Decoding Skills

LOOKING AT THE RESEARCH

Juel and Minden-Cupp (1999) studied the word learning instruction provided in four first-grade classrooms. The purpose of their research was to answer the question, "Which, and how many, word recognition strategies should teachers model for first-grade children?" (p. 1). For example, should teachers teach the strategy of sounding each letter in a word and then blending those sounds together to make the word? Should teachers teach a body of key words that make up a word wall, for example, and then teach children the strategy of decoding unfamiliar words by locating an analogous word on the word wall? Should teachers teach children the strategy of continual self-monitoring for meaning as reading proceeds? In this strategy the child checks the accuracy of a prediction for an unknown word by asking: Does it make sense? (in terms of meaning); Does it look right? (letters, sounds); and Can we say it that way? (structure, grammar). Finally, should teachers teach phonological awareness and then give children rich exposure to words so they learn them through repeated readings?

Source: From C. Juel and C. Minden-Cupp (1999). CIERA Report #1-008, Learning to read words: Linguistic units and strategies. Retrieved from www.ciera.org/library/reports/inquiry-1/1-008/Report%201-008.html. Reprinted with permission.

In each of the four first-grade classrooms observed by Juel and Minden-Cupp, children were placed in low, medium, and high achieving groups—a practice criticized by some in concern that once children are assigned to the low group, they are always in the low group (Barr & Dreeben, 1983; Juel, 1990). This practice in this study, however, permitted the researchers to look at the differences in instruction and performance for children operating at different levels.

While children in only four classrooms were the subjects, some interesting and useful conclusions were drawn, which may be used to inform practice. The more time incoming students with comparatively fewer early literacy skills spent in small, homogeneous group instruction—as opposed to whole class instruction—the better they learned.

In addition, children who entered first grade with minimal reading skill seemed to have the greatest success with the following classroom practices:

1. Teachers modeled word recognition strategies by chunking words into syllables, examining onsets (consonants preceding the vowel in a syllable) and rimes (vowel and any following consonants in a syllable), finding little words in big ones, encouraging blending of sounds in these chunks, and considering known letter sounds in a word and what makes sense.
2. Teachers encouraged children to finger point to words as text was read.
3. Teachers used hands-on materials such as pocket charts for active sorting of picture cards by sound and word cards by sound/letter patterns such as onset, rime or medial vowel sound.
4. "Writing for sounds" where children practice writing letters for sounds they hear in words was part of phonics instruction.
5. Instructional groups were small with lessons planned to meet the specific needs of children in the group.

Among other findings:

- The focus of instruction for the highest performing low group was phonics first and fast, but only until February when the focus of instruction became vocabulary and comprehension.
- Children who entered first grade with mid-range literacy skills benefited from a classroom with more trade book reading and time for writing text.
- Children who entered first grade with some reading ability did exceptionally well in a classroom that included a less structured phonics curriculum and more reading of trade books and writing of text.
- Children who possess some early literacy skills can become self-teaching; however, children who have few literacy skills on entering school benefit from initial teaching on how to approach unknown words before self-teaching is activated. The development of phonological sensitivity and lots of reading experience are not sufficient for some children. They need phonics instruction on onsets, rimes (including short and long vowel rimes), and short vowels coupled with demonstrations of how to approach unknown words.

Focus Questions

- What are decoding skills?
- How do children best learn to use decoding skills?
- How do I create an environment in which my students learn decoding skills?

REAL TEACHERS, REAL PRACTICE

Meet Stephanie Anders, *a K-1 multi-age teacher*

In my classroom, literacy instruction occurs mostly in small groups, according to individual student needs. I do not reteach letter sounds to children who already know all of their letter sounds. These children spend more time with vowel patterns. Students are required to complete some tasks during literacy center time and can choose other tasks they enjoy. I begin decoding instruction by allowing children to match pictures with the same beginning sounds on the pocket chart.

After I explicitly instruct them on each letter sound they do not know, I allow them to use these sounds during writing workshop through invented spelling. I take every opportunity to reinforce the sounds of the letters, using letter strips with pictures on each table to serve as a guide for those who need one to use sounds to write words. I also have alphabet charts, environmental print, and a word wall with pictures next to each letter to serve as guides. Student writing helps me see which sounds and patterns need reinforcing and which sounds are known.

To help children with blending and decoding, I use picture sorts from Words Their Way *(Bear, Invernizzi, Templeton, & Johnston, 1996) based on the sounds they hear at the beginning, middle, and end of words. We start reading using easy readers with decodable text along with high-frequency words. I also use predictable text, so that children can use meaning to figure out some words. Children must use meaning, visual, and semantic cues to become fluent readers, so I allow practice in all three strategies to help children become familiar with choosing the most appropriate strategy.*

If children are struggling with individual sounds, I take a different approach and teach them "word families" that are more easily recognized in text. I reinforce these concepts using text that focuses on specific phonograms. Lots of books have pictures to go with different phonograms, like bat, cat, mat, *etc. I begin phonogram instruction with these, to show how the same word pattern can be heard in words with varied beginning and ending sounds. Later, I introduce text that has the word family, along with basic sight words.*

I reinforce what students are learning through individualized spelling lists created from student writing and miscues in reading. We also use book baskets. Students have baskets of books that are designed to reinforce what they are learning. For example, students working on identifying the alphabet have lots of alphabet books. Students who are working on high-frequency words have books with specific words they are working on, and students who are working on word families have books with word families. Students can pick up their book basket any time they have an extra minute, as well as during nap/quiet reading time. It gives them an opportunity to make connections and also to take responsibility for their own learning, which always makes them feel confident and independent, no matter on what level they are working.

It is amazing to think about the number of words children are expected to read quickly and accurately. According to Adams (1990) if children are successful with all the texts they encounter by the end of third grade, they would learn more than 80,000 different words! The task of teaching children to decode words is daunting and important and generates some important questions.

WHAT ARE DECODING SKILLS?

As we read, we deal with words in print in essentially two ways. We employ word recognition or word identification. If we recognize a word, it is one we have already learned. It is in our sight vocabulary, and we can read it instantaneously. If we do not immediately recognize the word, we must employ strategies and skills to identify it. We have to decode it. To **decode** is to analyze spoken or graphic symbols of a familiar language to ascertain their intended meaning. In reading practice the term is used to refer to word identification (Harris & Hodges, 1995). To identify a word not immediately decodable, one must apply knowledge of cueing systems.

Cueing Systems

Cueing systems consist of the cues inherent in the printed text that readers may employ as they decode print into language. Readers bring their knowledge of print and how it works and their knowledge of language and how it works to bear on the task of making meaning from text. Consider the array of cues that exist on this page that you can draw on to decode the print into language and then make meaning with that language. Each letter represents a sound, a variation in sound, or the absence of sound. Each word represents meaning or signals aspects of the language structure. Each phrase has meaning. Each sentence has meaning. Skillful readers select from this myriad of cues to decode the print efficiently and effectively and make meaning. An informed reading teacher understands each of the cueing systems and has knowledge of a variety of ways to teach these understandings to readers.

The Graphophonic Cueing System. The graphophonic cueing system exists in the relationships between printed letters and the sounds they represent. The smallest sound units of speech are called *phonemes.* When one phoneme is contrasted with another phoneme, the meaning of words is affected. For example, /h/ in *hat* contrasts with /b/ in *bat* to make different words. A reader uses knowledge of the graphophonic cueing system when attempting to read a word not immediately recognized—a word not in his or her sight vocabulary. For example, a reader might encounter the word *hat.* Unable to recognize and decode it instantly, the reader then chooses to try sounding out each letter. She knows the /h/ sound from the word, *have.* She knows the /a/ and /t/ sounds from the word, *bat.* She sounds out the /h/ + /at/ sequence and then blend those sounds into the word *hat.* Perhaps the reader recognizes the common letter combination /at/. She might decode *hat* by recognizing the /at/ phonogram and then realizing she knows the sound of /h/ from *have.* She then blends these two word parts.

There are approximately 44 phonemes in American English with only 26 letters (*graphemes*) with which to represent them in print. This lack of phoneme/grapheme correspondence adds challenges to learning the graphophonic cueing system. The challenges of learning phonics suggest that we should carefully plan a sequence in which the graphophonic cueing system is taught. Consider this possible instructional sequence.

You might be interested in the symbols linguists use to record the 44 phonemes. Go to the Weblinks for Chapter 5 on our Companion Website at www.prenhall.com/harp to link to the International Phonetic Association's web site where the International Phonetic Alphabet is reproduced.

Graphophonic Instructional Sequence. There is no one agreed-upon instructional sequence for teaching the graphophonic cueing system. The one illustrated in Figure 5.1 is typical of the sequence used in many published instructional programs. You will want to consult your school's curriculum guide to determine the suggested sequence.

The Semantic Cueing System. *Semantic cues* are evidence from the general sense or meaning of a written or spoken communication that aid in the identification of an unknown

Figure 5.1
Graphophonic Skills Sequence

I. Letter names. Although it is not necessary for children to know letter names to learn to use the graphophonic cueing system, the ability to talk about letters facilitates instruction. It is important for readers to be able to distinguish between consonants and vowels. The consonants are all of the letters in the alphabet except *a, e, i, o,* and *u.*

II. Consonant sounds. Most publishers begin instruction with consonant sounds because the consonants in a sentence carry the bulk of the message. To illustrate this point, read the following sentences:

-e -oy -i- --e -a--.

Th- b-- h-t th- b-ll.

The sentence containing only consonants is much easier to decode than the sentence with only vowels.

A. Initial single consonants

B. Consonant clusters. Consonant clusters or blends are two or more consonants pronounced rapidly together. Examples: *bl, br, cr, dr, fl, pr, sk, sm, sp, st, str, scr*

C. Initial consonant digraphs. Digraphs are two consonants that represent only one sound. Examples: *ch, ph, sh, th, wh, gh*

D. Some instructional programs teach phonic elements in the three previous categories in initial positions in words and then repeat instruction with phonic elements in final positions in words.

III. Vowels. Vowel sounds are more variable and thus more difficult for children to learn than consonants.

A. Vowel sounds in syllable patterns.

1. VC and CVC. Syllable ends with a consonant; vowel sound is usually short.
2. VCe and CVCe. Syllable ends with an e preceded by a single consonant and a vowel sound is usually long.
3. CV and CVV. Syllable ends with a vowel; vowel sound is usually long.

B. Vowel sounds in other patterns.

1. Vowel digraphs. Two vowels, only one of which is sounded. Examples: *ai, ea, ee, oa, oo, au, wait, each, speech, oats, cool, auto*
2. Diphthong. Two vowels that make a new sound composed of the vowel plus glide. Examples: *ow, oi, oy, ou, how, oil, toy, out*
3. Consonant-controlled vowel. The sound of the vowel is distorted by the following consonant sound so the vowel sound is neither long nor short. Examples: *fir, far, call*

IV. Syllables. In the preceding section, we described the sounds of vowels predicted in certain syllable patterns. A set of generalizations describe how words may be divided into syllables. This information may be helpful to a reader in trying to decode an unfamiliar word because the structure of the syllable sometimes determines the sound of the vowel. Once an unknown word is divided into syllables, graphophonic analysis may be applied at the syllabic level. The following generalizations describe how words may be divided into syllables:

A. When two like consonants stand between two vowels, the word is usually divided between the consonants:

pup py   stag ger   pep per   com mon

(Continued)

Figure 5.1
Graphophonic Skills Sequence *Continued*

B. When two unlike consonants stand between two vowels, the word is usually divided between the consonants:
wal rus cir cus pic nic trum pet
C. When one consonant stands between two vowels, the consonant usually goes with the second syllable:
pi rate si lent pa per mi ser
D. When x is the consonant that is between two vowels, the x and the preceding vowel are the same syllable:
ex it Tex as max i mum
E. When a word ends in a consonant and le, the consonant usually begins the last syllable:
ea gle ta ble no ble ket tle
F. Compound words are usually divided between the parts and between syllables within those parts:
po lice man blind fold sun shine snow man
G. Prefixes and suffices are usually separate syllables:
dis own re sold swift ly re pay ment

word (Harris & Hodges, 1995). Suppose you read the sentence, "The frivolous girl was silly," and you didn't know *frivolous.* The general sense of the sentence is that the girl in question is silly. This would lead you to predict that *frivolous* must have something to do with lacking seriousness. Semantic cues exist in the understandings the reader brings to the text about word meanings and the meanings signaled by words around the target word. Knowledge of word meanings is fundamental to reading for meaning. Children come to school knowing 5,000 to 6,000 words (Clark, 1993). They learn more words as they are read to, as they read, and as they participate in discussions. Just as the general sense of a communication can help us unlock unfamiliar words, so can the grammatical structures we read.

The Syntactic Cueing System. Syntactic cues exist in the knowledge of language rules and patterns the reader applies to identifying an unknown word from the way it is used in a grammatical construction (Harris & Hodges, 1995). Suppose a reader encounters this sentence. "In their biting and tumbling, the rambunctious puppies overturned their water dish." The word *rambunctious* is not in the reader's sight vocabulary. She does not recognize it, but she can bring background knowledge and grammatical knowledge to bear on working out the word.

How could the structure of the sentence cue her to identify the word? The word before the target word in the sentence provides some help. *The* is a noun marker, indicating a noun follows. Other examples of noun markers are *those, this, that, some, his, her,* and *their.* When she sees a noun marker, she knows a noun will follow it next or very soon. In the sample sentence, she realizes that *puppies* is a noun. That means the unknown word has to be an adjective, a word that describes or modifies a noun.

She might recall how playful puppies look and envision these puppies tumbling over each other. She might then think about how some water dishes are made with wide bases to prevent tipping. This creates an image of pretty wild puppies being so active that they overturned a dish designed to be hard to tip. This understanding leads to the prediction that *rambunctious* describes the puppies because it comes in the sentence where an adjective would be, and it can't mean something like quiet, calm, or sedate. It must mean unruly.

At this point she probably would jump to the use of another cueing system and consider the beginning sounds in the unknown word to limit the possible puppy descriptors she will consider. As a start in identifying the unknown word, syntactic cues are helpful because of what the reader knows about how the language works.

Proficient readers have learned to be skillful in manipulating the cueing systems so they can decode and bring meaning to challenging texts. Because the term *skill* implies an ability to perform well, the term *decoding skills* refers to the ability to manipulate intellectually various linguistic components of each cueing system. Skills are the routinized, automatic procedures readers employ as they engage in the reading task.

Skill Automaticity. LaBerge and Samuels (1974) explain how *automaticity* applies to learning and applying skills: During the execution of a complex skill, it is necessary to coordinate many component processes within a very short period of time. If each component process requires attention, performance of the complex skill will be impossible, because the capacity of attention will be exceeded. But if enough of the components and their coordinations can be processed automatically, the loads on attention will be within tolerable limits. (p. 293)

An important instructional goal is to have learners develop automaticity in the ability to select and apply decoding skills. They will become so adept at using the graphophonic cues, semantic cues, and syntactic cues that they can do so virtually automatically. Proficient readers not only read accurately, but they recognize words automatically (Stanovich, 1980). When children develop automaticity in decoding, they require less cognitive attention directed toward decoding and therefore can direct more cognitive attention to comprehension—the ultimate goal of reading. This will require effective instruction in the use of the cueing systems and frequent opportunities to read increasingly more challenging texts.

Effective cueing system instruction involves making informed decisions about which decoding skills to teach. Your district's curriculum guide or the skills scope and sequence included in instructional materials will provide some guidance. However, one important consideration is the utility of a particular phonics generalization. Here, research conducted by three investigators in the 1960s (we have no reason to believe the data have changed) may be more helpful. Ted Clymer (1963), Mildred Bailey (1967), and Robert Emans (1967) independently conducted research to determine the utility of phonic generalizations (generalizations to guide pronunciation of written words such as, "When a word begins with *wr,* the *w* is silent"). Clymer examined primary-grade (1–3) materials, Bailey looked at first- through sixth-grade materials, and Emans studied intermediate-grade (4–6) materials. In each study the question was, "In what percentage of the time that a particular generalization could apply does it apply?" Of the 45 generalizations studied, only 10 applied in 100% of the instances in which they could apply. Many fell short of reasonable utility. For example, a generalization commonly taught in first grade is, "When two vowels go walking the first one does the talking" (another way to describe vowel digraphs). Many teachers have made this statement without thinking about the fact that a common word in the statement with two vowels together (does) does not follow the rule. In the primary materials this generalization held up 45% of the time; in grades 1 through 6, 34% of the time; and in intermediate-grade materials, only 18% of the time. A composite of these studies is found in Appendix C. We suggest that generalizations not be taught unless they have a minimal utility of 75%.

It is important to consider the utility of skill instruction because such instruction takes time away from real reading, which promotes the development of sight vocabulary.

Sight Vocabulary Development

Words a reader can decode instantly without any analysis are said to be in that reader's *sight vocabulary.* Reading teachers help learners develop large, meaningful sight vocabularies that lead to increasingly fluent reading. Ehri (1995) has described the stages children move through in developing a sight vocabulary. Figure 5.2 illustrates this process.

Figure 5.2
Ehri's Developmental Phases in Sight Word Recognition

Phase One: Prealphabetic

Beginning readers remember sight words by making a connection between some visual aspect of a word and its pronunciation or its meaning. Letter-sound relationships are not involved at this phase. A child might remember *tall* because it has so many tall letters or *look* because it has two eyes in the middle.

Phase Two: Partial Alphabetic

At this stage readers begin to attend to some of the sound-symbol relationships within the word—usually first and last letters and their sounds. Children are typically in kindergarten and first grade during this stage. For example, they might remember *books* by keying on the *b* at the beginning and the *s* at the end, paying little or no attention to the letters in between. Therefore, they might also decode *boots* as *books* or *banks* as *books.*

Phase Three: Full Alphabetic

At this stage readers have developed deeper understandings of the graphophonic cueing system. They recognize the ways in which phonemes are represented by graphemes in conventional spelling. This ease in decoding permits them to read words with similar spellings (books, banks, boots) and to decode unfamiliar words by sounding them out. With increased exposure, words enter the child's sight vocabulary and are recognized immediately, automatically. Words with irregular spelling that cannot be sounded out are also added to the sight vocabulary.

Phase Four: Consolidated Alphabetic

During this final phase readers begin to attend less to individual sound-symbol relationships and remember common spelling patterns. They begin to attend to onsets (consonants preceding the vowel) and rimes (the vowel and any following consonants in the syllable). Thus, they automatically recognize the /at/ sounds in words like *cat, bat,* and *hat.* They also develop the ability to recognize automatically syllables in multisyllabic words.

Source: Ehri, L. C. (1995). Phases of development in learning to read words by sight. *Journal of Research in Reading, 18,* 116–125. Reprinted with permission.

Note that at each of the last three stages readers attended more and more to sound/symbol relationships, that decoding becomes increasingly more accurate, and ultimately becomes automatic. At this stage, readers can coordinate their use of decoding skills and typically apply them in a predictable sequence.

Using Decoding Skills

Go to the Weblinks in Chapter 5 on our Companion Website at www.prenhall.com/harp for an illustrative list of reading skills organized by grade level.

As children become increasingly competent in applying decoding skills, they typically rely most heavily on their growing sight vocabulary to decode most words. They then use a sequence of syntactic cues, semantic cues, and finally graphophonic cues. Figure 5.3 illustrates the order in which developing and fluent readers typically use word recognition and word identification skills to decode and give meaning to words. Compare this sequence to the way in which you process text. It is interesting to note that while accomplished readers typically apply their knowledge of decoding skills in the order shown in Figure 5.3, the use of the cueing systems is usually taught in the reverse order. Reading programs either begin with teaching sounds in isolation and then teaching children to blend those sounds into words, which become their sight vocabulary, or they begin with

Figure 5.3
Order in Which Readers Typically use Decoding Skills

USE OF SIGHT VOCABULARY

Readers develop an increasingly large sight vocabulary. As we become more accomplished, we rely more and more on our sight vocabulary as our primary method of decoding text and making meaning.

USE OF SYNTACTIC CUES

When a word is not in our sight vocabulary, we typically skip it and read on, hoping to figure it out from the syntax of the sentence, the context in which the word sits. We may well combine our knowledge of syntax with our knowledge of phonics to ask ourselves, "Do I know a word that begins with this letter that would make sense in this spot in this sentence?"

USE OF SEMANTIC CUES

When we cannot decode a word using syntactic cues, perhaps combined with phonic cues, we then turn to semantic cues. We may examine the word to see if there is a prefix or suffix we recognize; we may try to see if there is a root word we know. We may combine our knowledge of semantic cues with our use of syntactic cues to attempt to decode the word and make some meaning.

↓

USE OF GRAPHOPHONIC CUES

When all else fails, we attempt to sound out the word—to systematically apply our knowledge of sound/symbol relationships to pronounce the word. Some readers attempt to identify syllables as an aid in decoding. Many readers look for familiar letter combinations in the challenging word.

teaching some sight words and then use those to teach phonics. In either approach the use of the graphophonic cueing system is taught ahead of use of the semantic and syntactic systems.

HOW DO CHILDREN BEST LEARN TO USE DECODING SKILLS?

Researchers have argued for the importance of early acquisition of decoding skills. Stanovich (1986) found convincing evidence that children who start slowly in acquiring decoding skills rarely become strong readers throughout their academic careers. Juel (1988) found that early acquisition of decoding skills leads to wider reading in and out of school. Wide reading in and out of school provides abundant opportunities for growth in vocabulary, concepts, and general knowledge (Lapp & Flood, 1997). With this research in mind and the following set of principles of good instruction, planning for skills lessons will become thoughtful and reasoned rather than mechanical.

Instruction Is Guided by Carefully Considered Principles

Teachers form their own philosophies about literacy instruction, what they value in instruction, how they view instructional materials and programs, and how they teach. Many teachers subscribe to a set of principles that guide their instruction (Stahl, 1992).

Following are five principles of instruction in the cueing systems. Carefully consider each of them and embrace or modify them as you choose.

Principle 1. Instruction in the use of the cueing systems should be seen as an aid to constructing meaning, not as an end in itself. Children are not taught the sound(s) represented by a certain letter because that knowledge is important. Sound/letter correspondences are taught so the process of constructing meaning may go on as effortlessly as possible.

Principle 2. Skills instruction should be as much like the reading act as possible. In skills instruction examples should be taken from meaningful texts, often texts written by children.

Principle 3. Before instruction of young children in the graphophonic cueing system can begin, four conditions must be met: The children must have (1) adequate phonemic awareness, (2) auditory discrimination (the ability to hear differences in sounds); (3) visual discrimination (the ability to see differences in letters and between words), and (4) the understanding that reading is a process of constructing or reconstructing meaning.

Principle 4. While engaging in instruction in the components of the reading process, the reading process must be respected. Having broken down the process to examine individual steps or pieces, we should put it back together before ending the instruction, so children can see the relationships between parts and the whole.

Principle 5. Cueing system instruction is useful only when the words identified are in the reader's listening or speaking vocabulary. The use of word identification cues will not be effective if children cannot recognize miscues when they make them and self-correct. Word identification is useless if readers do not know the words they have identified (Stahl, Duffy-Hester, & Stahl, 1998).

Children Develop Sight Vocabularies

Children in first grade should have explicit instruction in sound/symbol relationships and development of a sight vocabulary while reading a wide variety of well-written and engaging texts (Adams, 1990; Snow, Burns, & Griffin, 1998).

One of the best ways to develop children's sight vocabularies is to encourage them to read and read and read and read. Several studies have reported a relationship between the amount of classroom reading children do and their achievement in reading (Allington, 1977, 1980, 1983, 1984; Allington & McGill-Franzen, 1989). In these studies the average higher-achieving students read approximately three times as much each week as their lower-achieving classmates. These studies did not consider voluntary reading out of school. However, in another study that examined fifth graders' reading in and out of school, children were asked to keep reading logs documenting their out-of-school reading. The highest-achieving students read an average of 40.4 minutes per day, or about 2,357,000 words per year. The average-achieving students read 12.9 minutes per day, or about 601,000 words per year. The lowest-achieving students read 1.6 minutes per day, or about 51,000 words per year (Allington, 2001; Anderson, Wilson, & Fielding, 1988). It is no wonder the high-achieving students keep getting better at reading.

Children also develop sight vocabularies in activities out of school. A trip to Burger King teaches words like cheeseburger, fries, Coke, and ice. There are some additional instructional strategies for developing sight vocabulary that you will find helpful.

Sentence Strips. Use a piece of oaktag about 3" by 24". Using a felt marker, write a sentence from a story just read, from a language experience chart, or from a child's writing. Cut the words apart and scramble them on the table. Invite children to put the words back in order.

Repeated readings of text builds sight vocabulary.

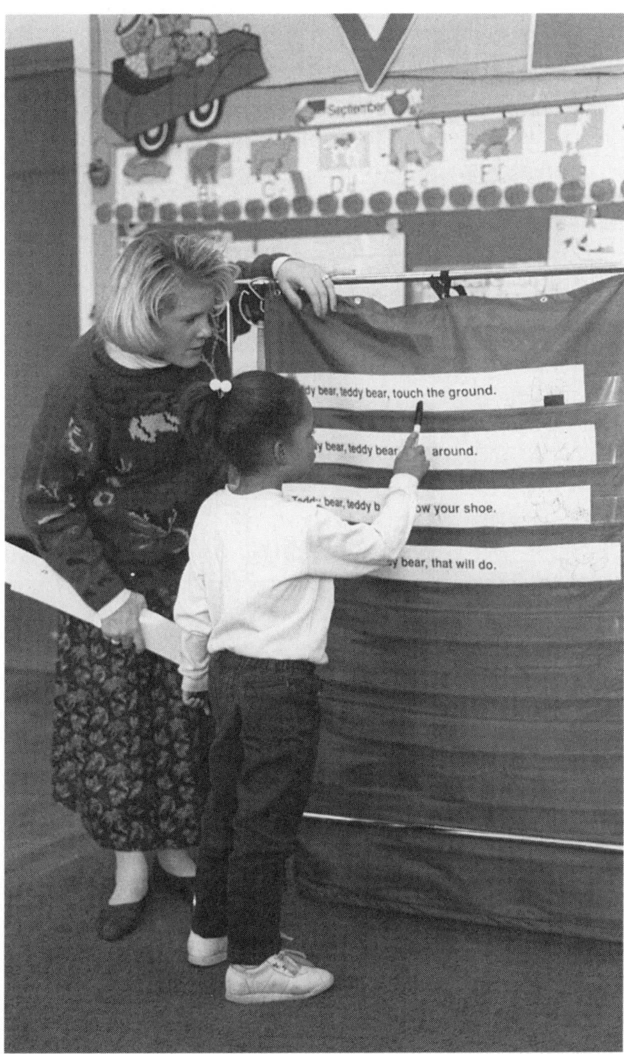

Word Walls. Word walls are used to display frequently used words as children learn to read them. The words are displayed on the wall in alphabetical order. Each list has words beginning with the same letter. Word walls are also used to display high frequency words found in books at the beginning levels. Another way to use the word wall is to display words according to the rime of the word, so all of the "ill" words would be displayed in a list. Even though you can purchase word wall kits, it is beneficial to construct them with the help of the children.

Word Banks. Word banks are typically used in classrooms where language experience is used as an instructional strategy, the approach to early literacy, or a technique for working with struggling readers. As children learn to read words they have dictated or written, they learn to recognize these as sight words. When you are certain that a word is in a child's sight vocabulary, you write it on a small card that the child then adds to his word bank, a personal collection of sight words. Children can practice reading and rereading their word bank words, find all words beginning with a certain sound, find all words with a certain vowel

Figure 5.4
WORDO Game

W	O	R	D	O
		Free Space		

Source: *Effective reading strategies: Teaching children who find reading difficult,* p. 97. 2e by Rasinski, T., & Padak, N. (2000). © Reprinted by permission of Pearson Education, Inc., Upper Saddle River, NJ.

sound, locate all words of a certain rime family, or make sentences. Repeated exposure to these word bank words reinforces the development of sight vocabulary.

Pocket Charts. Use pocket chart and word cards accompanying your literature anthology, a set of high-frequency word cards, cards you have made, or cards from your children's word banks. Keep a collection of sentence strips near the pocket chart. Have children arrange the cards in the pocket chart and then read them to a friend. Have the friend rearrange them and read them again.

Games. Games are an engaging way to reinforce sight vocabulary as well as phonics skills. Many commercial games are available, but you can adapt some of these ideas for classroom use. Rasinski and Padak (2000) describe their adaptations of some commercial games. They recommend Wordo, Concentration, and Scattergories.

Wordo. This is a form of Bingo, using Wordo cards (see Figure 5.4) that are almost identical to Bingo cards. Select 24 words to review. Have students randomly write one word in each square, leaving the center square free. You then select one word at a time, present the definition, an antonym, or a sentence with the target word missing (do not say the target word). Players then figure out the word and cover it with a marker. The player who gets a vertical, horizontal, or diagonal line of words covered first is the winner.

Figure 5.5
Scattergories Game

	CATEGORIES				
Initial Consonants & Blends					

Source: *Effective reading strategies: Teaching children who find reading difficult,* p. 145., 2e Rasinski, T., & Padak, N. (2000). Reprinted by permission of Pearson Education, Inc., Upper Saddle River, NJ.

Concentration. In this game you make two sets of cards. One set contains words to be learned and practiced; the other set contains definitions, synonyms, antonyms or some other way of matching the words. The cards are then laid out in a grid, face down. As in the television game of the same name, players or teams of players turn over pairs of cards trying to find a match. If a match is found, the player keeps the cards and continues to play. If no match is found, the next player takes a turn. The player with the most matches wins the game.

Scattergories. This game is an instructional adaptation of a commercial version. Select 5 to 10 letters or blends, and list them in the left hand vertical column. Please see the game sheet illustrated in Figure 5.5. Then select categories you want your students to focus on in this game. Draw these from a unit or theme you are studying. Write the category names in the large rectangles across the top of the game sheet. Duplicate the game sheets. Students are then given a time limit of several minutes to think of as many words as possible beginning with the designated letters in each of the categories. Players with the greatest number of unique words (words chosen by only one player or team) win that round.

You will discover that making games is time consuming. You may decide to seek the assistance of parent or grandparent volunteers or pursue the possibility that a local senior citizens center may be willing to help.

In addition to developing an ever-growing sight vocabulary, children must learn to use each of the cueing systems. Children must learn to pay attention to sounds in words and the letters that represent those sounds, but they also need to develop knowledge of the semantic and syntactic cueing systems of our language in order to make meaning and be good spellers (Nunes, Bryant, & Bindman, 1997).

Children Have Visual Discrimination, Auditory Discrimination, and Phonemic Awareness

In planning phonics instruction, you need to pay attention to understandings and abilities children need before they can be successful with phonics lessons. Three areas of concern are auditory discrimination, visual discrimination, and phonemic awareness.

Auditory Discrimination. If children cannot hear differences in letter sounds, the challenge of learning phonics increases dramatically. If you suspect a child has a hearing difficulty, bring this to the attention of the school nurse, school psychologist, or principal. A decision may be made to ask parents to have the child's hearing and auditory discrimination screened.

Visual Discrimination. For many children, learning phonics is the first time they have been in a situation where position in space determines object identity. No matter how they turn their fork, it is still a fork. No matter where they lay their toy, it is still that toy. Then they encounter letters and letter sounds. Turned one way this set of lines and circles is a *p* and says /p/, but turned another way it becomes a *d* and says /d/; yet another way a *q* says /qu/. *M, n,* and *w* require careful visual discrimination, as do other letters. Children need good visual acuity and discrimination to be successful in learning phonics.

Hopefully, your school will have both a Snellen Chart which screens for distance vision, and a Telebinocular, which screens for near and far point vision. Be certain to refer children who exhibit signs of visual limitations (red eyes, eye rubbing, squinting) for screening or referral to a vision specialist.

Phonological Awareness. Further, we need to be certain that children have phonological awareness, that they can hear sounds in spoken words. Cunningham (2000) defines phonological awareness as "the ability to recognize that words are made up of a discrete set of sounds and to manipulate sounds" (p. 3). In her book *Conversations,* Regie Routman (2000) confesses that she has taught many, many children to read without knowing anything about phonemic awareness. We make the same confession. However, several researchers have concluded that phonemic awareness is highly correlated with success in beginning reading experiences, and so we include it here. The performance of kindergartners on tests of phonological awareness is a strong predictor of their future reading achievement (Hoffman, Cunningham, Cunningham, & Yopp, 1998; Juel 1991; Lundberg, Frost, & Petersen, 1988; Scarborough, 1989; Stanovich, 1986).

It is not necessary to give phonemic awareness lessons to all kindergarten or first-grade children. Your job is to determine who is skilled in phonemic awareness knowledge and who might need some extra attention to become more skilled. Most children develop phonemic awareness as preschoolers.

Phonemic awareness is not a single skill; it is a cluster of skills that develops over a period of time. For example, recognizing rhyming words is one level of phonemic awareness, being able to distinguish the beginning sound of a word from the rest of the word is another level, and completely segmenting the word is another. Phonemic awareness is developed as a result of children's experience with oral and written language (Cunningham, 2000). Many children who have experience with nursery rhymes, chants, and listening to stories have become quite skilled at recognizing that words are composed of sounds and recognizing when two sounds are alike or different.

Many common preschool and kindergarten activities help children become more aware of sounds in words. Activities useful for developing phonemic awareness include: clapping the beats in children's names, completing the rhyming line of a nursery rhyme as the teacher says part of it and the children say the remainder, reading books with rhyming words, reading a wide variety of alphabet books, making a list of words that begin with the same sound as a given word, or dictating sentences in which all the words begin with the same sound (Novick, 1999/2000). Most children learn phonemic awareness through songs, rhymes, poetry, nursery rhymes, and raps. These activities are part and parcel of many activities throughout the day in preschool, kindergarten, and first grade. You can evaluate your learner's phonemic awareness by the ways in which they respond to these activities.

ssessment and Evaluation Toolbox

***TEST OF PHONOLOGICAL AWARENESS* (TORGESEN & BRYANT, 1994)**

The *Test of Phonological Awareness (TOPA)* is a standardized, norm-referenced test of children's sensitivity to, or explicit awareness of, the phonological structure of words in language. There are two versions, one for kindergarten and one for first grade. The greatest advantages of this tool are you get normative data and, if your students are able to handle it, you can test them as a whole group. The greatest disadvantage of the TOPA is that it measures awareness of sounds only at the beginning and ending of words (Harp, 2000).

If you have good reason to believe that a child needs additional practice with sounds, you might use an activity such as the Elkonin boxes (Elkonin, 1973). The child is given a card with boxes drawn on it—one box for each sound in the word—and markers (pennies or plastic chips). The instructions are to place a marker for each sound heard in a given word. The markers are for sounds, not letters. Four letter words such as cake would be marked with three boxes. However, most children develop phonemic awareness without specific instruction; they only need interesting language and teachers who help them focus on the sounds of words from their oral language.

ssessment and Evaluation Toolbox

YOPP-SINGER TEST OF PHONEME SEGMENTATION

If your observations and engagement with children leave you uncertain about their phonemic awareness ability, you might administer a phonemic awareness screening test such as the one developed by Hallie Yopp (1995). You will find it in Appendix D. You may decide to use it to determine which of your learners need phonemic awareness training and provide that training only to those who need it.

When you are confident that a child has adequate visual and auditory discrimination and phonemic awareness, you can move into phonics instruction.

Children Learn the Graphophonic Cueing System—Phonics

As children learn to use the graphophonic cueing system, their knowledge moves through developmental stages beginning with reading and writing "logographically" using images of whole words, moving to an alphabetic stance to both reading and spelling, and finally developing understandings that spellings often do not reflect word pronunciation and that they must pay close attention to the graphophonic cues (Frith, 1985; Ellis, 1997).

Assessment and Evaluation Toolbox

EKWALL/SHANKER READING INVENTORY

This informal reading inventory consists of 11 subtests. The subtests most directly related to decoding instruction are: Basic Sight Words and Phrases Test, Letter Knowledge Test, Phonics Test, Structural Analysis Test, Knowledge of Contractions Test, and the El Paso Phonics Survey.

Synthetic Versus Analytic Phonics. Let's follow up on our brief introduction to phonics in Chapter 2 with a more detailed discussion about phonics and teaching phonics. In preparing to teach phonics, you must make an instructional strategy decision between synthetic and analytic phonics. Synthetic phonics involves teaching sound-symbol relationships in isolation and then teaching children to blend the sounds into words. Analytic phonics involves teaching children sounds in the context of words and then blending sounds known from two or more words into the sounds of an unknown word.

Which of these approaches to use is a matter of considerable controversy. Research results have been used to bolster the claims for each of the approaches. In fact there is a great deal of controversy within the profession over phonics research.

ISSUES IN LITERACY

PHONICS RESEARCH CONTROVERSY

The National Institutes of Child Health and Human Development (NICHD) have sponsored research on phonics that has gained wide attention in the field. This research, which NICHD researchers call "scientific-based," has been held up by some as the only valid research on phonics.

However, many of these studies claiming to prove that direct, systematic phonics instruction results in higher achievement in reading have been criticized by other researchers. For example, Taylor (1999) examined the study by Foorman, Francis, Fletcher, and Schatschneider (1998) that supported direct phonics instruction for African American children and found that some of the results were based on a sample size of only five children. Generalization of the results of these studies to all children is impossible with such a small sample of subjects.

Reading research sponsored by the NICHD has been criticized by others (Allington, 2002; Coles, 2000; Krashen, 1999; McQuillan, 1998; Smith, 1999). Many of the NICHD studies were conducted on children with special learning needs and cannot be generalized to all children; others were conducted by researchers aligned with specific programs of instruction that would obviously benefit from findings recommending the type of instruction found in these programs. Many of the studies used the reading of isolated words as the measure of success, and there is no research to connect the success of reading isolated words with reading real, connected text. Use caution when you see calls for "scientifically based research" in reading instruction. If this means only experimental/control group studies are acceptable, this systematically excludes a large body of highly respectable research that should inform our instruction.

So which phonics instructional strategy should you select? While you need to know how to use each strategy, and you will use each strategy, the synthetic strategy has several disadvantages. Sounds in isolation have no meaning, look nothing like the reading act, and are the least important aspect of the reading process. Many consonant sounds produced in isolation are distorted because they must be voiced with a vowel sound. For example, the sound of *p* is rendered /puh/. Of great concern is the fact that drill on isolated sounds may well signal to young readers that the most important part of reading is making *sounds* rather than making *sense*. Children must learn that words have both meaning and sound in order to understand the alphabetic principle (Stahl & Murray, 1998).

Go to the Weblinks in Chapter 5 on our Companion Website at www.prenhall.com/harp for a link to the International Reading Association's *Position Statement on the Role of Phonics in Reading Instruction.*

While you will need to use both instructional strategies for phonics, the views of the International Reading Association (IRA) may provide guidance on which strategy to try first. The statement says, in part,

> When children engage with texts themselves, as readers or writers, they begin to orchestrate this knowledge of how written language works to achieve success. It is within these kinds of contexts of language use that direct instruction in phonics takes on meaning for the learner. When phonics instruction is linked to children's genuine efforts to read and write, they are motivated to learn. When phonics instruction is linked to children's reading and writing, they are more likely to become strategic and independent in their use of phonics than when phonics instruction is drilled and practiced in isolation.

Some children have a great deal of difficulty trying to decode words using the analytic method and therefore must be taught using the synthetic strategy (Bond & Dykstra, 1966–1967; Weaver, 1994). The position of the International Reading Association may persuade you to use the analytic method first and move to the synthetic method only as a last resort. Figures 5.6 and 5.7 are examples of a synthetic phonics lesson and an analytic phonics lesson. Notice the different kinds of graphophonic knowledge they require of children.

For many years phonics has traditionally been taught using either the analytic or synthetic approach or a combination of the two. However, in the last 15 years increasing attention is being drawn to the use of onsets and rimes to teach phonics.

Figure 5.6
Synthetic Phonics Lesson

Development of knowledge

1. Write the letters *sh, i,* and *p* on the board.
2. Say, "Today we are going to learn some new sounds. Listen as I read the sounds to you." Say each of the sounds in isolation.
3. Ask the children to repeat the sounds with you.
4. Write the word *ship* on the board. Say, "Now let's say the sounds together faster. Faster. Faster."
5. Say, "You now know all the sounds in the word *ship*."

Practice

1. Write the phonograms (clusters of letters) that the children know on the board, such as *ut, out,* and *ot.*
2. Write *sh* on the board. Have them practice the /sh/ sound and then add it to the front of each of the known phonograms.

Application

Give the children a test in which they must decode the /sh/ sound in nonsense words. Show them, for example, the letter groups bip and ship. Say, pointing to the first group, "If this says bip, what does this say?" (pointing to ship.)

Reinforcement

Repeat the practice portion of the lesson the next day.

Onset and Rime Instruction. Instead of teaching sounds in isolation or teaching phonics rules, teachers are moving to teaching the onset (the part of the syllable before the vowel—a consonant, consonant blend, or digraph) and the rime (the part of the syllable from the vowel onward). For example, in the word *cat,* the *c* is the onset and the *at* phonogram is the rime. With onset and rime instruction, children learn to decode unfamiliar words by analogy. They recognize onsets and rimes and reason, "If I know these letters and sounds in one word, I can recognize them in another word."

LOOKING AT THE RESEARCH

What the research says about phonemic segmentation and onset-rime segmentation

There appears to be a special link between early onset and rime awareness and reading development. Children with good rhyming skills prior to school entry tend to become better readers and spellers (Bradley & Bryant, 1983). Children who receive instruction in phonics as well as onset and rime training achieve significantly higher spelling and reading ability than children with phonics training alone (Goswami & Bryant, 1990). This suggests that if you are working with readers who are learning phonics, you will want to include carefully planned onset and rime instruction. However, more recent research by Nation and Hulme (1997) has indicated that phonemic segmentation is an excellent predictor of reading and spelling ability, whereas onset-

Figure 5.7
Analytic Phonics Lesson

Development of knowledge

1. From a recently read or dictated story, select sentences that use words containing the sounds on which you wish to focus.
2. Write the sentences on the board, underlining the target words.
3. Ask for volunteers to read the sentences, or have the children read each sentence after you.

   The shark has very sharp teeth.

   The shark flips its tail in the water.
4. Then ask them to read the underlined words with you. Ask them to listen carefully to the /sh/ sound in the underlined words.
5. Write *flips* on the board. Ask the children to read it to you. Remove the *fl* and replace it with *sh.* Say, "If you know the /sh/ sound in the underlined words and you know the /ips/ sounds in *flips,* then you can combine the /sh/ sound with the /ips/ sounds and make a new word [ships]. Can you read this new word to me?

Practice

1. Have the children repeat the underlined words with you.
2. Ask them to name other words that have the same sounds. Reinforce the sound-symbol relationship within each word correctly suggested.

Application

Write the words *shine* and *top* on the board. Say, "Can you replace the *t* in *top* with the *sh* in *shine* to make a new word? What is that word?

Reinforcement

1. Have children blend sounds from other words in their sight vocabularies.
2. Practice reading sentences containing the word *ship* from a real text.

rime segmentation is not. Clearly, phonemic segmentation and onset-rime segmentation both relate to success in reading and spelling, but phonemic segmentation is the best predictor of future reading and spelling success.

How are you to decide which research to use in planning instruction when findings from different studies vary? Is there helpful information for you in the combined work of Bradley and Bryant, Goswami and Bryant, and Nation and Hulme?

Go to our Companion Website at www.prenhall.com/harp and join the global discussion by adding your comments on these questions to the Threaded Message Board.

You will find it easy to help children identify the onset and rime in words. Once children have learned a common rime, they can substitute the initial consonant and delight in making many words they can read.

Onset and Rime Word Walls. You can reinforce these understandings by creating word walls of the rimes your children are learning. For example, when they study the *at* rime, have them make long lists of all the *at* words they know. Display these lists on the walls.

Onset and Rime Tiles. Fox (1996) offers a clever idea for learning and practicing onset and rime knowledge. She recommends cutting up sentence strips or index cards to make onset and rime tiles. Print the most common onsets and rimes on the cards and encourage the children to practice joining the tiles together to create words. Help the children to see how many words they can read once they have learned a rime.

Flip Books. Flip books are a good way to reinforce children's understandings of onsets and rime. When you have taught a rime such as *all,* cut a piece of oaktag about 2½″ by 8″. Write the rime with a felt marker on the right-hand side of the strip. Then cut strips about 2½″ by 3″ and write an onset on each one. Make as many onset strips as the children will know or need to practice. Staple the onset strips on top of the left-hand edge of the rime strip. Children can lift up each onset strip and read the word.

Onset and rime instruction is remarkably efficient. Donald Durrell (1963) discovered that 95% of the 286 rimes that appeared in primary grade reading materials were pronounced the same every time they appeared. Nearly 500 primary grade words can be made using only 37 consistent rimes.

Magnetic Sheets and Letters. Magnetic sheets and plastic magnetic letters are a wonderful way for children to manipulate sounds in words. Visit an auto supply store and purchase a large metal drip pan intended to catch oil drips under a car. Cover it with vinyl plastic, and use it as the base for manipulating magnetic letters. You may wish to acquire several metal cookie sheets for the same purpose. You can purchase magnetic letters that are single letters and sets of common rimes. The cookie sheets and magnetic letters can be used in a word study center during center time.

Chunking Words into Syllables. Once children understand the concepts of onsets and rimes within a syllable, you can move into instruction intended to help them hear syllables in words. Refer again to Figure 5.1 for an illustration of the generalizations describing how words may be divided into syllables. However, you may find it effective to help children hear the syllables in words as they pronounce them and to chunk the words into syllable parts rather than apply the generalizations. For example, if children were trying to identify the syllables in *bracelet,* they could see that the word is chunked into syllables between the first *e* and the *l* by applying the generalization that a single consonant between two vowels usually goes with the second vowel to form a syllable. They could also say the word several times, perhaps clapping hands for each part, and chunking the words that way.

Sorting Picture Cards and Sound Cards. Other effective ways to help children apply their phonics knowledge is to have them sort picture cards by the beginning or ending sounds in the words describing the pictures or to have them sort word cards by similar sound/letter patterns in the words. You might have them use a pocket chart for these activities.

Writing for Sounds. This activity involves modeling how to write sounds in words and then coaching children in the process. For example, you might have read a story with the word *fast* in it. You might say, "Let's write the word *fast.* What sound do you hear at the beginning?" The children say /f/. You ask, "How do we write the /f/ sound?" The children tell you *f.* You use a white dry erase board and demonstrate how to form the *f.* This process continues for all of the sound/letter correspondences in the word. Older children might have their own dry erase board and felt markers and do the writing themselves. The notion of carefully analyzing the sounds in words is at the heart of another strategy known as "making discoveries about words."

Making Discoveries About Words. Making discoveries about words is a five-day cycle of activities to be used during the word identification portion of literacy instruction (Gaskins, Ehri, Cress, O'Hara, & Donnelly, 1997). During this time young readers are introduced to three or four new key words and provided with reading and writing practice in addition to their daily literature-based reading and process writing. Activities may vary from day to day, but each day involves a lesson on analyzing words and discovering how our language works. The lesson has four parts: discussion, word analysis, guided practice, and spelling.

Discussion. The discussion phase clarifies goals, rationale, and strategies for analyzing and decoding words; increases students' awareness of how they can take control of making discoveries about the structure of their language and about learning words; and allows students to share discoveries from their work as "word detectives." The strategies that receive the most attention during discussion are learning words in a fully analyzed way, discovering consistencies, noticing spelling patterns in words, and using known words to decode unknown words. Students discuss what strategies they are learning, why they are important, when they can use them, and how to use the strategies.

Word Analysis. Students are provided guided practice in fully analyzing words. Words are chosen that have high-frequency phonograms, and students always follow three steps: stretch out sounds in words, analyze and talk to themselves about each sound-letter correspondence, and summarize the clues they have discovered about sound and letters in words. Often they share their discoveries with a partner.

Guided Practice. The teacher discusses the reasons for the activity and solicits from the children the rationale for fully analyzing words. Guided practice provides repeated encounters with words so that the number of fully analyzed words is constantly increasing for each child.

Spelling. To develop the ability to segment words into sounds and to match sounds and letters, children each day write key words from memory.

You may wish to locate the article by Gaskin and colleagues (1997) in your library and read much more detail about the making discoveries about words strategies.

LOOKING AT THE RESEARCH

What the research says about helping children make explicit connections between sound segments and letters

Longitudinal and experimental studies completed in England by Bradley and Bryant (1983, 1985) established a causal relationship between phonological awareness and reading/spelling acquisition and demonstrated the value of creating links between sound units and their corresponding printed symbol. The children experienced 40 lessons over two years in which they learned to group or categorize pictures on the basis of shared sounds. A feature of the instruction was playing "the odd one out." Here pictures of objects that rhymed or shared an initial, middle, or final sound were placed on the table, along with one picture that did not belong. Children were asked to identify the "odd one out."

Bradley and Bryant's results indicated that, although the children trained in sound categorization outperformed the children who did not receive this training, the

(Continued)

LOOKING AT THE RESEARCH Continued

most successful children were those who were trained in sound categorization and who also learned to represent the common sounds with plastic letters. The children who experienced this multisensory training had significantly higher reading and spelling scores than the control group children–and this superiority was in a follow-up study conducted four years after the original research. This study supports many of the multisensory activities suggested in this chapter.

What understandings about child development and learning do you have that might help explain the power of multisensory learning activities?

Go to our Companion Website at www.prenhall.com/harp and join the global discussion by adding your comments on this question to the Threaded Message Board.

Small Group, Focused Instruction. Instruction in phonics is most effective when it is conducted with small groups of children and focused on developing phonics knowledge you know they need. This means you will need to assess and evaluate their knowledge and provide carefully planned, deliberately sequenced instruction.

Purcell-Gates (1996) has described an instructional model that works well for teaching decoding skills (and most anything else) known as the whole-part-whole model. She uses the metaphor of teaching a child to ride a bike. The teacher directly instructs learners about processes he must engage in to "ride" as the bicycle is propelled forward: "put your feet on the pedals," "hold onto the handlebars," "move your hands so that your knuckles are on top of the bars," and so on. The teacher's support moves from a two-handed grip to a one-handed grip. Eventually the teacher releases the bicycle but so subtly that the rider is unaware of the change. The teacher may reduce the support to a mere presence running along beside the rider. As soon as the rider has the basic parts of the process under control, the teacher backs off, allowing experience over time with bike riding to complete the learning.

So it is with teaching reading and writing. A decoding lesson should begin in the environment where the skill will be applied—with reading or writing real, connected text. In other words, it begins with the whole. The teacher helps the child take the process apart and scaffolds learning of small pieces such as decoding a CVC pattern or adding descriptive words to a sentence. Learning proceeds part by part. The learner then returns to the connected text—the whole—to refine decoding knowledge as he gains experience with reading. Purcell-Gates describes this process:

> Reading and writing are both processes, and learning to read and write must be undertaken as one would any process: get on and try to do it. Teachers are most helpful to learners if they can provide the support called for at any given moment, perceive and respond to ways in which the learner is performing pieces of the process (while trying to accomplish the whole process), and provide feedback to the learner in ways intended to allow him/her to get on with it and gain mastery over the process, in this case reading and writing. (p. 108)

ssessment and Evaluation Toolbox

AN OBSERVATION SURVEY OF EARLY LITERACY ACHIEVEMENT

Marie Clay (2002) has developed a set of systematic observation measures you can use to guide your observations of students' work on tasks related to reading and writing. The survey consists of several tests. The ones most directly related to assessing and evaluating phonic knowledge are letter identification, word tests (recognition of high-frequency words), and hearing and recording sounds in words (you dictate a sentence and score performance on the number of correct letter/sound correspondences written).

We want to offer you one final thought on the teaching of phonics. We believe a great deal of phonics instruction occurs as a part of the writing curriculum. As children are struggling to encode the sounds they hear in words into printed letters, they are applying the same phonics knowledge they use when they decode words. Clay (1998) says writing slows readers down, enabling them to analyze more carefully language that is read or spoken. Most teachers do a great deal of phonics teaching when they are helping children with writing. When a child asks you how to spell a word, your first response should prompt the child to explore his or her knowledge of the sound/symbol relationships within the word. Your first prompt might be, "What sound do you hear at the beginning of that word? How do we spell that sound? What sound do you hear in the middle of the word? How do we write that sound? What sound to you hear at the end of the word? How do we write that sound?" Be sure to carefully reinforce the sound/symbol relationships you have been working on in reading when you are helping children with writing.

Children Learn to Use Syntactic Cues

Recall that the structure of the sentence in which the word occurs can sometimes cue us as to the identification of an unfamiliar word. The sentence about the rambunctious puppies was used to demonstrate this skill. Although children intuitively know syntax in their native language, they need to bring this knowledge to a conscious level to use it in decoding tasks. Carefully planned instruction in the use of syntactic cues is necessary before most children will be able to use this cueing system.

We help children develop their use of the syntactic cueing system in the following ways.

Word Deletion Activities. Put a sentence on the board with only the first letter of a selected word showing. Have the children brainstorm words that begin with that letter and would make sense in that slot. Talk with them about why they made their predictions.

Rearranging Sentence Strips. Make a sentence strip of a sentence from a story the children have read or a language experience story they have written or dictated. Cut the strip up and ask the children to put the words back in order. When they have completed that task, rearrange a pair of the words and ask the children if it could be arranged that way. Talk about word order and how the order we choose must sound right to our ears—and make sense to us. Again, talk with them about their thinking as they engaged in the tasks.

Using Think-Alouds. When you are reading to the children and you miscue, do a "think-aloud" in which you demonstrate your use of the syntactic cueing system to them. For example, suppose the text is "The boy skipped to the pretzel vendor's stand." Your think-aloud might sound like this: "I just read, 'The boy shipped to the pretzel vendor's stand.' That doesn't sound right to me. We wouldn't say *shipped* there. So I take a closer look at the word I made an error on, and I know that word has to be *skipped.*"

A Modified Cloze. Create a cloze activity in which you write a paragraph on the board or on chart paper leaving out selected words that are cued by the syntax. Have children predict the words they think might work in the empty slot. Talk about the syntactic cues they used to make these predictions.

Small Group Reading. When you are reading a text with a small group of children, teach and reinforce syntactic cue use when children have had difficulty with challenging words or phrases in the text.

Children Learn the Use of Semantic Cues

Words within a sentence often cue other words semantically. In the following examples, semantic cues occur in the same sentence as the unknown word:

His sock was worn through; the /// was growing larger with each step he took.

He put the milk in the /// to keep it cool.

It was an easy book, and reading it was not at all ///.

These sentences have such clear semantic cues that you probably correctly predicted the missing words to be *hole, refrigerator,* and *difficult.* Semantic cues are not always that clear, but they are still helpful in identifying an unknown word. Consider this example:

His favorite dessert was ///.

The semantic cues are not nearly as strong in this sentence, but you would know that the unknown word is the name of a dessert, which eliminates many possibilities. In the next example, semantic cues occur in a sentence that follows the unknown word:

The student, who was the team's best center, was supercilious. Some of the fans called him a supercilious jerk. In fact, he was the most haughty member of the team.

If you did not know the meaning of *supercilious,* how would the surrounding sentences help you identify the word? The idea that the player is supercilious is in essence repeated two sentences later with the word *haughty.* This would cue you that *supercilious* must have a meaning like *haughty.*

You can help children develop their use of the semantic cueing system in a variety of ways as the following examples illustrate.

Word Advocacy. Be a word advocate. Be excited about words. When you are reading to children or they are reading aloud, stop from time to time and celebrate a word. Point out an unusual use of a word or explain its meaning.

Lists of Words. Make a list of words the class has found interesting. Post it in the room and encourage children to use the words in their speech and writing.

Use Think-Alouds. Model the use of the semantic cueing system when you are reading to children using think-aloud techniques.

Small Group Reading. When you are reading a text with a small group of children, focus on word meanings. Explain how you used the semantic cueing system to unlock a difficult word and invite children to do the same.

Classrooms that foster decoding skill development are exemplars of high quality, carefully planned instruction. Good skill instruction is not delivered by way of worksheets or workbooks, but rather by informed teachers who are directing instruction to the learning needs of students. Children need carefully planned instruction, not seatwork consisting of worksheets.

The Components of Skills Lessons

An important consideration in helping children develop decoding skills is the nature of a skill(s) lesson. The lesson plan format presented here is one that has developed over time and worked well for many teachers. Revisit Figures 5.6 and 5.7 to see examples of the lesson plan format. The components of a skill lesson are presented here using graphophonic skills as examples.

The skill lesson format is appropriate for teaching any skill—a reading skill, a writing skill, a math skill—and it is also appropriate for teaching reading strategies. A skill or strategy lesson has four components: development of knowledge, practice, application, and reinforcement.

Development of Knowledge. To begin, the skill is demonstrated, explained, memorized, or discovered. You must decide whether to use an inductive teaching strategy or a deductive teaching strategy to develop knowledge. Deductive learning is rote learning. Inductive learning is discovery learning.

Using a deductive strategy, you make a statement such as, "The sound of *m* is the sound you hear at the beginning of *mommy, monkey,* and *make.*" You then present several examples of words that begin with /m/. Students are guided to state the sound/symbol relationship themselves. The deductive strategy is best employed in phonics instruction when you are teaching letter/sound relationships rather than generalizations such as "in a word or syllable with a consonant-vowel-consonant construction, the vowel sound is usually short."

Using the inductive strategy, you present several examples of words illustrating the skill (a pattern or generalization) and guide students' examination of the samples until they discover the pattern. To teach the generalization that a syllable formed by a consonant, vowel, and consonant (CVC) usually has a short vowel sound, you present examples of words (preferably from a story they have recently read), such as *cat, hid,* and *had.* The children are asked to read the words and then to describe how the words are alike.

After carefully guiding the children's observation, you encourage them to state the pattern in their own words. Clearly, inductive learning takes longer than deductive learning. The good news is that it is also longer lasting and more readily transferable. The time spent in inductive skill instruction is therefore worthwhile.

Practice. The children practice with words that are already in their sight vocabulary, looking for examples of the skill demonstrated in the development of knowledge stage. For example, they might search through stories they had recently dictated or written and peruse magazines or newspapers in search of instances of the pattern. They might suggest alternative ways to state the generalization they had just discovered.

Children may also practice with words that are not in their sight vocabularies, but you must take care to see they are not frustrated in their efforts. Practice activities could be planned on a continuum from very easy, using known words, to more challenging, using unfamiliar words. Often it is helpful for you to guide the children's practice, especially in initial or challenging activities.

Practice is important because it helps lock the use of a skill into long-term memory. Easy skills require relatively little practice. Complicated skills call for massed practice initially, followed by spaced practice. Massed practice means that the skill is practiced daily or even more than once a day for a period of time. Spaced practice means that beyond the initial practice, additional practice is planned on a regular basis, but not every day. For example, you might practice recognizing base words in multisyllabic words several times in a week and then once a week for several more weeks. Some practice activities can be presented in game format that groups of children can use. If you use learning centers in your classroom, your students are likely to enjoy a phonics games center where they can practice the skills they are learning.

Application. In the application phase of a lesson you assess the mastery of a skill by asking children to apply it to words not in their sight vocabulary. The only purpose for teaching decoding skills is to enable children to decode words not already in their sight vocabulary. Therefore, the ultimate application of any decoding skill is the decoding of an unfamiliar word. You must now make instructional decisions regarding how controlled or "strict" the application is to be.

Application activities can be distributed over a continuum from controlled to uncontrolled, or assumed. The most controlled application of a decoding skill would be decoding nonsense words: the least controlled would be to assume that sooner or later the child will come across an unfamiliar word in a text and be able to apply the skill knowledge. We are not comfortable working at either of these extremes. We dislike using nonsense words because we believe that everything we do in the name of skill instruction should look as much like the reading act as possible. We are not comfortable with assuming application that we cannot observe. Therefore, we work to observe children applying new skills in the context of guided reading activities (see Chapter 8).

Reinforcement. All teachers have had the painful experience of teaching a skill lesson they are certain would earn them the "Teacher of the Year Award," only to have the children return to school the next day and appear never to have heard of the skill! Skills instruction requires a great deal of patience from both the teacher and learners. Sometimes additional practice is all it takes for retention; at other times it is necessary to reteach a skill. The best way to ensure that children retain skill knowledge is to provide instruction

Reading is the best way to apply any reading skill.

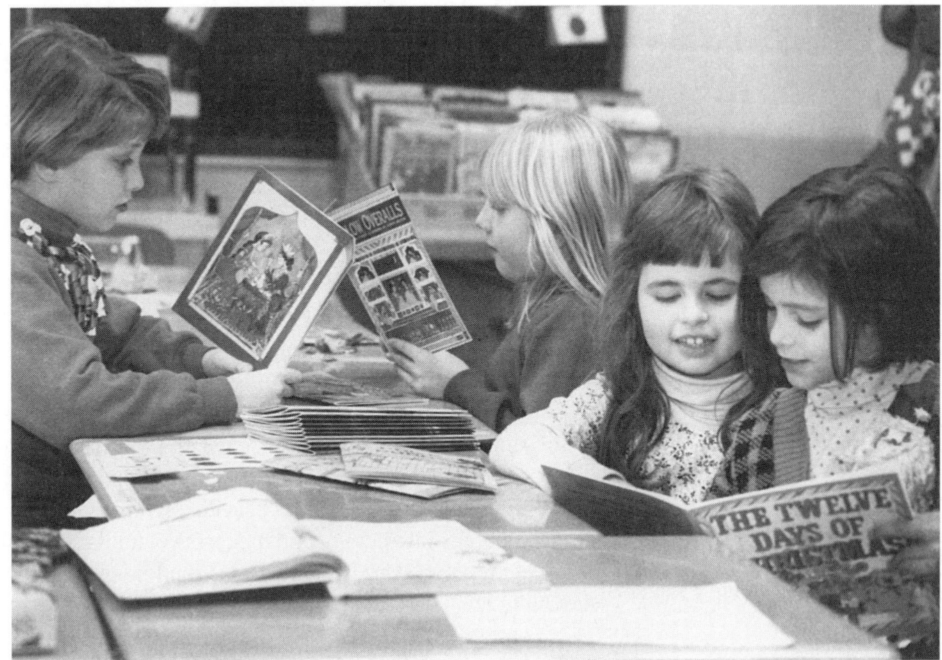

at the point at which the child needs the knowledge. Reviewing a skills lesson the next day and walking through practice activities with children is helpful. This review should usually be followed by opportunities to read. The more reading skillful readers do, the better they develop understandings of how spelling patterns correspond to possible word pronunciations and a sensitivity to the frequency of printed word forms (Snow, Burns, & Griffin, 1998).

Reading is clearly the best reinforcement for skill use. It is also important as you listen to a child read or as you conduct guided reading lessons that you highlight places in the text where the skills you have been teaching apply. Suppose you had taught a skill lesson on Tuesday that focused on the *ch* digraph. On Thursday two children who were in that skill group are in your guided reading group. When they successfully decode the *ch* digraph, you would remind them of the work they did on Tuesday on that skill and praise them for successfully applying that knowledge today. You will want to create an environment that celebrates literacy and each accomplishment that moves a child along the continuum toward skillful, independent reading.

HOW DO I CREATE AN ENVIRONMENT IN WHICH MY STUDENTS LEARN DECODING SKILLS?

The best way to answer this question is to turn to the research on effective practices. Some of these findings are very clear.

Consider how you might go about implementing some of the best practices described previously in your classroom, or how you might support a schoolwide effort to improve literacy instruction.

LOOKING AT THE RESEARCH

What the research says about best practices

Barbara M. Taylor (1999) examined the factors that best support primary grade reading achievement. She studied 14 schools across the United States with moderate to high numbers of students on subsidized lunch (children living in poverty). The schools were ranked as most, moderately, or least effective based on primary grade reading performance. A combination of school and teacher factors was found to be important in the most effective schools. These factors were: strong links to parents, systematic assessment of pupil progress, strong building communication, and a collaborative model for the delivery of reading instruction, including early interventions. Significant teacher factors included: time spent in small group instruction, time spent in independent reading, high pupil engagement, and strong home communication. The most effective teachers provided frequent coaching as children were reading, explicit phonics instruction, and higher-level thinking questions after reading. In all of the most effective schools, reading instruction was a priority at both the building and classroom level.

Do a self-assessment of your current understandings of these school and teacher factors. Which ones do you have solid understandings about, and which ones will you want to learn more about as you complete this course? Perhaps you should identify some specific goals for this learning.

Go to our Companion Website at www.prenhall.com/harp, join the discussion on the Threaded Message Board, and discover what other students are saying about these factors and their learning goals.

Systematic Assessment of Pupil Progress

Children move through developmental stages as they learn to use the cueing systems. Use a three-ring binder to create a record-keeping system, a monitoring book as described in Chapter 3, to track this progress. Place an index divider in the binder for each of your students. Behind the divider place a copy of a reading development checklist, a skills checklist, sheets for your anecdotal notes, and record sheets from other assessment and evaluation tools. Keep careful track of the progress of each of your learners.

A Collaborative Model for the Delivery of Reading Instruction

Find ways to open communication between yourself and other teachers at your same grade level. Offer to share effective teaching practices with your colleagues. When you have a child who is struggling as a reader, consult your colleagues, including the reading specialist, the Title I teacher, the special education teacher, the school psychologist, and the principal. Reading instruction is most effective when all of these players are contributing to the process and practicing open and frequent communication.

Build Strong Links to Parents

Invite parents to your school for a presentation on your reading program. Help them understand the goals, the nature of daily activities, and the importance of their support at home. Encourage them to spend time daily reading to their child, listening to their child read to them, and showing enthusiasm for the reading and writing their child does. You might even videotape some of your typical instructional activities to show them. Ask the bilingual teacher to serve as an interpreter at your meeting if you cannot provide this service yourself. Send home monthly newsletters highlighting literacy activities in your classroom. If you have a classroom telephone or web site, place information there about homework, and highlight literacy activities children could do at home. Make sure the activities you suggest are reasonable for parents to accomplish and are truly useful to the child as a reader. You cannot ask parents to engage in activities that are beyond the family budget or that involve too much time for limited outcomes. Parents often have to do assignments such as dioramas (a three-dimensional display) or other projects that are not especially productive. One family we know had to collect a spider's web when the teacher was reading *Charlotte's Web* (White, 1952). One has to wonder how such an activity promoted the development of literacy. Also, remember that reading books is not the only activity that can contribute to literacy skills. Some families engage in literacy building activities such as clipping and sorting coupons from the newspaper, translating for other family members, and telling family stories. Be sure that you appreciate what all families can do and that you do not expect that every family must be the same in order to help their children.

Foster High Pupil Engagement

Create a classroom climate where learning skills is celebrated, where children have a personal appreciation for what they are learning, and where accomplishments are celebrated. A supportive classroom climate also encourages children to help each other. Train your learners to turn to classmates for help before they come to you. Some teachers have a rule that a student must have asked at least two classmates for help before asking the teacher.

Be Well Prepared for Small Group Instruction

Create a place in your classroom where you have easy access to the tools of skill instruction. These might include magnetic plastic letters, small magnetic white boards, markers, sand paper alphabet letters, supplies of writing paper and pencils, white correction tape, cards for masking letters, sticky notes for covering up letters in words, tape that can be used to highlight words in text, and cards with movable letters for working with onsets and rimes.

In the area where you conduct small group instruction, place a large white board or chalk board, large chart paper, and a pocket chart. Have a supply of sentence strips and markers here as well. Keep everything organized so that whenever you need materials, they are within reach and you waste no instructional time looking for supplies.

Use every interaction you have with students to identify their strengths and next learning steps. Consult your district curriculum guide frequently so that you are clear on what you must teach at your grade level. Use the data in the monitoring notebook frequently. Set instructional goals daily for each of your learners. This is a much more manageable goal than it might appear at first. Whenever you provide instruction to a group of children, you will note what you need to do next for that group. As you go through each day, you will have opportunities to observe children as they engage in literacy and make notes that will help you set learning goals. For example, if you observe how the children select a book for independent reading, you can learn a great deal about their needs. Some young readers may lack the book handling skills to know the front of the book or how to turn the pages. Older students might flip through a book but fail to consider the difficulty of the text. Each of these learners needs instruction, and you can set learning goals while you are performing your supervision duty at the same time.

Provide Explicit Phonics Instruction

Children learn decoding skills best when they are taught directly in the context of meaningful text. The more reading children do, the better they learn skills such as phonics and spelling. Sight vocabularies increase with reading experience. Stock your classroom with a rich supply of books that are at children's instructional reading levels for guided reading and skill instruction, and at children's independent reading levels for practice in reading. Focus your skill instruction at times when children are engaged with meaningful text, and create browsing boxes of books that children may access for independent reading. Rather than boxes, some teachers prefer to use a large plastic bag with a zip top in which each child stores 10 or so books that are at his independent reading level. As the child gains skill as a reader, the books are systematically replaced with other, more challenging books. Create a classroom culture that says this room is a reading and writing place where we all are real readers and real writers.

Children need to learn to decode sounds in words. They also need to learn to use what they know about the morphology and syntax of their language to make meaning from print and to become good spellers. Materials and activities selected for instructional use must therefore sound like real language and have content that makes it possible for the reader to create meaning. Some materials have such highly controlled vocabularies that the sentences do not sound like real language and that do not make sense when they are read. If you asked a child where a fan could be sitting, most would be able to say on a desk, a dresser, or the floor, in a window, or in other reasonable places. But when the sentence they are asked to read says, "The fan sat on the van," they have no way to use what they know about language or the world around them to help them read. When you are doing shared writing and when you are reading with small groups of students, seize opportunities to ask, "Think of words that would make sense in this spot in the sentence. What are other words you know that would mean about the same thing? Look at the beginning letter of this word and think if you know a word that begins with that sound that would make sense in this sentence."

Provide Time for Independent Reading

Skill attainment is greatly supported by independent reading in and out of school. Work with your principal and school reading specialists to plan a way to support at-home reading and to give support and encouragement to parents in this endeavor. We know that the more children read in school, the more they read outside of school. Work to build a climate that so enthusiastically supports reading in school that it spills over to reading at home.

THINKING AS A TEACHER

1. A parent comes to you to explain that last year in first grade her child learned phonics in isolation, drilling on sounds with flash cards. This year you are teaching phonics using words from stories the children read. She is concerned that her child will be confused. What will you say?
2. Explore the teacher's edition of a literature anthology. Identify a skill lesson and compare its format to the format recommended in this chapter. Would you plan to make any changes in the lesson plan in the anthology in light of studying this chapter? If so, what changes would you make? If not, why not?

3. You are teaching on a second-grade team with three other teachers. One member of your group has been trained in a synthetic phonics decoding program and favors this approach. Others believe that children should be taught analytic phonics in the context of reading meaningful text. Strong opinions are held on both sides of this issue. What will you use to guide you in formulating your own beliefs, and how will you respond to your colleagues if they ask where you stand on this issue?

FIELD-BASED ACTIVITIES

1. Consider phonics instruction you have observed and compare that to the recommendations in the International Reading Association's Position Statement on the Role of Phonics in Reading Instruction.
2. Plan and teach two skill lessons to small groups of children. Plan to use an inductive teaching strategy in one and a deductive teaching strategy in the other. Reflect on these lessons and your understandings of the two instructional strategies.
3. Give the Yopp-Singer Phonemic Awareness Test to a group of kindergarten and first-grade children. Determine which of these children would benefit from phonemic awareness instruction. Plan and teach a lesson to help develop phonemic awareness.
4. Interview five first-grade teachers to learn their views on the phonics in isolation versus the phonics in context debate. Reflect on their responses and write a statement of your own position.
5. Plan and teach an onset and rime lesson. Include tiles or plastic letters in your plan. Reflect on your lesson in terms of what went well, what you would change if you could reteach the lesson, and what you learned about children, yourself, and teaching.

REFERENCES

Adams, M. J. (1990). *Beginning to read: Thinking and learning about print.* Cambridge, MA: MIT Press.

Allington, R. L. (1977). If they don't read much, how they ever gonna get good?, *Journal of Reading, 21,* 57–61.

Allington, R. L. (1980). Poor readers don't get to read much in reading groups. *Language Arts, 57,* 872–877.

Allington, R. L. (1983). The reading instruction provided readers of differing abilities. *Elementary School Journal, 83,* 548–559.

Allington, R. L. (1984). Content coverage and contextual reading in reading groups. *Journal of Reading Behavior, 16,* 85–96.

Allington, R. L. (2001). *What really matters for struggling readers. Designing research-based programs.* New York: Longman.

Allington, R. L. (2002). *Big brother and the national reading curriculum: How ideology trumped evidence.* Portsmouth, NH: Heinemann.

Allington, R. L., & McGill-Franzen, A. (1989). School response to reading failure: Chapter 1 and special education students in grades 2, 4, and 8. *Elementary School Journal, 89,* 529–542.

Anderson, R. C., Wilson, P., & Fielding, L. (1988). Growth in reading and how children spend their time outside of school. *Reading Research Quarterly, 23,* 285–303.

Bailey, M. H. (1967). The utility of phonics generalization in grades one through six. *The Reading Teacher, 20,* 413–418.

Barr, R., & Dreeben, R. (1983). *How schools work.* Chicago: University of Chicago Press.

Bear, D. R., Invernizzi, M., Templeton, S., & Johnston, F. (1996). *Words their way: Word study for phonics, vocabulary, and spelling instruction.* Upper Saddle River, NJ: Merrill.

Bond, G. L., & Dykstra, R. (1966–1967). The cooperative research program in first-grade reading instruction. *Reading Research Quarterly, 2,* 5–142.

Bradley, L., & Bryant, P. E. (1983). Categorizing sounds and learning to read: A causal connection. *Nature, 310,* 419–421.

Bradley, L., & Bryant, P. E. (1985). *Rhyme and reason in reading and spelling.* Ann Arbor: University of Michigan Press.

Clark, E. V. (1993). *The lexicon in acquisition.* Cambridge, England: Cambridge University Press.

Clay, M. M. (1998). *Different paths to common outcomes.* York, ME: Stenhouse.

Clay, M. M. (2002). *An observation survey of early literacy achievement.* Portsmouth, NH: Heinemann.

Clymer, T. (1963). The utility of phonic generalization in the primary grades. *The Reading Teacher, 16,* 252–258.

Coles, G. (2000). *Misreading reading: The bad science that hurts children.* Portsmouth, NH: Heinemann.

Cunningham, P. M. (2000). *Phonics they use: Words for reading and writing.* New York: Addison Wesley.

Durrell, D. D. (1963). *Phonograms in primary grade words.* Boston: Boston University Press.

Ehri, L. C. (1995). Phases of development in learning to read words by sight. *Journal of Research in Reading, 18,* 116–125.

Ekwall, E. E., & Shanker, J. L. (1993). *Ekwall/Shanker reading inventory* (3rd ed.). Boston: Allyn and Bacon.

Elkonin, D. B. (1973). Reading in the USSR. In J. Downing (Ed.), *Comparative reading* (pp. 551–579). New York: Macmillan.

Ellis, N. (1997). Interactions in the development of reading and spelling: Stages, strategies, and exchange of knowledge. In C. Pefetti, L. Rieben, & M. Fayol (Eds.), *Learning to spell: Research, theory and practice across languages.* Hillsdale, NJ: Lawrence Erlbaum.

Emans, R. (1967). The usefulness of phonic generalizations above the primary grades. *The Reading Teacher, 20,* 419–425.

Foorman, B. R., Francis, D. J., Fletcher, J. M., & Schatschneider, C. (1998). The role of instruction in learning to read: Preventing reading failure in at-risk children. *Journal of Educational Psychology, 90,* 35–55.

Fox, B. J. (1996). *Strategies for word identification: Phonics from a new perspective.* Columbus, OH: Merrill.

Frith, U. (1985). Beneath the surface of developmental dyslexia. In K. Patterson, J. Marshall, & M. Coltheart (Eds.), *Surface dyslexia: Neuropsychological and cognitive studies of phonological reading.* London: Lawrence Erlbaum.

Gaskins, I. W., Ehri, L. C., Cress, C., O'Hara, C., & Donnelly, K. (1997). Analyzing words and making discoveries about the alphabetic system: Activities for beginning readers. *Language Arts, 74,* 172–184.

Goswami, U. C., & Bryant, P. E. (1990). *Phonological skills and learning to read.* Hillsdale, NJ: Lawrence Erlbaum.

Harp, B. (2000). *The handbook of literacy assessment and evaluation* (2nd ed.). Norwood, MA: Christopher-Gordon Publishers.

Harris, T. L., & Hodges, R. E. (1995). *The literacy dictionary: The vocabulary of reading and writing.* Newark, DE: International Reading Association.

Hoffman, J., Cunningham, P. M., Cunningham, J. W., & Yopp, H. (1998). *Phonemic awareness and the teaching of reading.* Newark, DE: International Reading Association.

International Reading Association. (1997). The role of phonics in reading instruction. A position statement of the International Reading Association. Newark, DE: Author.

Juel, C. (1988). Learning to read and write: A longitudinal study of fifty-four children from first through fourth grades. *Journal of Educational Psychology, 78,* 243–255.

Juel, C. (1990). Effects of reading group assignment on reading development in first and second grade. *Journal of Reading Behavior, 22,* 233–254.

Juel, C. (1991). Beginning reading. In R. Barr, M. L. Kamil, D. B. Mosenthal, & P. D. Pearson (Eds.), *Handbook of Reading Research,* Vol. 2 Mahwah, NJ: Lawrence Erlbaum.

Juel, C., & Minden-Cupp, C. (1999). CIERA Report #1-008, Learning to read words: Linguistic units and strategies. Retrieved from *www.ciera.org/library/reports/inquiry-1/1-008/Report%201-008.html.*

Krashen, S. D. (1999). *Three arguments against whole language and why they are wrong.* Portsmouth, NH: Heinemann.

LaBerge, D., & Samuels, S. (1974). Toward a theory of automatic information processing in reading. *Cognitive Psychology, 6,* 293–323.

Lapp, D., & Flood, J. (1997). Where's the phonics? Making the case (again) for integrated code instruction. *The Reading Teacher, 50,* 696–701.

Lundberg, I., Frost, J., & Petersen, O. P. (1988). Effects of an extensive program for stimulating phonological awareness in preschool children. *Reading Research Quarterly, 23,* 264–268.

McQuillan, J. (1998). *The literacy crisis: False claims, real solutions.* Portsmouth, NH: Heinemann.

Nation, K., & Hulme, C. (1997). Phonemic segmentation, not onset-rime segmentation, predicts early reading and spelling skills. *Reading Research Quarterly, 32,* 154–167.

Novick, R. (1999/2000). Supporting early literacy development: Doing things with words in the real world. *Childhood Education, 76,* 70–75.

Nunes, T., Bryant, P., & Bindman, M. (1997). Spelling and grammar. In C. Pefetti, L. Rieben, & M. Fayol (Eds.), *Learning to spell: Research, theory and practice across languages.* Hillsdale, NJ: Lawrence Erlbaum.

Purcell-Gates, V. (1996). Process teaching with direct instruction and feedback in a university-based clinic. In E. McIntyre & M. Pressley (Eds.), *Balanced instruction: Strategies and skill in whole language.* Norwood, MA: Christopher-Gordon Publishers.

Rasinski, T., & Padak, N. (2000). *Effective reading strategies: Teaching children who find reading difficult.* Columbus, OH: Merrill.

Routman, R. (2000). *Conversations.* Portsmouth, NH: Heinemann.

Scarborough, H. S. (1989). Prediction of reading disability from familial and individual differences. *Journal of Educational Psychology, 81,* 101–108.

Smith, F. (1999). Why systematic phonics and phonemic awareness instruction constitute an educational hazard. *Language Arts, 77,* 150–155.

Snow, C. E., Burns, M. S., & Griffin, P. (1998). *Preventing reading difficulties in young children.* Washington, DC: National Academy Press.

Stahl, S. A. (1992). Saying the "p" word: Nine guidelines for exemplary phonics instruction. *The Reading Teacher, 45,* 618–625.

Stahl, S. A., Duffy-Hester, A. M., & Stahl, K. A. D. (1998). Everything you wanted to know about phonics (but were afraid to ask). *Reading Research Quarterly, 33,* 338–355.

Stahl, S. A., & Murray, B. A. (1998). Issues involved in defining phonological awareness and its relation to early reading. In J. Metsala & L. C. Ehri (Eds.), *Word recognition in beginning literacy* (pp. 65–87). Mahwah, NH: Erlbaum.

Stanovich, K. E. (1980). Toward an interactive-coompensatory model of individual differences in the development of reading fluency. *Reading Research Quarterly, 16,* 32–71.

Stanovich, K. E. (1986). Mathew effects in reading: Some consequences of individual differences in the acquisition of literacy. *Reading Research Quarterly, 21,* 360–407.

Taylor, B. M. (1999). CIERA Inquiry 2: Home and School. What schoolwide practices characterize schools in which at-risk learners are beating the odds? What instructional practices are used by the most accomplished primary-grade teachers and by teachers in the most effective schools? Ann Arbor: University of Michigan Center for the Improvement of Early Reading Achievement.

Torgesen, J. K., & Bryant, B. R. (1994). *Test of phonological awareness, Examiner's manual.* Austin, TX: Pro-Ed.

Weaver, C. (1994). *Reading process and practice: From sociopsycholinguistics to whole language.* Portsmouth, NH: Heinemann.

Yopp, H. K. (1995). A test for assessing phonemic awareness in young children. *The Reading Teacher, 49,* 20–29.

Children's Books

White, E. B. (1952). *Charlotte's Web.* New York: HarperCollins.

Chapter 6

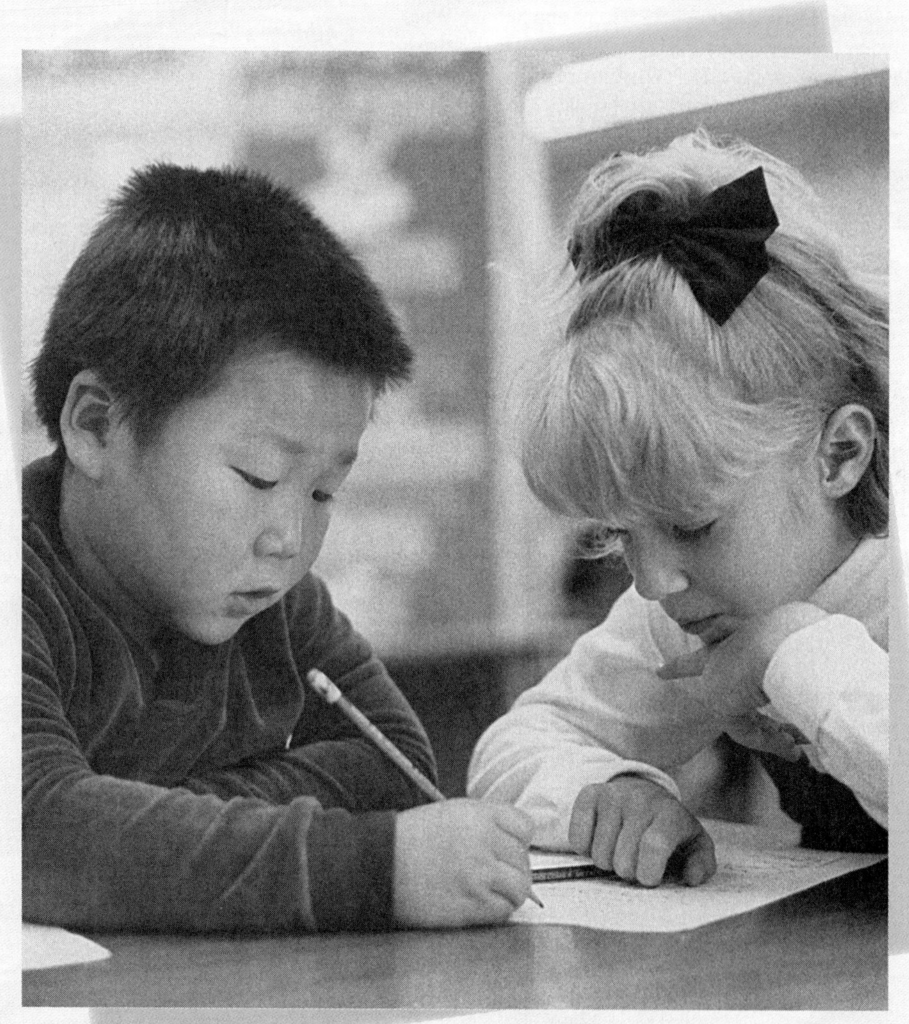

Guiding the Development of Reading Strategies

LOOKING AT THE RESEARCH

Nine-year-olds' ability to think about their own thinking as readers is quite variable. However, students rated as average or above average readers by their teachers have better knowledge of reading strategies (Hall, Bowman, & Myers, 1999). This means that teaching reading strategies is important work, and it can be done with young children.

Focus Questions

- What are reading strategies?
- How do children best learn to use reading strategies?
- How do I create a learning environment that supports the teaching and learning of reading strategies?

REAL TEACHERS, REAL PRACTICE

Meet Kate McLaughlin, ***a second-grade teacher***

Reading represents a major problem-solving situation for our students, probably the single most important one of their young lives. Just as we teach students specific strategies to solve real-world problems, we must teach students strategies so that they can directly meet the challenges of reading.

One strategy that has worked in my classroom is an obvious, but often overlooked, one. That reading strategies need to be introduced to students is a given, but I would argue that reading strategies need to be seen *by students as well. In my classroom, reading strategies are posted on the bulletin boards, written down by students in their guided reading folders, and listed on bookmarks used regularly throughout the day. The posting of reading strategies in a variety of places is important for many reasons. It sends a message to the students that reading strategies are important and useful. It gives students a common language for discussing and using reading strategies. It also serves as a guide for students to refer to on a regular basis.*

However, the mere listing of reading strategies is not sufficient. Students need numerous opportunities to learn and practice reading strategies. Guided reading affords the students in my classroom the chance to apply the strategies they have acquired. An agreement has been forged in my classroom; my students know they have the power to improve their reading. Having many opportunities to read books at their level and with just the right amount of challenge encourages students to use their strategies to make sense of the text.

We also spend a lot of time on what the word "helping" means. Students become aware that "giving the word" to other students does not help peers because telling takes away the chance to use strategies to figure out unknown words. In addition, students know they are expected to articulate their thinking, including the strategies they are using to decode and understand the text.

How do my students learn to articulate their strategy use? I consistently model the articulation of reading strategies through "think-alouds." When working with a shared reading group, I stop on a word students are thinking about, one that will foster discussion of reading strategies. Talking about how I would figure out the word shows my students what they should do as they read and how to explain their strategy use. I may ask students for advice and assistance so that they can practice articulating their reading strategies.

My thinking aloud also allows me to teach a more advanced use of reading strategies. After all, it is essential that students know and use reading strategies, but it is imperative for strong readers to use the most appropriate reading strategy for each situation that arises. For instance, in mathematics, students know that they can use an addition algorithm to solve a multiple digit multiplication problem, but we teach them that it is more efficient to use an algorithm for multiplication. We mirror that same idea when we teach students how to be good problem solvers in reading. Through regular modeling by teachers and consistent practice by students, young readers will develop a wealth of strategies from which to choose to solve every reading challenge resourcefully and accurately.

The importance of strategies in reading is a relatively new issue. We have come to deeper understandings about the importance of reading strategies in the last 10 to 15 years. The issues surrounding reading strategy instruction lead to several important questions.

WHAT ARE READING STRATEGIES?

To answer this question we need to review the nature of the reading process presented in Chapter 1. Informed teachers of reading who understand the reading process can help children become strategic readers.

The Reading Process

When a reader interacts with a piece of text, a transaction occurs between what the reader brings to the text and what the writer placed in the text. The reader's understandings of language and how it works, the reader's thoughts, and the reader's worldview transact with the writer's understandings of language and how it works, the writer's thoughts, and the writer's worldview. As we read, we consider the meaning the author is making while we are building meaning for ourselves (Goodman, Watson, & Burke, 1996).

Background Knowledge. Readers do not come to a piece of text as blank slates or empty vessels into which the ideas of the author are poured. When they interact with a text, readers bring background knowledge, knowledge of language and how it works, and questions they want to answer. The understandings, attitudes, and biases the author and reader bring to the text are influenced by personal and social histories. In other words, the meaning we make when we read is structured by the knowledge we bring to the text and the degree to which our knowledge matches that of the author.

Inquiry by the Reader. This model of the reading process suggests that reading begins with an inquiry by the reader. This inquiry is a critically important question asked by all readers: *What does what I'm reading mean to me?* A reader cannot create meaning with a text without sufficient background information to interact with the thoughts and language of the author. Readers use their purposes for reading, their knowledge about language and about the world to sample the text, to make inferences about the author's meaning, to answer their own questions, and to make predictions as they read. We approach text purposefully. We know what the author has written about, and we have reasons for wanting to engage with his or her ideas. Consider how futile the reading act can be when these conditions are not in place.

When Background Knowledge and Inquiry are Missing. Read the following paragraph. It would be very easy for you to make meaning if we cued you to activate your background knowledge before you read. However, we are not going to do that. Consider how difficult it is to make meaning when you don't know the topic in advance and cannot, therefore, activate your prior knowledge. Consider, too, how difficult it is to make predictions under these conditions.

> ***The procedure is not complicated, and you have to keep in mind that if you do it at all, you only do it once a year. Although some folks only do it once. Remove the storage device from the place it is kept. Open the device and carefully remove the pieces. If you have left the important pieces in place just check for damage. Remove and replace any damaged pieces. Once this phase of the operation is complete, carefully transport the pieces to the intended***

destination. You may find it easier to walk in circles as you do this. When you run out of pieces, you are finished. At the appropriate moment, reverse your direction and place the pieces, once again, in the storage container (modeled after Bransford & Johnson, 1973).

Did you read the paragraph with understanding? Probably not. See what happens to your understanding of the selection when we tell you it is a description of how to prepare and place lights on a tree. Now you can activate your prior knowledge about putting lights on a tree. Reread the paragraph and see how much easier it is to understand. Background knowledge is crucial to making meaning.

The Role of Prediction Making. As we read we make predictions on a variety of levels. We may predict that a text is fiction, what a story is going to be about, or that we can get answers to our questions by reading a certain text. We may predict what is going to happen next in a story. We may predict that the word we are uncertain of is a noun because of our knowledge of the structure of language. We might predict that the vowel sound in an unknown word is short because of our knowledge of phonic generalizations. We might combine our knowledge of language structure and phonics to make several predictions about what an unknown word might be that begins with a given letter and holds a given slot in a sentence.

Inferring and Sampling. According to Goodman and her coauthors (1996):

> In sampling, the proficient reader selects the least amount of print information necessary to make inferences and predictions. Inferring is coming to understandings based on informed predictions, and at the same time informed predictions are based on inferences. Inferring and predicting are not trial and error phenomena; these natural reading strategies are based on knowledge and background experiences. Sampling the text, inferring, and predicting are integral and cyclical. These reading strategies usually occur without conscious awareness. (p. 5)

Confirming and Integrating. The rest of the reading model suggests that when our sampling, predicting, and inferring work, we can confirm what we thought the text was saying to us. We ask ourselves if what we are reading sounds like language and makes sense. When we answer "yes" to these questions, we then integrate what we have read with what we know. If we cannot confirm our inferences and predictions, we must either rethink them or reread the text, perhaps paying closer attention to more of the cues and sampling more carefully. If this still doesn't work— if it doesn't result in meaning—we must either continue on hoping that we will be able to build meaning with more context or quit reading, concluding that the text is too difficult for our background knowledge.

Strategic Reading

The process we have just described is known as **strategic reading.** Reading strategies are the ways in which readers use, monitor, and manage the reading process. Strategic readers monitor their use of the reading process, know when the process breaks down, and can invoke an array of fix-up strategies when this happens. Strategy instruction once focused on teaching isolated strategies. This practice is being replaced by an emphasis on learning a repertoire of strategies and when and how to orchestrate their use to meet the reader's needs (Dowhower, 1999).

Go to the Weblinks in Chapter 6 on our Companion Website at www.prenhall.com/harp to link to a webquest on reading strategies.

Strategies Checklist. You will find an example of a checklist of reading strategies in Figure 6.1. This checklist was developed at the Horace Mann Elementary School in San Jose,

Figure 6.1
Horace Mann Strategies Checklist

Date	Observer	Name ______________________	Self-Assessed
		EXPECTS READING TO MAKE SENSE (Characterizes reading as meaningful, not simply decoding. Reads for a purpose, i.e., for enjoyment or information)	
		DRAWS ON PRIOR KNOWLEDGE (Indicates that what is already known about a topic will help in the process of gaining further information.)	
		MAKES REASONABLE PREDICTIONS (Samples, confirms, or disconfirms words and/or passages)	
		READS ON OR SKIPS (Comes back to a word when appropriate, i.e., when meaning is lost.)	
		USES PICTURES FOR CUES (Looks to them before/during reading)	
		SELF-CORRECTS (Consistently when meaning is lost; otherwise may not)	
		EXPECTS READING TO "SOUND RIGHT" (Knows the way English works; i.e., word order, parts of speech, sentence structure, grammar)	
		READS IN "CHUNKS" (Rapidly reads phrases such as "Once upon a time. . .")	
		USES KNOWLEDGE OF LETTER/SOUND RELATIONSHIPS (Uses decoding to confirm or disconfirm other strategies)	
		READS DIFFERENT WAYS FOR DIFFERENT PURPOSES (Skims, uses index or table of contents when reading for information)	
		VISUALIZES (Attempts to "paint a mental picture" of settings, characters)	

(A reading strategy is signed and dated when it is observed being used consistently.)
(A self-assessed strategy is one of which the child indicates awareness)

Source: Horace Mann Elementary School, San Jose Unified School District. Reprinted with permission.

California, and it is a good example of a useful strategies checklist. Use this checklist as a model that you and your colleagues can modify as you continue working on strategies with learners. Examine this checklist carefully to begin getting a deeper understanding of the nature of reading strategies. The deeper your understandings, the more skillfully you can plan strategy instruction, beginning in kindergarten.

HOW DO CHILDREN BEST LEARN TO USE READING STRATEGIES?

In the past teachers believed that teaching children about 150 reading skills would do the job of developing independent readers. Teachers now understand they must teach and evaluate the mastery of reading strategies as well as reading skills. This is not viewed as an either-or matter. Equal attention must be given to both reading skills and reading strategies. The goal is to teach children to use strategies with flexibility, appropriateness, and determination. To achieve this important goal, you will need to provide high quality strategy instruction.

High Quality Strategy Instruction

High quality reading instruction leads children to the point where they can quickly and flexibly select strategies to help them manage the reading process. Such instruction is characterized by:

1. descriptions of strategies that are sensible and meaningful to students
2. an understanding by students why the strategy should be learned and the potential benefit of using it
3. step-by-step explanations of how to use a strategy
4. students understanding the circumstances under which strategies should be employed
5. students learning to evaluate their use of strategies so that they can monitor and improve their own strategic reading.

With these characteristics in mind, you will have a wide variety of instructional techniques from which to choose.

Techniques for Teaching Reading Strategies

Reading strategies can be taught. Baumgart (1998) found that first graders can be taught to be strategic readers. Others have found that students who do not use reading strategies spontaneously can be taught to use them (Garner, 1992; Pearson & Fielding, 1991). Expert readers use many different strategies to process text (Pressley, Goodchild, Fleet, Zajchowski, & Evans, 1992). Strategies are used intentionally by readers to work through challenges in reading. Reading strategies may be classified as before-reading strategies, during-reading strategies, and after-reading strategies.

You will find detailed information about shared reading and guided reading in Chapter 8.

Teaching Before-Reading Strategies. You can develop children's knowledge of before-reading strategies by demonstrating them yourself when reading to children and by encouraging children to use them in shared reading and guided reading, beginning with children in kindergarten.

Consider these before-reading strategies:

Previewing the Text. Take a "picture walk" through the text looking at the title page, the pictures and illustrations, headings, and subheadings. Encourage children to think about what they can learn from this picture walk and to think about what they may discover in reading the text.

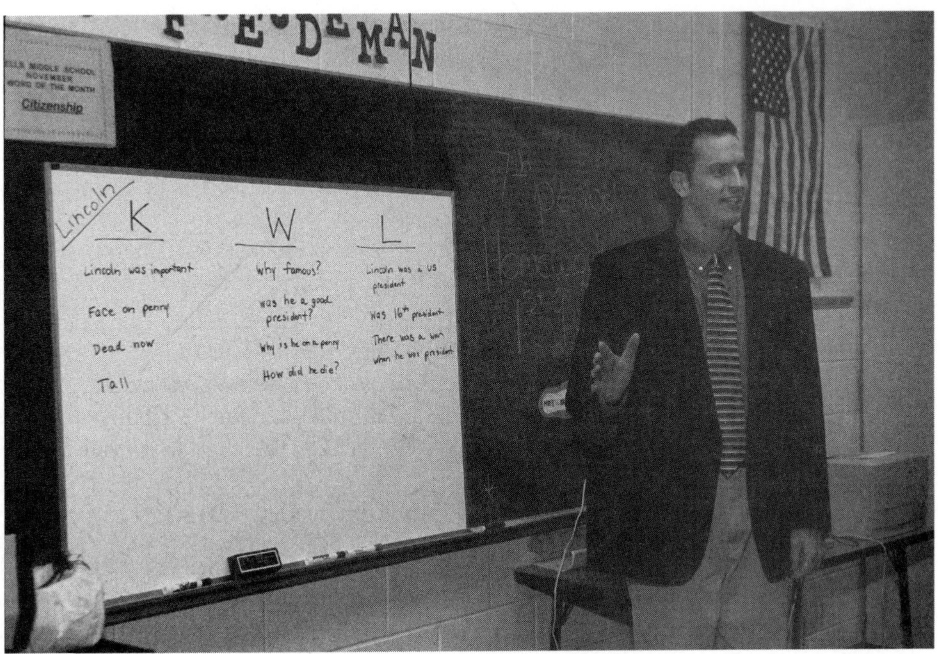

KWL is a way of organizing information before, during, and after learning experiences.

Activating Prior Knowledge. Encourage children to think about what they know about the topic of the text. What experiences have they had reading other texts like this one? What experiences have they had that will help make meaning with this text?

K-W-L Strategy. One well-established and well-researched form of engaging with text is Donna Ogle's (1986) K-W-L strategy. As you probably know, the K stands for "What do I know?" The W stands for "What do I want to know?" and the L stands for "What did I learn?" Thinking about what one knows about a topic and what one wants to learn from reading leads to increased comprehension and self-monitoring. Ogle's plan ends with readers recording what they learned from their reading. Jan Bryan (1998) has extended the K-W-L strategy in an interesting way. She has added a fourth category, "Where." Her categories, then, are "I know," "I want to learn," "Where I can learn this," and "I have learned." Dealing with "where I can learn this" would help children to think about resources for learning and lead to independence in learning.

Assessment and Evaluation Toolbox

K-W-L CHART

Ask students to make their own K-W-L chart before reading a piece of text. After reading the material, ask them to add to their L column of their chart in a different color marker or ink than they used originally. After reading yet another selected text, add to the chart once again in another color. You will be able to see at a glance what they have learned from the texts read.

Prediction Making. Prediction making is another useful before-reading strategy. Before-reading predictions probably will focus on what the story will be about or what can be learned from an expository text. When you are engaging children with a book they have not seen or heard read before, it is important to show them the title and cover and ask them to predict what they think the story will be about. Explain that our predictions help us think about our reading and that we are trying to make educated guesses about what the author wrote. Our predictions are not thought of as "correct" or "wrong," but rather as ways of thinking about what the author might have done in creating this text. Guiding and modeling prediction making with your learners will help them understand how to engage with a text when they are reading on their own.

Before-Reading Strategies in Action. Consider how before-reading strategies might be used in reading *Bats* by Gail Gibbons (1999) with first graders.

If the children had read other books by Gibbons, they could be asked what kind of books she writes (information). If they do not know her as an author, you might say "We are going to read this book by Gail Gibbons. Let's look at the front cover. The title of this book is *Bats.* We know it must be about bats, but do you think it is a story or is it an information book? Once you have gotten a response(s), then say, "Now let's look at the first couple of pages. On the first page, what is this picture? On the third and fourth pages, what do you see? (labels, scale legend). What does this tell you? Turn several more pages and point out the words in all caps (*migrate* and *hibernate*)." Discuss what these words mean. Look at several more pages to observe that each bat has a label and that each page tells something about bats. Ask the children to summarize what they think they will learn by reading this book.

Teaching children these before-reading strategies will help them to engage with texts independently. They will know how to move into a text with purpose and expectations. They will then be able to apply during-reading strategies.

Teaching During-Reading Strategies. During-reading strategies include predicting, sampling, inferring, confirming, and integrating. We discussed these strategies when we examined the reading process model at the beginning of this chapter. Each of these strategies is appropriately taught beginning in first grade. Some will be appropriate with some children in kindergarten.

Prediction Making. Prediction making during reading is quite different from prediction making before reading. Before-reading prediction involves thinking about what a story will be about or what can be learned from an expository text. These predictions will continue during reading and will be refined as a reader moves through text. In fact, you may find it unnecessary to ask comprehension questions of children after they have read a text because their predictions grew increasingly more accurate as they moved through text. You will have no doubt that they have comprehended the text.

During-reading prediction involves more than tracking the narrative plot or factual information. Readers make predictions on as small a scale as what a sound will be in a word. They also make predictions about unfamiliar words in a text. Teach children to ask themselves three important questions about their predictions. When they predict a sound in a word or the pronunciation of an unfamiliar word, they need to ask, "Does my prediction look right?" This question focuses attention on the graphophonic cues. Do the letters match the sounds I predicted? When they predict an unfamiliar word in a sentence, they need to learn to ask, "Does my prediction sound right?" This question focuses attention on the semantic and syntactic cueing systems. "Does my prediction sound like language I have heard or would say?" And finally, they need to learn to ask, "Does my prediction make sense?" Strategic readers understand they are constantly in search of meaning.

Using Phonics Skills. Sharpening their use of phonics skills is a during-reading strategy young learners must master. Emerging readers come to deeper understandings of the regularities of letter sound relationships though they may not be able to verbalize these relationships (Clay, 1991). You can facilitate this process by drawing attention to particular letters and letter clusters and by helping children decode challenging words by thinking of other, analogous words they know. As children are reading text, stop them periodically and ask if they have encountered any tricky words. Use this opportunity to reinforce the skills you have been teaching such as vowel generalizations, decoding blends or digraphs, or using onsets and rimes. This is also a time when you can reinforce other during-reading strategies such as rereading, reading ahead, or asking for help.

Using Syntactic Information. Using syntactic information during reading involves checking predictions a reader makes about unfamiliar words with his or her knowledge of grammar. The strategy of using syntactic knowledge is best taught as you think aloud during oral reading to children and in guided reading lessons with them. When you are reading to children and you make a miscue, share your thinking as you consider that the mistake you made does not sound right. Let them hear you work through untangling a word. Consider the beginning sound and think about a word that would make sense that begins with that sound; then ask yourself if the predicted word sounds right. Strategic readers combine information from all three cueing systems to monitor their use of the reading process. They need to see you model this behavior with think-alouds.

Drawing Inferences. Drawing inferences is another valuable during-reading strategy. Consider the following "story" about Evan and Rita on a shopping trip. As you read and reflect on your reading, think about the inferences you draw as you read. Think about the colorful images you make in your head as you read.

Evan and Rita walked into the town square. They looked into the display window at the drug store, but they didn't see anything they thought she would like.

"Let's look in Roger's window," said Rita. "They always have things she likes. It is one of her favorite stores."

As they examined the display in the window, Evan said, "I like the blue one. It looks fuzzy and warm. It would be good for cold mornings."

"No," replied Rita. "She doesn't like blue. Have you ever seen her wear blue? How about the gray one?"

"The gray one looks like an old lady's. You know how she is always worrying about looking older. I don't think the gray one is a good idea."

"There it is. I see the perfect one," exclaimed Rita. "She would love the yellow one. It is soft and warm and just the right length. And she will look beautiful in yellow. Shall we buy it?"

Reflect now on the inferences you drew as you read the piece about Evan and Rita shopping. What is the relationship between Evan and Rita? For whom are they shopping? What were they seeing in Roger's window? What size is the place they live? How old are Evan and Rita? These questions cannot be answered by reading what the author has written, but you have made inferences that would answer them for yourself. Not all readers would have made the same inferences. Do we know for sure that these inferences match what the author intended? No, but all of us read by creating images and applying our own experiences and background knowledge to the text we are reading.

Much of the meaning a reader makes is inferred from the text. The pictures in our heads are always richer and more colorful than the text alone could present. You will probably find that you have to teach children the concept of inference and help them understand how important inferences are in the reading process. Do this with think-alouds during reading to them and in shared reading. Reinforce it with discussions about inferences in guided reading. If you were thinking aloud about the previous vignette, you might be saying, "Oh, I think they are brother and sister, and they are shopping for a present for their mother. I think they live in a small town because it says town square, and they are shopping alone. I think Rogers is a store on the square, and it has clothing in its window. It could be sweaters or it could be bathrobes" and so on.

Identifying Important Ideas. Identifying important ideas is a during-reading strategy that will help readers stay focused on the topic and the purposes for reading a text. First graders can do this. Finding the important ideas is a complex process that requires readers to understand what is read, to make judgments about the importance of the information, and then to pare it down to the essentials (Harp, 1999). Teaching children to identify important ideas results in increased comprehension, but young children find this difficult. One way to help children understand that there are several important ideas in a text is to give each child three sticky notes to mark three important ideas in the text. Have them draw a big asterisk on each sticky to signify importance. After you model the process, have each child place the sticky notes on the text where they identify important ideas. Share these ideas in the group. Ask children to defend their choices and to explain why they made them. Discuss why they do not all agree on the specific important ideas and why that is okay (Harvey & Goudvis, 2000).

Cross-checking Sources of Information. Cross-checking sources of information is a during-reading strategy that helps readers combine sources of text-based information. Here they may use pictures to confirm a prediction, or they may reread text to try to figure out a difficult word. First graders can do this. About cross-checking Clay (1991) says,

> The child checks a character's name with the picture, re-reads the line when the number of words spoken does not tally with the number pointed to, comments when a singular noun suddenly becomes a plural, or that a phrase is repeated three times. The reader works at synchronizing the visual, directional and speech aspects of reading and this is evident in rather deliberate word-by-word reading and in self-correction strategies (p. 245)

Model these cross-checking behaviors, and reinforce them with individuals when you observe the behavior. This might occur while you are taking a running record or during a guided reading session.

Questioning. Questioning is a strategy that helps readers move through a text. Our observation is that children and adults are naturally curious. This curiosity leads to our asking many questions as we read. Searching for the answers to these questions moves us forward into the text, often deeper and deeper in search of our answers. We begin to develop this questioning strategy in our kindergarten readers by demonstrating it ourselves. Select a text to read aloud to your students. Let them actually hear you asking questions as you read and finding and celebrating the answers as you go. Let them see how this quest for answers excites you as a reader and keeps you moving through the text. Then, encourage children to share their questions as you conduct shared and guided reading activities with them.

Self-corrections. Self-correcting is a during-reading strategy that proves a reader is monitoring his or her use of the reading process and is taking corrective action when the process fails. When a reader self-corrects, it is likely that she considered a mistake and concluded that the miscue didn't look right, didn't sound right, or didn't make sense. The reader solved this problem by paying more detailed attention to some of the cues, and made the correction. Focus on self-corrections you make when reading aloud to children as early as kindergarten, discuss self-corrections with children in guided reading activities, and focus on self-corrections when you debrief running records.

Adjusting Strategy Use to Purpose. Adjusting strategy use to purpose is another important understanding. Children need to learn that when they are engaged in close reading to maximize recall, they will have to use strategies in quite different ways than when they are skimming for a date, name, or location, for example. Skimming and scanning are strategies that students will need to practice. For example, you might demonstrate to fifth graders how to skim the social studies book to find dates for a time line they are constructing. Model thinking about your purpose for reading and then demonstrate for your students the differences in your use of strategies depending upon your purpose. Encourage your learners, as early as second grade, to think about their purpose and how they will use strategies before they read.

Making Connections. Another important during-reading strategy is connecting what we are reading to what we know—the integrating part of the reading process. Even kindergarten readers can make connections between what they are reading and other texts, between what they are reading and themselves, and between what they are reading and the world. Harvey and Goudvis (2000) offer a clever way to help children begin to think about their connections to text. They give readers sticky notes and ask them to write a large R on each note for "reminds me of." When a child discovers a connection, he writes a few words on the sticky note describing the memory. Later, a group of children who have shared a text come together to create a chart with two columns, "What the Story Is About" and "What It Reminds Me Of." You could begin this activity with first graders.

As children become increasingly successful with making connections, Harvey and Goudvis suggest adding more codes to the sticky notes: T-T for text to text connections, T-S for text to self-connections, and T-W for text to world connections.

If your area has blizzards or nor'easters, then compare the information in newspaper reports of the storms to Murphy's *Blizzard* (2000) as an intratextual connection. Of course, if you live in an area where blizzards occur, then children would also have life connections to make to the book. In terms of connections between forms, children might read *The Amazing Impossible Erie Canal* (Harness, 1995) or *Erie Canal: Canoeing America's Great Waterways* (Lourie, 1999), learn to sing the song (Spier, 1970), and read an account of the building of the canal in an encyclopedia or a social studies text.

Again, let's look at a piece of text and think about during-reading strategies you could help children employ as they are reading. If your were reading *Because of Winn-Dixie* (DiCamillo, 2000) with your fifth graders, one of your prereading strategies might be to ask the children why they are reading this book. One of the answers might be to discuss it with their peers after reading it. Another answer might be for enjoyment or entertainment. You can help the children think about what they will attend to during reading such as important ideas, character traits, making friends, loneliness, and coming to grips with reality. As they read, you can ask them to think about the images they have created for the setting and/or the characters. You might have them discuss their images of the dog in their groups or draw their images of the dog. You might have them discuss the peculiar traits of each of the characters Opal meets. You might also have them compare how they read this novel with reading from their social studies text. Underscore the differences in reading for pleasure and reading to learn specific information.

ssessment and Evaluation Toolbox

VENN DIAGRAM

Ask children to complete a Venn diagram comparing the information on a given topic from one text to the information on the same topic from another source. Have them record the information unique to one text on the right-hand side, the unique information from the other text on the left-hand side, and the information common to both in the intersecting middle. This will help you check on their understanding of the big ideas and their ability to make connections between texts.

Many of the during-reading strategies described previously can be revisited after reading. Strategic readers revisit a text and extend and deepen understandings, amplify inferences, and reconnect what they read to background knowledge. They also revisit texts to work out confusion.

Teaching After-Reading Strategies. After-reading strategies include reviewing and reflecting, summarizing, repeated readings, and questioning. Most first graders are capable of these tasks with some modeling and coaching from you.

Reviewing and Reflecting. Reviewing and reflecting is an after-reading strategy that focuses on the meaning of a text and the ways in which a reader processed the text. Asking questions such as "Were my predictions accurate?" "Did I meet my reading goals?" "Did everything make sense?" and "Can I summarize the main ideas?" leads to an evaluation of the strategies used by a reader as early as first grade.

Summarizing. Summarizing is an effective way to enhance comprehension. Teaching children to summarize has two benefits. It improves the ability to summarize and it improves overall comprehension of text (Duke & Pearson, 2002). Summarizing involves reducing a text to its main points. Good summarizers guard against including information that is not important in their summaries. Teaching children a set of rules for making summaries (McNeil & Donant, 1982) has been proven more effective than having children write summaries based on the main ideas in the text (Bean & Steenwyk, 1984). The rules are:

Rule 1: Delete unnecessary material.
Rule 2: Delete redundant material.
Rule 3: Compose a word to replace a list of items.
Rule 4: Compose a word to replace individual parts of an action.
Rule 5: Select a topic sentence.
Rule 6: Invent a topic sentence if one is not available.

Begin by modeling the use of these rules and then move from large group practice to small group practice and finally to individual writing of summaries.

Repeated Readings. Repeated readings is a strategy some readers use to deepen understandings and increase fluency. Jay Samuels (1979) explored the value of repeated readings of the same text many years ago, and his article was reprinted in 1997 as a

For more information on repeated readings of text see Chapter 9.

Reading Teacher classic. Originally, it was thought the power of repeated readings was in increased ability in decoding. While this is true, repeated readings also improve fluency and comprehension. This is true for older readers as well as younger readers. The important lesson here is that teachers should be encouraging learners to visit and revisit texts they enjoy.

Questioning. Questioning is useful as both a during-reading strategy and an after-reading strategy. You could end a guided reading session or begin a reading conference by asking children to thumb through the text they just read and share questions they asked, important ideas they noted, and inferences they made. As they share, you have the opportunity to reinforce strategic behavior and celebrate their accomplishments. This practice helps you understand a child's evolving thinking during reading—a way for us to observe strategy use. As children share their questions with us, we need to be watchful that they are asking higher order questions and not always asking simple recall questions.

Strategy Use with Fiction and Nonfiction. A given strategy may not be applied in the same way when reading fiction as when reading nonfiction. The table in Figure 6.2 lists the before-, during-, and after-reading strategies about which you have just been reading. Then the strategy's application during fiction and nonfiction reading is described. Where the applications are the same, a check mark is placed in the box. As you study this figure, consider your own strategy use in reading fiction and nonfiction, and consider the degree to which you agree with our descriptions.

Using verbal prompts to teach strategy use. Irene Fountas and Gay Su Pinnell (1996, 2001) have helped teachers appreciate the value of using verbal prompts to help children become more strategic readers. This is a fine example of the coaching part of being a teacher of reading that begins in kindergarten. The verbal prompts we use guide and encourage children's strategic reading behaviors. With young, beginning readers you might encourage their one-to-one correspondence of finger, voice, print match by saying, "Read it with your finger. Did you have enough words?" After they have made an error you might prompt a more careful examination of the text with, "Where is the tricky word?" Asking, "Does it look right? Does it sound right? Does it make sense?" are excellent ways to prompt strategic reading.

With older, more fluent readers, you might prompt more strategic reading with, "What can you do to help yourself?" or "What do you know that might help?"

Clearly, the verbal prompts we use with learners will guide them toward using strategies effectively. Another way we can assist in the use of strategies is by asking our learners questions aimed at specific strategy use.

Go to the Weblinks in Chapter 6 on our Companion Website at www.prenhall.com/harp to link to a site offering lesson plans for reading strategies.

Questions Aimed at Strategy Use. Harvey and Goudvis (2000) adapted the work of Keene and Zimmermann (1997) in creating a set of generic questions for each strategy. These questions are illustrated in Figure 6.3. As you examine these questions, think about the ways in which each strategy could be helpful to a reader and think about how the questions could guide readers toward using a specific strategy.

After-reading strategies are important in helping children make sense of what they read in terms of the content and its personal meanings. To help children of any age become increasingly strategic readers, we need to give careful thought to the classroom environment we create to support strategy learning.

Figure 6.2
Strategy Use with Fiction and Nonfiction

STRATEGY	FICTION	NONFICTION
Before-Reading Strategies		
Previewing Text	Look at illustrations	Look at photos, charts, graphs, headings, and subheadings
Activating Prior Knowledge	✓	✓
K-W-L Strategy	(does not apply)	✓
Prediction Making	Focus on plot and characters	Focus on concepts and your reason for reading
During-Reading Strategies		
Prediction Making	Focus on plot and characters	Focus on concepts and your reason for reading
Using Phonics Skills	✓	✓
Using Syntactic Information	✓	✓
Drawing Inferences	More than with nonfiction	Less than with fiction
Identify Important Ideas	Related to story grammar and characters	Major ideas, supporting details; evidence and conclusions; qualifications of the author; author's purpose
Cross-Checking	✓	✓
Sources of Information	✓	✓
Questioning	✓	✓
Self-Corrections	✓	✓
Adjusting Strategy Use to Purpose	Purposes are usually related to being entertained or enjoyment	Purposes are usually related to gaining information
Making Connections	✓	✓
After-Reading Strategies		
Reviewing & Reflecting	Probably focused on character development and how the story conflict was resolved. Reader may reflect on important life messages and connections to self.	Probably focused on developing concepts and specific information related to the purposes for reading the text.
Summarizing	Not likely done for self, but may be done for others	Likely done both for self and others
Repeated Readings	✓	✓
Questioning	Less likely	More likely

Figure 6.3
Questions to Encourage Use of Strategies

Building Connections. Is there a part of this story or piece that reminds you of something in your own life? Of something that's happened to you?

Asking Questions. Can you show me a part of the text where you have a question? What were you wondering about as you read this part? Can you show me a part where you were confused? What was confusing about it?

Visualizing. Were there places in the text where you made a picture in your mind? What images or pictures did you see?

What specific words helped you create that picture in your mind?

Inferring. What do you predict will happen in this piece? Can you show me a place in the text where you found yourself making an inference? What do you think were the big ideas in the story?

Determining Importance in Text. What is this story or piece mostly about? Can you tell me about some of the important ideas that struck you? Any important themes you noticed? What do you think is most important to remember about this story/topic?

Summarizing. Can you tell me what the piece is about in just a few sentences?

Personal Reaction. Can you show me a place in the piece where your thinking changed? How did your thinking change? Do you have some new ideas or information?

Intratextual Connections. Does this piece remind you of any other books or stories you have read? Of any information books or reports? Of any poetry?

Adapted from *Strategies That Work: Teaching Comprehension to Enhance Understanding* by Stephanie Harvey and Anne Goudvis, copyright © 2000, with permission of Stenhouse Publishers.

HOW DO I CREATE A LEARNING ENVIRONMENT THAT SUPPORTS THE TEACHING AND LEARNING OF READING STRATEGIES?

In this chapter you have learned that first graders—and other students who do not use strategies spontaneously—can be taught to be strategic readers. You have also learned that expert readers use many strategies to process text, and our goal is to develop with each of our learners a repertoire of strategies to be invoked purposefully to meet reading needs.

LOOKING AT THE RESEARCH

What the research says about teacher behavior and children's learning of reading strategies

Teachers of underachieving readers in grades 6 through 11 were trained in transactional strategy instruction (TSI). The TSI approach includes teachers' explicit explanations of strategy use and the ability of teachers to facilitate discussion in which students collaborate on interpretations of text meaning as well as discussions of the mental processes and strategies involved in comprehension. The

(Continued)

LOOKING AT THE RESEARCH Continued

students in the treatment groups made significant improvements in such activities as treating reading problems openly, focusing on how to solve problems, and asking questions—all important reading strategies (Anderson, 1992). In another study with struggling second-grade readers, teachers trained in a TSI approach called SAIL (Students Achieving Independent Learning) achieved significant instructional results. The treatment students had better recall of text details, they used more strategies on their own, and they performed significantly better on the *Stanford Achievement Test* (Brown, Pressley, Van Meter, & Schuder, 1996). This means that you can be effective in teaching strategies if you carefully explain strategies to learners and engage them in discussions of the thinking they do as they read. Strategic processing, the ability to control and manage one's own cognitive activities in a reflective, purposeful way, is possible with students with learning disabilities (Williams, 2000).

What questions might you ask a group of readers to get them to collaborate on interpretations of text meaning and to talk about the strategies they used as they read?

Go to our Companion Website at www.prenhall.com/harp and join the global discussion of this question by adding your responses to the Threaded Message Board.

You know what constitutes effective strategy instruction. What might the classroom environment look like that supports these important efforts?

Visual Reminders

As evidence of a focus on strategies, create wall charts that remind students of reading strategies. One such chart might read:

All good readers think about making meaning.
All good readers make mistakes when they read.
All good readers notice and fix some mistakes.

Another wall chart might be written on a long piece of butcher paper listing all of the reading strategies the children in the class have learned to use. You could draw on the Reading Strategies Checklist illustrated in Figure 6.1 where you record individual successes with strategy use to create a class composite of strategies learned. Encourage children to refer often to this class list and celebrate their success with them daily.

A second piece of evidence that strategies are being taught is bookmarks. Nancy Charron, a teacher we know, made bookmarks for her students on which recently learned reading strategies were listed. She typed the text for two bookmarks on an 8½"× 11" sheet of paper, duplicated them on colored card stock, and then laminated them. Nancy found the idea in a chapter written by Kathleen Visovatti (1998). Figure 6.4 illustrates the first bookmark Nancy made for her children. As children learn new strategies, the bookmarks are redone to reflect new learning.

Buddy reading is a way to share understandings of reading strategies.

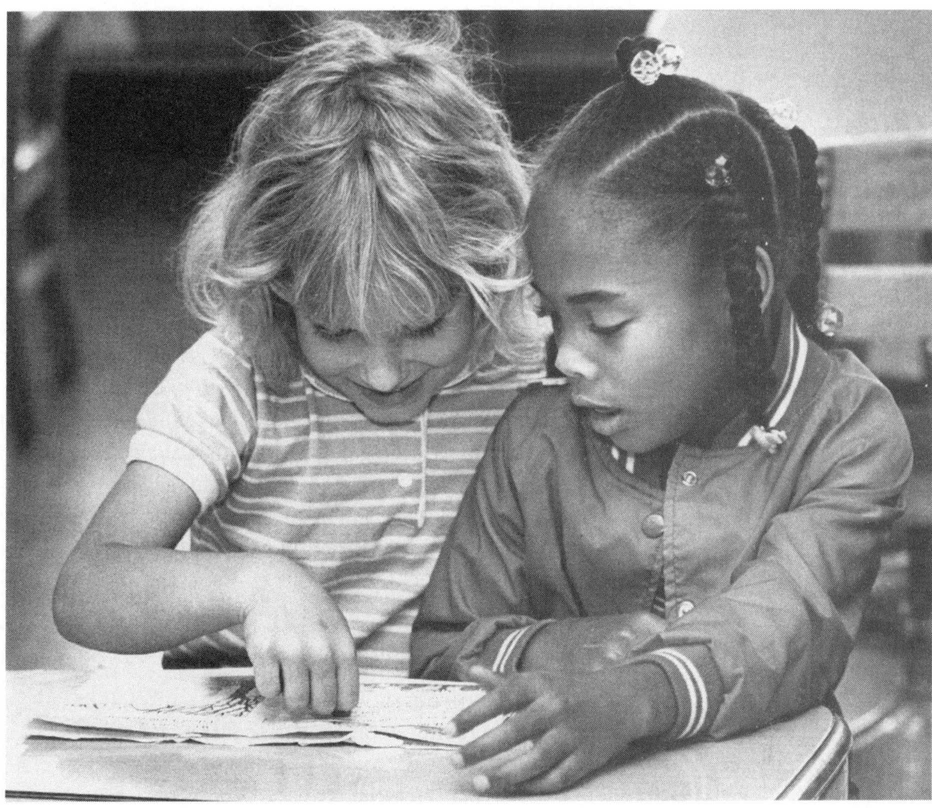

Figure 6.4
Strategy Bookmark

STUCK?

WHAT CAN

I DO?

SKIP IT AND

KEEP GOING.

REREAD (MAYBE I

MISSED SOMETHING).

PUT IN SOMETHING

THAT MAKES SENSE.

SOUND IT OUT.

ASK SOMEONE.

Source: Visovatti, K. (1998). Developing primary voices. In C. Weaver (Ed.), *Practicing what we know: Informed reading instruction.* Urbana, IL: Copyright © 1998 by the National Council of Teachers of English. Reprinted with permission.

Demonstrations

A classroom environment that supports strategy learning will have visual reminders of strategies readily apparent. This environment will also encourage strategy use through the demonstrations you offer when you are reading to children and when you are reading with children. For example, if you make a mistake as you are reading a text to your class, pause and say, "Did you hear what I just read? The text says *fright* but I read *height.* That doesn't sound right to me, and when I look at the text the word on the page doesn't look right. I think I need to think of another word to try in this spot." In other words, use think-alouds to model strategy use with your children during times you are reading to them and times you are reading with them both in shared reading and guided reading. However, we suggest you not do this every time you read to your students, or they may run for the door each time you pick up a book!

Strategy instruction is most effective when it begins with you modeling and thinking aloud as you use a strategy, showing students how to apply that strategy. This is followed by the students' practice of strategies while reading meaningful texts. You monitor this practice and coach your students in the use of strategies, reducing your feedback as they become more accomplished (Pressley, 2000). Through these experiences children come to be able to talk with you about their strategy use.

Children Learn the Language of Miscue Analysis

*Y*ou may want to revisit Chapter 3 to review running records.

Our friend Mary Giard, when teaching first grade in Maine, took running records on her first-graders' reading often enough that she had a new running record on every child within any three-week time span. She also debriefed running records with her students immediately after taking the running record and sometimes later during reading conferences. She would select a miscue or two, or perhaps a self-correction, and ask the child to talk with her about what he or she was thinking at that point in the reading. Mary's students became so familiar with the language of miscue analysis and strategy use that they began using the terms themselves.

One day when Mary was working with a small group of learners at a table in the front of the room, she had the rest of the class doing buddy reading. She overheard one reading buddy say to another, "Why do you think you made that insertion?" Mary suddenly realized that her children were taking running records on each other and engaging spontaneously in miscue analysis. This same group of first graders asked Mary if she would help them make a strategy checklist because they were having difficulty remembering all of the reading strategies they had learned. Their checklist (Giard, 1993) is illustrated in Figure 6.5. Please use this list as an inspiration to have your students create their own strategies checklist with your help.

When readers employ strategies efficiently and effectively, these procedures are facilitative, promoting deeper and better understanding of text (Pressley, Goodchild, Fleet, Zajchowski, & Evans, 1989). One instructional strategy that has proven to be especially effective with a wide variety of learners, including students with learning disabilities and limited English proficient students, is collaborative strategic reading (CSR) (Klingner and Vaughn, 1999).

Children Learn Collaborative Strategic Reading

This research-validated approach combines comprehension strategy instruction and cooperative learning, and is intended for use with expository text found in content area textbooks, beginning about fourth grade. CSR has improved reading comprehension, content learning and vocabulary acquisition of Spanish/English bilingual learners in science (Klingner, 1997; Klingner & Vaughn, 1998b), and it has improved comprehension in social

Figure 6.5
First Graders' Strategy Checklist

Reader: ________ Date: ________

Partner: ________ Title: ________

Strategies	Yes, it worked	No, it didn't
1. Does it make sense?		
2. Does it sound right?		
3. Does it look right?		
4. Finger Point		
5. Picture Clue		
6. Read something you Know		
7. Use your experiences		
8. Reread a book		
9. Rerun, start over		
10. Find word, self correct horse/house		
11. Rhyming Pattern cat fat		
12. Repeating Pattern Brown Bear Brown Bear		
13. Skip it, Come back		
14. Length of Word cat Caldecott		
15. Beginning sound cat come		
16. Give a hint		
17. Ask Someone Help		
18. Make predictions What do you think?		
19. Title The Very Hungry Caterpillar		
20. Small Word in a Big Word		
21. Insertion The fat cat...		
22. Omission The — cat is on the mat		

Did the reader understand the piece? How do you Know?

Giard, 1991

Source: From M. Giard. (1993). Bringing children to literacy through guided reading. In B. Harp (Ed.), *Bringing children to literacy: Classroom at work.* Norwood, MA. Christopher-Gordon. Reprinted with permission.

studies with struggling readers, English language learners, and average and high-achieving students (Klingner, Vaughn, & Schumm, 1998). Figure 6.6 illustrates the components of collaborative strategic reading.

Preview. The first part of CSR is preview. The goals of previewing are generating interest and questions about the text they will read, stimulating background knowledge, and facilitating their ability to make predictions about what they will read. Klingner and Vaughn (1998a & b) encourage readers during preview to look for what the passage is about, who

Figure 6.6
CSR's Plan for Strategic Reading

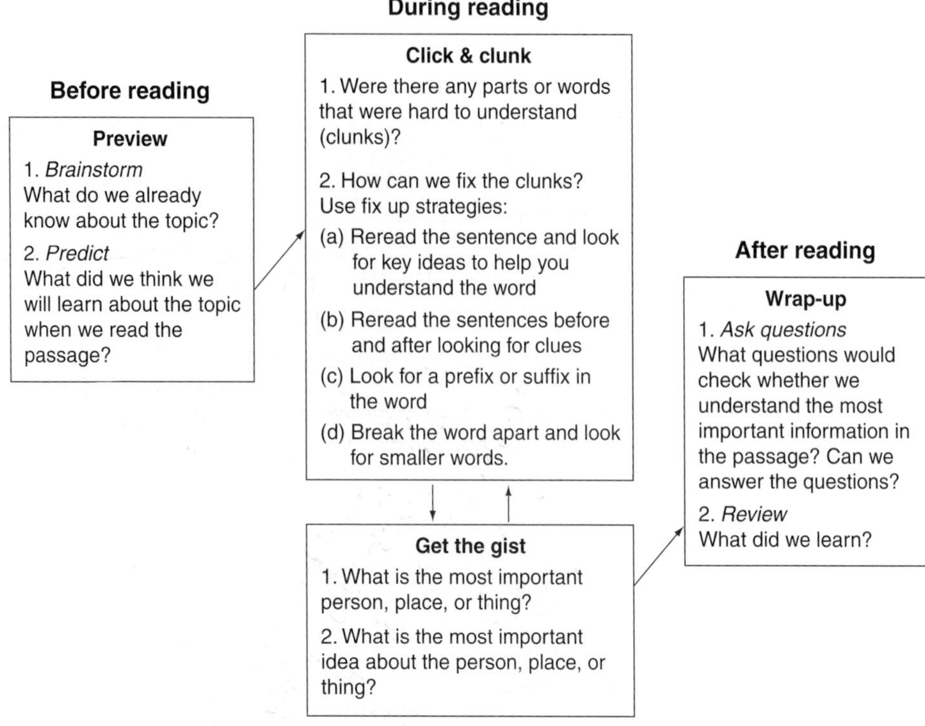

Source: Figure from Klingner, Janette Kettmann, & Vaughn, Sharon. (1999, April). Promoting reading comprehension, content learning, and English acquisition through Collaborative Strategic Reading (CSR). *The Reading Teacher, 52(7),* 738–747. Reprinted with permission.

is described in the text, when the passage takes place, and where the text is describing information they already know about the topic.

Click and Clunk. Clicking and clunking describe the self-monitoring strategy students are taught to use in CSR. When their reading is "clicking," they are recognizing information that they know well and understand. They are clicking along smoothly through the text. When they "clunk," they have identified words, concepts, or ideas they don't understand and about which they need to know more. They are taught to use fix-up strategies to declunk words. Klingner and Vaughn give students clunk cards with strategy suggestions for declunking words:

- Reread the sentence with the clunk and look for key ideas to help you figure out the unknown word.
- Think about what makes sense.
- Reread the sentences before and after the clunk looking for clues.
- Look for a prefix or suffix in the word that might help.
- Break the word apart and look for smaller words you know.

Get the Gist. Here students identify the main idea or the most critical information in a one- or two-paragraph section. The challenge is to state the gist in as few words as possible while conveying the most meaning.

Wrap-Up. Students learn to get the gist from every paragraph or two in the text they read. They wrap up only at the end of the material, usually about 12 to 14 paragraphs. Wrap-up involves formulating questions and answers about what they have read and reviewing key ideas. The purpose of wrap-up is to teach students to identify the most important ideas across the entire text they read.

Cooperative Learning Roles. Each member of a cooperative learning group has a designated role. The roles rotate so that over time each student gets experience carrying out each role. Klingner and Vaughn describe five roles within a CSR group:

Leader. Leads the group in implementing CSR by saying what to read next and what strategy to apply next.

Clunk Expert. Uses clunk cards to remind the group of the steps to follow when trying to figure out a difficult word or concept.

Gist Expert. Guides the group toward the development of a gist and determines that the gist contains the most important idea(s) but no unnecessary details.

Announcer. Calls on different group members to read or share an idea. Makes sure everyone participates and only one person talks at a time.

Encourager. Watches the group and gives feedback.

LOOKING AT THE RESEARCH

What the research says about how effective teachers use instructional time

In observing more and less effective elementary teachers, the amount of time children actually spent reading was a distinguishing feature of high-achievement classrooms (Allington & Johnston, 2000; Pressley et al., 2001; Taylor, Pearson, Clark, & Walpole, 2000). The most effective teachers had children reading for 40 to 45 minutes of each hour allocated to reading instruction. These teachers spent 5 to 10 minutes preparing the children to read the material and another 5 to 10 minutes in follow-up activities after reading. While the children were reading, the teacher worked with individuals or small groups (Allington, 2001). Allington recommends, and we agree, that children through grade six should spend 90 minutes a day actually reading.

In a typical elementary classroom, what changes would be needed to ensure that children are reading for 90-minute blocks?

Go to the Weblinks in Chapter 6 on our Companion Website at www.prenhall.com/harp to link to sites presenting research on effective teachers; then go to the chapter's Threaded Message Board to add your comments to the global discussion.

To have your students become skillful at using reading strategies, you need to create a learning environment in which:

- You are carefully teaching strategies by modeling them, helping children understand them, helping children see why they are helpful, and helping children think about using them.
- Students are learning and practicing collaborative strategic reading.

- Visuals keep children reminded of the strategies they are learning.
- You use running records, checklists, and reading conferences to evaluate children's use of strategies.
- You teach and reinforce strategy use during guided reading lessons and, to a lesser degree, during shared reading and reading to children.

Assessment and Evaluation Toolbox

METACOMPREHENSION STRATEGY INDEX

The *Metacomprehension Strategy Index (MSI)* is a 25-item, multiple-choice questionnaire designed to assess students' awareness of reading strategies they use before, during, and after reading a narrative text selection. The index is suitable for use with middle through upper elementary children. It is reprinted in Appendix E (Schmitt, 1990).

THINKING AS A TEACHER

1. You are teaching first grade and working to balance skill instruction and strategy instruction. A concerned parent makes an appointment to see you. He expresses his concern over "why you are spending all this time on reading strategies, whatever they are, when my son should be learning phonics in first grade." How will you respond?
2. A colleague who has become a good friend overhears you talking with another teacher about reading strategies. Your friend quietly comes to you and explains that she took her coursework in teaching reading some time ago and doesn't recall any mention of reading strategies. She asks you to explain the difference between reading strategies and reading skills. How will you respond?
3. In Chapter 5 we presented a model of a skill lesson. Review the components of that lesson format and determine whether you could use it to plan strategy instruction. If you determine that you would need to modify the format, what modifications would you make and why?
4. Articles critical of whole language often stated that teachers advocating whole language taught strategies but not skills. Think carefully about this. Could a good teacher teach strategies without teaching skills? Defend your answer.

FIELD-BASED ACTIVITIES

1. Explore the teacher's edition of a literature anthology. Identify a strategy lesson and compare it to the qualities of strategy instruction we recommended in this chapter. Would you plan to make any changes in the strategy instruction presented in the anthology in light of studying this chapter? If so, what changes would you make? If not, why not?
2. Arrange to observe a teacher engaging in strategy instruction with a group of learners or arrange to teach a strategy lesson with a group of learners. Reflect on your experience by thinking about what you learned about children, yourself, and/or teaching. What questions arise from this experience, and how will you get your questions answered?

3. Take a running record on a child's oral reading and then meet with the child to debrief his or her miscues and self-corrections that indicate the use of strategies. Reflect on this experience in terms of what you learned about teaching, children, or yourself.
4. Interview a first-grade teacher and a fifth-grade teacher about their views and practices on strategy instruction. Reflect on these interviews by comparing and contrasting their views and drawing your conclusions about the differences in strategy instruction for younger and older learners.

REFERENCES

Allington, R. L. (2001). *What really matters for struggling readers: Designing research-based programs.* New York: Longman.

Allington, R. L., & Johnston, P. (2000, April). *Exemplary fourth-grade reading instruction.* Paper presented at the American Educational Research Association, New Orleans.

Anderson, V. (1992). A teacher development project in transactional strategy instruction for teachers of severely reading-disabled adolescents. *Teaching & Teacher Education, 8,* 391–403.

Baumgart, A. (1998). Improving beginning first graders' reading strategies. M.A.Research Project, Saint Zavier University, ERIC#: ED420050.

Bean, T. W., & Steenwyk, F. L. (1984). The effect of three forms of summarization instruction on sixth graders' summary writing and comprehension. *Journal of Reading Behavior, 16,* 297–306.

Bransford, J. D., & Johnson, M. K. (1973). Considerations of some problems of comprehension. In W. C. Chase (Ed.), *Visual information processing.* New York: Academic Press.

Brown, R., Pressley, M., Van Meter, P., & Schuder, T. (1996). A quasi-experimental validation of transactional strategies instruction with low-achieving second-grade readers. *Journal of Educational Psychology, 88,* 18–37.

Bryan, J. (1998). K-W-W-L: Questioning the known. *The Reading Teacher, 51,* 618–624.

Clay, M. M. (1991). *Becoming literate: The construction of inner control.* Portsmouth, NH: Heinemann.

Dowhower, S. L. (1999). Supporting a strategic stance in the classroom: A comprehension framework for helping teachers help students to be strategic. *The Reading Teacher, 52,* 672–683.

Duke, N. K., & Pearson, P. D. (2002). Effective practices for developing reading comprehension. In A. E. Farstrup & S. J. Samuels (Eds.), *What research has to say about reading instruction.* Newark, DE: International Reading Association.

Fountas, I. C., & Pinnell, G. S. (1996). *Guided reading: Good first teaching for all children.* Portsmouth, NH: Heinemann.

Fountas, I. C., & Pinnell, G. S. (2001). *Guiding readers and writers grades 3–6: Teaching comprehension, genre, and content literacy.* Portsmouth, NH: Heinemann.

Garner, R. (1992). Metacognition and self-monitoring strategies. In S. J. Samuels & A. E. Farstrup (Eds.), *What research has to say about reading instruction* (2nd ed., pp. 236–252). Newark, DE: International Reading Association.

Giard, M. (1993). Bringing children to literacy through guided reading. In B. Harp (Ed.), *Bringing children to literacy: Classroom at work.* Norwood, MA: Christopher-Gordon.

Goodman, Y. M., Watson, D. J., & Burke, C. L. (1996). Reading strategies: Focus on comprehension (2nd ed.). Katonah, NY: Richard C. Owen.

Hall, K., Bowman, H., & Myers, J. (1999). Metacognition and reading awareness among samples of nine-year-olds in two cities. *Educational Research, 41,* 99–107.

Harp, B. (1999, May). Developing strategic readers: The key to comprehension. *Reading Forum NZ,* 6–13. Auckland, NZ: New Zealand Reading Association.

Harvey, S., & Goudvis, A. (2000). *Strategies that work: Teaching comprehension to enhance understanding.* York, ME: Stenhouse Publishers.

Keene, E. L., & Zimmermann, S. (1997). *Mosaic of thought: Teaching comprehension in a reader's workshop.* Portsmouth, NH: Heinemann.

Klingner, J. (1997, March). *Promoting English acquisition and content learning through collaborative strategic reading.* Paper presented at the annual meeting of the American Educational Research Association, Chicago.

Klingner, J. K., Kettmann, J., & Vaughn, S. (1998a). *The helping behaviors of bilingual fifth-graders during collaborative strategic reading (CSR) cooperative learning.* Unpublished manuscript.

Klingner, J. K., & Vaughn, S. (1998b). Using collaborative strategic reading. *Teaching Exceptional Children, 30,* 32–37.

Klingner, J. K., Vaughn, S., & Schumm, J.S. (1998) Collaborative strategic reading during social studies in heterogeneous fourth-grade classrooms. *Elementary School Journal, 99,* 3–21.

Klingner, J. K., & Vaughn, S. (1999). Promoting reading comprehension, content learning, and English acquisition through collaborative strategic reading (CSR). *The Reading Teacher, 52,* 738–747.

McNeil, J., & Donant, L. (1982). Summarization strategy for improving reading comprehension. In J. A. Niles & L. A. Harris (Eds.), *New inquiries in reading research and instruction* (pp. 215–219). Rochester, NY: National Reading Conference.

Ogle, D. M. (1986). K-W-L: A teaching model that develops active reading of expository text. *The Reading Teacher, 39,* 564–570.

Pearson, P. D., & Fielding, L. (1991). Comprehension instruction. In R. Barr, M. Kamil, P. Mosenthal, & P. D. Pearson (Eds.), *Handbook of reading research, Vol. II* (pp. 815–860). New York: Longman.

Pressley, M. (2000). What should comprehension instruction be the instruction of? In M. L. Kamil, P. B. Mosenthal, P. D. Pearson, & R. Barr (Eds.), *Handbook of reading research, Vol. III.* Mahwah, NJ: Lawrence Erlbaum.

Pressley, M., Goodchild, F., Fleet, J., Zajchowski, R., & Evans, E. D. (1989). The challenges of classroom strategy instruction. *Elementary School Journal, 89,* 301–342.

Pressley, M., Allington, R. L., Wharton-McDonald, R., Block, C. C., & Morrow, L. M. (2001). *Learning to read: Lessons from exemplary first grade classrooms.* New York: Guilford Press.

Samuels, S. J. (1997). The method of repeated readings. *The Reading Teacher, 51,* 376–381.

Schmitt, M. C. (1990). A questionnaire to measure children's awareness of strategic reading processes. *The Reading Teacher, 43,* 632–638.

Taylor, B., Pearson, D., Clark, K., & Walpole, S. (2000). *Beating the odds in teaching all children to read* (Report #2-006). East Lansing, MI: Center for Improving Early Reading Achievement.

Visovatti, K. (1998). Developing primary voices. In C. Weaver (Ed.), *Practicing what we know: Informed reading instruction.* Urbana, IL: National Council of Teachers of English.

Williams, J. P. (2000). Strategic processing of text: Improving reading comprehension of students with learning disabilities. ERIC/OSEP Digest #599. ED449596.

Children's Books

DiCamillo, K. (2000). *Because of Winn-Dixie.* Cambridge, MA: Candlewick.

Gibbons, G. (1999). *Bats.* New York: Holiday House.

Harness, C. (1995). *The amazing impossible Erie canal.* New York: Simon & Schuster.

Lourie, P. (1999). *Erie canal: Canoeing America's great waterway.* Honesdale, PA: Boyds Mills Press.

Murphy, J. (2000). *Blizzard! The storm that changed America.* New York: Scholastic.

Spier, P. (1970). *The Erie canal.* Garden City, NY: Doubleday.

Chapter 7

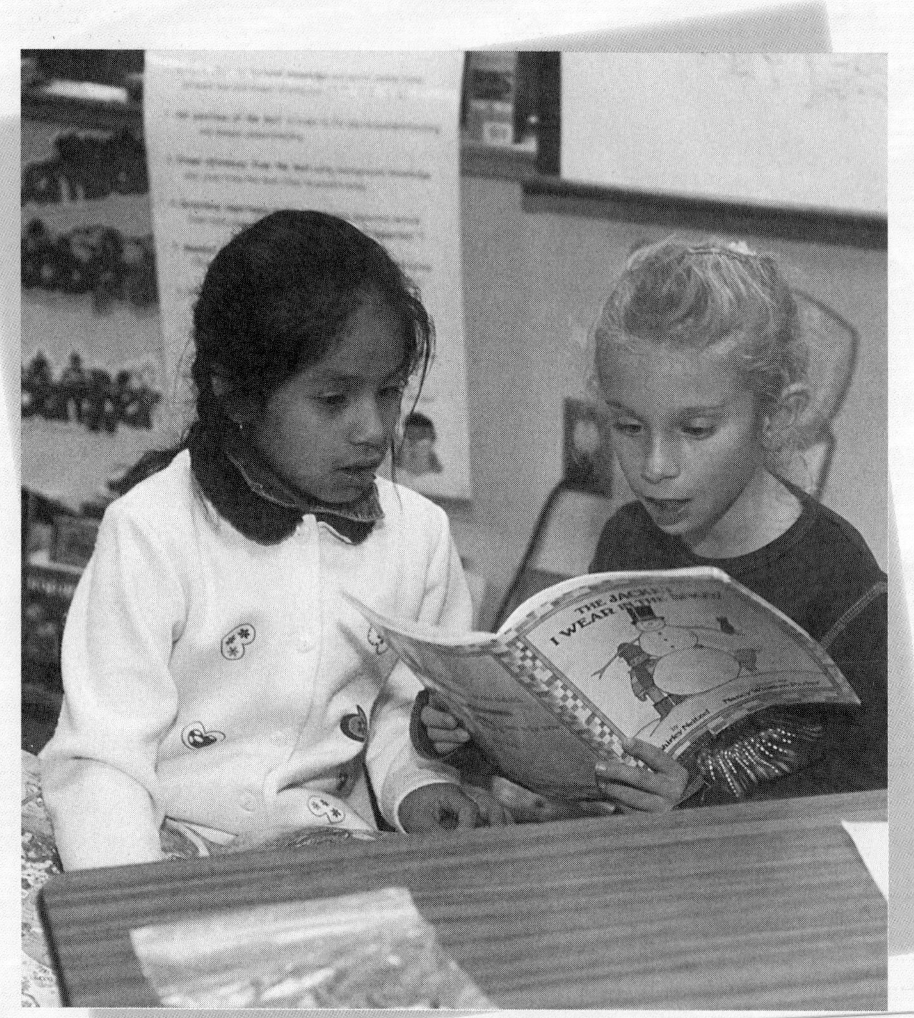

Guiding the Development of Vocabulary

LOOKING AT THE RESEARCH

Students learn approximately 3,000 to 4,000 words each year, resulting in a vocabulary of approximately 25,000 words by the end of elementary school and approximately 50,000 words by the end of high school (Anderson & Nagy, 1992; Anglin, 1993; and White, Graves, & Slater, 1990). We clearly cannot teach students 50,000 or more individual words. Word consciousness—an awareness of words around us; a celebration of words in reading, writing, speaking, and listening; an intrigue with the use of one word over another; an awareness of first encounters with words—plays a critical role in learning vocabulary (Anderson & Nagy, 1992).

Focus Questions

- How complex is the task of vocabulary learning?
- How do I guide the development of word consciousness in my students?
- What other components shall I include in my vocabulary curriculum?
- How will I know a good vocabulary program when I see one?

REAL TEACHERS, REAL PRACTICE

Meet Leah Alvarado, *a fifth-grade teacher*

My fifth-grade class at Mayer Elementary is made up of 27 students who come from a variety of ethnic, racial, and economic backgrounds and have a wide range of skills. I believe and instill in my students that each of them has the ability to learn and succeed. I try to foster development in all areas, especially language development. Vocabulary is an integral part of our everyday lives, and giving children exposure and practice with different words is a necessary component of any reading program. I set up my classroom so that it is rich with language. I want it to be clear that reading and vocabulary are skills that are highly valued in my room as well as in the real world.

I teach vocabulary based on the idea that I need to provide as many opportunities as possible for my students to use the words they learn. They do not just learn the definition and put a new word away in a notebook. Each day students enter in the same way. As they come into the room, I greet them and they use a vocabulary word we have learned in a sentence that shows me they understand its meaning. I do this to provide a chance for them to practice using a new word and become familiar enough with it so that they begin to incorporate it into their everyday language.

One way I introduce new words to the students is through a word of the day, two or three times a week. On these days, there is a new word on the overhead with its part of speech, a definition, and an example of its use in a sentence. Then the students select synonyms or antonyms or give examples of the word, depending on the instructions. Next is a short writing activity that requires students to show an understanding of the word. After each student has completed the writing, we discuss the word and share responses. The word is then added to the word wall, so that it can be referenced for future use.

Many times students come to a word they don't understand in their book and write the word down. That way, as a group we can choose some to learn together. The students enjoy this because it provides a sense of ownership and gives them an opportunity to share. These are frequently the words that get incorporated into their vocabulary first.

I believe that in teaching vocabulary, modeling is extremely important. When I use the words we have studied, the students usually recognize them right away, even if they are not familiar with the meaning. This practice allows the students to hear the words and become more comfortable using them. This helps build their confidence.

When my students realize how important I think it is to learn new words, they begin to pay more attention to words they don't know in their reading. I frequently have students call me over to show me a vocabulary word we have learned in something they are reading. Their excitement in finding one of "our words" in a book is rewarding.

I truly believe that the most important part of teaching vocabulary is to make the students feel comfortable using new words. The more practice and exposure they have to different words, the more they will begin to use them. Vocabulary is an essential building block to lifelong learning and an important element of a successful reading program.

Building enthusiasm for vocabulary learning as Leah describes it, and the enormity of the task of learning 50,000 or more words in 12 years of schooling, leads to some important questions about teaching and learning vocabulary.

HOW COMPLEX IS THE TASK OF VOCABULARY LEARNING?

Word knowledge could be thought of as a continuum. Dale (1965) proposed four stages along this continuum:

Stage One: I never saw this word before.
Stage Two: I've heard that word, but I don't know what it means.
Stage Three: When I see it in context, I know it has something to do with . . .
Stage Four: I know the word well.

We would add to the end of the continuum: I can use this word in a sentence, or I can use variations in this word's meaning with accuracy.

In order to facilitate learners' growth along this continuum, it is useful to deepen one's understanding of the complexity of vocabulary learning. Nagy and Scott (2000) have described five aspects of this complexity:

- Word learning is incremental.
- Word learning requires understanding multiple meanings.
- Word learning is multidimensional; the meaning of one word is related to the meanings of other words.
- What it means to know a word depends on the kind of word one is talking about.

Word Learning Is Incremental

Word learning is not an all-or-nothing process. Children learn the meanings of words in many incremental steps moving from incomplete understandings toward adult understandings (Clark, 1993). Children have learned many of the words in their 5,000 to 6,000 word vocabulary when they begin school from direct experience. The incremental nature of this learning is apparent when we observe a young child call every animal with four legs "doggie" and then gradually learn to discriminate among cats, horses, cows, and other four-legged animals. We are probably fortunate that much vocabulary learning is incremental. This helps explain how a great deal of vocabulary knowledge can be gained from context without direct instruction. It also underscores the importance of providing children with frequent exposures to text and to as many real objects as possible. We know that children learn words when they are read to (Eller, Papas, & Brown, 1988), and they learn words when they read (Herman, Anderson, Pearson, & Nagy, 1987). Children also learn words during discussions in the classroom (Stahl & Vancil, 1986) and around the dinner table (Snow, 1991).

Word Learning Requires Understanding Multiple Meanings

Many words have multiple meanings. Children must learn to deal with small variations in meaning such as in "*play* the piano" and "*play* the CD" as well as significant variations in meaning such as in "the *bear* is in the tree" and "I cannot *bear* the thought of cleaning the garage."

Word meanings are often flexible and influenced by the context in which they are encountered (Green, 1989; Nagy, 1997). Dealing with multiple meanings of words becomes even more challenging when children encounter figurative language such as metaphors, idioms, and similes that have meanings different from the literal. You may want to help your learners celebrate the adventure of dealing with expressions such as "he is as straight as an arrow," "she is as tight as the bark on a tree," "he is a silver-tongued scoundrel," "a family tree," and "he is a wolf in sheep's clothing."

Instructional strategies to aid children in understanding words used in nonliteral ways cannot usually begin until about second grade. You can determine if the children have recognized that words can be used nonliterally with a quick read of *Amelia Bedelia* (Parrish, 1963). Most kindergartners think Amelia Bedelia is just fine and fail to catch on to the double meanings of the words. By the time they reach age 8, most children think Amelia Bedelia is hilarious because they have learned that words can have double meanings.

Second and third graders can create a dictionary of phrases with the literal meanings illustrated. You could read Gwynne's *The King Who Rained* (1970) or *A Chocolate Moose for Dinner* (1988) as models for making their own books. Older students could be encouraged to collect words and phrases that fit into various categories. For example, you might put up three large charts, one headed *metaphors,* one headed *similes,* and one headed *idioms.* As children find examples of these in their reading, they can copy them on the correct chart, and once a week or so, the lists can be reviewed in a class discussion.

Poetry is an especially good source for figurative language examples. In dealing with poetry your task will be twofold. You will need to help children understand poetic language at the same time you are helping them learn to celebrate it.

Lyon (1999) has created a book of metaphors for "book," which she says may be a house, a chest, a farm, filled with leaves, and a boon companion. After several readings and discussion, children could be encouraged to write about other objects that are personally important to them using metaphor. Children in fourth grade and up could collect similes from books they are reading and discuss the judicious use of similes to help the reader create mental images. Be prepared for a little purple prose; writers just learning any strategy tend to overuse it at first.

Word Learning Is Multidimensional

If vocabulary learning were one-dimensional, it would be easier to think about how vocabulary instruction should look. We could think of a child's vocabulary knowledge as somewhere between "nonexistent" and "fully developed." However, vocabulary instruction is complicated by the multidimensionality of word learning. Children must learn the spoken form of a word, the written form of the word, the grammatical slots in which the word can exist, other words with which this word commonly appears, the concepts the word represents, and the word's multiple meanings. Word learning involves learning new concepts, learning new labels for known concepts, and bringing words into students' productive vocabularies (Graves, 1986).

Researchers and curriculum designers distinguish between receptive vocabularies and productive vocabularies. Our receptive vocabulary is all the words we can understand when we read or listen to a speaker. Our productive vocabulary is all the words we use in writing or speaking to others. Our receptive vocabularies are usually larger than our productive vocabularies. That is to say, we recognize more words in listening and reading than we can produce in speaking or writing. When choosing material to be read aloud, one rule is to choose something with a vocabulary a little more complex than that of the children who will listen because children can understand more words than they can say or write. You will also want to make sure that reading material offers some vocabulary challenges.

Word Meanings Are Related

Nagy and Scott (2000) explain this relationship as follows: How well a person knows the meaning of *whale* depends in part on their understanding of *mammal.* A person who already knows the words *hot, cold,* and *cool* has already acquired some of the components of the word *warm,* even if the word *warm* has not yet been encountered. (p. 272)

Words are so closely interrelated that reading and understanding some words can result in deepening understanding of words that were not even in the text.

ssessment and Evaluation Toolbox

THE PEABODY PICTURE VOCABULARY TEST–III

The Peabody Picture Vocabulary Test–III (PPVT – III) is normed for ages 2–6 (2 years, 6 months old) through adulthood. The PPVT–III is a test of listening comprehension for the spoken word in standard English. It may be used to evaluate a child's receptive vocabulary against the norming sample. A low score would indicate a limited hearing vocabulary and might indicate limited verbal ability (Dunn & Dunn, 2003).

The Relationship Between Learning a Word and the Kind of Word Being Learned

Linguists make a distinction between structure words and form class words. **Structure words** are the words that have no inherent meaning but keep the structure of sentences together. **Form class words** are more interesting than structure words because they have inherent meaning. Knowing the meaning of structure words requires a different understanding than knowing the meaning of form class words.

Structure Words. Structure words are words such as *am, is, are, was, the, and, of,* and *is* (just a few examples). These words are difficult for children to learn and remember in reading because they lack meaning, often look similar to other words, and are not very interesting. But they must be taught because decoding and understanding them permits the reader to deal with more interesting sentences. Consider the variations in sentence structure afforded by *structure words:*

Billy asked Susan to come* and *play.
Susan,* who *was too busy, said, "No."
Billy* and *Tom played together.
They *threw snowballs* at *Susan.*

Because structure words include prepositions, conjunctions, pronouns, articles, auxiliary verbs, and forms of the verb *to be,* they present challenges to children early in their reading lives. Structure words make texts authentic (like real spoken language) because they permit the creation of compound sentences, compound subjects, phrases, and clauses.

Form Class Words. Form class words are easier for children to learn and to remember because they are more meaningful. Some form class words require a context in order to be understood. The ones requiring a context are homonyms, homographs, and homophones. We will explore these later in this chapter.

LOOKING AT THE RESEARCH

What the research says about types of words and learning them

In a study of fourth-grade students, certain word characteristics had an impact on the vocabulary learned from reading stories. Verbs, adverbs, and adjectives were learned better than nouns, and words that easily create mental images were learned more readily than less easily imageable words. The characteristics of vocabulary words are more important variables in learning of vocabulary from stories than are the number of word repetitions or the amount of contextual support (Schwanenflugel, Stahl, & McFalls, 1997). This suggests that when you are teaching children the meaning of nouns, you need to help them create strong mental images of the words.

Suppose you are teaching fifth graders the meaning of *pastoral* (relating to the countryside, not urban). What questions would you ask to help them create mental images? What thinking aloud could you offer them to help them appreciate the mental images you are creating?

Go to our Companion Website at www.prenhall.com//harp and add your thoughts on these questions to the discussion on the Threaded Message Board.

Nagy and Scott (2000) conclude their discussion of the complexity of word learning with the following critical understanding.

> The knowledge that students have for many words is far more complex than could be attained through instruction that relies primarily on definitions. Not only are there too many words to teach them all to students one by one; there is too much to learn about each word to be covered by anything but exceptionally rich and multifaceted instruction. Hence, the complexity of word knowledge further bolsters the argument that much of students' vocabulary knowledge must be gained through means other than explicit vocabulary instruction. In those cases when students are dependent on instruction to learn a word, if they are to truly gain ownership of that word, the instruction must provide multiple and varied encounters with the word. (p.273)

Understanding the complexity of word learning lends credibility to the notion that we must help our learners develop word consciousness.

HOW DO I GUIDE THE DEVELOPMENT OF WORD CONSCIOUSNESS IN MY STUDENTS?

In the research summary that opened this chapter, we described students with word consciousness as being aware of words around them, as celebrating the use of words, and as noticing first encounters with words. Word consciousness is the motivational and affective component of a vocabulary program (Graves & Watts-Taffe, 2002). We have known for many years that vocabulary knowledge is a powerful contributor to comprehension (Davis, 1942). This means that teachers need to be word advocates and pull their learners into their enthusiasm for words. Your students will benefit from seeing your excitement about words, your thrill for a phrase well turned, and your enjoyment in playing with words.

Word Play

Word play involves an array of activities, each designed to invite learners into the fun of exploring, manipulating, and celebrating words. These include using games and puzzles; riddles, jokes, and puns; and books that play with language.

Games and Puzzles. You can make games and puzzles yourself or find commercially available versions. You may find that your students will get so involved in games and puzzles they will want to create some on their own.

Concentration. This is a variation on the old television show of the same name, and it is appropriate for children beginning in second grade. We described the game in Chapter 5. You may want to revisit that description. Concentration is effective in teaching both decoding skills and vocabulary.

Bingo. Second grade is a good time to introduce this game, which requires a set of word cards and corresponding sets of cards with matching definitions. Each player lays his or her word cards on the table in a 5 × 5 grid with a "free" space in the middle. One person,

Word games help children develop vocabulary.

the caller, draws a card from the definition pile and reads it aloud. Each player who has a matching word on the table covers the word with a piece of paper, a plastic tangram, or a poker chip. The first person to have all of the words covered in either a vertical, horizontal, or diagonal row is the winner and becomes the caller for the next game. You could vary this game by placing definitions on the table and drawing word cards, or by substituting synonyms or antonyms for the definition cards.

Categories. Categories is a good pencil and paper game (Blachowicz & Fischer, 2002), which many children can enjoy toward the end of first grade. Students draw a grid. You decide how challenging you want the game to be. You might specify a 2 × 2 grid for young children and a 5 × 5 grid for older children. One child in the group finds a word in a book or in the classroom with the same number of letters as there are vertical columns in the grid. Each player writes this word across the top of the grid, one letter for each column. You or the children then assign a category to each horizontal row on the grid.

Players are given a designated time limit to find as many words as they can to fill in the squares. The word must fit the category for the row and begin with the letter at the top of the column. When the time is up, the points are totaled. Players get 5 points for every category square they fill in, but that no other player has filled; 2 points for every category square filled in that others have filled in, but with other words; and 1 point for every category square filled in where someone else has the same word. An example of a 5 × 5 grid is illustrated in Figure 7.1.

Blachowicz & Fisher (2002) offer a variation on Categories they call Word Challenge. Each horizontal row on a grid contains a challenging word. Each of the vertical columns is headed with a category describing a characteristic of words such as "synonym//similar," "antonym//different," "example," and "related word." Play is the same as described for Categories, and is appropriate for children in fourth grade and up.

Balderdash. This game is available commercially, but you can have your fourth-grade and older children play it by just giving them dictionaries and explaining the game. It works best in a group of about six children. Each child selects an unusual word from the dictionary. Each child writes down the definition from the dictionary or a made-up definition. In turn, each child reads his or her chosen word and the definition they have written. The other children in the group guess whether the definition read is the real definition according to the dictionary or a made-up definition. Each child who guesses correctly gets a point. The child with the most points is the winner.

Figure 7.1
Categories Grid

P	L	A	N	E	
					FRUITS
					WAYS TO TRAVEL
					ANIMALS
					CITIES
					NAMES OF BOYS

Riddles, Jokes, and Puns. You will discover that students not only enjoy the riddles, jokes, and puns you share, but they will also enjoy making up their own. Young children seem to enjoy riddles and jokes, and middle grade children love puns.

Word riddles. Blachowicz and Fisher (2002) draw on the work of Thaler (1988) to describe a process for creating word riddles with pun-like responses. First, you choose a subject and generate a list of related terms. For example, if your subject is *pig,* your list might contain the words:

ham	pork
pen	grunt
hog	oink

Second, you take the first letter off one of the words and make a list of words that begin with the remaining letters. If you choose *ham,* you would make a list of words that begin with *am* such as:

ambulance	amnesia
amphibian	America

Then you put back the missing letter:

Hambulance	Hamnesia
Hamphibian	Hamerica

And make up riddles for the words.

Riddle: How do you take a pig to a hospital?
Answer: In a hambulance!
Riddle: What do you call it when a pig loses its memory?
Answer: Hamnesia!

Tom Swifties. The name comes from the verbal manipulations of a fictional character who appeared in books written for boys in the early 1900s. Enjoyed by children in upper elementary grades, Tom Swifties are created by writing a quotation followed by a descriptive verb or adverb that has some relationship to the quotation.

"Let's hurry," said Tom swiftly.
"Your sewing is extremely sloppy," she needled.
"Catch that stray dog!" he barked at the bystanders. (Blachowicz & Fisher, 2002)

The world of children's literature is rich with books of riddles, jokes, and puns. In fact, you can use a wide variety of children's books that involve very playful use of language.

Go to the Weblinks in Chapter 7 on our Companion Website at www.prenhall.com//harp to link to sites supporting vocabulary instruction.

Using Books that Play with Language. In a classroom where words matter, children will be more likely to attend to the unusual words they find in the books they are reading. However, you will want to collect and present books with a particular focus on words on a regular basis. Many kindergarten and first-grade teachers have watched children delight in the books of Denise Fleming. The books have repetitive language patterns and interesting vocabulary. The titles are: *Time to Sleep* (1997); *Pumpkin Eye* (2001); *Count!* (1992); *Lunch* (1992); *In the Small, Small Pond* (1993); *Alphabet Under Construction* (2002); *Barnyard Banter* (1994); *In the Tall, Tall Grass* (1991); *Where Once There Was a Wood* (1996); and *Mama Cat Has Three Kittens* (1998).

For younger readers, *Quick as a Cricket* (Wood & Wood, 1989) is an example of similes. Other books for younger readers just have fun with language such as *Rain Makes*

Applesauce (Scheer, 1964), where silly statements such as "My house goes walking every day" end with "and rain makes applesauce" (unpaged). In *Pickles Have Pimples and Other Silly Statements* (Barrett, 1986), the author notes Beds have sleeps. Chicks have peeps. Sniffles have sneezes. Crowds have squeezes" (unpaged). Another example is *The Absolutely Awful Alphabet* (Gerstein, 1999), which begins "A is an awfully arrogant amphibian annoyed at . . . B who is a bashful, belching bumpkin bullied by . . . " (unpaged); the book continues through the alphabet. Some younger readers can appreciate books using idiomatic language such as the books by Gwynne that were mentioned previously. A third title by Gwynne is *A Little Pigeon Toad* (1990).

Second and third graders can appreciate *Donovan's Word Jar* (DeGross, 1994), a book about a third grader who collects words that he likes in a big jar and has to decide what to do with them when the jar is full. Fourth graders (and older) can enjoy *Miss Alaineus: A Vocabulary Disaster* (Frasier, 2000), which tells of a fifth-grade girl who misunderstands the meaning of the word *miscellaneous* and therefore feels really foolish until she decides to make the joke on herself.

Intermediate grade readers can enjoy other examples of books that focus on words such as *So Many Dynamos! And Other Palindromes* (Agee, 1994), *Hog on Ice & Other Curious Expressions* (Funk, 1948), *Heavens to Betsy & Other Curious Sayings* (Funk, 1983), and *Horsefeathers & Other Curious Words* (Funk, 1986) are all books that explain the origin of some of the odd or unusual phrases that we use in English. Children might collect other phrases that they wonder about and try to research the origins of those phrases. *Letter Jesters,* (Falwell, 1994) tells about fonts and letters and explains the origin of their names. Even though it is a book about letters, it can certainly help children with the vocabulary of letters and fonts we see every day.

Intermediate grade readers will also enjoy an alphabet book that plays with language, Hepworth's (1992) *Antics!*. For each letter entry, she chose a word with the little word "ant" in it and then pictured the words with ant characters. For example, she uses "Brilliant" for B, and the illustration depicts an ant with Einstein hair working a laboratory. *Walking the Bridge of Your Nose: Wordplay Poems and Rhymes* (Rosen, 1995) is another example for this age group. In the introduction to this book, Rosen "warns" the reader to be prepared to be baffled, bamfoozled, bewitched, and bedazzled. Some of the rhymes are attributed to a source, but many have no known author; they are just the result of language play over the years.

Certainly, you would not want to miss the books on parts of speech by Ruth Heller and Brian Cleary. Heller has written eight of these books, all done with lovely illustrations and clever rhymes to explain the parts of speech and to use them in creative ways. The titles are as follows: *Merry-Go-Round: A Book About Nouns* (1990); *Up, Up and Away: A Book About Adverbs* (1991); *Mine, All Mine: A Book About Pronouns* (1997); *Kites Sail High: A Book About Verbs* (1988); *Fantastic! Wow! And Unreal! A Book About Interjections and Conjunctions* (1998); *A Cache of Jewels and Other Collective Nouns* (1987); *Behind the Mask: A Book About Prepositions* (1995); and *Many Luscious Lollipops: A Book About Adjectives* (1989). Each of these books is an interesting, colorful, and playful look at the parts of speech. Cleary's books also help readers become more aware of parts of speech. His titles include: *Hairy, Scary, Ordinary: What Is an Adjective?* (2001); *A Mink, a Fink, a Skating Rink: What Is a Noun?* (2000); *To Root, to Toot, to Parachute: What Is a Verb?* (2001). He has other titles forthcoming.

Books are wonderful sources for building vocabulary, encouraging attention to words, and finding examples of word choices that are interesting enough to emulate.

There are clearly many ways to use word play to build the word consciousness of your students. But word play is only one avenue. Another important strategy is for you to model enthusiasm for words in your own speaking and writing and in the speaking and writing of your learners.

Modeling Enthusiasm for Words in Your Own Speech and Language

Sometimes we use "easy" language purposefully motivated by our desire to be sure our learners understand. The task here is to do just the opposite of that. Use rich and exciting language. Use language that challenges and stimulates inquiry. Use language deliberately chosen to cause your students to ask you "What does that mean?" Such modeling also requires that you are willing to take the time to explain word meanings to children, to explore variations in meanings, and to invite them to use the words as well.

Using Rich Oral Language. One strategy for using language well is to use the vocabulary of each discipline as much as possible. For example, it is not more difficult for a child to learn *rhombus* for the name of a shape than to learn *diamond.* In mathematics, children can learn the correct terms for both plane and solid shapes, for lines and segments, and for the operations they are learning. In social science, children can learn the vocabulary used by historians, such as *primary document,* the terms of physical and social geography, and the meanings of words used in anthropology. For example, when kindergarten children are learning to test their hypothesis, they can call what they do an experiment to test their hypothesis. Older children can talk about variables, species, phylums, and other terms used in the scientific community.

The arts provide another source of rich vocabulary learning as children learn about musical phrases, painting techniques (brush strokes, spatter), art materials (velum, gouache), the words for colors (magenta, chartruse), and the words to describe movements in dance. Just as teachers want children to be able to discuss literature in terms of its genre and characteristics, so can they add the vocabulary of other arts to help children express their understandings and feelings.

Word of the Day. Each day select one word you are going to deliberately use as often as is reasonable. Challenge your students, as young as kindergarten, to try to identify the word. Have them write the word on a piece of paper with their name, collect these papers at the class meeting at the end of the day, and celebrate the number of children who identified the word. Talk about the word's meanings and discuss when they first realized it was the word of the day. For example, you may have chosen *electrify* as the word of the day. You might share with the children a discussion that you and two other teachers were having before school about the newest Harry Potter film. You might say, "But Mrs. Swenson's comments tended to electrify the discussion when she boldly stated that she was finding the Harry Potter phenomenon equal to the impact that *Lord of the Rings* had on her when she was in high school." While discussing the morning assembly, you might tell your students that you observed the suspense over the "mystery guest" seemed to electrify the atmosphere in the cafeteria. Perhaps you will find other times to use the word of the day in debriefing a literature study circle or discussing revision in writing with individual children. Noticing children's use and discovery of electrifying language is another way to build word consciousness.

Celebrating Children's Discovery and Use of Language

As you know, our hope is that your classroom will be one in which children are immersed in language and texts. Teachers need to be watchful for opportunities to celebrate language in the reading and writing children do.

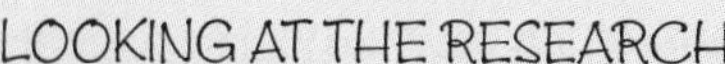

LOOKING AT THE RESEARCH

What the research says about encounters with words

Instruction of word meanings has been found to be highly effective for vocabulary learning (Tomeson & Aarnoutse, 1998; White, Graves, & Slater, 1990). The more connections learners make with a word the better. Making connections with other reading material or oral use of the same words in other contexts improves vocabulary learning (Dole, Sloan, & Trathen, 1995; Rinaldi, Sells, & McLaughlin, 1997). This means that we need to celebrate language when we are reading with children, when we are talking with children, and when we encourage children to write. We don't assign the use of certain words, but we encourage children to use interesting and exciting words they have encountered in reading in their speech and in their writing. We also model this for them.

Can you think of a teacher you once had who loved language and it showed? How did this person share his or her excitement for words with you?

A Variation on Word of the Day. A variation on the word of the day is to create a Word of the Day chart on which children, from first grade on, can write interesting words they have found in their reading, in the news, or elsewhere in their daily lives. They write the word on the chart, and during a class meeting they are asked to explain where they found the word, why they chose the word, and what it means. Children are encouraged to use words from the chart in their writing and speaking.

Literature Study Groups. When you organize your students in literature study groups (third grade and above), appoint one person in each group to be the word finder whose job it is to look for and record particularly interesting language. During a class meeting call on each word finder to share one or two of the words identified, to read the context in which the word was used, and perhaps to record the words on a large chart. You then lead a discussion with the class about the word choice the author used. Recording these words on a large chart keeps them accessible to your students who may wish to use them in their own writing.

Independent Reading. Provide your children, as early as first grade, with 3×5 index cards for use during independent reading. Encourage them to look for particularly interesting, lively, colorful uses of language. Record the sentence in which they found a word. Share these sentences and discuss the word meanings at the end of the independent reading period, or have children gather in small groups to share their chosen words.

Independent reading is one of the best ways to expand vocabulary, according to a research-supported theory espoused by Stephen Krashen (1985). His Input Hypothesis (IH) assumes that we acquire language by understanding messages. He argues that comprehensible input is essential—along with our brain's internal language acquisition device (Chomsky, 1975)—to vocabulary development. Research support for Krashen's theory is strong. The more children read, the better they perform on vocabulary tests (Anderson, Wilson, & Fielding, 1988; Greaney, 1980; Greaney & Hegarty, 1987; Krashen, 1985). This is also true for second language learners. Wells (1985) reported that children who heard more stories during preschool years had larger vocabularies. It is important for you to spend time reading to children and encouraging children to read on their own.

Revising Groups. Revising groups are relatively stable groups of approximately six children, second grade and older, who meet on a regular schedule to give each other verbal feedback on the writing members bring to the group to share. You could assign revising groups to search for particularly well-crafted, interesting use of language in the writing of group members. Members of the group are encouraged to point out such language, to engage the author in a discussion of his or her word choice, and perhaps to share some of these discoveries with the whole class. You must model this process during meetings with editing groups or during writing conferences before the children will be able to do it on their own.

We have suggested an array of possibilities for developing word consciousness in your learners. Our assumption is that you will pick and choose from these activities over time as you build other aspects of your vocabulary curriculum.

Assessment and Evaluation Toolbox

FIRST STEPS ORAL LANGUAGE DEVELOPMENTAL CONTINUUM

First Steps Oral Language Developmental Continuum is one part of a set of resources that provide you a framework for observing children as users of language and planning for their instruction. The oral language developmental continuum describes oral language development through eight stages. Key indicators are described for each phase. Included in the key indicators are criteria for vocabulary development such as: develops specific vocabulary to suit different purposes, uses appropriate specialized vocabulary and structures, and shows sophisticated understanding of the power and effect of spoken language. The First Steps continua are most effectively used when all of the teachers in a school are using them (Allen, 2001).

WHAT OTHER COMPONENTS SHALL I INCLUDE IN MY VOCABULARY CURRICULUM?

The research on vocabulary learning informs our answer to this question. Graves and Watts-Taffe (2000), in reviewing this research, propose a four-part vocabulary program: wide reading, teaching individual words, teaching strategies for learning words independently, and fostering word consciousness. The National Reading Panel (2000) concluded its review of the research with a set of implications for teaching vocabulary:

1. Vocabulary should be taught both directly and indirectly.
2. Repetition and multiple exposures to vocabulary items are important.
3. Learning in rich contexts is valuable for vocabulary learning.
4. Vocabulary tasks should be restructured when necessary.
5. Vocabulary learning should entail active engagement in learning tasks.
6. Computer technology can be used to help teach vocabulary.
7. Vocabulary can be acquired through incidental learning.
8. How vocabulary is assessed and evaluated can have differential effects on instruction.
9. Dependence on a single vocabulary instruction method will not result in optimal learning.

The work of Graves and Watts-Taffe and the work of the National Reading Panel have defined the parameters of a good program of vocabulary instruction.

Wide Reading

Wide reading means extensive reading. Wide reading means spending time each day engaged in reading with a variety of texts. In a sense, this whole textbook is about wide reading! Here we wish to underscore the importance of extensive reading to the development of vocabulary without repeating ideas we have included elsewhere in this text. We know that students learn vocabulary from their reading (Anderson, 1996). It is critically important that children read and read and read. Since many children do not read at home, it becomes imperative that we create time for them to read in school from kindergarten on.

Learners are more highly motivated when they are working on school activities that tap into their interests. Interest inventories are a tool that can help us reach this goal. Interest inventories are questionnaires developed by teachers to tap into children's interests. You can use this information to help learners select books for wide reading. Figures 7.2 through 7.4 illustrate three kinds of interest inventories. Use them as models and adapt them to your needs (Harp, 2000). Techniques for encouraging wide reading will be discussed in detail in Chapters 9 and 11.

Teaching Individual Words

One issue that immediately arises when one thinks about teaching individual words is what words to choose. Some of the best ways to deal with this dilemma are to look for vocabulary challenges in texts you are going to have children read, ask children which words are giving them difficulty, use graphic organizers, create word walls, teach words with special characteristics, and teach high-frequency words.

Previewing Texts for Challenging Vocabulary. As you are reading a text in preparation for sharing it with children, carefully consider terms that will be new to your students. Consider whether or not the term is a new label for a concept the children already have or if the term represents a new concept.

New Labels for Existing Concepts. If the vocabulary term under consideration is simply a new label for an existing concept, you may need only to explain the meaning of the term, perhaps have students read the dictionary definitions, and then decide which definition fits the current context. For example, suppose one of the characters in a book you are planning to use is discussing studying for a final exam. You know the children have the concept for something that is final, because they have talked about *final* in the context of races in physical education. You could discuss the relationship between the final heat in a race and a final exam in a course. You could have the children check the dictionary listings for *final:* something that is final (a) the deciding match, game, heat or trial; (b) the last examination in a course. In this case it should be fairly easy to expand their understanding of *final* because they already have a concept for it.

Labels for New Concepts. If you discover terminology in a text for which your learners do not have a concept, then you have a clear choice. Do not use the text at this time, or teach the children the concept. It is reasonable to decide that children do not yet have adequate background knowledge to make meaning from a text and that you should delay introducing it to them. If you decide to use the text, then an instructional procedure known as the Frayer Method may be useful (Frayer, Frederick, & Klausmeier, 1969). The

Figure 7.2
General Interest Inventory

Name ______________________________ Date ______________

1. What hobbies do you have?

2. Do you have any collections of things? What are they?

3. What are your favorite things to do after school? On weekends?

4. When you have free time, who do you like to spend it with?

5. How do you use your computer at home?

6. What are your favorite television programs?

7. What are your favorite movies?

8. If you could travel anywhere, what would be the three places you would go? Why?

Source: Harp, B. (2000). *The handbook of literacy assessment and evaluation.* Norwood, MA: Christopher Gordon. Reprinted with permission.

Figure 7.3
Reading and Writing Interest Inventory

Name ______________________________ Date ________________

1 What are your favorite books?

2. What kinds of books do you like to read?

3. When you write, what kinds of things do you most like to write about?

4. When do you like to write?

5. When do you like to read?

6. What do you think you should do to become a better reader?

7. What do you think you should do to become a better writer?

Source: Harp, B. (2000). *The handbook of literacy assessment and evaluation.* Norwood, MA: Christopher Gordon. Reprinted with permission.

Figure 7.4
School Interest Inventory

Name ______________________________ Date ______________

1. Which school subjects do you find most interesting?

2. If you could study anything you wanted in school, what would it be?

3. Of all the school subjects, which is your least favorite? Why?

4. Which subject would you most like to have homework in? Why?

5. Which subject would you least like to have homework in? Why?

6. If you could select themes to study in school (like mystery, adventure, ecology), which ones would you select and why?

7. Which section of the school library is your favorite?

8. Which computer software programs are your favorites? Why?

Source: Harp, B. (2000). *The handbook of literacy assessment and evaluation,* Norwood, MA: Christopher Gordon. Reprinted with permission.

Frayer Method is designed to teach new concepts. Assuming that the fourth graders you teach did not know the concept of pyramid, then you would follow the following procedure.

1. Define the concept of pyramid, giving it specific attributes. For example, you might say "A pyramid is a four-sided geometric shape composed of four triangles that meet in a point. The triangles are attached to a flat, square base. Demonstrate the pyramid shape with solid geometric blocks and with a paper cutout so that you can show the triangles and the flat base.
2. Distinguish between a pyramid and other shapes that are similar but different. For example, you could compare it to a cube, a cylinder, and a triangular prism.
3. Give examples of the concept and explain what makes them good examples. For example, you could show photos of the pyramid at the entrance to the Louvre and the Egyptian pyramids.
4. Provide nonexamples of the concept. For example, you might use plane geometric shapes and other solid geometric shapes that are not pyramids.
5. Present examples of the concept and nonexamples and ask the children to distinguish between them. You could present cubes, cylinders, triangles, and pyramids of different sizes.
6. Ask students to find examples and nonexamples and explain why they are examples or nonexamples. Provide feedback on their examples and explanations.

Helping children learn concepts is an important component of vocabulary instruction.

Asking Children Which Words Are Challenging. This may sound overly simple, but it can be effective, even with first graders. If you create a classroom climate that views mistakes as opportunities to learn, that rejects immediately "jumping on" someone's error, you will create a climate where children are comfortable saying, "This was a tricky word for me."

Writing Down Tricky Words. Whenever children are reading silently, give them 3 × 5 cards and ask them to write any "tricky" words they find on the card. When the children have silently read the assigned pages, have them share the tricky words with the group. Lead a discussion about the pronunciation and meaning of the words. Have each child write the definition and/or a sentence using the word on the back of the card.

LOOKING AT THE RESEARCH

What the research says about learning words

The best instructional techniques for learning new words are combinations of learning definitions, using context to understand new words, and the keyword method for remembering words (Stahl & Fairbanks, 1986).

After you read the section on the keyword method that follows, think of examples of learning activities you could design for learning definitions, using context to understand new words, and the keyword method.

Go to our Companion Website at www.prenhall.com//harp to add your ideas to the global discussion on the Threaded Message Board.

The Keyword Method. Studies have found the keyword method to be effective with children in grades three through eight. The studies have compared the keyword method with teaching meanings, using context, using pictures, and free study. In each case the keyword method proved superior, especially for at-risk students (Levin et al., 1984; Levin, McCormick, Miller, & Berry, 1982; Levin, Levin, Glasman, & Nordwall, 1992; McGivern & Levin, 1983). In the keyword method students create mental images to help them remember word meanings. You will need to guide younger learners in this process. Older children can learn to create the images independently. At first glance, the keyword method seems like a lot of effort to try to remember a word, but it is difficult to ignore the support this method has in the research.

The process begins by examining the word to be learned. Suppose a child is trying to remember the meaning of *aficionado* (a person who likes, knows about, appreciates, or feverently pursues an interest or activity). He examines the word to find a word of part of a word in the target word that can become the keyword. This may actually be a word or a group of letters. He selects as the keyword *fish.* He then forms a rich, detailed mental image that incorporates and key word and the meaning of the target word. In this example the student forms a mental image of a man who loves fishing so much that he carries his tackle box and fishing pole with him everywhere he goes. He carries them on the subway, to his office, to meetings, to the park—everywhere—just in case he will have a chance to fish. Another student is using the method to remember the meaning of *ameliorate* (to make better or more tolerable). She selects *a meal* as the keyword. Her mental image is of herself preparing a gourmet meal in her family's kitchen where she is using wonderful spices and excellent ingredients to make the meal better.

If you are having students make Important Word Books of the new words they are learning, they might include the keyword they have chosen for the target word with each of their entries. They could even draw an illustration of the mental image.

Teaching Words with Graphic Organizers. Two popular kinds of graphic organizers (useful in kindergarten and beyond) are semantic maps and structured overviews. **Semantic maps** use circles connected with lines to a central circle containing the target word. The connecting circles show the relationship of the words contained in them to the target word. **Structured overviews** are schematics that illustrate the relationships between concepts and related ideas. We will illustrate both of these graphic organizers in the next chapter on comprehension. Here, in the context of vocabulary development, we explore Venn diagrams and semantic feature analysis as ways to deepen understandings of word meanings.

Venn Diagrams. Venn diagrams are used to compare and contrast two concepts or subjects with children as young as first grade. They are overlapping circles. The characteristics unique to one concept are written in the left-hand circle, the characteristics unique to the other concept are listed in the right-hand circle, and the characteristics shared by the two concepts are written in the overlapping circles. Figure 7.5 illustrates a Venn diagram created by a group of third graders comparing airplanes and helicopters as part of a transportation unit.

Semantic Feature Analysis. A semantic feature analysis compares characteristics of items within a related group. The semantic feature analysis could be used before students read a selection to help activate background knowledge and focus on word meanings, or it could be used to review information after reading a text (Pittleman, Heimlich, Berglund, & French, 1991). The semantic feature analysis in Figure 7.6 illustrates a partially completed analysis done by a group of second graders after reading several books about bats.

A concept map helps build and reinforce vocabulary.

Figure 7.5
Venn Diagram for Airplanes and Helicopters

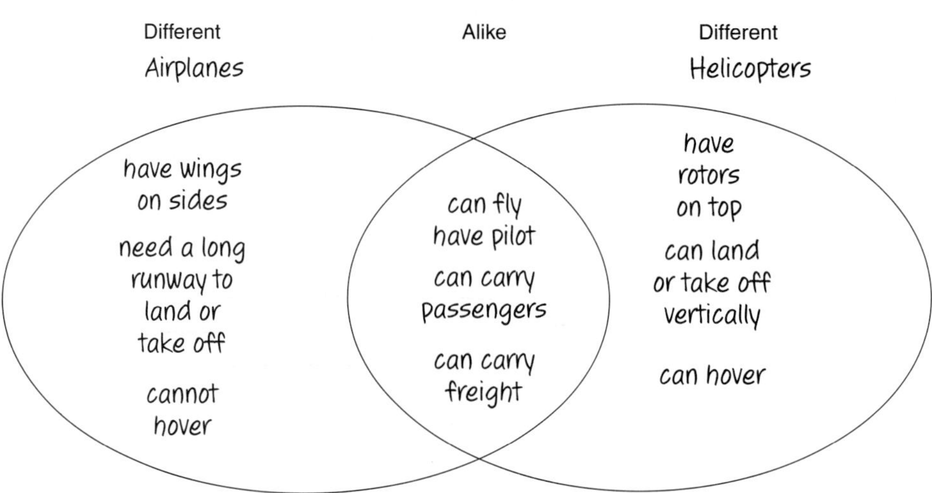

Creating Word Walls. Word walls, found in kindergarten classrooms and beyond, are displays of collections of words organized by some common criteria or characteristics. For example, a word wall could be created of interesting words encountered during a study of transportation. You and the children could share in the selection of words to be added to the wall. Another possibility is having children select a particularly interesting word encountered in a small group reading of a text. Each child in the group is invited to select a word from the reading selection he or she thinks is important enough for the whole group to learn. The group discusses the meaning of the word and uses the text to explore the context in which the word was used. The group may consult a dictionary, if necessary, to further understand the word's meaning. When the group has agreed on the meaning, the person selecting the word adds it, and a sentence using it, to the word wall. Students may also add the words and sentences to their Important Word Books.

Figure 7.6
Semantic Feature Analysis

	Mammal	Nocturnal	Hibernate	Eat Insects	Migrate
Little Brown Bat	✔				
Jamaican Fruit Bat	✔				
Mexican Free-Tailed Bat	✔			✔	✔
Giant Flying Fox	✔				
Epaulet Bat	✔				
Nectar Bat	✔				
Vampire Bat	✔				

Teaching Words with Special Characteristics. To understand the meanings of some words, children from second grade on must understand the special characteristics of those words. This applies to homonyms, homophones, and homographs.

Homonyms. Homonyms are words that are spelled the same but have different meanings.

> ***I've lost my* ring.**
> ***I guess you didn't hear the phone* ring.**
> ***You could run a* ring *around me as fast as you work.***
> ***Please clean the* ring *off the tub.***

Homographs. Homographs are words that are spelled the same but have different meanings and possibly different pronunciations. The context determines both pronunciation and meaning.

> ***Susan lives* close *to Juan.***
> ***Please* close *the door behind you.***
> ***The cold* wind *is blowing off the ocean.***
> ***Please be sure to* wind *the clock.***

Homophones. Homophones are words that are pronounced the same but have different spellings and meanings.

> ***The* deer *at the petting zoo were darling.***
> ***You are a darling, my* dear.**
> ***I* would *come see you if I could, but I have to chop* wood.**
> ***In that tuxedo he certainly* complements *his wife.***
> ***One secret to their success: he* compliments *his wife daily.***

You are likely to discover that you will need to teach carefully the concepts of homonym, homograph, and homophone and reinforce this instruction frequently. The subtle distinctions between these groups of words are difficult for children to grasp. Teach the concept by explaining, for example, what a homonym is and then create a spot in the classroom to list homonyms as children discover them in reading. Guide the children's discovery of them in text by pointing out that there is a homonym on the page they are reading and challenge them to find it. Remember the research says it is best for children to have multiple encounters with words in meaningful contexts. This is why it is good to reinforce this teaching time and again as children are reading. Another category of language with special characteristics is figurative language.

Figurative Language. Figurative language includes figures of speech and idiomatic expressions. Idioms are peculiar to a given language and cannot be translated literally (Harris & Hodges, 1995). **Figures of speech** are expressive, nonliteral uses of language for special effects and idiomatic expressions are statements that do not mean what they literally say. Figures of speech are often either **similes** (a comparison of two things that are unlike, usually using the words *like* or *as*) or **metaphors** (a comparison implied by analogy, but not stated).

A simile would be, "The willow is like an etching, fine-lined against the sky" (Merriam, 1973, p. 43) or "I could feel the cold, as if someone's icy hand was palm-down on my back" (Yolen, 1987). An example of a metaphor is, "But I was a shadow as we walked home" (Yolen, 1987).

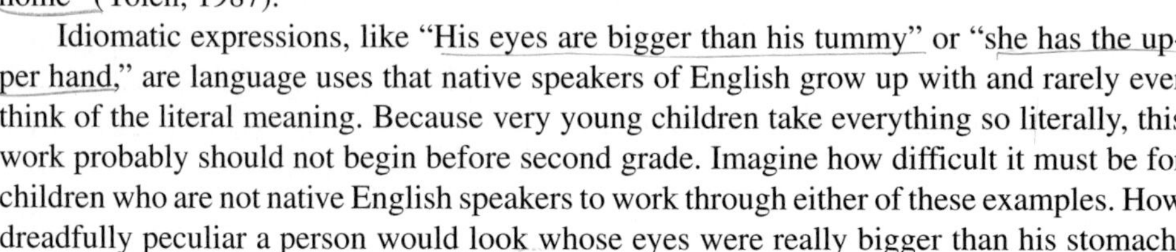

Idiomatic expressions, like "His eyes are bigger than his tummy" or "she has the upper hand," are language uses that native speakers of English grow up with and rarely ever think of the literal meaning. Because very young children take everything so literally, this work probably should not begin before second grade. Imagine how difficult it must be for children who are not native English speakers to work through either of these examples. How dreadfully peculiar a person would look whose eyes were really bigger than his stomach, and having the upper hand has absolutely nothing to do with hands.

You can introduce children to the fun of double meanings and the notion of "she doesn't really mean what she said" by introducing them to the *Amelia Bedelia* books by Peggy Parrish. Children delight in Amelia's literal interpretations of Mrs. Roger's instructions to draw the drapes and dress the chicken. You can introduce them to similes and metaphors by sharing favorite poems with them and helping them understand particularly beautiful uses of figurative language. You will have to take careful pains (there is an example) to help nonnative speakers of English deal with figurative language. Some teachers keep lists of figures of speech posted on the wall and add to the list as children make new discoveries.

Paying Attention to Word Genres. One way of collecting and learning words is to make collections on charts of words that belong to different categories or genres. This work is probably best begun at about fourth grade. For example, portmanteau words are words that are made of two other words such as combining *breakfast* and *lunch* to make *brunch,* or *motor* and *hotel* to make *motel.* The category of acronym words includes words made from the first letters of their descriptions such as *scuba* (**s**elf-**c**ontained **u**nderwater **b**reathing **a**pparatus) and *radar* (**ra**dio **d**etecting **a**nd **r**anging). Borrowed words are words taken directly from other languages and used in English. Examples include *café, lariat, pretzel, ambiance,* and *lingerie.* Oxymorons are phrases in which the words seem to contradict themselves such as *student teacher* and *plastic silverware.* Palindromes are words or phrases that read the same forwards and backwards such as *mom* and *dad.* Eponyms are words that originated from a person's name such as *diesel, silhouette, sandwich,* and *leotard.* Onomatopoeia are words whose sounds are related to their meanings such as *buzz* or *gulp.* Collective words are words that label a group, usually a group of animals, such as *gaggle, pride,* or *covey.*

Teaching High-Frequency Words. There is risk in including a subheading on high-frequency words in this chapter. One might mistakenly conclude that we could help children achieve vocabulary mastery if we were to teach them a given set of high-frequency words. We know that children learn vocabulary better when they encounter vocabulary

words frequently and in various ways. They need to encounter vocabulary terms across a variety of meaningful contexts (National Reading Panel, 2000). We also know that much vocabulary learning is incidental and that children learn many more words than we alone can teach them.

ssessment and Evaluation Toolbox

COMPREHENSIVE RECEPTIVE AND EXPRESSIVE VOCABULARY TEST (CREVT)

The CREVT is a norm-referenced test suitable for use with children between 4 years of age and 17 years, 11 months. The CREVT tests receptive vocabulary by showing children pictures and asking them to point to a picture of the spoken word. Expressive vocabulary is tested by asking children to describe stimulus words in some detail. The test is used to identify students significantly below their peers in oral vocabulary proficiency (Wallace & Hammill, 1994). Low scores on either receptive or expressive vocabulary would alert you to take this information to the Student Assistance Team (as described in Chapter 4).

Yet, it seems worthwhile to note that some vocabulary words occur more often than others in the reading and writing children do. Edward Fry (1980) has compiled a list of 300 words that make up about 65% of all written material. The first 10 words make up about 24% of all written material, and the first 100 words make up about 50% of all written material. Fry's New Instant Word List is displayed in Figure 7.7.

We include this word list for two reasons. You may be surprised that so few words comprise so large a portion of written material, and you may want to consult this list when you are selecting words to teach.

Another well-known list of high-frequency words is the Dolch Basic Sight Word List. It was published by Edward Dolch in 1936, so some of the words (*shall,* for example) are out of date. It lists 220 words common to beginning reading instruction broken down into 11 lists by frequency.

Teaching Strategies for Learning Words Independently

If children's vocabularies are to grow, we must motivate them to want to learn new words, and we must give them the tools necessary for learning words independently. This includes teaching them how to use dictionaries and other reference aids to learn new words, how to use word parts, and how to use context clues to determine word meanings.

Using Dictionaries and Other Reference Aids. What do you do when you are reading and you come to a word you don't know, a word that is not in your sight vocabulary? If you are like most readers, you ignore the word hoping that you can still make meaning without it. When you discover that you can no longer ignore the word, you probably try to use cues in the text to figure out the word and its meaning. If this still does not work, you probably turn to the dictionary. In fact, next to the use of text-based cues, the use of the dictionary

Figure 7.7
Fry's New Instant Word List

The first 10 words make up about 24% of all written material, the first 100 words about 50% of all written material, and the first 300 about 65%.

1. the
2. of
3. and
4. a
5. to
6. in
7. is
8. you
9. that
10. it
11. he
12. was
13. for
14. on
15. are
16. as
17. with
18. his
19. they
20. I
21. at
22. be
23. this
24. have
25. from
26. or
27. one
28. had
29. by
30. words
31. but
32. not
33. what
34. all
35. were
36. we
37. when
38. your
39. can
40. said
41. there
42. use
43. an
44. each
45. which
46. she
47. do
48. how
49. their
50. if
51. will
52. up
53. other
54. about
55. out
56. many
57. then
58. them
59. these
60. so
61. some
62. her
63. would
64. make
65. like
66. him
67. into
68. time
69. has
70. look
71. two
72. more
73. write
74. go
75. see
76. number
77. no
78. way
79. could
80. people
81. my
82. than
83. first
84. water
85. been
86. called
87. who
88. oil
89. its
90. now
91. find
92. long
93. down
94. day
95. did
96. get
97. come
98. made
99. may
100. part
101. over
102. new
103. sound
104. take
105. only
106. little
107. work
108. know
109. place
110. years
111. live
112. me
113. back
114. give
115. most
116. very
117. after
118. things
119. our
120. just
121. name
122. good
123. sentence
124. man
125. think
126. say
127. great
128. where
129. help
130. through
131. much
132. before
133. line
134. right
135. too
136. means
137. old
138. any
139. same
140. tell
141. boy
142. following
143. came
144. want
145. show
146. also
147. around
148. form
149. three
150. small
151. set
152. put
153. end
154. does
155. another
156. well
157. large
158. must
159. big
160. even
161. such
162. because
163. turned
164. here
165. why
166. asked
167. went
168. men
169. read
170. need
171. land
172. different
173. home
174. us
175. move
176. try
177. kind
178. hand
179. picture
180. again
181. change
182. off
183. play
184. spell
185. air
186. away
187. animals
188. house
189. point
190. page
191. letters
192. mother
193. answer
194. found
195. study
196. still
197. learn
198. should
199. American
200. world
201. high
202. every
203. near
204. add
205. food
206. between
207. own
208. below
209. country
210. plants
211. last
212. school
213. father
214. keep
215. trees
216. never
217. started
218. city
219. earth
220. eyes
221. light
222. thought
223. head
224. under
225. story
226. saw
227. left
228. don't
229. few
230. while
231. along
232. might
233. close
234. something
235. seemed
236. next
237. hard
238. open
239. example
240. beginning
241. life
242. always
243. those
244. both
245. paper
246. together
247. got
248. group
249. often
250. run
251. important
252. until
253. children
254. side
255. feet
256. car
257. miles
258. night
259. walked
260. white
261. sea
262. began
263. grow
264. look
265. river
266. four
267. carry
268. state
269. once
270. book
271. hear
272. stop
273. without
274. second
275. later
276. miss
277. idea
278. enough
279. eat
280. face
281. watch
282. far
283. Indians
284. really
285. almost
286. let
287. above
288. girl
289. sometimes
290. mountains
291. cut
292. young
293. talk
294. soon
295. list
296. song
297. being
298. leave
299. family
300. it's

Source: Word list from Fry, Edward B. (1980, December). The New Instant Word List. *The Reading Teacher, 34* (3), 284–289.

may be the most helpful route to the pronunciation and meaning of an unfamiliar word (when there is no one to ask).

Helping Young Children Appreciate Dictionaries. It is important that children see the dictionary as a valuable tool early in their reading and writing experiences in the hope that its use will pose no threat in later grades. Here are some ways to help young children become comfortable with the dictionary:

1. Make alphabetized Important Word Books or language-experience dictionaries in which to record words that children have wanted to use in their writing. Working with these projects, children become accustomed to alphabetical order early.
2. Place picture dictionaries and beginning dictionaries in the classroom reading corner and model their use with young readers and authors.
3. Share larger dictionaries in the media center with children and talk about their use.
4. Help children see that words have more than one meaning and that those meanings are defined in the dictionary.

Dictionary Skills Lessons Versus Integrated Use. How should dictionary use be taught? Should you plan isolated lessons in dictionary skills, or should reference to the dictionary be integrated with real reading and writing activities? In a sense, the answer is yes to both alternatives. Use of the dictionary should be integrated with reading and writing activities through carefully planned lessons on dictionary use. When an unknown word turns up while you are sharing a reading experience with children, that is the time for you to help children turn to the dictionary. Keeping dictionaries on the reading table or in the writing center facilitates this integration. Consulting the dictionary for real purposes in real situations will foster its use far better than skill-and-drill activities in workbooks or with worksheets.

Dictionary Skills. The skilled use of the dictionary is a developmental process that continues throughout the grades. Consulting the curriculum guide for a given grade level will determine the skills to be taught at the grade level. Most elementary school programs include the following goals for dictionary use:

1. Use alphabetical order for everyday things; at first, go only by initial letter, and later add second, third, and more letters.
2. Learn to open the dictionary near the word sought.
3. Use guide words to find the page on which the desired word is located.
4. Use diacritical marks to produce the correct pronunciation of words.
5. Use the pronunciation key and phonetic respellings of words.
6. Identify several meanings of words.
7. Be able to select the meaning that fits the text being read.
8. Develop an attitude that says, "Let's look it up!"

Using a Glossary. That "Let's look it up" attitude will extend to the use of glossaries if you model this behavior. At the same time you are teaching children to use the dictionary, locate some texts that include a glossary in the back. Show your students the similarities between the dictionary and the glossary. When your whole class is writing a class book or a small group of children is writing an expository book together, encourage them to include a glossary of important terms.

Using the Thesaurus. By the time children are in the third grade, it is appropriate to introduce them to the use of the thesaurus. You may find it most useful to introduce your students to the thesaurus as a function of editing written drafts. Children tend to use repeatedly the same comfortable or familiar word without thinking about alternatives. When you see this in a piece of writing, demonstrate the use of a thesaurus or the thesaurus function in the word processing program. When children begin writing dialogue, they typically overuse the word *nice.* By activating the thesaurus function in the word processing program the following synonyms for *nice* were identified: pleasant, good, kind, polite, and fine. Using the thesaurus will help children choose more interesting, descriptive language as writers and aid their independent vocabulary growth.

An interesting way to get children thinking about using alternative language in their writing is to engage them in brainstorming all of the words they can think of to occupy a given slot in a sentence. Select a sentence from your own writing or have children volunteer a sentence they have written. Write it on the board, and list all of the words you and the class can think of that might occupy a given place in the sentence. Children enjoy keeping a graph of the number of words they were able to generate each time they engage in this activity.

Another thesaurus activity is to rewrite a known nursery rhyme with more complex language. For example, given Three Blind Mice, one fifth grader wrote:

> *A trio of visually impaired rodents,*
> *Observe how they ambulate,*
> *The group chased the agrarian workers spouse,*
> *She amputated their rear appendages with a sharpened blade,*
> *Did you ever visualize such an apparition in your existence as a trio of visually impaired rodents?*

Using the thesaurus is also a good time to teach children about synonyms and antonyms. Synonyms are words that have highly similar meanings, as *sadness, grief,* and *sorrow.* Antonyms are words that are opposite in meaning.

Using Electronic Dictionaries and Thesauruses. The skills needed for using a traditional dictionary and thesaurus are not needed when students use the electronic versions. In most word processing programs, one can highlight a word and click on either the dictionary or the thesaurus to get information about the spelling and definitions or about synonyms and antonyms. Since the electronic versions are what most of the children will be using most of the time, do not spend too much time on traditional dictionary skills. The thrust of your instruction should be to help children write well and comprehend their reading, so spend most of the instructional time in activities that will achieve this goal.

An activity to help fourth graders learn more about synonyms from the thesaurus is to examine the sports headlines from the newspaper for several days. Sports writers tend to avoid the use of win or lose, but have wonderful synonyms for winning and losing in the headlines. Consider these examples all from *The Boston Globe* in August 2002: "Missing their mark," "Soriano sparks Yankees past A's," "Postseason tuneup goes the Starzz' way," "New York turns back Middlesex in shootout," and "Sox take a fall."

Using Word Parts. Using word parts to unlock word meanings entails using prefixes and suffixes (together known as *affixes*) as well as root words and compound words. This work begins at second grade. Affixes are word parts that are attached to either the beginnings of words (prefixes) or the endings of words (suffixes). Prefixes modify the meanings of words to which they are attached. Suffixes either alter the meaning or the grammatical function of the words to which they are attached.

Compound Words. Compound words are a combination of two or more words that function as a single unit of meaning. Compound words are written as a single word (booklist), hyphenated words (books-on-demand), or separately (book report) (Harris & Hodges, 1995). The teaching task with compound words is to help children see the separate words that make up the compound, to understand the individual meanings, and then to be able to

Figure 7.8
Most Frequently Occurring Prefixes

Prefix	Number of Words with the Prefix
un-	782
re-	401
in-, im, ir, il- (not)	313
dis-	216
en-, em-	132
non-	126
in-, im- (in or into)	105
over-	98
mis-	83
sub-	80
pre-	79
inter-	77
fore-	76
de-	71
trans-	47
Total	2,686

Source: White, T. G., Sowell, J., & Yanagihara, A. (1989). Teaching elementary students to use word-part clues. *The Reading Teacher, 42,* 302–308. Reprinted with permission.

explain the combined meanings. Choose with care the words you use to illustrate compound words. A student teacher was flummoxed one day when she used *hangup* to illustrate compound words and she took the meaning to be placing a phone on its cradle. This term is not a single compound word; it can be used as a hyphenated word or as a two-word descriptor (that call was a hang up).

Prefixes. Prefixes are added to the beginning of words to alter their meaning. Our experience suggests that it is easier for children to learn prefixes than suffixes. White and his colleagues (1989) have identified the most commonly occurring prefixes in English used in school. These prefixes are used in 2,686 words, and the four most frequently appearing occur in 65% of these words. This list is exhibited in Figure 7.8. You could use this research to inform your instruction. Beginning in about third grade, select the most frequently occurring prefixes to teach, and gradually work your way down the list.

Prefix instruction is similar to the strategy instruction we described in Chapter 6. We need to show children how the information will be helpful to their quest of becoming better readers as we teach them, in this case, about prefixes. A prefix introductory lesson might look like the following.

1. Explain the concept of prefix, which is added to the beginning of a word to alter its meaning.
2. Explain how understanding this can help a reader unlock the meaning to an unfamiliar word.
3. Demonstrate prefix function. In the case of prefix *un-* show children how adding this prefix to words they know alters the meaning. Write *happy* on the board or overhead projector. Talk with children about the meaning of *happy.* Then ask them to watch what you do as you add *un-* to the beginning of the word. Ask if anyone can explain the meaning of the revised word. Point out that the prefix, *un-,* altered the meaning.

4. Reinforce this understanding with other words, some you offer and some the children may suggest. You might begin with *friendly, likely, American,* and *tie.*
5. Encourage children to identify *un-* words in their reading. Perhaps you will want to make a collective class list of the discoveries or have children add them to their personal dictionaries or Important Word Books.

The key to good instruction about prefixes is that children come to recognize the prefix visually—almost like a sight word. They come to understand the meaning of the prefix and therefore can explain how the prefix alters the meaning of the word to which it is attached. You will likely find a scope and sequence chart for common prefixes in your school district's literacy curriculum guide.

Suffixes. Suffixes are more complicated than prefixes because there are two forms: derivational suffixes and inflectional suffixes. Derivational suffixes change the words to which they are added into another part of speech. For example, *-some* forms adjectives as in changing the noun *trouble* into an adjective, *troublesome.* And *-age* forms nouns as in changing *post* to *postage.* Inflectional suffixes express plurality or possession when added to a noun (*boys* or *boy's);* tense when added to a verb (*hopped* or *hopping);* and comparison when added to an adjective and some adverbs (*funnier, funniest, hesitantly, quickly*) (Harris & Hodges, 1995).

The process of teaching suffixes is similar to the process we described previously for teaching prefixes. One significant difference is that while prefixes rarely change the part of speech a word reflects, suffixes frequently do. Or suffixes change the inflected ending. Learning suffixes not only involves recognizing the suffix as a visual entity, but knowing how the suffix acts on the word. You can follow the process we described previously for teaching prefixes to teach suffixes. It would be effective to add a think-aloud demonstration by you of how to use suffixes to unlock word meanings.

Suppose you were reading the sentence: *The boy's uncle was his legal guardian.* Your think-aloud demonstration might sound like this: "Students, I am going to do a think aloud for you to demonstrate how to use the suffix *-ian* and root word *guard.* Suppose I was reading the sentence on the board and was not sure of the meaning of *guardian.* I might use my knowledge of suffixes to help me work it out. I see the *-ian* at the end of the word. I recognize that as a suffix. I know the meaning of *-ian.* It means 'one who.' So in the word *guardian* I predict the meaning to be 'one who guards.' When I think of one who guards, my first thought is a guard at the gate to an airplane, or the guard at the entrance of City Hall. But I don't think that meaning of guard fits in this sentence: The boy's uncle was his legal guardian. So I am going to predict that guardian means a person who takes care of the boy rather than someone who is a guard. I am going to reread the sentence and see if the meaning I have worked out makes sense, and if it continues to make sense as I read further." This kind of thinking aloud of your use of word parts is exactly the kind of demonstrations children need as they are learning to make meaning of suffixes. Repeat this kind of demonstration until you determine that your students can do this thinking themselves.

You can draw on the research of White, Sowell, and Yanagihara (1989) in deciding which suffixes to teach if you don't have a curriculum guide. They determined the most frequently occurring suffixes. Their list, represented in Figure 7.9, may be useful to you in making instructional decisions. However, the best way to decide what suffixes to teach may be to preview the texts your students will read and identify suffixes you wish to teach.

Root Words. The root of a word is the basic part of the word that usually carries the main component of meaning and that cannot be further analyzed without loss of identity (Harris & Hodges, 1995). For example, *happy* is a root word that, if analyzed further, would lose its meaning. If you remove the *py* from *happy* you no longer have the word. One may

Figure 7.9
Most Frequently Occurring Suffixes

-er (one who);	-ity (state of);
-(t)ion (act of);	-ment (state of);
-able (is or can be);	-ic (like, having the nature of);
-ible (is or can be);	-ous or -ious (having or being);
-al (having);	-en (made of);
-ial (function of);	-ive (of, belonging to, quality of);
-y (being or having);	-ful (full of or having);
-ness (having);	-less (without).

Source: White, T. G., Sowell, J., & Yanagihara, A. (1989). Teaching elementary students to use word-part clues. *The Reading Teacher, 42,* 302–308. Reprinted with permission.

add affixes to *happy* to create *un-happy* or *happ-ily,* for example. A root word to which affixes may be added to create other forms of the word is also known as a *base word.* Another example of a base word would be *think,* as in *re*think, *re*think*ing,* or *un*think*able.*

Root words may be either free or bound. A free root word is a base word that stands alone to communicate meaning but may be altered with the addition of affixes. Examples are words such as *happy* and *think.* A bound morpheme does not stand alone as a word, but is useful only when it is part of a larger word. These are typically Greek and Latin roots. Examples are *tele* (which means distance) as in *telephone, telegraph,* or *television* and *ology* (which means the study of) as in *biology, geology,* and *pharmacology.*

Seize every opportunity to help your learners deepen their understandings of root words. Teach them the concepts of free and bound roots. Preview text before you assign its reading, looking especially for root words that may be new or that will provide an opportunity for review. The chapter appendix on pages 245–251 displays Greek and Latin affixes and roots. Consult your school's curriculum guide to discern which roots and affixes to teach, or select from the lists in the chapter appendix. Perhaps your best guide to the word parts to teach are the words found in the materials your students are reading.

Using Context Cues. You learned at the beginning of this chapter that students learn between 3,000 and 4,000 words per year. Most of the words they learn, they learn without our direct intervention. Most of the words they learn, they learn from listening. Some of the words they learn, they learn from reading. The more they read, the more words they learn. The use of cues resident in the text helps readers unlock unfamiliar words. These are called **context clues.**

There are some general understandings children can learn about context cues.

- Context cues can help me learn words I do not know. They may help me pronounce the word, but they will probably be more helpful in discovering the word's meaning.
- Words, phrases, and sentences around the unknown word may tell me something about it.
- Really helpful cues are close to the unknown word, usually in the same sentence.

Children need repeated exposures to seeing how context cues can be helpful. Recall that in Chapter 6 you learned that quality strategy instruction (and using context cues is certainly a strategy) involves making certain that the strategy is sensible to students, that they understand why the strategy should be learned, and that they receive a step-by-step explanation of the strategy. Your demonstrations of the use of context cues when you read to your learners, using think-alouds, and your coaching them in using context cues when you are sharing reading experiences with them are two powerful teaching opportunities.

Types of Context Cues. We introduced the idea of using the syntax of a sentence to help decode unfamiliar words in Chapter 5. Recall the sentence: *In their biting and tumbling, the rambunctious puppies overturned their water dish.* We identified *rambunctious* as an adjective modifying the noun *puppies.* We used the knowledge that the dish was overturned to further add meaning to *rambunctious.* The syntactic cues are useful in both decoding and comprehending words. Many other clues to word meaning are imbedded within text.

Another form of context cue is definition. The definition of a word or term is presented in a sentence following the use of the word. For example:

A good way to help children develop the use of context cues is to use think-alouds. This is a demonstration by you of your thinking as you work through getting the meaning of the word.

Another form of context cue is appositives. The definition of the word is supplied immediately after the unknown word. For example:

The Developmental Reading Inventory, a form of miscue analysis, is a sound way to measure a child's reading success.

Synonyms are another context cue. The synonym usually appears following the unknown word. Note the use of the synonym, *context cues,* in the second sentence:

Using syntax, looking for words in apposition to other words, and searching for synonyms are all useful ways to assign meaning to a word. These context cues require careful teaching and repeated practice.

Writers sometimes place examples in a text to help the reader bring meaning to the text. In the following sentence the author provides an example for *strategies.*

We know that learning skills such as decoding sound symbol relationships help readers develop fluency, but so does the use of strategies, such as asking "Does that look right?"

This chapter has identified many ways you can teach your students word meanings and ways in which they can learn to be independent in bringing meaning to unfamiliar words. One last possibility bears mention: the possible use of computers to teach vocabulary.

LOOKING AT THE RESEARCH

What the research says about using computers to teach vocabulary

The National Reading Panel recommends the use of computers to teach vocabulary, and the research of Reinking and Rickman (1990) supports this approach. In their study of sixth graders, Reinking and Rickman provided three forms

LOOKING AT THE RESEARCH Continued

of vocabulary instruction. One group of students read passages printed on paper and had available standard dictionaries and a glossary. One group of students read passages on a computer screen with a program designed to give optional assistance to the reader as the reader commanded. Another group of readers used a computer program that provided mandatory assistance on the meanings of targeted words. The results revealed that students who used the computer programs scored significantly better on vocabulary tests than did the students who read printed text and had dictionaries and glossaries available to them. The computer group using the mandatory, automatic assistance outperformed the paper-text group on a measure of comprehension. These results suggest that you may want to search for computer programs that provide students with text to read and automatic vocabulary assistance.

Software is available for handheld computers with which students can read whole books on the screen. With some software, when the reader taps an unknown word with the stylus, the dictionary definition of the word appears on the screen. This may be an exciting way to encourage children to do more independent reading, which you know increases vocabulary knowledge. In what ways can you imagine e-books increasing enthusiasm for independent reading?

HOW WILL I KNOW A GOOD VOCABULARY PROGRAM WHEN I SEE ONE?

To answer this important question we turn to the work of Blachowicz and Fisher (2002). They have created a classroom checklist for teachers to use in evaluating their vocabulary instruction. The checklist is presented in Figure 7.10. We hope you will find this useful in your classroom and modify it as you gain more experience and greater knowledge about vocabulary development.

THINKING AS A TEACHER

1. You remember vocabulary work as copying definitions from the dictionary and then having a test on the words. You have learned that this is still a common assignment for elementary teachers to make even if the evidence is clear that it is not an effective practice. With your group, discuss the reasons why this kind of instruction continues in schools and how you can help make a change in this instruction when you have your own classroom.
2. In most classrooms, children groan when the teacher mentions vocabulary work. How will you overcome these negative feelings in your own classroom?
3. Make a list of activities for learning vocabulary words that you remember from your own elementary years. Compare your list with the lists of your peers. Are some activities common to most lists? If you like these activities, think about what made them enjoyable and effective. If you did not like these activities, think about what it was that made you have negative feelings about them. What do your answers tell you about vocabulary instruction?

Figure 7.10
How Will I Know a Good Vocabulary Program When I See One?

Word-Rich Environment

Teacher shows enthusiasm for words and word learning:

_____ Daily read-aloud
_____ Word of day or word activity of day
_____ Students indicate teacher *loves* word and word play
_____ Understand differences and connections between spelling, phonics, and vocabulary

Classroom shows physical signs of word awareness:

_____ Word charts or word walls (showing student input)
_____ Books on words, word play, specialized dictionaries (where students can easily access them)
_____ Labels in classroom
_____ Word games
_____ Puzzle books and software
_____ Student-made word books, alphabet books, dictionaries

Builds the Base for Independence

_____ Students show enthusiasm for words and word learning and are responsible for their own learning
_____ Spend part of each day reading on appropriate level
_____ Can name a favorite word book, puzzle activity, and/or game
_____ Have personal dictionaries or word logs
_____ Can use dictionary on appropriate level
_____ Have a strategy for dealing with unknown words
_____ Have strategies for self-selection and self-study
_____ Develop a knowledge base for independent strategies (word parts, context, word references, and so on)
_____ Develop strategies for using knowledge base

Models, Supports, and Develops Good Strategies

_____ Rich instruction on content area vocabulary words where definitional and contextual information provided
_____ Use of mapping, webbing, and other graphics to show word relationships
_____ Multiple exposures to see, hear, write, and use new words
_____ Wide reading with follow-up discussion of new words
_____ Emphasis on students using strategies
_____ Word play and motivation activities

Uses Varied Assessment

_____ Differ depending on goal
_____ Differ depending on entry knowledge level of learners
_____ Assess both depth and breadth

Source: Blachowicz, C., & Fisher, P. J. (2002). *Teaching vocabulary in all classrooms.* Upper Saddle River, NJ: Merrill//Prentice Hall, p. 15.

FIELD-BASED ACTIVITIES

1. Visit with a computer teacher who works with children in fifth through eighth grade. Investigate the software this teacher uses to teach vocabulary. Ask if you can see some of the software in operation. Inquire about the teacher's opinion of the software currently available and what he or she hopes future software will present.
2. Show the checklist in Figure 7.11 to several teachers. Try to include a third-grade, fifth-grade, and seventh- or eighth-grade teacher in the group. Ask each teacher to review the checklist with you in terms of the appropriateness for his or her assigned grade level. Compare and contrast their reactions.
3. Plan a vocabulary lesson for a group of young children in which you use a real object or objects. Plan a similar lesson for older children in which you could use actual objects.

REFERENCES

Allen, L. (2001). *Oral language developmental continuum.* Port Melbourne, Victoria, Australia: Rigby Heinemann.

Anderson, R., Wilson, P., & Fielding, L. (1988). Growth in reading and how children spend their time outside of school. *Reading Research Quarterly, 23,* 285–303.

Anderson, R. C., & Nagy, W. E. (1992, Winter). The vocabulary. *American Educator, 16,* 14–18, 44–47.

Anderson, R. C. (1996). Research foundations to support wide reading. In V. Greaney (Ed.), *Promoting reading in developing countries* (pp. 55–77). Newark, DE: International Reading Association.

Anglin, J. M. (1993). Vocabulary development: A morphological analysis. *Monographs of the Society for Research in Child Development, 58*(10), 1–186.

Blachowicz, C., & Fisher, P. J. (2002). *Teaching vocabulary in all classrooms.* Upper Saddle River, NJ: Pearson Education.

Chomsky, N. (1975). *Reflections on language.* New York: Pantheon.

Clark, E. V. (1993). *The lexicon in acquisition.* Cambridge, England: Cambridge University Press.

Davis, F. B. (1942). Two new measures of reading ability. *Journal of Educational Psychology, 33,* 365–372.

Dolch, E. W. (1936). A basic sight vocabulary. *Elementary School Journal, 36,* 456–468.

Dole, J. A., Sloan, C., & Trathen, W. (1995). Teaching vocabulary within the context of literature. *Journal of Reading, 38,* 452–460.

Dunn, L. M., & Dunn, L. M. (2003). *The picture vocabulary test–III.* Circle Pines, MN: American Guidance Service.

Eller, G., Pappas, C. C., & Brown, E. (1988). The lexical development of kindergartners: Learning from written context. *Journal of Reading Behavior, 20,* 5–24.

Frayer, D. A., Frederick, W. D., & Klausmeier, H. J. (1969). *A schema for testing the level of concept mastery* (Working Paper No. 16). Madison, WI: Wisconsin Research and Development Center for Cognitive Learning.

Fry, E. (1980). The new instant word list. *The Reading Teacher, 34,* 284–289.

Graves, M. F. (1986). Vocabulary learning and instruction. In E. Z. Rothkopf & L. C. Ehri (Eds.), *Review of research in education* (Vol. 13, pp. 49–89). Washington, DC: American Educational Research Association.

Graves, M. F., & Watts-Taffe, S. M. (2002). The place of word consciousness in a research-based vocabulary program. In A. E. Farstrup & S. J. Samuels (Eds.), *What research has to say about reading instruction.* Newark, DE: International Reading Association.

Greaney, V. (1980). Factors relating to amount and type of leisure time reading. *Reading Research Quarterly, 15,* 337–357.

Greaney, V., & Hegarty, M. (1987). Correlations of leisure-time reading. *Journal of Research in Reading, 10,* 3–20.

Green, G. M. (1989). *Pragmatics and natural language understanding.* Hillsdale, NJ: Lawrence Erlbaum.

Harp, B. (2000). *The handbook of literacy assessment and evaluation.* Norwood, NA: Christopher Gordon.

Harris, T. L., & Hodges, R. E. (1995). *The literacy dictionary: The vocabulary of reading and writing.* Newark, DE: International Reading Association.

Herman, P. A., Anderson, R. C., Pearson, R. D., & Nagy, W. E. (1987). Incidental acquisition of word meaning from expositions with varied text features. *Reading Research Quarterly, 22,* 263–284.

Krashen, S. (1985). *The input hypothesis: Issues and implications.* New York: Longman.

Levin, J. R., Levin, M. E., Glasman, L. D., & Nordwall, M. B. (1992). Mnemonic vocabulary instruction: Additional effectiveness evidence. *Contemporary Educational Psychology, 17,* 156–174.

Levin, J., Johnson, D., Pittelman, S., Levin, K., Shriberg, L., Toms-Bronowski, S., & Hayes, B. (1984). A comparison of semantic-and mnemonic-based vocabulary-learning strategies. *Reading Psychology, 5,* 1–15.

Levin, J., McCormick, C., Miller, G., & Berry, J. (1982). Mnemonic versus nonmnemonic vocabulary-learning strategies for children. *American Educational Research Journal, 19,* 121–136.

McGivern, J. E., & Levin, J. R. (1983). The keyword method and children's vocabulary learning. An interaction with vocabulary knowledge. *Contemporary Educational Psychology, 8,* 46–54.

Nagy, W. (1997). On the role of context in first- and second-language vocabulary learning. In N. Schmitt & M. McCarthy (Eds.), *Vocabulary: Description, acquisition and pedagogy* (pp. 64–83). Cambridge, England: Cambridge University Press.

Nagy, W. E., & Scott, J. A. (2000). Vocabulary processes. In M.L. Kamil, P. B. Mosenthal, P. D. Pearson, & R. Barr (Eds.), *The handbook of reading research, Vol. III* (pp. 269–281). Mahwah, NJ: Lawrence Erlbaum.

National Reading Panel. (2000). *Report of the national reading panel.* Washington, DC: Author.

Pittleman, S. D., Heimlich, J. E., Berglund, R. L., & French, M. P. (1991). *Semantic feature analysis: Classroom applications.* Newark, DE: International Reading Association.

Reinking, D., & Rickman, S. S. (1990). The effects of computer-mediated texts on the vocabulary learning and comprehension of intermediate-grade readers. *Journal of Reading Behavior, 22,* 395–409.

Rinaldi, L., Sells, D., & McLaughlin, T. F. (1997). The effects of reading racetracks on the sight word acquisition and fluency of elementary students. *Journal of Behavioral Education, 7,* 219–233.

Schwanenflugel, P. J., Stahl, S. A., & McFalls, E. L. (1997). Partial word knowledge and vocabulary growth during reading comprehension. *Journal of Literacy Research, 20,* 531–553.

Snow, C. E. (1991). *Unfulfilled expectations: Home and school influences on literacy.* Cambridge, MA: Harvard University Press.

Stahl, S. A., & Fairbanks, M. M. (1986). The effects of vocabulary instruction: A model-based meta-analysis. *Review of Educational Research, 56,* 72–110.

Stahl, S., & Vancil, S. (1986). Discussion is what makes semantic maps work in vocabulary instruction. *Reading Teacher, 40,* 62–69.

Thaler, M. (1988, April–May). Reading, writing, and riddling. *Learning,* 58–59.

Tomesen, M., & Aarnoutse, C. (1998). Effects of an instructional programme for deriving word meanings. *Educational Studies, 24,* 107–128.

Wallace, G., & Hammill, D. D. (1994). *Comprehensive receptive and expressive vocabulary test.* Examiner's manual. Austin, TX: Pro-Ed.

Wells, G. (1985). Preschool literacy-related activities and success in school. In D. Olson, J. Torrance, & A. Hilyard (Eds.), *Literacy, language and learning.* Cambridge, England: Cambridge University Press.

White, T. G., Graves, M. F., & Slater, W. H. (1990). Development of recognition and reading vocabularies in diverse sociolinguistic and educational settings. *Journal of Educational Psychology, 82,* 281–290.

White, T. G., Sowell, J., & Yanagihara, A. (1989). Teaching elementary students to use word-part clues. *The Reading Teacher, 42,* 302–308.

Children's Books

Agee, J. (1994). *So many dynamos! And other Palindromes.* New York: Farrar, Straus & Giroux.

Barrett, J. (1986). *Pickles have pimples and other silly statements.* New York: Atheneum.

Cleary, B. (2000). *A mink, a fink, a skating ring: What is a noun?* Minneapolis, MN: Lerner.

Cleary, B. (2001). *Hairy, scary, ordinary: What is an adjective?* Minneapolis, MN: Carolrhoda Books.

Cleary, B. (2001). *To root, to toot, to parachute: What is a verb?* Minneapolis, MN: Carolrhoda Books.

DeGross, M. (1994). *Donovan's word jar.* New York: HarperCollins.

Falwell, C. (1994). *Letter jesters.* New York: Ticknor and Fields.

Fleming, D. (1991). *In the tall, tall grass.* New York: Henry Holt.

Fleming, D. (1992). *Count.* New York: Henry Holt.

Fleming, D. (1992). *Lunch.* New York: Henry Holt.

Fleming, D. (1993). *In the small, small pond.* New York: Henry Holt.

Fleming, D. (1994). *Barnyard banter.* New York: Henry Holt.

Fleming, D. (1996). *Where once there was a wood.* New York: Henry Holt.

Fleming, D. (1997). *Time to sleep.* New York: Henry Holt.

Fleming, D. (1998). *Mama cat has three kittens.* New York: Henry Holt.

Fleming, D. (2001). *Pumpkin eye.* New York: Henry Holt.

Fleming, D. (2002). *Alphabet under construction.* New York: Henry Holt.

Frasier, D. (2000). *Miss Alaineus.* San Diego, CA: Harcourt.

Funk, C. E. (1948). *A hog on ice & other curious expressions.* New York: Harper and Row.

Funk, C. E. (1983). *Heavens to Betsy! & other curious sayings.* New York: HarperCollins.

Funk, C. E. (1986). *Horsefeathers & other curious words.* New York: Harper and Row.

Gerstein, M. (1999). *The absolutely awful alphabet.* San Diego, CA: Harcourt Brace.

Gwynne, F. (1970). *The king who rained.* New York: Simon & Schuster.

Gwynne, F. (1988). *A chocolate moose for dinner.* New York: Aladdin.

Gwynne, F. (1990). *A little pigeon toad.* New York: Aladdin.

Heller, R. (1990). *Merry-go-round: A book about nouns.* New York: Grosset & Dunlap.

Heller, R. (1991). *Up, up and away: A book about adverbs.* New York: Grosset & Dunlap.

Heller, R. (1997). *Mine, all mine: A book about pronouns.* New York: Grosset & Dunlap.

Heller, R. (1988). *Kites sail high: A book about verbs.* New York: Grosset & Dunlap.

Heller, R. (1998). *Fantastic! Wow! And Unreal! A book about interjections and conjunctions.* New York: Grosset & Dunlap.

Heller, R. (1987). *A cache of jewels and other collective nouns.* New York: Grosset & Dunlap.

Heller, R. (1995). *Behind the mask: A book about prepositions.* New York: Grosset & Dunlap.

Heller, R. (1989). *Many luscious lollipops: A book about adjectives.* New York: Grosset & Dunlap.
Hepworth, C. (1992). *Antics!* New York: G. P. Putnam's.
Lyon, G. E. (1999). *Book.* Illus. by P. Catalanotto. New York: DK Publishing.
Merriam, E. (1973). Simile: Willow and Ginkgo. *A sky full of poems.* New York: Dell.
Parrish, P. (1963). *Amelia Bedilia.* New York: HarperCollins.
Rosen, M. (1995). *Walking the bridge of your nose: Wordplay poems and rhymes.* New York: Kingfisher.
Scheer, J. (1964). *Rain makes applesauce.* New York: Holiday House.
Yolen, J. (1987). *Owl moon.* New York: Philomel Books.
Wood, A., & Wood, D. (1989). *Quick as a cricket.* Swindon, United Kingdom: Child's Play.

CHAPTER 7 APPENDIX

Appendix: Greek and Latin Affixes and Roots

Base	**Meaning**	**Origin**
ab	away	Latin
acro	top, tip, end	Greek
ad, ac, at, as, ap, am, an, ar, ag, af	to, toward, at	Latin
ambi	around, both	Latin
amphi	both, of oth sides, around	Greek
ant, anti	against	Greek
ante	before	Latin
apo, ap, aph	away from, off	Greek
archa, arshae	old, ancient	Greek
auto	self	Greek
ben, bon	good, well	Latin
bi	two	Latin
co, con, com	together, with	Latin
contra, contro	against	Latin
de	from, away, off	Latin
deca, dec, deka	ten	Greek
di, dis	two, twice	Greek
dia	through, across	Greek
dis, dif	apart, away, not, to deprive	Latin
du	double, two	Latin
dys	difficult, bad	Greek
e, ex, ec	out, beyond, from, out of, forth	Latin
ecto	outside of	Greek
en	in give [intensifier]	Latin
endo, ento	within	Greek
ep, epi	upon, at, in addition	Greek
eu	good, well	Greek
extra	beyond	Latin
fore	before	Anglo-Saxon
hemi	half	Greek
hetero	various, unlike	Greek
hier	sacred	Greek
holo	whole	Greek
homo	same	Greek

(Continued)

Source: Kent School District. Kent, WA., Successfully Preparing All Students for their Future. Retrieved from *www.kent.wednet.edu/KSD/MA/resources/greek_and_latin_roots/prefix_l.html*

Base	Meaning	Origin
hyper	above, beyond	Greek
hypo, hyp	under, less than	Greek
ideo, idea	idea	Greek
in, ir, im, il	not, without	Latin
in, im	in,on, upon, into, toward	Latin
inter	between	Latin
intro	within	Latin
iso	equal	Greek
kilo	thousand	Greek
macro	long, large	Greek
magn, mag, meg, maj	great	Latin
mal	bad, ill	Latin
mega	great	Greek
met, meta, meth	among,with, after, beyond	Greek
micro	small	Greek
migr	to move, travel	Latin
mill	thousand	Latin
mis	less, wrong	Latin
mono	one	Greek
multi	many, much	Latin
neo	new	Greek
non, ne	not	Latin
o, ob, oc, of, op	against, toward	Latin
omni	all	Latin
paleo	long ago, ancient	Greek
pan, panto	all, every	Greek
para	beside, beyond	Latin
penta	five	Greek
per	through	Latin
peri	around, about	Greek
pre	before	Latin
pro	before, forward, forth	Latin
pronto	first	Greek
poly	many	Greek
post	after	Latin
pseudo	false, counterfeit	Greek
quad, quatr	four	Latin
re	again, anew, back	Latin
retro	back, backward, behind	Latin
se, sed	apart, aside, away	Latin
semi	half	Latin
sover	above, over	Latin
sub	under, below, up from below	Latin
super, supra	above, down, thoroughle	Latin
syn, sym, syl	together, with	Greek
tele	far off	Greek
trans	over, across	Latin
tri	three	Latin
un	not	Latin
uni	one	Latin

SUFFIX LIST

Noun forming suffixes

Suffix	Meaning	Origin
age	belongs to	Latin
ance	state of being	Latin
ant	thing or one who	Latin
ar	relating to, like	Latin
ary	relating to, like	Latin
ence	state, fact, quality	Latin
ent	to form	Latin
ic	like, having the nature	Latin & Greek
ine	nature of-feminine ending	Latin
ion, tion, ation	being, the result of	Latin
ism	act, condition	Latin & Greek
ist	one who	Latin
ive	of, belonging to, quality of	Latin
ment	a means, product, act, state	Latin
or	person or thing that	Latin
ory	place for	Latin
ty	condition of, quality of	Latin
y	creats abstract noun	Greek & Anglo-Saxon

Adjective forming suffixes

Suffix	Meaning	Origin
able	capable of being	Latin
al	like, suitable for	Latin
ance	state of being	Latin
ant	thing or one who	Latin
ar	relating to, like	Latin
ary	relating to, like	Latin
ate	to become associated with	Latin
ent	to form	Latin
ial	function of	Latin
ible	capable of being	Latin
ic	like, having the nature of	Latin & Greek
ine	nature of-feminine ending	Latin
ive	of, belonging to, quality of	Latin
ory	place for	Latin
ous	characterized by, having quality of	Latin
y	quality, somewhat like	Greek & Anglo-Saxon

Verb forming suffixes

Suffix	Meaning	Origin
ate	to become associated with	Latin
fy	make, do	Latin
ise, ize	to become like	Latin

Adverb forming suffixes

Suffix	Meaning	Origin
ic	like, having the nature of	Latin & Greek
ly	like, to extent of	Latin

(Continued)

Greek and Latin Roots

BASE	MEANING	ORIGIN
act	to act	Latin
acu, acr, ac	needle	Latin
alt	high	Latin
anima, anim	life, mind	Latin
ann, enn	year	Latin
anthrop	man	Greek
aqua	water	Latin
arch, archi	govern, rule	Greek
arm	army, weapon	Latin
arbitr, arbiter	to judge, consider	Latin
art	craft, skill	Latin
arthr, art	segment, joint	Greek
aud	to hear	Latin
bell	war	Latin
biblio, bibl	book	Greek
bio	life	Greek
capit, cipit	head	Latin
caus	cause, case, lawsuit	Latin
cede	to go, yield	Latin
cele	honor	Latin
cell	to rise, project	Latin
cent	one hundred	Latin
cept, capt, cip, cap, ceive, ceipt	to take, hold, grasp	Latin
cert	sure, to trust	Latin
cess, ced	to move, withdraw	Latin
cid, cis	to cut off, be breif, to kill	Latin
circ, circum	around	Latin
civ	citizen	Latin
claud	close, shut, block	Latin
clin	to lean, lie, bend	Latin
cog	to know	Latin
column	a column	Latin
comput	to compute	Latin
cont	to join, unite	Latin
cor, cord, cour, card	heart	Latin
corp	body	Latin
cosm	world, order, universe	Greek
crac, crat	rule, govern	Greek
cred	believe, trust	Latin
crit, cris	separate, discern, judge	Latin
culp	fault, blame	Latin
curs, curr, corr	to run	Latin
custom	one's own	Latin
dem	people	Greek
dent, odon	tooth	Latin
derm	skin	Greek
dic, dict	to say, to speak, assert	Latin
duct, duc	to lead, draw	Latin
dur	to harden, hold out	Latin

More Greek and Latin Roots

BASE	MEANING	ORIGIN
ego	I	Latin
ethn	nation	Greek
equ	equal, fair	Latin
fac, fic, fect, fact	to make, to do	Latin
famil	family	Latin
fen	to strike	Latin
fer	to carry, bear, bring	Latin
fid	trust, faith	Latin
fin	to end	Latin
flu	to flow	Latin
form	shape, form	Latin
fort	chance, luck, strong	Latin
frig	cool	Latin
fum	smoke, scent	Latin
gam	marriage	Greek
gen	race, family, kind	Latin
geo	earth	Greek
gno, kno	to know	Greek
grad, gred, gress	step, degree, rank	Latin
graph, gram	write, draw, describe, record	Greek
grat	pleasure, thankful, goodwill, joy	Latin
grav, griev, grief	heavy	Latin
gymn	naked	Greek
hab	to have, hold, dwell	Latin
hom	man, human	Latin
hosp	guest, host	Latin
host	enemy, stranger	Latin
hydro	water	Greek
hygiene	the art of health	Greek
hypno	sleep	Greek
init	to begin, enter upon	Latin
jur, jus, jud	law, right	Latin
juven	young	Latin
labor, lab	work	Latin
lat	lateral, side, wide	Latin
laud	praise	Latin
leg, lig	law, to chose, perceive, understand	Latin
lev	to make light, raise, lift	Latin
liber, liver	free	Latin
lingu, langu	tounge	Latin
lith	stone	Greek
loc	place	Latin
locu, loqu	word, speak	Latin
log	idea, word, speech, reason, study	Greek
luc, lum	light	Latin
man	hand	Latin
mar	sea	Latin
med, medi	middle	Latin
medic	physician, to heal	Latin

(Continued)

More Greek and Latin Roots

BASE	MEANING	ORIGIN
memor	mindful	Latin
men, min, mon	to think, remind, advise, warn	Latin
ment	mind	Latin
meter, metr	measure	Greek
migr	to move, travel	Latin
mim	copy, imitate	Greek
mit, mis	to send	Latin
mor	fool, manner, custom	Greek
morph	form	Greek
mort	death	Latin
mov, mob, mot	to move	Latin
mus	little mouse	Latin
mut	change, exchange	Latin
necess	unavoidable	Latin
neur, nerv	nerve	Greek
noc, nox	night, harm	Latin
nomen, nomin	name	Latin
null, nihil, nil	nothing, void	Latin
nym, onym, onom	name	Greek
opt	eye	Greek
ord, ordin	order	Latin
ortho	straight	Greek
par, pair	arrange, prepare, get ready, set	Latin
part, pars	portion, part	Latin
ped, pes	foot	Latin
pend, pond, pens	to weigh, pay, consider	Latin
phe, fa, fe	speak, spoken about	Greek
phil	love	Greek
phon	sound, voice	Greek
photo	light	Greek
pler	to fill	Latin
plic	to fold	Latin
plur, plus	more	Latin
pneu	breath	Greek
polis, polit	citizen, city, state	Greek
port	to carry	Latin
pos	to place, put	Latin
pot	powerfull	Latin
prim, prin	first	Latin
priv	seperate	Latin
prob	to prove, test	Latin
psych	mind, soul, spirit	Greek
pyr	fire	Greek
reg, rig, rect, reign	government, rule, right, straight	Latin
respond	to answer	Latin
rupt	break, burst	Latin
sacr, secr, sacer	sacred	Latin
sat	to please	Latin
sci	to know	Latin
scope	to see	Greek

More Greek and Latin Roots

Base	Meaning	Origin
scrib, script	to write	Latin
sed, sid, sess	to sit, to settle	Latin
sent, sens	to feel	Latin
sequ, secut	to follow, sequence	Latin
simil, simul, sembl	together, likeness, pretense	Latin
sol, soli	alone, lonely	Latin
solus	to comfort, to console	Latin
somn	sleep	Latin
son	sound	Latin
soph	wise	Greek
spec, spect, spic	to look at, behold	Latin
spond, spons	to pledge, promise	Latin
tac, tic	silent	Latin
techn	art, skill	Greek
temp	time	Latin
ten, tain, tent	to hold	Latin
tend, tens	to give heed, stretch toward	Latin
term	boundary, limit	Latin
test	to witness, affirm	Latin
the, them, thet	to place, put	Greek
theatr	to see, view	Greek
theo	god	Greek
topo	place	Greek
tract	to pull, draw	Latin
trib	to allot, give	Latin
vac	empty	Latin
ven	to come	Latin
ver	truth	Latin
vers, vert	to turn	Latin
vest	to adorn	Latin
vestig	to track	Latin
via	way, road	Latin
vir	manliness, worth	Latin
vis, vid	to see, to look	Latin
viv, vit	life	Latin
voc, vok	voice, call	Latin

Chapter 8

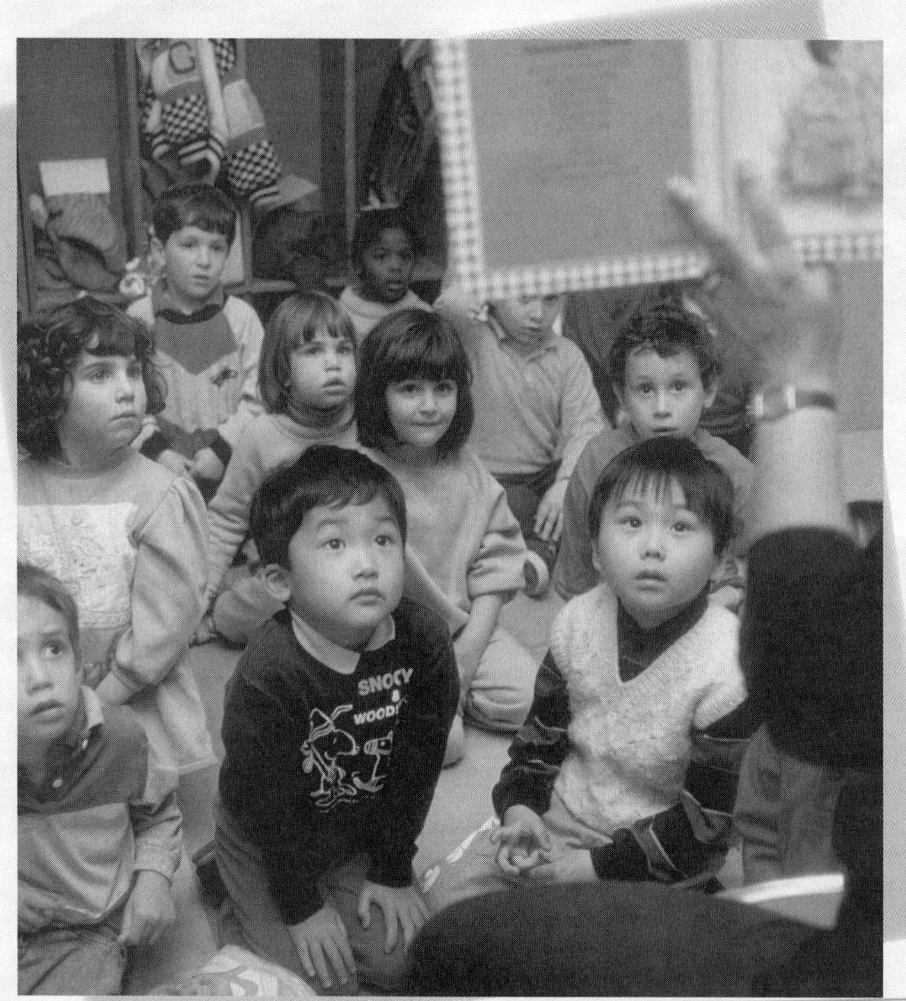

Guiding the Development of Comprehension

LOOKING AT THE RESEARCH

Researchers have identified cognitive processes good readers use before, during, and after reading.

Processing Before Reading

- Good readers have clear reading goals.
- They overview the text with the following goals before reading:
  - ✔ to determine whether the text is worth reading
  - ✔ to identify goal-relevant sections
  - ✔ to develop a reading plan

Processing During Reading

- Reading generally progresses from beginning to end.
- There is differential attention to information relevant to the reader's goals.
- Good readers sometimes jump forward and backward to find particular information and to clarify confusions that arise during reading. They are aware of such confusions, because they do much monitoring as they read.
- Good readers anticipate what might be said, updating their predictions and hypotheses as reading proceeds.
- Good readers relate their prior knowledge to the ideas in text and relate ideas in the text to one another. Sometimes old knowledge is revised in light of information in the text. Many inferences are made during reading.

- Good readers sometimes use strategies as they read, for example, to determine the meanings of unknown words or to remember particular ideas.
- Good readers demonstrate passion for certain ideas presented in the text.
- Good readers construct interpretations and conclusions as reading proceeds.

Processing After Reading

- Sometimes good readers reread or reskim text just read.
- Good readers sometimes attempt to restate important ideas from the text. If notes might help later recall, they make them.
- Good readers continue to reflect on the text after they have finished reading. (Pressley, 1997; Pressley & Afflerbach, 1995).

Focus Questions

- What is meant by the term *reading comprehension?*
- How can I help children develop reading comprehension abilities?
- How do I guide the development of comprehension ability before reading a text?
- How do I guide the development of comprehension ability during the reading of a text?
- How do I guide the development of comprehension ability after reading a text?

REAL TEACHERS, REAL PRACTICE

Meet Judy Snetsky, *a first-grade teacher*

The purpose of guided reading instruction is to help children learn how to use reading strategies successfully so that they can become independent readers. Therein lies the challenge for teachers in the early grades. For while these strategies may be obvious to us, they are not so to beginning readers.

In my first-grade classroom, I begin the school year by modeling these strategies during shared reading time. We discuss the strategies used and begin a "Reading Strategies List." During the first six weeks, I observe the children to see where they are in terms of reading development. From these observations and through the use of running records, I determine a reading level for each child and form guided reading groups. Each group is made up of children who are at the same stage of reading development. Groups of four to six children seem to work best. Placement in these groups is fluid and changes throughout the school year.

A guided reading lesson usually lasts about 20 minutes per group unless we do an extension activity. I begin by showing the group the cover of the book, reading the title and inviting the children to share what they think the story will be about. I try to relate the story to something in their lives. For example a story about pets would generate a discussion about their pets. Some educators sug-

gest previewing all the illustrations, but I do not do this unless it is a complicated piece. Previewing all the illustrations takes away the important opportunity for the children to predict what will happen. During the discussion I use as much language from the piece as possible.

I listen as the children "whisper read" the first pages. A few questions are asked to check their comprehension and to be sure that this is indeed the right match for their instructional reading level. The children share how they dealt with unfamiliar words. Any new strategies are added to our "Reading Strategies List."

The children continue reading quietly almost to the end of the piece. I ask the group if anything they have read has made them want to change their earlier predictions. We then finish the piece and talk about how it ended. I often ask the children if anything in the piece reminds them of something in their own lives.

I ask the children to choose a passage to read aloud. This gives me a chance to check on their pacing, fluency, and intonation.

Guided reading demands a great deal from the teacher. The teacher must be constantly observing and assessing the children's reading behaviors. The teacher needs to be flexible in grouping and moving students as the need arises. A wide variety of books on different levels need to be available. As great as the demands are, so are the results. The children will be able to read progressively more difficult pieces with accuracy and fluency. They will be able to solve problems with confidence. They will become readers.

Comprehension is what reading is all about. In fact, if comprehension has not occurred, nothing has been read. We often have students return from a practicum in schools saying, "I'm working with this child who can read anything I give him, but he doesn't understand it." If children haven't read with meaning, they haven't read; they have only decoded. Helping learners improve their comprehension ability across increasingly more difficult texts and genres is one of our most important responsibilities as informed reading teachers. We must address some challenging questions about comprehension instruction.

WHAT IS MEANT BY THE TERM READING COMPREHENSION?

In order to define *comprehension* it may be useful to review some of the key understandings we discussed in Chapters 1 and 6. In Chapter 1 we discussed the work of Louise Rosenblatt (1978), who provided us with the notions of the reader, the text, and the poem as a description of the reading process.

- The reader is the person seeking to make meaning by transacting with (actively reading) a text, of whatever kind.
- The text is the collection of word symbols and patterns on the page, the physical object you hold in your hand as you read.
- The poem is the literary work created as the reader transacts with the text.

These descriptors help us to define reading as a process resulting in meaning created by the blending of the author's ideas and the background knowledge of the reader.

In Chapter 6 we further explored the transaction that occurs when a reader engages with a piece of text. The transaction occurs between the reader's thoughts, language, and questions and the author's thoughts, language, and questions. Readers do not come to a piece of text as blank slates or empty vessels into which the ideas of the author are poured. Readers, when they engage with a text, bring background knowledge, knowledge of language and how it works, and questions they want to answer. Frank Smith (1978) says we cannot read what we do not already have in our heads. In other words, we cannot read something about which we have no knowledge at all and expect to comprehend it. We call this idea the *Velcro theory:* If we do not have at least some prior knowledge to bring to the reading experience, the new words and ideas do not stick.

Comprehension is the application of our background knowledge to the act of reading. We comprehend when we can combine the words (ideas) of the author with our own background knowledge (mini-theories about the world). Interaction is central to the process. Thus **comprehension** is defined as the interaction of the author's ideas and the reader's background knowledge that results in the creation or re-creation of meaning. We cannot identify any aspect of teaching children to read upon which we place more importance than helping them develop reading comprehension abilities.

HOW DO I HELP CHILDREN DEVELOP READING COMPREHENSION ABILITIES?

You can invoke many instructional strategies to help children develop comprehension abilities. We will share many of them with you throughout the rest of this chapter and elsewhere in this text. A powerful instructional strategy you can use to develop comprehension abilities is called *guided reading.* **Guided reading** is a relatively short, highly intense instructional episode in which you, as a more senior member of the Reading Club, coach your students, as junior members of the Reading Club, in becoming increasingly more strategic, self-monitoring, comprehending readers. Your coaching duties include carefully observing each reader in the group. You intervene in their use of the reading process when you see an opportunity to help them work out a confusion, untangle a tricky word, apply a skill, or apply a strategy.

LOOKING AT THE RESEARCH

What the research says about your role in guiding the reading of children

When teachers demonstrate, guide, and model comprehension strategies, helping readers take incremental next steps, even students who are adequate decoders but poor in comprehension become better readers (Palinscar & Brown, 1984; Rosenshine, Meister, & Chapman, 1996). This underscores the importance of your role in helping your learners master comprehension strategies.

The teacher's role described as "demonstrating, guiding, and modeling" may be quite different from your memories of your teachers giving you workbooks or worksheets. What are some of the major differences you can envision?

Go to our Companion Website at www.prenhall.com/harp and contribute your answers to this question on the Threaded Message Board. How do your responses compare to those of other students?

Your interventions will often involve asking a question, giving a direction, or using a verbal prompt to help children move along in their reading. Guided reading instruction, while sometimes spontaneous in response to children's actions, requires a great deal of careful planning on your part.

Planning for Guided Reading Instruction

Planning for guided reading requires that you think about the grouping of children, the instructional objectives, the selection of an appropriate text, the segmentation of the text, the selection of instructional strategies, evaluation of the activity, and planning for the next learning steps.

The Grouping of Children. Because your job is to watch each child carefully as a reader before, during, and after reading the chosen text, guided reading is best done in groups of no more than six children. It is difficult to observe and respond to more than six children at one time. During guided reading you will want to get predictions from children and encourage their valuable contributions as you discuss the text. More than six children in the group may preclude such sharing.

How Do You Determine Which Children Should Be in Each Group? You must carefully consider the basis on which you are grouping particular children. Two considerations you will want to make are (1) to group children who are reading at the same instructional level and (2) to group those who have similar reading abilities and instructional needs. One of the greatest challenges in conducting effective guided reading instruction is constantly maintaining a watchful posture so that you are continually evaluating whether or not to regroup your students. Your goal is to move them to increasingly more difficult texts as their reading abilities improve. This way grouping does not become static, and you can be confident that you are appropriately challenging each of your readers with the texts you select for guided reading.

Guided reading is the heart of the reading program.

Let's revisit Kelly King, who contributed the "Real Teachers, Real Practice" essay in Chapter 1. *In this section, we will follow parts of a guided reading lesson with Kelly and her first graders. Her guided reading lesson using* City Mouse–Country Mouse and Two More Mouse Tales from Aesop *(Wallner, 1987) will serve as the model for the following discussions of guided reading. You may recall in this fable a City Mouse goes to visit his cousin, the Country Mouse. The City Mouse rudely rejects the Country Mouse's offer of simple food. They go to the City Mouse's home where they find wonderful food but are nearly killed by mean dogs. The Country Mouse decides to return home that very night realizing that finding food isn't good for much if you can't enjoy eating it. He decides it is better to eat plain food in peace.*

Planning the Instructional Objectives. Figure 8.1 illustrates a guided reading planning document you may find useful. Kelly completed this form as she made plans for using an insect book and a fiction book called *City Mouse–Country Mouse and Two More Mouse*

Figure 8.1
Guided Reading Planning Form

Students: Carly, Monirot, Nate, Katelyn

Week of: 1/13

Books(s): Insects (non-fiction) City Mouse-Country Mouse (fable)

Level: J

Goals for week:

1. Be able to answer, How are fiction & nonfiction books different?
2. Practice phonics skills (small words in big words, consonant blends, common endings)
3. Comprehension—understanding literary language: once upon a time, fine food, turned up his nose, no sooner said than done, fine feast, all at once

Plans:

Monday: Preview Insects • ask what about? • look through without reading • review strategies of Goal 2 • Read as a group (particular attention to pg. 6)

Tuesday: Reread insects independently. Take Running Record on Nate and Katelyn.

Wednesday: Preview City Mouse same as Monday. Read story with a focus on literary language: Once upon a time, p. 6; no sooner said than done, p. 10; at last, p. 11. Check understanding of fine food, turned up his nose, and fine feast.

Thursday: Review City Mouse and discuss moral. Do children agree with it? Compare the nonfiction book with the fable. Assign one of the books for homework.

Ideas for next week: Reinforce Nate's self-correcting behavior. Review magic e with Carly and Nate.

Tales from Aesop. In the "Goals for the Week" section she has listed three objectives for the group. At other times, she might have objectives for individual students as well as the general objectives for the group.

There are several data sources for determining instructional objectives. One is the observations you make during a guided reading session. You will want to keep careful notes of these observations. Another is children's performance on running records and other measures of oral reading performance. Note that Kelly plans to take a running record on Nate and Katelyn's reading of the insect book. Yet another is the conversations you have with children during reading conferences. A fourth source is the curriculum guidelines of your district or state. Many teachers make checklists of strategies and comprehension processes required for their grade level; such lists will be helpful as you plan for guided reading instruction.

Selection of Appropriate Texts for Guided Reading. Each day you teach you will be confronted with a persistent and critical question: How do I engage this child (these children) with this text at this time? Matching children with texts is a daily challenge. Margaret Mooney (1990) has deepened our understandings of how to meet this challenge. She suggests that the answer to the question "How do I engage these children with this text at this time?" is reading it to children, reading it with children, or asking children to read it independently.

When a book presents many challenges (difficult concepts, challenging vocabulary, complicated sentences, few illustrations, for example), you may decide to read it to children. When a book presents fewer challenges, you may decide to read it with your children, either in shared reading or guided reading. In this context *shared reading* implies that each child has visual access to the text and you lend your voice support to their oral reading of the text. You increase or decrease the volume of your oral reading as they need more or less support from you. If you decide the book is an appropriate guided reading text, you give each child in the small group a copy and coach them as they read through the text with you. For guided reading the text should provide some challenges, but children should be able to read it orally with 90% to 95% accuracy and good comprehension. Finally, if the text provides so few challenges that it is easy for children to read, you may assign it as a "read by yourself" book. A book that at one time is a "read-to" book may later become a guided reading book (with some modifications of the usual procedure) and ultimately become a "read-by-myself" book.

When selecting a book for use with a guided reading group you need to consider three important reading teacher basics: (1) supports and challenges in the text, (2) the current reading capacities of the children in the group, and (3) what you learned in your last guided reading session with them.

Using Leveled Book Libraries. When teachers taught with basal readers, there was no need for leveling books because the difficulty level of the pieces of text had been determined by the publisher. Today's teachers who want to rely on real books for reading instruction need a system for judging which books their children can read and what makes a book more difficult. Hence, many books have been "leveled." **Leveled books** are books that someone has examined and then determined how difficult it would be for a reader to read each book. Several authors have described systems for leveling books (Fountas & Pinnell, 1999; Weaver, 2000), and some publishers claim their books are leveled for the teacher. Each of these systems marks the books with a symbol that the teacher uses to gauge how well a given child might be able to read the book. If the system uses numbers beginning with the easiest text as 1 and a child could read all the "1" books easily, then the teacher would choose a "2" book for that child.

Basically, leveling programs help teachers examine the text in books for features that support the reader and are therefore easier to read or for features that make the text more difficult for the reader. For example, if the font size is larger, there is less text to read. Predictable text, text that repeats in a predictable pattern such as the pattern in *Over in the Meadow* (Keats, 1971), is easier to read than text that is not predictable. Other factors include length of the book, number of illustrations and how well the illustrations match the print, content (topics that most children are familiar with are easier than uncommon topics), text structure (narrative or expository), and the complexity of vocabulary and sentence structures. Leveling books, then, is a process of thinking about the features of various books and how they support or challenge the reader. Most teachers work together to level the books in their collections and then code the books in a way that all teachers can use. Most teachers begin with lists established by one of the leveling programs and then add their own books to these lists.

In addition to leveling books by difficulty, you will want to include books that cover a range of interests and genres. Not to be overlooked are books of poetry and nonfiction. These books can be leveled with other books for reading instruction. You will also need a wide range of books for browsing boxes. **Browsing boxes** contain books that have been used in guided reading and are now at the children's independent level. These boxes can be arranged by topic (dinosaurs or cats, for example), by author (Keats or Carle), or by genre (poetry or biography). You will want to change the books in the boxes at regular intervals so that you can reinforce topics of study and respond to changing student interests and growing reading ability. One teacher uses empty cereal boxes to hold the books. This way children are presented with text to read even on the browsing boxes themselves!

Using leveled books requires great care in planning. You are the only one who really knows your children and their needs. Not every leveled book will be accurately leveled for your readers. For example, one of the criteria used in leveling books is the likelihood that the child will have the background knowledge needed to understand the book. How will any person leveling the books really know that about your readers? Interest is also a factor in selecting reading materials for a specific reader. Some children will work and work to read material that they find extremely interesting even though it might be too difficult according to the leveling system used. On the other hand, a book that a child finds uninteresting will likely be difficult for them even if it is at an easy level. Leveled books do not relieve the teacher of the responsibility for selecting materials for each reader, but they do give the teacher some guidelines for groups of books from which to choose.

Assessment and Evaluation Toolbox

THE LEXILE FRAMEWORK FOR READING (LFR)

The Lexile Framework was developed under a grant from the National Institute of Child Health and Human Development. The framework has been marketed since 1996 by MetaMetrics, Inc., in Research Triangle Park, North Carolina. This assessment and evaluation tool can be used to evaluate a child's reading comprehension and the vocabulary and syntactic complexity of texts. Both evaluations result in a Lexile score ranging from 200 to 1700 Lexiles. The newest Harry Potter book, *Harry Potter and the Order of the Phoenix,* has a Lexile level of 950L, which equates to approximately fifth- or sixth-grade level. The framework includes a database in which texts have been assigned Lexile levels.

You may access the Lexile Framework web page by going to the Weblinks for Chapter 8 on our Companion Website at www.prenhall.com/harp.

Planning How to Segment the Text. In planning guided reading you need to read carefully the book you select. Think about how you will introduce the book to children, and then identify where you will have children pause to discuss their reading. Decide whether you will show them only the cover to prompt their initial predictions or whether you will have them discuss the cover and then take a picture walk partway through the story. Try to have children read segments of the story that end with an interesting turn in the plot. If you choose a nonfiction text, think about reasonable amounts of text for your students to read at one time, or look for ways in which the author segmented the text with headings. As you examine each segment, you will want to think about what you will say to children or ask the children about that part. You will need to be flexible and ready to change your plans for each section in response to the children's ideas, comments, or questions. However, it is useful to go into the guided reading session with plans for each segment.

Kelly decided to have Carly, Monirot, Nate, and Katelyn read only the first of three fables in the book. The first fable, as you can predict from the title of the book, is about the country mouse and the city mouse. The book has mice characters and uses some language that will be familiar to children with experience with traditional literature. For example, when the mice decide to go to the city, the next sentence reads, "No sooner said than done." Before the children read the book for a guided reading experience, Kelly read them some fables from other sources. For example, *Aesop's Fables* (Hague, 1985) contains a selection of short, one-page fables that would help the children learn what to expect in reading a fable. She would not have read the same fables that are included in this book.

Go to the Weblinks in Chapter 8 on our Companion Website at www.prenhall.com/harp for links to sites from which you may download Aesop's fables.

Selecting Instructional Strategies. You will need to select instructional strategies you think will best meet the objectives you have described for your guided reading lesson. You may decide to activate children's background knowledge, to explore their reasons for reading the text, and to examine the patterns of text organization used by the author. You may choose to create a prediction map or use another graphic organizer. You might decide to use think-alouds to model certain strategies or to encourage the children to collaborate in working through reading challenges. Please remember that the goal of this lesson and others like it is to help children gain comprehension skills. This range of possible instructional strategies will be explored in the remainder of this chapter.

Return to Figure 8.1 and note the goals Kelly has chosen. Her goals are all related to comprehension as she helps children think about the elements of fiction compared to nonfiction, focuses on literary language, and helps children gain more skill in decoding.

Evaluating the Guided Reading Lesson and Planning Next Learning Steps. In the crush of a busy school day, it is difficult to find time to do this, but evaluating each guided reading lesson—with an eye toward identifying the next learning steps for children—is of paramount importance. You probably will not have time to do this immediately following the guided reading session, but before you go home at the end of the day, return to your planning sheets to complete this work. If you wait long before recording what you have learned, you will not be able to remember the details that are so important for future planning. Note that Kelly took a running record on Nate's reading of part of the insect book on Tuesday. She noticed that he was self-correcting more often and so made a note to reinforce that with Nate next week.

Remember, during a guided reading lesson you will take an active role in helping children process text before reading, during reading, and after reading. Another scheme for guided reading is the experience-text-relationship (ETR) approach.

Experience-Text-Relationship (ETR) Approach

The ETR was developed by Kathryn Au in 1979 to give students a general strategy for text comprehension, including the use of background knowledge. When you use this approach, you lead your students in a discussion of the text and text-related topics. You also model the process an expert reader uses to construct meaning. You plan the ETR experience by previewing the text and deciding how to segment it. ETR is divided into three phases: experience phase, text phase, and relationship phase (Au, Mason, & Scheu, 1995).

Experience or E Phase. In the E phase you lead the students into a discussion about their background experiences relative to the topic of the text. As the discussion proceeds, you may ask questions to encourage them to make tighter connections between their background experiences and the text. You may ask children to make predictions about the text.

Text or T Phase. As students finish reading each section of the text, engage them in a discussion of their feelings and ideas. Have them check to see if predictions were confirmed, and focus on plot, setting, and characters and their motivation. Encourage them to discuss the problem in the story and its resolution as well as any interesting language they uncovered.

Relationship or R Phase. In the R phase you ask students to think of relationships between the story and their own lives. Encourage children to explore the theme or author's message and how it connects to their lives.

HOW DO I GUIDE THE DEVELOPMENT OF COMPREHENSION ABILITY BEFORE READING A TEXT?

Taking an active role in helping learners develop comprehension ability *before reading* a text involves helping them activate background knowledge, make predictions, think about purposes for engaging with the text, and exploring the structure of the text. It is also important to invoke the research findings described in this chapter's opening by engaging children in a discussion of the goals for reading the chosen text and examining the text to determine whether the children deem it worth reading. (Be sure to have a back-up text chosen in case they say "No"!).

LOOKING AT THE RESEARCH

What the research says about explicit instruction of text comprehension

The National Reading Panel (2000) states,

> The idea behind explicit instruction of text comprehension is that comprehension can be improved by teaching students to use specific cognitive strategies or to reason strategically when they encounter barriers to comprehension when reading. The goal of such training is the achievement of competent and self-regulated reading. (Chapter 4, p. 40)

This explains why it is so important for you to engage your learners in quality guided reading instruction. Guided reading is where you deliver explicit comprehension instruction and coach learners in their use of the reading process.

Identify a reading strategy you learned about in Chapter 6. How can you imagine delivering explicit instruction and coaching that strategy in a guided reading situation?

Activating Background Knowledge

Helping children become aware of what they know about a topic before they read is a helpful prereading activity. Fourth-grade children who were instructed in activating prior knowledge, making predictions, and examining purposes for reading over a full year scored significantly better on the *Metropolitan Achievement Test* than a control group (Payne & Manning, 1992).

You can activate learners' prior knowledge by showing them the cover illustration of a book and asking them to talk about what they see there, what similar experiences they have had, and what they know about the topic. You can also conduct a picture walk. A picture walk is conducted by slowly turning to each picture or illustration and asking the children to describe what they see in the illustrations, but without mentioning the text. However, if you are preparing to read a story, you may need to stop looking at the pictures before the end of the story in order not to reveal all of the plot. The point of a picture walk is to help children gain knowledge of the setting, characters, and plot that will help them understand the text as they move into it and through it.

Selectively use the language of the text as you discuss the pictures so that children will become familiar with challenging language in the text. While engaging in the picture walk, decide if you need to discuss the meaning of selected vocabulary words. This is critical if you think students lack sufficient background knowledge to make sense of this vocabulary. On the other hand, if you teach all the vocabulary words before reading the book, the students will have no opportunity to practice their decoding skills, and you will not know which of the skills they can apply.

If you are preparing them to read an expository piece, it may be helpful to show them all the illustrations. Finally, use the picture walk to motivate their prediction making about the text. Try to get predictions from as many children as possible. If any child in the group does not make a prediction, revisit all the predictions and ask for a show of hands to get a commitment to a prediction from each child. You can record these predictions on a class chart.

Here is how Kelly's introduction of *City Mouse–Country Mouse* sounded:

Kelly: Children, do you remember the short stories I read to you yesterday? Do you remember what that kind of story is called?

Carly, Monirot, Nate, and Katelyn all raise their hands. Kelly points to Carly.

Carly: Yes, they are called fables. They mostly have animals.

Kelly: Yes, they are called fables, and the characters are usually animals. Do you remember anything else about fables? Katelyn's hand shoots up.

Katelyn: They teach you a lesson that you find out at the end of the story.

Kelly: You remembered important things about fables. Today we are going to read one of the fables in this book (holds up book). We are going to read *City*

Mouse–Country Mouse. A man named John Wallner drew the pictures. See, his name is right here. What reasons might we have for reading this fable? Katelyn's hand goes up again.

Kelly: Katelyn, what reasons might you have for reading *City Mouse–Country Mouse?*

Katelyn: One reason might be because it is a fable and it will teach us a lesson.

Monirot raises her hand, and Kelly recognizes her.

Monirot: Another reason would be because it might be fun to read.

Kelly: Those are good reasons for reading *City Mouse–Country Mouse.* Shall we do it? (Nods of agreement.) Good. Look closely at the cover, and tell me what you see and what you think this fable will be about.

Monirot: One mouse is all dressed up, and the other one has a patch on his pants.

Nate: It looks like one mouse is sitting on a broken cup and the other one has real furniture. Maybe one mouse doesn't have any money.

Katelyn (her hand waving wildly in the air): I get it. This mouse (pointing to the right), this mouse lives in the country. See he doesn't have fancy clothes and if he walked up this path he would go home in the woods. This mouse (pointing to the one on the left) lives in this great big house up here.

Kelly: So which one do you think is the city mouse and which one is the country mouse?

All hands go up.

Monirot: The one with the big house lives in the city and the other one lives in the country.

Everyone agrees.

Kelly: What do you think would be different about the mouse who lives in the city and the mouse who lives in the country?

Nate: I think the city mouse is going to have real good stuff, and the country mouse is going to have broken things. Carly, Monirot, and Katelyn all nod in agreement.

Kelly: So you all agree with that. Can you think of any other differences?

Carly: Well, they wear different clothes, and the country mouse looks fatter than the city mouse.

Kelly (turning to a third title page): Look at this picture. (An illustration of a trail across a bridge from the city house to the country.) What predictions do you have about this story from this picture?

Katelyn: I know. I know.

Kelly: What, Katelyn?

Katelyn: The city mouse and the country mouse are going to visit each other. They are going to go over that bridge and go to their houses.

Kelly (turning to pages 6 and 7): What predictions can you make from these pictures?

All hands shoot up.

Monirot (laughing): Oh, look. The city mouse is going to see the other mouse, and a squirrel is pulling him. He doesn't have a car!

Carly: See, the country mouse is waving to him. He lives in a tree!

Kelly (turning to the next two pages): What do you think is happening in these pictures?

Nate: Now they are in the tree house. Look. There is the broken cup we saw on the cover. See, the country mouse does have broken things for furniture.

Kelly: What do you think is going to happen here?

Monirot: Look (pointing to the picture on page 9). The city mouse doesn't like the food the other mouse gave him. He is dropping the plate. I think they are going to have a fight.

Kelly: Let's review the things you have predicted so far, and I will write them on the chart. What was your first prediction?

Nate: I said that maybe one mouse wouldn't have any money. The mouse I was talking about is the country mouse.

Kelly (writing on the chart): So I'll write Nate's prediction here. What was the next prediction?

Nate: I said that the city mouse would have good stuff, and the country mouse will have broken stuff.

Kelly: So I will write that the city mouse will have nice things in his home and the country mouse will have broken things. Is that alright? (Everyone nods in agreement.) What was our next prediction?

Nate: We said the city mouse and country mouse are going to visit each other. They were going to walk on that bridge.

Kelly: So I will write 'visit each other' on the chart. Any other predictions?

Monirot: Yes. I said the city mouse isn't going to like the food the country mouse gives him.

Kelly (writing the last prediction on the chart): Let's read to the bottom of page 9 to see if we can prove any of our predictions. You can read in quiet voices so I can hear you.

You can also activate prior knowledge by building collections of artifacts that provide information about a subject, a time period, or ideas children will encounter in texts. Rasinski and Padak (2000) call these collections *jackdaws,* named for a British bird, similar to the American grackle, that picks up brightly colored, interesting, and attractive objects and carries them off to its nest. Rasinski and Padak recommend the creation of such collections, noting that the number and types of items are limited only by one's imagination and creativity. Figure 8.2 illustrates the kinds of artifacts your might collect.

Figure 8.2
Possible Jackdaws for a Book

1. Clothes of the type worn by particular characters in a book—actual clothing examples or catalog pictures, paper dolls, collages, old photos, etc.
2. Songs or music from a period or event depicted in a book—sheet music, recordings, demonstrations, titles, or musical instruments
3. A news article from the period, real or a facsimile
4. Photographs from the time period or geographical area depicted in the book
5. Household items from the period depicted in the book
6. A time line depicting the occurrence of events in a book (may also include real-world events not mentioned in the book)
7. A map showing any journey the main characters make
8. Recipes and food dishes typical of the time period or the geographical area depicted in the book
9. Selected poems that reflect the theme of the book
10. A glossary of interesting or peculiar words or their origins in the book
11. Dioramas that illustrate particular scenes from the story
12. A biographical sketch of the book's author
13. A list of other related books (by story, theme, characters, and so on) that students can read to extend their literacy experience
14. Videos, sound recordings, or web sites that allow students to see or hear people or places similar to those in the book

Source: *Effective Reading Strategies: Teaching Children Who Find Reading Difficult.* 2/E by Rasinski/Padak, ©. Reprinted by permission of Pearson Education, Inc., Upper Saddle River, NJ.

Exploring the Reasons for Reading a Text

Research supports engaging children in a discussion before they read about the reasons for reading a particular text. Students may be reading a text to be entertained, to be informed, to get answers to specific questions, or to find interesting information. They may be reading a text because they know and like the author, appreciate the work of an illustrator, or are particularly fond of a genre. Whenever you introduce a text you plan to read aloud to your students, be sure to share with them the reason(s) you have selected that particular text. In addition to activating background knowledge and exploring reasons for reading a text, we enhance children's comprehension when we help them examine the structure of a text before they read.

Exploring Text Structures

An extensive review of the research on text organization and comprehension reveals that the organization of text, students' awareness of that organization, and students' strategic use of text organization affect their comprehension (Dickson, Simmons, & Kameenui, 2001). Good texts are always written with an identifiable organizing structure. However, expository texts and narrative texts are organized in distinctly different ways. Children's comprehension of text is improved when they explore and understand these patterns of text structure.

Narrative Text Structures. Authors of narrative texts have a choice of organizational patterns as they construct their stories. Knowledge of story structure, or *story grammar* as some refer to it, involves an understanding of the setting, the main characters, the problem, attempts to solve the problem, and the resolution. Recognizing this pattern in narrative texts can help children make predictions and apply previous experience as they read. Folktales are often excellent examples from which to teach story structure because their structure is so transparent. Think about your favorite fairy tale as you read about story maps and how to create one.

Story Maps. Story maps are heuristics to help children understand the components of a story. A variety of studies have shown the value of using story maps as an aid to comprehension with young children, intermediate grade to high school students, struggling readers, and children with special needs (Duke & Pearson, 2002). As each element of the story is discovered during reading, the story events are added to the map. The use of story maps has been shown to aid both able and less able readers in writing and reading narrative texts (National Reading Panel, 2000). Figure 8.3 is a story map for *City Mouse–CountryMouse.* As you review this story map, consider how illustrating the structure of a story on a map could aid student's comprehension. A variation on the story map is the story cube.

Story Cube. Story cubes are appropriate for students in third grade and up. Students use a paper, unfolded (flattened) cube to illustrate elements of the story. Each of the six sides of the cube is used. After students have drawn or written the story elements on each side, they fold the paper to form a cube.

Simplified Drawings. Another good device for helping children analyze the structure of stories is a simplified drawing of a nursery rhyme, such as Figure 8.4, "Little Miss Muffet" (Gatheral, 1984). Each box represents a story element: main character, setting, exposition, introduction of the antagonist, conflict or problem, and resolution of the story. In the first box, the circle represents Miss Muffet, the main character. In the second box, the tuffet represents the setting. The exposition tells us what is going on as Miss Muffet is eating her curds and whey. The spider is the antagonist, and sitting down beside her is the problem. Resolution

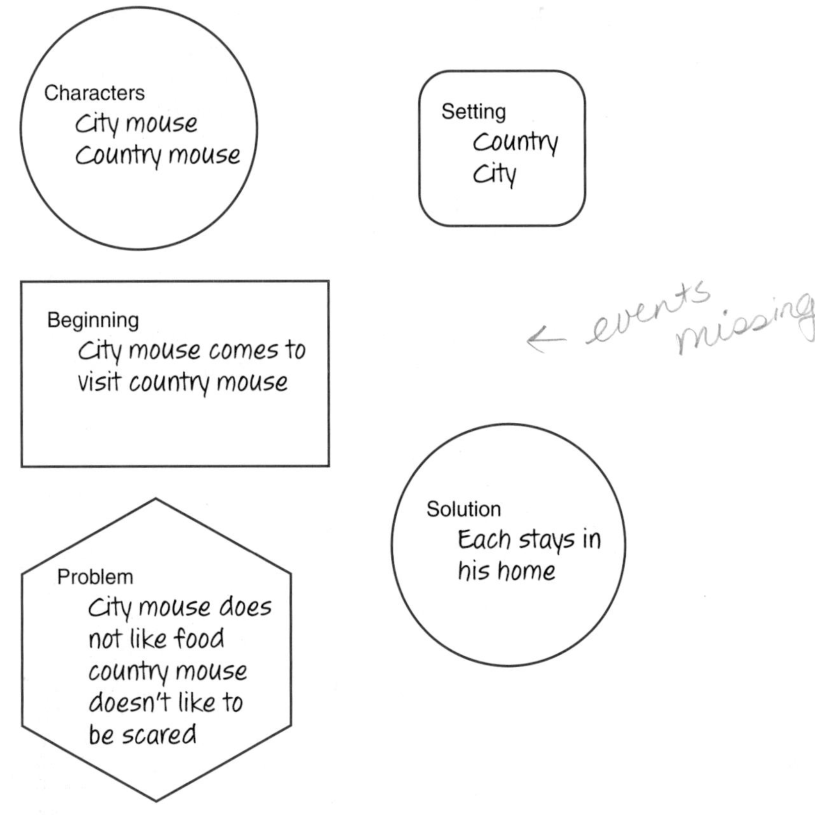

Figure 8.3
Story Map for *City Mouse–Country Mouse*

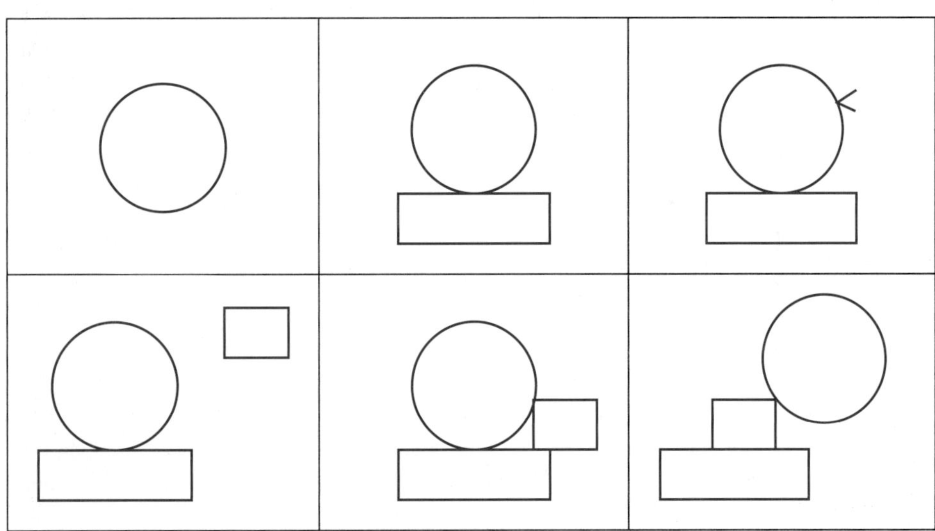

Figure 8.4
Simplified Drawing of "Little Miss Muffet"

comes when Miss Muffet runs away. It is best to draw these pictures on separate 8 × 10 cards so they can be rearranged to match each story. Even young children can begin to recognize the parts of the story and relate them to story structure in general. This skill is important for both reading and writing. As children read, they form expectations about what will happen next; as they write, they need to think about story elements and the arrangement of these elements in their own stories.

Charles Temple (1990) has argued that we need to coach readers in digging deeper and deeper into stories. He calls structuralism an "enchanted roadmap" (p. 56) for helping us think about stories both as readers and writers. **Structuralism** is the literary study of the structures that we can use to write and read literature. Here we look at two additional examples of ways to analyze story structure: dramatic roles and structured opposites.

Dramatic Roles. Temple (1990) reports on the work of Etienne Souriau who described a set of roles that could be occupied by the characters in any one scene of a play. Souriau described only six such roles, but argued that their various combinations could yield 210,141 different dramatic situations. The first four of the six roles are simple enough to explain to first graders who can then use them to identify the roles played by characters and the characters' motives. Temple's description of Souriau's roles follows. Souriau assigned each character a sign from the Zodiac to make them easier to remember.

- *The Lion Force.* The Lion Force is the hero, the protagonist, the person whose will directs or centers the events of the story. In "Jack and the Beanstalk," for example, Jack is the Lion Force.
- *The Sun, or Object.* The object is the thing or quality that is desired. In "Jack" the object might be adventure or the wherewithal to survive. As this case illustrates, who or what the objects are is more often than not the subject of interesting debate.
- *Mars, the Rival.* Some person or force usually opposes the Lion Force and stands as someone to be contended with, or as a trial to be overcome. Children are tempted to simplify the rival by calling it "the bad guy" or "the enemy," but this isn't always accurate. In many stories, rivals can turn out to be a friend of the Lion Force, as does Little John in the story of Robin Hood.
- *Moon, the Helper.* There is often a character in a story who helps the Lion Force, especially at those times when he or she has reached the limits of his or her own powers. In "Jack," the helper's role is played by the man with the beans, and also by the giant's wife. Helpers can serve other characters in stories, too, but those who are most developed as characters usually serve the Lion Force.

When we have introduced these roles to children, we deal only with the first four roles at first: the Lion Force, the Sun-Object, Mars the Rival, and Moon the Helper. Souriau had two further roles, which we sometimes introduce later:

- *Earth, the Receiver.* The receiver is the person or persons who receive the good things sought by the Lion Force. In the story of the hole in the dike, for example, the boy wanted to save the dike to prevent a flood, and he wanted this protection for his community. The community thus is the receiver of the goods of this story. In "Jack," if you accept that the Sun-Object is the wherewithal to survive, then Jack shares the role of receiver with his mother. But usually the receiver is the Lion Force, so this role is not critical in many stories.
- *Libra, the Arbiter or Judge.* The Arbiter decides whether or not the Lion Force will receive the object she or he seeks. If there is a separate character occupying this role, we call this character Libra, the Judge. In *The Wizard of Oz,* the wizard seems to play this role when he tells the cowardly lion, the tin woodsman, and the scarecrow what they must do in order to learn courage, intelligence, and a heart. (p. 34)

Temple (1990) asserts that analyzing the roles in a story leads readers to a discussion of the most important issues in a story. Another scheme for analyzing story structure is structured opposites.

Structured Opposites. Temple (1990) described the work of Claude Levi-Strauss who believed that the human mind finds it most natural to think of the world in terms of hot and cold, east and west, good and bad, light and dark. Thus, a useful way to look at stories is to find the contrasts within them. Temple recommends the following questions to get your students thinking about the contrasts in a story:

- What does the main character really want? What does the main character really not want?
- What is the character trying to do or to make happen in the story? What is the character trying not to do or not make happen?
- What do other people expect the character to be like? What is she or he really like? (p. 39)

Expository Text Structures. Just as narrative texts are written with identifiable patterns of organization, so are expository texts. However, authors of expository material rarely confine themselves to a single organizational pattern; a text normally reveals several. Students who are more knowledgeable about text structures recall more of the information they read than students who are less knowledgeable about text structures (Bartlett, 1978; Meyer, Brandt, & Bluth, 1980). The following list describes some common patterns of text organization. Help your learners understand each of these patterns first by pointing them out in texts you read to your students, then by helping them identify the patterns in texts they are reading, and finally in using the patterns in text they write themselves.

1. *Major idea/supporting details:* Author states the major idea or conclusion and then offers the evidence to support it.
2. *Details/conclusion:* Author offers the data first, then draws conclusions.
3. *Time order:* Author relates events in the sequence in which they occurred, using chronological order or ordinal markers such as "first, second, third" or "then, then, and finally."
4. *Cause/effect:* Author explains events or phenomena in terms of conditions that create them and follow from them.
5. *Compare/contrast:* Author examines similarities and differences between things.
6. *Question/answer:* Author asks a question and then answers it, perhaps repeating the device throughout the text.

Children understand these patterns best if they use them in their own writing after studying them. When do they study them? As you are assigning an expository selection, you point out the organizational patterns the author uses. For example, discuss the pattern of organization based on cause and effect before the students read a text arranged that way. Then have the students perform a science experiment that demonstrates a cause-effect relationship and write about it using the model you have provided. Practicing the use of various patterns in class discussions of topics important to the children is another helpful strategy. When a class discussion exhibits a particular pattern, be sure to point that out to your students.

Len Unsworth (1999), an Australian linguist, has helped us understand expository text structures from a grammatical perspective. By comparing the differences between oral language grammar and the grammar of science and social studies texts, Unsworth has demonstrated the significantly greater complexity of expository text. He has done this using a measure of lexical density.

Lexical density is calculated by counting the number of lexical items (content words) in comparison with grammatical items (structure words) per clause. Spoken English typically has a lexical density of 1.4—that is, 1.4 content words per clause. In written texts where the language is more planned and more formal, the lexical density is usually about 4 to 6 lexical items per clause (Halliday, 1993, in Unsworth, 1999). Unsworth stresses that this greater complexity of school texts can contribute to comprehension difficulties. We need to help learners deconstruct expository texts, sometimes a sentence at a time, to help them understand the complex language. Comprehension is improved when you spend time helping children understand the way(s) in which a text is organized before they read it and as they are reading it.

Assessment and Evaluation Toolbox

EXPOSITORY RETELLING CHECKLIST

Here is a checklist you can use as a student retells an expository text (Harp, 2000).

Check appropriately: _____ aided _____ unaided (Did the student retell without prompting from you?) _____ written _____ oral

Check One:

_____ All important facts are recalled.
_____ Most of the important facts are recalled.
_____ Some of the important facts are recalled.
_____ None of the important facts are recalled.
_____ Supporting ideas are recalled.
_____ Ideas recalled in logical order.
_____ Reader made use of charts, graphs, illustrations.
_____ Reader recalled important conclusions.
_____ Reader stated valid inferences.
_____ Reader read critically.

Comments:

Prediction Making

Another good prereading strategy that advances comprehension is charting readers' predictions. You can do the prediction charting on a chalkboard or white board, overhead projector, or chart paper. You have children make their predictions for a section of the story before they read it, and then modify their predictions as they move through the text. Figure 8.5 is an illustration of a prediction chart made when Kelly's first graders moved into *City Mouse–Country Mouse.* This prediction chart served the children well as they read to learn if their predictions were verified and as they discussed their predictions during the reading.

The National Reading Panel (2000) identified seven categories of comprehension instruction that appear to have a "firm scientific basis for concluding that they improve comprehension in normal readers" (chap. 4, p. 42). These categories are: cooperative learning, comprehension monitoring, graphic and semantic organizers (including story maps), question answering, question generation, and summarization. Invoking these instructional strategies during the reading of text will enhance your guided reading instruction.

Figure 8.5
Prediction Chart for *City Mouse-Country Mouse*

one mouse is dressed up/the other has a patch on his pants

one mouse doesn't have any money

the city mouse is going to have real good stuff and the country mouse is going to have broken things

city mouse and country mouse are going to visit each other

the city mouse does not like the food the other mouse gave him

~~the mice are going to have a fight about the food~~

~~the country mouse is going to be mad about the broken plate~~

they are going to the city mouse's house and eat good food

~~they are going to a restaurant~~

the two dogs will find them

~~they will be too full to run~~

something scary is going to happen

they will save their lives

home is the best place to be

LOOKING AT THE RESEARCH

What the research says about story mapping before reading

A study compared the effects of two teacher-directed prereading instructional procedures on literal and inferential reading comprehension. Literal comprehension is recalling details in the words of the author. Inferential reading comprehension is "reading between the lines," creating mental images more detailed than the words of the author alone permit. One strategy was the traditional directed reading activity (developing background, creating interest, introducing vocabulary, and establishing purpose for reading). The other strategy was a teacher-prepared story map the children studied with the guidance of the teacher prior to reading. The story mapping procedures resulted in significantly better inferential and literal comprehension than did the directed reading activity at the third-grade level (Davis, 1994). This research supports your use of story maps to introduce a text. Why do you think studying a story map would increase literal comprehension? How might it increase inferential comprehension?

HOW DO I GUIDE THE DEVELOPMENT OF COMPREHENSION ABILITY DURING THE READING OF A TEXT?

Once you have investigated the cover illustration and title, completed a picture walk, activated background knowledge and discussed predictions, it is time to move the children into reading the text. At this point you carefully observe children's reading behavior and coach them toward more strategic reading with greater comprehension. Comprehension is improved when children support each other as readers.

Cooperative Learning—Cooperative Support

Children helping each other and interacting over the use of reading strategies improve the learning of the strategies, promote intellectual discussion, and increase reading comprehension (National Reading Panel, 2000). Recall our description of Mary Giard's first graders in Chapter 6 in which we described the strategy checklist Mary's students asked her to help them create so they could monitor their strategy use when they were doing buddy reading. You can promote this kind of cooperative support during guided reading.

Suppose you are watching children read and you notice one child tracking with his finger and rereading the same line. You might say, "Joshua, I see you are having some difficulty with a word on that line. Can you tell us about that?" If you have modeled this kind of language often, children will respond readily. To encourage discussion among children about their reading, you might say instead, "Joshua, I saw that you were having some difficulty with a word on that line. Let's see if Josh can think of one fix-it action he can take, and then let's see if others in our group can make other suggestions for Josh." In other words, try to encourage interaction among the children in a guided reading group about the story and about the process of reading the story as well. Let's return to Kelly's guided reading lesson as the children are completing the first round of reading. Recall that Kelly had made a prediction map and then invited the children to whisper read the first nine pages.

Kelly (watching Carly finger point and frown as she is working on a word): Carly, have you found a tricky word?

Carly: Yes, I thought (pointing to *fine* in "The Country Mouse did not have fine food") this was saying free, but it doesn't look right. The *f* and *e* are right, but I'm stuck on the middle of this word. It says *in,* but *fin* doesn't make any sense.

Kelly: Can you show me the first vowel? (Carly points to the *i.*) Now look at the last vowel. Do you remember what the *e* does to the *i?*

Carly: Oh yes, it makes the *i* say its name.

Kelly: Yes, it makes the *i* sound long. Can you sound and blend the word now?

Carly: Yes, it is /f/i/n/—fine.

Kelly: You are right. Now read the line again and see if *fine* makes sense there.

Carly: "The Country Mouse did not have fine food." Well, I guess that makes sense, but I'm not sure what "fine food" means.

Kelly: You did a good job working out "fine," and you read the line correctly. We will talk about the meaning of "fine food."

Kelly: I see everyone is finished now. Thank you for turning your books over when you got to the end of page 9. That helps me know you are ready to discuss the story. Turn your books to page 8. Carly did nice work on a word she found tricky in the first line. Did anyone have trouble with the word just before *food?*

Nate raises his hand.

Kelly: Nate, what happened when you came to that word?

Nate: I wasn't sure what that word said, so I saw the word *in* in the middle of it and tried reading it *fin.* But that didn't make any sense, "fin food." So then I saw the *e* at the end of the word and remembered about the *e* making the first vowel long, I think—anyway, say its name. So then I tried "fine" and it sounded right."

Kelly: But did it make sense?

Nate: Well, I saw "fine food" on a sign at a restaurant one time. So I know you can say that, but I don't really know what "fine food" means.

Kelly: Let's talk about the meaning of "fine food." Does anyone have an idea?

Monirot: I think it means special food, like we have for a party like a birthday or maybe a holiday like Thanksgiving.

Katelyn: Yeah, like when we had my daddy's birthday dinner, we had steaks. That was special. I think that's what "fine food" means.

Kelly: I think you understand the meaning of "fine food." Any other ideas?

Katelyn: I think it means food that costs lots of money.

Kelly: Yes, fine food usually does cost more than plain, everyday food. I think you understand. Let's turn to page 6.

Kelly leads the children through a discussion of the meaning of "Once upon a time" on page 6, and "cousin" on page 7. When she was satisfied they had adequate understanding, she asked for volunteers to reread the sentences containing these words emphasizing reading with expression. She then asked them to turn to page 9.

Kelly: What is happening on this page?

Monirot: The city mouse is dropping his plates, and the country mouse is maybe saying "Oh, no!"

Kelly: Monirot, can you read the first sentence on this page to us? (Monirot fluently reads the sentence). Can anyone explain the meaning of "turned up his nose at the country food"? (Carly and Nate raise their hands.) Nate what do you think?

Nate (looking at the illustration): I think it means the city mouse turned his head away. See, he isn't looking at his cousin or the food.

Kelly: You are correct about the picture, but "turned up his nose" means more than looking away. Any more ideas? (Carly raises her hand again.) Carly, what do you think?

Carly: I think it means he doesn't like the food. If you turn up your nose at something, you don't like it. Like when my mom wants me to eat broccoli.

Kelly: That's correct, Carly. Do any of you ever turn up your noses at something? (laughter from the children)

Katelyn: My mommy made liver one night for dinner. Boy! I turned up my nose at that. It was yuck!

The children each took their turn at offering an example.

Kelly: What do you think will happen next in this story? (Hands go up). Carly, what do you think?

Carly: I think the mice are going to have a fight about the food. The country mouse is going to be mad about the broken plate.

Monirot: I don't think that. I think they are going to go to the city mouse's house and eat good food. See, it says, "And he invited his cousin to have dinner with him in the city."

Nate: I think they are going to go to a restaurant in the city.

Kelly: Let's add those three predictions to our chart. Are there any more predictions? (No response from the children). Then turn the page and read to the end of page 13.

After they read the next section, Kelly and the children revisit their predictions and read aloud the text that confirms predictions. They cross off the predictions about having a fight and going to a restaurant. Kelly revisited "No sooner said than done" to confirm their understanding, and then she invites the students to make a new round of predictions following the line about hearing growling and barking.

Kelly: What do you think will happen next? (Hands fly up.) Katelyn, what do you think?

Katelyn: I think a big dog is going to come and find them on the table. And . . . and they are too full to jump off the table and run away.

Carly: Yeah, and something really bad is going to happen.

Kelly: Carly, what bad thing do you think will happen?

Carly: I don't know. It is going to be scary.

Nate: I think they are going to get away from the dog just in time to save their lives.

Kelly: Okay, we will add to our prediction chart that the dog will find them and the mice will be too full to run, something scary is going to happen, and they will save their lives. Let's read the next two pages. Turn your book over when you finish page 15.

When the children finish reading, Kelly revisits the predictions. They discuss crossing off the scary prediction, but the children decide that the two dogs chasing the mice is pretty scary. They change the one dog prediction to two dogs and cross off the idea that the mice would be too full to run. Kelly confirms understanding of "all at once," and then they focus on the idea that the country mouse made up his mind to go back to the country that very night. They agree that he was probably really scared and was ready to go home.

Kelly: I will tell you the next page is the last page of the story. You told me earlier that fables always have a lesson to teach us at the end. Do you have any ideas about what the lesson of this fable will be? (Nate's hand goes up.) Nate, what do you think?

Nate: I think the Country Mouse is going to decide that home is the best place to be.

Kelly: Nate, I think that is a lesson we could draw from this story. Are there any more? (No response.) Let's turn and read the last page. (The children read.) Is Nate's prediction the lesson the author chose to teach?

Nomirot: The author is saying that it is better to eat plain old food if eating fancy food is going to get you in trouble.

Carly: Yeah, but I think Nate was mostly right because it is peaceful at the country mouse's house. So he was saying just about the same thing.

Kelly: I think you have understood the moral of this fable. Did you enjoy it? (Enthusiastic indications of agreement.) Good. We will revisit it tomorrow, and then you may choose to take it home.

Comprehension Monitoring

In Kelly's work you saw that as children are moving through a text in guided reading, you improve their comprehension by helping them to monitor how well they comprehend. One way to do this is to revisit the prediction map and talk about which of their predictions match what the author did with the story. Another way to help students monitor their comprehension is to ask them to draw or describe the mental images forming as they read.

Describing Mental Images. For young children it is best to ask them to draw a picture of a scene or character. Older children can learn to make vivid oral descriptions of their mental images. Students enjoy comparing their images. That affords you the opportunity to reinforce that we don't all make exactly the same mental images even though we all comprehend the text.

Using Think-Alouds. Another device for helping readers monitor their comprehension is think-alouds (Bereiter & Bird, 1985). Think-alouds require a reader to stop reading from time to time, reflect on how the reading is going, and orally describe what reading strategies are being used. Baumann, Seifert-Kessell, and Jones (1992) studied the effect of think-alouds by teaching one group of fourth-grade students a variety of comprehension monitoring and fix-up strategies through the think-aloud technique. Students in comparison groups read the same stories but did not have the think-aloud training. The researchers concluded that the think-aloud instruction was highly effective in helping students improve comprehension.

In subsequent work Baumann, Jones, and Seifert-Kessell (1993) described an effective instructional sequence of activities that began with the teacher sharing think-alouds and moved to the teacher suggesting that children create their own think-alouds. The sequence concludes with children collaborating in small groups to share, discuss, and create think-alouds. In reporting their research the authors share transcripts of two groups of children who were reading Laura Ingalls Wilder's *On the Banks of Plum Creek,* in which Laura, playing in the fast-running waters of Plum Creek, rolls off a footbridge and nearly drowns. As the students read the story aloud, the researchers stopped them periodically and asked, "Can you tell me what you were doing or thinking about as you read this part of the story?"

As you read the following transcripts, notice the striking differences in the children's responses.

Children's Responses # 1

Ann: I was asking questions, and I asked questions like "Why did she go to the creek when her mother told her not to?" And "Why did Laura take her shoes and socks off when she knew the creek was going to be rocky and muddy on the bottom?"

Kim: I was asking myself, "Is this making sense?" and I was asking if like do I think what would happen next without reading the next page—just reading that [the present] page."

Children's Response # 2

Kate: Nothing. [**Researcher:** Nothing? What kind of ideas did you have as you read?] **Kate:** *That her mom was very nice and understood that it could have killed her.* [**Researcher***:* Any other ideas you had?] **Kate:** *She was nice.* [**Researcher***:* Anything else?] **Kate:** *No.*

Lynn: Oh, trying to stop at every period and trying to pause at the commas. [**Researcher***:* Is there anything else you were trying to do as you read?] **Lynn:** *I was trying to read loud like instead of talking real soft and you couldn't hear me.* [**Researcher***:* What else? Anything else you did or thought about as you were reading this section?] **Lynn:** *Not really.*

The readers quoted in the first example had think-aloud training. They were clearly more strategic in monitoring their comprehension than the readers quoted in the second example who had not had think-aloud training. Think-aloud instruction clearly promotes comprehension monitoring.

Figure 8.6
Structured Overview of Westward Expansion

As you introduce the text ("Today we are going to read a piece about westward expansion"), the diagram might look like this:

- Westward Expansion
  - Vast amounts of land
  - Desires of the people

As the children read about Manifest Destiny, the diagram might look like this:

- Westward Expansion
  - Vast amounts of land
  - Desires of the people
    - Manifest Destiny
      - God's will
      - Good for people
      - Right of the people

As they read about the incentive to move westward created by the offer of free land, your structured overview might look like this:

- Westward Expansion
  - Vast amounts of land
    - Free parcels
    - Stake claim
    - Farm success
    - Homestead
  - Desires of the people
    - Manifest Destiny
      - God's will
      - Good for people
      - Right of the people
    - New home

As children discuss what they read about modes of travel used by the pioneers, your structured overview might look like this:

- Westward Expansion
  - Vast amounts of land
    - Free parcels
    - Stake claim
    - Farm success
    - Homestead
  - Travel
    - Conestoga wagons
    - Teams of oxen
    - 10 miles per day
  - Desires of the people
    - Manifest Destiny
      - God's will
      - Good for people
      - Right of the people
    - New home

As children discuss their understandings of the hardships suffered by the pioneers, your diagram might look like this:

- Westward Expansion
  - Vast amounts of land
    - Free parcels
    - Stake claim
    - Farm success
    - Homestead
  - Travel
    - Conestoga wagons
    - Teams of oxen
    - 10 miles per day
  - Hardships
    - Illness
    - Indians
    - Weather
  - Desires of the people
    - Manifest Destiny
      - God's will
      - Good for people
      - Right of the people
    - New home

Graphic and Semantic Organizers

Graphic and semantic organizers have proven useful in helping students comprehend expository texts (Armbruster, Anderson, & Ostertag, 1987). Story maps have been proven helpful in comprehending narrative texts (Pearson, 1981). During a guided reading session, you can assist children in creating a schematic or graphic organizer as their comprehension of the piece unfolds.

Structured Overview. One form of graphic organizer is the structured overview. Structured overviews show the relationships between vocabulary terms and concepts. If you were leading a guided reading session using a text on Westward Expansion, your growing structured overview might look like the one illustrated in Figure 8.6. This overview is a collaborative effort involving the children in its construction.

Semantic Map. Another form of graphic organizer is the semantic map. Semantic maps, less complex than structured overviews, are likewise intended to show the interrelationships among ideas. Introduced as a note-taking and study technique by Hanf (1971), the semantic map can provide a way for children to organize what they know about a topic before the reading. It also can be developed during the reading of a selection or can follow it as a part of a group discussion. Teaching students to represent the ideas that they are reading about in a graphic organizer benefits the ability of the students to remember what they read and may transfer to better comprehension in social studies and science content areas (Alvermann & Boothby, 1986). Figure 8.7 is a semantic map based on a piece about sandhill cranes.

Knowledge of word meanings is an important contributor to comprehension.

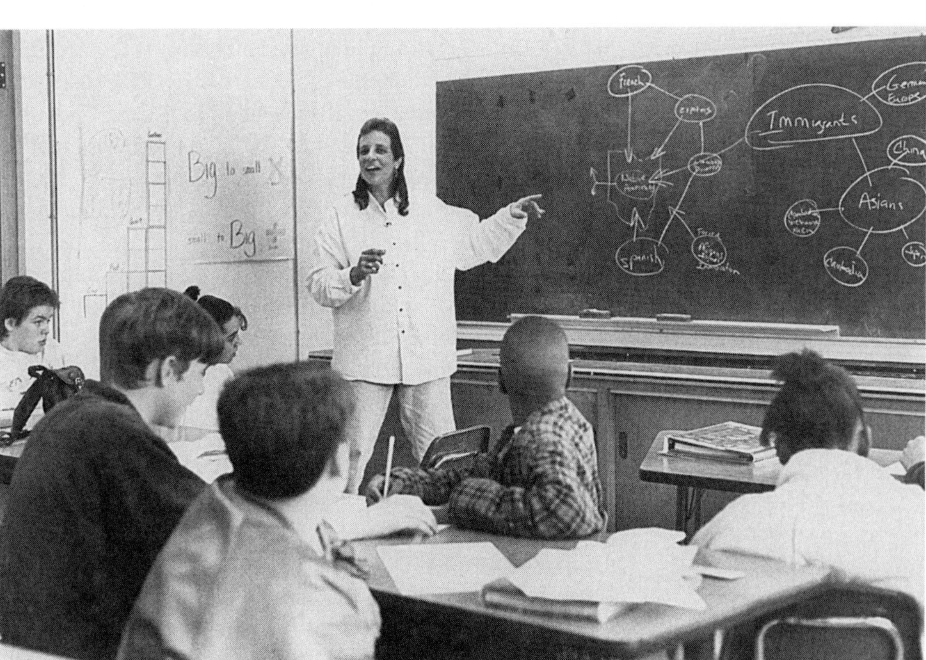

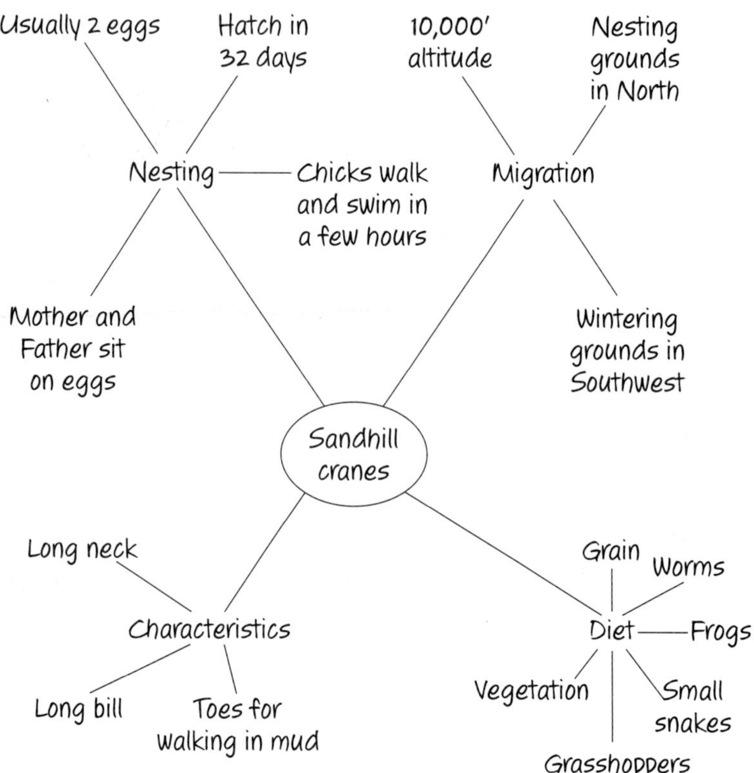

Figure 8.7
Semantic Map for *Sandhill Cranes*

Question Answering

In 1978 Dolores Durkin published a famous study about what classroom observations revealed regarding comprehension instruction. She discovered that little if any comprehension was being taught; teachers tended to ask comprehension questions that were *testing* comprehension, not *teaching* it. We have learned a great deal about teaching comprehension in the years since Durkin did her research. The National Reading Panel (2000) concluded that there was value in asking learners comprehension questions to monitor their comprehension. What is different about the questions of today and the questions that Durkin noted is that the recommended questions today are not simply literal recall questions. Literal recall questions are those that have only one answer and require readers to remember isolated bits of information. Better are questions that require readers to focus on concepts and connections.

Attending to the Kinds of Questions We Ask. We have also learned that readers' understanding and recall of their reading can be shaped by the kinds of comprehension questions their teacher asks (Anderson & Biddle, 1975). If you predominately ask your learners recall questions, they will learn to focus their attention in future reading encounters on recalling details. If your questions tend to be inference questions, your students will tend to focus on making inferences. Research suggests you need to be mindful to ask a variety of comprehension questions. For example, after reading *The Three Little Pigs,* you might ask,

How is this story like other stories that we have read? What do you think is the lesson of this story? What did the wolf do to try to solve the problem of getting the third little pig? The specific answer to any given question is not as important as knowing your learners can answer questions that reflect a specific kind of thinking. The decisions you make about the kinds of comprehension questions to ask can be greatly informed by the work of Frederick Davis and Judith Irwin.

Frederick Davis's Analysis of Comprehension. Davis was a pioneer in researching the components of reading comprehension. He began working in the 1940s. His suggestions for points of emphasis in comprehension instruction are still useful today. Davis (1968) identified the following five components of reading comprehension:

- knowledge of word meanings
- ability to draw inferences
- ability to follow the structure of a passage
- finding answers to questions answered explicitly or in paraphrase in the material read
- recognizing the author's attitude, tone, mood, and purpose

Judith Irwin's Comprehension Processes. Irwin (1991) identified five distinct comprehension processes. Understanding each of these processes will inform your asking of comprehension questions. Irwin defines these processes as:

- Microprocesses—dealing with the "micro" levels of information, or individual phrases and sentences
- Integrative processes—understanding and inferring the relationships between clauses and sentences
- Macroprocessing—ongoing process of creating or selecting an organized set of summary ideas, presumably for the purpose of organizing recall and reducing the number of ideas to be remembered
- Elaborative processes—the process of making inferences that enrich and extend comprehension; elaborations on the text
- Metacognitive processing—selecting, evaluating, and regulating reading comprehension strategies

Bloom's Taxonomy. Benjamin Bloom created a classification of cognitive tasks. Teachers have long found his scheme helpful in formulating questions for class discussions. You may wish to draw on this work to formulate comprehension questions. Figure 8.8 illustrates the classifications in Bloom's Taxonomy (1956) as applied to *City Mouse–Country Mouse.*

Remember that asking comprehension questions is testing comprehension, not teaching it. Using questions to teach comprehension will require that you use think-alouds to model for your students how you work your way through answering a certain kind of comprehension question. You will find it necessary to monitor the kinds of comprehension tasks each of your students has learned. The Comprehension Checklist illustrated in Figure 8.9 is adapted from the work of Davis (1968) and Irwin (1991). Keep a copy of this checklist in your monitoring notebook for each of your students. Although it is a challenge to keep checklists updated for all of your students, teachers we work with have found it useful to identify a small group of five or six children each Monday (maybe a guided reading group) and then carefully observe just these children during one week to update each of their checklists.

Figure 8.8
Bloom's Taxonomy of the Cognitive Domain. Sample Questions for *City Mouse–Country Mouse*

Evaluation: making critical judgments (Decide who had the best life, the city mouse or the country mouse, and tell why you think so.)

Synthesis: coming up with something new (Can you think of a time in your life when something you had or something you did was better than you had thought it was?)

Analysis: breaking information into simpler parts to see the relationships among the parts (What information can you find in the story to show that the city mouse and country mouse liked each other?)

Application: using information to solve problems (If the city mouse and the country mouse visited a cousin who lived in a church, would they have liked it there?)

Comprehension: translating, interpreting, or extrapolating information (What does it mean to be a "city mouse" and a "country mouse"?)

Knowledge: recalling information (Who comes to visit the country mouse?)

Assessment and Evaluation Toolbox

RETELLINGS

Irwin and Mitchell (1983) long ago established the power of retellings. Their research demonstrated that retellings reveal not only that a reader has comprehended but has made inferences. You prompt a retelling by asking the child to tell you everything he or she can recall from reading the story. If the child stops short of retelling the whole story, you can them prompt for more detail by asking questions. You saw a rubric for evaluating oral story retelling in Chapter 3, Figure 3.11. Here is a rubric for a written retelling from Rickards and Cheek (1999):

SCORE POINT 4

The student correctly writes the characters and setting and fully describes the story's problem and solution. Events are described thoroughly and sequenced accurately.

SCORE POINT 3

The student correctly identifies the characters and setting and explains the story's problem and solution. Events are described and sequenced accurately.

SCORE POINT 2

The student identifies the characters, setting, problem, solution, and events, though the information is minimal and may contain slight inaccuracies.

SCORE POINT 1

The student does not identify the necessary story elements, and/or the information contains significant inaccuracies.

Figure 8.9
Comprehension Checklist

Name ______________________________

Word Meanings
- ☐ By definition
- ☐ By synonym
- ☐ Create a sentence

Microprocesses
- ☐ Understands ideas in sentences
- ☐ Reads aloud with phrasing
- ☐ Recalls ideas stated in the text
- ☐ Recalls ideas paraphrased in the text

Integrative Processes
- ☐ Can identify pronoun referents

Macroprocesses
- ☐ Summarizes with a new title
- ☐ Summarizes main ideas
- ☐ Identifies the structure of narrative text
- ☐ Identifies the structure of expository text
- ☐ Synthesizes:
  - ☐ Text to Self Connections
  - ☐ Text to World Connections
  - ☐ Test to Text Connections

Elaborative Processes
- ☐ Makes inferences
- ☐ Makes predictions
- ☐ Integrates information with knowledge
- ☐ Forms and describes mental images
- ☐ Responds affectively
- ☐ Uses higher-level thinking processes

Metacognitive Processes
- ☐ Knows when comprehension fails
- ☐ Takes remedial action when necessary
- ☐ Uses study strategies purposefully

Question Generating

The research on students generating their own comprehension questions is not definitive, but it is encouraging. The National Reading Panel (2000) recognized the value of question generating as a part of a multiple strategy instruction program. Duke and Pearson (2002) concluded that question generation activities should not be used as a steady routine repeated for every text encountered, but as an activity that is regularly but intermittently scheduled into guided or shared reading. One such strategy is analyzing the relationship between the type of question being asked and where the answer may be found.

Question-Answer-Relationships (QAR). This procedure for helping students analyze the type of question being asked and where the answer may be found was developed by Taffy Raphael (1982, 1986). Raphael identified four QARs to help learners uncover the connections between questions and answers. The four relationships (two in the text, and two in the reader's head) are: (1) right there, (2) think and search, (3) author and you, and (4) on my own. "Right there" answers are easily found in the text in the words of the author. These are the answers to what we typically think of as recall questions. "Think and search" answers are in the text, but the reader must combine ideas from different parts of the text or read between the lines.

"Right there" and "think and search" are the answers to what we typically think of as inference questions. Let's use *Ira Sleeps Over* (Waber, 1972) here as an aid to understanding these two kinds of information sources. You may recall that this is the story of the night Ira's neighbor, Reggie, invites him to sleep over at his house. Ira's sister taunts Ira about taking his Teddy bear. Ira decides not to take his bear, but changes his mind after the telling of scary stories when Reggie gets out of bed and gets his own bear out of a drawer. A "right there" question would be, "What was the name of Ira's next-door neighbor?" A "think and search" question would be, "How did Ira feel as he was trying to decide whether or not to take his bear to Reggie's house?"

"Right there" and "think and search" questions are based on information that is in the text; "author and you" and "on my own" questions are not. To answer these questions readers must combine what they already know with what the author is telling them. These are the answers to what we typically think of as synthesis questions. "Was it right or fair for Ira's sister to treat him the way she did?" is an "author and you" question. "On my own" answers can be drawn entirely from readers' own experiences; they don't have to read the text to answer them. These are the answers to what we typically think of as critical thinking or evaluative questions. "When have you had to make a difficult decision?" is an "on my own" question.

Raphael's research has shown that training in QARs increases student confidence in the ability to answer different types of questions and to generate questions. You could make use of both Bloom's Taxonomy and QARs to analyze the questions you ask during shared and guided reading and when you are leading class discussions. This way you can be sure to ask a wide range of question types.

Another effective way to train readers to ask questions of text is to set up situations in which you and the students take turns generating questions as you move through a text.

Reciprocal Questioning (ReQuest). ReQuest is an instructional strategy for helping your students learn to generate questions and to answer questions about a text. The procedure was developed by Anthony Manzo (1969) to be used one on one, but it can be easily adapted to a group. You could use ReQuest as part of a guided reading session. The procedure involves:

1. You and your students read an identified section of the text silently. With very young readers, struggling readers, or students new to the process, you might select only a sentence to be read. Later, with more experienced readers, this could be expanded to a paragraph or two.
2. When the assignment has been read, everyone closes their books. The students then ask you questions about the selection. You will want to pay particular attention to the types of questions they are asking you, and you may need to coach them to ask more or different questions. Soon you will have the opportunity to model question asking for them.

3. You all read the next assigned piece of the text and close your books when finished.
4. Now you ask questions of the students. This may be a good opportunity for you to talk about the kinds of questions you are asking, thus modeling for them the thinking you want them to do when they generate questions.
5. Steps 2, 3, and 4 may be repeated for as much of the text as you choose to read this way.
6. You ask students to make predictions about how the last section of the text will end. When students complete the reading, you revisit these predictions. You may ask children to read aloud pieces of the text that confirm or disconfirm the predictions.

Questioning the Author (QtA). We know that skillful readers are actively engaged with the ideas of the author when they read. Questioning the author is an instructional strategy that reinforces this active dialogue between the reader and the author by encouraging readers to ask questions of the author as they read. QtA was devised by Beck, McKeown, Hamilton, and Kucan (1997) to assist readers in maintaining this active connection between reader and author. You may find this instructional strategy particularly helpful when you are doing guided reading with expository text. The planning process for QtA entails three steps. First, you carefully read the text you are planning to share with children. Identify the particular challenges offered by the text. These might be a complex technical vocabulary, unusually complex sentences, paraphrasing to build in redundancy, a challenging pattern of text organization, or limited explanation of new concepts, for example. Note the major understandings you want children to take from the text and the challenges you will highlight. Second, decide how you will segment the reading of the text. Third, note the questions you will ask during the reading of the selection to model questioning the author. Such questions might include: "What is the author trying to say here?" "Does she go on to explain this further?" "This is a technical term. Does the author define it or give examples?" At the end of a passage or the selection, you may want to ask questions that follow up on the reading. Such questions are "Does this make sense with what the author said earlier?" "Why do you think the author is telling us this now?"

QtA can also be used with narrative text, although the questions change some. You would focus your questions on setting, character, and plot development. Such questions would include: "How is the author helping us see where this story is taking place?" "How is the author letting us know there is an impending problem?" "How is the author leading us to see how this character may resolve the difficulty?"

Students reading persuasive writing as in newspaper editorials or magazine ads can be helped to recognize the words and techniques that are used to lead readers to agree with the position of the writer or to believe that the product is necessary for our lives. Help the children look for loaded words, testimonials, and other persuasive strategies, and discuss why the author would want readers to believe a certain way or to buy a certain product.

The research on QtA demonstrates that when you implement this strategy successfully, students nearly double their contributions to discussions while improving comprehension and comprehension monitoring (Beck, McKeown, Hamilton, & Kucan, 1997).

Facts, Questions, Responses (FQR). Facts, questions, responses is an instructional strategy we have been using successfully with primary grade children in our work in schools. Developed by Harvey and Goudvis (2000), the strategy begins with children identifying important and interesting facts in their nonfiction reading. They then generate questions they have about those facts and responses they have to their reading. Prepare for this activity by preparing a three-column chart with the columns headed "facts" "questions" "responses." During guided reading, assign the silent reading of a section of text. After the

Figure 8.10
An FQR completed for *An Extraordinary Life*

Facts	Questions	Responses
multiplied her weight 2500 times in 2 weeks	is this usual for insects?	wow! think how big people would be if they did that
caterpillar changed into a chrysalis	do all caterpillars change like this?	the tools for hanging on are built in - that is amazing
it takes 5 monarchs to equal the weight of a penny	are they very fragile?	they travel so far and they are so tiny

children have read, ask "What are some interesting facts you read in the text?" Record the children's responses in the "fact" column. Then ask them what questions or "I wonders" they have about the facts. Record these in the "questions" column. Finally, ask the children what responses they have to the facts, and record them. We have enjoyed using this strategy with children because it focuses on identifying important facts; invites the generation of questions, which is known to enhance comprehension; and acknowledges the value of our responses to reading. Figure 8.10 is an example of an FQR completed by fourth graders after having read *An Extraordinary Life: The Story of a Monarch Butterfly* (Pringle, 1997).

Assessment and Evaluation Toolbox

CLOZE PROCEDURE

Many teachers, especially from third grade on, find that expository texts are frequently too difficult for many learners. The cloze procedure provides a quick and easy way to assess for which of your learners expository texts, such as your science, social studies, or health text, are too difficult. To create a cloze, select a passage of about 250–300 words. Type the selection, leaving the first and last sentences intact but omitting every fifth or seventh word in the rest of the text. Insert a blank line of about 15 spaces where each word is omitted. Proper nouns are not omitted. To score the cloze, count the number of blanks in which the student replaced the exact word that had been omitted. If the student exactly replaces 45% to 59% of the words, the selection is probably at the student's instructional reading level; if 60% or more, at the independent level. If the correct replacements amount to less than 45%, the text is at the reader's frustration level (Bormuth, 1968).

HOW DO I GUIDE THE DEVELOPMENT OF COMPREHENSION ABILITY AFTER READING THE TEXT?

Good readers continue to reflect on text after reading. Your job as a teacher is to guide this reflection. This instruction is informed by looking at the work of Louise Rosenblatt (1982) on reader response. She has helped teachers understand that readers make two kinds of responses to texts. One response she calls an *aesthetic stance,* and the other she calls an *efferent stance.* Usually readers do not take just one of these stances in responding to a text. These responses are on a continuum, and our response to any text has some of both stances, with one of the stances being dominant.

Aesthetic Stance to Text

When a reader adopts an aesthetic stance, the focus is on what was being created as the reading occurred. Here reading is appreciated for the emotional impact it has on the reader. The reader is attending to the personal, private feelings, perceptions, and attitudes that the text creates *in the reader.* Rather than using the text, the reader is attuned to the affective response to the piece as he or she celebrates the work of the author.

Rosenblatt (1982) has described the aesthetic stance as follows:

> In aesthetic reading, we respond to the very story or poem that we are evoking during the transaction with the text. In order to shape the work, we draw on our reservoir of past experiences with people and the world, our past inner linkage of words and things, our past encounters with spoken or written texts. We listen to the sound of the words in the inner ear; we lend our sensations, our emotions, our sense of being alive, to the new experience which, we feel, corresponds to the text. We participate in the story, we identify with the characters, we share their conflicts and their feelings. (p. 270)

The discussion questions we ask after reading a text will guide children's aesthetic responses. Thinking again about *Ira Sleeps Over,* we might ask, "Is there any place in this book where Waber used language that you really liked—that really grabbed your attention?" "How did you feel when Ira had so much trouble deciding whether or not to take his Teddy bear?" "What did you think when you learned that Reggie had a favorite stuffed animal?"

Teachers often invite children to respond to texts through what are called *enrichment activities,* which build bridges between reading and other curricular areas and offer students opportunities to enrich and extend their comprehension. These activities might be art, drama, or musical experiences. For example, a small group might produce a reader's theater production from *Voices of the Alamo* (Garland, 2000), or some children might like to try making some pottery after reading *A Single Shard* (Park, 2001). After reading *Bobbin Girl* (McCully, 1996), students could participate in a field trip to a mill, learn about the early textile mills on the Internet, or try their hands at weaving something simple. Enrichment activities can be important in aiding comprehension, but teachers need to think about the results in terms of the time invested. Often enrichment activities can contribute to goals in other curriculum areas such as social studies. In planning enrichment activities, think about what will help the children become more skilled as readers and writers and will integrate literacy with instructional goals you have in other disciplines. Do not waste your or your children's time on activities that are "cute" but do not make a contribution to their literacy development (Pressley, 2000; Roser, 2001).

A word of caution seems appropriate here. When teachers determine the activities through which children will respond to a text, those activities are often inauthentic responses. Take the example of children reading *The Very Hungry Caterpillar* (Carle, 1969) and then being assigned to make a caterpillar out of the leg of pantyhose, tissues, string, and construction paper. This activity, if assigned by the teacher, cannot be an authentic response for all of the children who read the text. Authenticity of response is characterized by the honest choice of the readers and by an activity that a real life-long reader would select as a response to a text. We have never been motivated to make a pantyhose caterpillar despite the countless times we have read *The Very Hungry Caterpillar.* This is not to say an art activity cannot be an authentic response to a text. It simply must be the honest response of the reader.

We can gain much more authentic responses to texts when we give children the choice of how they wish to respond. Texts "speak" to each of us in different ways. Individual response may vary greatly. The greater range of responses a teacher encourages, the more personal the responses are likely to be. Some examples of responses are discussion, telling a classmate why he or she should read a book, a journal response about a book that the writer wants to remember, writing a book review for the school newspaper, and finding another book with a similar plot, theme, or style.

Efferent Response to Text

When a reader adopts an efferent stance to a text, he or she is focused on what can be taken from the text. Here reading is done to obtain information: to learn the steps in a process, to learn facts for a test, to seek a conclusion to a debate. In an efferent stance the reader is *using the text* to meet specifically identified needs.

The questions we pose after children have read a text will guide their efferent responses. For example, if children were reading with an efferent stance, they presumably stated such purposes before reading. We could revisit these purpose statements after the reading to determine which have been met, and to help children reenter the text to satisfy unmet purposes. One instructional strategy supporting an efferent stance is summarization. Instruction in summarization improves memory for what is read, both in terms of free recall and answering questions (Armbruster, Anderson, & Ostertag, 1987).

Summarization. Kintsch and Van Dijk (1978) are generally credited with some of the most helpful work on teaching summarization. They analyzed the process used by persons who write good summaries and created a set of guidelines for summarization. Their steps are:

1. *Include no unnecessary detail.* Teach your students to identify the most critical information and delete trivial and redundant information.
2. *Collapse lists.* Teach your students to examine lists of actions, traits, and components, and identify one or two words that describe the list. For example, if the list included Dell, Sony, Gateway, and Apple, they could collapse this to "computer companies."
3. *Use topic sentences.* Teach your students to identify and use topic sentences in their summaries. If the text lacks topic sentences, teach students to create them for their summary.
4. *Integrate information.* Teach students to use important words, phrases, and topic sentences and to polish their summary so that the ideas are integrated into a cohesive summary.
5. *Polish the summary.* Teach students to take their summary through an editing and polishing process to make it better.

Figure 8.11
Possibilities for Guided Reading

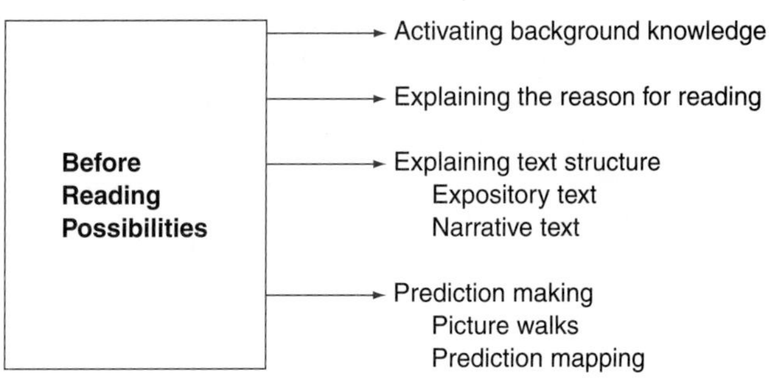

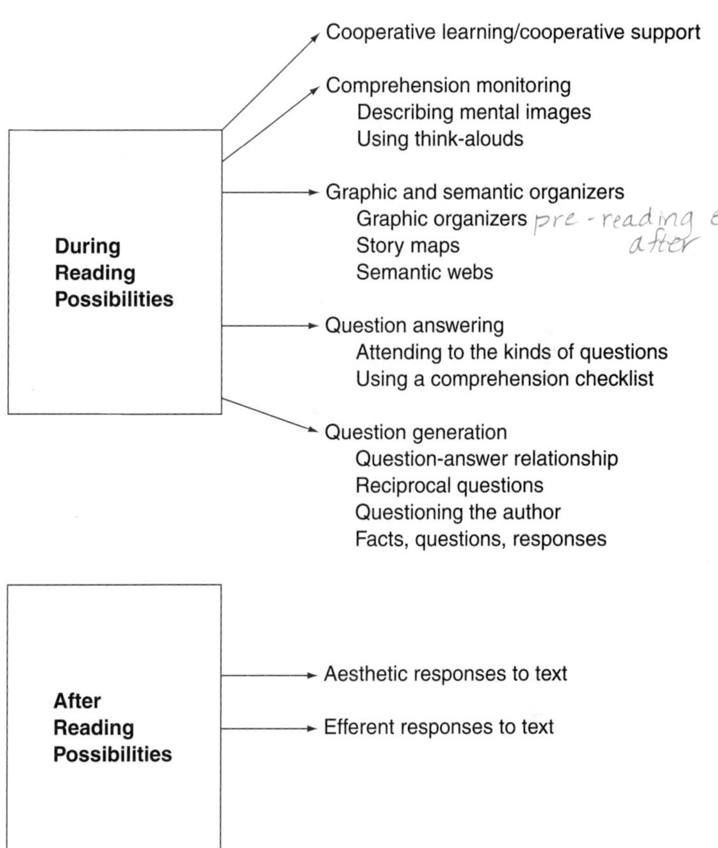

You have carefully considered issues surrounding guiding the development of comprehension before reading, during reading, and after reading. It may be helpful to review the components of guided reading we have described throughout this discussion. Figure 8.11 illustrates the key understandings we have developed about guided reading. We have organized this overview around before, during, and after reading **POSSIBILITIES** because in each case you select from an array of possible instructional strategies.

Assessment and Evaluation Toolbox

COMPREHENSION STRATEGY CHECKLIST

Guiding the development of comprehension is one of the most important aspects of your literacy instruction. Many of the teachers with whom we work express more concern about this aspect of the curriculum than any other. They are continually evaluating their work and seeking to do an ever better job in guiding the comprehension development of their learners. We offer the following checklist for assessing comprehension instruction in your classroom. This checklist is not intended to overwhelm you, but to guide you in monitoring your work.

About Comprehension Strategy Instruction

- Are students taught to . . .

Yes No

_____ _____ identify their purpose for reading?
_____ _____ preview texts before reading?
_____ _____ make predictions before and during reading?
_____ _____ activate relevant background knowledge for reading?
_____ _____ think aloud while reading?
_____ _____ use text structure to support comprehension?
_____ _____ create visual representations to aid comprehension and recall?
_____ _____ determine the important ideas in what they read?
_____ _____ summarize what they read?
_____ _____ generate questions for text?
_____ _____ handle unfamiliar words during reading?
_____ _____ monitor their comprehension during reading?
_____ _____ take corrective action when comprehension fails?

- Does instruction about these strategies include

_____ _____ an explicit description of the strategy and when it should be used?
_____ _____ modeling of the strategy in action?
_____ _____ collaborative use of the strategy in action?
_____ _____ guided practice using the strategy?
_____ _____ independent practice using the strategy?

_____ _____ Are students helped to orchestrate multiple strategies rather than using only one at a time?
_____ _____ Are the texts used for instruction carefully chosen to match the strategy and students being taught?
_____ _____ Is there concern with student motivation to engage in literacy activities and apply strategies learned?
_____ _____ Are students' comprehension skills assessed on an ongoing basis?
Adapted from Duke & Pearson (2002).

Source: Adapted from N. K. Duke & P. D. Pearson. (2002). Effective practices for developing reading comprehension. In A. E. Farstrup & S. J. Samuels (Eds.), *What Research Has to Say About Reading Instruction* (pp. 235). Newark, DE: International Reading Association.

Many of the strategies described in this chapter require that the teacher and children read a few lines or paragraphs of text and then talk about that text in some way. You must keep in mind that the purpose of comprehension instruction is to help children learn to understand what they are reading so that they will read more widely and more often. Katherine Paterson (1989) says it best:

> For a long time we have been trying to train *stoplight* readers. We ask children to read a bit of a story, stop, and talk about it. But what we should be working for is *flashlight* readers—readers who take a book under the blanket with a flashlight, because they cannot bear to stop reading what may very well be the best book they have ever read. If you want illumination, friends, a flashlight will beat a stoplight every time. (pp. 137–138)
>
> Please make sure that most of the reading your children are doing is of the flashlight variety, and they are getting stoplight reading only as it is needed to help them become flashlight readers.

THINKING AS A TEACHER

1. With a group of your peers, make a list of the comprehension strategies that each of you employs to comprehend the text as you are reading it. How does this list compare to the strategies recommended in this chapter?
2. Many readers have been discouraged by their inability to answer literal recall questions. If you had such a reader in your class, what would you do to help that child feel more successful in reading?
3. Make a list of the strategies you would use to help a reader who could call the words, but did not understand the material. Compare your list with those of your peers and discuss why each of you selected the strategies on your list.

FIELD-BASED ACTIVITIES

1. For a small group, select a tradebook and plan for before, during, and after reading strategies that would be useful in comprehending the book. After you have taught the children this book, evaluate the strategies you selected. Did they meet the needs of the readers? Did they take more time than the results justified? Would they have been more effective at another point in the reading experience?
2. Choose a tradebook that you think is appropriate for the readers in your group, and plan two or three enrichment activities that you could offer to the children as choices after they had read the book.
3. Create a plan for assessing comprehension of a given story other than asking children questions and then evaluate your plan. How much did you learn about each child's comprehension? Was this experience one that offered children choices in their responses? Was this experience closely related to the development of literacy abilities?

REFERENCES

Alvermann, D. E., & Boothby, P. R. (1986). Children's transfer of graphic organizer instruction. *Reading Psychology, 7,* 87–100.

Anderson, R. C., & Biddle, W. B. (1975). On asking people questions about what they are reading. In G. H. Bower (Ed.), *The psychology of learning and motivation* (Vol. 8, pp. 9–129. New York: Academic Press.

Armbruster, B. B., Anderson, T. H., & Ostertag, J. (1987). Does text structure/summarization instruction facilitate learning from expository text? *Reading Research Quarterly, 22,* 331–346.

Au, K. H. (1979). Using the Experience-Text Relationship Method with Minority Children. *Reading Teacher, 32* (6), pp. 677–79.

Au, K. H., Mason, J. M., & Scheu, J. A. (1995). *Literacy instruction for today.* New York: Harper Collins College.

Bartlett, B. J. (1978). *Top-level structure as an organizational strategy for recall of classroom text.* Unpublished doctoral dissertation, Arizona State University, Tempe.

Baumann, J. F., Seifert-Kessell, N., & Jones, L. A. (1992). Effect of think-aloud instruction on elementary students' comprehension monitoring abilities. *Journal of Reading Behavior, 24,* 143–172.

Baumann, J. F., Jones, L. A., & Seifert-Kessell, N. (1993). Using think alouds to enhance children's comprehension monitoring abilities. *The Reading Teacher, 47,* 184–193.

Beck, I. L., McKeown, M. G., Hamilton, R. L., & Kucan, L. (1997). *Questioning the author: An approach for enhancing student engagement with text.* Newark, DE: International Reading Association.

Bereiter, C., & Bird, M. (1985). Use of thinking aloud in identification and teaching of reading comprehension strategies. *Cognition and Instruction, 2,* 131–156.

Bloom, B. (1956). *Taxonomy of educational objectives.* New York: David McKay.

Bormuth, J. R. (1968). The cloze readability procedure. *Elementary English, 45,* 429–436.

Davis, F. B. (1968). Research in comprehension in reading. *Reading Research Quarterly, 3*(4), 499–545.

Davis, Z. T. (1994). Effects of prereading story mapping on elementary readers' comprehension. *Journal of Educational Research, 87,* 353–361.

Dickson, S. V., Simmons, D. C., & Kameenui, E. J. (2001). *Text organization and its relation to reading comprehension: A synthesis of the research.* Washington, DC: National Center to Improve the Tools of Educators. Retrieved from *http://idea.uoregon.edu/~ncite/documents/techrep/tech17.html*

Duke, N. K., & Pearson, P. D. (2002). Effective practices for developing reading comprehension. In A. E. Farstrup & S. J. Samuels (Eds.), *What research has to say about reading instruction.* Newark, DE: International Reading Association.

Durkin, D. (1978). What classroom observations reveal about reading comprehension instruction. *Reading Research Quarterly, 14,* 481–533.

Fountas, I. C., & Pinnell, G. S. (1996). *Guided reading: Good first teaching for all children.* Portsmouth, NH: Heinemann.

Fountas, I. C., & Pinnell, G. S. (1999). *Matching books to readers: Using leveled books in guided reading, K–3.* Portsmouth, NH: Heinemann.

Gatheral, M. (1984). *Teaching gifted children in the regular classroom.* Paper presented at a meeting of the Mid-Valley Reading Association, Albany, OR.

Halliday, M. A. K. (1993). Some grammatical problems in scientific English. In M. A. K. Halliday & J. R. Martin (Eds.), *Writing science: Literacy and discursive power.* London: Falmer.

Hanf, M. B. (1971). Mapping: A technique for translating reading into thinking. *Journal of Reading, 30,* 415–422.

Harp, B. (2000). *The handbook of literacy assessment and evaluation.* Norwood, MA: Christopher-Gordon.

Harvey, S., & Goudvis, A. (2000). *Strategies that work: Teaching comprehension to enhance understanding.* York, ME: Stenhouse Publishers.

Irwin, J. W. (1991). *Teaching reading comprehension processes.* Boston: Allyn & Bacon.

Irwin, P. A., & Mitchell, J. N. (1983). A procedure for assessing the richness of retellings. *Journal of Reading, 26,* 391–396.

Kintsch, W., & Van Dijk, T. A. (1978). Toward a model of text comprehension and production. *Psychological Review, 85,* 363–394.

Manzo, A. V. (1969). The request procedure. *The Journal of Reading, 13,* 123–126.

Meyer, B. J. F., Brandt, D. M., & Bluth, G. J. (1980). Use of top-level structure in text: Key for reading comprehension of ninth-grade students. *Reading Research Quarterly, 16,* 72–103.

Mooney, M. E. (1990). *Reading to, with and by children.* Katonah, NY: Richard C. Owen.

National Reading Panel. (2000). *Report of the National Reading Panel: Teaching children to read. Reports of the subgroups.* Washington, DC: National Institute for Literacy, National Institute of Child Health and Human Development.

Palinscar, A. S., & Brown, A. L. (1984). Reciprocal teaching of comprehension-fostering and comprehension-monitoring activities. *Cognition and Instruction, 2,* 117–175.

Paterson, Katherine. (1989). *The spying heart.* New York: Lodestar.

Payne, B. D., & Manning, B. H. (1992). Basal readers instruction: Effects of comprehension monitoring training on reading comprehension, strategy use and attitude. *Reading Research and Instruction, 32,* 29–38.

Pearson, P. D. (1981). Asking questions about stories. In *Ginn Occasional Papers: Writing in reading and language arts* (Monograph No. 15). Lexington, MA: Ginn and Co. Reprinted in A. J. Harris & E. R. Sipay (Eds.), *Readings in reading instruction* (3rd ed.). New York: Longman, 1984.

Pressley, M. (1997). Skilled comprehension and its development through instruction. *School Psychology Review, 26,* 448–467.

Pressley, M. (2000). What should comprehension instruction be the instruction of? In M. L. Kamil, P. D. Pearson, & R. Barr (Eds.), *Handbook of reading research, Vol. III* (pp. 545–561). Mahwah, NJ: Erlbaum.

Pressley, M., & Afflerbach, P. (1995). *Verbal protocols of reading: The nature of constructively responsive reading.* Hillsdale, NJ: Erlbaum.

Raphael, T. E. (1982). Question-answering strategies for children. *The Reading Teacher, 36,* 186–191.

Raphael, T. E. (1986). Teaching question-answer relationships, revisited. *The Reading Teacher, 39,* 516–523.

Rasinski, T., & Padak, N. (2000). *Effective reading strategies: Teaching children who find reading difficult.* Columbus, OH: Merrill.

Rickards, D., & Cheek, E. (1999). *Designing rubrics for K–6 classroom assessment.* Norwood, MA: Christopher-Gordon.

Rosenblatt, L. M. (1978). *The reader, the text, the poem: The transactional theory of the literary work.* Carbondale, IL: Southern Illinois University Press.

Rosenblatt, L. M. (1982) the literacy transaction: Evocation and response. *Theory into Practice, 21*(4), p. 268–278.

Rosenshine, B., Meister, C., & Chapman, S. (1996). Teaching students to generate questions: A review of the intervention studies. *Review of Educational Research, 66,* 181–221.

Roser, N. L. (2001). A place for everything and literature in its place. *The New Advocate, 14,* 211–221.

Smith, F. (1978). *Reading without nonsense.* New York: Teachers College Press.

Temple, C. (1990). How literary theory expands our expectations for children's reading and writing. In T. Shanahan (Ed.), *Reading and writing together: New perspectives for the classroom.* Norwood, MA: Christopher-Gordon.

Unsworth, L. (1999). Developing critical understanding of the specialized language of school science and history texts: A functional grammatical perspective. *Journal of Adolescent & Adult Literacy, 42,* 508–521.

Weaver, B. M. (2000). *Leveling books K-6: Matching readers to text.* Newark, DE: International Reading Association.

Children's Books

Carle, E. (1969). *The very hungry caterpillar.* New York: Philomel.

Garland, S. (2000). *Voices of the Alamo.* New York: Scholastic.

Hague, M. (1985). *Aesop's fables.* New York: Holt, Rinehart, & Winston.

Keats, E. J. (1971). *Over in the meadow.* New York: Scholastic.

McCully, E. A. (1996). *The bobbin girl.* New York: Dial.

Park, L. S. (2001). *A single shard.* New York: Clarion.

Pringle, L. (1997). *An extraordinary life: The story of a monarch butterfly.* Illus. by Bob Marstall. New York: Orchard Books.

Waber, B. (1972). *Ira sleeps over.* New York: Scholastic.

Wallner, J. (1987). *City mouse–country mouse and two more mouse tales from Aesop.* New York: Scholastic.

Wilder, L. I. (1953). On the Banks of Plum Creek. NY: Harper Collins.

Chapter 9

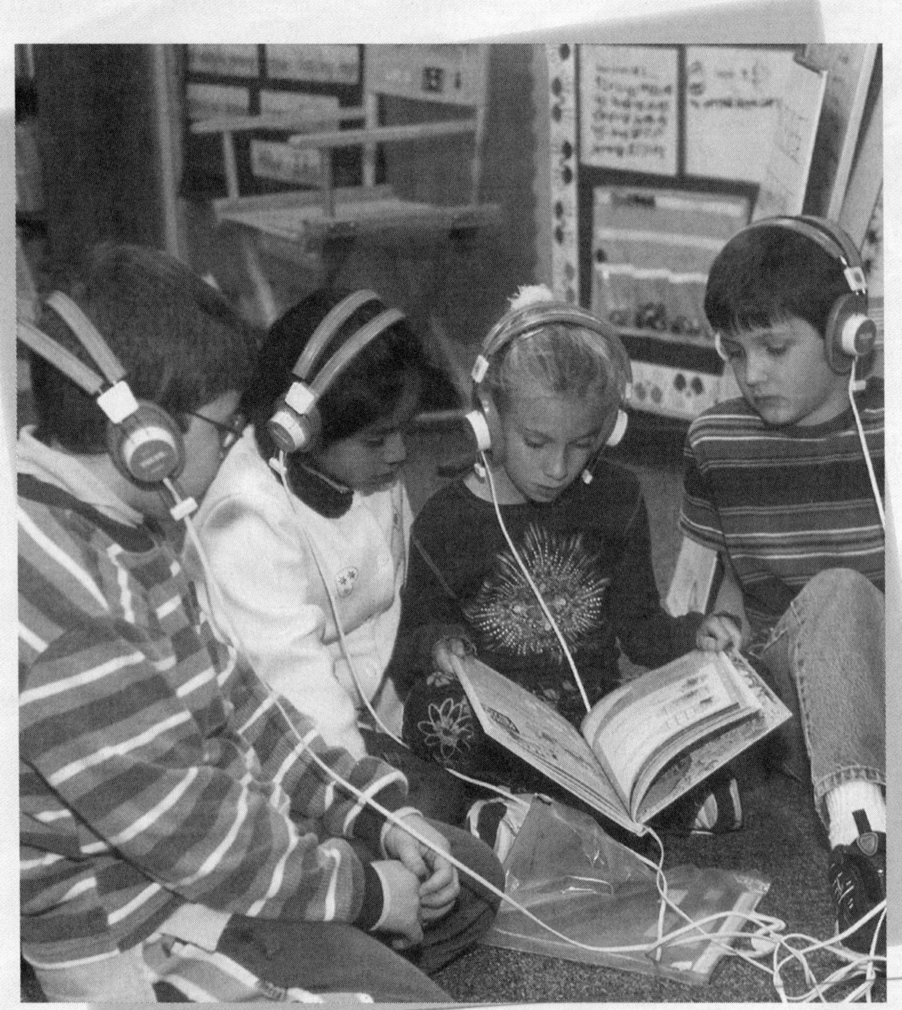

Guiding the Development of Reading Fluency

LOOKING AT THE RESEARCH

Melanie Kuhn and Steven Stahl (2000) carefully reviewed an extensive array of research on fluency. They drew important conclusions about fluency instruction for children in late first and second grades and older children with reading problems who are not fluent:

> From this review, we have come to view fluency instruction as successful in improving the reading achievement of children at a certain point in their reading development. However, we have seen relatively little of this instruction in the schools. To help more readers move from labored decoding to the construction of meaning, we consider it to be important that educators integrate these techniques in the classroom more frequently. (p. 27)

Focus Questions

- What is reading fluency?
- What are effective classroom strategies for helping children achieve fluency in reading?
- Do I need to be concerned about reading rate with my learners?

REAL TEACHERS, REAL PRACTICE

Meet Susie Gummere, ***a first-grade teacher***

Fluency instruction can take a variety of forms in an elementary school classroom. In my class, the children seem particularly engaged by reader's theater and poetry reading. Both activities provide viable and manageable ways to promote fluency in children.

When working on a reader's theater piece, students read and reread a particular text multiple times. While reader's theater pieces are available commercially, a series (e.g., Fox on Stage, Fox in Love*) with interesting characters and a clear dilemma can be recast as a reader's theater piece (Martinez, Roser, & Strecker, 1998/1999). In my class, children practice different "mini-plays" in small groups. They rotate the parts until every child in the group has had a chance to read each one. While rehearsing their parts, the children work on developing appropriate expression for their character. Because children become so familiar with the text in reader's theater, they can read with more automaticity (Samuels, 1994). After a few days of practice and rereading, the children present their reader's theater piece to the class. They never seem to tire of performing. Reader's theater appeals to all levels of reading ability.*

Children also benefit from repeated readings of poetry. Poetry reading is a practical way for even a struggling student to participate in fluency work. In my classroom, the children are introduced to the "Poem of the Week" on Monday. The weekly poem reflects an upcoming special event, holiday, or unit of study. The children read the poem every morning as part of the calendar time routine. Like reader's theater, we focus on reading smoothly and with appropriate expression. On Friday, the children receive their own personal copy of the poem to illustrate. Once the illustrations are complete, children add the poem to their poetry notebook. The poetry notebook is a collection of all of the poems from the year. Over the weekend, the children take their poetry notebooks home to share with their families. By the end of the school year, the children have acquired a sizable collection of poems.

It is vitally important that children learn reading skills, and it is equally important that they learn reading strategies. However, when children are skilled strategic readers, they also need to read with fluency. Most of the work on fluency has focused on either of two theories about how fluency contributes to comprehension. One of these theories examines the role of automaticity (remember our discussion in Chapter 5), and the other theory examines the role of prosody in fluency (Kuhn & Stahl, 2000). **Automaticity** refers to effortless decoding and word recognition, and **prosody** refers to the effective use of stress, pitch, and juncture when reading aloud. **Stress** refers to the amount of emphasis given to pronouncing some words over others. **Pitch** refers to the rising and falling intonation we use to differentiate statements from questions or exclamations. **Juncture** refers to the phrasing we produce when we read aloud. The goal is to help children produce oral reading that sounds like rich language production in which decoding is automatic, speed is adjusted to purpose, and meaning making is of great importance.

WHAT IS READING FLUENCY?

Think about some skill you have learned. Perhaps it is playing the piano or another musical instrument. Perhaps it is skiing or swimming, maybe sewing or cross-stitch, or even driving a car. In any case, you were slow and halting at it at the beginning. With practice you got better. Then came a day when you could execute this skill virtually without thinking about it. You became a pro! Eventually it seemed almost impossible to think about how "clumsy" you had been, now that you could perform the skill(s) almost automatically.

So it is with learning to read. Once your ability to read becomes virtually automatic; once you have learned to read with expression, with excellent comprehension, with appropriate rate, you are a fluent reader. You have developed a strong sight vocabulary, have well-developed schema for the words in your sight vocabulary, and have learned to read both orally and silently with rich, language-like expression. You are a confident reader who can monitor your use of the reading process and take corrective action when you run into difficulties. In a word, you understand reading.

WHAT ARE EFFECTIVE CLASSROOM STRATEGIES FOR HELPING CHILDREN ACHIEVE FLUENCY IN READING?

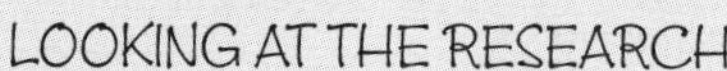

LOOKING AT THE RESEARCH

What the research says about sight vocabulary

Direct instruction of sight vocabulary results in enhanced reading rate and reading fluency (Frantantoni, 1999). Without accuracy and fluency at the level of the word, there will always be constraints on comprehension (Adams, 1990; Adams & Bruck, 1995).

Can you think of a college text you read that presented many unfamiliar words as labels for new concepts? Recall how much more difficult comprehension was on that text than on one with which you were highly familiar. A well-developed sight vocabulary—words you can read accurately and fluently—is essential to good reading performance.

Development of Sight Vocabulary

The development of a large sight vocabulary is essential to reading fluency. You may want to review the discussion on the development of sight vocabulary in Chapter 5. There we recommended the use of sentence strips, pocket charts, word walls, word banks, and games to develop children's sight vocabularies. However, the most powerful way to develop children's sight vocabularies is to have them read, read, read, and read books at their independent reading level. Extensive reading promotes fluency, vocabulary, and background knowledge (Pressley, 2000). While repeated reading of the same text results in increased fluency, repeated oral readings done along with a taped version of the text are even more effective (Dowhower, 1987). Repeated home readings with audio tapes improve the reading fluency, monitoring, and motivation of second language learners in first grade (Blum et al., 1995). Clearly, repeated readings promote fluency.

Repeated Readings of Text

Some teachers with relatively little teaching experience seem to think they must be delivering instruction to children all the time or they aren't doing a good job. These teachers sometimes worry that if the principal came to their classroom and saw the children just reading, this would reflect badly on the teacher. Yet the comprehension and fluency benefits of students' own repeated reading of texts have been well documented (Dowhower, 1994). When you engage in repeated read-alouds of favorite books, children's understandings of literature deepen (Dowhower, 1987; Rasinski, 1990). Repeated readings result in responses from children that are more in-depth interpretations of literature (Morrow, 1988). The National Reading Panel (2000) concluded "that classroom practices that encourage repeated oral reading with feedback and guidance lead to meaningful improvements in reading expertise for students—for good readers as well as those who are experiencing difficulties" (p. 3-3). There are many compelling reasons for using repeated readings. Children can repeatedly engage with a text individually, in pairs, in small groups, or even larger groups. Consider some of these possibilities. This list is not exhaustive, and as you think about it you will think of ways to add to the list.

Classroom Library. Create a classroom library by arranging some low bookshelves together in a corner of your classroom. Stock this library with books from the school's media center, the city or state library, your own library; include books the children have published. You might want to include copies of books children have written in your classroom in previous years. Spend some time the first day of school helping your students know when and how they may access the classroom library, and encourage them to visit it often when reading and rereading favorite books.

Browsing Boxes. Browsing boxes are collections of books children have read in guided reading activities. These books were at the children's instructional reading level when they were used for guided reading (see Chapter 8). Now that they have read them at least once, the books may be reread independently. You will need to remove books from the browsing boxes as new ones are added.

You may have to be creative in finding containers for the books. Some teachers have used plastic "milk crates" purchased at an office supply store. Others have covered cardboard boxes with peel and stick vinyl. Some have used flip-top file boxes or small plastic baskets. The important thing is for each guided reading group to have their own collection of books that can be easily accessed for independent reading.

Plan times in your day when children can read freely from the boxes or library. These might be a before-school activity, an activity to turn to when other work is complete, or an activity during center time. Please refer to Chapter 12 for a discussion of centers in primary grade classrooms.

We visited Ann Conant's first-grade classroom recently. As we approached the room, our attention was drawn to two girls in the hallway with pointers. They were using their pointers to underscore the text in reports about Artic tundra the class had written and displayed on the walls. They were enthusiastically and fluently reading the stories aloud with each other. They also were "reading around the room."

Some of the goals of independent reading can be met at the computer terminal.

Reading Around the Room. This technique is described by Fountas and Pinnell (1996). It is an invitation for children to read all of the print displayed in the classroom, or in Ann's case, in the hallway as well. You need to amass a collection of pointers. Some teachers use rulers, some use chop sticks, others cut dowel rods into varying lengths and put a protective cover on the tip such as an eraser or pom pom. As Fountas and Pinnell note,

> Every rich literacy classroom is "loaded" with print that is meaningful to children. Children can read their own group-written versions of favorite stories or their own variations on texts and poems. Young children enjoy reading the alphabet charts, word wall, lists and the name chart. Even children who can read very little can read around the room when their own names as well as the number and alphabet charts are displayed. One may argue that the activity is not 'real reading,' but they are getting a feel for reading while pointing and matching. (p.59)

The day we visited Ann's class, the children were reading a wide variety of texts displayed in and out of the room.

Drop Everything and Read (DEAR); Uninterrupted Sustained Silent Reading (USSR); Sustained Silent Reading (SSR); and Super, Quiet, Uninterrupted Independent Reading Time (SQUIRT). Each of these acronyms describes the same activity—a time during the day when everyone, including the teacher, reads silently from texts of their choice. Hopefully, there will be many times in the day when your learners may choose to read. But SSR is a time when everyone, at the same time, stops all other activity and READS! If you make a point of reading during this time, it will signal to your students how important this time is and how important reading is to you.

Some teachers end the sustained silent reading periods by inviting students to share a few words about what they are reading or to read an interesting part of their book aloud. Over time all of the children have an opportunity to participate in this activity if they wish.

If you are working with very young children, you might schedule SSR for only 5 minutes at the beginning of the year and then extend the time to up to 20 minutes as the year progresses. With older students you can have productive SSR times of up to 30 minutes or longer. Rasinski and Padak (2000) report that even the most reluctant readers eventually find success with sustained silent reading:

> They begin trying to read because they know that reading is what they're supposed to be doing. As they experience success, their interest in reading grows, as does their confidence in themselves as readers. (p. 27)

Take-home Book Bags. A wonderful way to encourage children to read at home is to ask the parent association to buy or make canvas bags that children can use to carry books from school to home and back, or you can use large plastic bags with zippers. These books can be chosen from the browsing boxes, classroom library, or school's media center. Some teachers put a stenographer's pad in each book bag so that after they read the book, children may write a response and then ask their parents or caregivers to write a response as well. When Hillary, a first grader, took home *The Napping House,* she wrote: "I like how each one got on top of the others and went to sleep. Then each one woke up." Her father wrote, "We are going to the library on Saturday and look for another book by Audrey and Don Woods. We had so much fun reading this book together!"

Go to the Weblinks for Chapter 9 on our Companion Website at www.prenhall.com/harp to link to sites of publishers who produce trade books and accompanying audiotapes or CDs.

Audiotapes for Reading Along. Because the research supports reading along with an audiotape of a text, we recommend that you find ways for your school to purchase a set of tape recorders that could be added to the take home book bags. You might be able to get funds from your parent association, local businesses, or a foundation. Helen Waller, a first-grade teacher we know, wanted to have an audio library of favorite books for her classroom. She invited parents to an evening workshop in which she explained the value of audio books and invited families to choose a title, take it home with tapes and recorders she provided, and make a family-read audio tape. Helen and her family had made a demonstration tape she played at the workshop. Families became so excited about the project that all but one of them made tapes, and several asked if they could make subsequent tapes of other books.

Buddy Reading. Buddy reading implies that you pair learners up to read to one another. This strategy takes two forms. You can pair a younger reader with an older reader, or you can pair peers.

Younger and Older Reading Buddies. Deborah Manning and Jean Fennacy (1993), both second-grade teachers, say that pairing a younger reader with an older reader helps the novice reader over some of the hurdles along the path toward independent reading. The major benefit they found in children reading with older buddies is that the younger children come into contact with reading materials they find especially compelling. Here the basic skill of enjoying reading is highlighted and modeled. Manning and Fennacy underscore the importance of novice readers engaging in reading-like behavior when sharing reading with a more experienced member of the literacy club. Basic skills that are taught or reinforced in this situation include: turning pages at appropriate times; relying on previous knowledge and illustrations; using the context as well as a story's syntactic and semantic cues to support meaning; paying more attention to print; identifying specific words and phrases in context; using picture cues, matching oral production to the text; and finally coming to control the whole of reading.

Buddy Reading Peers. Another form of buddy reading is pairing children of like reading achievement to share books. They may choose books from an assigned book box, or you may identify a book for them to read together. The important consideration here is that the book is one that each of the children can read. The children may take turns reading aloud or they may share read a book or a part of a book. Mary Giard (1993), when teaching first grade in Maine, had an experience that underscores the value of buddy reading:

> I see real changes as children work with one another. Sometimes following a guided reading lesson, the children like to reread the text in pairs to practice. I see very different kinds of behavior and activity as the children have more guided reading practice. I see children taking pride in helping their friends be successful as readers rather than making fun of the errors made. The individuals who do the oral reading begin to monitor themselves more carefully and effectively. The partners, or buddies as we call them, begin to take on the role I have in guided reading lessons. They ask probing questions to get at strategies rather than give all the answers requiring no thinking or work on the part of the reader. (p.80)

Concern for Prosody

Prosody, as defined in the opening research piece, is the ability to read text orally using appropriate pitch, stress, and juncture. These features of oral reading produce language that sounds like real, expressive language. Texts have prosodic cues built into them such as exclamation points, question marks, periods, italicized text, and enlarged fonts. There are also prosodic cues within the syntax of a sentence. However, these signs can be elusive to some students (Allington, 1983).

Richards (2000) has developed a teaching strategy she calls the *oral recitation lesson (ORL)* to help readers deal with prosodic cues. First, select a text and model its fluent reading. Continue with a discussion of the prosodic elements and cues found within the text. Students are then asked to practice the oral reading of the text with particular attention paid to the prosodic elements. Finally, students perform the reading for an audience. The ultimate goal is that students will begin to preview texts for prosodic elements before they read. Previewing text is another way to support the development of fluency.

Previewing Text

The purpose of previewing a text is to become familiar enough with it to think about how to interact with it as a reader and to think about purposes for reading. Previewing permits children to anticipate what will happen in a story or the way information will be presented in an expository piece.

Thinking About Questions. A good way to begin teaching previewing is to help your students think about the kinds of questions they might ask about a text as they are preparing to read it. The questions they ask will vary depending on whether the text is narrative or expository. Previewing questions for a narrative text might include: What do I think will happen in this story? Is this text going to entertain me? What do I know about the kinds of stories this author writes? What is my purpose for reading this story? Previewing questions for an expository text might include: What is my purpose for reading this text? What information do I expect to gain from reading this text? Do I need to read slowly and carefully for details and ideas, or may I skim for certain facts? We know that previewing activities increase reading fluency (Rose, 1984; Sindelar, 1987).

Modeling Previewing Activities. A good way to teach previewing strategies is to model them for your learners. You could easily do this when you are reading to them or engaging them in shared reading. As you move into text, let them hear you generating questions. It works well to demonstrate previewing by taking a picture walk through an enlarged print text with a group of children. Begin by looking at the title and cover picture and asking questions about these. Then turn the pages slowly and examine each picture as you move through the text. Talk about what you think the pictures tell you about the story and what questions or predictions you have.

You can reinforce previewing behavior in guided reading lessons, in literature discussion groups, during reading conferences, and when you read to your students. Observe your children during buddy reading or SSR to see if you can verify that they are previewing.

Reader's Theater and Choral Reading

Reader's theater and Choral Reading techniques are good ways to have children practice oral reading and to do it for an audience. Reader's theater experiences develop fluency in reading (Martinez, Roser, & Strecker, 1998-1999), and they are wonderful ways to have children practice oral reading by dramatizing a story they have read. Reader's theater bypasses all the hassles of sets, costumes, and memorization. Often students who have enjoyed a story in guided reading or a literature study group may decide they want to perform the story or a part of a story for the whole class. Reader's theater is informal even though it is usually planned and practiced.

Reader's theater, which requires repeated readings, promates fluency.

Preparing for Reader's Theater. To prepare for reader's theater, duplicate the story pages and have children use highlighters to mark their parts, writing in additions on the duplicated copy. This way you can get from story reading to performance quickly without having to create scripts. Although creating the script can be an important writing experience. If your purpose is developing fluency, then you will want to focus the process on the reading at this time. You will need to explain carefully how to choose parts for both characters and narrator(s), how to work with each member of the group, how to rehearse, and how to deliver an enthusiastic, fluent performance. Soderman, Gregory, and O'Neill (1999) have offered some specific suggestions for organizing reader's theater, which are adapted here.

1. Choose a favorite narrative story that contains a relatively simple story line, preferably one with a variety of speaking/acting parts or characters.
2. Read the original story and follow up with guided discussion and other related reading strategies to foster a good understanding of the story line and characters.
3. Discuss the various roles that people play in producing a play, including those of the narrator, characters, prop person (if you are going to use props), and musical director.
4. Have the children choose a part they might like to play, including that of a prop person or other backstage worker. Show them how to highlight their parts on the scripts. Have them practice their parts with the intention of presenting the story to the rest of the class, another class in the school, and/or family members. Make sure children understand they are to read their parts fluently, not memorize them.
5. Discuss ways in which they can use their voices, gestures, and body language to make their person more believable.
6. Hold rehearsals until the presenters are comfortable, and then invite real audiences, including parents and other classes, to the performance.

Go to the Weblinks in Chapter 9 on our Companion Website at www.prenhall.com/harp for links to sites about reader's theater. Of special interest will be the Aaron Shepard site where many scripts are available for classroom use.

Others (Young & Vardell, 1993) have suggested that nonfiction material is also suitable for reader's theater. Nonfiction could include biography and informational literature. Adapting biography for reader's theater might mean having people who had experiences with the subject of the biography tell the story of the person in their own voices. Content material in social studies and science also lends itself to reader's theater productions. For example, a script for the event of settling Plimoth could be prepared easily, or students could present information about the rainforest. Think of content material as sources for reader's theater material and you will be helping children become more fluent readers and learning content material well.

Preparing for Choral Reading. Choral reading is another form of audience reading, but it is more simply done than reader's theater. It is a way to engage children with print with an emphasis on interpretation and expression of meaning. In choral reading a poem or short story is read with attention to how best to use voices to orchestrate the reading. Some lines or parts will be assigned to a single voice, others to a small group, and still others to a larger group of voices. You may wish to add sound effects or gestures, and attention should be paid to delivery in terms of reading fast or slow, loud or soft, or with high or low voices (Pappas, Kiefer, & Levstik, 1999).

You can select various formats for choral reading depending on the age and experience of your readers. One format is speaking in unison. Another is called "line a child," meaning that each reader reads one line. Another is a style with a refrain, where one reader reads a line or a verse, and the whole group reads the refrain. Antiphonal readings rely on one group to read a section of a piece and a response by another group. The content of the material will usually dictate how a piece can be performed, but pieces can be rearranged to meet the needs of your learners.

Children's books and rhymes are excellent sources of material for choral readings. For example, Fleischman's book of poems about insects, *Joyful Noise: Poems for Two Voices* (1988) is written to be performed by two readers. Children in second or third grade can read these, but the format is a little challenging for very young readers. Fleischman also created *I Am Phoenix: Poems for Two Voices* (1985) (about birds) and *Big Talk: Poems for Four Voices* (2000). This one is more difficult, but would appeal to middle school readers. Many choices for choral reading are available, from Mother Goose to Prelutsky or Silverstein.

For choral reading to be successful, you must help your children develop rhythmic sensitivity (Tierney, Readence, & Dishner, 1995). You will need to demonstrate proper phrasing, tempo, and enunciation with the selections chosen for choral reading. Help your students see that a poem may be interpreted in different ways. It would be interesting to have two or three groups prepare the same poem for choral reading and then examine their different interpretations. Choral reading activities will naturally lead to using music as part of the reading curriculum.

LOOKING AT THE RESEARCH

What the research says about the music/reading connection

Limericks and rhymes set to the melody of well-known songs facilitated students' vocabulary learning (Baechtold & Algier, 1986). When music teachers and classroom teachers collaborated to infuse songs into themes, students' reading and writing abilities improved (Collett, 1991).

Could it be the multisensory nature of singing and reading that facilitates literacy learning? What speculation do you have about why the connection between music and reading is so strong?

Go to our Companion Website at www.prenhall.com/harp to add your comments on these questions to the Threaded Message Board.

Activities Using Songs

Teachers of young children and struggling readers have long recognized the value of predictable, patterned literature (Heald-Taylor, 1987). The characteristics that make predictable books inviting—repetition, pattern, and rhythm—can also be found in chants and songs. The use of songs strengthens children's reading skills (Algozzine & Douville, 2001).

Teachers find songs helpful in dealing with concepts in literature and social studies. In a third-grade class children had read *The Lucky Stone* (Clifton, 1979) as part of a study on slavery. Their teacher played spirituals from that period, which deepened children's understandings about how slaves used the songs to pass messages. In this same teacher's classroom a group studying the theme of ugly ducklings and acceptance of self chose music and created a dance to illustrate their understandings (Short, Kauffman, & Kahn, 2000). Smith (2000) documents the support provided by singing and songwriting in the areas of learning letter names and sounds, phonemic awareness, print conventions, background knowledge, vocabulary, decoding, and writing.

Activities that use songs to teach reading fall into four categories: learning favorite songs, meeting the lyrics in print, reading song charts and booklets, and engaging in comprehension extension activities. Even if you do not think of yourself as especially musical, you can find suggestions here that will work for you.

Learning Favorite Songs. The first step in using singing to help children develop their ability to read is filling the classroom with songs that will quickly become favorites. Bringing favorite songs to the classroom requires only that you be willing to spend some time selecting the songs and employ compact discs, tapes, or an instrument in teaching the songs to children. Because of the ready availability of recorded music, one need not be an accomplished musician to use singing to teach reading. You can also seek the music teacher's help or use songs the children are learning in music class. Folksongs, raps, rhymes, nursery songs, and other simple songs are all suitable for teaching young children. For now, the important point is that children should have repeated exposure to songs so rote learning of lyrics occurs.

The songs should be sung over and over again so the language becomes as familiar to the children as if it were their own. A total of 15 exposures to the words and music of a song over a two- or three-day period is not excessive. Learning to read by singing will be successful only if the children are totally familiar with the lyrics they will eventually meet in print.

Meeting the Lyrics in Print. When children have sung a song enough times to be comfortable with the tune and lyrics, they are ready to meet the lyrics in print. The easiest language for children to read is language with which they are familiar. They delight in seeing the songs they know in print, and you will truly be rewarded when the children shout, "I can read this!"

Prepare for this activity by printing the song lyrics on large lined chart paper with a dark marker. The chart stand can hold your growing library of songs. You can also print the lyrics on large pieces of tagboard that can be placed on an easel or chalk tray for presentation.

Introduce the song charts by explaining to the children they are now going to read the words to the song they have been singing. Show them the chart, and invite them to sing along as you move your hand or a pointer under each line of print. After singing the song once or twice using the chart, stop and encourage the children to celebrate the fact they can read the words with such expression.

Using Song Charts. In addition to promoting fluency, you can use song charts to reinforce word identification skills. Here are some word identification activities you can do with song charts:

1. Invite individual children to come up to the chart to point to words you pronounce.
2. Invite individual children to come to the chart and identify words they recognize.
3. Encourage children to locate words that appear in more than one place on the chart.
4. Write individual words of the song on separate pieces of tagboard, using the same size print as on the chart. Have children match the words on the cards with the words on the chart.
5. Using highlighting tape, have the children cover words that have the same beginning sound, words that have the same vowel sound in the middle, or words that rhyme.

Using Song Booklets. Once children have learned to sing the songs with confidence from the song charts, they may be introduced to individual song booklets. Make the booklets by duplicating the lyrics on sheets of 8 ½″ × 11″ paper, cut in half, folded, and stapled along the fold. Print only a few lines of lyrics on each page, leaving plenty of space for the children's illustrations.

Children seem to enjoy singing from their own booklets as much as they enjoy reading their own storybooks. You can be confident that the children are developing a sight vocabulary and reading fluency when they point to words or phrases accurately as they sing along in their booklets. The booklets lend themselves to many activities that reinforce fluency. Here are some possibilities:

1. Sing (read) the song lyrics while sharing the song booklet with a friend.
2. Sing (read) the lyrics to a friend who does not know the song.
3. Follow the lyrics in the booklet while listening to the recorded song at the listening center.

Engaging in Comprehension Extension Activities. Throughout this text you have been developing the understanding that reading has not really occurred until the reader interacts with the ideas represented by the text. Knowing the meaning of words read is one of the most valuable contributors to comprehension. It is, therefore, appropriate to ask children about the meaning of words or phrases in the songs they have learned to sing and read. After children have enjoyed a song, select key words or phrases that are essential to understanding the ideas in the song, and ask children to tell what the words mean. Be certain they can explain the word meanings in their own words and are not simply parroting back the definition you gave them. Given the importance of memory for the meaning of words to overall comprehension, it is essential to spend time ensuring that children understand the songs they learn to sing and read.

Comprehension can be extended through drawing illustrations for songs, dramatizing phrases in songs, creating puppets of characters in songs, and creating motions to accompany a song. You can engage children in discussions about how fast they should sing the songs, and encourage them to play with different tempos. This will afford you the opportunity to underscore that fluency does not always mean speed.

The use of song lyrics to help children learn to read is not limited to younger children. Third graders and older learners could also use song lyrics to good advantage. You would not follow the steps as outlined for young beginning readers, but song lyrics make excellent sources of text for older readers. You could have the children select a song they would like to include in a class booklet (you will want to approve the selections to make sure the lyrics are appropriate for classroom use), or you could ask individual children to select two or three songs that they especially like and make their own individual booklet. Reading song lyrics can lead to improvement in fluency as well as other reading skills, and knowing the song well before attempting to read it is a scaffold that works well for struggling readers. Song lyrics are of interest to older readers, and if the songs selected are songs the students like and listen to on their own, they are a relevant text for reading.

DO I NEED TO BE CONCERNED ABOUT READING RATE WITH MY LEARNERS?

Our observations indicate that little is done in most elementary school classrooms with reading rate, but it bears attention because of research documenting links to fluency.

LOOKING AT THE RESEARCH

What the research says about the connection between reading rate and fluency

Reading rate is correlated with reading comprehension and reading fluency. A reduced reading rate means students read less text in the same amount of time as more fluent readers. Slower reading rates suggest that students may be putting more cognitive effort into identifying words than students who read with more automaticity (Mastropieri, Leinart, & Scruggs, 1999).

You have encountered the term *automaticity* several times in this book. What does the term now mean to you? What is the relationship between the goal of automaticity and the goal of comprehension? How might you work a measure of oral reading rate into a running record? How frequently would you want to take a measure of oral reading rate? How could you take a measure of silent reading rate? Would your decision to assess and evaluate oral versus silent reading rate be influenced by the age of your learners?

Go to our Companion Website at www.prenhall.com/harp to add your comments on these questions to the Threaded Message Board.

The research supports teachers being concerned about rate as it relates to both fluency and comprehension. In what is now considered a classic study, Clay and Imlach (1971) studied the reading behaviors of 100 beginning readers and concluded that early readers making the greatest progress read faster and more accurately with better phrasing and intonation than more slowly progressing students. High-progress students read in five- to seven-word phrases, while low-progress students read in one- and two-word segments. When you discover children in your classes whose reading rate is noticeably slower than that of their classmates, you will want to investigate the causes. In a study of fourth graders accurately reading easy text, rate and fluency were critical factors in comprehension (Pinnell et al., 1995). This suggests that rate cannot be ignored.

In building a case that speed does matter in reading, Rasinski (2000) asserts that excessively slow, disfluent reading leads to less overall reading, to poor comprehension, and to reading frustration. He recommends the following for helping disfluent, slow readers improve:

1. Focus on increasing sensitivity to meaningful phrasing and syntax.
2. Improve word recognition efficiency.
3. Be certain the reader has an appropriate text.
4. Integrate poetry reading into the reading program.

You may wish to have some understanding of what constitutes "typical" reading rates at various grade levels. Figure 9.1 presents data on typical reading rates. This summary was prepared by Harris and Sipay (1990) and included in Allington's (2001) book on working with struggling readers.

Figure 9.1
Reading Rates

Grade	WPM	Grade	WPM
1	60–90	6	196–220
2	85–120	7	215–245
3	115–140	8	235–270
4	140–170	9	250–270
5	170–195	12	250–300

Source: From Albert J. Harris, Edward R. Sipay. *How to Increase Reading Ability: A Guide to Development and Remedial Methods,* 9/e. Published by Allyn and Bacon, Boston, MA. Copyright © 2003 by Pearson Education. Reprinted by permission of the publisher.

Assessment and Evaluation Toolbox

DYNAMIC INDICATORS OF BASIC EARLY LITERACY SKILLS (DIBELS)

The DIBELS measures were designed at the University of Oregon to measure phonological awareness, alphabetic principle, and fluency with connected text. This popular assessment and evaluation tool is used in many schools that have been awarded Reading First Grants. The Measure of Fluency with Connected Text is a standardized, individually administered test of accuracy and fluency with connected text. The student reads a passage aloud for one minute. Words omitted, substituted, and hesitations of more than three seconds are scored as errors. Words self-corrected within three seconds are scored as accurate. The Oral Reading Fluency Rate is the number of correct words read within the minute. Comprehension of the passage is evaluated with a retelling.

Go to the Weblinks in Chapter 9 on our Companion Website at www.prenhall.com/harp to link to sites describing DIBELS in greater detail. 

Allington cautions that reading rate guidelines must be applied with care because a number of factors will influence rate. Oral reading is slower than silent reading. Rates for younger children are usually established from oral reading, while rates for older children are established from silent reading.

Consider including measures of reading rate as one form of data you collect on your learners. When you discover a child is reading much more slowly than others,

- check to see that you have this child placed in text at his or her instructional reading level (90–94% accuracy with reasonably good comprehension) for guided reading.
- check to see that you have this child placed in text at his or her independent reading level (95–100% accuracy with good comprehension) for independent reading.
- maximize this child's opportunities to read both at school and at home.
- maximize the child's opportunities to engage in many of the activities described in this chapter.

Assessment and Evaluation Toolbox

GRAY ORAL READING TESTS (GORT)

The *GORT* is a norm-referenced, oral reading test that measures a reader's speed, accuracy, and comprehension. Analysis of performance involves both computation of scores and analysis of miscues. Comprehension is assessed in response to multiple-choice questions. The *GORT* affords you the opportunity to compare how well a student is reading in terms of rate, accuracy, and comprehension with others in a national sample. The test is normed for students 7 years, 0 months, through 18 years, 11 months (Wiederholt & Bryant, 1992). You could administer the *GORT* in the fall and in the spring to monitor progress in reading speed, which is one factor in fluency.

THINKING AS A TEACHER

1. A parent, well versed in the popular message in the media about failing schools, sees you in the grocery store and says, "I understand that my child is enjoying what she calls 'reader's theater' in your classroom, but really, don't you think with all we hear about how our schools are failing our children that frills of this kind are out of place?!" How will you respond?
2. Allington (2001) reviews the research on fluency and struggling readers and concludes that instructional practices for struggling readers are very different than instructional practices used with better readers. He says struggling readers are:
   - more likely to be reading material that is difficult for them
   - more likely to be asked to read aloud
   - more likely to be interrupted when they miscall a word
   - more likely to be interrupted more quickly
   - more likely to pause and wait for a teacher to prompt
   - more likely to be told to sound out a word

   By comparison, better readers are:
   - more likely to be reading material of appropriate difficulty
   - more likely to be asked to read silently
   - more likely to be expected to self-monitor and self-correct
   - more likely to be interrupted only after a wait period or at end of sentences
   - more likely to be asked to reread or to cross-check when interrupted (pp. 73–74)

   What is your reaction to Allington's conclusions? What do you see as the instructional implications here?
3. Your principal is aware of the benefits of peer tutoring as supported in the research. She asks you and your fellow third- and fourth-grade teachers to implement this practice. What considerations will you need to make? What preparation will be necessary before beginning this practice? How will you measure the effectiveness of this practice? What communication needs to be shared with parents before and during the implementation of this practice?

FIELD-BASED ACTIVITIES

1. Interview teachers at grades one, three, and five. Ask them how they define fluency and how they go about developing fluent reading with their students. Compare what you learn with the recommendations we have made in this chapter. Identify some important understandings you gained from the interviews and your reading of this chapter that you want to be sure to consider when you begin teaching.
2. Work with a group of children in preparing a reader's theater presentation or a choral reading. Carefully plan your activities, conduct them, and then write a reflection on the experience. Include your thoughts on what you learned about reader's theater, choral reading, children, teaching, and yourself.
3. Create a board game such as Wordo or Scattergories and try it out with children. Try the same game format with children at different ages, and compare their responses to the game. What did you learn about using games to promote fluency? What did you learn about children, teaching, and/or yourself?

REFERENCES

Adams, M. J. (1990). *Beginning to read: thinking and learning about print.* Cambridge, MA: MIT Press.

Adams, M. J., & Bruck, M. (1995). Resolving the "great debate." *American Educator, 19,* 10–20.

Algozzine, B., & Douville, P. (2001). Tips for teaching. *Preventing School Failure, 45,* 187–188.

Allington, R. L. (1983). Fluency: The neglected reading goal. *The Reading Teacher, 36,* 556–561.

Allington, R. L. (2001). *What really matters for struggling readers: Designing research-based programs.* New York: Longman.

Baechtold, S., & Algier, A. (1986). Teaching college students vocabulary with rhyme, rhythm, and ritzy characters. *Journal of Reading, 30,* 240–253.

Blum, I. H., Koskinen, P. S., Tennant, N., Parker, E. M., Straub, M., & Curry, C. (1995). Using audiotaped books to extend classroom literacy instruction into the homes of second-language learners. *Journal of Reading Behavior, 27,* 535–563.

Clay, M. M., & Imlach, R. H. (1971). Juncture, pitch and stress as reading behavior variables. *Journal of Verbal Learning and Verbal Behavior, 10,* 133–139.

Collett, M. J. (1991). Read between the lines: Music as a basis for learning. *Music Educators Journal, 77,* 42–45.

Dowhower, S. L. (1987). Effects of repeated reading on second-grade transitional readers' fluency and comprehension. *Reading Research Quarterly, 22,* 389–406.

Dowhower, S. L. (1994). Repeated reading revisited: Research into practice. *Reading and Writing Quarterly: Overcoming Learning Difficulties, 10,* 343–358.

Fountas, I. C., & Pinnell, G. S. (1996). *Guided reading: Good first teaching for all children.* Portsmouth, NH: Heinemann.

Frantantoni, D. M. (1999). The effects of direct instruction of sight vocabulary and how it can enhance reading rate and fluency. M.A. Research Project, Kean University. ERIC: ED427302.

Giard, M. (1993). Bringing children to literacy through guided reading. In B. Harp (Ed.), *Bringing children to literacy: Classrooms at work.* Norwood, MA: Christopher-Gordon.

Harris, A. J., & Sipay, E. R. (1990). *How to increase reading ability* (8th ed.). New York: Longman.

Heald-Taylor, G. (1987). How to use predictable books for K-2 language arts instruction. *The Reading Teacher, 40,* 656–661.

Kuhn, M. R., & Stahl, S. A. (2000). *Fluency: A review of developmental and remedial practices.* CIERA Report #2-008. Ann Arbor: University of Michigan Center for the Improvement of Early Reading Achievement.

Manning, D., & Fennacy, J. (1993). Bringing children to literacy through shared reading. In B. Harp (Ed.), *Bringing children to literacy: Classrooms at work.* Norwood, MA: Christopher-Gordon.

Martinez, M., Roser, N. L., & Strecker, S. (1998–1999). I never thought I could be a star: A Readers Theatre ticket to fluency. *The Reading Teacher, 52,* 326–334.

Mastropieri, M. A., Leinart, A., & Scruggs, T. E. (1999). Strategies to increase reading fluency. *Intervention in School & Clinic, 34,* 278–285.

Morrow, L. M. (1988). Young children's responses to one-to-one story readings in school settings. *Reading Research Quarterly, 23,* 89–107.

National Reading Panel. (2000). *Report of the National Reading Panel: Teaching children to read. Reports of the subgroups.* Washington, DC: National Institute for Literacy, National Institute of Child Health and Human Development.

Pappas, C. C., Kiefer, B. Z., & Levstik, L. S. (1999). *An integrated language perspective in the elementary school: An action approach.* New York: Longman.

Pinnell, G. S., Pikulski, J. J., Wixson, K. K., Campbell, J. R., Gough, P. B., & Beatty, A. S. (1995). *Listening to children read aloud: Data from NAEP's integrated reading performance record (IRPR) at grade 4.* Report No. 23-FR-04, prepared by the Educational Testing Service. Washington, DC: Office of Educational Research and Improvement, U.S. Department of Education.

Pressley, M. (2000). What should comprehension instruction be the instruction of? In M. L. Kamil, P. B. Mosenthal, P. D. Pearson, & R. Barr (Eds.), *Handbook of reading research, Vol. III.* Mahwah, NJ: Lawrence Erlbaum.

Rasinski, T. V. (1990). Effects of repeated reading and listening-while-reading on reading fluency. *Journal of Educational Research, 83,* 147–150.

Rasinski, T. V. (2000). Speed does matter in reading. *The Reading Teacher, 54,* 146–151.

Rasinski, T., & Padak, N. (2000). *Effective reading strategies: Teaching children who find reading difficult.* Columbus, OH: Merrill.

Richards, M. (2000). Be a good detective: Solve the case of oral reading fluency. *The Reading Teacher, 53,* 534–539.

Rose, T. L. (1984). The effects of two prepractice procedures on oral reading. *Journal of Learning Disabilities, 17,* 544–548.

Samuels, S. J. (1994). Toward a theory of automatic information processing in reading, revisited. In R. Ruddell, M. R. Ruddell, & H. Singer (Eds.), *Theoretical models and processes of reading* (pp. 864–894). Newark, DE: International Reading Assocation.

Short, K. G., Kauffman, G., & Kahn, L. H. (2000). I just need to draw: Responding to literature across multiple sign systems. *The Reading Teacher, 54,* 160–171.

Sindelar, P. T. (1987). Increasing reading fluency. *Teaching Exceptional Children, 19,* 59–60.

Smith, J. A. (2000). Teaching reading: Singing and songwriting support early literacy instruction. *The Reading Teacher, 53,* 646–649.

Soderman, A. K., Gregory, K. M., & O'Neill, L. T. (1999). *Scaffolding emergent literacy: A child-centered approach for preschool through grade 5.* Boston: Allyn and Bacon.

Tierney, R. J., Readence, J. E., & Dishner, E. K. (1995). *Reading strategies and practices* (4th ed.). Boston: Allyn and Bacon.

Wiederholt, J. L., & Bryant, B. R. (1992). *Gray oral reading tests, examiner's manual (3rd ed.).* Austin, TX: Pro-ed.

Young, T. A., & Vardell, S. (1993). Weaving readers theatre and nonfiction into the curriculum. *The Reading Teacher, 46,* 396–406.

Children's Books

Clifton, Lucille. (1979). *The lucky stone.* New York: Delacorte.

Fleischman, P. (1985). *I am Phoenix: Poems for two voices.* New York: Harper & Row.

Fleischman, P. (1988). *Joyful noise: Poems for two voices.* New York: Harper & Row.

Fleischman, P. (2000). *Big talk: Poems for four voices.* Cambridge, MA: Candlewick.

Wood A. & Wood D. (1984). *The napping house.* Orlando, FL: Harcourt Brace Jovanovich.

Chapter 10

Writing in the Reading Program

LOOKING AT THE RESEARCH

In a 1998 survey, 57% or more of the teachers reported that writing process instruction and integrated reading and writing were central to their teaching. At least another 51% reported similar emphasis on grammar or skill-based instruction. Rather than treating writing process approaches and skill-based instruction as in opposition to one another, all but a handful of the teachers surveyed reported some emphasis on both. The 1998 NAEP assessment also found that attention to spelling, grammar, and punctuation exercises was highest in the lower grades and for low-achieving students within each grade (Applebee, 2000, p. 92)

Focus Questions

- Why is there a chapter on writing in a book devoted to teaching reading?
- What is the writing process?
- What are the components of quality writing instruction?
- What is writer's workshop?
- How do I help young writers learn to write?

REAL TEACHERS, REAL PRACTICE

Meet Susan Smith, ***an eighth-grade English teacher***

Will the real "Dear Abby" please stand up? As my middle school students look at me quizzically, I explain that they will become advice givers to their classmates and answer real challenges posed by members of the class. I begin by reading to them some problems posed to Auntie Frazzle (Peak Potential, 1993). Students brainstorm answers to the problems and a list of feeling words such as anxious, upset, lucky, *or* annoyed.

Next I ask the students to write their own anonymous letters to Auntie Frazzle or Uncle Frazzle expressing one of the challenges they face in their own lives. These letters are written on index cards and placed in a special mailbox. Each day one card is taken from the mailbox and read by a student volunteer. Then the students write their answers for five to seven minutes. I choose one or two answers to read to the class from their responses. Since everyone wants to know all the peer responses, the card containing the letter and all the responses are posted on the bulletin board. I check them just to make sure they are appropriate before they are posted. The following is one example of a student problem and response.

Dear Auntie Frazzle,

I am new to my middle school, and I am shy and not sure how to make friends. What should I do?

Signed, Feeling Lonely

Dear Feeling Lonely,

Please do three things to make friends. One, sit with a group in the lunchroom. Talk to them. Two, talk to the people who sit by you in class. If they don't act friendly, keep smiling and they will. Three, join one of the after-school clubs. These clubs will have people who like some of the things you like. I think you will feel less lonely soon.

Auntie Frazzle

I have found this to be a successful reading/writing/thinking/listening project and I am impressed that there is such a high level of participation and interest. In addition to improving their writing abilities, this project helps students develop genuine empathy for each other.

Do you remember writing experiences in elementary school? For most of you, that memory would include writing papers assigned by the teacher (as in the "what did I do on my summer vacation") followed by the return of the paper with either a good mark at the top or covered with the red ink of the teacher's corrections. Most of the teacher's corrections were concerned with the mechanical correctness of the sentences. Rarely was voice or style even mentioned. Organization might be mentioned as a lack, but there was typically no explanation of what might be done to improve organization.

In the 1970s educators started to look at the instruction of writing in the school setting and determined that teachers were not teaching writing very well. Part of the problem was that teachers were not writers and could not teach what they themselves had never experienced. Summer writing projects sprang up all over the country, and teachers were invited to participate in these projects. From these projects and the continuing research on the development of writing abilities in children came the ideas of implementing the writing process in schools. In the hands of some teachers, the process became lock step, beginning with prewriting on Monday, drafting on Tuesday, revision on Wednesday, editing on Thursday, and final draft on Friday. These procedures do little to help children learn to write any better than the writing and grading of papers that most of us experienced as students. In the following pages, we will discuss strategies for implementing the writing process in ways that help children learn to write, not just complete assignments.

WHY IS THERE A CHAPTER ON WRITING IN A BOOK DEVOTED TO TEACHING READING?

LOOKING AT THE RESEARCH

What the research says about the importance of writing in a reading program

Learning to write assists children in their reading; in learning to read, children also gain insights that help them as writers. But writing is more than an aid to learning to read; it is an important curricular goal. Through writing children express themselves, clarify their thinking, communicate ideas, and integrate new information into their knowledge base (Hiebert et al., 1998, unpaged).

Writing experiences provide children with the chance to study not only words, but also sentence structures and text structures. Students who write regularly are more likely to read better as well as write better.

What might you do as a teacher to help students examine their writing in ways that promote reading skill, and how might you encourage them to look at the texts they are reading that would help them with writing?

Go to our Companion Website at www.prenhall.com/harp and contribute your answers to these questions on the Threaded Message Board. How do your responses compare to those of other students?

Reading and writing are closely connected. It is almost impossible to write without reading. Think about a paper you wrote that took several days to complete. Probably the first thing you did whenever you sat down to work on it again was to read what you had already written. You could not compose new sentences without reading what you had written previously. When a child writes, he must read what he has written. Listen to children as they write, and you will hear them reading what they have put down on paper, sometimes a letter at a time. Writing is essential in any reading program because it supports growth in reading.

Contributions of Writing to Learning to Read

Clay (1998) has summarized some of the important contributions of writing to the learning of reading. She states:

"Writing fosters slow analysis." Spoken language is very fast, and language that is read can be fast or slow. Writing is necessarily slow. The motor act of forming the letters forces the writer's careful analysis of the print.

"Writing highlights letter forms, sequences, and letter clusters." Children writing are forced to attend to the differences in letters that are in reality very similar. Think about the detailed analysis necessary to determine the differences in *b, d, q,* and *p.* Writers must also attend to the sequence of letters in words. The analysis of letters is "detailed and unavoidable."

"Writing seduces the learner into switching between different sources of knowledge (that is, levels in the hierarchy of information in print)." The writer learns that words must be composed letter by letter and that phrases, sentences, and stories are composed word by word. The learner who is aware of the reciprocal nature of writing and reading can foster competence in reading by writing and competence in writing by reading.

"Cognitive advantages can be predicted." As writers learn to monitor their writing, they become more accomplished as learners and more able to monitor their reading behaviors (p. 139).

Other Studies of the Effect of Writing on Learning to Read

Others have also studied the effect of writing on learning to read. In 1971, Carol Chomsky wrote an article entitled, "Write First, Read Later." She described the benefits of a child learning to read from learning to write at the same time. She was writing for an audience of teachers, most of whom had been taught that reading began in first grade and followed a highly sequenced instructional pattern. Writing, for most of these teachers, was not to be taught until many of the reading skills had been mastered. Her work forced many teachers to rethink their concept of teaching reading and writing as separate constructs.

A great many researchers in the 1980s looked at the relationship between reading and writing and found that students who read widely gain a sense of genre features that are useful in writing (Bereiter & Scardamalia, 1984); children reading children's literature tend to write more maturely (Eckoff, 1983); children borrow structures from their reading to use in their writing (McConaghy, 1985); and even young children demonstrate knowledge and use of appropriate text structures in reading and writing (Newkirk, 1982; Pappas, 1991, 1993). Shanahan (1988) noted that instruction should enable students to transfer knowledge from their reading into their writing and that understanding the writing process enhances the writer's ability to communicate and the reader's ability to create meaning from text. Graves (1983) found that the process of writing caused students to read for varied purposes. Students read and reread their written drafts to ensure clarity. They read to acquire additional information, to discover style and form, to learn organizational techniques, and to ensure correct use of language conventions.

It is clear that writing benefits the process of learning to read and that a reading program should include writing as an integral part of the program. The writing that we are describing as having benefits for reading instruction is composition and is generally referred to as the *writing process.*

ssessment and Evaluation Toolbox

THE TEST OF WRITTEN LANGUAGE–3

The *Test of Written Language–3* is a norm-referenced test designed to evaluate abilities in written language production in children from 7 years of age to 17 years, 11 months. It is administered one on one. Subtests include: vocabulary, spelling, style, logical sentences, sentence combining, contextual conventions, contextual language, and story construction (Hammill & Larsen, 1996).

WHAT IS THE WRITING PROCESS?

Although the writing process is often described as prewriting, drafting, revising, editing, and publishing, it is not a linear process with the steps always following in just that order.

A Recursive Model of the Writing Process

Graves (1983) and Calkins (1994) are among those who described the writing process in ways that focused on helping children learn to write and not just follow the steps of the process. Based on their work and the work of others, New Zealand educators (Ministry of Education, 1992) wanting to help teachers provide the most useful instruction for young writers developed a model of the writing process that was not linear, but recursive. This model is illustrated in Figure 10.1.

Please notice that the lines from each step are not simply from one step to the next but indicate that the writer may go back and forth between the steps. Recall a previous writing experience. You probably thought about what to write over a period of time and changed your mind several times in the process. Part of your decision making included the audience for the piece: Was it going to be read by a teacher, a committee that would determine if you could be admitted to graduate school, or your friends? Once you started the writing, you might have changed your mind several times. Perhaps you wanted to write a poem to a friend who had suffered a loss but found that a letter would work better for you.

As you composed the draft, you marked out words (or hit delete on the word processor) and made changes. You probably moved sentences around or maybe even rearranged the order of the paragraphs. You might have read the whole thing and made some additional changes. You might have decided at this point to scrap the whole thing and start again or, depending on what you were writing, you might have asked someone to read your piece and give you advice. Then you might have incorporated their suggestions or decided not to do so. When you were satisfied with the product (or were out of time to work on it), you wrote the final draft.

If you think about your own writing, it will probably match the recursive model of forming intentions, composing and drafting, proofreading and publishing, and finally outcomes or sharing the work and getting a response.

Forming Intentions. Forming intentions in the New Zealand model consists of choosing topics; determining the audience; finding out, selecting, and ordering information; and

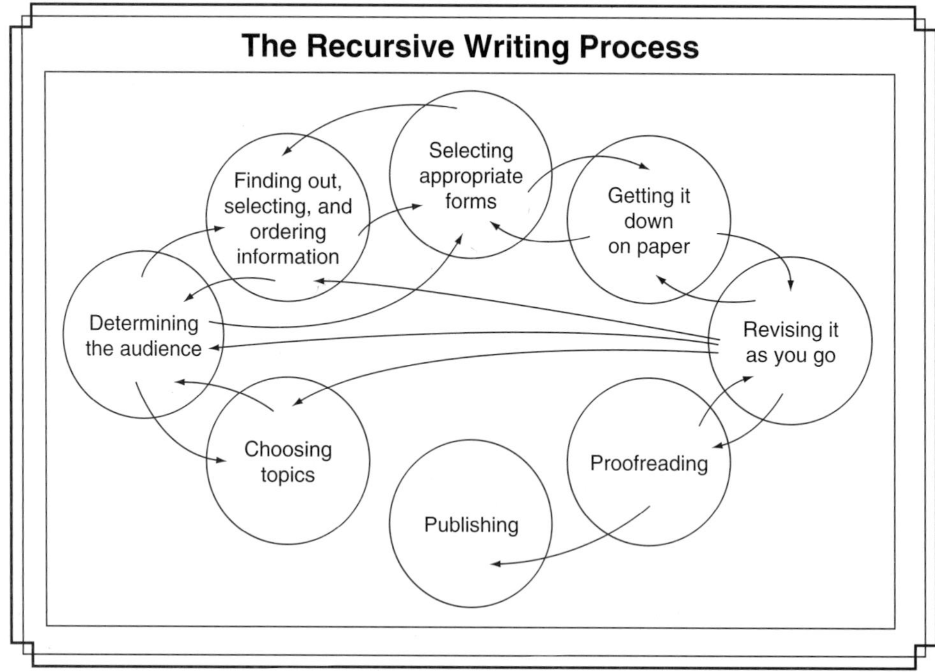

Figure 10.1
Recursive Model of the Writing Process

selecting appropriate forms. Teachers honor their students as writers when they encourage them to make their own topic decisions and to ask their own research questions. In choosing topics, you may want to engage children in conducting research, brainstorming, and looking at books, films, or drama to help them make a selection and foster a growing sense of "I know what I want to say" about that topic.

In addition, real writers do not write without knowing the audience. Children should never write without the audience in mind (even if it is only self or teacher). When we are discussing children's purposes for writing, we should challenge them to consider their audience. In fact, by teaching children to respect their audience, we build the foundation for concern about clarity and mechanics.

Once students have determined what they want to write about and to whom they will write, they can select and order the information they know about the topic, determine what further research needs to be done about the topic, and how they can best organize the information to make it clear to their audience. Here children should be encouraged to get assistance from classmates, you, the librarian, the Internet, parents, and others in finding answers to their questions and thinking about how to organize that information.

Children must be helped to ask an all-important question, "Given my purpose and audience, what is the best form for my writing to take?" The ability to answer this question in a variety of ways develops slowly over time in a text-rich environment. As a teacher you will want to introduce your students to many different forms of writing. Often this is done through sharing many genres of literature and discussing the various writing forms or through focus lessons. You will need to provide age-appropriate formats, demonstrate the writing of each format, and encourage your students to expand their repertoire. Mooney (2001) details approximately 78 different text forms that elementary and middle school students can write. Examples of the more unusual forms are almanacs, letters to the editor, minutes, feature articles for a newspaper, and magazine articles.

Composing and Drafting. In the composing and drafting stage, writers must think about the meaning of their words and the words themselves and ways to get their ideas onto paper quickly. Clearly, in this view of the writing process, the writer is not simply drafting but is considering the unfolding of the piece as the drafting is going along. The writer must be willing to make changes in this process. An author will naturally switch back and forth between rehearsal (trying the words out mentally) and composition (writing them down). The writing is often tentative and exploratory: "How do I want to say that? I'll try it like this. No, I don't like the sound of that. Here, let's try it this way." If you model this process over and over again, children will see how the shifting works: thinking, writing, crossing out, writing again, thinking, changing, and finally accepting or celebrating what you have written.

The recursiveness of the writing model is apparent as children begin a piece that they think will take a given form, then realize that another form might suit their purposes better, discover that they need to do more research or gather more information, then begin to write again. It is also apparent that changes are made constantly as the draft is underway. It would be rare to write a complete draft without any revisions in the process.

Proofreading and Publishing. In the proofreading stage the focus shifts from making the meaning clear to correcting mistakes in the conventions of punctuation and spelling. The writer checks on facts, quotations, references, and diagrams to be sure all are correct. Writing to be read by others should be as correct as it is possible to make it.

With today's word processing programs, most of the simple editing tasks such as spelling are caught automatically by the computer's spell check program. However, students must learn to proof their work even after it has been checked by a computer program. Words that are real words, but not the *correct* word, are not detected by any checking program. For example, if one means *or* but types *of,* the spell checking program will not highlight the word. The same is true of weather/whether, their/there, two/too, and other words. Grammar checkers may highlight sentences that are too long to meet the criteria in the checker program or such words as "which" and "that" if the program suggests that the author confirm the correctness of the use of these words. Grammar checkers can also recognize when the subject does not agree with the verb in number or when an infinitive has been split. These programs are not infallible as you may have learned from experience, but they do help catch major glitches.

The publishing stage is the "getting it perfect" stage. Here the author takes into consideration any editorial recommendations made by the teacher or classmates, and the final polished draft is prepared. The author makes final decisions about how the work will appear on the page, then carefully copies the work and proofreads the copy. This draft represents the author's very best work.

Outcomes. This final stage of the New Zealand model is sharing audience response. It is important for young writers to see their writing reach its intended audience and to get feedback from that audience. Here the author seeks the response of readers. Writers learn to accept constructive criticism of their work, and readers learn to respond to the writing of others without offending. The goal is for writers to look forward to the responses of their readers, to know they will grow as writers, to feel good about their writing, and to see communication improve.

Writing is an important part of the reading program. Further, writing is a process—an ongoing, recursive process—in which children have many opportunities to select what they write and then polish and publish that writing. Children need frequent constructive feedback on their writing from a variety of audiences if their writing is to improve. The writing program must focus equally on process and product.

Figure 10.2
Student Writing Sample

Frog and and Toad are friends.
Tdad is very silly. One at silliest things
that Toad does is when he sings songs
to his seedsand fcads poems to his seeds
and playmusic for his seeds. He alsoreads
books to his seeds.

Assessment and Evaluation Toolbox

ANALYZING STUDENT WRITING

Examine the writing in Figure 10.2. This is the writing of a second grader who has mastered many elements of the written system of English. List as many of these elements as you can. If you were conferencing with this child, what might be an appropriate goal for his writing? Try to go beyond just the spacing of the words in your goal. Some possible answers are listed at the end of the chapter.

WHAT ARE THE COMPONENTS OF QUALITY WRITING INSTRUCTION?

LOOKING AT THE RESEARCH

What the research says about children learning to write

Children across the primary grades learn the social and personal power of print. They create a personal system for generating and encoding written text by learning about their own purposes for writing and the expectations and needs of others (Flood & Lapp, 2000).

How would the decision to allow children to make their own choices of writing topic influence their feelings about the personal significance of their work? How would the disposition of their work, publishing or grading and returning, influence these feelings?

Go to our Companion Website at www.prenhall.com/harp and contribute your answers to these questions on the Threaded Message Board. How do your responses compare to those of other students?

The question for teachers is how to make the writing process work in an elementary classroom. Writing instruction is included in every elementary school curriculum, but quality writing instruction can be defined by the characteristics of adequate time for writing, a classroom environment conducive to writing, clear writing goals, authentic writing experiences, appropriate assessment, and comprehensive reading experiences. Not all writing programs look exactly alike, but programs that encourage the most growth in writing are marked by having these elements.

Teacher Modeling

Let your students see you working as a writer. You can model your own thought process as you compose a short text by projecting it with an overhead projector and thinking aloud about what you are writing and the changes you are making. Over a period of time, you will want to model all the various stages of the writing process. In one lesson, for example, you might want to model writing a friendly letter (a common requirement in state writing frameworks). You would talk the students through the composition of a real letter, thinking out

Teachers can model writing skills for the whole class using an overhead projector.

loud about the person to whom you are writing and then drafting, modeling making changes in words, phrases, or sentences as you go. Ask for student advice about your choices, make any corrections, and finally copy the letter and send it.

Go to the Weblinks for Chapter 10 on our Companion Website at www.prenhall.com/harp to find links to sources that discuss writing, writing assessment, and/or that publish children's writing.

When Zaragoza and Vaughn (1995) asked second graders about the elements of writing, one child suggested that teachers "tell us what you are writing about, even at home." Another child said, "The teacher should write every day and share every day." These students recognized that they could learn much about writing from the modeling provided by the teacher.

Time to Write

Another component of a quality writing program is adequate time for writing. The research (Edwards et al., 1995) supports the engagement of writers in writing in order to increase both their skill and motivation to write. Graves (1994) argues that writing instruction requires a minimum of 45 minutes four times a week and that more time is better. Edwards and colleagues (1995) found that increasing the writing experiences of children not only increased their writing skills, but also resulted in more positive attitudes toward writing. Calkins (1994) also argues that teachers must learn to give children time to learn to write—not just in minutes per day, but over time as they develop. She also argues that teachers must give themselves time to learn to provide the kind of instruction that is most helpful to children as writers and to talk with children about their writing in ways that help them become better writers.

Authentic Writing Experiences

Another component of a quality writing program is that writing in the classroom is authentic writing. Calkins (1994) recommends that the genres chosen for instruction in school be genres that are really useful in life. Graves (1994) and many others recommend that children write for authentic reasons. Writing assignments such as learning how to write a report are necessary because children are making reports on their projects. Learning how to collect information and organize it as a contribution to a class information book on the theme of whales is an authentic reason to write. Writing a letter to get information or to voice an opinion are valid reasons for learning to write letters. The point is that writing in school should have a purpose and be useful to the child.

Choice in writing is important to all writers, but Marchisan (2001) states that children with learning disabilities may need authentic writing activities even more than more typical students. She suggests that students with learning disabilities have great difficulty connecting to artificial writing situations.

Classroom Environment

Another critical element of writing instruction is a supportive classroom environment. Children must have interesting things about which to write. An interesting and relevant curriculum with projects that children have selected is likely to provide opportunities for children to engage in writing that really interests them than a more rigid curriculum. If, for example, your children are doing research on penguins and writing research reports, you might set up the environment so that each pod of desks is an "ice floe" and each group of students is reporting on a different species of penguins. Such projects yield authentic reasons for children to write.

See Chapters 12, 13, and 14 for more descriptions of projects that involve authentic and interesting writing experiences.

The psychological environment must also be supportive in that the teacher and the children feel they are all learners. They should feel that helping each other is not only important but also expected.

Assessment and Evaluation Toolbox

WRITING RUBRIC

One form of assessment for writing is a rubric as described in Chapter 3. The following is an example of a rubric that might be used for the penguin reports described previously. Each statement would be followed by a frowning face, a neutral face, and a smiley face.

1. My report had a title.
2. I told three facts about my penguin.
3. I started each sentence with a capital letter and ended with a period.

Access to the Tools of Writing

In addition to interesting activities about which to write, children need the tools of writing close at hand. They need easy access to paper, markers, pencils, and pens. They need appropriate periods of time on the computer and access to dictionaries, thesauruses, and other reference texts. Some teachers choose to use a writing center in which to store the materials for writing, even if the writing is actually done in other places. In addition to supplies, the writing center could display posters, photographs, student work, or other inspirational displays. Other centers that support writing might include a listening center, a viewing center, and a resource center. Of course these centers support the learning of reading as well.

Clear Writing Goals

Another critical element of good writing instruction is that the teacher and the children are clear about the goals of the writing experience. It is difficult to know if you are getting anywhere without knowing where you are trying to go. Writing goals should always be made clear, and they should be individualized for each child. Typical goals for writing include the following:

- Students will write with a clear focus, coherent organization, and sufficient detail.
- Students will write for different audiences and purposes.
- Students will demonstrate appropriate organization, content, paragraph development, level of detail, tone, and word choice in their compositions after revising them.
- Students will use knowledge of standard English conventions in their writing, revising, and editing.
- Students will organize ideas in writing in a way that makes sense for their purpose.
- Students will gather information from a variety of sources, analyze, and evaluate the quality of the information they obtain, and use it to answer their own questions.

These broad goals must be interpreted for students at various levels of ability and experience. For example, a beginning writer would not be expected to know all the rules of standard English usage, but a student graduating from high school should know them. Beginning writers would learn to begin sentences with capital letters and end them with a punctuation mark. Middle grade writers would learn the rules for capitalization other than at the beginning of a sentence and to recognize sentence fragments. Beginning writers would learn how to organize their writing in simple ways. An example is the rubric introduced earlier; writers were expected to include a title followed by at least three facts about their penguins. In gathering information, young writers would gather information from books, films, the Internet, and perhaps interviews. Older writers would be expected to conduct research using library resources and to evaluate the information acquired as to its value and authenticity.

Appropriate Assessment

Assessment of writing is also a critical component of an effective writing curriculum. Assessment must help the child improve as a writer. A letter grade on a paper does not inform the writer about what should have been done or what was done well. Therefore, assessment must be based on the child's work over a period of time, and both the teacher and the child should be able to point to the child's growth in specific terms and illustrate that growth with samples of writing taken over time. Assessment is critical to improving writing; a novice writer cannot improve without feedback and suggestions. Inscribing "good work" or "you can do better work" on the top of a paper does not help the writer know how to improve the writing or what parts were successful. A conference in which the teacher reads the piece, asks questions to guide the writer, and makes suggestions that may help the writer understand the role of organization in helping the reader understand the content of the writing is infinitely better than writing "needs organization" on a paper.

Figure 10.3 is an example of a checklist for writing behaviors (Hill, 2001). Keeping this checklist (or the appropriate portion of it) in the child's writing folder can help both the teacher and the child check accomplishments and set future goals.

Figure 10.4 is an example of the kinds of questions you might want children to answer on periodic self-evaluations and some questions you might want to use as you develop a questionnaire about writing. Both self-evaluations and attitude surveys help you to know how the child is feeling about her writing and will give you information for judging what changes you might need to make in your writing instruction.

The best assessment of a child's growth in writing is a portfolio focused on writing. The portfolio can contain the checklist described previously, samples of writing that illustrate growth in writing ability, summaries of focus lessons, and reports of conferences. These portfolios are open to the student and are kept over the course of the year. The selection of pieces for the portfolio may be guided by the school curriculum frameworks and your judgment about the importance of different kinds of writing. For example, if the district frameworks require that children write a personal communication, a piece of poetry with a specific format, a personal narrative, and an expository piece, then those pieces would be kept in the portfolio. A portfolio differs from the child's regular writing folder in that it does not contain all the child's work. Pieces from the writing folder can be photocopied for the portfolio to make management easier.

Writing Proficiency Tests. Many states now require a writing proficiency test of children in 4th, 8th, and 10th grade (and sometimes other grades as well). These tests supply children with a prompt, and they are required to write to that prompt. On our state test, a recent fourth-grade prompt was to select one of the seasons of the year and explain why it was your favorite season. The tests are scored in terms of how well the answer is organized, the paragraph structure, the sentence structure, and the mechanics of grammar and spelling. You can help your students to score well on these tests through the use of the writing process and writing workshop experiences.

First, help your children treat writing to a prompt as a problem-solving situation by frequently discussing the questions they can ask themselves to get started with the writing.

Figure 10.3
Writing Continuum Checklist

Preconventional

			Makes marks other than drawing on paper (scribble writing)
			Primarily relies on pictures to convey meaning
			Sometimes labels and adds "words" to pictures
			Tells about own writing
			Writes random recognizable letters

Emergent

			Sees self as writer
			Copies names and familiar words
			Uses pictures and print to convey meaning
			Pretends to read own writing
			Prints with upper-case letters
			Uses beginning/ending consonants to make words

Developing

			Takes risks with writing
			Begins to read own writing
			Writes names and favorite words
			Writing is from top-bottom, left-right, front-back
			May interchange upper- and lower-case letters
			Begins to use spacing between words
			Uses beginning, middle, and ending sounds to make words
			Begins to write noun-verb phrases
			Uses appropriate tone and mood for a variety of purposes
			Experiments with complex sentence structure
			Connects paragraphs in logical sequence
			Uses an increased repertoire of literary devices
			Revises for clarity by adding reasons and examples
			Includes deleting in revision strategies
			Edits with greater precision (spelling, grammar, punctuation, capitalization)

(Continued)

Source: B. C. Hill. (2001). *Developmental Continuums: A Framework for Literacy Instruction and Assessment K–8.* Norwood, MA: Christoper-Gordon Publishers, Inc.

Figure 10.3
Writing Continuum Checklist
Continued

Proficient

			Adapts style for a wide range of purposes
			Varies sentence complexity naturally
			Uses literary devices effectively
			Integrates information from a variety of sources to increase power of writing
			Uses sophisticated descriptive language
			Uses many revision strategies effectively

Independent

			Writes cohesive in-depth pieces
			Internalizes writing process
			Analyzes and evaluates written material in-depth
			Perseveres through complex writing projects

Figure 10.4
Self-Evaluation of Writing

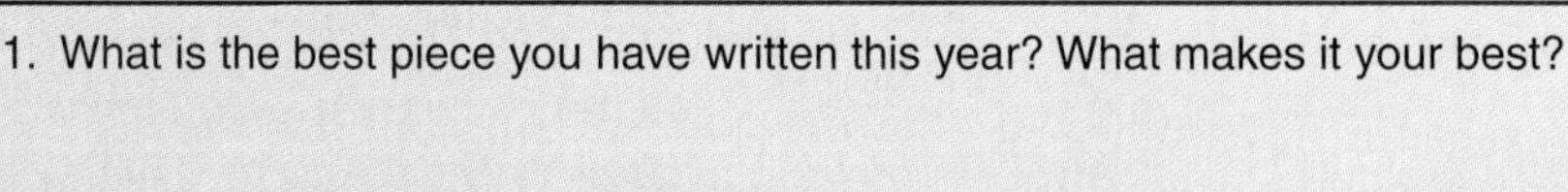

1. What is the best piece you have written this year? What makes it your best?

2. What do you do best as a writer?

3. What do you need help with as a writer?

4. Do you enjoy writing? Why or why not?

5. Do you write outside of school? What was the last thing you wrote outside of school? Why did you write it?

Questions would include: Who will be the audience for the answer I write? What do I know about writing that will help me do well on this task? Help them learn to analyze carefully the prompt to determine exactly what is being requested.

Second, help your writers learn to proofread their work carefully for grammar and spelling errors. Most state tests allow the child to write a rough draft and then a final copy. Make sure that your students have experience in finding their own errors and correcting them.

Third, writing, like reading, is learned by doing. You cannot teach students how to write well without engaging them in writing experiences. Children in schools where writing is important in the curriculum and who have many writing experiences from the time they enter school will do well on proficiency tests.

Some teachers view the state tests as having both positive and negative outcomes (Strickland et al., 2001). The positives may be more focus on writing instruction and goals that are more clearly understood by the teachers, administrators, and students. The negative may be the complaint that there is little time to devote to writing because there are state tests in other content areas as well as writing. Another issue is "teaching to the test," as only the writing genres tested are likely to be taught in the classroom.

Comprehensive Reading

Writers must read. As King (2000) notes, "If you want to be a writer, you must do two things above all others: read a lot and write a lot" (p. 145). Writers must read widely to learn more about writing, but teachers can help readers learn what to look for as writers in the reading they do. For example, if children are expected to learn to write poetry, they must read and discuss a great deal of poetry, looking specifically at word choice, rhythm, and other techniques of writing. You cannot expect children to write in any genre they have not read and discussed. Writers need to learn the rules for each genre and be able to recognize the characteristics of the genres in which they will be required or want to write. Some teachers choose the pieces of literature they want to use as writing examples early in the year and read those pieces aloud. Children who are skilled readers can read many examples independently, of course, but often the examples we want to offer children are too difficult for independent reading.

The most effective strategy for writing instruction that includes the critical components discussed previously is writing workshop.

WHAT IS WRITER'S WORKSHOP?

Writer's workshop is a planning and teaching strategy for promoting the development of writing. A specific time is scheduled for writer's workshop, usually 45 minutes to an hour, and during this time the typical schedule of events includes a short directed lesson focusing on a specific need exhibited in the children's work. Often this lesson is followed by a short status of the class report when the teacher determines where each child is in the writing process. For example, some may be forming intentions, some composing and drafting, and some proofreading and publishing. During this time, some children may ask for a conference with you, or you may determine who is ready for conferencing. The body of the writing period is spent writing and conferencing. Some conferencing may be student to student(s), and some will be one-on-one with you. The workshop period ends with a short sharing session with one or two students invited to share a completed piece or a portion of their writing.

This description may make writer's workshop sound easy, but it requires a great deal of consistency in organization and instruction on the part of the teacher to make it successful. Let us examine this workshop idea in more detail with more examples of what could be done to make its use successful for you.

LOOKING AT THE RESEARCH

What the research says about managing writing instruction

Grouping for instruction is reported as being one of the barriers to the implementation of process writing. With more research, Flood and Lapp (2000) report:

> Changes in classroom practice will occur that offer children many opportunities to write, to confer, to share, and to publish. Writing instruction is a highly complex phenomenon; it requires us to integrate what we know about cognitive processes and curriculum resources into classroom programs that are well managed and well structured. (p. 247)

Is it necessary to group students by ability for effective writing instruction? Should there be some common writing assignments so that student's performance in writing can be compared with that of their classmates?

Go to our Companion Website at www.prenhall.com/harp to add your comments on these questions to the global discussion on the Threaded Message Board.

Organizing and Planning Focus Lessons

A focus lesson is a short, 10- to 15-minute period of instruction on a specific topic. These topics are selected by assessing the children's needs in terms of improving their writing. In a second-grade classroom, you might respond to some children's desire to record dialogue by teaching how to use quotation marks to mark speech. You might use the overhead projector to demonstrate how to mark speech with quotation marks on several examples. You might then make a copy of the "rules" that the class dictates about using quotation marks to go in the children's writing folders. Older children might make an entry in their writing journals to summarize the content of the lesson. Atwell (2000) often types the content of the focus lesson, and her middle school students paste these sheets into their writing notebooks. These lessons are intended to focus on one aspect of writing at a time and to be short and to the point. Figure 10.5

Figure 10.5
Rules for Using Capital Letters

1. Use a capital letter at the beginning of every sentence.
2. Use a capital letter for a person's name.
3. Use a capital letter for the names of days of the week and months of the year.
4. Use a capital letter on Mr. and Mrs.

illustrates an example of a summary that might be prepared after a focus lesson on using capital letters. Notice that this focus lesson only covered four rules for the use of capital letters, not every rule.

One way to organize the focus lesson is to begin with an example from familiar literature, followed by examples from children's writing, then an example from your own writing, and closing with an extension to some other type of writing in which the skill or strategy is used. Literature examples should be selected from books you have read aloud in class. The following description offers one example of a focus lesson. This lesson is an example of applying the research that demonstrates how strategies used by authors can help children improve their own writing.

Almost all second graders write "the end" at the end of their writing, but think little about an ending beyond that. To help them write better endings, the teacher might choose to read from the beginning and ending of a book such as *Owl Moon* (Yolen, 1987). In the beginning, the text reads,

> It was late one winter night, long past my bedtime, when Pa and I went owling. There was no wind. The trees stood still as giant statues. And the moon was so bright the sky seemed to shine. Somewhere behind us a train whistle blew, long and low, like a sad, sad song.

The end reads,

> When you go owling you don't need words or warm or anything but hope. That's what Pa says. The kind of hope that flies on silent wings under a shining Owl Moon.

Help the children recognize that some of the beginning words and ideas are repeated in the ending. From a child's writing and from your own writing, select two or three words or ideas at the beginning that could be repeated in the ending.

Finally, use another example to illustrate the strategy. For example, *What Zoo-Keepers Do* (Hanna, 1998) is a nonfiction book that begins,

> Ever since I was a little boy, I have loved being around animals big and small. That's why I work in a zoo now.

The children could predict which of the words or ideas might be repeated at the end. The ending reads,

> Maybe you will want to work with animals one day. If you do, you will help other people learn about animals. I think that's the best job there is!

Selecting Topics for Writing

Some focus lessons, especially at the beginning of the year, may be used to help children learn how to select topics for their writing.

A common question from teachers is whether they should assign topics or allow children to select their own topics for writing. Most writers would agree that children should choose their own topics because they will have some knowledge and interest in topics they select. When interviewed by their teacher recently, a group of third graders unanimously agreed that it was easier to write on their own topics than on those selected by the teacher. The children interviewed by Zaragoza and Vaughn (1995) agreed; one said, "Teachers should not give ideas for what to write about. Students think of their own ideas." Forcing children to write on topics without considering their interests and knowledge is not likely to lead to the best writing. However, simply telling children to "just write about anything" may also fail to lead to the best writing. If you allow the children to choose their own topic, then how do you get that child who never has an idea about what to write to select a topic and get to work on the writing?

The following suggestions for helping children with topic selection will aid you in planning for writer's workshop:

- Calkins (1994) supports the use of a writer's journal in which the children record ideas, observations, pieces of dialogue, and other bits that can then be mined for writing topics. Students can also brainstorm lists of topics that would be good topics for writing and keep these lists in their writing notebooks.
- As the research suggests, writing topics may also be selected from content needs and discussions. McMackin and Siegel (2001) connected research on curriculum topics to writing experiences and found that such experiences supported children's writing. Children wrote about the topics of their research in authentic ways.
- Other teachers have asked students to write on given topics such as to interview a person about his or her life and write a brief biography of that person. Often these topics are required by state mandates.
- When teaching a specific format or genre of writing, children will need to write in that format or genre to learn to use it. The point of teaching formats is to build a repertoire of formats from which the student can choose the one they think will be best for a particular writing task.
- If one must assign topics, leave room for the child to make choices within the assignment. For example, the curriculum might dictate that children be asked to write a cinquain, but children can choose the topic of that poetry. Children may need to learn to write a report, but they can choose the subject of the report. Standards in most states require that students write narratives, summaries, essays, letters, directions, and other genres. If the curriculum frameworks dictate a specific genre of writing, you must assign that genre. However, teachers can still encourage students to write about topics of interest to them. For example, in writing summaries, children could choose to write a summary of material they select from a given set of sources.

Second graders created a list of suggestions for helping students think about topics that would be good choices for writing (Zaragoza & Vaughn, 1995). This list is presented in Figure 10.6.

ISSUES IN LITERACY

HOW MUCH IS ENOUGH WRITING?

Teachers sometimes worry about how many pieces a child should take through the complete writing process. All writers know that not everything an author begins ends up being published. Most writers have a box or a drawer with half-finished pieces or ideas for pieces that are not appealing at all now. Teachers at each grade level might get together and determine how many finished pieces make sense for their students. Maybe the third graders will complete one piece every month; maybe the fifth graders can complete one piece every two weeks. The teachers must determine what requirements make sense in terms of the writing experiences of the children and the curriculum requirements for their state or district.

Figure 10.6
Ideas for Writing Topics from Second Graders

1. Think about things you've done.
2. Think about things that aren't real.
3. Ask others (students, friends, parents) for ideas.
4. Did you do something on the weekend? You can use that.
5. Ask someone to share a story and then you'll get an idea.
6. Think of a title and a problem.
7. Ask your teacher if you can go to another classroom and interview a student.
8. Think about things you already saw and put it together with friends in the story.
9. Look in a book.
10. Get ideas from places you go.
11. Get a piece of paper and make a list of things you could write about.

Source: Zaragoza, Nina & Vaughn, Sharon, (1995, September). Children teach us to teach writing. *The Reading Teacher, 49* (1), 42–47.

Status of the Class

A status of the class report (Atwell, 1998) is usually kept on a clipboard or in a folder. This report is a list of the class down the side and the days of the week across the top with boxes to be completed each day. If a child says he is thinking about what to write on Monday, again on Tuesday, and again on Wednesday, the teacher might schedule some time with that child to find out what he is trying to do and what difficulties he is encountering. Other children may report that they are proofreading and publishing. The status of the class report helps the teacher track the progress of each child and make note of any problems that need attention.

Some teachers call each child's name and the child responds with what he or she is doing; others walk around the classroom and take the status report quietly from each child. A large coathanger can be used as a status record. Laminated squares are hung in a vertical row and each square is labeled choosing topics/determining audience, finding out, selecting and ordering information, selecting appropriate forms/getting it down on paper, revising, proofreading, and publishing. Each child has a clothespin with his/her name on it and clips the pin on the edge of the appropriate card as writing workshop begins or ends. The teacher can then make a quick note of each child's working plans for that day. This system is illustrated in Figure 10.7.

Figure 10.8 is an example of a portion of a status of the class report kept on a clipboard. This chart reflects the reality of a classroom in which the children are at different points in their writing. However, the status report can help the teacher form small groups that might need help solving a common problem. Note that in this chart, four children are working on editing. This might be a good time to have these four children help each other with editing.

Writing Conferences

Conferences are the heart of writing workshop. During conferences teachers teach individual children. During the body of the workshop time, you will engage in numerous individual conferences. Most teachers keep a list on which they mark the dates of their conferences with each child to make sure that no child is ignored. Some teachers designate a place in the classroom, and children are invited to come to that place for their conference. Others do roving conferences in which they walk around the room stopping to work with individual children for short periods. There is no formula for a good conference, but the following descriptions of conferencing will help you think about structuring effective conferences.

Figure 10.7
Coat Hanger Status of the Class

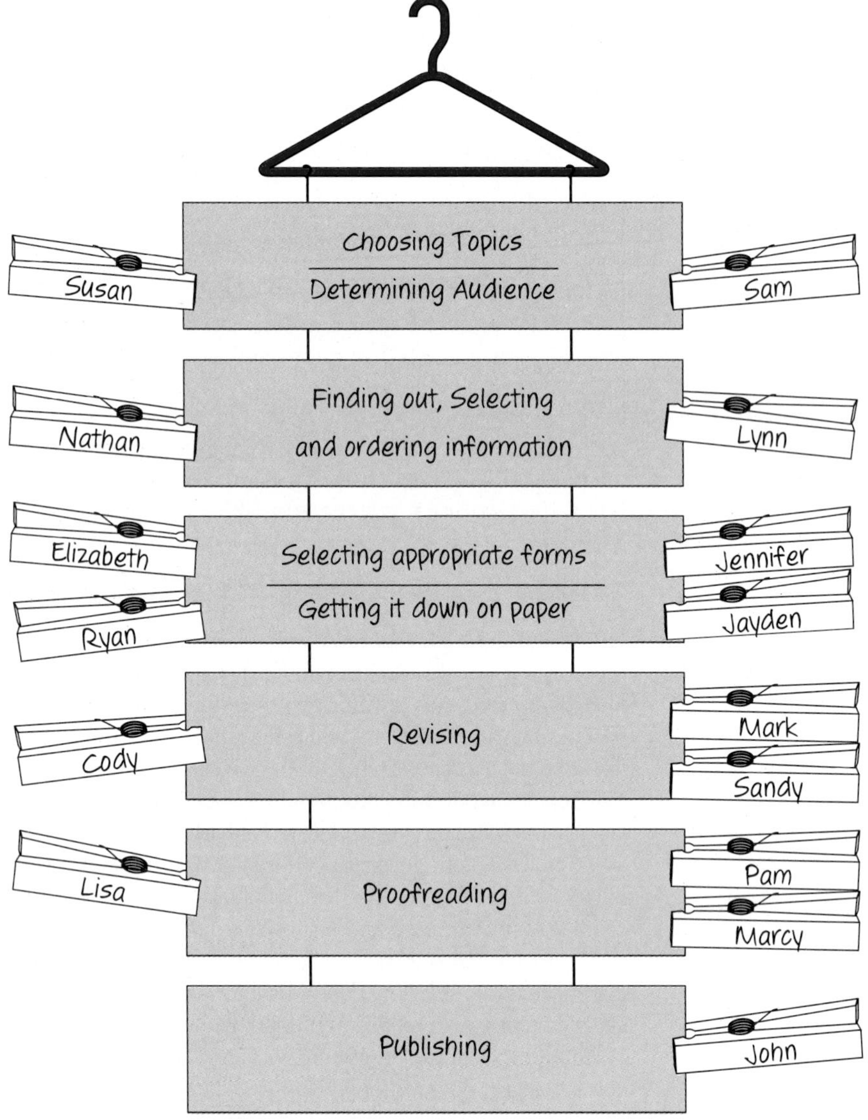

Figure 10.8
Clipboard Status of the Class

Children	Monday	Tuesday	Wednesday	Thursday	Friday
Alonzo	Editing	Publishing	Thinking		
Brigette	Thinking	Thinking	Thinking		
Brenda	Editing	Editing	Publishing		
Carlos	Editing	Publishing	Thinking		
Davio	Publishing	Thinking	Thinking		
Daniel	Editing	Editing	Publishing		
Demitri	Drafting	Drafting	Drafting		

Assessment and Evaluation Toolbox

PLANNING FORMS FOR BEFORE-WRITING CONFERENCES

BEFORE OUR WRITING CONFERENCE

_____ Select a piece of writing you want to take to the conference.
_____ Be prepared to explain why you selected this piece.
_____ If you have taken this piece of writing to an editing group or committee, be prepared to explain what happened there.
_____ Collect drafts of the piece and think about why you made changes. Be ready to talk about these decisions.
_____ Update your list of "Things I Am Doing Well as a Writer" and your list of "My Next Learning Goals as a Writer."
_____ Prepare to talk about what you plan to do with this piece next and why.
_____ Think about other things about your writing that you want to talk about with me.

Source: B. Harp. (2000). *The Handbook of Literacy Assessment and Evaluation.* Norwood, MA: Christopher-Gordon Publishing.

Ray (2001) reminds teachers that conferencing is teaching, not just troubleshooting. Her advice is to keep conferences short. Ray describes conferences as having four parts. The first is "research," trying to find out what the writer is trying to do and how things are going for him. The beginning of the conference can be general, as in "Tell me about how your writing is going," or specific, as in "Tell me what kinds of crafting techniques you are trying in your writing." (p. 160). Expecting children to tell you about their writing encourages them to think about the writing in a metacognitive way and helps them to be aware of their own responsibility in the conferencing process.

The second part of a conference is the decision-making part. Here the teacher must decide what she could teach this writer at this moment. Ray (2001) suggests several questions for teachers to ask themselves as they make decisions about what to do in the conference.

> What would help most at this time?
>
> What would bring quick success?
>
> What would be a stretch, a risk, or a challenge?
>
> What is not likely to come up in whole-class instruction?
>
> Is this something I need to reteach or extend?
>
> What is the balance of curriculum I have offered this student?
>
> What kind of teaching would this student like me to offer? (pp. 165–166)

Of course all these questions can help guide our decisions about what to teach only if we know our students well and have been working with them thoughtfully. Good conferencing requires that the teacher know about writing and about each child as a writer.

The third part of the conference is the actual teaching. Once you have decided what to teach, then the conference turns into a short focus lesson in which you teach the child one thing about writing. Ray (2001) recommends that you conclude this part of the conference by saying, "Say back to me what I just talked to you about" (p. 168). She finds that this request gets much better results than asking children if they have any questions.

Finally, you must make a record of each conference. Write down a summary of what was taught in the conference so that you can use that information for further planning, for student accountability, and for planning units of study that many children in the class need. Some teachers prefer to write a brief summary of the teaching on a sticky label and paste it in the child's writing notebook. Others keep their records for each child in a binder that they review at the end of the day. Whatever system of record keeping you use, taking the time to make a record of each conference before moving on to another conference is critical. You may find it useful to review the discussion of anecdotal records in Chapter 3.

Fletcher (2001) agrees with Ray that conferences should be short and should focus on only one issue at a time. He reminds teachers that the conference is for "teaching the writer, not the writing." That means helping the child learn something that can be used in many pieces of writing, not just helping her correct her current piece of writing.

Conferencing Beginning Writers. Preschoolers and kindergartners need to talk about their own intentions in writing, and you will have to use good judgment to help them learn what makes sense to them at the moment. For example, some young learners will be able to make corrections to their letter forms (such as reversals) while others cannot use that information at the time. Others will be able to make changes in their grammatical forms such as hearing the difference in "me and my brother went . . . " as compared to "my brother and I went . . . " Until a child can make sense of corrections, they are not helpful to growth in writing.

Conferencing Early Writers. For second or third graders, the conference might involve the teacher asking the child what is going well in the writing, if there are any problems, or what kind of help she could use. Conferencing as described by Thomason (1998) is not a time for editing but a time for coaching. Try to talk less and listen more. Telling writers what to do to improve is not nearly as effective as helping them to think through the process themselves. Coaching is helping, demonstrating, providing specific praise, and supporting the writer's efforts to accomplish his own goals.

Conferencing Older Writers. For older writers, you might expect more specific responses when students tell you about their writing, such as a description of a crafting technique they have been trying. These conferences are more like those between an author and a professional editor in that the teacher might point out parts of the writing that work well and parts where improvement is needed to achieve the writer's goals. Professional editors do not focus on editing in the sense of correcting mechanical problems; that is the job of another person, the copyeditor. The writer's goals must always be respected in a conference. The teacher's job is to help students achieve their own writing goals and provide guidance and support, but not to take over the writing. When we talk about the art of teaching, this is one place where that art of helping and supporting without overpowering is critical.

LOOKING AT THE RESEARCH

What the research says about revision

Revision in reading and writing requires readers and writers to reconsider and evaluate meaning, a form of critical understanding (Fitzgerald, 1989).

How can you help your students learn that revision is not simply copying over the piece in neater handwriting? What kind of modeling of revision would you plan?

Advising Writers About Revisions

During revision writers cycle back to what they have written to reenvision meaning and check for their success in meeting the communication goals they had for the piece. The writer must decide if the piece as it is now written expresses the original intent or if the meaning conveyed by the piece is not what they intended to say. There are not rules to tell you how much revision is necessary. The criteria should be that revision is purposeful and that the writer sees how the revision is important to the work. Requiring a certain number of drafts or revision of every piece of writing does not make sense. Revision for the purpose of improving organization, paragraph and sentence structure, word use, or other improvements to the writing that are appropriate for the individual learner does make sense.

Each author has an individual style for revisions that works for him or her. Mem Fox (1999) revised *Possum Magic* 49 times. Katherine Paterson (1996) has said that a draft is like the block of granite on which a sculptor begins polishing and chipping away to bring out the final form. Stephen King (2000) reports that he writes a complete draft, shares it with a few trusted readers, and then revises the whole thing. Byrd Baylor (1992) says she writes each page until it is perfect. The point is that no rules apply to all writers in terms of revision.

Your goal as a teacher is to help young writers see that revision is what has been happening as the draft has been composed (changing words, marking out sentences, and so on) and that the purpose of revision is not just to copy over the piece but to make it better in some significant way.

Peer Conferences. Peer interaction plays an essential role in the development of writing. These interactions provide valuable support as children write texts of their choosing. These interactions are influenced by the child's personal style, the nature of the task, and the norms for writing established in the classroom (Yaden, Rowe, & MacGillivray, 2000). Because peer conferences are an important component of the workshop, students should have the option of talking to one or more of their peers at any point in the writing process. Peers can learn to listen and help their classmates think through writing problems. Sometimes teachers use focus lesson time to help children learn what to do to help each other write more clearly.

Sharing Time

The time for sharing at the end of the period is a short time of 5 to 10 minutes in which one or more students share their writing, either a completed piece or a portion of a piece they choose to share. There may also be times when you will choose to share the child's work (with the child's permission, of course). Greenberg (1986) has found that some children become silly when they get up to share work. You will have to use your own judgment about how to arrange the sharing. A common feature of sharing time is the author's chair, a chair designated as a place where authors sit to share their work.

Author's Chair. Most teachers set up the author's chair early in the year and model how the sharing of material is to be done. For example, you might share a piece of your own work and help the children with possible responses such as commenting on what they liked about the piece, what part of the piece they liked best, or how the piece made them feel. Together you and the class will decide on the rules for sharing such as (1) Listen when someone is reading. (2) Make only positive comments. (3) Ask questions about the process the writer went through to get the piece done." The point of sharing is to celebrate the writing accomplishments of the children, so there are no specific rules about how to organize it.

Publication as Sharing. Another form of sharing is the publication of children's work for their peers and others. Publishing can mean that the work is displayed on a bulletin board, collected for a class book, printed in the school newspaper, or any number of other options. "Publication" should be as authentic as you can make it; it is difficult to require revisions and editing without a real reason for doing them. None of us would be interested in polishing and editing our grocery list.

Some publication possibilities are so logical; for example, it makes such good sense that children would learn to write an explanation of their entry to the science fair and that the publication would be the presentation of the text beside their display. Other publication may not be so logical, and you may have to spend more time thinking about the reasons for completing a piece of work. Sometimes children are asked to share their work with their family, with other children via the Internet, with younger children in the school, or some other format that provides an authentic reason to take their work through a full writing cycle. Students may also need to demonstrate mastery of a given format for their portfolio. This, too, is an authentic reason for "publishing" work.

HOW DO I HELP YOUNG CHILDREN LEARN TO WRITE?

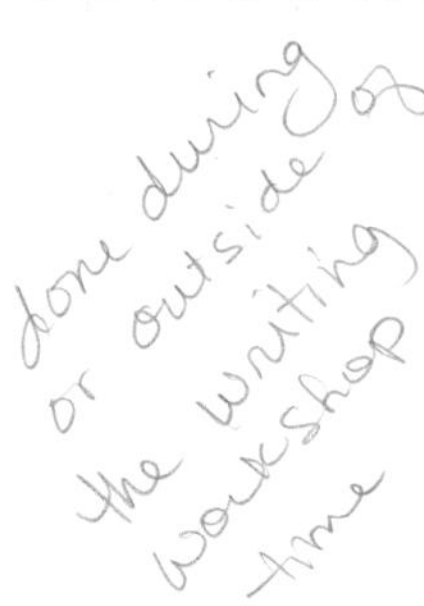

A good program of writing instruction will offer opportunities for independent writing, demonstrations of writing, and interactive writing experiences. Once you have determined what the children need to know, writing experiences can be planned. Most of the writing will take place during writing workshop but sometimes journal writing is done outside the workshop time. Journal writing is a common form of independent writing.

Journal Writing

At least several times a week, if not daily, children will need time to write in their journals. Most teachers plan journal writing for every child every day.

First Thing in the Morning. Journal writing is often available to the children as they come into the room first thing in the morning. Other teachers plan journal writing for another quiet time of day, perhaps immediately after lunch. Whenever it is planned, the time is short, but may be extended as the children gain experience as writers.

Time for Teacher Responses. Many teachers use journal writing as an opportunity to respond to children's writing and model writing forms. For example, if the child writes, "My pupe chws on my shus," the teacher can respond, "My puppy chews on my shoes, too. I try to give him something else to chew on." Often the "writing" in children's journals is drawing.

Journal writing provides an opportunity for students to express their ideas and feelings.

LOOKING AT THE RESEARCH

What the research says about drawing in the reading program

Research demonstrates that drawing is an important step for some children in organizing their thoughts. Sidelnick and Svoboda (2000) noted that opportunities to draw are useful to children as they move into writing. Millard and Marsh (2001) agree that drawing is important in the developing literacy of children. Some researchers believe that schools limit the visual and graphic literacy of children to only letters and that such limitations fail to recognize the importance of children's visual representation of their knowledge (Kress, 1997).

Is there an age when it is appropriate to ask children to stop drawing as part of their writing experiences?

Is representing through drawing as valuable as representing through words?

Go to our Companion Website at www.prenhall.com/harp and contribute your answers to these questions on the Threaded Message Board. How do your responses compare to those of other students?

Drawing in the Writing Program

Kindergarten and first-grade teachers need to accept the drawing of children as their writing. As children gain more experience with writing, they will begin to add letters and words to their drawings and then move toward writing that may be illustrated but drawing is not the focus of the child's writing. Children often treat their drawing as part of the text they are creating, much like a picture book page where the picture and the text are arranged to produce a response. Much that young children understand, but cannot yet write about, can be recorded through drawing. For some older children, drawing will continue to be a way to organize their thinking and represent what they know.

Interactive Writing

Interactive writing is defined as writing in which the teacher guides the children in recording the sounds they hear in words (McCarrier, Pinnell, & Fountas, 2000).

Hearing and Writing Sounds. Button, Johnson, and Furgerson (1996) relate their experiences in asking children in a small group to record the word *Goldilocks* as they create a story map of the story of the Three Bears. You ask the children to say the word slowly and report what sounds they hear. As a child reports the sounds, she comes to the chart and writes the letters in order. The teacher supplies the letters that cannot be heard in a word.

Values of Interactive Writing. The Ohio Early Learning Literacy Initiative (Button, Johnson, & Furgerson, 1996) describes the values of interactive writing as:

1. Demonstrating the concepts of print, early strategies, and the way words work
2. Providing opportunities to hear sounds in words and connect with letters
3. Helping children understand "building up" and "breaking down" processes in reading and writing.
4. Providing opportunities to plan and construct texts (p. 448)

Interactive writing is a strategy that promotes the learning of sound/letter relationships. Most teachers of young children would agree that they teach phonics more in writing than in reading.

Interactive Writing as Assessment and Evaluation. Participation in interactive writing also provides information about which sounds a child can represent with a letter or letters and which ones still need instruction. The teacher makes a real effort to support and scaffold for a child, but tries not to take over the writing or force the child into a direction of the teacher's choice.

You add what the children cannot yet do in interactive writing, but as the children gain experience and skill, you switch to adding what the children can do easily and asking them to fill in the more challenging parts. For example, kindergarten children might be asked to add letters for sounds that are easily heard and have a single choice for representing that sound (not the sound at the beginning of *cake,* for example, which can be represented with either a *c* or a *k*) with the teacher filling in the remainder of the letters. By the time the children are in second grade and are writing most sounds easily, you would fill in all the easy letters and ask the children to fill in new combinations such as *-tion* in *nation.*

Demonstrating Writing

In addition to modeling writing through journal responses, you can find many other opportunities for modeling during the course of the day. If the children need to write a thank you note to a speaker, you would model how to write a thank you note by talking through the thinking that one does in composing a thank you note. You might help the children write a note to invite their parents to attend a short program at the school. You will model how to write a report on the growth of the seeds or another science experiment. Many opportunities to model and demonstrate are presented throughout the school day.

Guided Writing

In guided writing as in guided reading, the teacher sets the stage for success, but the children do the actual writing. For example, with a small group, you might help them write a report by first reading several reports, then discussing the parts of a report, and then talking the children through the writing of their reports and discussing what parts were difficult and how they solved their writing problems.

Go to the Weblinks in Chapter 10 on our Companion Website at www.prenhall.com/harp to find links that access details about trait writing programs.

ISSUES IN WRITING INSTRUCTION

TRAIT WRITING SCHEMES

Over the last few years, several people (Northwest Regional Educational Laboratory, 2001; Spandel, 2001) have proposed schemes to help teachers talk to children about their writing and to know what elements of writing are appropriate for instruction. Even though we would not advocate a six-trait writing program that focused on teaching the traits in a lock-step fashion, we do think that knowledge of the traits is valuable information for the teacher and sometimes for the children. For example, if you are familiar with the traits, both planning focus lessons and conferencing can be improved as you use the traits to explain to children the elements of writing that will help them achieve their writing goals.

The six traits usually are defined as ideas and content, organization, voice, word choice, sentence fluency, and conventions. The Northwest Regional Laboratory writing program also includes presentation or the appropriateness of form, spacing, handwriting or fonts, and use of headings or subheadings.

The original goal of developing trait writing was to provide teachers and students with the language for discussing writing and a vision of what good writing looks like in order to implement fully the writing process. Helping children achieve excellence in their writing is a worthy goal. The question is, can a writing program with predetermined content and implementation on a specific schedule of drafting, revising, editing, and publishing that is identical for every child meet the needs of developing writers? You have a critical decision to make: Will you let your learners' writing needs determine your instruction, or will you follow a predetermined scope and sequence?

Writing is important for learning to read and supports and encourages reading. Writing also provides opportunities for children to express knowledge and feelings and to communicate with others. Teaching writing is a challenge, but it is worth the effort in helping children become literate.

THINKING AS A TEACHER

1. You want to implement a writing workshop time in your classroom. How will you introduce it to your children? How will you explain it to the parents? How will you assess the value of the workshop in teaching writing?
2. Your state frameworks require that fourth-grade children write a response to a prompt. If you are allowing children to choose their own topics for writing, how will they learn to write to a prompt on a writing proficiency test?
3. You know that teaching writing is difficult at times, but when one of your fourth graders writes, "Comet, comet, it makes me vomit" as poetry, you are undone. What can you do to help children write meaningfully for themselves when they have such an attitude about writing?

FIELD-BASED ACTIVITIES

1. Find a piece of children's literature that has traits you would like children to learn to use in their own writing. Plan how you might use this book in a focus lesson.
2. Ask three children of different ages to complete the attitude survey from Kear, Coffman, McKenna, and Ambrosio (2000). What did you learn from their answers that would help you plan instruction for your classroom?
3. Plan a focus lesson that you could teach to third graders on voice in writing. How would you adapt this lesson for older children? How might you adapt this lesson for less experienced third graders?

Possible Responses for the Writing Assessment in Figure 10.2

Elements Mastered:

Capital letters on personal nouns
Periods at the ends of sentences
Conventional spelling

Suggestions in Conference:

This piece begins with a statement about frog and toad, but tells only what toad does.
Can you tell the reader something about why frog and toad are friends?
Can you tell the reader why Toad sings to his seeds?

REFERENCES

Applebee, A. N. (2000). Alternative models of writing development. In R. Indrisano & J. R. Squire (Eds.), *Perspectives on writing* (pp. 90–110). Newark, DE: International Reading Association.

Atwell, N. (1998). *In the middle.* Portsmouth, NH: Heinemann/Boynton-Cook.

Atwell, N. (2000). Writing lessons I have learned. Presentation at New England Reading Association, Portland, ME.

Baylor, Byrd. (1992). A workshop for teachers. Beaverton Public Schools. Portland, OR.

Bereiter, C., & Scardamalia, M. (1984). Learning about writing from reading. *Written Communication, 1,* 163–188.

Button, K., Johnson, M., & Furgerson, P. (1996). Interactive writing in a primary classroom. *The Reading Teacher, 49,* 6, 446–454.

Calkins, L. M. (1986, 1994). *The art of teaching writing.* Portsmouth, NH: Heinemann.

Chomsky, C. (1971). Write first, read later. *Childhood Education, 47,* 296–299.

Clay, M. M. (1998). *By different paths to common outcomes.* York, ME: Stenhouse.

Eckoff, B. (1983). How reading affects children's writing. *Language Arts, 60,* 607–616.

Edwards, L., Walsh, R., Mackert, J., Hancock, S. (1995). Improving student writing skills and attitudes thorough the increase of writing experiences. ERIC Document Reproduction Service 386 750.

Fitzgerald, J. (1989). Enhancing two related thought processes: Revision in writing and critical reading. *The Reading Teacher, 43,* 42–48.

Fletcher, R. (2001). The writing conference: Breaking the silence. *School Talk, 6,*(2), 1–2.

Flood, J., & Lapp, D. (2000). Teaching writing in urban schools: Cognitive processes, curriculum resources, and the missing links—management and grouping. In R. Indrisano & J. R. Squire, (Eds.), *Perspectives on writing: Research, theory and practice* (pp. 233–250. Newark, DE: International Reading Association.

Fox, M. (1999). Writing picture books. Presentation at National Association for the Education of Young Children Conference. New Orleans, LA.

Gilhool, M., Byer, J., Farmer, L., Dean, M., & O'Hare, A. (1996). A qualitative study: The effect of modeling nonfiction text strategies on third and fourth grade student's nonfiction writing. ERIC Document Reproduction Service Number 403 589.

Graves, D. (1983). *Writing: Teachers and children at work.* Portsmouth, NH: Heinemann.

Graves, D. H. (1994). *A fresh look at writing.* Portsmouth, NH: Heinemann.

Greenburg, D. (1986). *Teaching poetry to children.* Portland, OR: Continuing Education Publications.

Hammill, D. D., & Larsen, S. C. (1996). *Test of written language examiner's manual* (3rd ed.). Austin, TX: Pro-ed.

Harp, B. (2000). *The handbook of literacy assessment and evaluation.* Norwood, MA: Christoper-Gordon.

Hiebert, E. H., Pearson, P. D., Taylor, B. M.; Richardson, V., & Paris, S. G. (1998). Topic 6: Writing and reading. *Every child a reader.* Unpaged.

Hill, B. C. (2001). *Developmental continuums: A framework for literacy instruction and assessment K–8.* Norwood, MA: Christoper-Gordon Publishers, Inc.

Kear, D. J., Coffman, G. A., McKenna, M. C., & Ambrosio, A. L. (2000). Measuring attitude toward writing: A new tool for teachers. *The Reading Teacher, 54,* 1, 10–23.

King, S. (2000). *On writing: A memoir of the craft.* New York: Scribner.

Kress, G. (1997). *Before writing: Rethinking the paths to literacy.* London: Routledge.

Marchisan, M. L. (2001). The write way. *Intervention in school & clinic, 36,* 154–163.

McCarrier, A., Pinnell, G. S., & Fountas, I. C. (2000). *Interactive writing: How language & literacy come together, K-2.* Portsmouth, NH: Heinemann.

McConaghy, J. (1985). Once upon a time and me. *Language Arts, 62,* 349–354.

McMackin, M., & Siegel, B. (2001). Integrating research projects with focused writing instruction. *Reading Online, 4,* 7.

Millard, E., & Marsh, J. (2001). Words with pictures: The role of visual literacy in writing and its implication for school. *Reading, 35,* 54–62.

Ministry of Education. (1992). *Dancing with the pen.* Wellington, New Zealand: Author. (Distributed in the United States by Richard C. Owens, Katonah, NY).

Mooney, M. E. (2001). *Text forms and features: A resource for intentional teaching.* Katonah, NY: Richard C. Owens.

Newkirk, T. (1982). Young writers as critical readers. *Language Arts, 59,* 451–457.

Northwest Regional Educational Laboratory. (2001). *Six trait writing.* Portland, OR: Author.

Pappas, C. (1991). Young children's strategies in learning the book language of information books. *Discourse Processes, 14,* 203–226.

Pappas, C. (1993). Is narrative "primary"? Some insights from kindergarteners' readings of stories and information books. *Journal of Reading Behavior, 25,* 97–129.

Paterson, K. (1996). Writing for children. A speech at a conference for teachers sponsored by the Tsongas Historical Center, Lowell, MA.

Peak Potential. (1993). *Dear Auntie Frazzle: Creative–ready to use–prompts for problem solving.* Loveland, CO: Author.

Ray, K. W. (2001). *The writing workshop: Working through the hard parts (and they're all hard parts).* Urbana, IL: National Council of Teachers of English.

Shanahan, T. (1988). The reading-writing relationship: Seven instructional principles. *The Reading Teacher, 41,* 636–647.

Sidelnick, M. A., & Svoboda, M. L. (2000). The bridge between drawing and writing: Hannah's story. *The Reading Teacher, 54*(2), 174–184.

Spandel, V. (2001). *Creating writers through 6-trait writing assessment and instruction.* New York: Longman.

Strickland, D., Bodino, A., Buchan, K., Jones, K., Nelson, A., Rosen, M. (2001). Teaching writing in a time of reform. *The Elementary School Journal, 101,* 385–397.

Thomason, T. (1998). *Writer to writer: How to conference young authors.* Norwood, MA: Christopher-Gordon.

Yaden, D. B., Jr., Rowe, D. W., & MacGillivray, L. (2000). Emergent literacy: A matter (polyphony) of perspectives. In M. L. Kamil, P. B. Mosenthal, P. D. Pearson, & R. Barr. (eds.) *Handbook of Reading Research Vol. III.* Mahweh, N.J.: Erlbaum. p. 425–454.

Zaragoza, N., & Vaughn, S. (1995). Children teach us to teach writing. *The Reading Teacher, 49,* 42–47.

Children's Books

Hanna, J. (1998). *What Zoo-Keepers Do.* Illus. by Rick A. Prebeg. New York: Scholastic.

Yolen, J. (1987). *Owl Moon.* Illus. by John Schoenherr. New York: Philomel.

PART

3 PLANNING FOR BALANCED LITERACY PROGRAMS

We defined the balanced approach to literacy instruction in Chapter 2. There you also discovered the rationale behind taking a balanced approach to literacy. You may find it helpful to review Chapter 2 before studying Part Three. In Part Three, we begin by looking closely at the role wonderful children's literature plays in supporting the literacy program. Then we will turn our attention to applying the information you have learned to building literacy programs at three levels of school: PreK–2, grades 3–5, and grades 6–8. Our intent in creating these chapters is to give you clear, practical illustrations of literacy instruction in action at various grade levels. We hope that, whatever grade you teach, you will find these chapters especially helpful in planning and executing informed literacy instruction.

Chapter 11

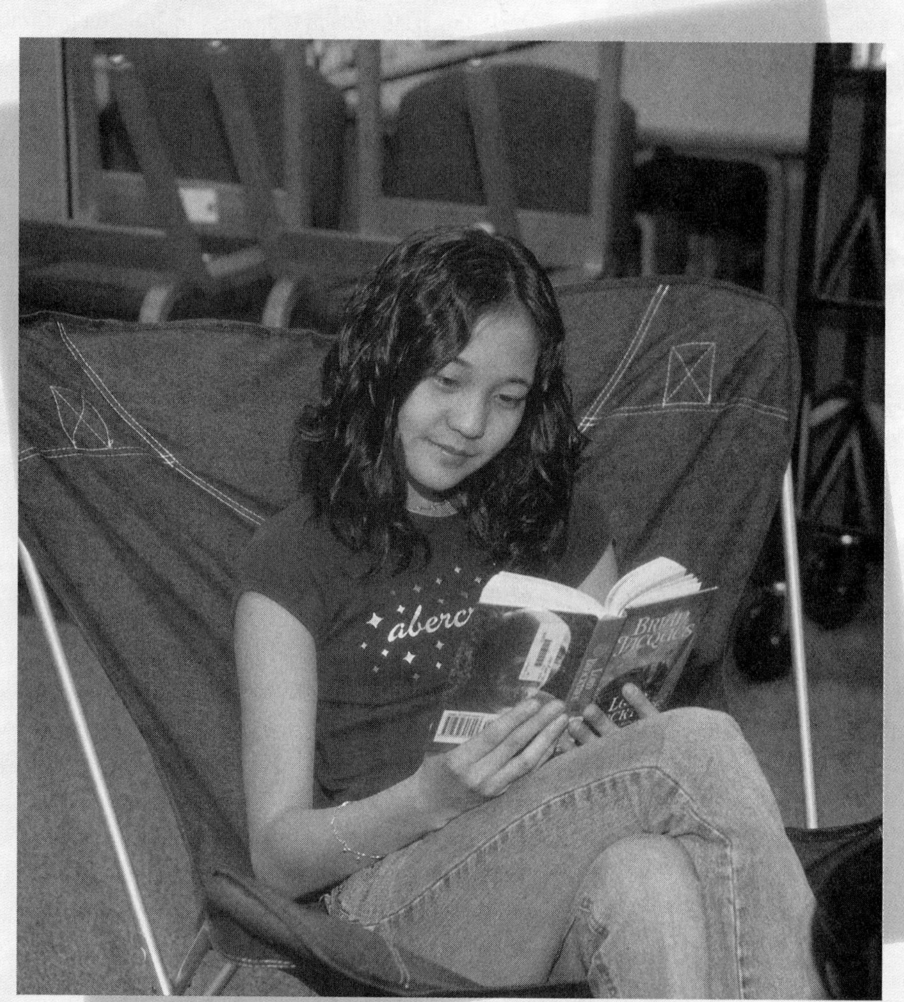

Supporting Literacy with Literature in the Classroom

LOOKING AT THE RESEARCH

A rich diet of children's literature helps students become more strategic readers (Dahl & Freppon, 1995), provides material for practice in reading (Morrow, Presley, Smith, & Smith, 1997), has a positive effect on content area learning (Gussetti, Kowalinksi, & McGowan, 1992), and has a positive influence on children's knowledge of written language (Purcell-Gates, McIntyre, & Freppon, 1995).

Focus Questions

- How do I select good literature for the classroom?
- How can I organize instruction in literature?
- How does using literature encourage growth in literacy?

REAL TEACHERS, REAL PRACTICE

Meet John Clark, ***a middle school teacher***

One of the activities that helps my students learn literacy skills is the creation of a book of Navajo stories heard in the students' homes. I believe it is important to include the literary traditions of a student's first language when teaching literature. Using the literary traditions of my students helps to validate their culture and promote their self-image. Culture-based stories also help to lower the cognitive load my students face by accessing their shared background knowledge. One of the problems with basing instruction on culturally appropriate stories is finding relevant Navajo literature. Although I have used some quality books in my class, the literary traditions that come from the homes of my students are richer and more authentic than published texts. Navajo stories that have been published by commercial publishing houses have been adapted to fit a more European American storytelling model and are never as authentic as the stories the children hear at home. Writing their own stories engages children in learning literacy skills in a meaningful context as this book is an authentic reason to learn to communicate effectively. When students read and write on topics that are a part of their culture and home, they are more open to learning the language typically used in literature.

I use extensive prewriting activities during this project. I read to my students and focus on books that reflect the Navajo people. The Navajo have a vast oral tradition, but few of their written literary pieces are readily available. Books such as Monster Birds *retold by Vee Browne,* Sunpainters: Eclipse of the Navajo Sun *by Baje Whitethorne,* Navajo Wedding Day: A Dine Marriage Ceremony *by Eleanor Schick are some examples of picture books that I read during this prewriting period. These books focus on the Navajo people in an authentic manner, and they are beautifully illustrated. Discussion of Navajo culture is a natural extension of these readings. My students enjoy the discussions and are soon willing to clarify aspects of Navajo culture that remain unclear to me. Navajos will normally not engage in discussion on a topic unless they have had plenty of time to think about what they will say. I therefore provide plenty of prewriting time when working with my students. A valuable ongoing activity during these class discussions is the brainstorming of possible writing topics related to Navajo culture.*

It is important to involve the family in the creation of the book of stories, so families are encouraged to participate in helping their children. Many of the stories are considered private to some Navajo families, and they must clearly understand that the stories they contribute will be published in a class book. Traditional Navajo culture teaches that some stories can be told only in the winter (after the first snow and until the snakes come out of hibernation in the spring). Coyote stories and the string game are a few examples of cultural traditions that are restricted to winter. I often wait until the first snow or the first Yei-Be-Chei ceremony to start this project as these indicate to traditional Navajos that winter has begun. Several families in the past have been unwilling to al-

low their stories to be published, and that wish is always respected. During the draft period, the book is divided into sections based on the topics shared. Families offer literary pieces that include traditional Navajo recipes, ceremonies, family histories, stories, and games. Students also include original artwork and photography as part of their rough drafts.

The process of revision is difficult for all writers, and that is true in this activity as well. I must keep in mind that good Navajo writing does not conform to traditional European American traditions because traditional stories are often circular and do not always have a clear beginning, middle, and end. I always make a point of allowing the cultural identity of the child to take shape while maintaining a piece of work that communicates the story to the reader.

I remember one year when a student started writing about his pride in being a Navajo. The young boy wrote a few sentences about what he did but soon began to write about his grandfather. The story ended up being a tribute to this young boy's grandfather, a medicine man. This boy's pride in himself was expressed best through his love and respect for his grandfather. It was not necessary for him to talk just about himself, and any revision to a more linear European American tradition would have been inappropriate. Word processing programs and spell checkers can help as students revise their work, but I must always keep in mind that the main purpose of this project is to allow the students to see the literacy traditions of their culture as an important reason for learning to read.

Students spend quite a bit of time learning word processing skills during our final stage of writing. Most students can complete their typing in a few weeks. Scanning pictures and taking time to include last-minute stories always delay the final printing of the book for a little time. When students finish typing, they turn their work in electronically to a master file. I use the master file to organize the book into sections, add student artwork and photographs, and print the finished book. Students help with collating and binding the book once it is printed. The book is usually finished by our winter break, and the students enjoy taking the book home as a gift. My students also read their culture book during our silent reading time throughout the year. Creating a book of stories from the cultures of the students in any class can be a challenging and rewarding experience. I always feel that I have learned more from this project than have my students.

Children learning to read must have something to read. That something, we would argue, should be the very best in children's literature. Good stories that catch the interest of the reader and keep him turning the pages to see what happens can add motivation and interest to any reading program. It is hard to imagine any child putting forth the effort to learn to read without the desire to read great stories and to learn about interesting things in the world.

As you will want to use the best in literature in your program, this chapter will provide a basis for selecting literature for use in the classroom and some examples of authors and/or illustrators to get you started in your study of children's literature. About 6,000 books for children are published each year and since there are only about 185 school days, good selections are critical.

HOW DO I SELECT GOOD LITERATURE FOR THE CLASSROOM?

When selecting books for classroom use, you need to think about the intended purpose for the books. Do you plan to read these books aloud? Will the children read them independently? Will they be used to achieve curricular goals? There are some general guidelines for selecting quality literature and specific guidelines for each intended use of the books. All books used for instruction in the classroom should be of high quality. Quality is determined by the skill of the author as a writer, use of language and writing techniques that can be emulated by the children, illustrations that are artistically valuable if the book is a picture book, and a book design that provides an attractive and interesting presentation to the reader. In addition to these general characteristics, both fiction and nonfiction have more specific qualities that are important in selecting books.

LOOKING AT THE RESEARCH

What the research says about books in the curriculum

"Books can play a significant role in the life of the young, but the extent to which they will do so depends upon the adults surrounding them. Books and children aren't made of Velcro; they don't stick to each other without a little help from significant others." (Galda & Cullinan, 2002, p. 24)

What kind of "help" do you think these authors mean? Is the help you think they mean possible for a teacher with a large class?

Who provided the help that guided your interest in books? Could these people be recruited to help in the classroom?

Go to our Companion Website at www.prenhall.com/harp to join the discussion of this question by adding your response to the Threaded Message Board.

Selecting Fiction for Classroom Study

Books of fiction you will use to read aloud or to ask the children to read for their literary qualities must have

- an appropriate theme
- an interesting plot
- memorable characters
- a setting that is easily interpreted
- a style that appeals to the reader

Theme in Children's Fiction. Frequent themes in children's books include family relationships, friendship, honesty, perseverance, growing up, justice, integrity, or acceptance of self or others. The theme should not be so obvious that it overpowers everything else about the book. For example, some books preach so much about the message of the book that characters and plot become secondary. A quality book can be read with many layers of meaning depending on the previous experiences of the reader. In *Shiloh* (Naylor, 1991), some readers would interpret it as a story of a boy and a dog, while others might recognize the importance of honesty as a theme in the story. As you would expect, middle grade readers can comprehend symbols and recurring motifs in text that younger readers are not likely to see. For example, most middle grade readers understand that the wheel in *Tuck Everlasting* (Babbitt, 1975) represents the cycle of life and death.

Plot in Children's Fiction. In addition to an appropriate theme, a quality book must have a plot that is well constructed and develops logically without dependence on coincidence and contrivances. Plot is what first appeals to a child; it is what happens in the story. Plots should not be trite or too predictable. Examples of plots that are too predictable are the series books such as *Babysitter's Club.* A second-grade reader picked up one of these books, read the first page, and said, "Oh, I know what is going to happen." Such predictability may appeal to relatively unskilled readers for a time, but developing readers want more challenge in their reading material. Poorly plotted books have characters who engage in actions that would be impossible for real children of their age or that solve difficult problems quickly and easily. Even in fantasy and science fiction, the plot must reflect the realities of the world the author has created. Most plots in children's books are linear as multiple plot lines or flashbacks may make comprehension of the story more difficult.

Setting in Children's Fiction. Setting includes the geographical place and the time period in which the story takes place. Some settings are integral to the story: It could not have happened in another time or place. An example is *Minty* (Schroeder, 1996). This story of the childhood of Harriet Tubman could not have taken place in the present time when slavery is not a common feature of the culture. Sometimes place is deliberately vague so that the story could have taken place in any city or anywhere in a rural place.

Often the people and actions in a story are influenced by the setting. Karen Hesse's (1997) Newbery award book, *Out of the Dust,* is an example of the force of the setting on the action and people of the story. The wind and dust of the dust bowl days in Oklahoma are critical to the story. Some settings in historical fiction are difficult for very young children to understand because these youngsters have a poorly developed sense of long ago. You may need to supply more information to help children with the comprehension of these books. Some older children may need help with understanding changing social mores and changing rules for appropriate language use in books set in historical times.

Characterization in Children's Fiction. Well-written books have characters that ring true; readers will feel that these characters could be real people. These characters are multidimensional and are presented to the reader bit by bit through thoughts, actions, thoughts of others, and dialogue. Characters must also be consistent and behave in ways that would be expected for their age, education, and social status. The best characters are those who stay in our memories long after we have forgotten other elements of the story. Even as adults we remember Wilbur, Peter Rabbit, Lancelot, Madeline, and Babar. Tomorrow's adults are not likely to forget Harry Potter.

Style in Children's Fiction. Style is difficult to define. It means the author's choice of words, the arrangements of words into sentences, the pace at which the story moves, and the structure of the story. The style should fit the story in terms of plot, characters, and setting. An example of style that adds to the meaning of the story is found in Lois Lowry's (1993) *The Giver.* This is a story of a community where everything about life is controlled for members of the community—their choice of mate, their food, their life's work, even their memories. In the beginning when the community is being described, Lowry's sentences are short and controlled. Nothing is loose or random. As the control begins to unravel, the sentences and paragraph structures become looser and more open.

Several of Avi's books are good examples of style differences. For example, in *Nothing but the Truth* (1991), the story is told through the use of documents; in *Who Was That Masked Man Anyway?* (1992) the story is told entirely through dialogue. Style should enhance the story and not distract the reader. Beautiful language that paints a picture we can see, dialogue that reveals character, and precise vocabulary are elements of style we can admire.

Go to the Weblinks in Chapter 11 on our Companion Website at www.prenhall.com/harp to find links to the Children's Literature Assembly of the National Council of Teachers of English and the Children's Literature and Reading Special Interest Group of the International Reading Association. Both of these groups are comprised of people who are especially interested in children's literature and the classroom.

Selecting Poetry for Study in the Classroom

Selecting poetry that children like and using it in ways that encourage their continued interest in poetry are crucial. Classroom poetry can be about topics of interest such as school experiences found in *Lunch Money and Other Poems About School* (Shields, 1995) or *School Supplies* (Hopkins, 1996); dinosaurs such as *Dinosaurs* (Hopkins, 1987) or *Tyrannosaurus Was a Beast* (Prelutsky, 1992); insects and spiders such as *The Little Buggers* (Lewis, 1998) and *Spiders Spin Webs* (Winer, 1998); or the experience of being black such as *My Black Me* (Adoff, 1994). Poetry also makes sense in the classroom when it is coordinated with curriculum topics. It is difficult to imagine an acceptable topic of study for which no poetry would be available. Children prefer action, humor, and strong rhythms in poetry.

Go to the Weblinks in Chapter 11 on our Companion Website at www.prenhall.com/harp to find links to poetry sites that have resources and suggestions for poetry in the classroom.

Selecting Biography for Study in the Classroom

Good biography contains enough detail about the individual, but not so much that the reader loses interest. Authors of biographies must clearly document their sources of information, and they must make clear if portions of the book are fictionalized (such as conversations between characters). As in fiction, biography should have a strong theme and a style that is appropriate for the subject. Among the outstanding authors who write biography for children are Russell Freedman, Jean Fritz, David Adler, Milton Meltzer, and Diane Stanley.

Biography comes in a variety of forms for young readers. Some biographies are snapshots of part of the person's life. These are frequently found in picture book biographies. Some are in collections that put together short summaries about people who had some elements of their lives in common. An example would be stories of African American inventors. Biographies are also available about popular movie, music, or sports stars. In general, these are not especially well written and they are dated quickly. Last year's winner is not interesting for long. However, some of these biographies are written at a low level of difficulty and may be what is needed at a high-interest, low-difficulty level for some students.

Selecting Information Books for Study in the Classroom

In selecting information books, one must consider the accuracy of the information and whether it is up to date. One must also consider the qualifications of the author to write the book. Authors of good information books make clear distinctions between facts, theories, and opinions. The style selected by the author is also important in information books; lists of dry facts are not very interesting. Style in information books includes the vocabulary and sentence structure that are important in fiction, but it also means how the text is arranged on the page; how graphs, illustrations, and charts are incorporated; and how headings and subheadings are employed to help the reader. The organizational pattern selected by the author is also important. Finally, one must evaluate the quality of the illustrations and other graphic material.

Good sources for titles of nonfiction are the lists of outstanding trade books for science and social studies. The lists are published in *Science and Children* and *Social Education* each year and are also available on the web. The reviews on these lists indicate a grade level for which the books would be most appropriate. Both the National Council of Teachers of English (NCTE) and the American Library Association (ALA) have awards for the best information book each year.

Poetry, biography, and information books are often excellent choices for reading aloud, for critical study, and for enhancing the exploration of various curriculum topics. Studies (Duke, 1998) confirm that informational texts are scarce in the early grades. Young children can interact productively with expository texts (Duke & Kays, 1998), which should be included in literacy programs.

Go to the Weblinks in Chapter 11 on our Companion Website at www.prenhall.com/harp to find links to lists of Outstanding Books in the Social Studies, Outstanding Science Books for Children, the Orbis Pictus Award (NCTE), and the Siebert Award (ALA) winners.

Selecting Alphabet Books for Study in the Classroom

Alphabet books are often classified with picture books, but they may also be information books in the sense that they convey information about the letters and objects that begin with a given letter. Two concepts about alphabet books are important as you consider selecting them for use in the classroom. First, many alphabet books are not for young children. An example is the Caldecott winner, *Ashanti to Zulu* (Musgrove, 1976). This is an alphabet book with information about 26 African tribes. The text is much too complex for young learners. The fact is that many alphabet books are written for middle and older readers, and some are for adults.

Secondly, many alphabet books are not useful for teaching children about sound/letter relationships. Many alphabet books picture objects on the pages that begin with the letter represented, but the sound is not the sound usually taught for that letter. For example, in Graeme Base's wonderful *Animalia* (1986), the G page reads, "Great green gorillas growing grapes in a gorgeous glass greenhouse." On the page are pictures of a gibbon, a gong, a guitar, a gnome, a giraffe, a garage, a gazebo, and a gendarme, among others. Obviously *gnome* and *gendarme* do not begin with the sound typically taught for /g/ and *great, green, grapes,* and *greenhouse* begin with the /gr/ blend. Glass begins with the /gl/ blend, so the sounds are not really the sound of /g/.

In evaluating alphabet books for the classroom, look for a clear organizing principle. Some alphabet books just feature the letters with a variety of objects pictured for each letter, some are arranged sequentially to tell a story, and some are organized around themes so that each letter is connected to the theme. An example of a themed book is *What Pete Ate* (Kalman, 2001), a book in which a variety of items are consumed by Pete the dog (most are far-fetched!). Another criteria should be that the intended audience can recognize the pictures. In addition, the illustrations should match the tone of the book. If the book is whimsical and light, the illustrations should convey that tone. Alphabet books can be useful in extending topics of study (*Geography from A to Z,* Knowlton, 1988), in learning about other cultures, (*A is for Africa,* Onyefulu, 1993), or in focusing on language such as homophones or spelling patterns (*The Alphabet from Z to A,* Viorst, 1994). They are also useful models for writing. Creating an alphabet book can be a very appropriate culminating activity for a study of whales, insects, or other topics.

Selecting Books for Independent Reading

Teachers selecting books for independent reading often relax the standards for quality to some extent to provide books that will catch the interests of all children. Most notably, this happens with books in a series. Often books like the Goosebumps series would not be selected for study or for read-alouds, but they are an important part of the library for independent reading. Many

Independent reading is the time when children choose their own books.

teachers understand that getting children to read is a primary goal and that teaching taste and appreciation for literary quality must come after a child is hooked on reading.

The point in any classroom library is to have books that children are anxious to read so there must be books with a wide range of reading difficulty, coverage of many topics, and many types of books, including fiction, poetry, and nonfiction. Cunningham and Allington (2003) note that often there is nothing in the classroom that struggling readers can read or would want to read. It is crucial that every child be able to find reading material that is interesting and readable. Remember that many children prefer information books to fiction. One seven-year-old we know was not interested in the incredibly popular Harry Potter books because he liked books "that help you learn something." Scary books, comics, and magazines usually top the lists when students are surveyed about their reading preferences (Worthy, Moorman, & Turner, 1999). A classroom library needs to meet many reading needs and interests.

ISSUES IN LITERATURE

COMICS IN THE CLASSROOM

Should children be allowed to read comic books in the classroom? What about the Goosebumps books? Would you plan to have these materials in your classroom library? Would you expect children to give up reading materials with little literary value at a certain time? What would you say to the parents of children who are choosing such materials?

Go to our Companion Website at www.prenhall.com/harp to join the global discussion by adding your comments on these questions to the Threaded Message Board.

Selecting Multicultural Literature

Teachers need to establish selection criteria that include not only literary quality and children's interests, but also issues of diversity and representation (Jipson & Paley, 1991) when choosing fiction and nonfiction for the classroom. It is important to select multicultural books for at least two reasons. One is that all the children in your class should be able to see themselves in the books read in the classroom. One Latino fifth grader whose teacher was deliberately using multicultural literature stated in his journal that he had never read a book that had Latino characters before. All children should have books that represent their culture in the classroom.

Ours Is a Multicultural World. The second major reason for selecting multicultural literature is that all children live in a multicultural world. Even if you have a class of children who all share the same cultural and ethnic heritage (not likely to happen), they need to know and understand as much as possible about other cultures. In most communities today, many different cultures and ethnicities are represented. Knowledge and understanding can go a long way in promoting respect for others and the ability for different groups to live peacefully together. Norton (2003) has compiled a checklist, presented in Figure 11.1, that will help you in evaluating multicultural books.

Go to the Weblinks in Chapter 11 on our Companion Website at www.prenhall.com/harp to find a link to the Coretta Scott King, Pura Belpré, and the Notable Books in a Global Society award lists and to other sites that list recommended books for various cultural or ethnic groups.

Aids in Selecting Multicultural Literature. For African American literature, the Coretta Scott King awards are a good beginning point in selecting literature for classroom use. The winners of the Pura Belpré award are a good beginning point in selecting Latino literature. In addition, Norton (2001), Corliss (1998), and Harris (1997) offer suggestions for choosing books appropriate for presenting many cultures/ethnic groups to children. The list of Notable Books in a Global Society is another source of information about multicultural books. This list is compiled by a committee from the Special Interest Group in Children's Literature of the International Reading Association.

Illustration in Children's Books

Illustration is, of course, critical to the quality of picture books and can add to other works as well. Picture books are defined as books in which the illustration is as necessary for full comprehension of the story as is the text. Picture books often fit into the various genres of literature. There are picture books of poetry, biography, and information as well as fiction. Because the text is limited in picture books, it is often the illustration that helps develop the characters, delineate the setting, and add detail to the narrative. Therefore, picture books must be evaluated on their literary qualities and on the quality of their illustrations. The questions in Figure 11.2 will be helpful to you in evaluating picture books (Jalongo, 1988).

Picture Books for Many Audiences. Picture books are not limited to an audience of the youngest children in our schools. Great picture books are for all ages, even for adults. Some excellent examples of picture books for younger readers include *Where the Wild Things Are* (Sendak, 1963), *Sylvester and the Magic Pebble* (Steig, 1969), *Owl Moon* (Yolen, 1987), *Joseph Had a Little Overcoat* (Taback, 1999), and *And the Dish Ran Away with the Spoon* (Stevens & Crummel, 2001). For intermediate readers, selections might include *Rapunzel* (Zelinsky, 1997), *Lon Po Po: A Red Riding Hood Story from China* (Young, 1989), *Maii and Cousin Horned Toad* (Begay, 1992), and *The Dinosaurs of Waterhouse Hawkins* (Kerley, 2001). For grade 6–8 readers, selections might include *Golem* (Wisniewski, 1996), *Snowflake Bentley* (Martin, 1998), *The Butterfly* (Polacco, 2000), and *Behold the Trees* (Alexander, 2001). Some of these books are old favorites that children have loved for years; some are newer examples of truly outstanding picture books.

Figure 11.1
Evaluation Criteria for Multicultural Literature for Children

1. Are the characters portrayed as individuals instead of as representatives of a group?
2. Does the book transcend stereotypes?
3. Does the book portray physical diversity?
4. Will children be able to recognize the characters in the text and illustrations?
5. Is the culture accurately portrayed?
6. Are social issues and problems depicted frankly, accurately, and without oversimplification?
7. Do nonwhite characters solve their problems without intervention by whites?
8. Are nonwhite characters shown as equals of white characters?
9. Does the author avoid glamorizing or glorifying nonwhite characters?
10. Is the setting authentic?
11. Are the factual and historical details accurate?
12. Does the author accurately describe contemporary settings?
13. Does the book rectify historical distortions or omissions?
14. Does dialect have a legitimate purpose and does it ring true?
15. Does the author avoid offensive or degrading vocabulary?
16. Are the illustrations authentic and nonstereotypical?
17. Does the book reflect an awareness of the changing status of females?

Source: *Through the Eyes of a Child: An Introduction to Children's Literature,* 6/e by Norton/Norton/McClure, © Reprinted by permission of Pearson Education, Inc., Upper Saddle River, NJ.

Figure 11.2
Evaluation of Illustrations

1. Are the illustrations and text synchronized?
2. Does the mood conveyed by the artwork (humorous/serious, rollicking/quiet) complement the story?
3. Are the illustrative details consistent with the text?
4. Could a child get a sense of the basic concepts or story sequence by looking at the pictures?
5. Are the illustrations or photographs aesthetically pleasing?
6. Is the printing (clarity, form, line, color) of good quality?
7. Can children view and review the illustrations, each time getting more from them?
8. Are the illustrative style and complexity suited to the age level of the intended audience?
9. If the book is a hardcover edition, how have the endpapers been treated? Do they add to the aesthetic balance of the book?

Source: M. J. Jalongo. (1988). *Young Children and Picture Books: Literature from Infancy to Six* (p. 22). Washington, DC: National Association for the Education of Young Children.

ISSUES IN USING CHILDREN'S BOOKS

CENSORSHIP

Teachers usually censor books in the sense of selecting books that meet their own standards of what should and should not be discussed in the classroom. Some teachers balk at any language they consider profanity, while others refuse to use books that deal with racism or other sensitive issues. No one would suggest that pornography or gutter language be included in the curriculum, but teachers should think about why some books make them uncomfortable and try to examine the needs of their students for books that deal with real life in all its messiness. Or should all the books be those with happy endings and no controversial elements?

Censorship may also be an issue with parents or the community. Some parents, for example, have wanted to keep the popular Harry Potter books out of the classroom because they contain references to witchcraft and spells. How would you answer a parent who wanted to remove a book from the classroom reading list or ask that you not read a given book aloud to the class?

Go to the Weblinks in Chapter 11 on our Companion Website at www.prenhall.com/harp to find links to the home pages of the journals that review children's books and to the various children's and teachers' award lists.

Book Selection Aids

No teacher has time to read and evaluate all the books published for children, so most teachers rely on book reviews for help in choosing good books. Reviews of children's books are published in *Horn Book, The Reading Teacher, Booklist, Young Children, Childhood Education, Language Arts,* and other journals. *Book Links* features bibliographies to support themes and topics for classroom study. *The Reading Teacher* publishes lists of books selected by child readers (Children's Choices) every October and lists of books selected by teachers (Teachers' Choices) every November. The books that win the Caldecott and Newbery awards, the Coretta Scott King award, the Pura Belpré award, the Globe/Hornbook award and that are selected for the Notable Children's Books in the Language Arts are always good starting points. Another source of help is your school librarian or the children's librarian in your local public library. Librarians know which books are popular with children and which ones have particular qualities that might be useful as you plan your program.

HOW CAN I ORGANIZE INSTRUCTION IN LITERATURE?

Once good literature has been selected, teachers have many options when making decisions about how to present literature to students. One choice is reading aloud. Other choices include the study of a book or books in various ways, including individualized reading, literature circles, genre studies, theme studies, author or illustrator studies, or the study of a core book. We will discuss each of these options, provide examples that illustrate how each looks in the elementary classroom, and discuss the advantages and disadvantages of each choice. However, reading aloud is important regardless of which other organizational strategy is selected.

LOOKING AT THE RESEARCH

What the research says about literature-based programs

In a comparison of several different approaches to reading instruction, Eldredge and Butterfield (1986) found that students who read literature as opposed to basal readers

> . . . not only made significantly higher achievement gains than children using basals, but their attitudes toward reading also improved significantly. Attitudes toward reading decreased among those children using basal readers during this same period of time. Materials do make a difference. (p 36)

Modern basals have more real literature than the basals that were probably used in this study. Would you think that having real literature in a basal would change the results of this study? Why or why not?

If you were going to read an excerpt from a piece of literature in a basal anthology, would it be the same experience as reading the same pages from the original book?

Organizing for Reading Aloud in the Literature Program

Reading to children is a critical element in any reading program; the reading aloud discussed in this chapter refers to an adult or more experienced reader doing the reading. Reading to children serves multiple purposes and provides opportunities for the development of skills directly related to success in reading. Reading aloud is much more than simply an enjoyable and pleasurable activity, although that alone would be enough to justify its inclusion in the reading program. Reading to children is an important strategy for motivation, skill building, comprehension, listening, and understanding text structures.

LOOKING AT THE RESEARCH

What the research says about reading aloud

Children in classrooms "who were read to daily over long periods of time scored significantly better on measures of vocabulary, comprehension, and decoding ability than children in control groups who were not read to by an adult" (Morrow & Gambrell, 2000, p. 568).

Other researchers (Meyer & Wardrop, 1994) reported that reading aloud sometimes has negative effects on literacy development because sessions in classrooms are often not of sufficient quality to engage students fully and to maximize literacy growth.

How would you describe the qualities of a read-aloud experience that would lead to growth as reported by Morrow and Gambrell?

Go to the weblinks for Chapter 11 on our Companion Website at www.prenhall.com/harp to link to sites for Mem Fox and Jim Trelease, and read their suggestions for positive read-aloud experiences.

Motivating/Stimulating the Desire to Read on One's Own. As children listen to a skilled reader read aloud, they develop more interest in reading independently and develop interest in reading the material being read aloud. Most of the time, the book that has just been read aloud is the most popular book in the classroom. Reading aloud can spark interest in a new genre, a new author, or a new style of book. Material that is easy enough for children to read independently is not likely the kind of material that will challenge and intrigue students. If children are to know that the world is full of really wonderful stories that are worth the effort it takes to learn to read, then they must get that knowledge through read-alouds.

Building Skills Through Read-Alouds. Children listening to a good selection read aloud are likely to hear and understand words that they might not have met in other ways. For example, in Henkes's popular book *Chrysanthemum* (1991), he includes the words *scarcely, winsome, envious, begrudging, discontented, jaundiced,* and *indescribable.* Children learning vocabulary in the context of a good read-aloud will be able to understand such vocabulary when they meet it in their independent reading. In addition to new words, children will learn how authors structure their sentences and how word choice changes the reader's or listener's perception of a piece of text.

Comprehension Skills. In addition to vocabulary skills, children participating in read-alouds develop comprehension skills. The skill of comprehending is basically the same skill whether a child is listening to a text read to her or reading it independently. If the child listens carefully to the story and understands it, she will be much more able to comprehend stories she reads independently. Comprehension means getting the sense of the story, and it will be quite obvious to the reader if the audience is not "getting" it. Comprehension can also mean learning how to listen for information that is contained in the reading.

Listening Skills. Obviously listening skills are developed during read-alouds. Listening can be either efferent or aesthetic (Rosenblatt, 1978). *Efferent listening* is listening to get information as in listening to directions for how to do or to make something. *Aesthetic listening* is listening to appreciate the words, sentences, phrases, or writing techniques used by the author. Aesthetic listeners pay attention to the mood created and to the tone of the writing. When children are good listeners in read-aloud experiences, they develop both their efferent and aesthetic listening abilities. Listening, just as reading, may switch from one stance to the other in the course of a listening experience. A listener might be listening to a text and learning factual information about snakes and also admiring the author's use of language to describe snakes.

Understanding Text Structure. Good read-aloud experiences can also help children develop their understanding of text structure. Knowing how pieces of text are put together and the rules for various genres is a useful skill in both reading and writing. In reading, if the reader knows what to expect, at least in general terms, it makes the reading of the piece much easier. Knowing what to expect from a college textbook makes such a text more comprehensible to you just as knowing what to expect from a fairy tale makes it easier for the child to read one. In writing, knowing story structure helps children know what parts they must include in order to write a story, report, or any other piece of text. Read-aloud experiences can help children become familiar with narrative and expository text structures.

Selecting Books for Read-Alouds

Books selected for reading aloud must be of outstanding literary quality. In addition to meeting the basic criteria for good literature, books to be read aloud need to meet some additional standards. Reading aloud is a performance art in which you share your interest and love for a book with others.

Appropriate for Audience. A selected book should be appropriate for reading aloud in a school setting. It should be a length that is comfortable for reading in its entirety or for reading a chapter at one sitting to the selected age group and a size that makes sharing it with a group possible. For example, the tiny versions of the Beatrix Potter books are not designed for read-alouds as they are too small to be seen by a group.

Language Qualities. A read-aloud book should have language that is slightly above the instructional reading levels of the class. Children are capable of comprehending books that are more complex than their instructional reading levels, and read-aloud books should be challenging enough to evoke interest and admiration of the author's work.

Interesting to the Audience. A chosen book should be interesting to the intended audience. Young children appreciate adventure stories such as those with a circular structure in which the character begins at home, has adventures, and returns home. Examples would include *The Snowy Day* (Keats, 1962) and *Rosie's Walk* (Hutchins, 1968). They also like animal stories such as *The Stray Dog* (Simont, 2001), folktales such as The Three Bears and The Three Billy Goats Gruff, family stories such as *The Relatives Came* (Rylant, 1985), and humorous stories such as *Baloney (Henry P.)* (Scieska & Smith, 2001) and *A Fine, Fine School* (Creech, 2001). They enjoy stories about children like themselves such as *Madlenka* (Sis, 2001), who lost her tooth, and animals who act like children such as *Bunny Cakes* (Wells, 1997).

Intermediate grade readers usually like stories about children involved in experiences like theirs such as going to school, moving, and friendship. They also enjoy more complex folk stories. Examples would include *Ramona Forever* (Cleary, 1984), *The Whipping Boy* (Fleischman, 1986), *John Henry* (Lester, 1994), and *Hurry Freedom* (Stanley, 2000).

Older elementary readers appreciate those stories of adventure that illustrate independence and "growing up" stories in which characters face and overcome their problems. Examples include *Julie of the Wolves* (George, 1972), *Bridge to Terabithia* (Paterson, 1976), *Bud, not Buddy* (Curtis, 1999), and *Black Potatoes: The Story of the Great Irish Famine, 1845–1850* (Bartoletti, 2001).

Personal Appeal. A read-aloud book choice should be one that you truly like. There are too many great books to read one that is not personally appealing and run the risk of modeling disinterest in the book. You should also consider that younger children will request the same book over and over, and the book should be worthy of spending time on it for repeated readings.

Genres for Reading Aloud. Poetry and information books should not be overlooked as read-aloud choices.

Poetry. Often poetry is written to be read aloud; therefore it is a natural choice. Many teachers like to choose poems that relate to curriculum themes, such as *Hand in Hand* (Hopkins, 1994) when studying American history. Some pair fiction and poetry read-alouds, as in selecting the baseball poems in *Extra Innings* (Hopkins, 1993) to accompany the reading of *Bat 6* (Wolfe & Layden, 1998). Poetry selections may supply humor in the classroom, such as *Riddle-icious* (Lewis, 1996). Other examples include *Black Earth, Gold Sun* (Hubbell, 2001), an anthology about gardening; *Chicka Chicka Boom Boom* (Martin & Archambault, 1989), a classic chant about the alphabet; and *Songs for the Seasons* (Highwater, 1995) and *Awful Orge's Awful Day* (Prelutsky, 2001). Other good examples of appropriate poetry are *Honey, I Love* (Greenfield, 1978), *Dancing Teepees* (Sneve, 1989), and *My Sister's Rusty Bike* (Aylesworth, 1996).

Biography. Nonfiction also provides good read-aloud material. Biography often meets the criteria for read-aloud in terms of dialogue, interest, and literary quality. For example, younger readers will appreciate *Duke Ellington* (Pinkney, 1998) or *Satchel Paige* (Cline-Ransome, 2000). Older readers would respond to *Leonardo de Vinci* (Stanley, 1996) or *Abigail Adams: Witness to a Revolution* (Bober, 1998).

Information Books. Information books may also be good choices for read-alouds. For example, if you were studying eggs, you could read *Chickens Aren't the Only Ones* (Heller, 1981). If you were studying insects, you could read *Bugs* (Parker & Wright, 1987). You could also read *Bats* (Gibbons, 1999) or, for older readers, *An Extraordingary Life: The Story of a Monarch Butterfly* (Pringle, 1997). Nonfiction provides an opportunity to help children expand their knowledge in topics related to science or social studies or to introduce a topic that will be explored in depth in the following days or weeks.

Preparing for a Read-Aloud

Once you have selected the book you want to read, you will need to prepare to read it by thinking about your purpose and goals for reading it.

Setting a Purpose. The purpose is always enjoyment of literature, but most teachers also have other purposes as they choose books for reading aloud. Your purpose might be to introduce an author, a genre, or a style. You might read a selection because you want children to attend to the writing techniques used by the author. You might want to emphasize prediction skills or help the listeners to understand such literary techniques as foreshadowing or to focus on sensory details or figurative language.

Introduction. Once a purpose has been determined, then you will decide how to introduce the book to the readers. One key is to keep the introduction short; do not say too much about the book before getting on with the reading. One or two sentences such as, "This is a story about going to school." Or "This is a story about moving. How many of you have moved?" Then ask one or two children what it was like to move. Try not to tell children what to think as in, "This is the funniest story you have ever heard." You can, however, share what you think, "I really like this story because ________________." For books other than stories, you might say, "This book tells us about ants. I learned some new information about ants when I read it." Poems might be introduced by saying, "Since it is ________________ outside today, I want to read this poem about ________________." Whatever you choose, the introduction must be short. Sometimes teachers like to offer a prop to accompany a story. Perhaps you have a model or a toy that would help to focus the children's attention on the story about to be read.

A well-planned, short introduction draws children into books.

Decisions About Vocabulary. Once you have thought about the introduction, you must think about the vocabulary. If the book includes words you think most of the children do not know and will not be able to figure out from the context and if those words are critical to understanding the story, then you might introduce those words. Otherwise, read the story and then discuss the vocabulary. Most vocabulary can be comprehended from the context of the sentences. You will want to discuss the vocabulary after the reading, perhaps focusing on what choices the author might have had when selecting a particular word or phrase.

Practice Reading. The next step is to practice reading the story. Just as we do not ask children to read orally material that they have not had a chance to practice silently, you also need to practice. At least read the story through silently so that you know where to emphasize certain words or phrases and how to use your voice to help the listener comprehend the text. You should also know the story well enough to make adjustments as needed. For example, if the children get restless, where can you cut without losing the sense of the story? You also need to be able to read well enough that you can read while holding the book sideways so that the children can see the illustrations or when you turn the book to show the illustrations you will not lose the thread of the story. Reading aloud well is a skill that is worthy of the time it takes to develop it.

Follow-up Activities. As you read, you must pay attention to audience response. If the story is not being well received, you must decide what to do. Can you shorten it? Can you change some of the words to a more comprehensible vocabulary? Can you speed up the reading or slow down the pace with more emphasis on certain parts of the story? In other words, your job is to help the listeners enjoy and comprehend the story, and you may need to make adjustments as necessary to accomplish this goal. Most teachers of young children are more successful in accomplishing their read-aloud goals if the children are seated physically near the reader. They need to be able to see the pictures and not be distracted by items on their tables. A small chair for the reader with the children sitting around on the floor within touching distance is ideal.

After you have read the text, you must decide what to do next. Sometimes, the correct response is nothing, at least for a few minutes. Carol Hurst, a well-known storyteller, has said she likes to leave a good story "shimmering on the air" while children have a few moments to think about the story and respond to it. After these moments, you may want to read the book again (or promise to do so at another time). You might also have available materials from which children can choose to do follow-up activities such as drawing, writing, or constructing. Just remember that follow-up activities should be a choice, not a required activity for every child. We do not wish to do anything that makes children think that reading or listening to good stories is always followed by a chore. You will want to make the book available to children to look at the illustrations more closely or to page through the book again or to read it themselves if they can. Perhaps you will want to have a specific spot where the books you read aloud are kept for a few days or weeks after the reading.

In making decisions about what should come after a story reading, think about role play or drama as follow-up choices. Roser (2001) contends that writing as a response to literature is in danger of being overused, while responses featuring drama are rarely employed but can be useful in helping children solidify their understandings of text.

Go to the Weblinks in Chapter 11 on our Companion Website at www.prenhall.com/harp to find links to articles supporting reading aloud in the classroom and lists of books that are good choices for read-alouds.

Research has confirmed the value of reading aloud for developing literacy skills, increasing reading achievement, promoting interest in reading, developing oral language skills, positively influencing children's writing, and providing opportunities for social interaction (Galda & Cullinan, 1991). Repeated readings of text have been found to increase the amount, form, and focus of student talk about a text and the depth of processing text (Martinez & Roser, 1985).

Reading aloud is only one part of the program you will plan. You will also want to think about how to organize reading experiences around children's literature. Possible organizational patterns include individualized reading, genre studies, literature study groups, author/illustrator studies, and core books. Chapter 2 presented individualized reading as one example of literature-based instruction. In this chapter, we will discuss the other choices for organizational patterns.

All of the choices for literature-based reading instruction require that teachers conference with children about their reading. The reading conference outline in the accompanying Assessment and Evaluation Toolbox would work equally well for all the patterns of instruction.

Organizing for Reading Instruction Using Genre Studies

Genre studies offer almost as much choice as individualized reading. In organizing by genre, the teacher would determine the genre to be read, and students would choose a book from that genre and participate in appropriate follow-up activities. Because each child would be reading a different book, much of the reading instruction would be individualized. Children would need instruction in making a good selection and would need individual or small group instruction in skills and strategies. Children would need to write response logs, and you, as the teacher, would need to keep excellent records of the child's growth as a reader and the type of instruction offered.

Genre studies provide more opportunities for both large and small group work than individualized reading. In organizing for genre studies, most teachers determine the time frame for the reading. For example, children might be expected to read a book in two weeks.

Assessment and Evaluation Toolbox

A READING CONFERENCE PLANNING FORM

_____ Practice a piece of reading silently that you will read to me during the conference.
_____ Update your reading folder and reading record.
_____ Select a passage that gave you difficulty and be prepared to discuss how you handled it.
_____ Be prepared to retell what you have read.
_____ Prepare a list of words you have not been able to figure out yet.
_____ Be prepared to describe a part of the reading you found particularly interesting, exciting, or humorous and be ready to tell why.
_____ Be prepared to describe a happening in the book that reminded you of an experience you have had.
_____ Be prepared to discuss why you think the author wrote this piece and to discuss the writing.
_____ Update your list of "Things I Am Doing Well as a Reader" and your list of "My Next Learning Goals as a Reader."
_____ Think of other things about your reading that you want to talk about with me.

Source: B. Harp. (2000). *The Handbook of Literacy Assessment and Evaluation* (2nd ed., p. 102). Norwood, MA: Christopher-Gordon.

During the reading and after the reading is completed, children could be asked to participate in small or large group activities related to the genre. Examples include the following:

- ✔ Historical fiction
  - Place characters on class time lines.
  - Create puppets to introduce their characters with written descriptions of the characters.
  - Write the script to role-play an incident from history.
- ✔ Science fiction
  - Produce a mini-museum of objects used in the world of the book and compose cards explaining each item.
  - Create a chart to explain phenomena from the book that are not possible in this world.
- ✔ Mystery stories
  - Watch a mystery on television and compare the plot structure to that of the book.
  - Learn about fingerprints, solve a "crime" using fingerprints as evidence, and write a logical solution to the "crime."
  - Contribute to a mystery bulletin board with mysterious items that are connected to the books being read—drawings or clues can be covered with flaps to add to the mystery.

You can specify the genre restrictions to meet curriculum needs. For example, if the class were studying animals, children could choose an information book about an animal.

The advantages of genre studies include:

- choice for the readers
- wide range of reading levels in any genre

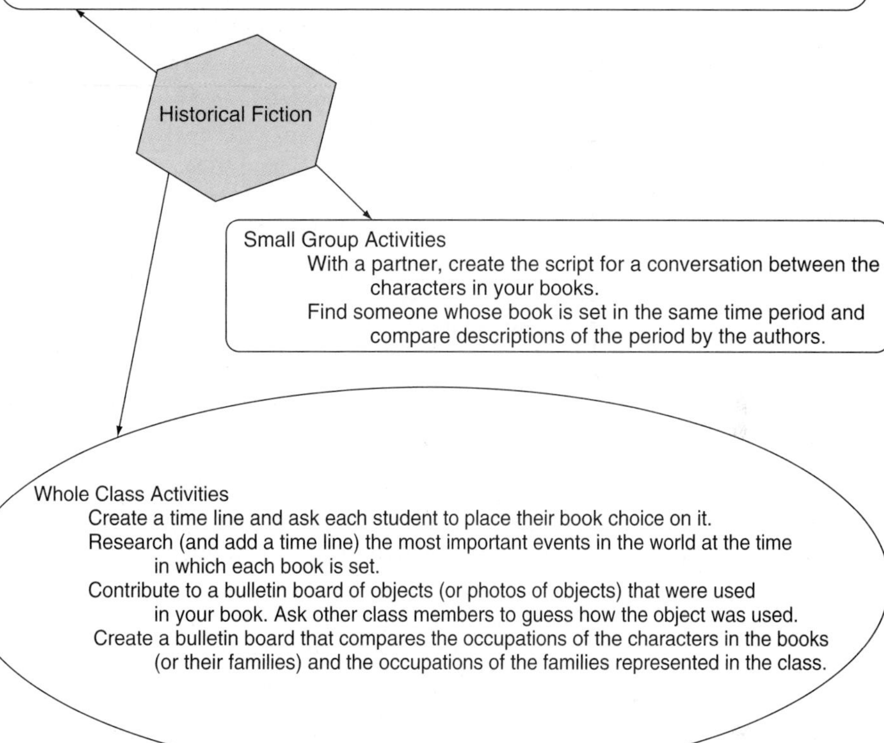

Individual Activities
Compare your daily life to that of the main character in the book you selected.
Make a list of words that were used in the book that are not used now.
Make a map of the setting and the travels of the characters.
Create a list of common objects that would have been unknown to your character.
Research the clothing of the time period.
Research the music of the time period.
Create a script for a news report of an important event described in your book.
Evaluate your book against a list of criteria for good historical fiction.
Create a time line of the life of your character.
Create a character sketch of the main character.
Historical Fiction
Small Group Activities
With a partner, create the script for a conversation between the characters in your books.
Find someone whose book is set in the same time period and compare descriptions of the period by the authors.
Whole Class Activities
Create a time line and ask each student to place their book choice on it.
Research (and add a time line) the most important events in the world at the time in which each book is set.
Contribute to a bulletin board of objects (or photos of objects) that were used in your book. Ask other class members to guess how the object was used.
Create a bulletin board that compares the occupations of the characters in the books (or their families) and the occupations of the families represented in the class.

Figure 11.3
Web of Possible Activities Based on Historical Fiction

- an opportunity to learn to appreciate genres that might never have been read before
- the ease of tying reading instruction to other areas of the curriculum
- ease of planning meaningful group activities.

The challenges include:

- access to the number of books needed
- record keeping for each child
- providing appropriate instruction for each child
- supporting learners as they develop as readers
- finding books appropriate for each child's instructional reading level

In Figure 11.3, we have webbed some possibilities for a genre study of historical fiction. Each genre would present opportunities to engage the children in a variety of reading and writing activities.

Organizing for Reading Instruction Using Literature Study Groups

Another common organizational pattern is literature study groups or literature sets. Literature study groups offer the reader a choice of what to read within the limits set by the teacher. Study groups or book club groups read a book in common, keep a response journal of their reading individually, discuss their book together as they read it, and participate in some follow-up activity following the reading.

Steps in Planning Literature Study Groups. Although literature study groups have been used in a variety of ways, the most common pattern is as follows:

1. The teacher selects five or six books as choices for the reading groups and presents a short book talk about each book.
2. The children choose one of the books as a first choice and another as a second choice. A second choice is indicated so that there is some flexibility in forming the groups. If too many children choose one book for a group, then one or two children can read their second choice book, but with the promise of having their first choice during the next round of reading.
3. Groups are formed from the children selecting a book. Groups should be about five to eight children. Less than five does not offer enough stimulation for the exchange of ideas; more than eight makes it difficult for every child to get a chance to participate. If many children choose the same book, two groups can read it at the same time if there are enough copies, or one can read it now and the other group can read it in the next cycle.
4. The group determines the schedule for reading within a time frame you specify. You might say that the book needs to be finished within two weeks. Within that time, the group can determine how much will be read before each meeting of the group. Each child would write in their response log on a schedule that you and the group set; it could be daily, every other day, or weekly.
5. The groups meet, usually every other day, to discuss their reading. They often mark points in the book or bring their response journals to the discussion to help them focus on their concerns about the reading. Usually, you meet with the group as a facilitator. (We will discuss your role in more detail later.)
6. When the book is finished, you may ask the group to share the book with the class in some way, such as a skit, a short reader's theater piece, a mural, or other art. Assessment is based on the learner's self-evaluation, records you keep, the quality of the response journal, and/or other measures.

Assessment and Evaluation Toolbox

LITERATURE CIRCLE INDIVIDUAL EVALUATION

The sample checklist reproduced in Appendix F provides an opportunity for both the student and the teacher to mark the various components of successful participation in literature circles.

Source: L. Gilbert. (2000). Getting Started: Using Literature Circles in the Classroom. *Primary Voices,* 9(1), 9–15.

Adapting Literature Study Groups for Young Children. For young children, the teacher may read the book to the children, or the children may engage in buddy reading in which students read the book in pairs. Other options include echo reading, in which the teacher reads a section and the child then reads that section, or assisted reading, in which the child follows along as the book is read on audio tape. If they can read the book independently, they would do so. The group may read the book many times, and you may focus on different instructional tasks with each rereading. However, even young children can learn to discuss what books mean and how they relate to their own experience. You will need to keep excellent records of each child's increasing ability as a reader. For example, you will note which children are focusing on the print or features of the print, which can match the words you say to the print, and which can recognize given words by sight.

Assessment and Evaluation Toolbox

LITERATURE CIRCLE SELF-EVALUATION

This is a sample of a self-evaluation form that can be used with younger readers.

Literature Circle Self-Evaluation

Name ______________________________ **Date** ______________

Title ______________

1. I read my book	yes	no
2. I marked places in my book.	yes	no
3. I brought my book on Monday.	yes	no
4. I shared my book with others.	yes	no
5. I thought this book was		

Not so Good   O.K.   Very Good

Source: B. C. Hill, N. J. Johnson, & K. L. S. Noe. (1995). *Literature Circles and Response.* Norwood, MA: Christopher-Gordon.

The advantages of literature study groups include:

- children's choice of reading, but within limits that you set to control the quality and content of the books offered for reading
- discussion of books and their personal meanings with the group, which aids the social construction of meaning
- ease of planning group activities

Challenges in literature study groups include:

- providing eight copies of every book to be read
- teaching the children how to participate in the groups in a productive manner (just saying anything that pops into their heads will not benefit learning)
- keeping excellent records

Since class size is not likely to change appreciably in the near future, the small groups of literature studies can help you know each child and meet his or her individual needs. The group interaction is important in the social construction of meaning (Vygotsky, 1986). Meaning does not reside in the text alone, and it is important that children have the opportunity to construct meaning with other learners.

Teacher's Role in Literature Study Groups. You will not be able to assume that the children know how to do any of the elements of literature study and must plan for instruction and modeling on how to write a response log and how to participate in a discussion group.

Your role in literature study groups is critical to their success. When you sit with the groups, you can offer questions or ideas that help the group stay on track, but your role is not to interrogate the children. The teacher must work hard to break the discourse pattern that is common in schools and is labeled I-R-E (McMahon & Goatley, 1995). I-R-E is the pattern of the teacher initiating a question, the student responding to the question, and the teacher evaluating the answer. For example, the teacher might ask, "In what part of the story did the character exhibit the most growth?" The child responds, "The part where he found the old boat." The teacher responds, "How did his finding the boat have anything to do with character development?" As teachers sit with literature groups, they must break that pattern and encourage children to talk to each other rather than simply answer questions.

Some teachers handle this initial period of teaching the children how to discuss a book by assigning roles to each child in the group. Daniels (1994, 2002) suggests that summarizer, discussion leader, passage master, word wizard, connector, and artist are good beginning roles. These roles are defined as follows:

- The *summarizer* provides the summary of what has been read.
- The *discussion leader* makes sure that everyone participates and prepares some questions to ask.
- The *passage master* chooses a passage that is especially significant for reading aloud or careful scrutiny.
- The *word wizard* makes a list of words that are especially interesting or challenging.
- The *connector* finds ways the book relates to other books or real life.
- The *artist* makes some visual representation of the book.

After the teacher has demonstrated each role, every student would take a turn at each role until all roles have been learned. Most teachers find that after the children become skilled in discussing a book, the assigning of roles can be dropped. If you use these roles, you may need to alter them or use different roles for different material. In the newest edition of his book, Daniels (2002) suggests that a researcher who provides background information might be a useful role; for some books, a scene setter who helps the group keep up with where the action is taking place might be valuable. For reading nonfiction material, the role of word wizard might be adapted to vocabulary enricher. The message from Daniels and others is that teachers and children must try out various strategies and evaluate them to make decisions for their classrooms.

Organizing for Reading Instruction Using Author/Illustrator Studies

Another organizational pattern is author or illustrator studies. Such studies are often undertaken in small groups much like the literature groups described previously or the whole class may study one author or illustrator. The basic pattern is that an author or illustrator is chosen for intensive study. Children choose a book by the author, read it, and discuss it with a group of readers reading other books by the same author. With younger children, the teacher may read aloud the books and discuss them with the children. Charts or records of various elements may be completed by the teacher as the children dictate the information from the reading. For example, the children might note the characters that are found in the Ezra Jack Keats books. The teacher would help record the children's observations that many of the characters are in several of the books.

Go to the Weblinks in Chapter 11 on our Companion Website at www.prenhall.com/harp to find links to information about authors and illustrators on the web.

Author studies lend themselves to deep discussions of themes and styles. As children learn about the life of the author, they may find connections between the author's work and the landscape or culture of the place where the author grew up or reflections of childhood experiences in the work of the author.

Group activities can be planned, such as bulletin boards or displays that children construct to represent the whole body of an author's work. If the author writes in different genres, children would automatically compare the work in one genre to the work in another genre. The work of some authors will lend itself to reader's theater or other dramatic performances. Illustrator studies would naturally lead to explorations of the media used by the illustrator and perhaps demonstrations of media by local artisans.

The advantages of author/illustrator studies include:

- choice within the body of the author's work
- ease of planning meaningful activities
- the depth possible in the children's discussions

Challenges include:

- finding enough books for the class to read
- the relatively small number of authors and illustrators who have a large enough body of work to be used in the classroom

In any of these organizational patterns, children are asked to choose their own books. One strategy for helping them assess the difficulty of books is called the *Goldilocks strategy.* It means helping children learn how to select books that are just right for them, not too easy and not too hard. In the accompanying Assessment and Evaluation Toolbox are some possible questions to guide children. These could be mounted on a poster after you have demonstrated to the children how to use these questions.

Assessment and Evaluation Toolbox

ASSESSING THE DIFFICULTY OF TEXT (GOLDILOCKS STRATEGY)

Too Easy Books

Have you read it lots of times before?
Do you understand the story well?
Do you know almost every word?
Can you read it smoothly?

(Continued)

Assessment and Evaluation Toolbox Continued

Just Right Books

Is this book new to you?
Do you understand some of the book?
Are there just a few words per page that you don't know?
When you read, are some places smooth and some choppy?
Can someone help you with this book? Who?

Too Hard Books

Are there more than a few words on a page that you don't know?
Are you confused about what is happening in most of the book?
When you read, does it sound pretty choppy?
Is everyone else busy or unable to help you now?

Source: Based on M. Ohlhausen & M. Jepsen. (1992). Lessons from Goldilocks: Somebody's Been Choosing My Books But I Can Make My Own Choices Now! *The New Advocate, 5,* 31–46.

Organizing for Reading Instruction Using Core Book Experiences

A core book approach means choosing one book that everyone in the class reads. It is easy to imagine that a core book approach is not the first choice of most teachers because of the various reading levels in every class. The children have the least choice in this pattern, as the teacher selects the book. The challenges are in choosing a book that will meet the reading level needs for all the children and obtaining enough copies of the book for every child.

In rare circumstances, a teacher might choose a core book if one book was so important to the curriculum goals that other books could not be used. In that case, the teacher would be responsible for helping all readers succeed with the text through such strategies as tape recordings for struggling readers and finding additional materials for advanced readers.

Combining Organizational Patterns

Most experienced teachers use a combination of organizational patterns to meet the curriculum demands and the needs of all their learners. You might begin your planning by putting on your calendar the authors/illustrators you want to study. If you used author/illustrator studies exclusively, you would have to ignore new authors who did not have enough work to study. Next you might want to decide which genres would be most important for your learners to study in depth and add those to your calendar. In both the author studies and genre studies, the format you use could be either individualized reading or literature study groups. You could then fill in the other weeks in the school year with individualized reading. Figure 11.4 is a calendar suggesting a reading year for a third-grade class.

Figure 11.4
A 36-Week Calendar for Third Grade

Week 1 & 2	Individualized reading (you will need to be involved with assessments)
Week 3, 4, & 5	A study of our state Information books, biography of important people in state history, fiction set in the state
Week 6 & 7	Author study of Jack Prelutsky
Week 8 & 9	Individualized reading
Week 10 & 11	Genre study of mystery books
Week 12 & 13	Information books about plants
Week 14 & 15	Individualized reading
Week 16 & 17	Genre study of biography
Week 18 & 19	Author study of David Adler
Week 20 & 21	Individualized reading
Week 22 & 23	Genre study of realistic fiction Theme: family issues
Week 24 & 25	Illustrator study of Leo & Diane Dillon
Week 26 & 27	Individualized reading
Week 28 & 29	Genre study of tall tales
Week 30 & 31	Author/illustrator study of Demi
Week 32 & 33	Genre study of poetry
Week 34, 35, & 36	Individualized reading

HOW DOES USING LITERATURE ENCOURAGE GROWTH IN LITERACY?

The goal of every teacher is to help children become more literate, more skillful users of reading and writing, and to develop the dispositions to continue to be readers and writers. This goal can only be achieved through engaging children with books and helping them develop skills and strategies they can apply in their own reading. Two factors are critical here—that children have books to read and that they have the opportunity to read and to write. Teachers must arrange for an adequate classroom library, and they must determine the literacy needs of each child to plan instruction for that individual.

Literature in the Reading Program

Studies (Reutzel, Oda, & Moore, 1989) have found that literature-based programs had a positive effect on the print awareness and word-reading acquisition of kindergarten children. Students in a year-long study of second graders in a literature-based program "demonstrated high levels of engagement with books, developed skill in word identification, fluency, and comprehension; and grew in written-composition abilities" (Gambrell, Morrow, & Pennington, 2001, p. 6). In a literature-based program implemented with second graders, Roser, Hoffman, and Farest (1990) found significant growth in children's scores on state-mandated basic skills tests. This study supports the implementation of literature-based instruction with children from economically disadvantaged homes who were primarily limited speakers of English.

Literature-based programs lead to a more positive attitude toward reading (Goatley, Brock, & Raphael, 1995; Goatley & Raphael, 1992) and to more reading (Dahl & Freppon, 1995; Stewart, Paradis, Ross, & Lewis, 1996). Children allowed to choose what they will read have the opportunity to interact with others to discuss what they have read, feel successful about reading, and want to read more often (Gambrell, Palmer, & Coding, 1993).

Literature in the Writing Program

Reading provides the models and inspiration for writing. Gilhool and colleagues (1996) found that using literature examples of how authors use various text strategies such as varying sentence patterns has a positive effect on the quality of children's writing. Others have noted that children exposed to literature reflect this exposure in their writing. Galda & Cullinan (2002) state, "Literature helps students become better writers. When students read a lot, they notice what writers do. They see that writers use structured patterns in their writing. When readers write, they borrow the structures, patterns, and words from what they read" (p. 8). Reading and discussing books and their own compositions can help children become more critical consumers of text and increase their store of words and structures to use in their own writing.

LOOKING AT THE RESEARCH

What the research says about the influence of reading material on writing

The language used in reading materials significantly influences the language used in composition (Deford, 1981; Eckhoff, 1983). These findings suggest that it is essential when selecting books for reading aloud and classroom study that the choices provide language models worth emulating.

We know from the research that what children read influences their writing (Galda, 2001). As children build a storehouse of words, phrases, and sentence structures from their reading, they can then employ those in their writing. If we want children to write in any genre, they must first read that genre, with a focus on the writing so that they can use the models in their own writing. For example, if children are to write personal narratives, then they must read personal narratives from the literature, discuss the elements of writing a personal narrative, discuss what makes a personal narrative interesting to the reader, and have time to write their own narratives. They must write with the reader in mind, and they must read with an eye to the author's craft.

If you want children to write more descriptively, you would ask them to think about descriptive words as they read some examples of extraordinary descriptive writing such as Eve Bunting's *Secret Place* (1996). On the first page of the book, Bunting writes, "There are warehouses with windows blinded by dust and names paint-scrawled on their brick walls.

The lines on the telephone and electric poles web the sky. Smokestacks blow clouds to dim the sun" (unpaged). Or you read Yolen's *Welcome to the Greenhouse* (1993), in which she writes, "a slide of coral snake, through leaves, a glide of butterflies through air, past crimson flowers, past showy orchid bowers. Everywhere color threads through, spreads through the hot green house" (unpaged). Discuss with students the words the authors had chosen and how those words helped to create clear pictures in readers' heads and how the author can help readers by using such language.

You might also want children to attend to character descriptions. If you read a Harry Potter book with an eye to the language that describes each of the characters, you can help children understand the need to make a character so memorable that readers feel that they had really met the person. Ask students to keep character descriptions in their reading logs for a period of time, and then the class can share and discuss the descriptions that worked for them.

As you work to help children improve their writing, you can choose pieces of good literature to serve as models and examples. At times, you will want to use these examples in whole class instruction, such as in the focus lessons of the writing workshop. At other times, you will want to have individual children look at a specific piece of literature as an example of how the author solved a writing problem that the child is now facing.

Literature in Independent Reading

The amount of independent, silent reading children do is significantly related to gains in reading achievement (Taylor, Pearson, Clark, & Walpole, 2000). Anderson, Wilson & Fielding (1988) found that the children studied averaged 130 minutes of television viewing per day. They also found that avid readers in this study did as much as 20 times more reading than the children who chose to read less. Even reading the comics was positively related to reading achievement (Greaney, 1980). Children can be motivated to read more by providing class time for reading and allowing choice in what to read (Smith, Tracy, & Weber, 1998).

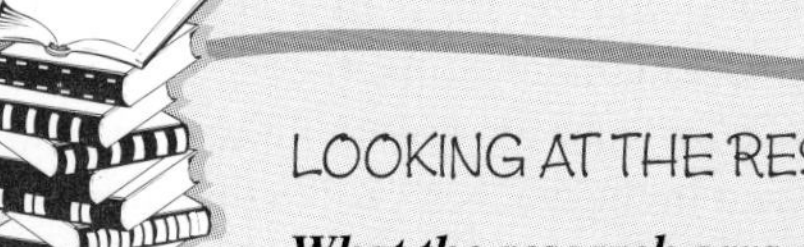

What the research says about time spent in reading

Anderson, Wilson, & Fielding, (1988) found that 50% of the children studied reported reading books for an average of four minutes or less each day, 30% read books for two minutes or less per day. For the majority of children, reading books occupied less than 1% of their free time. Since reading ability does not improve without engaging in reading, children must read at school and be encouraged to read at home as well.

What would you plan to do if you interviewed your students and found that they were reading as little as the students who were subjects in this research? What are the implications for instruction of these research findings?

Go to our Companion Website at www.prenhall.com/harp to join the global discussion of these questions by adding your comments to the Threaded Message Board.

Classroom Environment for Independent Reading. You must arrange the time in the classroom so that children have the opportunity to read. They must be reading real books, not excerpts from an anthology, and they must have the choice of what to read. This period of reading may be longer for older readers, but must be provided for all K-12 grades. Children who read more in school are more likely to read more outside of school (Kameenui, 1998). If reading is important, then children must know that there is time in the school day for reading. Please recall the discussion in Chapter 9 about independent reading in SSR, DEAR, or other formats.

Tension Between Competing Goals. When you select books for reading and studying in the classroom, there will always be a little tension. Should you choose books for the lessons you can teach from the books? Or should you choose books for their literary qualities so you and your students can discover together the "lessons" in a good book? For example, many fourth graders read Lois Lowry's *Number the Stars* (1989), a book about the Danish resistance during World War II. Would you begin your planning with thinking about what the children could learn in terms of social studies lessons? We would recommend that your planning be focused on helping children make connections with the characters and think about the larger meanings in the book. We believe that if you do this and discuss the book with children as they read it, you will find that the social studies lessons—and much more—are learned. Children who have read this book and had a chance to explore its meanings with guidance from a skilled teacher will learn the meaning of courage and friendship, and without a "lesson" they will absorb the content knowledge about the war. The story should take precedence over any content lesson. If you focus on the content lessons of good books, then you will have lost the opportunity to help children move beneath the surface structure of a text and really think about its meaning.

When you love literature and help children learn to love it as you do, you will be on your way to helping children become successful readers and writers.

THINKING AS A TEACHER

1. You have been hired to teach first grade at XYZ School. This school is in an urban neighborhood, and there is much concern about reading instruction. You are busy selecting books for your classroom library and thinking about your read-aloud program when you hear in the teacher's room that all the instructional time in language arts will be devoted to skill instruction and that all frills such as reading aloud are to be eliminated. What resources will you gather to make your case in support of real books and real reading to the parents and the principal?
2. You have never been a "reader" yourself in the sense that you think you should be as a teacher. You know that you will need to inspire children to become readers by your own behavior. What can you do now to begin growing as a reader so that you can model for children?
3. Your school has little money for buying books for either the school library or for classroom libraries. What can you do to help acquire books? What can you say to parents and to administrators to gain their support for acquiring books?

FIELD-BASED ACTIVITIES

Go to the Weblinks in Chapter 11 on our Companion Website for a link to a list of Caldecott winners and honor books.

1. Examine 10 picture books that have won the Caldecott medal. Please choose books you like and you think should have received the medal. What do you think are common characteristics of these books? Could children recognize these common features? Plan how you would introduce these books to readers in either the primary or intermediate grades.

2. Select an information book. Evaluate the book and make a plan for introducing it to either primary or intermediate students. Be sure to include what you might teach about structure of the text as well as content.
3. Observe three or four elementary classrooms in terms of their classroom libraries. Would you rate these libraries as adequate in terms of topic coverage, range of reading difficulty, and range of interests for the children in the class? If they are not adequate, how could they be improved?

REFERENCES

Anderson, R. C., Wilson, P. T., & Fielding, L. G. (1988). Growth in reading and how children spend their time outside of school. *Reading Research Quarterly, 23,* 285–303.

Corliss, J. C. (1998). *Crossing borders with literature of diversity.* Norwood, MA: Christopher-Gordon.

Cunningham, P. M., & Allington, R. L. (2003). *Classrooms that work: They can all read and write.* Boston: Allyn and Bacon.

Dahl, K. L., & Freppon, P. A. (1995). A comparison of innercity children's interpretations of reading and writing instruction in the early grades in skill-based and whole language classrooms. *Reading Research Quarterly, 30,* 50–74.

Daniels, H. (1994). *Looking into literature circles.* York, ME: Stenhouse.

Daniels, H. (2002). *Voice and choice in book clubs and reading groups.* York, ME: Stenhouse.

Deford, D. E. (1981). Literacy: Reading, writing, and other essentials. *Language Arts, 58,* 652–658.

Duke, N. K. (1998). Empirical confirmation of the scarcity of informational text in the early grades. Paper presented at the Harvard Graduate School of Education Research Conference, Cambridge, MA.

Duke, N. K., & Kays, J. (1998). "Can I say 'once upon a time'?": Kindergarten children developing knowledge of information book language. *Early Childhood Research Quarterly, 13,* 295–318.

Eckhoff, B. (1983). How reading affects children's writing. *Language Arts, 60,* 607–616.

Eldredge, J. L., & Butterfield, D. (1986). Alternatives to traditional reading instruction. *The Reading Teacher, 40,* 32–37.

Galda, L. (2001). High stakes reading: Articulating the place of children's literature in the curriculum. *The New Advocate, 14,* 223–228.

Galda, L., & Cullinan, B. E. (1991). Literature for literacy: What research says about the benefits of using trade books in the classroom. In J. Flood, J. M. Jenson, D. Lapp, & J. R. Squire (Eds.), *Handbook of research on teaching English language arts* (pp. 529–535). New York: Macmillan.

Galda, L., & Cullinan, B. E. (2002). *Literature and the child.* Belmont, CA: Wadsworth.

Gambrell, L. B., Morrow, L. M., & Pennington, C. (2001). Early childhood and elementary literature-based instruction: Current perspectives and special issues. Reading Online. Retrieved from *www.readingonline.org.*

Gambrell, L. B., Palmer, B. M., & Coding, R. M. (1993). *Motivation to read.* Washington, DC: Office of Educational Research and Improvement, U.S. Department of Education.

Gilbert, L. (2000). Getting started: Using literature circles in the classroom. *Primary Voices, 9* (1), 9–15.

Gilhool, M., Byer, J., Parmer, L., Howe, M., Dana, M., & Cliburn, A. (1996). The effect of modeling nonfiction text structures on third and fourth grade student's nonfiction writing. Eric Document Reproduction Service ED 403589.

Goatley, V. J., Brock, C. H., & Raphael, T. E. (1995). Diverse learners participating in regular education "book clubs." *Reading Research Quarterly, 30,* 352–380.

Goatley, V. J., & Raphael, T. E. (1992). Non-traditional learners' written and dialogic response to literature. In J. Zutell & S. McCormick (Eds.), *The fortieth yearbook of the National Reading Conference* (pp. 313–322). Chicago: National Reading Conference.

Greaney, V. (1980). Factors related to amount and type of leisure time reading. *Reading Research Quarterly, 15,* 337–357.

Guzzetti, B. J., Kowalinski, B. J., & McGowan, T. (1992). Using a literature-based approach to teaching social studies. *Journal of Reading, 36,* 114–122.

Harp, B. (2000). *The handbook of literacy assessment and evaluation* (2nd ed.). Norwood, MA: Christoper-Gordon.

Harris, V. J. (1997). *Using multiethinic literature in the K-8 classroom.* Norwood, MA: Christopher-Gordon.

Hill, B. C., Johnson, N. J., & Noe, K. L. S. (1995). *Literature circles and response.* Norwood, MA: Christopher-Gordon.

Jalongo, M. J. (1988). *Young children and picture books: Literature from infancy to six.* Washington, DC: National Association for the Education of Young Children.

Jipson, J., & Paley, N. (1991). The selective tradition in teachers' choices in children's literature: Does it exist in the elementary classroom? *English Education, 23,* 148–159.

Kameenui, E. J. (1998). Diverse learners and the tyranny of time: Don't fix blame; fix the leaky roof. In R. L. Allington (Ed.), *Teaching struggling readers* (pp. 10–18). Newark, DE: International Reading Association.

Martinez, M., & Roser, N. (1985). Read it again: The value of repeated readings during storytime. *Reading Teacher, 38,* 782–786.

McMahon, S. I., & Goatley, V. J. (1995). Fifth graders helping peers discuss texts in student-led groups. *Journal of Educational Research, 89,* 23–34.

Meyer, L. A., & Wardrop, J. L. (1994). Effects of reading storybooks aloud to children. *Journal of Educational Research, 88,* 69–86.

Morrow, L. M., Pressley, M., Smith, J. K., & Smith, M. (1997). The effect of a literature-based program integrated into literacy and science instruction with children from diverse backgrounds. *Reading Research Quarterly, 32,* 54–76.

Morrow, L. M., & Gambrell, L. B. (2000). Literature-based reading instruction. In M. L. Kamil, P. B. Mosenthal, P. D. Pearson, & R. Barr, (Eds.), *Handbook of reading research, Vol. III* (pp. 563–586). Mahwah, NJ: Lawrence Erlbaum.

Norton, D. E., Norton, S. E., & McClure, A. (2001). *Multicultural children's literature: Through the eyes of many children.* Columbus, OH: Merrill.

Norton, D. E. (2003). *Through the eyes of a child.* Columbus, OH: Merrill.

Ohlhausen, M., & Jepsen, M. (1992). Lessons from Goldilocks: Somebody's been choosing my books but I can make my own choices now! *The New Advocate, 5,* 36.

Purcell-Gates, V., McIntyre, E., & Freppon, P. A. (1995). Learning written storybook language in school: A comparison of low-SES children in skills-based and whole language classrooms. *American Educational Research Journal, 32,* 659–685.

Rosenblatt, L. M. (1978). *The reader, the text, and the poem.* Carbondale, IL: Southern Illinois University Press.

Roser, N. L. (2001). A place for everything and literature in its place. *The New Advocate, 14,* 211–221.

Roser, N. L., Hoffman, J. V., & Farest, C. (1990). Language, literature and at-risk children. *Reading Teacher, 43,* 554–559.

Reutzel, D. R., Oda, L. K., & Moore, B. H. (1989). Developing print awareness: The effect of three instructional approaches on kindergartners; print awareness, reading readiness, and word reading. *Journal of Reading Behavior, 21,* 197–217.

Smith, C., Tracy, E., & Weber, L. (1998). Motivating independent reading: The route to a lifetime of education. Eric Document Reproduction Service ED 422559.

Stewart, R. A., Paradis, E. E., Ross, B. D., & Lewis, M. J. (1996). Student voices: What works in literature-based developmental reading. *Journal of Adolescent & Adult Literacy, 39,* 468–477.

Taylor, B. M., Pearson, P. D., Clark, K., Walpole, S. (2000) Effective schools and accomplished teachers: Lessons about primary-grade reading instruction in low-income schools. *Elementary School Journal, 101,* pp. 121–166.

Vygotsky, L. (1986). *Thought and language.* Cambridge, MA: MIT Press.

Worthy, J., Moorman, M., & Turner, M. (1999). What Johnny likes to read is hard to find in school. *Reading Research Quarterly, 34,* 12–27.

Children's Books

Adoff, A. (1994). *My black me.* New York: Dutton.

Alexander, S. (2001). *Behold the trees.* New York: Scholastic.

Avi. (1991). *Nothing but the truth.* New York: Orchard.

Avi. (1992). *Who was that masked man, anyway?* New York: HarperCollins.

Aylesworth, J. (1996). *My sister's rusty bike.* New York: Atheneum.

Babbitt, N. (1975). *Tuck everlasting.* New York: Farrar Straus & Giroux.

Bartoletti, S. C. (2001). *Black potatoes: The story of the great Irish famine, 1845–1850.* Boston: Houghton Mifflin.

Base, G. (1986). *Animalia.* New York: Abrams.

Begay, S. (1992). *Maii and cousin horned toad.* New York: Scholastic.

Browne, V. (1993). *Monster birds: A Navajo folktale.* Illus. by B. Whitethome. Flagstaff, AZ: Rising Moon.

Bober, N. S. (1998). *Abigail Adams: Witness to a revolution.* New York: Aladdin.

Bunting, E. (1996). *Secret place.* Illus. by T. Rand. New York: Clarion.

Cleary, B. (1984). *Ramona forever.* New York: Camelot.

Cline-Ransome, L. (2000). *Satchel Paige.* Illus. by J. E. Ransome. New York: Simon & Schuster.

Creech, S. (2001). *A fine, fine school.* Illus by H. Bliss. New York: HarperCollins.

Curtis, C. P. (1999). *Bud, not Buddy.* New York: Delacorte.

Fleischman, S. (1986). *The whipping boy.* New York: Greenwillow.

George, J. C. (1972). *Julie of the wolves.* New York: Harper & Row.

Gibbons, G. (1999). *Bats.* New York: Holiday House.

Greenfield, E. (1978). *Honey, I love and other poems.* Illus by D. & L. Dillon. New York: HarperCollins.

Heller, R. (1981). *Chickens aren't the only ones.* New York: Grosset & Dunlap.

Henkes, K. (1991). *Chrysanthemum.* New York: Greenwillow.

Hesse, K. (1997). *Out of the dust.* New York: Scholastic.

Highwater, J. (1995). *Songs for the seasons.* Illus. by S. Speidel. New York: Lothrop, Lee, & Shepard.

Hopkins, L. B. (1987). *Dinosaurs.* San Diego: Harcourt Brace Jovanovich.

Hopkins, L. B. (1993). *Extra innings: Baseball poems.* San Diego: Harcourt Brace Jovanovich.

Hopkins, L. B. (1996). *School supplies.* New York: Simon & Schuster.

Hopkins, L. B. (1994). *Hand in hand: An American history through poetry.* New York: Simon & Schuster.

Hubbell, P. (2001). *Black earth, gold sun.* Illus. by M. Newell DePalma. New York: Marshall Cavendish.

Hutchins, P. (1968). *Rosie's walk.* New York: Scholastic.

Kalman, M. (2001). *What Pete ate from A-Z.* New York: Putnam.

Keats, E. Z. (1962). *The snowy day.* New York: Scholastic.

Kerley, B. (2001). *The dinosaurs of Waterhouse Hawkins.* New York: Scholastic.

Knowlton, J. (1988). *Geography from A to Z: A picture glossary.* New York: HarperCollins.

Lester, J. (1994). *John Henry.* New York: Dial.

Lewis, J. P. (1996). *Riddle-icious.* New York: Knopf.

Lewis, J. P. (1998). *The little buggers: Insect & spider poems.* New York: Dial.

Lowry, L. (1989). *Number the stars.* Boston: Houghton Mifflin.

Lowry, L. (1993). *The giver.* Boston: Houghton Mifflin.

Martin, B., Jr., & Archambault, J. (1989). *Chicka chicka boom boom.* Illus. by L. Ehlert. New York: Simon and Schuster.

Martin, J. B. (1998). *Snowflake Bentley.* Boston: Houghton Mifflin.

Musgrove, M. (1976). *Ashanti to Zulu: African traditions.* New York: Dial.

Naylor, P. R. (1991). *Shiloh.* New York: Antheneum.

Newton, J. (1992). *Cat-Fish.* New York: Lothrop, Lee & Shepard.

Onyefulu, I. (1993). *A is for Africa.* New York: Dutton.

Parker, N. W., & Wright, J. R. (1987). *Bugs.* New York: Greenwillow.

Paterson, K. (1976). *Bridge to Terabithia.* New York: Crowell.

Pinkney, A. D. (1998). *Duke Ellington.* Illus. by B. Pinkney. New York: Hyperion.

Polacco, P. (2000). *The butterfly.* New York: Philomel.

Prelutsky, J. (1992). *Tyrannosaurus was a beast.* New York: Mulberry.

Prelutsky, J. (2001). *Awful ogre's awful day.* Illus. by P. O. Zelinsky. New York: Greenwillow.

Pringle, L. (1997). *An extraordinary life: The story of a monarch butterfly.* New York: Orchard.

Rylant, C. (1985). *The relatives came.* New York: Bradbury Press.

Schick, E. (1999). *Navajo wedding day: A Dine marriage ceremony.* Vaughn, Ontario: Marshall Cavendish.

Schroeder, A. (1996). *Minty: A story of young Harriet Tubman.* Illus. by J. Pinkney. New York: Dial Books.

Scieska, J., & Smith, L. (2001). *Baloney (Henry P.).* Illus. by L. Smith. New York: Viking.

Shields, C. D. (1995). *Lunch money and other poems about school.* New York: Dutton.

Simont, M. (2001). *The stray dog.* New York: HarperCollins.

Sis, P. (2001). *Madlenka.* New York: Farrar Straus & Giroux.

Sendak, M. (1963). *Where the wild things are.* New York: Harper & Row.

Sneve, V. D. H. (1989). *Dancing teepees: Poems of American Indian youth.* New York: Holiday House.

Stanley, D. (1996). *Leonardo de Vinci.* New York: Morrow.

Stanley, J. (2000). *Hurry freedom: African Americans in gold rush California.* New York: Crown.

Steig, W. (1969). *Sylvester and the magic pebble.* New York: Simon & Schuster.

Stevens, J. & Crummel, S. S. (2001). *And the dish ran away with the spoon.* San Diego, CA: Harcourt.

Taback, S. (1999). *Joseph had a little overcoat.* New York: Viking.

Viorst, J. (1994). *The alphabet from Z to A.* New York: Atheneum.

Wells, R. (1997). *Bunny cakes.* New York: Dial.

Whitethorne, B. (1994). *Sunpainters: Eclipse of the Navajo sun.* Flagstaff, AZ: Northland Publishing.

Winer, Y. (1998). *Spiders spin webs.* Waterton, MA: Charlesbridge.

Wisniewski, D. (1996). *Golem.* New York: Clarion.

Wolff, V. E., & Layden, J. (1998). *Bat 6.* New York: Scholastic.

Yolen, J. (1987). *Owl moon.* New York: Philomel.

Yolen, J. (1993). *Welcome to the greenhouse.* Illus. by L. Regan. New York: Putnam.

Young, E. (1989). *Lon Po Po: A Red Riding Hood story from China.* New York: Philomel.

Zelinsky, P. (1997). *Rapunzel.* New York: Dutton.

Chapter 12

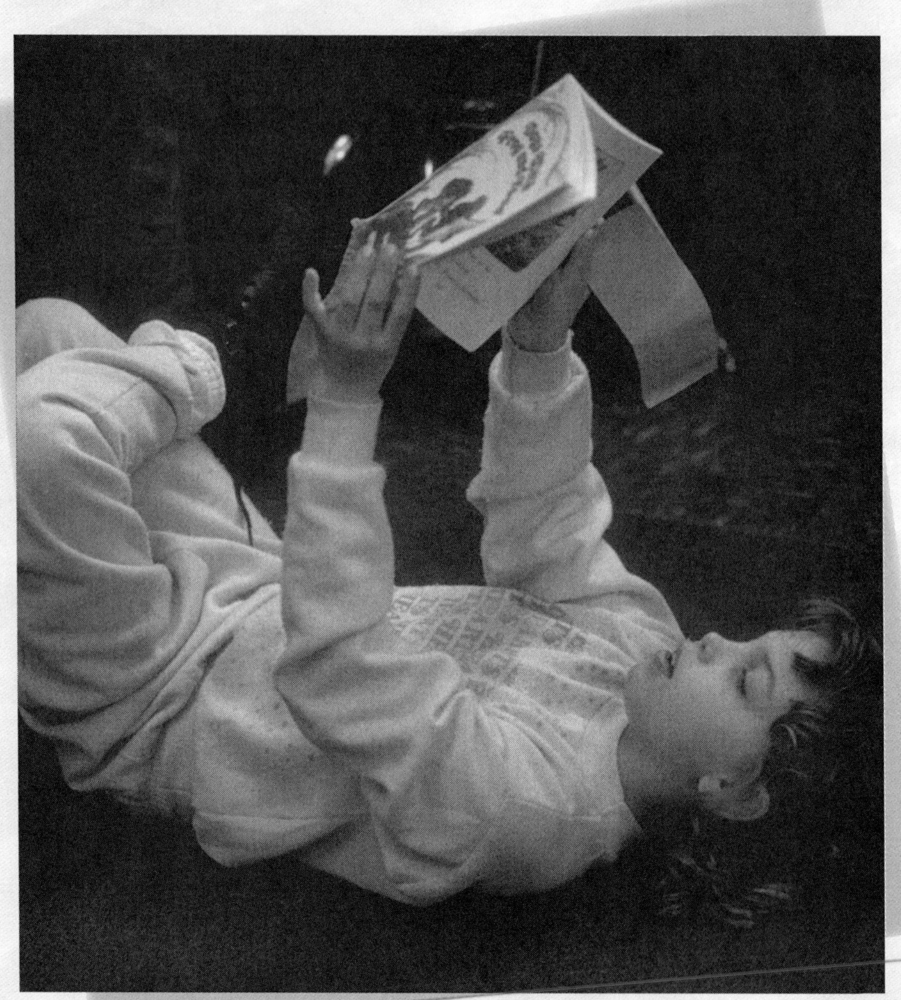

Building a K-2 Reading Program

Teaching the youngest children is always a wonderful challenge, especially when we think about helping these children become more literate. Young children are excited about learning in general and most excited about learning to read and write. The challenge to us as teachers is to make the best decisions we can possibly make and design programs that will be beneficial for all children. This chapter will serve as a beginning point in building your program for young learners. The classroom environment, the daily schedule, the assessments, and the literacy activities are all important elements in creating a program for young children that will help you to guide the literacy development of each learner.

Focus Questions

- How do I create a classroom environment that will help me be an effective teacher?
- What assessments will I use to get started in the instructional program?
- What are the essential elements of a quality instructional program?
- How do I handle management and record keeping?
- How do I capitalize on diversity in the classroom?

HOW DO I CREATE A CLASSROOM ENVIRONMENT THAT WILL HELP ME BE AN EFFECTIVE TEACHER?

Montessori (1967) believed that a "prepared environment" is essential for effective teaching; educators at the famous Reggio Emilia schools of northern Italy call the environment "the third teacher" (Edwards, Gandini, & Forman, 1993). These statements reflect the importance of an environment for learning that encourages certain kinds of behavior and sends messages to children that certain kinds of learning are valued in this place. Materials and furniture in a Montessori program are carefully selected and arranged so that children are encouraged to engage with the materials and participate in the individual learning experiences prevalent in Montessori classrooms. For example, once the teacher in a Montessori classroom has demonstrated the "pink tower" (a tower to be constructed of blocks that are graduated in size) for a child, the child will be encouraged to find a mat, a place on the floor to work, and take the pink tower from the shelves and work with it. Materials are stored so that children can remove them from the shelves, work with them, and return them to the shelves without adult assistance.

In the Reggio Emilia schools, the environment is planned to stimulate children's explorations and to display children's work and stories of their work in a such a way as to encourage reflecting on what has been done and learned and to inspire further study and exploration. For example, the children have made drawings of a poppy. These drawings are displayed along with the children's descriptions of the poppy and their process for making the drawing. The displays help children recall their experiences so that they can revisit their thinking and think of poppies in new ways. They might create a poppy from clay next. The display of their work in clay would then encourage more exploration of poppies. The displays and thinking continue until the children have exhausted their interest in one subject and want to go on to something else.

A room environment that supports learning and invites children to participate in activities can be achieved with some planning on your part and a regular evaluation of the room arrangements and materials. Think about the room's aesthetics, including the lighting, use of color, and use of space. Hopefully, your classroom will have natural light, which can be adjusted, and adequate ventilation, which the adults can control. Displays of the children's work can add color if you use colorful backgrounds of paper or fabric. You can also add color with plants. Space needs to be arranged so that children can move about the room without squeezing between pieces of furniture or crossing areas where children are busy at work.

Room Arrangement

Figure 12.1 is a diagram of a possible room arrangement for a primary classroom. As you examine the diagram, we will explain the rationale for the major components. To begin just inside the door, the back of the shelf unit is used for the sign-in board, the lunch count board, and announcements and notices. Going around the room to the right, there is a large area with a rug for comfortable seating on the floor. This area has shelves on two sides for book storage, an easel for holding big books or charts, and a comfortable chair for the teacher. This area is used for whole group activities such as reading aloud, focus lessons in writing, or word study lessons. The listening center is placed here because it is a quiet area during work time.

The wall next to the computer and writing centers is used as a word wall so that children can consult it easily when they write, and shelves above the word wall provide additional storage space. The math area with storage shelves is placed next. A large cabinet with

Figure 12.1
Possible Room Arrangement

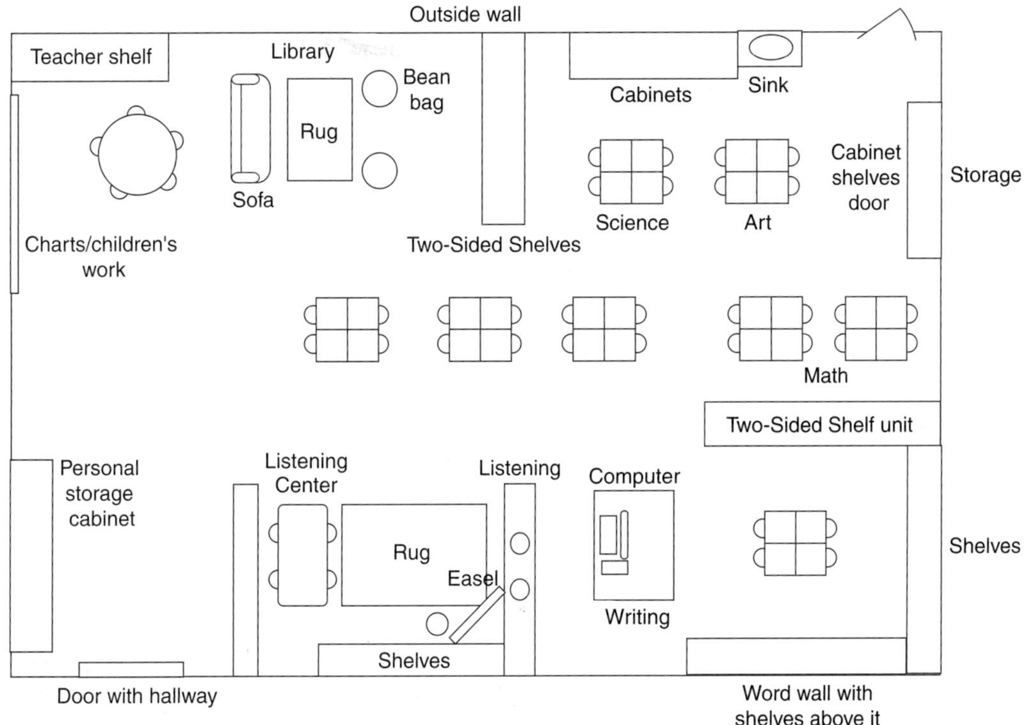

doors and shelves inside is used for storage. Beyond the door to the outside area, the sink and storage cabinets are under the windows on the outside wall. Art and science materials are stored in the cabinets, and a two-sided shelf unit divides this area from the library. These areas need to be near the sink and away from the quieter areas. The library has a sofa for comfortable seating, two bean bag chairs or floor pillows, a small table, and a rug on the floor.

The teacher's table is in the corner with shelf units along the wall. From this corner, the teacher can scan the room for supervision while conferencing with individuals or small groups. This is also the place for small group instruction, so storage for small chalkboards and/or white boards is located here. The children's reading folders are also stored in this area. Everything the teacher needs for instruction is on the shelf behind the table, including markers, blank cards, masking tape, highlighting tape, correcting tape, and sticky labels.

The final wall has space for a chart wall, displays of children's work, and storage of the children's personal tubs. A few additional tables are arranged in the middle of the room for children to use as needed.

Kindergarten teachers can use the large meeting area as a block area during work time and one of the shelf units for block storage. In this case the listening center might need to be moved to a quieter spot near the library area. The large group meeting area can be used for music and movement activities as well as reading activities. Kindergarten teachers may also want to add a creative dramatics area that could be arranged in the center of the room with bookshelf dividers.

Learning Centers

One way of organizing the classroom environment is to use learning centers. Calling these areas *learning centers* does not imply that they are the only places learning takes place, just that the materials for completing various kinds of activities are stored together so that children can get them easily and use them without adult assistance. In our floor plan, we have planned for a listening center, a computer/writing center, a math center, an art center, a science center, and a library center. Children will have access to the materials they need for their work at these centers, but they may move from the center to another place in the classroom as they do the work.

You will need some management system for which children work in which area each day. Some teachers rotate the groups through the areas and use a circle chart such as the one illustrated in Figure 12.2. One turn of the inner circle moves a group to another center. Other teachers prefer to encourage children to make their own choices and use some system similar to the one illustrated in Figure 12.3. This is a pegboard labeled with the center areas; the children each have a circle with their name on it to hang on the pegs when they have selected a center area. The pegboard allows the teacher to decide how many children can use each area by controlling the number of pegs available. Once all the pegs in the row for the art area have a name on them, a child must make another choice.

Daily Schedule

The daily schedule needs to be consistent yet flexible. Children need to know that certain activities will happen every day and that they can depend on having time to complete activities. Figure 12.4 is an example of a daily schedule for kindergarten and first and second grades.

Figure 12.2
Circle Chart

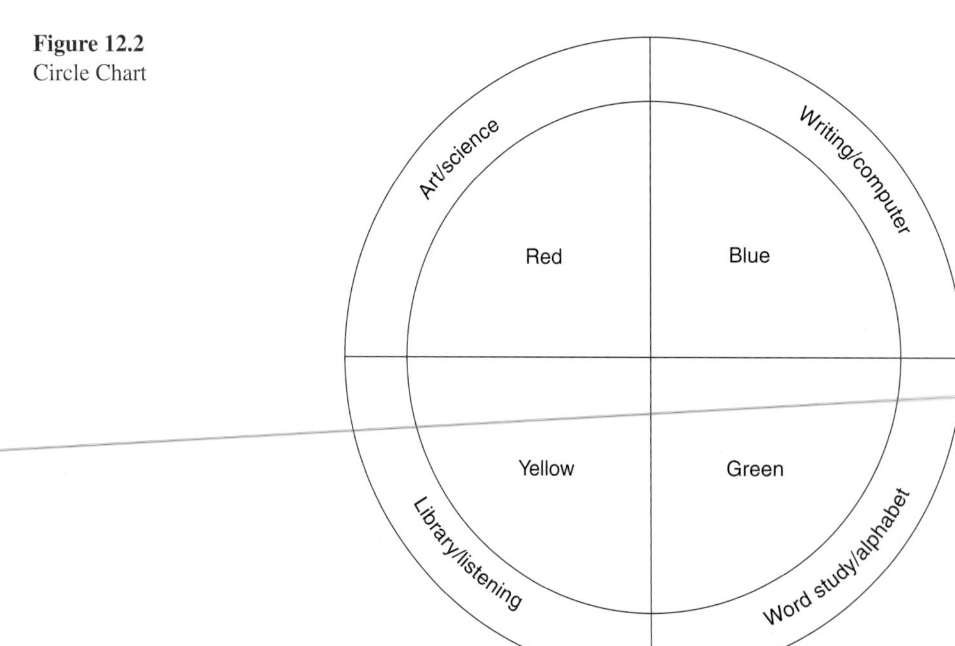

Figure 12.3
Center Pegboard

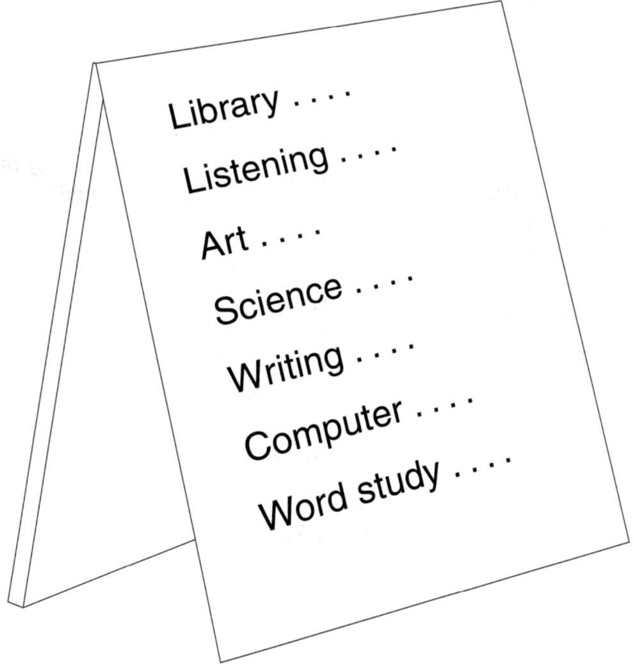

Library . . . .
Listening . . . .
Art . . . .
Science . . . .
Writing . . . .
Computer . . . .
Word study . . . .

Figure 12.4
Daily Schedules

Kindergarten

9:00–9:15	Book browsing/journal writing
9:15–9:35	Read aloud
9:35–10:15	Work time
10:15–10:35	Recess/break
10:35–11:00	Work time
11:00–11:30	Word study
11:30–12:15	Lunch
12:15–12:30	Sharing time

If you have a full-day kindergarten, additional work, story, and outdoor play times would be added.

First and Second Grade

9:00–9:15	Book browsing/journal writing
9:15–9:35	Read aloud
9:35–10:15	Reading workshop
10:15–10:35	Recess/break
10:35–11:00	Reading workshop
11:00–11:30	Word study
11:30–12:15	Lunch
12:15–1:00	Writing workshop
1:00–2:30	Math, science, social studies (usually related to current theme)
2:30–3:15	Specials. Obviously you will not be able to schedule all the specials at one period of the day. However, as the specials are inserted in the schedule, you will arrange the work periods around them. Of course, when it is time for a special, the children can leave what they are doing and return to pick up where they were.

Figure 12.5
Word Cards/Flip Chart

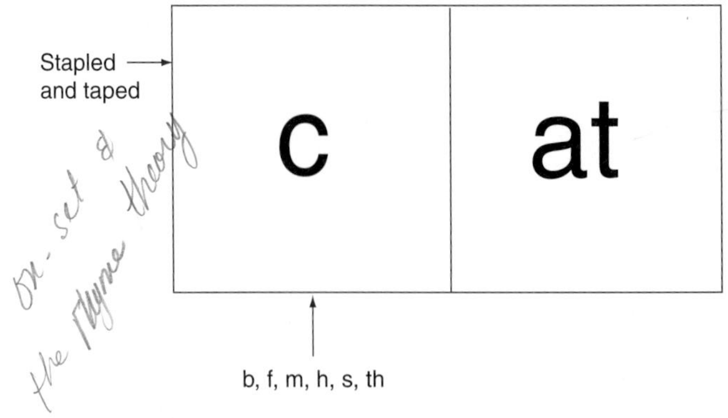

As you can see on these schedules, blocks of time are planned for both reading and writing workshops or work time in kindergarten. Kindergarten teachers can plan choices of activities for children during this time, including the library, listening center, writing, and activities that incorporate literacy such as setting up the creative dramatics area as an office, a restaurant, or a doctor's office. Real literacy materials should be used in these areas, such as real-file folders, order pads, and patient information sheets. During this work time, the teacher works with individual and/or small groups in shared reading, acting out stories and rhymes, and other literacy activities, along with talking with individual children about their writing.

Word Study. During the word study period, the focus is on words taken from the shared reading books, features of print, chants, rhymes, and phonemic awareness activities. The sharing period at the end of the schedule can be another time for reading aloud poetry and for allowing the children to choose their favorite pieces to be repeated.

For example, you have been reading stories about cats in the read-aloud time such as *Cat-Fish* (Newton, 1992), *Six-Dinner Sid* (Moore, 1991), and *The Cat and the Rooster* (Malkovych, 1995). You choose *Greedy Cat* (Cowley, 1995) as a shared reading text for a small group. After reading it several times, you choose *cat, look,* and *bag* as words for focus in the word study time. You make cards for these words and ask children to match them to the words in the text. Once the children know these words as sight words, you help them see that if they know how to spell and read *cat,* they can read and spell *hat, bat, sat, fat,* and *that* by substituting the initial consonant of the word. You can make magnetic letters available to build these and other words. You can make word cards or flip charts such as the one illustrated in Figure 12.5 to practice these words. Use the same strategy with *look* and *bag.* With the children helping, construct a word wall that contains *cat, look,* and *bag* across the top and the words the children dictated under them.

Each time you read *Greedy Cat,* point out different print or text features. For example, you can help children attend to rhyming words, capital letters, or the way the print is arranged on the page with any print features the children have not yet mastered. Once they know about capital letters and punctuation marks, they should be encouraged to use these marks in their own writing. Figure 12.6 is an example of a lesson plan for a shared reading experience for early readers. The assumption of this plan is that assessments have been done, and a small group of children has been selected who have a strong concept of word, can retell stories read to them, and have a sight vocabulary of several words.

Figure 12.6
Lesson Plan for Shared Reading

Goal: Children will be able to use the picture clues to help decode the text and to use their knowledge of predictable text to help them decode the rhyming words.

Text: Fleming, D. (1991). *In the tall, tall grass.* New York: Henry Holt.

Procedures:

1. Introduce the book by showing the cover, reading the title and the author/illustrator aloud, and asking the children to predict what this book is about. Record these predictions on a white board. After the predictions are made, tell children that one strategy they can use to help them read is to listen for rhyming words at the ends of the line. Tell them that we are going to try that strategy and see how it works as we read this book today.
2. As you read the text, use a pointer or your hand to emphasize the word you are reading. Read the first page and allow children to examine the illustration carefully. Turn to the next page and read this page. Ask the children to think about the rhyming words *crunch* and *lunch.* On the next double page spread the rhyming words are *dip* and *sip.* Read "dart, dip, hummingbirds _____" (unpaged), and pause to see who can fill in *sip.* Continue through the book, allowing the children to read the final words on each spread. On the final double page spread and the final page, the pattern changes. Help the children notice the change.
3. List the pairs of rhyming words on the white board and read them with the children. Ask the children to supply other rhyming words and record them. Make sure to point out the change in the onset of the pairs of rhymes.
4. Read the entire story again without stopping but at a pace that will allow children to join in when they can.
5. Recall the original predictions of what the book would be about and compare them to what the book was about. Discuss the clues they used to make good predictions. For some groups, it would be useful to talk about this book as poetry.

Evaluating the Environment

On a regular basis you will want to evaluate the learning environment and determine if changes need to be made in it. One strategy for evaluation is to draw a map of the children's movements during a 30-minute period of the day. On a map of the classroom showing the placements of the furniture and equipment, draw a line each time a child moves from one place to another. If all these lines cross and converge in one place, you will want to think about what is in that place that is causing congestion. For example, if all the children are moving to get paper for their work and all need to go to the same spot, perhaps you could find a way to store paper on each table or move the paper storage to a central spot where it will not cause congestion.

Another strategy is to ask the children if they have had problems with moving where they need to move and getting the supplies they need. If they agree that an area is a problem, let them help you problem solve a solution.

You will also want to examine your schedule on a regular basis. Are you allowing enough time for children to work on their projects so that they do not feel rushed or hurried? Are you allowing them to move about enough? Is there enough change of pace that the day is interesting, but not harried?

Finally, you may want someone to help you look at your environment with a checklist that will give you good feedback about the effectiveness of the learning environment. One such checklist is found in *Assessment of Practices in Early Elementary Classrooms*

(Hemmeter, Maxwell, Ault, & Schuster, 2001). This checklist contains a seven-point rating scale on three different areas: physical environment, instructional context, and social context. The physical environment is rated on room arrangement, display of child products, classroom accessibility, and health and classroom safety. Although you could use the checklist for self-evaluation, it would be good to ask someone else to look with other eyes at your room at least occasionally.

Materials for Instruction

You will need a wide selection of books for reading instruction. Taberski (2000) recommends that a primary classroom have about 1,500 books. That does not mean that each teacher must own that many books. Often teachers pool their sets of books and keep them in a central room. Most of these books have been leveled so that it is easier to match books to developing readers. Many of the schools we work in have leveled book libraries where teachers can check out sets of six or eight copies of a given title. (Please recall the discussion of leveled books in Chapter 8.)

In addition to leveled books, you will want a large selection of trade books. At a minimum, you will want about 10 trade books for each child. From these books children will select their books for independent reading, along with the leveled books that have been taught. As useful as leveled books can be for reading instruction, they are not likely to have the literary qualities of outstanding trade books, so you need both for the classroom.

Other Materials Needed. In addition to books, you will need a good supply of chart tablets (24″ × 36″), one or two pocket charts, an ample supply of sentence strip paper, rolls of 36″ butcher paper, newsprint, and various other kinds of paper. You will also need whiteboards, a large one for you to use in instruction and small ones for children to use individually.

WHAT ASSESSMENTS WILL I USE TO GET STARTED IN THE INSTRUCTIONAL PROGRAM?

The first few days of school will be spent in observations of the children's reading and writing behaviors. As you read aloud, how do individual children respond? How do they select a book for browsing? What do they write? Do they choose books and writing activities eagerly? You will also want to use informal interviews about reading, writing, and interests with individual children as discussed in Chapter 3. After a few days, you will want to begin more formal assessments to determine more precisely what the children can do in reading and writing.

Kindergarten Assessment

For kindergartners, use Clay's (2002) *An Observation Survey of Early Literacy Achievement,* specifically the concepts about print, letter identification, word test, writing vocabulary, and dictation task. You will also want to use the Yopp Singer Test of Phonemic Awareness (1995). While all students are engaged in activities such as browsing in the library, drawing, listening at the listening center, and working with the math manipulatives, you can ask a child to sit with you for a few minutes to complete the assessments. You can assess each child individually on these tasks over several days. Keep your anecdotal observations and the score sheets for the tasks in a folder for each child. When you have completed these assessments, you will have a fairly good picture of each child's abilities and can form some small groups for instruction.

You can use what you learned on the concepts about print task to help you guide the focus of your shared reading experiences. For example, if you were to read *The Doorbell Rang* (Hutchins, 1986) and you know that none of the children in the group know what a period is, then on the second, third, or fourth reading, you can point out the periods at the end of the sentences. If all the children know about the period and other features of print, you might focus on the inferencing skills of figuring out the weather from the illustrations even though the weather is never mentioned in the text. You would also use what you learned in planning other learning experiences. If you learned that some children lacked the ability to segment words into sounds, then as you work with various books, poetry charts, or other texts, you can focus on the sounds in words, rhyming words, and words that begin with the same sound.

For children skilled in identifying the sounds in words, you would plan instruction that allows them to use what they know, such as writing experiences and reading experiences where they can decode some words because they rhyme with known words.

First- and Second-Grade Assessment

For first and second graders, use running records, samples of writing, Clay's word identification task, and Clay's dictation task (Clay, 2002). As children work over the first few days of school, carefully observe their interactions with books and their writing. As you complete these observations, you begin making predictions about the reading abilities of each child and finding material that will be at both their instructional levels and their independent reading levels.

As you conduct the shared reading sessions, make more observations about which children recognize which print features and which can identify words and spelling patterns. These observations can help you plan more instruction. After a few days, you can begin guided reading instruction with small groups, but it will take some time to be as accurate as you would like to be in judging what instruction is needed for each child.

For kindergartners and first and second graders, you must carefully analyze samples of the children's writing in addition to the Clay observation tasks. Careful analysis of children's writing will provide information about letter/sound knowledge, knowledge of directionality of print, their concept of writing, and spelling knowledge. Once you have a good beginning on these assessments, you will be ready to implement a quality instructional program.

Technological Aids in Assessment and Record Keeping

As we discussed in Chapter 3, software for handheld computers is available for completing running records on the spot. The texts of many books are available for downloading. As children read these books, the teacher records the oral reading in very much the same way as a paper record would be marked. At the end of the day, the handheld can be connected to a desktop computer and all the calculations for the running record will be automatically completed and stored.

Many teachers are using electronic portfolios as a technique for sharing information with parents. The materials selected for the portfolio can be scanned and mounted on a web site parents can access with a password. These electronic portfolios can help parents feel that they have current information on their child at all times. Samples of reading aloud and video clips of children engaged in various activities can also be placed on the web site. The teacher can provide written explanations or a voice-over to explain what is being included in the portfolio and why it is significant.

WHAT ARE THE ESSENTIAL ELEMENTS OF A QUALITY INSTRUCTIONAL PROGRAM?

Good instructional programs for young learners include several critical elements: reading aloud, shared reading, guided reading, writing, word study, phonemic awareness activities, response activities, and independent reading activities.

Short (1999) has described a balanced literacy program and illustrated her concept with the graphic featured in Figure 12.7. The three overlapping circles of this graphic help to clarify the interrelatedness of literacy experiences and how all these experiences focus on

Figure 12.7
Balanced Literacy Program

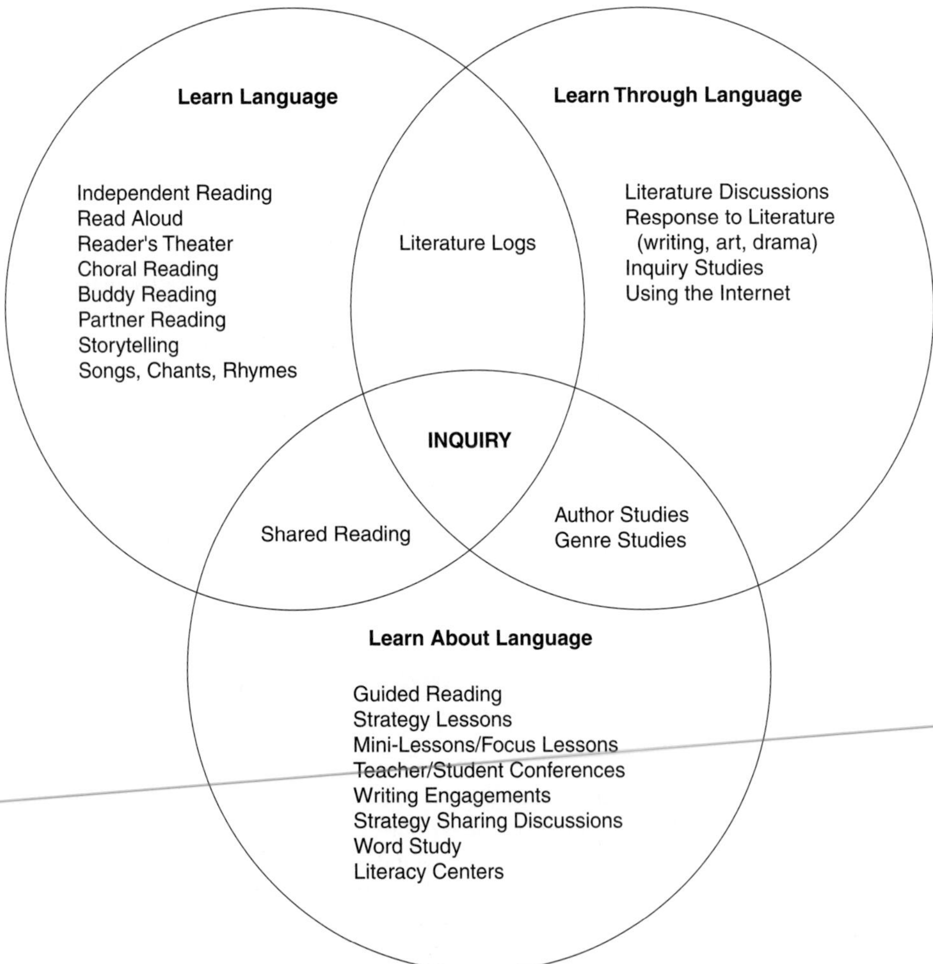

Source: Adapted from Short, K.G. (1999). The Search for "Balance" in a Literature-Rich Curriculum. *Theory Into Practice, 38*(3), 130–137. Copyright by the College of Education, The Ohio State University. All rights reserved.

inquiry. Please examine this graphic carefully. As you will note, circle 1 is labeled "Learn Language," circle 2 "Learn Through Language," and circle 3 "Learn About Language." Learning language is meant to help you think about all that could be done to help children develop their vocabularies and become more skillful users of language. Learning through language includes the activities that will be implemented to help children learn more about how language can be used to help learners clarify and consolidate content knowledge. Learning about language includes activities that help children use language, especially printed language, more effectively. Note that on the graphic all the activities rotate around "Inquiry," the point at which this discussion will begin.

Inquiry in the Literacy Program

One of the key elements in organizing a curriculum for young children is a topic useful for inquiry. Most literacy experiences in a comprehensive program focus on a topic that is carefully selected and implemented. A topic of study is usually selected as a subtopic of a broad, useful theme. Therefore, selecting an appropriate theme is critically important.

Selecting a Theme. First, a good theme must have intellectual worth. It is not appropriate to be spending the children's time on "fluff" studies unlikely to result in real learning that will last a lifetime. Some examples of themes for younger children include patterns, changes, and animals. Note that each theme is broad and offers many possible subtopics that would fit under each broad theme. At the subtopic level, input from the children and consideration of their interests are really important in selecting the best topics of study for a particular group.

Secondly, the theme should be a study in which children can participate actively. What interesting activities might include construction, experiments, or other hands-on opportunities? In addition to activities, the topic must provide authentic reasons for the children to apply the skills they are learning. If children are learning note taking, report writing, or scientific documentation, they need studies that require the use of these skills. Teachers must also determine that they can meet the curriculum requirements through the selected topic of study. If the requirements in your district dictate that all children have experience in presenting a topic orally to their classmates, the topic selected should be one in which an oral presentation would make sense. Of course, not every standard would be met with every topic, but over the course of the year all standards must be met.

Third, the topics should be relevant to the students' lives. This does not mean that a student who lives in the desert should never study the ocean, but it does mean that the connections to their lives should be genuine. If the theme were regions of the world, then you would begin with the most familiar region where the children live and then move to neighboring regions. If the children have no understanding of the ocean or experience with it, then one would not begin with a study of ocean life.

Finally, the theme should be one that both the students and teachers find interesting and engaging. Learning in the classroom can be effective, meet high standards for achievement, and result in the growth of individual skills and abilities when learners and the teacher want to know about the topics of study.

A well-selected theme helps the children make connections between the many different experiences and activities in the classroom and provides coherence for the curriculum. Theme studies are intended to help children achieve a depth of understanding that is not possible when activities are not related and when too many topics are "covered." Some state tests are based on given topics of instruction, such as a study of ancient civilizations in fourth grade. If your state requires a certain topic of study at your grade level, then that topic will be the focus of your inquiry studies for some time in the year. The steps for implementing a theme remain the same no matter what the content of the theme.

Implementing a Theme. Once the topic is selected, you must decide how long the topic will last, how many of the wonderful activities you have imagined can actually be done, and in what sequence you will present the activities. For example, in a study of plants, you might take a field trip to a greenhouse as an opening activity to create interest and help children formulate their questions, or you might take the field trip at the end of the study in order to consolidate the students' knowledge. You will also need to determine the materials and resources you will need and how you will organize the schedule so that the studies can be completed.

An Inquiry Study in Action

In our hypothetical classroom the theme selected is "Everything Grows." Several subtopics have been developed during the year, beginning with personal (human) growth, plant growth cycles, the life cycles of frogs and toads, and the hatching and growth of chicks; now the class is ready to learn about the life cycles of insects. Their inquiry will focus on how insects grow and change and how insect life cycle patterns compare and contrast with the other life cycles they have studied.

For inquiry experiences that are central to the plans, examples of many kinds of real insects, insect larvae, insect cocoons, and materials for creating habitats for several kinds of insects will be provided. For research on insects, you will have collected a wide range of expository books about insects and evaluated the many informational sites about insects on the Internet. You will also explore community resources for insect displays at the museums or entomologists who could speak to your class and help them with their research questions.

As children observe the insects, you will guide them to discover the common characteristics that define insects and to appreciate the many forms that insects take. Each child will choose a research project that will include studies of the life cycles of selected insects, insects that help us, insect pests, social insects, and unusual insects. The products of their projects might be a poster, a paper or clay model, or a labeled drawing. As a class project, you might compile a field guide to the insects chosen for study and ask each child to complete one entry for the field guide. Each day the children have time to pursue their individual or small group projects related to insects. In the afternoon block of time for theme work, the children participate in many activities related to the study of insects. For example, they could use a hoola hoop to mark an area of the playground and count and classify all the insects found within that area (after instruction on safety and not touching biting or stinging insects).

In addition to individual project work, you will want to plan some group experiences, such as viewing videos about insects, read-alouds chosen from books about insects, presentations by guest speakers, and appropriate field trips. One field trip could be to a butterfly place; several zoos also have insect collections or butterfly exhibits.

On the day you introduce the study of insects to your students, ask them to complete a KWWL chart. Ogle (1986) first introduced the KWL chart as one technique for introducing a new topic of study. (We introduced this strategy in Chapter 6.) A KWL chart has three columns, one labeled *K,* one labeled, *W,* and one labeled *L.* The *K* stands for *Know;* the children either write or dictate what they know to fill in this column. The *W* stands for what they *want* to know; the children write or dictate their questions for this column. The *L* stands for *Learned;* as the study unfolds, information learned is added to the chart. A *W* for a fourth column is for adding the *where* of the information can be learned. For example, children might learn new information from a video, books, the web, and a guest speaker, and those source would be listed in the *S* column.

KWL charts are commonly used as graphic organizers, either as a class or for individual study projects. The children provide the information they know about insects and the questions they have about insects. This chart remains in the classroom for the entire study and is expanded and reviewed regularly. On the second day, a video is shown that illustrates the life of a common insect such as an ant. On the third day, children have adequate time to examine real insect specimens and write or dictate their observations about them. These observations may take several days to complete if you have a large variety of insects. On a following day, children select their topics for research, either individually or, if several are interested in the same topics, in small groups. In Figure 12.8 we have illustrated a KWLS chart that is partially completed. After the children completed any activity such as watching the video, they would add information to the chart or mark through information that they have put on the chart that they thought they knew and have now discovered is not true.

Research for kindergartners may mean observing carefully and recording their observations with drawings. For first graders, it may mean that you supply them with charts created on 11″ × 17″ paper and marked with three columns and three rows. In the rows, the child lists the source of the information. The columns are labeled "What they eat," "Where they live," and "Pest/helper." Second graders may be able to collect all the information they need for a field guide page. A research center will help keep the materials and supplies that are needed for research together and accessible. Figure 12.9 is an example of how a research center might look in a primary classroom.

As we begin this discussion of the activities listed on the graphic, remember that both reading workshop and writing workshop are in place and that it is in the framework of these workshops that all the instruction described here takes place.

Figure 12.8
KWLS Chart

K	W	W	L
cockroaches are insects	is a spider an insect?		
insects bite	what do insects eat?		
some insects eat plants	how do insects stay warm in winter?		
ants are insects	where do insects go when it rains?		
	what insects live in houses?		

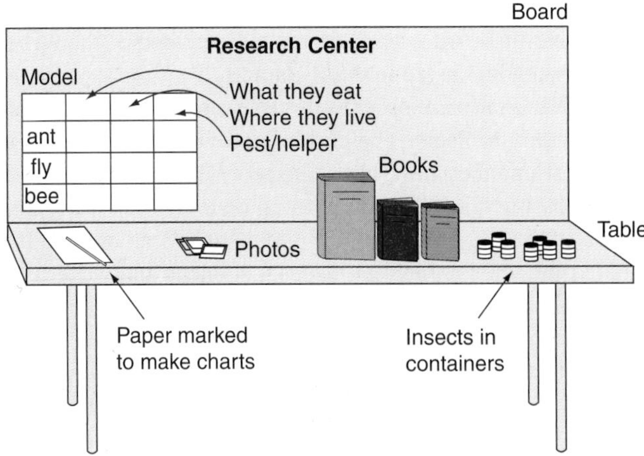

Figure 12.9
Research Center

Learning Language

In the organizational diagram, circle 1 is "learn language," and in Figure 12.10 we repeat it. Please note that this circle includes independent reading, read-aloud, book share/book talks/displays, reader's theater, choral reading, buddy reading, partner reading, storytelling, and songs, chants, and rhymes. The following are descriptions of what could be done with the topic of insects for a week.

Independent Reading. In arranging for independent reading during book browsing, you put out one or two tubs of books related to insects. These books are at many different levels of difficulty. Direct each child to select one book that is interesting to them and that they can read on their own (independent reading level). This book is placed in their individual book bag to be available during reading workshop time.

Read-Aloud. Read-aloud book choices should be selected from books and poetry that are too difficult for the children to read independently (as we discussed in Chapter 11). For the week, the read-alouds could include *Ladybug at Orchard Avenue* (Zoehfeld, 1997); *Will You Sting Me? Will You Bite? The Truth About Some Scary-Looking Insects* (Miller, 2001); *ABC of Crawlers and Flyers* (Ryden, 1996); *Monarch Butterfly of Aster Way* (Ring et al., 1999); and selected poems from *Insectlopedia* (Florian, 1998).

Reader's Theater. Because reader's theater requires dialogue to be successful, there are not many choices about insects for reader's theater that would be at the reading level of most primary children. One choice might be to select a fable such as "The Grasshopper and the Ant" and help the children write additional dialogue for the parts. Another choice for able second-grade readers would be *Joyful Noise: Poems for Two Voices* (Fleischman, 1988). The best choice might be for the children to write their own script.

Choral Reading. There are many, many poems and chants to use for choral reading experiences. Choral reading makes a great beginning for read-aloud time as you get everyone together and ready to listen at the same time with no nagging. In addition to choral reading, use chants such as "The Ants Went Marching One by One" to begin the read-aloud time. The songs, chants, and poems for choral reading should all be printed on large chart

Figure 12.10
Learn Language

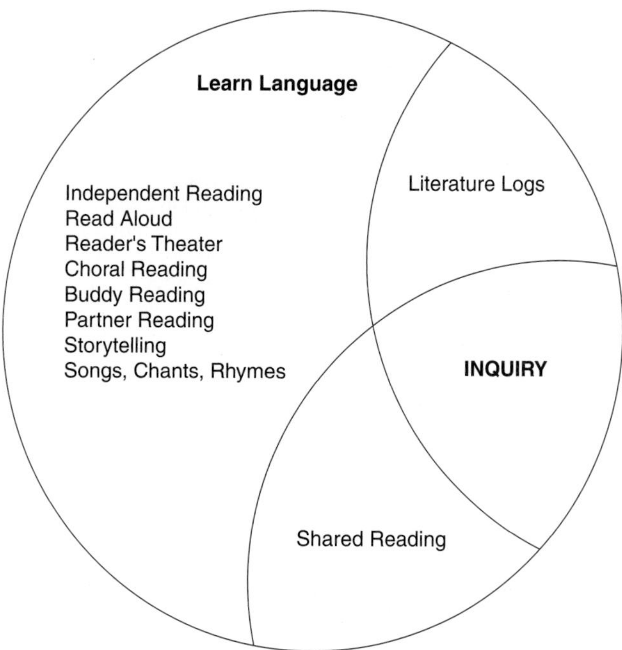

Source: Adapted from Short, K.G. (1999). The Search for "Balance" in a Literature-Rich Curriculum. *Theory Into Practice, 38*(3), 130-137.

paper and hung so that children can see them easily and use them as meaningful text when they practice reading. Some teachers like to print a copy of each poem or chant that the children have learned and put these into a poem book for each child.

Learning Through Language

Figure 12.11 is the second of the organizing circles. This one is "Learn Through Language" and includes literature discussions, response to literature (writing, art, drama), and the work children do on their inquiry studies.

Literature Discussions. Literature discussions are meant to be discussions, not interrogations. They are listed under learning *through* language because as children have the opportunity to talk about what they have read, they can clarify their own understandings and build new mental connections. Literature discussions often follow read-alouds for the youngest readers, and one of the roles the teacher must assume for these young learners is to supply the words the children need to express their thoughts. That is not to say that the teacher tells them what to say, but when children are talking about books and their connections to what they have heard read, they may need the teacher to help them. Once while observing a group of kindergartners discuss several books about the moon, we noticed one child was struggling with trying to express her observation that the illustrations in some of the books were round like the moon. She was searching for the word *circular,* and the teacher failed to supply it for her. The teacher's job is to supply the vocabulary and monitor the child's contributions so that each child has a chance to participate.

Figure 12.11
Learn Through Language

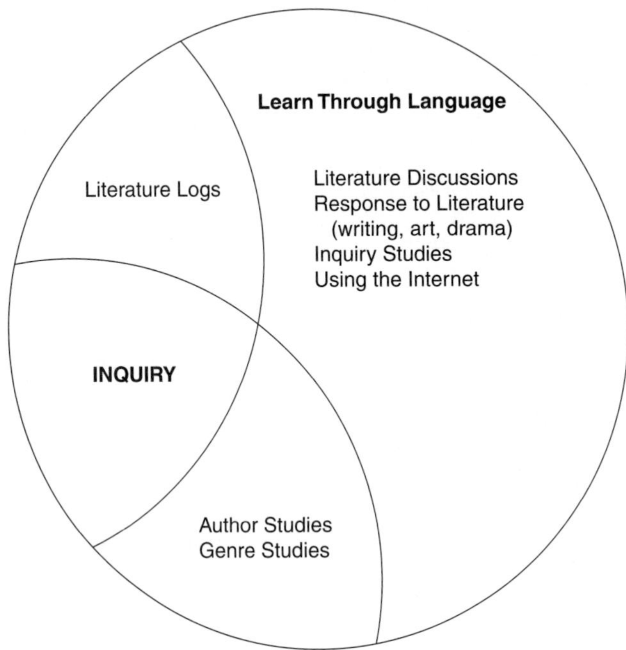

Source: Adapted from Short, K.G. (1999). The Search for "Balance" in a Literature-Rich Curriculum. *Theory Into Practice, 38*(3), 130-137.

Literature Logs. Literature logs are in the intersection between circle 1 and circle 2. For very young children, these logs may be a recording of the titles of the books they have read and/or a sentence or two about the book. As children grow to be more skillful as writers, these logs become another avenue for expressing what the reader felt and learned from the reading experience.

Responses Other Than Writing. Responses other than writing are also important as children learn through language. Many children can create art pieces that reflect their feelings about their reading. Assigning a "craft" project such as making a spider from a circle of black construction paper and eight accordion folded legs is not what we mean by art as a response to reading. If a child wants to create a painting of a butterfly or moth after watching one emerge from a cocoon and reading about the process of changing from a caterpillar to a butterfly, that would be an artistic response. If the response is assigned and everyone must make a butterfly, then it is not a personal response.

Many young children especially enjoy drama and the opportunity to recreate a story with puppets, flannel board pieces, or creative drama. During this study of insects, flannel board pieces representing an egg, a caterpillar, a chrysalis, and a butterfly should be available. Puppets of insects can help children express their understandings of how insects move, what noises they make, or how they might relate to other insects. Children learn a great deal when they must create the dialogue or narration to retell a story or recall an event.

Inquiry Studies. If students are engaged in a variety of research activities, they will be reading and writing widely and deeply about insects. If you select a class project of making a field guide to insects, you should read examples of field guides over several days and spend some

Drama is an often overlooked response to literature.

time deciding with the group what information must be included on each page. Once your class has decided what should be included, a rubric for a field guide page can be developed.

Using the Internet. As children do their independent research activities, they need access to some of the web sites that contain pictures and information about various insects. You can bookmark the sites that you deem appropriate for the children to use. Most teachers find that it works best to have children begin their research with questions, find some answers in books, magazines, and reference materials before they start to look on the web. Then they can use the web to complete or extend their information. There is so much information on the web and it is often so dense that children who begin on the web may never get focused enough to complete their research.

Learning About Language

Our third and final circle, illustrated in Figure 12.12, is labeled "Learn about Language." In the intersection of circle 2 and circle 3 are author studies and genre studies. In Chapter 11 we discussed both author studies and genre studies. Many of the books about insects are nonfiction, and if the children have not been engaged in a study of information books before, you should spend some time in read-alouds and in guided and/or shared reading, reading information books, and learning about how such books can be structured. Information books have features such as tables of content, indexes, headings and subheadings, and source lists that are not usually found in works of fiction. Even young children can learn to use these text features to help them find information they need and to help them comprehend the information.

Shared Reading. The intersection of circle 3 with circle 1 contains shared reading. Shared reading was defined and explained in Chapter 8. For this study of insects, you would select several books for shared reading. These books are selected for shared reading because

Figure 12.12
Learn About Language

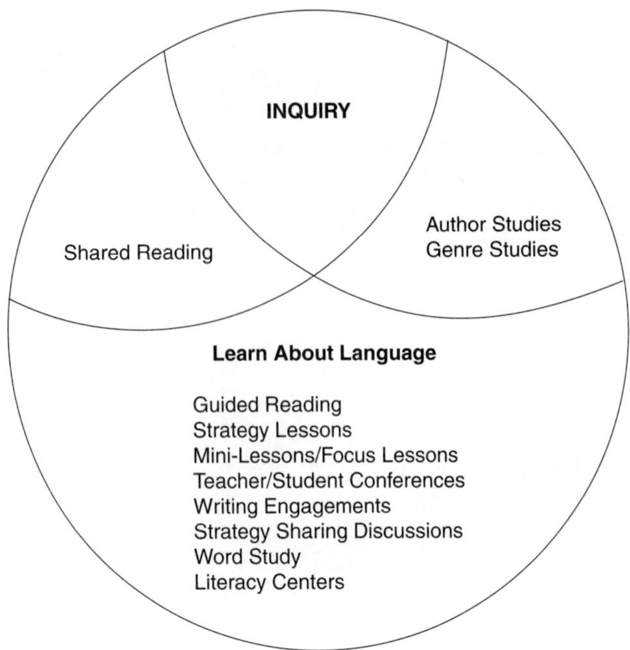

Source: Adapted from Short, K.G. (1999). The Search for "Balance" in a Literature-Rich Curriculum. *Theory Into Practice, 38*(3), 130-137.

they are too difficult for independent reading at this time, but in a few weeks—with more study about insects to provide more background information—these books may be used for guided or independent reading. Shared reading is in the intersection between learning language and learning about language because children learn both during shared reading. They might be learning new vocabulary or they might be learning how words they know can be used in different ways, such as in writing poetry.

Guided Reading. Guided reading was described in Chapter 8 as the heart of reading instruction. For guided reading groups, select insect books to meet the instructional needs of each small group. This means that you need multiple copies of some books for use in guided reading. Fountas and Pinnell (1999) list several books on insects at several different reading levels. For example, *Bugs!* (Rookie Readers), *Bumble Bee* (Ready to Read), *Bumble Bees* (Pebble Books), *Butterflies* (Pebble Books), *Butterfly Eggs* (Pebble Books), *A Buzz is Part of a Bee* (Rookie Readers), *Buzzing Flies* (Sunshine), *Caterpillars* (Book Shop), *Insects* (MacLulich), *Insects All Around* (Early Connections), and *Insects that Bother Us* (Foundations) are just a few. In the Fountas and Pinnell system, these books range from Level C (K or 1) to Level M (end of second, early third). Of course, insect books are available at more difficult levels if you need them.

Strategy Lessons. Strategy lessons for information books focus on the strategies for reading nonfiction. For example, you can copy the table of contents from one of the books onto a transparency and teach children how to use it. You can also teach children how to use an index from one of the books. In addition, you might want to demonstrate how headings and subheadings help the reader find information quickly and relate pieces of information.

You can be sure to help children ask themselves questions before reading, such as "What will I learn about in reading this book?" "How can I know if this information is true?" Other strategy lessons include how to read the charts and graphs included in some of the texts.

Mini-Lessons or Focus Lessons. A focus lesson may be part of reading workshop or writing workshop. In reading workshop, the focus lessons about insect books might include strategy lessons as described previously or other lessons that would help children read information books more easily. The writing workshop focus lessons might be devoted to helping children write reports or the format for writing the field guide. Begin with reading reports or field guides over a period of several days; discuss the information contained in the reports or guides, and then compose a field guide page as a whole group. Children would follow up on these experiences by working in small groups to complete the field guides for the class project.

Conferencing with Students. As we described in Chapter 10, conferencing with students during writing workshop focuses on what the children are trying to achieve as writers and what kind of help they need to achieve their goals. For example, students might draw a picture of an insect, and you can provide help by assisting them as they sound out words they want to write. For other primary students, you might need to help them put their facts into sentences or help them learn how to make a bulleted list of facts. During reading workshop, talk with students about their choices of books and any difficulties with insect names. Make sure they can match the real insect with the book description and talk about why the illustrator used a labeled drawing rather than a photograph, for example. Of course, conferences would be used for ongoing assessments of student progress.

Strategy-Sharing Discussions. As children read and write about insects, they will make discoveries that will be useful to others in the class. Providing a short sharing time every few days for discussing how a problem was solved can help other children learn to use a strategy. For example, a reader might discover that she can compare the information found in three different books about bumblebees. A writer might find that keeping a list of words about insects in his writing folder is helpful. Once children share these strategies, other children can use them.

Centers in the Literacy Program

Different points of view arise over literacy centers and their use in the elementary literacy program. Some teachers prefer that when they are not engaged with the teacher, children spend their reading workshop time actually reading. These teachers ask children to keep a relatively large number of books in their individual book bags so they read these books whenever they are not working with the teacher. There is evidence that the more children read at school, the more they will read outside school (Krashen, 1999). This is logical, as children will not value an activity the teacher does not value. These teachers ask children to keep daily records of what they have read by genre (fiction, nonfiction, and poetry) and write brief responses to their reading. They do not want children to spend too much of their reading time engaged in writing activities. Their reasoning is that children will not become better readers without reading and that the 30 to 40 minutes of reading workshop is definitely not too much time to be reading seriously (not just thumbing through a book or looking at the pictures). Some of this reading time can be spent in partner or buddy reading, but most of it is in individual reading practice.

Other teachers like to have literacy centers where the children can practice various reading skills. There is no simple formula for what kinds of reading activities are useful and actually produce increased learning. For nine years, Cambourne (2001) studied teaching learning activities in elementary classrooms and found that some activities worked in some classrooms with some teachers while the same activity in another classroom was ineffective. One key to effective activities was that the children could understand the relationship of the activity to learning to read and write. Another criteria was that the activity engaged the child through more than one modality. For example, if you asked children to sequence a set of pictures into a story, the child is only required to read silently. If the sequencing activity is assigned to a group of four children who must agree on the sequencing, explain why they chose the order they chose, and then write a story to go with the pictures as a group, the child must read, write, and talk. If the child also knows how sequencing will contribute to his reading skill, it is even better.

The point is that there is no easy answer about what you should do with centers and center activities. You must give careful thought to what you ask children to do in the classroom and why you ask them to do it. If you decide that literacy centers would benefit your students, the following suggestions will be helpful.

Possibilities for Literacy Centers

The following suggestions for literacy centers are not meant to imply that all these centers must be available all the time. At times you might want one or two centers available, and you would select the activities that would be most appropriate for your learners at that time.

ABCs. Centers devoted to the alphabet can provide a wide range of activities, such as the following:

- Magnetic letters and boards on which to construct words, such as the side of a filing cabinet or cookie sheets.
- Objects to classify into containers labeled with the letters of the alphabet, such as strawberry baskets or milk cartons. These objects can be models, such as plastic models of animals or insects or small real objects collected from the classroom or from home (pencil, tape, ruler, or toy cars and spools, for example).
- Alphabet letters on cards made of materials with texture, such as sandpaper, velvet, or string glued down; wicki sticks or pipe cleaners to construct letters.
- Newspapers or magazines to use in searching for letters to cut out and compare styles and fonts.
- Letters and pictures to use in making an alphabet book. These books could range from environmental print to books on a topic such as insects.

Word Study. Word study can be designed so that the activities are fairly simple or quite complex. The following are a few of the possibilities:

- Words on cards to be arranged into sentences or sorted in many different ways such as by beginning sounds, parts of speech, spelling pattern, words that have the same number of syllables, words that are theme related, or words that could describe a character
- Words that can be sorted by onsets and rimes
- Words that can be constructed given a set of letters
- Words that can be used to create alliterative sentences
- Words that can be pictured (sketch a meaning)

Building words is a helpful part of word study.

- Words that have multiple meanings
- Words to be arranged into similes and metaphors

Listening Center. The listening center can be stocked with audiotapes (both commercially produced tapes and tapes you or a volunteer have created). These tapes allow children to listen to the story as they follow along with the print. Audiotapes are one means of making materials that some children cannot read independently available to all children. If you find books with information you think is basic to understanding insects, then you could tape that material. Audiotapes can support readers who are having difficulty with a text, and they can provide models of fluent reading for children.

Art center. Art is a useful response to literature, and you can supply materials that will help children create images that are meaningful responses to their reading. For insects, you would want to make sure that the art center was supplied with tissue paper in many colors, black markers, and pipe cleaners, in addition to the usual paper, crayons, and paint.

Writing Center. The writing center is always available to children, but during this study of insects you might want to put field guides, reference materials, and lists of insect words that the children might need in their writing in this center. Some shape book covers could be available for the children to select if they chose. For example, a ladybug and a butterfly template would be good choices for shape books (books in which the covers and the pages are cut into a shape, then stapled together).

Computer Center. Even though the computer is another center that is always available, you can focus its use on specific topics of study. During a study of insects, you can bookmark web sites of special interest. The word processing program is available for children who want or need to compose on the computer.

Overhead Projector. The overhead projector is a popular center. Children love seeing the images they have created enlarged on the screen or wall. Possibilities for insects include silhouettes of insects to tell about, fact sheets about different insects to be reviewed, and labeled illustrations of insects to be shared with a group.

Pocket Charts. Pocket charts can be used to hold various rhymes and chants about insects. Children can arrange the words to make new poems and can add illustrations to the lines of a poem. Other words can be made available so that children can construct their own poems, chants, or descriptions of insects.

Read Around the Room. Children use this center by selecting a pointer and moving around the room to point at and read all the accessible print. The task can be varied by having the children work in pairs, by asking children to find certain kinds of words (describing words, for example), by asking children to record the words they find, by giving children a frame (hole cut in a fly swatter for example) and asking them to find all the words in the room with the rime /ing/, or by asking children to find all the words in the room that are two- or three-syllable words. As you can see, the task can be varied to meet the needs of various children and to provide practice for many different reading skills.

HOW DO I HANDLE MANAGEMENT AND RECORD KEEPING?

Young children are not likely to come to school knowing exactly how to do everything the teacher might expect. From the first day of school, teachers will be helping children learn what is expected in school and how children can meet these expectations.

Getting Started

It is not likely that children will come to school knowing how to use the centers in your classroom. If they have had experience working in centers before, then the introduction to center use will be shorter but still necessary. If you want children to use the centers, you must teach them how to use each one. Choose one center, take the group to that area, and show them step by step how to use the area. If you started with the listening center, you would show them how to turn on the tape player (and code the buttons with green for on, red for stop), how to adjust the volume, how to stop the player, and what to do with the books and headphones when they are finished. Put these directions on a poster and number the steps. Put in pictures to help clarify the directions. After a few days, introduce another area and so on until the children can manage all the areas of the classroom. Be prepared to help children get started with the centers for a day or two after they are introduced.

During the initial introduction period of the work areas, you will not be able to schedule reading or writing workshop for as long as will be possible after the children can manage all the centers or can read independently for longer. You can use many activities to keep children engaged while you are working with assessments or small groups for brief times. Children can draw, look at books, use puzzles, play matching games like concentration or lotto, or create pictures to go with a few key words to make themselves a personal dictionary, for example. You will probably do two or three whole group experiences each day, such as extra story times and music times when you teach songs and chants they will be able to read later. You can also teach a variety of other classroom skills, such as where to place their name cards when they are going to buy a lunch.

Efficient Organization

A key lesson is to help children learn where to keep their folders for reading and writing and how to find their own folder. Make sure they return the folders to the storage box whenever they have finished with them for the day. Get children started using their journals and help them find and replace their own journal. Help children learn where to find the tools they will need to do their work without interrupting the teacher. For example, on each of the work tables, keep a container of pencils. Markers, scissors, tape, correction tape, rulers, and other supplies also should be kept so that they are easy to reach and easy to replace. You might want to begin with either signs or symbols to designate the proper place for different supplies.

Monitoring Learning

You will want to implement the monitoring notebook discussed in Chapter 3. Create a section for each child, and place all the assessments that you complete for that child in the notebook. A front page in the notebook with a class list and columns for each of the assessments can give you a quick overview so that you will know at a glance which children you have assessed on what measures. You will also want to place the anecdotal observations you are recording in the course of every day in this notebook. Part of your daily planning will be to check your lists and plan for assessments you will need to do the next day. You may want to place this page on a clipboard with fresh sticky labels for writing notes at the beginning of each day. Assessments cannot be divorced from planning. Only when you attend carefully to your assessments can you purposefully plan appropriate instruction for each child.

HOW DO I CAPITALIZE ON DIVERSITY IN THE CLASSROOM?

Diversity is a matter of fact in almost every school in America. Diversity means more than simply differences in skin color; it means that significant differences exist in any classroom population. These differences may be in skin color, native language, ethnic heritage, gender, socioeconomic family status, family structure, cultural group, and life experiences. For many years, teachers were advised to be "color blind," meaning that they were to treat each child the same, no matter what color their skin was. The problem is that some children of color have a set of cultural beliefs, family interaction patterns, and life experiences that are different from those of other children. Some children who are not children of color also have differences from what is generally considered mainstream American culture. Treating every child the same ignores real, meaningful differences and fails to provide experiences that are appropriate for every child.

Learning About Your Students

Our job as teachers is to learn as much as we possibly can about each of our students, their families, and their previous experiences. For example, let's say two children in your classroom are Cambodian; one from a family that has been living in the United States for 15 years and the other from a family that has been here for 15 days. These students have different needs even though they share the same culture and language.

One element of learning about the child is learning about the culture of the child's family. You probably will not be an expert on every child's culture, but you can learn enough not to be unwittingly insulting to children or their families or not to assign tasks that families would consider inappropriate. You will be able to find much information in books and on the Internet, and you may want to consult people who are familiar with the cultures of your students.

Armed with this knowledge, you should be able to make better plans for the children in your classroom. For example, if you know that a child does not speak English, try to learn a few words of the child's language. Post signs in more than one language, and try to send home parent information in a language the parents can read. If you know that a child has not had many experiences with reading books, try to learn how the family uses literacy in the home. Some families may read the newspaper to cut and organize grocery coupons, some may correspond with relatives in their country of origin, some may teach their children traditional tales and nursery rhymes, and some may read the holy books of their religion. All these experiences, and more, can be the basis for helping children come to understand the importance of literacy in their own lives and to move gradually into more academic literacy for school. To assume that children who are poor and do not speak English have no literacy experience is not usually accurate.

Helping Children Learn in English

Once you learn about your students, their culture, and their experience with literacy, you will know what must be done to help them gain literacy experiences in English. If a child has no experience listening to storybooks being read by an adult, then you may need to begin with telling stories rather than reading them. After telling stories a few times, you can accompany the telling with several illustrations that can be used to help the child develop the vocabulary to talk about the story. After the child is comfortable listening to stories and knows what it means to listen and be able to tell what the story was about, then you can transition to reading stories from books. Helping children make their own books helps them develop a concept of what a book is and how books are made. They might dictate a book for you to record.

Some children respond better as members of a group than as individuals. Some cultures promote the success of the group and expect individuals to contribute to the group success, but do not encourage individuals to speak out about their learning. Other cultures help children learn acceptable behavior as their culture defines it through stories that are told and retold until the child understands the meaning. Some cultures expect that their children will not be expected to display their abilities until they have had a private time to practice and feel that they are ready to perform the skill being learned. All of this means that you must try to plan experiences so that individual children can learn what is expected in a variety of ways and that you respect the style of learning preferred by the child's culture.

Involve the Family and Their Culture

Some teachers have been successful in involving the children's families and learning a great deal about the families by having a family tree project in which the child and the family create a book to share with the class about their family. These books are often works of art decorated with traditional materials and colors, and they help children tie together what the school demands and what their families know. Some teachers furnish the basic materials for making these books because it would be a strain on family resources to produce such a book on their own. You may also want to have a workshop in which parents could come to learn about what they could put in their books and see samples of other books to give them ideas. These books need not be produced in English, but if they are not, you may want to create a translation to be attached at the end.

Families can also be invited to share favorite stories or foods with the class, and a book could be put together recording these experiences. Some families are reluctant to come to school for a variety of reasons: some work several jobs and don't have time, some may feel they lack acceptable clothing, and some lack transportation or worry that their English is not good enough to communicate with teachers. It takes a great deal of effort and usually a schoolwide effort to convince all parents that they are welcome in school and appreciated for what they have taught their children.

CONCLUSION

Putting together a literacy program for young children is an exciting and rewarding task. It is always challenging even for experienced teachers because the children are different each year, the resources change, and their own knowledge level changes. The challenges are to create a comfortable, but interesting, work environment for the children and create manageable record-keeping systems for yourself. You will also want to make sure that even though the focus is always on meaning in literacy, the learners who leave your classroom have a wide array of useful skills and strategies that will serve them well for a lifetime of continued learning.

Juel (1988) found that children who were poor readers at the end of first grade were still poor readers at the end of fourth grade. The probability of a poor reader becoming a good reader was very low. Knowing that the abilities of children as readers and writers in these beginning years are critical to their later success is reason enough to make these beginning experiences useful and productive for children.

THINKING AS A TEACHER

1. You have been hired to teach first grade in a school that is fairly traditional. The literacy program at this school is based on a published set of materials. How will you implement the elements of a good program as described in this chapter?
2. You very much want to implement an inquiry-based program of literacy development, but you are worried about what the parents will say if you do not use standardized tests to measure the competencies of the children. How will you explain to parents how you know the children are learning?
3. You want all the teachers at your grade level to share their books for reading instruction. If some of the teachers are not using leveled books, how will you convince them to participate in book sharing for the benefit of all children?

FIELD-BASED ACTIVITIES

1. Interview a kindergarten, first-grade, and second-grade teacher about how they organize the literacy experiences in their classrooms. If they use a thematic organization, record the themes and topics they have found useful. If they do not use a thematic approach, compare their organizational scheme to a thematic approach.
2. Interview a child in kindergarten, first grade, and second grade. Ask them what topics they want to learn about in school, and when they have identified a topic, what would they like to know about that topic. Compare what you learn to the results of your classmates and create a list of topics that are interesting to young children.
3. Administer one set of assessments recommended in this chapter to a kindergartner, a first grader, or a second grader. Evaluate what you have learned in terms of how you would plan literacy instruction for that child.

REFERENCES

Cambourne, B. (2001). What do I do with the rest of the class? The nature of teaching-learning activities. *Language Arts, 79,* 124–135.

Clay, M. M. (2002). *An observation survey of early literacy achievement* (2nd ed.). Portsmouth, NH: Heinemann.

Edwards, C., Gandini, L., & Forman, G. (Eds.). (1993). *The hundred languages of children: The Reggio Emilia approach to early childhood education.* Norwood, NJ: Ablex.

Fountas, I. C., & Pinnell, G. S. (1999). *Matching books to readers: Using leveled books in guided reading, K–3.* Portsmouth, NH: Heinemann.

Hemmeter, M. L., Maxwell, K. L., Ault, M. J., & Schuster, J. W. (2001). *Assessment of practices in early elementary classrooms (APEEC).* New York: Teachers College Press.

Juel, C. (1988). Learning to read and write: A longitudinal study of 54 children from first through fourth grade. *Journal of Educational Psychology, 80,* 437–447.

Krashen, S. B. (1999). *Three arguments against whole language & why they are wrong.* Portsmouth, NH: Heinemann.

Montessori, M. (1967). *The absorbent mind.* New York: Dell.

Mooney, M. E. (2001). *Text forms and features: A resource for intentional teaching.* Katonah, NY: Richard C. Owens.

Moore, L. (1975/1993). Move over. In J. Taxel (Ed.), *Fanfare: The Christopher-Gordon children's literature annual* (p. 22). Norwood, MA: Christopher-Gordon.

Ogle, D. (1986). KWL: A teaching model. *The Reading Teacher, 30,* 564–571.

Short, K. G. (1999). The search for "balance" in a literature-rich curriculum. *Theory into Practice, 38,* 130–137.

Taberski, S. (2000). *On solid ground.* Portsmouth, NH: Heinemann.

Yopp, H. K. (1995). A test for assessing phonemic awareness in young children. *The Reading Teacher, 49,* 20–29.

Children's Books

Carle, E. (1969/1987). *The very hungry caterpillar.* New York: Philomel.

Cowley, J. (1995). *Greedy cat.* Illus. by R. Belton. Wellington, New Zealand: Learning Media.

Fleischman, P. (1988). *Joyful noise: Poems for two voices.* New York: Harper & Row.

Fleming, D. (1991). *In the tall, tall grass.* New York: Henry Holt.

Florian, D. (1998). *Insectlopedia.* San Diego, CA: Harcourt.

Hutchins, P. (1986). *The doorbell rang.* New York: Mulberry Books.

Malkovych, I. (1995). *The cat and the rooster.* Illus. by K. Cavro. New York: Knopf.

Miller, S. S. (2001). *Will you sting me? Will you bite? The truth about some scary looking insects.* Illus. by R. Chrustowski. Stemmer House Publishers Audio.

Moore, I. (1991). *Six-dinner Sid.* New York: Simon & Schuster.

Newton, J. (1992). *Cat-fish.* New York: Lothrop, Lee, & Shepard.

Ring, E. (1999). *Monarch butterfly of Aster Way.* Norwalk, CT: Soundprints Corporation Audio.

Ryden, H. (1996). *ABC of crawlers and flyers.* New York: Clarion.

Zoehfeld, K. W. (1997). *Ladybug at Orchard Avenue.* Illus. by T. Buchs. Norwalk, CT: Soundprints Corporation Audio.

Chapter 13

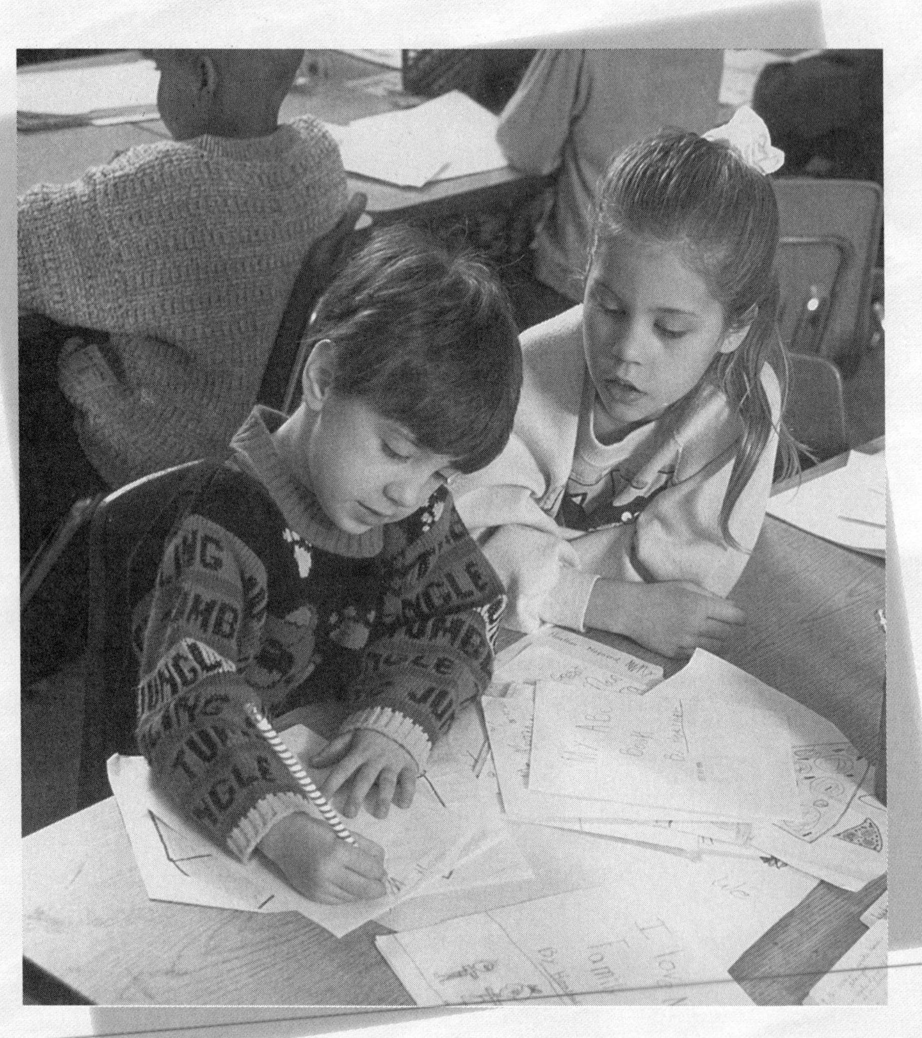

Building a Literacy Program Grades 3–5

For many teachers, the intermediate grades of third through fifth are choice teaching assignments because the children have a great deal of independence and can do so many interesting activities. These children need so much less help from the teacher, but they still seek the teacher's approval. As a teacher of this age group, you needn't spend time wiping their noses or tying their shoes, but they miss you when you are absent and still seek your approval.

Focus Questions

- What is the nature of third, fourth, and fifth graders?
- How do I challenge unmotivated readers at this level?
- How do I create a classroom environment that will help me be an effective teacher?
- What assessments will I use to get started in the instructional program?
- How do I plan instruction for grades 3–5?
- How do I handle management and record keeping?

WHAT IS THE NATURE OF THIRD, FOURTH, AND FIFTH GRADERS?

Children in this age group are difficult to classify. In a third grade class, you might find some children who are so small they would not stand out in a first-grade class and some who would look at home in a sixth grade class. Some intermediate girls are wearing bras and some are still thin as rails. Their level of physical activity varies a great deal over these intermediate grade years: third graders tend to be very active and moving, while fourth graders and fifth graders can sit still for longer periods of time and are less active than third graders (Howe, 1993). They choose same sex friends almost exclusively; to have to hold the hand of a person of the opposite sex is torture. They have much more ability to control their own behavior and are much less impulsive than younger children.

Peer groups become important during these intermediate years. The importance of the child's peers begins in third grade and grows stronger in fourth and fifth grades. It is important to children that they are accepted by their peers, that they dress like their peers, and that they read what their peers read or recommend (Howe, 1993). Reading interests in animals continues. Romance is mentioned for the first time by girls in third grade and is more common in fourth and fifth grades. Many boys like sports, mysteries, and books of lists. Both sexes express interest in reading about the people and food of other cultures (Howe, 1993).

Peer pressure can be a positive influence if the peers are good models for school behavior and school achievement. Teachers can make use of this need for peer acceptance by organizing group work and encouraging students to share their reading and writing interests.

The cognitive development of intermediate students is as variable as their physical development. Most children of this age have made the discovery that teachers and parents do not know everything. They love playing with language and laughing at the double meanings of words and at silly jokes. They can also focus on topics of interest for extended periods of time and have strong individual preferences for what they want to learn. They tend to be curious and eager in their approach to learning. They particularly like to find out how things work and do experiments. For example, third graders enjoy using the microscope in science, participating in dramatics, and measuring and weighing things. Fourth and fifth graders can usually engage in more long-term projects than before, are better at finding out things on their own, are better at research, but may be inconsistent in doing their work (Howe, 1993).

In terms of academic abilities, the gaps in achievement among intermediate children may be quite startling. Some children read so well at this age that they can read almost anything. The challenge is finding material that will offer them a reading challenge and be appropriate for their emotional and social developmental stages. Others will not be beyond the beginning stages of reading. Achievement in writing will also vary greatly. Planning and implementing a program for these children will require careful thought and advanced skills in organization.

HOW DO I CHALLENGE UNMOTIVATED READERS AT THIS LEVEL?

A common problem that intermediate grade teachers worry about is the lack of interest in reading by some intermediate grade boys. Some boys of this age love reading and read often and widely. Others, while they can read, do not, and some cannot read well and do not read much at all. For children who cannot yet read, encouraging students to explore a wide variety of texts in different ways and for different purposes and continuing to provide teacher-structured instruction have proven to be useful (Moss, 2000). Different texts could mean using graphic formats, newspapers, magazines, and web formats as texts for reading. Odean (2001) believes boys are more likely to be interested in nonfiction than fiction. Reading an exciting first book in a quality series aloud can spark interest in the series for these readers. In addition, introducing exciting and current topics with photos or models and then offering books on those topics will stimulate interest, and many boys respond well to recommendations from their peers.

O'Reilly and Alexander (1998) studied the impact of using newspapers as texts for reading. They concluded that the newspaper helped balance the reading of girls who tended to read more fiction and less nonfiction, and many boys reading the newspaper continued to read the paper after the school project ended. For many boys, newspaper reading fits their interest in sports and cars. As another strategy for identifying books that boys would enjoy, Walter (1998) suggests finding books related to video games that boys enjoy.

Allington, Johnston, and Day (2002), in a large study of teacher behaviors in classrooms in five states, noted that exemplary fourth-grade teachers encouraged students to talk to each other and the teacher in conversational styles rather than giving information and asking students to repeat it on tests. A common feature of these teachers was asking "how," such as how could we find out or how could we answer that question. These teachers had students engaged in reading and writing all during the day and went beyond textbook assignments. They used graphic organizers to help students understand concepts and texts rather than as assessments, and they provided as many choices in reading material as possible. They also gave long-term assignments as opposed to short, isolated tasks. Exemplary teachers create "instructional plans based on their best analysis of student's needs and interests rather than from an externally imposed framework" (p. 466). These qualities of exemplary teachers are common to outstanding teachers of the intermediate grades.

HOW DO I CREATE A CLASSROOM ENVIRONMENT THAT WILL HELP ME TO BE AN EFFECTIVE TEACHER?

In this chapter, we will rely on the same organizing graphic that we used in Chapter 12. Please recall that this graphic (illustrated in Figure 13.1) describes curriculum through activities designed to help children learn language, learn through language, and learn about language. We will offer examples of activities that could be part of an appropriate curriculum for the intermediate grades and suggestions for how to adapt instruction for those children who are second language learners or who need support for their learning to be successful. A good place to begin planning for successful learning is with the physical arrangement of the classroom.

Classroom Arrangement

The physical arrangement of the classroom needs attention in every grade level. In Figure 13.2 we offer an example of an arrangement and a rationale for the choices in this example. In any classroom, the point is to have supplies that children will need readily available so that they can get them and put them away without disturbing other children. In the intermediate years, much of the children's work will be done independently and in small groups, and the room arrangement should facilitate such work. Examine the room arrangement illustrated in Figure 13.2 as we describe the details of the arrangement.

Beginning at the entrance to the room, the back of a shelf unit serves as a place for the attendance board, announcements, reminders, and lunch information, all of which the children are expected to complete independently. Children can move their names from one side of the board labeled "not here" to the side labeled "present today." A calendar can be placed

Figure 13.1
Balanced Reading Program

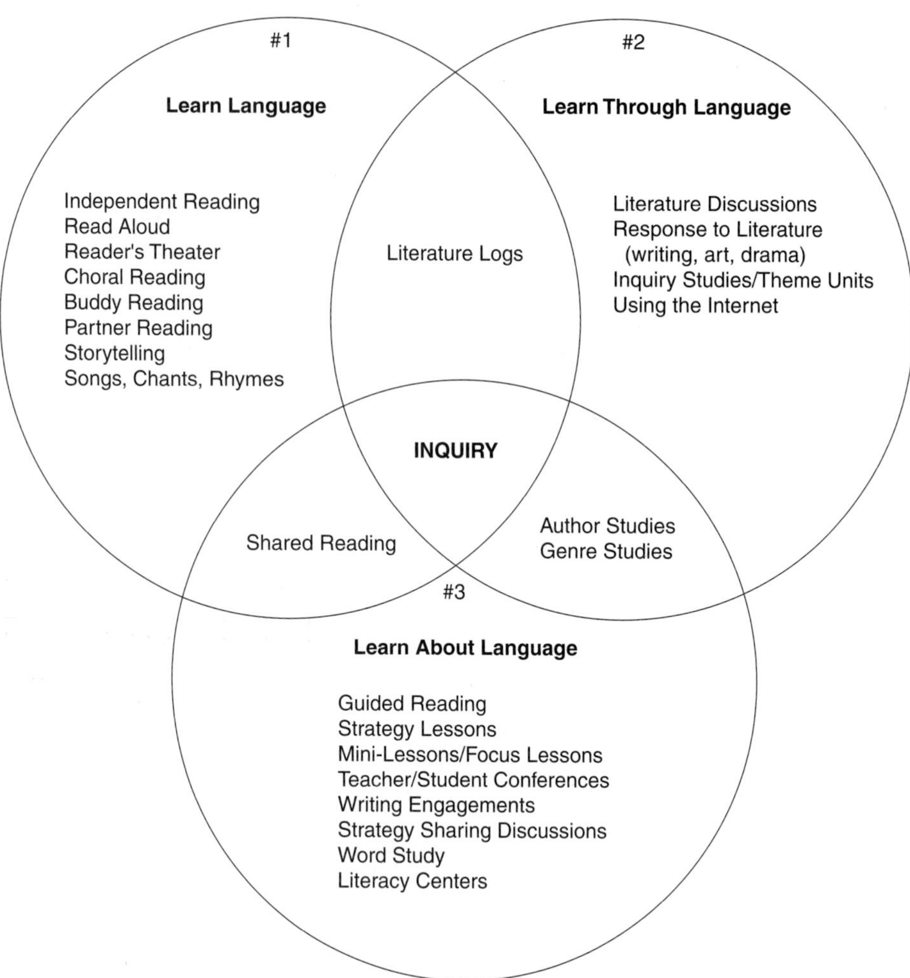

Source: Adapted from Short, K.G. (1999). The Search for "Balance" in a Literature-Rich Curriculum. *Theory into Practice, 38*(3), 130–137.

here, marked with important dates or reminders of special events. The lunch information may be collected by asking children to place a tongue depressor with their name on it in the pockets marked "brought lunch," "milk only," or "hot lunch" (depending on the information needed at your school).

Continuing on to the right is the computer and writing center. Supplies such as paper and dictionaries are stored on the shelves. The computers are available for each child to use at least one hour each week. The space under the shelves in this area is used for various word wall projects or charts of words the children collect.

The next area is the library with shelves on two sides and a sofa on the third side. Several comfortable beanbag chairs or large floor pillows should be available for comfortable reading. The listening center is located behind the sofa. The corner shelf unit is for storing the teacher's supplies and records. Please notice that this room plan does not have a teacher's desk. Teacher's desks are large and take up too much floor space to justify having one when the space could be used to accommodate the children's needs.

The classroom wall at the end of the classroom is covered with corkboard for mounting various charts and the children's work on various topics. The table here is for topical

Figure 13.2
Room Arrangement

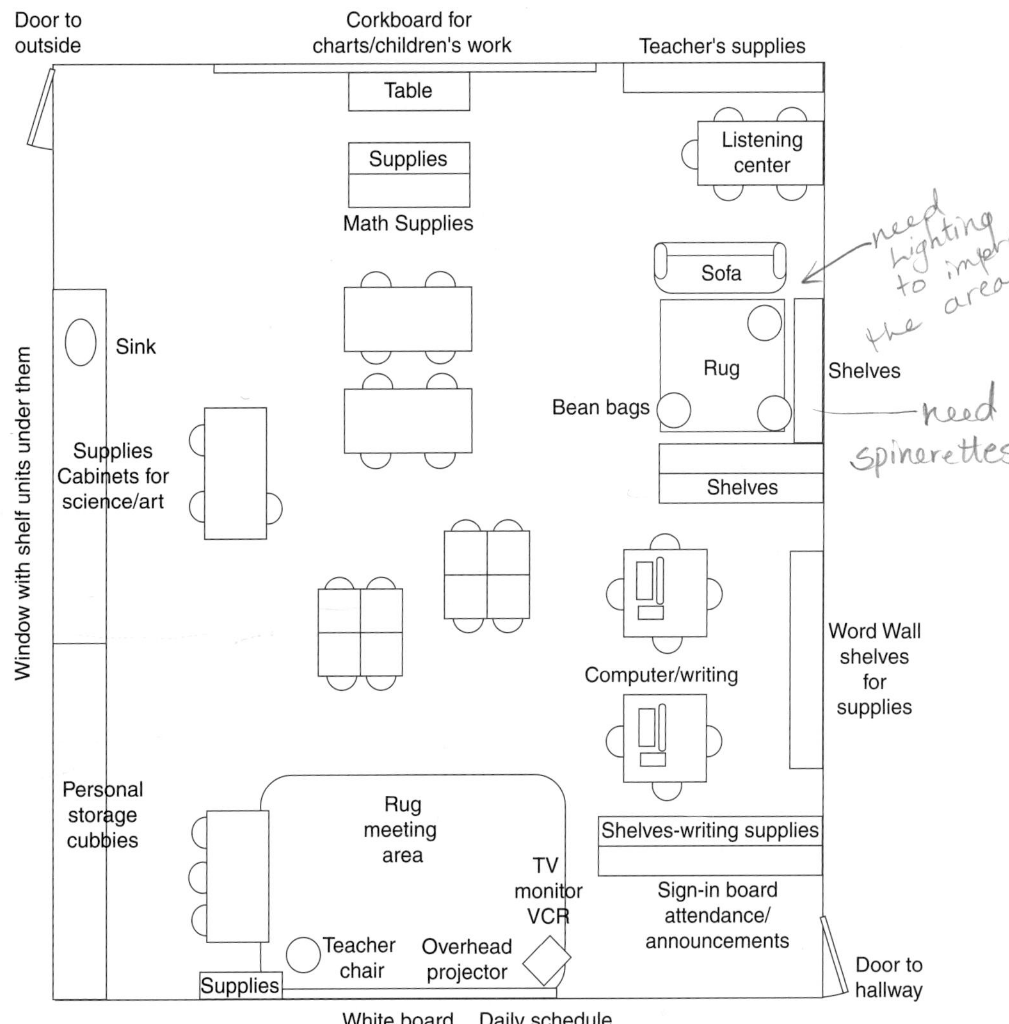

projects, research projects, or other projects related to the curriculum. A double set of shelves across from the table allow for storage of materials for any of these projects on one side and of math materials and games on the other side.

The outside classroom wall has windows with shelves underneath. These shelves are used for storage of art and science materials and the remainder for personal storage cubbies. A table near the sink and the cabinet where art and science materials are stored provide working space for projects that require water or other messy materials that will need to be cleaned up in the sink.

The fourth wall of the classroom contains a large dry erase board and a smaller dry erase board for the daily schedule of activities. In front of these boards is a large rug on which the children can gather for whole group activities or smaller groups can gather for instruction. An overhead projector, TV monitor, and VCR are kept in this area. Along one side of the area is a table for small group instruction such as guided reading. A small shelf unit holds all the teacher supplies for such instruction so that they are readily available.

Additional tables and chairs are arranged in the middle of the classroom and can be used for small group work or individual work. The expectation is not that all writing work

Figure 13.3
Daily Schedule

9:00–9:15	Silent Reading/Journal Writing
9:15–9:35	Morning Meeting, Read Aloud
9:35–10:15	Reading Workshop
10:15–10:35	Recess
10:35–11:00	Reading Workshop (Sharing for last few minutes)
11:00–11:30	Word Study
11:30–12:15	Lunch
12:15–1:15	Writing Workshop
1:15–2:00	Math
2:00–2:45	Social Studies/Science
2:45–3:30	Specials

would be done in the writing area, for example. Students might get the materials they need there and then move to one of these tables to do their work. Baskets or bins for holding writing folders and reading folders would be stored on the shelves in the writing center or library for easy access by the children. The tops of the shelves under the windows could be used for storing browsing boxes, displays related to topics of study, or other materials needed by the children.

Evaluating the classroom arrangement should be an ongoing activity. You will want to observe the children as they use the space and materials and make changes if there are problems. If you discover that children cannot reach some materials, that more work space is needed at a particular time of day, that too many children need to be in one area of the classroom at one time, then you and the children should talk about what changes could be made. Remember that the room arrangement is supposed to serve the needs of the learners in the classroom and that finding the best arrangement may take some experimentation.

Daily Schedule

Schedules for the day's activities need to be consistent, yet flexible. Consistent means that the children can count on regular times when they will have opportunities to do their work. On the other hand, teachers must be able to take advantage of special opportunities for teaching and learning that might arise in any day. An example of a possible schedule is illustrated in Figure 13.3.

Obviously all the specials cannot be scheduled for every class at the time period on the sample schedule. As specials are inserted into the day, you will arrange the work periods around them. Often teachers complain that they do not have enough time in the day for such long instructional periods, but children can stop what they are doing, leave their materials where they are, go to a special, then return and pick up their work where they left it.

Managing the Work Areas

Managing the work areas requires less control on the part of the teacher than is required for younger children. The children know how to get their reading folders for reading workshop and their writing folders for writing workshop, find a comfortable place to work, and get busy. They can make decisions about where they work without disturbing others and with

Figure 13.4
Daily Checklist

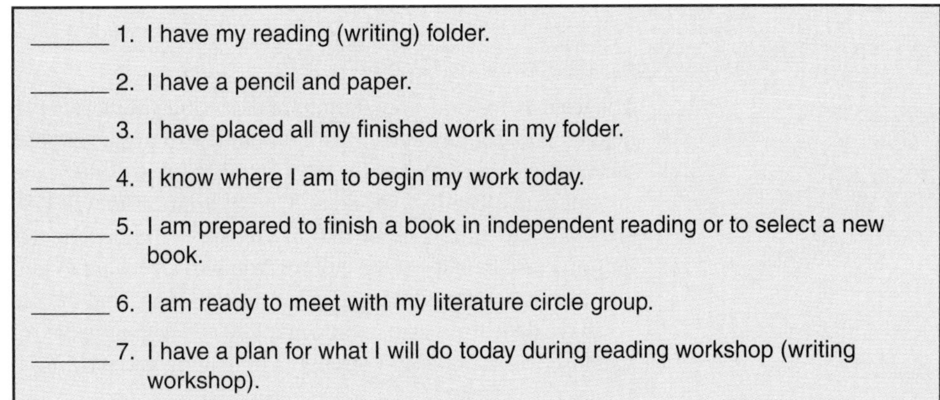
______ 1. I have my reading (writing) folder.

______ 2. I have a pencil and paper.

______ 3. I have placed all my finished work in my folder.

______ 4. I know where I am to begin my work today.

______ 5. I am prepared to finish a book in independent reading or to select a new book.

______ 6. I am ready to meet with my literature circle group.

______ 7. I have a plan for what I will do today during reading workshop (writing workshop).

only minimal guidance. One possibility for helping children make good choices in getting their work started is to use a self-checklist to list responsibilities. One example of questions to be checked is illustrated in Figure 13.4. This form could be used for either reading or writing workshop. When the children have demonstrated that these behaviors are automatic, you could discontinue use of the forms.

Another important management strategy is to go over the daily schedule so the children can help you decide what would be an appropriate noise level for each of the planned activities. Some activities will require quiet voices, such as writing workshop. Some can be a little louder such as completing projects in social studies or science, and some may require silence such as when a test must be administered. If children have some say in determining the appropriate noise level, they are much more likely to be cooperative about being quiet when quiet is needed. A classroom "rule" that has worked well for many teachers is "you cannot do anything in this class that interferes with someone else's learning." Children at these ages can understand this policy and monitor their behavior accordingly.

Instructional Materials

Middle grade classrooms need large classroom libraries that cover a wide variety of genres and a wide variety of reading levels (as described in Chapter 11). Books for guided reading or literature circles need to be in sets of six or eight, and many books must be available for independent reading. Krashen (1999) has stated that the number of books available to students is highly correlated with high achievement in reading. If children do not have access to a wide choice of reading materials, then they will read less and not improve their reading as quickly as children who read more.

In addition to books, intermediate grade students should have access to magazines such as *Ranger Rick, Boy's Life, National Geographic, Sports Illustrated for Kids,* and *Newsweek Junior.* Newspapers offer reading that appeals to a broad range of interests such as sports stories, fashion stories, and human interest stories, so classrooms need subscriptions to local newspapers.

In addition to reading materials, classrooms for children of this age group need charts, chart paper, sentence strips, paper for constructing bulletin boards or displays, butcher paper, newsprint, and various other kinds of paper. They also need a variety of markers, crayons, pencils, colored chalk, and other writing instruments. Individual white boards with dry erase markers and erasers are very helpful for whole or small group instruction.

WHAT ASSESSMENTS WILL I USE TO GET STARTED IN THE INSTRUCTIONAL PROGRAM?

You need to do some preparation for assessing your learners before school starts. Check student records for any students for whom IEPs have been developed and note the goals from the year-end conferences for these students. Also, check the records for any students who are not native English speakers. One of your tasks will be to determine what language is spoken in the child's home and, if you are not knowledgeable about the child's culture, to do some research about the culture. You will also want to know if any of your students were enrolled in a summer reading program, and if so, find the records from that program. Once you have done this basic homework, you can begin to plan for the assessments that will help you discover each child's strengths in reading and writing.

Assessing Reading

On the first day of school, provide a large number of books of many levels of difficulty and about many topics from which the children may select a book to begin reading independently. You can observe carefully how the children make their selections and if they find a satisfactory book quickly. Record which children start to read several books before they finally find one to read, and note the children who do not find a book at all. Attend to those children who know what they are looking for and select an appropriate book quickly.

Be prepared with several books, riddles, jokes, selections of poetry, news items, or other material that you want to read aloud in the first few days. You may begin with picture books, even though you will probably select a novel to read by chapters after a few days. Picture book reading can help you judge interests and past reading experiences. For example, if you read *Fortune-Tellers* (Alexander, 1992), you would be able to determine from the discussion if the children understood the theme of hearing what you want to hear and if they understood the humor in the story. If the children can discuss the setting and style of a book, then this helps you judge their experience with reading and their experience with discussions following reading.

Ask the children to complete a *Motivation to Read Profile* Reading Survey (Gambrell, Palmer, Codling, & Mazzoni, 1996) and the general reading conversational interview from the same source. During independent reading time, you can administer the *Qualitative Reading Inventory III* (Leslie & Caldwell, 2000) to several children each day until you have assessed all students. With your observations, the children's responses to the QRI and their responses to the Motivation to Read interviews, you are ready to start selecting children for various small group instructional activities, such as shared and guided reading.

Assessing Writing

Ask children to do some writing so that you can get an idea about their writing abilities by the end of the first week. Some teachers write a letter to the students telling about themselves before school begins, and they ask the students to write a letter to them on the first day of school. If you have not written such a letter, you can take a box of artifacts that represent important aspects of your life, personal photo albums, and anything else that you think will help the children know about you and then introduce yourself using what you have brought. You could ask the children to write a letter to you about themselves, bring a box of artifacts about themselves, or create a short report about themselves to share with the class.

Analyze carefully the writing from the letters or reports described previously, and ask the children to complete the *Writer Self-Perception Scale* (Bottomley, Henk, & Melnick, 1997). After several more writing samples have been obtained from the children, you might want to administer the *Test of Written Language 3* (Hammill, & Larsen, 1996) to those two or three children about whom you are puzzled and unsure of what they can do as writers. A careful examination of children's writing reveals their strengths in composition, the use of mechanics, and spelling. From these writing samples, you can select appropriate content for the focus lessons in writing workshop. For example, if you find that most of your students know how to use quotation marks appropriately, then you might select learning to use apostrophes to mark possession as a focus lesson. The curriculum guide spells out what skills and abilities are expected of children in your grade level, and you can select from those goals the one you believe is most reasonable to begin with given your students' current abilities.

Assessing English Language Learners

Although you must pay attention to the oral language development of all your students, those who are not native speakers of English will require specific observations. Try to learn about the children's oral language through observation of their interactions with others in the classroom and in instructional experiences rather than relying on standardized tests of language that test parts of language and not the whole of it. Try to learn what kinds of scaffolds children will need to become successful in different tasks. For example will they need pictures of some vocabulary terms, or will they need to buddy read with a native English speaker for a specific task?

Most importantly, you should maintain an attitude that being bilingual is an advantage rather than a deficit. If you look for what these children can do and can bring to the classroom as learners, rather than at their lack of English language skills, you will find much that will help you think of them as capable learners who can succeed. The observations you make should be of authentic language use across a variety of situations. Classroom language, playground language, and home language use may all present different views of how a child uses language for real communication purposes. Halliday's work (1973) on the functions of language can guide your observations in the classroom. Figure 13.5 is a chart that can help you assess the use of language in the classroom.

Instrumental language refers to the language used in order to achieve one's goals. For example, a child might ask for a piece of paper or a quiet place to work. Regulatory language refers to the language used to control the behavior of others such as saying, "Please stop leaning on my desk while I am writing." Interactional language is the whole category of language used to continue interactions such as "please," "thank you," "can I ask you a question," "can you do me a favor," and so on. Personal language is that which is used to express one's thoughts about content topics, classroom environments, and so on. One might say, for example, "I like the research center over in the corner because it is quieter there." Imaginative language is the language used in poetry or in playful experiences. One might say, "The snow was as white as milk," or, "The sky is the home for the fog." Heuristic language is the language used to get information such as the why questions children ask so often. Informative language is language used to provide information such as an oral report or the language of show and tell.

Just as you look for strengths in all your students, you will look for strengths in your English language learners.

Figure 13.5
Assessing Language Use

Name: ____________________
(individual, small group, large group observed)

Time: ____________________
(time of day)

Setting: ____________________
(physical setting and what happened prior to observation)

Activity: ____________________
(activity, including topic/subject area)

LANGUAGE FUNCTION	EXAMPLES
Instrumental	
Regulatory	
Interactional	
Personal	
Imaginative	
Heuristic	
Informative	

Note: Check each time a language function is heard and/or record examples.

Source: From Pinnell, G. S.: Ways to look at the functions of children's language (2002) in Power, B.M., Hubbard, R.S.: *Language Development: A Reader for Teachers* © 2002. Reprinted by permission of Pearson Education, Inc., Upper Saddle River, NJ.

HOW DO I PLAN INSTRUCTION FOR GRADES 3–5?

Planning the instructional program for the intermediate grades is always an interesting challenge. Children in these grades have mastered many literacy skills, such as basic reading, writing, responding to what they have read, listening, and viewing for enjoyment or for learning. As the graphic at the beginning of the chapter indicates, the curriculum revolves around inquiry. Such a focus on inquiry helps teachers to plan authentic skill and strategy instruction and helps children to make the connections between what they are learning to do in school and their interests and needs, both in school and out of school.

Topics for Inquiry

Many topics of inquiry can be useful for organizing curriculum in the intermediate grades. Some examples are rivers, pathways, communication, space, and the human body. Each of these themes would provide many authentic learning experiences and opportunities to meet the district curriculum standards. However for the beginning inquiry cycle, a study of folk literature has been selected. This topic provides numerous possibilities for instruction. For example, there are folk stories at all levels of reading difficulty, such as novel length stories and epic poems or short, easy-to-read fables. These stories will appeal to both boys and girls (stories are not usually labeled boy stories or girl stories, but some boys of this age would not read what they considered to be a girl story). Folk literature was originally told to audiences of all ages and certainly was not considered to be just for children, so it offers many possibilities for a mixed ability group.

Folk stories can be romantic, such as the stories of princesses rescued by Prince Charming, or action adventures, such as the tall tales. A study of folk literature can be organized in multiple ways. For example, variants of one story from different cultures could be compared, or children could study the subgenres of folk literature such as fables, myths, and legends. Another choice might be to study the stories by motif, such as transformation stories or magical object stories. Other choices might be to study the basic stories and then the tongue-in-cheek variations of some of them or to study folk tales from around the world. Each of these options has advantages. For example, if the curriculum called for learning the geography of the world, then choosing folk literature from around the world would be a good choice. If the social studies guidelines called for a study of the regions of the United States, then a focus on tall tales from the various regions would be a good choice, as would Native American stories from the different regions of the country. For this example, the study will be organized around the subgenres of folk literature.

Inquiry: Folk Literature

Introduce the study of folk literature by developing a concept map on the board beginning with folk literature in the center and subgenres around the outside edge. Ask children what stories they know that they consider folk stories and add these titles in the categories of folk literature such as fables, myths and pourquoi stories, legends, beast tales, tall tales, wonder tales or fairy tales, cumulative tales, noodlehead stories, trickster stories, and realistic tales. At this point, some categories may not have titles listed under them. Leave this map up in the classroom so that students can add titles as they read. An example of the concept map is illustrated in Figure 13.6.

Help the children define folk literature and share examples of stories from the various categories over several days. Emphasize the oral beginnings of folk tales, and note that the authors of the stories are unknown. In modern books of traditional stories, the title page often lists a reteller rather than an author. An opening note may explain the source of the story from which the person retold the story, and sometimes the authors explain how many sources were consulted before they adapted the tale for the book.

Learning Research Skills

Folk literature can be the topic of study as children learn various research skills, such as selecting appropriate sources of information, note taking, organizing information, and presenting information in a variety of formats. Before children undertake independent research, you might want to conduct one project as a whole class so that you can teach all the parts of a research project. The first task in conducting research is to choose a good research question.

Selecting the Research Question. It takes time and instruction for children to learn to ask a good research question. They often begin with questions that require only a yes or no answer and therefore fail to provide any in-depth knowledge. Such a question related to folk

Figure 13.6
Concept Map for Folk Literature

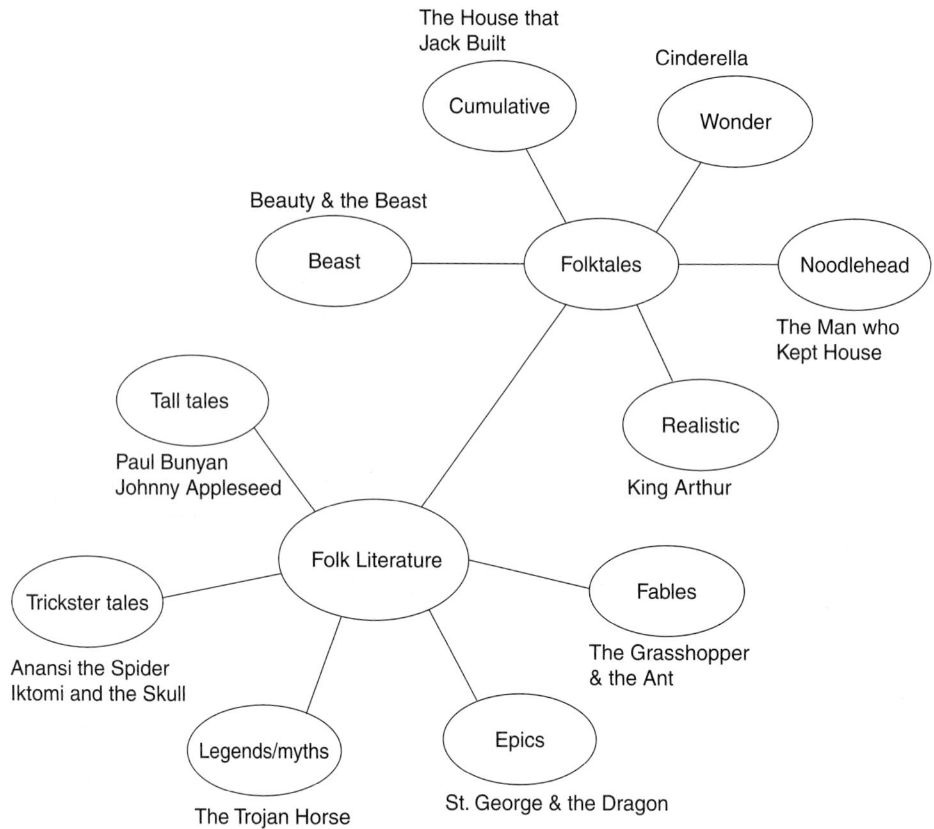

literature might be, "What kind of story is _____?" Other questions are so broad that it is impossible to answer them. An example would be "Why do people like folk literature?"

For this project, you would offer several questions and then help children select three or four questions to answer. Possible questions might include: Who were the Brothers Grimm? Who was Hans Christian Anderson? Who was Charles Perrault? What are the characteristics of a pourquoi tale? What are the characteristics of a trickster tale? How are beast tales and wonder tales alike and different? How are stories from Puerto Rico like stories from Mexico (or any two cultures represented in your classroom), and how are they different? Where did we get the names of the constellations, the days of the week, and the months of the year? How are symbols and names from mythology used in modern marketing?

If you have completed a classroom research project and you think the students are prepared for individual projects, they would select research questions of their own.

Gathering Information. Children seeking information on a topic must learn how to predict what resources will be helpful in finding the information and how to use the resources once they have found them. This might be a good time for focus lessons on using the table of contents and the index of various kinds of reference books. Many teachers have discovered that allowing children to go to the web in the beginning of their research is too overwhelming. There is so much material and it is so difficult to evaluate that these teachers ask their students to begin their studies with print searches for information. When they have narrowed their topic sufficiently, they can use the web for additional re-

Using the library is a critical part of learning to do research.

search. In using print and Internet resources, children need to learn how to take notes rather than copying the information verbatim from the source. Note-taking skills require several focus lessons with demonstrations of how good note taking is critical for collecting information.

Many teachers have recommended that children using the web are not allowed to print the information from a site in their initial research (unless a child has special needs that would make reading on screen difficult). They can note the URL and take notes on the content, but are much less likely to copy the content if they are not allowed to print it. Figure 13.7 is an example of a page that could be used for recording notes from several sources that relate to the questions being researched. Others prefer having children use small index cards for this recording step. If you give children only a small space to write, they will not be tempted to copy too much information.

Another research skill that is important in the information gathering stage is the triangulation of data. In other words, do the various sources agree or disagree on a given topic? If they disagree, can you find a third source to help answer the question? This step is part of the evaluation of a data source. Children need to learn to question the knowledge and background of the author of the material, the author's purpose in writing the material, and the publication date of the material.

Creating Final Questions. As children engage in research, they may find that their questions need to be revised in light of information they have found. If they had started with a question that asked about the elements of a trickster story, they might decide after some investigating that it would be better if they compared trickster stories from two or more countries of origin. Some guidance here will help children select higher-level thinking questions that will provide depth to their study.

Writing, Revising, and Polishing Information. At this stage, children evaluate their information, select the most important information, and write a rough draft of their findings.

Figure 13.7
Recording Form for Research

Name ______________________ Date ____________

Topic of Study ______________________________

	Resource 1	Resource 2	Resource 3
Question 1			
Question 2			
Question 3			
Question 4			

As with any other writing, they need to revise and polish the draft until it is the best product possible. They may make a decision here about how to present the information they have found, and the draft will reflect that decision. For example, if they are going to create a PowerPoint presentation, their draft might be written with the headings as the lines on the presentation and the information under each heading in the notes section of the presentation.

Learning How to Credit the References They Have Used. An important skill to be learned is making sure that readers know from where the information came. They should be able to retrieve that reference if they want to read more about a topic. Provide children with a model for citing a book and a web site and fill in the model with several examples. This is a difficult skill for novice researchers, so plan to take plenty of time to help children learn to do it well. Duffield (1997/1998) has summarized the stages of a research project in Figure 13.8. This summary outlines the four stages of a research project. You might want to reproduce this summary on a large chart to help students see what the major steps are in completing a good research project, and you might also want to create a checklist from this summary that will help students keep track of progress on their projects. You might leave enough space on the checklist to have students enter a few words to make a record of what they have accomplished.

Presenting the Final Project. To complete their research project, students need to select a format for presenting what they have learned. Some possible projects related to folk literature include the following:

- Creating a diorama representing an important scene in a story
- Creating a PowerPoint presentation for the class

Figure 13.8
Summary of Steps in Research

A Student-Centered Research Model

Goals—Objectives—Standards

Presearch

RESEARCH QUESTIONS	SEARCH STRATEGY	REPORT FORMAT	EVALUATE
What is the topic? What do you want to know? What questions are to be answered?	Where could you find the information? How could you find it?	What will you do with the information? What type of report? Judging criteria?	Do your plans go together? Revise as required.

Search

LOCATE	ANSWER	EVALUATE
Use the search strategy to find the information.	Use the information to answer the research questions.	Was the information adequate? Revise as required.

Interpret

EVALUATE	ANALYZE	EVALUATE
What are the sources? Is the information credible and valid?	Do the sources agree? What are the differences and why?	How does the information fit together? Can differences be resolved?

Report

PREPARE AND PRESENT	EVALUATE
Prepare the report according to the report form. Present the report.	Does the report answer the research questions? Does it meet the report criteria?

Source: J.A. Duffield. (1997/1998). Conducting Research: A Student-Centered Model. *Childhood Education, 74*(2), 67.

Figure 13.9
Self-Assessment in Research

Name ______________________ Date ____________

How Am I Doing?

Self-Reflection

1. An interesting fact I learned today was ______________________

2. A book I found helpful today was ______________________

3. I'm having trouble ______________________

4. Next time I'm going to ______________________

5. I use my research time: (circle one)

(A) wisely on task (B) I am wasting my time

(C) a little of both

Source: J. Servis. (1999). *Celebrating the Fourth: Ideas and Inspiration for Teachers of Grade Four.* Portsmouth, NH: Heinemann.

- Writing a song and sharing it with the class
- Writing a script for a skit and producing it for the class
- Writing an article for the school newspaper
- Creating an interactive bulletin board
- Creating an Imovie that summarizes their research
- Creating a videotape of a report on their research
- Creating a museum exhibit accompanied by explanatory cards

The choice of a project will depend on the kind of research done, but children need to know that researchers present their findings to other audiences or use their research in some way, such as in describing the setting or historical details of a book, movie, or theater production; publishing their research in a book or magazine; and sharing their findings orally.

A self-reflection assessment will help children think about what they did well and what they could improve for the next round of research. One example of such a form is illustrated in Figure 13.9.

Figure 13.10
Curriculum Graphic, Circle 1

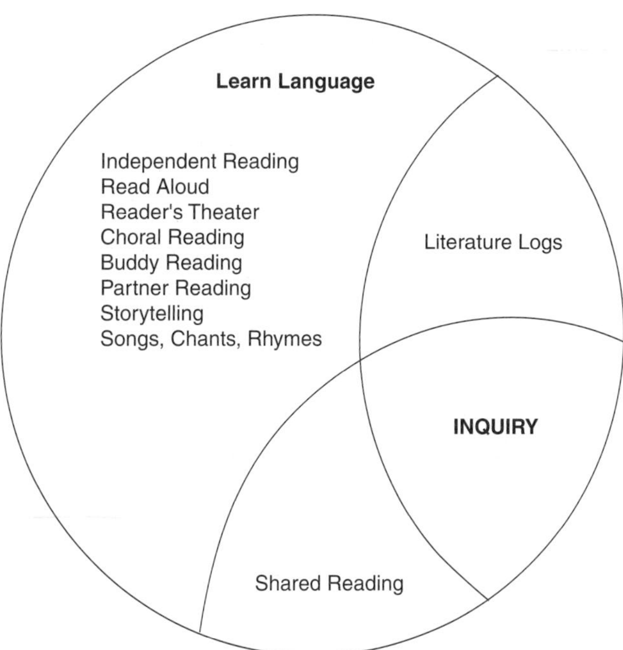

Source: Adapted from Short, K.G. (1999). The Search for "Balance" in a Literature-Rich Curriculum. *Theory into Practice, 38*(3), 130-137.

Inquiry is at the hub of the three circles in the graphic. As the graphic at the beginning of the chapter indicates, the first circle will focus on learning language.

Learn Language

Beginning with the first circle of the graphic (which is repeated here in Figure 13.10), you will notice that this circle labeled "Learn Language" contains independent reading, reading aloud, book talk, reader's theater, choral reading, buddy reading, partner reading, storytelling, and songs, chants, and rhymes. As a topic of study, folk literature will provide numerous opportunities for learning language.

Independent Reading. Folk literature is a rich source of material for independent reading. Such literature is available for all levels of reading ability. Aesop's fables may be read by readers who are just becoming independent readers. Many of the tall tales and wonder stories offer a challenge to intermediate grade readers, but the predictable form helps readers cope with the vocabulary demands. For very skilled readers, the Greek and Roman myths (with their difficult names) and book-length versions of some of the stories, such as *Ella Enchanted* (Levine, 1997) or *Beauty* (McKinley, 1978) offer an appropriate challenge.

Read-Aloud. Teachers can read aloud a selection from each of the categories on the concept map and then discuss with the children how that selection is classified as a particular kind of story. For more mature readers, you would note that stories can be classified in several ways. For example, if you read "Beauty and the Beast" as a wonder tale, you would note that it could also be classified as a transformation tale. For older readers in this group, you might also note the origins of the story in the myth of *Cupid and Psyche* (Mayer, 1996).

Choral Reading and Chants. Many of the traditional folk stories have repeated chants and poetry embedded in them. For example, in the story of the "Fisherman and His Wife," the verse that the fisherman says to the fish is repeated throughout the book. In Easton's (1992) retelling of the Grimm version of this story, the old man says. "Flounder, flounder of the sea, Come, for I am calling thee! My wife, whose name is Isobil, Has a wish against my will!" In Spear's (1992) retelling, the verse is "Dolphin, dolphin in the sea, Swim close by and speak to me, For my wife, sweet Isabil, Wills not as I'd have her will." In Stewig's (1988) retelling, the verse is, "Oh man, oh man, if man you be, Or flounder, flounder in the sea. Such a tiresome wife I've got. For she wants what I do not." In Bells's (1989) version, the rhyme is, "Flounder, flounder in the sea, Swim to shore and speak to me. For my good-wife Isabel/ Asks for more than I dare tell." These chants could be performed by one reader or by a group of readers speaking in unison in a telling or reading of the story.

Storytelling. One of the advantages of folk literature is that the stories have been honed to their essential elements over the centuries, so they provide excellent sources for story-telling and reader's theater. Storytelling is a skill that can be learned and can help children develop poise and confidence in speaking in front of a group that is rarely achieved with

Sharing a story builds skills in language use and in understanding story structure.

other types of oral performance. First, we are all storytellers as we recount our daily lives to others, and secondly, learning what will interest the audience and mastering the timing in the delivery that good storytellers exhibit can be useful skills throughout life. One young lady of our acquaintance was quite comfortable visiting a college classroom and telling a story to college students when she was a middle school student. She explained how much the storytelling training that she had as an intermediate grade student helped her feel self-confident in front of an audience.

Reader's Theater. Folk literature is an excellent source of material for reader's theater experiences. Reader's theater (described in Chapter 9) is an important strategy for building fluency, vocabulary skills, and knowledge of story structure. Many folk tales have wonderful dialogue and would lend themselves to adaptations for reader's theater. Some examples are *The Four Gallant Sisters* (Kimmel, 1992), *Jack and the Beanstalk* (Beneduce, 1999), and *The Shark God* (Martin, 2001).

Language Patterns. Another quality of good folk literature retellings is the use of interesting language, not simplified too much. In Kellogg's (1991) retelling of *Jack and the Beanstalk,* he uses *peltered* as a synonym for *dashed, larder* in describing the kitchen storage areas, and *start shop* meaning to go into a business of some kind. Marcellino's (1990) *Puss in Boots* uses *legacy, sow thistle, harebrained, warren, rascal, preserve,* and *affably.* The reading of folk literature offers opportunities for vocabulary development.

In addition, folk literature can help young readers recognize the uses of figurative language and language that is meant to present a signal to the reader. Remember that these learners are close to a completely literal use of language and that they are just realizing that language can be used in nonliteral ways. For example, the beginning of fairy tales "Once upon a time" is a deliberate invitation to suspend reality and attend to magic. Endings often serve the same purpose in reverse. "They lived happily ever after" or "My tale's told out" are stock phrases that signal to the reader or listener the story is over and now we are back in real time in a real world.

Folk literature often presents challenges in language patterns that children may need to reread before they can make sense of them. Please recall the examples of the lines from the "Fisherman and his Wife," when the fisherman says of his wife, "Wills not as I would have her will" or the sentence in *Herschel and the Hanukkah Goblins* (Kimmel, 1985) that reads, "Well could he believe that goblins lived here." The use of language in figurative rather than literal ways is also an element of reading folk literature that may demand strategy instruction before children can comprehend the stories. In *Herschel and the Hanukkah Goblins* (Kimmel, 1985), one sentence reads, "Herschel's blood turned to water, but he did not lose courage." Another example is found in *Pandora* (Burleigh, 2002); when describing her curiosity, the sentence reads, "Instead, it grew, like a clinging vine. Tighter and tighter around her waking thoughts" (unpaged).

Other reading challenges are presented by such books as Pullman's (2000) version of *Puss in Boots* in which speech balloons in the illustrations and several panels of illustration on some pages must be interpreted in order to understand the story.

Literature Logs. Literature logs, which are records of what has been read and responses to that reading, help children make the transition from what they read to learning to write about their reading experiences. One outcome of good discussions and literature response  logs is that children can begin to make connections between their present reading and other reading or experiences. For example, if children know what it means when we label a story a tall tale, then they will recognize that *Maniac Magee* (Spinelli, 1990) is a tall tale. To read

Figure 13.11
Curriculum Graphic, Circle 2

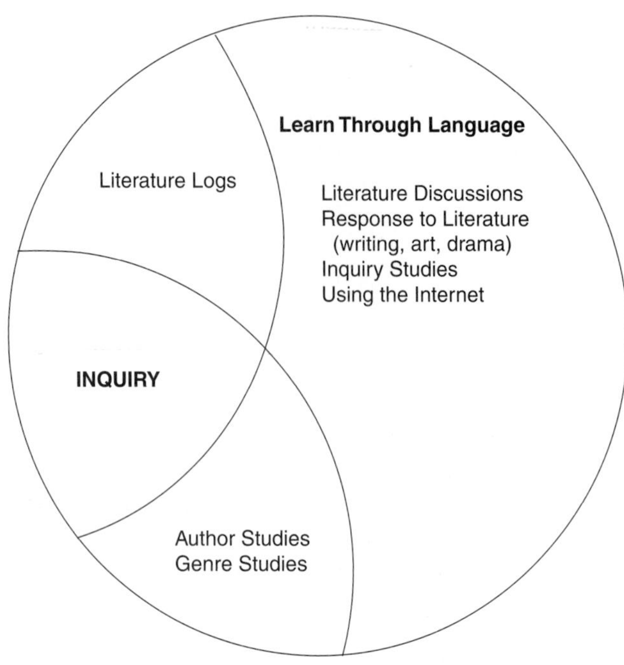

Source: Adapted from Short, K. G. (1999). The Search for "Balance" in a Literature-Rich Curriculum. *Theory into Practice, 38*(3), 130-137. Copyright by the College of Education, the Ohio State University. All right reserved.

Maniac Magee as a realistic story would make it difficult to comprehend. The Caldecott winner *Hey Al* (Yorinks, 1986) is a fable, and if children are familiar with the structure of a fable, they will use that information as an aid in comprehending the story.

Studies of folk literature can help young readers understand that the characters in folk stories are flat and typically represent only one character trait. The usual characters in folk literature are so good that they are perfect, so bad that they are readily classified as evil, or so stupid that they make us laugh at their moronic behavior. Many authors who write in genres other than folk stories have found it convenient to use a flat character while other characters in a story are developed and rounded. Fern in *Charlotte's Web* (White, 1952) is a relatively flat character so that the attention is given to the development of Wilbur and Templeton.

Literature logs are in the intersection between circles 1 and 2, learn language and learn through language. Learn through language includes literature discussions, responses to literature (writing, art, drama), inquiry studies, and theme units. The second circle is reproduced in Figure 13.11.

Learn Through Language

Good literature discussions of folk literature will help children recognize the patterns found in folk stories. For example, many European stories have three incidents in them, while a fable typically has only one incident. Folk stories were told to help codify the mores of the culture, and children can begin to recognize what was important in a culture by comparing the themes of the stories. Folk tale themes are so apparent that young learners can recognize them easily. This recognition of theme will help children recognize themes in other literature when the theme is usually not so obvious. Folk literature is very important in connecting to content material. Many of the myths that explain natural phenomena can be used to connect to the modern scientific explanation for things we observe in nature. For example, the myth of Arachne explains why spiders spin (Simons & Simons, 1991b) and Dionysus is featured in a myth that explains the calling of dolphins (Simons & Simons, 1991a). Of course there are many other connections, such as explanations for the seasons, day and night, and names of the constellations.

Social Studies Connections. For social studies connections, mythology can help children sort out what values were held by the ancient Greeks and Romans and how those values match (or fail to match) the values held in American society today. For example, what kinds of behaviors were punished (greed or jealousy), and what were rewarded (kindness and honesty)? The content of many Greek and Roman myths is not suitable for young children, and you must be selective about which myths you ask children to read and the web sites you might use in a study of myths.

Another social studies connection is creating a map of the United States and locating the origins of various folk tale characters on the map. Children could draw the characters, cut them out, and mount them on the map in the proper locations. Of course, the features of the regions are related to the characters whose stories originated there. Paul Bunyan would not have been a part of the folklore in the southwest where there are no huge forests.

Writing as a Response to Folk Literature. Folk literature is especially useful as a stimulus for writing. Children who are reading fables can learn to write their own fables. As with any writing experience when you wish to teach a particular format of writing, you would want to follow these steps to build success into the writing experience.

1. The first step is to read many examples. You might choose some fables for read-alouds, and students could read others independently.
2. After reading the examples, lead the children to discover the form of a fable (animal characters, one short incident, and a stated moral).
3. Write a fable as a whole group. Act as scribe while the children dictate what to write. You might put three boxes on the whiteboard and label them *characters, incident,* and *moral.* Often the writer of a fable begins with the moral and then thinks of characters and incidents to illustrate the moral. Children can write morals about school, friendship, or any number of other "lessons."
4. Write a fable as a small group. If some children have not quite understood the fine points of writing a fable, they can get help from their peers without anyone knowing that they were feeling unsure about their ability to write a fable.
5. Write a fable individually. After the small group experience, you may feel that you need to repeat the activity in a small group one more time before you ask children to complete a fable individually. Make sure every child is successful in completing this writing task.

Other types of folk literature are also wonderful examples for writing that the children could complete successfully. An example is the writing of a short myth to explain some natural phenomena. Children can follow the same steps described previously to create a myth that explains some intriguing element of nature. Of course, you might want them to follow up with the scientific reasons why the phases of the moon exist, but the explanation myths are interesting and will actually help children remember the scientific facts.

Children will also enjoy writing tall tales. The characters in tall tales are so exaggerated that students can write great character descriptions, poetry (Shel Silverstein wrote a poem about Paul Bunyan), or tall tales of their own. One way of publishing the tall tales is in a zig-zag book that opens vertically. When the book is unfolded, the tale is really "tall." The directions for making such a book are illustrated in Figure 13.12.

Figure 13.12
Directions for Tall Tale Zig-Zag Book

Zig-zag Book

A zig-zag book is one made from a long strip of paper folded in a zig-zag fashion. It requires no sewing, but the folding must be very carefully done if a neat result is to be achieved.

Zig-zag books have many uses:

1. Sequential stories
2. Autobiographies, showing stages of the person's life
3. Life cycles of plants and animals
4. Panels combining picture and description, such as of favorite animals
5. Cyclical events, like seasons
6. And many other possibilities.

Books, of course, can be made in any size. The dimensions used in these directions are included just as an example:

White construction paper: 2 sheets originally 12″ × 18″, cut to 6″ × 18″ with folded panels to 4½″ × 6″

Cardboard covers: 2 pieces 5½″ × 6½″

Cover paper or fabric: 2 pieces 7½″ × 8½″

1. Cut 2 pieces of cardboard for the book covers. These pieces will need to be 1″ larger on all four sides than the inside writing paper.
2. Cut 2 pieces of construction paper or fabric (designed with original artwork) at least 1″ larger on all four sides than the cardboard. Using original artwork as the design on the cover paper or fabric affords the book's creator a much greater sense of pride in authorship.
3. Glue the construction paper or fabric onto the cardboard. Use wallpaper paste for the glue. Wallpaper paste works better than glue because it spreads more easily and smoothly, is less expensive, and is more "forgiving" if a mistake occurs and the paper has to be pulled apart. Spread clean newspaper on a flat work surface. (Plain newsprint is even better, to avoid having black ink come off on the covers.)
   a. Turn construction paper or fabric upside down on a clean piece of newspaper.
   b. Use a wide brush to spread the glue evenly. Wide brushes are best because the glue dries so quickly. Spread the glue evenly over all the paper.
   c. Place the cardboard in the center of each glued paper or fabric. Do each cover one at a time because the glue dries so quickly.
   d. Turn in each corner and glue onto the cardboard. Don't pull too hard or the corners will puncture because they're wet from the glue and are weak.

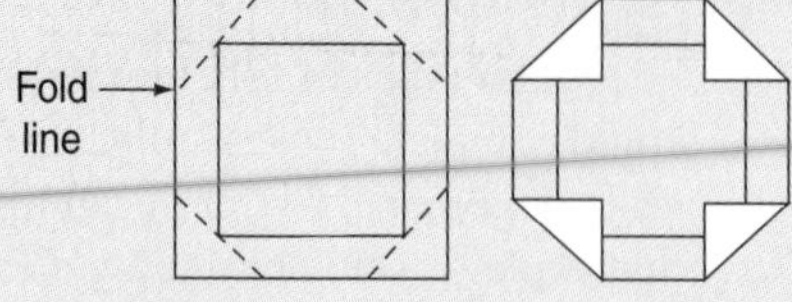

Source: Harp, B. & Brewer, J. A. (1996). *Reading and Writing: Teaching for the Connections.* Ft. Worth: Harcourt.

Figure 13.12
Continued

e. Lightly glue each turned down corner, since there has not yet been any glue on these corners.

f. Turn down each side panel onto the cardboard. Use the clean newspaper underneath to press over the paper that is being glued on the cardboard. This will help keep the paper and fingers clean. Remove the newspaper.

g. Repeat Steps a–f with the second piece of cardboard and the cover paper or fabric.

4. Set the paper- or fabric-covered cardboard pieces aside on a flat surface. Place heavy books on top of them so they don't permanently warp.

5. Fold two pieces of 12″ × 18″ white construction paper into four zig-zag accordion-pleat folds. Refold one piece into a stack. Trim down this rectangular stack so that it is ½″ smaller than the three sides of the cardboard. Then trim the other stack of white paper to the same size. The pages, of course, do not have to be white. "White" is used in these directions just to distinguish the writing pages from the other paper of the cover.

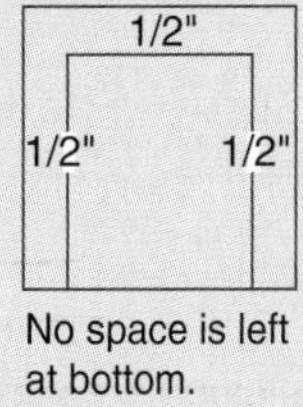

No space is left at bottom.

6. On a table, stand up the two folded stacks of white pages. Arrange them in an accordion-pleated way. Where the two pieces meet, overlap the two middle panels.

7. Smoothly glue or paste the two middle panels together, being *sure* all the pages are still arranged in an accordion-pleated manner.

8. Cut off and discard *one* end panel. That will leave six panels on each side. This will make the completed book open properly. (The last panel is cut off whenever there is an odd number of writing surfaces so the back opens properly. If three sets of folded papers are used, for example, there are ten writing panels. Since this is an even number, no panel needs to be cut off.)

9. Glue the two end panels of white construction paper onto the insides of the cardboard covers. Place the white pages on the cardboard so the ragged edges of the artwork paper or fabric are neatly covered. However, it is important to have one end *even* with the bottom of the cardboard so the book can stand up open for a display.

10. Place waxed paper or foil between the covers and the dry pages at both ends of the book for the 5 days the book is drying. If the foil or waxed paper is not placed in the book, the dampness from the glue will go through to the other pages and they will permanently wrinkle.

(Continued)

Figure 13.12
Directions for Tall Tale Zig-Zag Book *Continued*

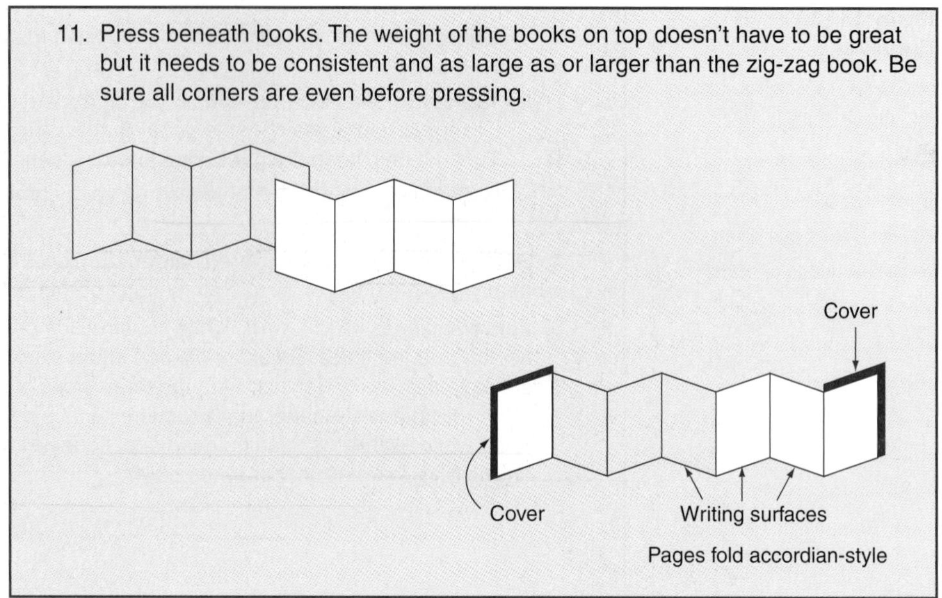

11. Press beneath books. The weight of the books on top doesn't have to be great but it needs to be consistent and as large as or larger than the zig-zag book. Be sure all corners are even before pressing.
Cover
Cover
Writing surfaces
Pages fold accordian-style

Go to the Weblinks in Chapter 13 on our Companion Website at www.prenhall.com/harp to find links to authors of folk stories and examples of Kamishibai.

Kamishibai. Another possibility for an activity based on folk literature is the Japanese storytelling form called *Kamishibai,* in which picture story cards are made that tell the story and a minimal text is written on the back of the card. The storyteller shows the cards one by one as they tell the stories. The audience cannot see the text. The storyteller has a minimal text to make sure that none of the story is left out, but it is told, not read.

Go to the Weblinks in Chapter 13 on our Companion Website at www.prenhall.com/harp to find links to pourquoi tales and sites where fourth graders have posted pourquoi tales they have written.

Go to the Weblinks in Chapter 13 on our Companion Website at www.prenhall.com/harp to find links detailing how to create a web quest as well as a sample web quest on female characters in tall tales.

Folk Literature on the Web. Internet projects are defined in many different ways. Some projects are huge and teachers from many locations participate in them by posting materials to a given site. Others may be projects such as tracking the progress of the Monarch butterflies on the web or following the course of a character that is mailed from school to school such as Flat Stanley (Leu, 2002). Internet projects are defined as projects in which a child has an assignment to complete each week and is prepared to share in a discussion of that project at the end of the week. For this topic, each child could be required to read a pourquoi tale of their choice from the web and share one or two facts about their tale with the group at Internet workshop time. In Figure 13.13, the schedule illustrates how each child in a class of 25 can have a half-hour of time alone on the computer and a half-hour with a partner.

Multiple resources can add variety and interest to a study of folk literature. For example, a web quest on the tall tale Paul Bunyan could be developed. In completing this web quest, students could learn about the setting, about the work of a lumberjack, and about Babe the Blue Ox through various sites on the web. They could compare whatever version of Paul Bunyan they are reading to other versions or compare the illustrations of several versions. They might make a chart of what a real lumberjack could do as compared to Paul Bunyan or find songs and/or poetry about lumberjacks and their work. Their project might be a skit, a poster, an Imovie, a PowerPoint presentation, or some other summary of their work.

Dramatic Responses to Folk Literature. Folk literature by definition has been passed down through the medium of oral storytelling and drama. Good storytellers add drama

Figure 13.13
Use of Internet Schedule

	Monday	Tuesday	Wednesday	Thursday	Friday
8:30-9:00	Michelle	Michelle/ Becky	Miguel/Emily	Shannon/ Cara	Cynthia/ Maria
9:00-9:30	Miguel	John/ Peter	Jeremy/Dave	Kati	Patti
9:30-10:00	***Class Meeting***	Ben	Aaron	Lisa	Rocca
10:00-10:30	Shannon	***PE***	Paul	***PE***	Andy
10:30-11:00	*Library*	Mike	Julio	Faith	Melissa
11:00-11:30	Cynthia	Eric	James	Linda	Sara
11:30-12:30	***Lunch***	***Lunch***	***Lunch***	***Lunch***	***Lunch***
12:30-1:00	Maria	Dave	Peter	Cara	Emily
1:00-1:30	Becky	Jeremy	Ben/Sara	Mike/Linda	John
1:30-2:00	Eric/James	Aaron/ Melissa	***Music***	Paul/Julio	***Internet Workshop***
2:00-2:30	Kati/Lisa		Faith/Andy	Patti/Rocca	

Source: D. J. Leu. (2002, November). Preparing Students for Their Literacy Future: Five Easy Steps to Integrating the Internet into Your Literacy Curriculum. Paper presented at New England Reading Association Conference, Newport, RI.

through their voices and the use of pacing and pauses to add flair to the story. Dramatic interpretations of folk literature are easy to plan and can be rewarding to participants. In addition to storytelling techniques, drama as a response to folk literature can include adaptations of stories and creative drama in which the actors invent the dialogue and actions to tell the story. Intermediate grade readers can dramatize fables like "The Boy Who Cried Wolf" and scenes from longer fairy tales, such as the scene in Cinderella when Cinderella confronts her stepsisters at the wedding. As they create dialogue for these dramatizations, they practice with a vocabulary and a register that are not their own, but drama can help them make it their own. Many students whose first language is not English credit drama with giving them a chance to learn vocabulary and to practice the pragmatic rules of speaking English.

Resources for studying folk literature include videotapes of many folk stories. These tapes can support readers who may need some help in reading the stories, or they can help children compare the reading of a folk tale and viewing a folk tale. They could select a story and think about how they would present it as a video by planning the background music, the voices of the readers, and visual effects that would add to the story. Of course, producing the video or an Imovie of their selection would be a valuable learning experience.

Learn About Language

Moving from learn through language to the third circle, learn about language, author studies and genre studies are in the intersection of these two circles. Folk literature is a genre study, of course, but many authors have significant collections of folk literature that would be interesting for an author study. You might choose an author who tells stories from a particular

Figure 13.14
Curriculum Graphic, Circle 3

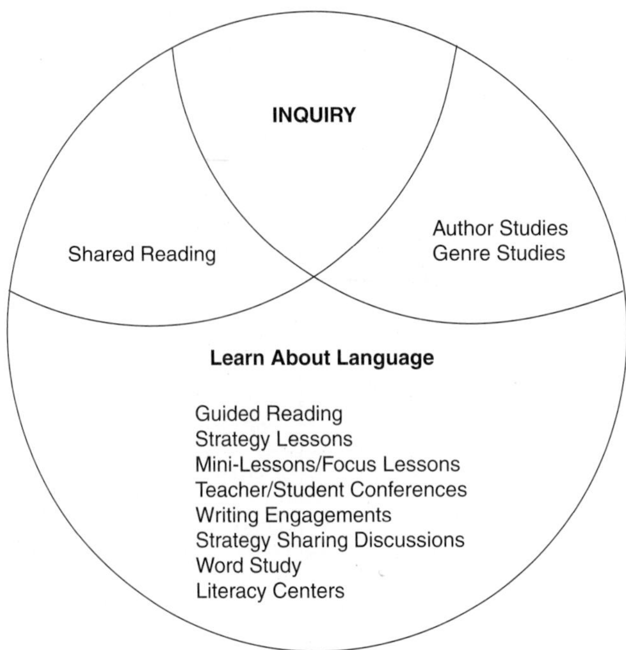

Source: Adapted from Short, K. G. (1999). The Search for "Balance" in a Literature-Rich Curriculum. *Theory into Practice, 38*(3), 130-137. Copyright by the College of Education, The Ohio State University. All right reserved.

culture, such as Paul Goble whose stories are from the Sioux nations, or you might choose an author with a variety of stories, such as Eric Kimmel who often retells Jewish stories, but also has retold stories from many countries. Other prolific retellers of folk tales are Robert San Souci and Rafe Martin. The authors listed here are careful researchers who try to retell their stories in authentic styles and who provide readers with information about their research into the sources of the stories. Studying any one of these authors would provide information about folk literature that would be interesting to the students and would help them understand the necessity of good research habits regardless of the topics they want to write about themselves.

In the third circle, learn about language (reproduced in Figure 13.14), the topics are guided reading, strategy lessons, mini-lessons/focus lessons, teacher/student conferences, writing engagements, and strategy sharing discussions. Each of these experiences will help students learn more about how language is used, what functions language serves, and how authors use language when they write.

Guided Reading

Using folk literature as the content for reading instruction provides many opportunities for guided reading experiences that can help students learn more about reading and how to read. Because folk literature can be accessible to a wide range of readers, it is relatively easy to find materials that will be appropriate for use with readers at all ability levels. Guided reading experiences can help students learn how to handle the structure of folk literature, how to recognize the author's use of storytelling language in a printed version of a story, how to tackle the sometimes difficult names encountered in folk literature, and how to appreciate the skill of telling a complex story with limited words.

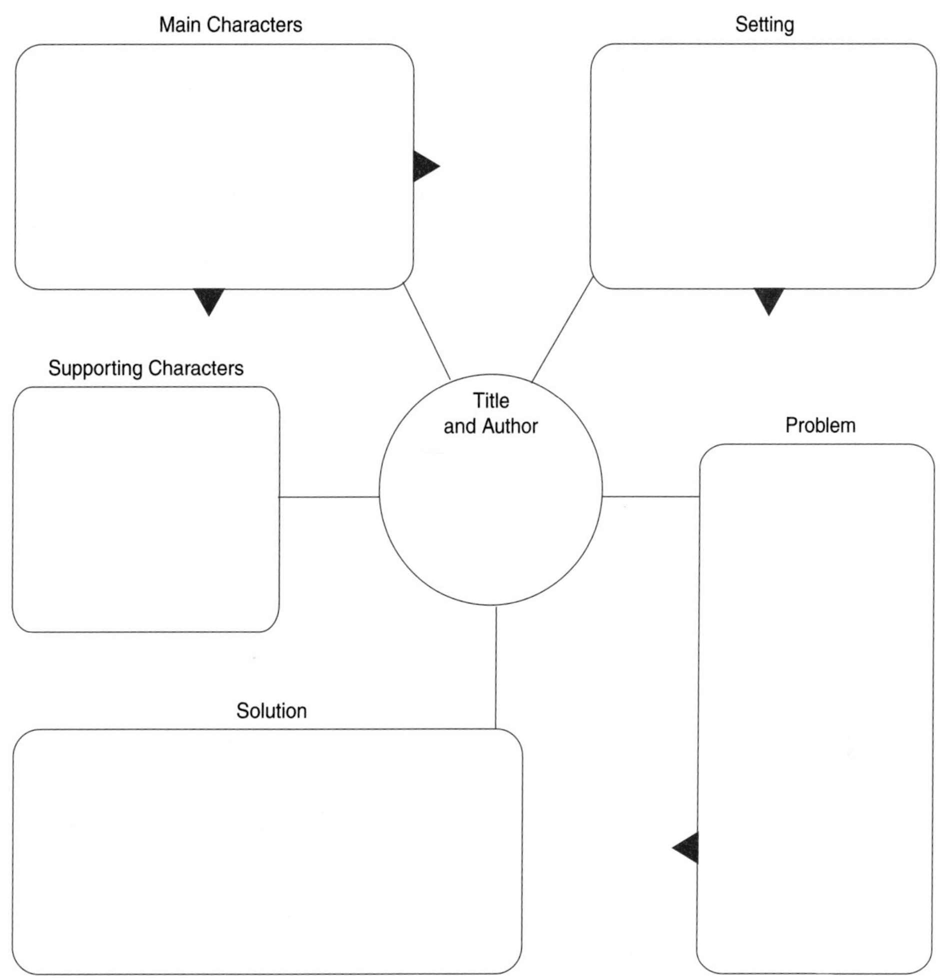

Figure 13.15
Story Map

Focus lessons that help children learn the structure of folk stories, the use of figurative language, and the connections between modern fantasy and traditional tales would be possibilities for instruction. For example, after reading *Foolish Rabbit's Big Mistake* (Martin, 1985), you could teach the children to use a Venn diagram to compare the plot of Henny Penny or Chicken Little with *Foolish Rabbit's Big Mistake.*

Strategy Lessons

Strategy lessons with folk literature would be selected on the basis of what students need. Only you can know what reading strategies your students can use confidently and which ones you need to model and discuss with them. In reading folk literature, as in any other kind of literature, you would want to help children learn how to monitor their own comprehension of the stories and what steps to take if they are failing to comprehend.

Structure of Folk Stories. In learning the structure of folk stories, story maps that children complete and then compare would be useful. The story map in Figure 13.15 could be used to help children visualize the structure of a given story. If we complete this map for *The Firebird* (San Scouci, 1992), then we can compare this map to a map of *The Tale of the*

Mandarin Ducks (Paterson, 1990). Children can complete maps of other stories they are reading as well and then in a focus lesson compare the story maps from several stories to reveal the common structures.

Folk Literature and Modern Fantasy. To help children understand the connections between traditional literature and modern fantasy, Steig's (1967) *Sylvester and the Magic Pebble* would be one good choice for comparing the structure of the story to a folk story. Children could complete a Venn diagram to compare this story with one of the folk literature selections, or they could complete the story map described previously and discuss how this modern story shares the same structure as folk stories. Another story of modern fantasy that would be a good example of folk literature structure would be *Chato's Kitchen* (Soto, 1995).

Transformation Stories. Other focus lessons in your study of folk literature might be structured around learning about the various transformation stories or stories that provide a new twist on old tales. Using transformation stories requires that the children know well the basic story on which the transformation is based. For example, *Sleeping Ugly* (Yolen, 1981) does not work unless the reader knows the story of Sleeping Beauty. Some of the transformations rely on a change in characters, some on a change in setting, and some on a change in language. *Snow White in New York* (French, 1986) is an example of a change in setting and characters as the dwarfs are now jazzmen. *Yo Hungry Wolf* (Vozar, 1993) is "The Three Little Pigs" written in rap. *Somebody and the Three Blairs* (Tolhurst, 1990) is a twist on "The Three Bears"; a bear goes to the home of the Blairs.

Transformations give students a chance to rewrite an old story with some of the structure and details provided by the traditional story. It is difficult to write a transformation that changes too many elements at once, but students can begin with changing only one element of the story in their retelling. Students have rewritten Goldilocks as a newspaper report of a burglary in which Goldilocks is portrayed as the "alleged perpetrator" or suspect in the crime. Some of the transformations use rhyme to tell the stories while others could be told in a modern setting, such as *Three Cool Kids* (Emberley, 1995). *The True Story of the Three Little Pigs* (Scieszka, 1989) is a popular transformation story. You could read several versions of "The Three Little Pigs" and then discuss and compare the various versions before reading Scieszka's version.

Go to the Weblinks in Chapter 13 on our Companion Website at www.prenhall.com/harp for a bibliography of transformation stories that can serve as writing models for children.

After children understand what the author did to the old story to create a new version, they could study other folk tales and write a new version by changing one element. Changing the gender of the main character is one change that could be explored. Osborne has written two such stories: *Kate and the Beanstalk* (2000) and *The Brave Little Seamstress* (2002). Other recent transformation stories that would be of interest are *The Wolf Who Cried Boy* (Hartman, 2002) and *The Three Billygoats Gruff and Mean Calypso Joe* (Youngquist, 2002). The important point here is that the children have the framework of a story that they know well to support their writing of a changed version.

Other Writing Possibilities. Additional writing possibilities include creating an alphabet book of folk tales, folk tale characters, or folk tale elements such as magic objects. An alphabet book summarizing the study of a particular kind of folk tale could also be constructed. For example, the children could make an alphabet book of tall tales or of myths. Encyclopedias of folk literature would also be appropriate for writing projects. In creating an encyclopedia, children would have to read the entries in an encyclopedia (either in print or on the web) to determine the writing style and the content of such entries.

HOW DO I HANDLE MANAGEMENT AND RECORD KEEPING?

One of the goals of school is that children become self-motivated, independent learners. Children in the middle elementary grades are capable of achieving these goals when given choices and opportunities to learn about topics that interest them. In offering a study of folk literature as an example, the children's choices are always most important in guiding the direction of the study and the projects or outcomes. If some children are really uninterested in folk literature, then you must think about their interests and how those interests can be honored through a broad topic of study. If you find two or three children whose interests are in scientific areas of study, they can report on the scientific reasons why the moon has phases and compare that to the myths that explain the phases of the moon by claiming that a monster eats the moon each month.

Go to the Weblinks in Chapter 13 on our Companion Website at www.prenhall.com/harp to find links to various publishers and sources of children's literature in two languages.

If some students are struggling with learning English, you can find folk literature that is printed in English and in other languages. If they can read in their native language, these books can be useful as they learn English. If they cannot read in their native language, these books can help all class members appreciate the fact that all cultures have folk stories. Pacific Asia Press produces some books available in Hmong/English, Khmer/English, Vietnamese/English, Lao/English, and English only. Milet Press produces books in many languages coupled with English. This press also has dictionaries for children in a long list of languages. Shen's Books and Children's Press are also a good source of folk literature printed in two languages.

Folk tales are also available as easy reading books, so that students who are struggling readers can participate in various class activities such as reader's theater even though the text they read might be a simplified version of the tale. If children are familiar with a tale, that knowledge can be a scaffold as they read these tales. Audiotapes can also be used to support struggling readers. As we have described previously, a project that involves parents and children in creating these tapes can be useful. If you cannot ask the families to participate in a taping project, groups of children in the class could certainly produce tapes and share them with other groups.

These ideas for differentiating instruction depend on the teacher's knowledge of the child, his needs, and the available literature. If the instructional day is organized into reading and writing workshop periods, all modifications to a study of folk literature described previously can be managed fairly easily. However, keeping good records remains as a critical skill in making this organization work. The monitoring notebook (described in Chapter 3) will continue to be an important tool as you work with individuals and small groups in skill and strategy instruction and as you help children gain writing ability. Children continue to need instruction in reading and writing at all levels of school. Even skilled readers need instruction and guidance. At no point can we say readers no longer need instruction. There is always something to learn about interpreting and responding to literature, no matter how skilled readers become.

THINKING AS A TEACHER

1. You know that some parents are concerned about the violence and sexism of some folk literature. In a small group of your peers, plan how you would explain to parents why you are using folk literature and how you plan to deal with the violence or apparent sexism in some of the stories.
2. You want to create a research center in your classroom that will house supplies needed for research activities. With your group, plan the contents of this center and the placement of this center in your classroom.
3. With your class, examine several skill lists from basal readers for the middle grades. How many of the skills could you teach during the study of folk literature? If some skills would not be taught during this study, what other topics would allow you to cover those skills?

FIELD-BASED ACTIVITIES

1. Interview three teachers of middle grade students and ask them to describe the big topics of study they find interesting to these children. When given these topics, think about how they could be developed using the model for learn language, learn through language, and learn about language.
2. Visit two or three classrooms and make notes about the arrangements of furniture and supplies. Observe the children long enough to get a sense of how well the room arrangement is working (no crowding, not everybody needing to be in one place at one time, no interruptions from people trying to use the pencil sharpener, etc.). Evaluate the arrangements and make notes of positive qualities you will want to include in your own classroom.
3. Interview a school librarian who works with the middle grade classes and ask her what kind of books are most popular with these readers. When you have a list of the most popular books, plan how you might include them in your classroom as independent reading, books for literature study, books for stimulating writing, or books that would stimulate research topics.

REFERENCES

Allington, R. L., Johnston, P. H., & Day, J. P. (2002). Exemplary fourth-grade teachers. *Language Arts, 79,* 462–466.

Bottomley, D. M., Henk, W.A., & Melnick, S. A. (1997). Assessing children's views about themselves as writers using the Writer Self-Perception Scale. *The Reading Teacher, 51,* 286–296.

Duffield, J. A. (1997/1998). Conducting research: A student-centered model. *Childhood Education, 74,* 66–72.

Gambrell, L. B., Palmer, B. M., Codling, R. M., & Massoni, S. A. (1996). Assessing motivation to read. *The Reading Teacher, 49,* 518–533.

Halliday, M. A. K. (1973) *Explorations in the functions of language.* London: Edward Arnold.

Hammill, D. D., & Larsen, S. C. (1996). *Test of written language examiner's manual* (3rd ed.). Austin, TX: Pro-ed.

Harp, B. & Brewer, J. A. (1996). *Reading and Writing: Teaching for the Connections.* Ft. Worth: Harcourt.

Howe, F. C. (1993). The child in the elementary school. *Child Study Journal, 23,* 227–363.

Krashen, S. D. (1999). *Three arguments against whole language & why they are wrong.* Portsmouth, NH: Heinemann.

Leslie, L., & Caldwell, J. (2000). *Qualitative reading inventory 3.* Boston: Allyn and Bacon.

Leu, D. J. (2002, October). The Miss Rumphius effect: Integrating literature and the Internet into the one-computer classroom. Presentation at New England Reading Association conference, Newport, RI.

Mogello, L. (executive editor). (2003). *Elements of literature: Second Course.* Austin, TX: Holt, Rinehart & Winston (pp. 507–508).

Moss, G. (2000). Raising boys' attainment in reading: Some principles for intervention. *Reading, 34,* 101–107.

Odean, K. (2001). How to keep boys interested in books. *NEA Today, 19,* 27.

O'Reilly, J., & Alexander, J. (1998). Newspapers as a reading resource: Their impact on boys and on parental involvement. *Reading, 32,* 21–27.

Pinnell, G. S. (2002). Ways to look at the functions of children's language. In B. M. Power & R. S. Hubbard (Eds.), *Language development: A reader for teachers* (pp. 110–117). Columbus, OH: Merrill.

Servis, J. (1999). *Celebrating the fourth: Ideas and inspiration for teachers of grade four.* Portsmouth, NH: Heinemann.

Short, K. G. The search for "balance" in a literature-rich curriculum. *Theory into Practice, 38*(3), 130–137.

Walter, V. A. (1998). Leading boys from bytes to books. *Book Links, 7,* 53–57.

Children's Books

Alexander, L. (1992). *Fortune-tellers.* Illus. by T. S. Hyman. New York: Dutton.

Bell, A. (1989). *The fisherman and his wife.* Illus. by A. Marks. Saxonville, MA: Picture Book Studio.

Beneduce, A. K. (1999). *Jack and the beanstalk.* Illus. by G. Spirin. New York: Philomel.

Burleigh, R. (2002). *Pandora.* Illus. by R. Colon. San Diego: Silver Whistle.

Easton, S. (1992). *The fisherman and his wife.* Illus. by M. Scanlan. Kansas City, MO: Andrews and McMeel.

Emberley, R. (1995). *Three cool kids.* Boston: Little Brown.

French, F. (1986). *Snow White in New York.* Oxford, England: Oxford University Press.

Hartman, B. (2002). *The wolf who cried boy.* Illus. by T. Raglin. New York: Putnam.

Kellogg, S. (1991). *Jack and the beanstalk.* New York: Morrow.
Kimmel, E. A. (1985). *Hershel and the Hanukkah goblins.* Illus. by T. S. Hyman. New York: Holiday House.
Kimmel, E. A. (1992). *The four gallant sisters.* New York: Henry Holt.
Levine, G. C. (1997). *Ella enchanted.* New York: Harper Trophy.
Marcellino, F. (1990). *Puss in boots.* M. Arthur, Trans. New York: Farrar, Straus, & Giroux.
Martin, R. (1985). *Foolish rabbit's big mistake.* Illus by E. Young. New York: Putnam.
Martin, R. (2001). *The shark god.* New York: Scholastic.
Mayer, M. (1996). *Cupid and Psyche.* New York: William Morrow.
McKinley, R. (1978). *Beauty: A retelling of the story of beauty and the beast.* New York: Harper Trophy.
Osborne, M. P. (2000). *Kate and the beanstalk.* Illus. by G. Potter. New York: Atheneum.
Osborne, M. P. (2002). *The brave little seamstress.* Illus. by G. Potter. New York: Atheneum.
Paterson, K. (1990). *The tale of the Mandarin ducks.* Illus. by L. Dillon & D. Dillon. New York: Lodestar.
Pullman, P. (2000). *Puss in boots.* Illus. by I. Beck. New York: Knopf.
San Souci, R. D. (1992). *The firebird.* Illus. by K. Waldherr. New York: Dial.
Scieszka, J. (1989). *The true story of the three little pigs!* Illus. by L. Smith. New York: Viking Kestrel.
Simons, J., & Simons, S. (1991a). *Why dolphins call: A story of Dionysus.* Englewood Cliffs, NJ: Silver Press.
Simons, J., & Simons, S. (1991b). *Why spiders spin: A story of Arachne.* Englewood Cliffs, NJ: Silver Press.
Soto, G. (1995). *Chato's kitchen.* Illus. by S. Guevara. New York: Putnam.
Spear, L. (1992). *The fisherman and his wife.* New York: Rizzoli.
Spinelli, J. (1990). *Maniac Magee.* Boston: Little Brown.
Steig, W. (1969). *Sylvester and the magic pebble.* New York: Simon & Schuster.
Stewig, J. W. (1988). *The fisherman and his wife.* Illus. by M. Tomes. New York: Holiday House.
Tolhurst, M. (1990). *Somebody and the three Blairs.* Illus. by S. Abel. New York: Orchard Books.
Vozar, D. (1993). *Yo, hungry wolf! A nursery rap.* Illus. by B. Lewin. New York: Doubleday.
White, E. B. (1952). *Charlotte's web.* Illus. by G. Williams. New York: HarperCollins.
Yolen, J. (1981). *Sleeping ugly.* New York: Coward-McCann.
Yorinks, A. (1986). *Hey, Al.* Illus. by R. Egielski. New York: Farrar, Straus, & Giroux.
Youngquist, C. V. (2002). *The three billygoats Gruff and mean Calypso Joe.* Illus. by K. Sorra. New York: Atheneum Books.

Chapter 14

Building a Literacy Program Grades 6–8

Teaching in the middle grades is challenging—and rewarding when it is done well. The middle grades are challenging because the students are so varied in all areas of development. Some may be going through puberty and are immersed in hormones and displaying their effects physically, emotionally, and socially. Others are not yet going through the physical changes of puberty, but are facing some of the social challenges of these grade levels such as the interest girls have in boys and the need by both sexes for peer approval.

The differences noted in children in third through fifth grades are more pronounced in middle school. Middle school teaching is never easy, but good teachers can make a real and lasting difference in the lives of young people.

Although the emphasis is often on academic achievement for middle school students, teachers must also pay attention to their social and emotional development if they wish to achieve academic goals with all students. Goleman (1995) identified five competencies that he labeled *emotional intelligence:* self and other awareness, mood management, self-motivation, empathy, and management of relationships. What is learned is filtered through what we feel at the time. Therefore, teachers of middle school must plan for a classroom climate that will help students become more able socially and emotionally as well as academically skilled. If teachers think about the emotional and social growth as part of their teaching responsibilities, academic learning also improves. The criteria for a caring environment include promoting "self-reflection and empathy for others, teaching kids how to set goals and solve problems, being flexible and imaginative, teaching kids how to learn, how to be generative and creative, and how to get along with each other" (Stern & Rosenzweig, 1999, p. 3).

These children are varied academically and physically. Some are excellent readers and writers, highly motivated to participate in literacy activities, while others are unable to read or write well and are not motivated to engage in academic work. Middle school teachers must establish an environment that encourages and supports growth in all areas. Teachers must also learn about each student, skills, abilities, motivations, and interests.

Focus Questions

- How do I create a classroom environment that will help me to be an effective teacher?
- What assessments will I use to get started in the instructional program?
- How will I plan instruction for the middle school classroom?
- How will I modify instruction for struggling readers?

HOW DO I CREATE A CLASSROOM ENVIRONMENT THAT WILL HELP ME TO BE AN EFFECTIVE TEACHER?

The classroom environment is important because it sends a message to students about expectations for their behavior and because it needs to be a calm and appealing place to be for several hours a day. The physical arrangement of the furniture, the schedule of activities, and the materials needed to help the instruction run smoothly and achieve program goals are all part of the classroom environment.

Classroom Arrangement

Many middle school programs are based on grouping children for instruction in the language arts and social studies and for math/science. This classroom plan is for language arts and social studies. One teacher teaches all the language arts and social studies for two groups; another teacher teaches all the math/science for the same two groups. Other instruction, such as art or phys ed, takes place in special rooms with special teachers.

In the floor plan in Figure 14.1, a rug for group meetings is placed at the front of the room. An easel and a chair for the teacher are kept here for read-alouds and whole group discussions. Also in this section is the overhead projector and the VCR. A large dry erase board is mounted on the wall in this area. The remainder of this wall would be used for displaying children's work on various projects or group-constructed bulletin boards. In the front corner of the room is a table and shelves for individual or small group instruction. The teacher stores her materials on these shelves. The outside wall of the room is windows with shelves below them. These shelves hold tubs with various books and writing materials for student use. At the back of the classroom are the computers and storage for games or other materials. Over the computers would be cork boards for posting instructions or time assignments for the computers, student work, or project work.

Along the fourth wall are shelves for storing the classroom library and other teaching materials. One of the pods of tables is designated as a listening center. It is possible to combine any of the pods for literature discussions or work on projects done in groups larger than four. Goals of a classroom arrangement are to make the distribution of materials efficient and to be flexible, so that different grouping arrangements can be accommodated with little disruption or expenditure of time.

Schedule

One of the advantages of block scheduling in the middle grades is that you will have a two and one-half hour block of time to use for language arts and social studies. As you plan for this time block, think about reader's workshop, writer's workshop, and inquiry work all focused on social studies themes. Integrating the literacy instruction and social studies content will free up more time for in-depth inquiry and for projects that need extended time to

Figure 14.1
Room Arrangement

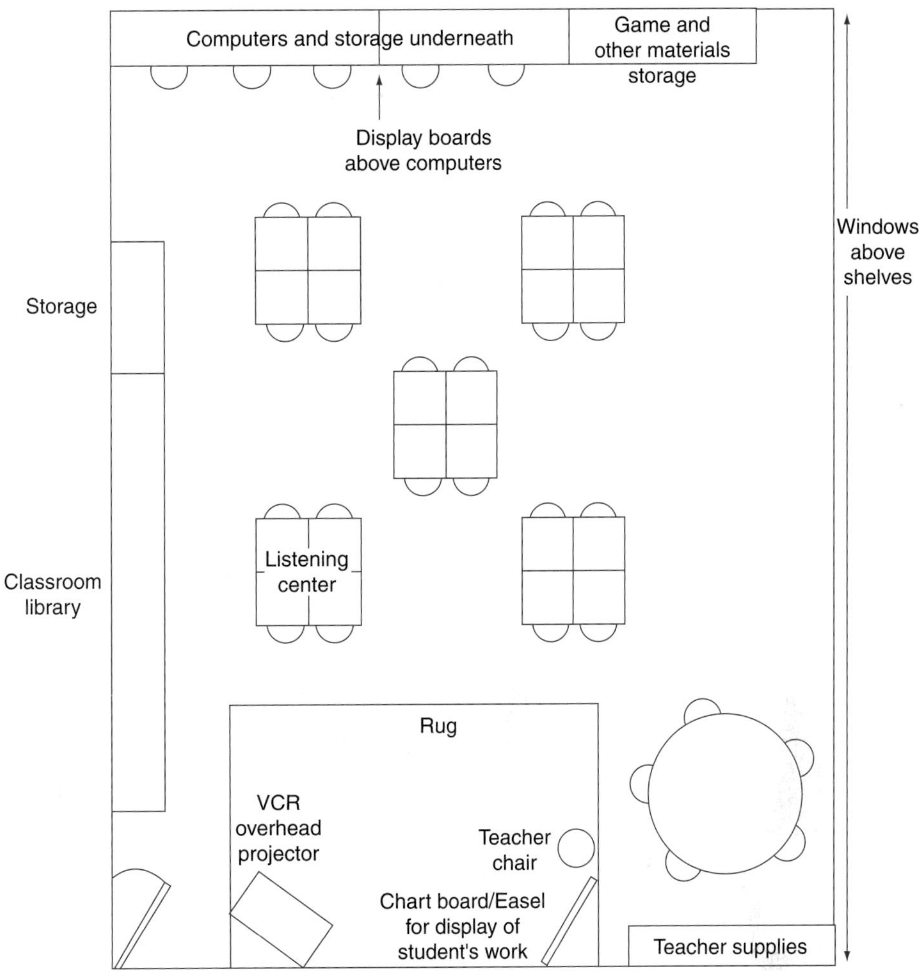

complete. Of course, not all schools have moved to block scheduling that combines language arts and social studies; if your school has a different schedule, you might be able to work with the social studies teacher to collaborate on projects.

Instructional Materials

The resources needed for teaching language arts and social studies include chart paper, sentence strips, many kinds of paper and pens, pencils, and markers of various kinds. Each student needs at least two folders, one for writing and one for reading. You may want to use loose leaf notebooks in place of folders so that materials can be added, removed, and rearranged easily. Social studies also requires up-to-date maps and globes. For both language arts and social studies, you need a wide variety of books, both fiction and nonfiction. Your classroom library should include text sets of several books you think will be interesting for study and many books for independent reading. These books should cover a wide range of reading abilities and many interests. Comic books, newspapers, magazines, and other materials will interest students. Some readers may prefer how-to manuals for constructing things or magazines for early teens such as *Teen Newsweek.*

WHAT ASSESSMENTS WILL I USE TO GET STARTED IN THE INSTRUCTIONAL PROGRAM?

Before school starts, review the children's records from previous years as a starting point. Some teachers feel that looking at previous records might bias their view of the children, but you do need to know which children have IEPs and the year-end goals on their learning plans. For the first day of school, plan reading and writing activities that will help the children begin to form a community and help you analyze their skills and abilities.

Informal Assessment

One possible activity would be to ask children to choose a book from the library for their independent reading. As small groups go to the library area, observe who chooses a book easily and who has difficulty in finding something to read. Be willing to make suggestions for books if the students are having too much difficulty in finding a book they can read.

A writing activity might be to teach the children the steps for writing a bio-poem and then ask them to write a bio-poem about themselves. The students can then be asked to introduce themselves to the class or to introduce a classmate using the information in the bio-poem. You will also want to complete a bio-poem to introduce yourself to the class.

A Bio-Poem Template

Line 1 = Your first name
Line 2 = Four adjectives that describe you
Line 3 = Son/daughter of. . . (or sibling, grandson, etc.)
Line 4 = Lover of. . .(three things, people or ideas)
Line 5 = Who feels. . . (up to three items)
Line 6 = Who needs. . . (up to three items)
Line 7 = Who fears. . . (up to three items)
Line 8 = Who would like to see. . . (up to three people, ideas or places)
Line 9 = Your family name

Interest Inventory

Ask your students to complete an interest inventory. Matching the interests of middle schoolers to topics of study and to books available for independent reading is critical to success. Figure 14.2 is an example of a useful school information/interest inventory, although you may want to adapt some of the questions to meet your own needs for specific information.

Self-Evaluation

In addition to the interest and information inventory, students should complete a self-evaluation of their skills and abilities in literacy. They might answer questions such as what they are best at as readers and writers, or they could write a paragraph explaining what they feel are their strengths as learners and what are their goals for this new school year.

Formal Assessments

Based on your observations and analysis of the student's reading and writing abilities, you may want to administer more formal assessments to some children, such as the *Test of*

Figure 14.2
Information/Interest Inventory

Name ______________________________ Date ______________

What was the best activity you have ever done in school? ______________
____
____

Why? ____
____

The best things about you are ______________________________
____
____

How do you like to spend your free time? ______________________
____

What is your favorite kind of book to read?

Fiction that could be true Biography Poetry Adventure
True Adventure Horror Science Fiction Romance Fantasy
Superhero Other ______________

About how much time do you spend reading each day during the school year? ______
______________ During summer vacation? ______________

What is your favorite book? ______________________________

What is your favorite TV show? ______________________________

Why? ____

What kind of music do you like? ______________________________

What is your favorite musical group? ______________________________

What is your favorite sport? ______________________________

Do you participate in a sport? ______________________________

Tell me about your hobby ______________________________
____

Do you have responsibilities other than school? If yes, please describe them. ______
____
____

What would you like to do after you finish high school? ______________
____
____

(Continued)

Figure 14.2
Continued

My biggest problem at this time is ______________________________

____

I speak and understand English:
Not at all A little Enough for a conversation Very well

My parents speak and understand English:
Not at all A little Enough for a conversation Very well

What languages other than English do you speak? ____________________

____

How well do you speak another language? __________________________

How long have you lived in the United States? _______________________

On the back of the page, write three questions you would like to ask me.

Written Language-3 (Hammill & Larsen, 1996) and the third edition of the *Test of Reading Comprehension* (Brown, Hammill, & Wiederholt, 1995). For your English language learners, schedule individual conferences in which you ask students about their experiences learning English and how they assess their own level of competence in English and in their native language.

HOW WILL I PLAN INSTRUCTION FOR THE MIDDLE SCHOOL CLASSROOM?

The Center for Early Adolescence (1987) lists seven key components for quality schools for adolescents:

1. diverse learning experiences and relationships
2. opportunities for self-exploration and self-definition
3. meaningful participation in their school and community
4. positive social interaction with peers and adults
5. physical activity
6. competence and achievement
7. structure and clear limits

We believe that including these components is best achieved through a curriculum that is integrated and interesting to learners. Through student choice and multiple ways to achieve learning goals, the curriculum is most likely to meet the needs of early adolescents.

In this chapter, we will rely on the same organizing graphic that we used in Chapter 12 and Chapter 13. This graphic (Figure 14.3) describes curriculum through activities designed to help children learn language, learn through language, and learn about language, all of which center on inquiry. We will offer examples of activities that could be part of an appropriate curriculum for middle school learners and suggestions for how to adapt instruction for those children who are second language learners or who need other supports for their learning to be successful. Because this graphic illustrates curriculum as centered on inquiry, we will begin with inquiry, the center of the circles.

Figure 14.3
Balanced Reading Program

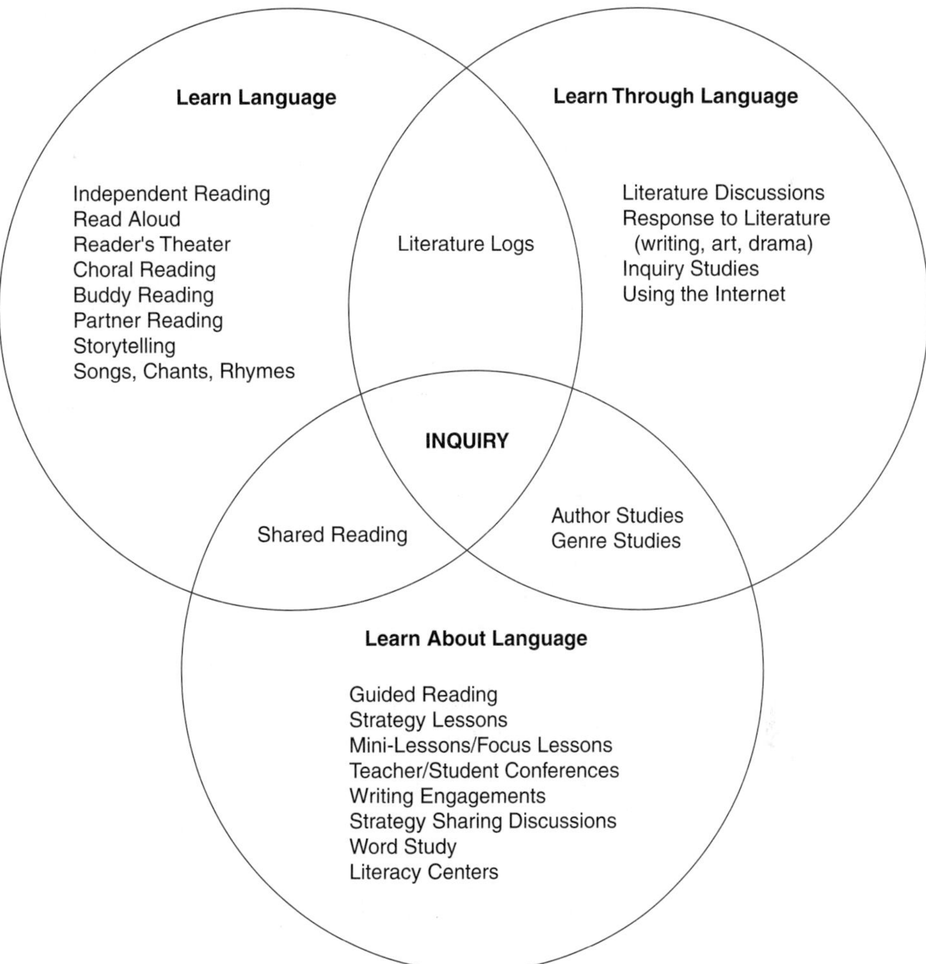

Source: Adapted from Short, K.G. (1999). The Search for "Balance" in a Literature-Rich Curriculum. *Theory into Practice, 38*(3), 130–137.

Planning Inquiry

Planning inquiry experiences is an appropriate beginning point, as these experiences influence all other curriculum choices. Because this inquiry is planned for a block that integrates social studies and language arts, a social studies theme is important. For this illustration, we have chosen "Heroes and Heroines: Past and Present" as a topic of study. There are many other excellent choices for topics of inquiry in the middle school. Pate, Homestead, & McGinnis (1995) recommend human migration, human interactions and the environment, civil rights and responsibilities, and communities of the future. The planning process for any one of these ideas would be similar.

Before beginning this study of heroes and heroines, collect the print resources you will use. Ask your librarian to help you find biographies of heroes and heroines. In addition, collect short biographical sketches from magazines and newspapers. With the ability to search the archives of most newspapers and magazines on the web, your search should not be too difficult. Some teachers mount these sketches on construction paper so that they are easier to store and will withstand the wear of student use better. You might decide to define selected vocabulary words on the back of the paper. Video and film resources also can help students explore the topic more fully. With all these materials ready, you can begin your study.

In introducing the topic, ask students to write a definition of what a hero or heroine is. In small groups, they would then compare their answers and create a group definition. These definitions would be shared with the whole class and recorded on chart paper. Once the class has discussed the definitions, they could begin to list people they believe are heroes or heroines. As they name people, lists can be compiled of heroes and heroines of the past and present and heroic fictional characters.

Students could then select a hero or heroine about whom they wish to learn. As the study proceeds, lists of traits common to heroes or heroines can be identified, time lines can be developed for those subjects from the past, and maps can be created to illustrate where the subjects lived or did their work. Events through which the subjects gained their status can be summarized, traits necessary for heroic behavior in the past can be compared to traits necessary for heroic behavior today, and a list of heroes or heroines of today who will be in the history books of tomorrow can be prepared (with justifications for their inclusion). Most of the activities in this inquiry study are language based and depend on learning language for their success.

Learn Language

The first circle of the graphic, labeled *learn language,* is reproduced in Figure 14.4. These ideas will guide our planning in meeting both language arts and social studies goals. This circle begins with independent reading, a daily occurrence in the classroom.

Figure 14.4
Learn Language

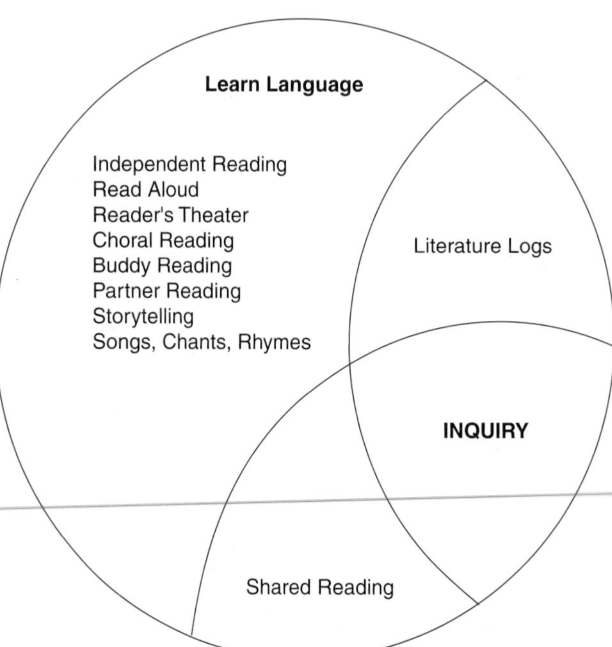

Source: Adapted from Short, K.G. (1999). The Search for "Balance" in a Literature-Rich Curriculum. *Theory into Practice, 38*(3), 130–137.

Independent Reading. Every student should have material they can read successfully and with interest readily available for independent reading. For some students, intensive research may be required to find such material. Some of this material may be periodicals, newspapers, and books. For the study of heroes and heroines, include as much material as possible about the people the students have listed.

By the time students are in the eighth grade, they want reality in their stories. Even if teachers would prefer stories with more ideal families and ideal teenage characters, most students prefer books such as *Drive-By* (Ewing, 1998), *Scorpions* (Meyers, 1990), *A Child Called "It"* (Pelzer & Pelzer, 1995), *The Lost Boy* (Pelzer & Pelzer, 1997), *Speak* (Anderson, 2001), and *Go Ask Alice* (Anonymous, 1998). These books deal with the problems teens face in today's world. (Note: These titles were suggested by three middle school reading teachers as books their students preferred to read.)

Reading Aloud. Reading aloud for middle school students is an important and appropriate strategy. Read-alouds can be planned for chapter books, poetry, and nonfiction. One goal of read-alouds is to present material that is too difficult for most of the students to read independently. This may be material from a new or challenging genre or with a vocabulary that will need to be unpacked. For example, you might choose to read the Gettysburg Address and guide a discussion of the meaning of this speech and its importance in history. Another example of a read-aloud choice might be some of the writing of Martin Luther King, Jr., or selections from *We Were There Too: Young People in U. S. History* (Hoose, 2001).

A strategy recommended by Hoyt (2002) is to stop at selected points during the reading and ask the students to turn to a partner and "say something." You must model what kinds of things could be said such as mentioning an important idea, phrase, word, or language structure. This strategy helps students comprehend the content of what they are hearing and negotiate meaning with a partner as they move through a piece of text.

Reader's Theater. Many pieces of poetry and scenes from books can be adapted for reader's theater productions for middle schoolers. The advantages of these group productions are the safety of performing in a group rather than individually and the necessity to reread the material to be performed many times to produce a skillful presentation. The rereading with the support of the group can aid the development of fluency and help with comprehension as the performer must attend to the meaning of material in order to read it appropriately.

Books such as Taylor's (2001) *The Land,* Delacre's (2000) *Salsa Stories,* and Bruchac's (2000) *Sacajawea* have scenes that would lend themselves easily to theater productions. As these pieces are read, students could be asked to determine whether the information is historically correct. Such inquiry would encourage them to use various sources to check the historical accuracy of the pieces. They will learn that a poet or storyteller often begins with fact, but may combine more than one historical incident in a story or may combine some fact and some fiction to create an interesting piece. Other pieces of nonfiction such as *Forging Freedom* (Talbott, 2000) and *Hurry Freedom* (Stanley, 2000) have scenes that could be converted into successful reader's theater productions. Having to create the scripts and dialogue provides other opportunities for reading and writing as well as all the benefits of Reader's Theatre.

Choral reading can serve some of the same purposes as reader's theater. Examples include poetry such as *The Midnight Ride of Paul Revere* (Longfellow, 2001), some of the orations and poetry in John Bierhorst's (1971) collection, *In the Trail of the Wind: American Indian Poems and Ritual Orations,* or selections from *Carver: A Life in Poems (Nelson, 2001).*

Storytelling. Middle school students often respond well to storytelling instruction. After all, they love to tell stories when they are with their friends. Storytelling instruction can encourage students to gain control of their voices, learn to pay attention to the audience, and learn how to present information in a way that is both entertaining and informative. Storytelling experiences can help students develop lifelong speaking skills that will serve them well. Stories about heroes and heroines lend themselves to telling, because most of them have some dramatic elements to emphasize. For example, the stories about Harriet Tubman are fascinating and dramatic. Preparing for a storytelling experience requires repeated practice to master both the content of the story and the style of delivery that best conveys the meaning of the story.

Songs, Chants, and Rhymes. At the middle school level, songs, chants, and rhymes are often used more to add interest and depth to the study of a topic or to help students learn to comprehend the genre of poetry. Such songs as those of Woody Guthrie (*This Land was Made for You and Me* (Partridge, 2002) can be used to help students understand the challenges of living in the depression times and the heroism Woody found in the lives of working men and women.

Finders and Hynds (2003) have created a list of forms for oral language and listening activities in the middle grades, which is reproduced in Figure 14.5. This list will be helpful as you think of oral activities that can meet your curriculum goals.

Literature Logs. The intersection between circle 1 and circle 2 in our organizing graphic is labeled *literature logs.* Such logs are useful both for learning language (learning how to express feelings and understandings) and learning through language as they help students examine the language authors use. Students can write logs of conversations about their reading that are shared with the teacher or with a small group of peers. Some teachers encourage response logs on the web in either a discussion group or a list-serve group where only the members of the group exchange responses. Response logs can also be completed as double entry journals. In a double entry journal, the student writes before reading and then again after reading. The before reading piece is usually a prediction about the content

Figure 14.5
Techniques and Forms of Oral Language and Listening

group discussions	interviews
debates	mock student congress
dramatic improvisations	memorized speeches
extemporaneous speeches	recitations
dramatic enactments	oral interpretations of literature
panel discussions	dramatic monologues
conversations	choral reading
"pair-shares"	poster sessions
collaborative learning groups	oral demonstrations
jokes	skits
storytelling	problem-solving groups
scripted dialogues	oral reports

Source: Literacy Lessons: Teaching and Learning with Middle School Students by Finders/Hynds, © Reprinted by permission of Pearson Education, Inc., Upper Saddle River, NJ.

of the piece or what the reader expects to feel about the reading. The after reading piece discusses the content and the response to the content of the reading piece.

Regardless of how they are completed, such logs can help you assess both reading and writing abilities. If a student fails to comprehend the material, this problem will be revealed in the literature log responses. On the other hand, an excellent grasp of the meanings of given materials will also be evident. The writing in the logs is unstructured enough to provide solid information about students' abilities to express themselves and about the mechanical needs of individual students. Literature logs are usually not graded but can be used to help determine needs for instruction in interpreting literature and in mechanical writing skills.

If logs are to be shared with peers, you will need to model appropriate responses. Positive comments with impact and good questions to ask the author can be modeled. A response of "Good" does not carry any impact, nor does it help the writer think more deeply about the work. Peer responses are notoriously bad, but they can be improved with modeling and encouragement over a long period of time.

Learn Through Language

The second circle of the graphic is labeled *learn through language* and is reproduced in Figure 14.6. This set of activities focuses on using language as a vehicle for learning content. The second circle includes literature discussions, responses to literature, and using the Internet as useful activities for learning through language.

Figure 14.6
Learn Through Language

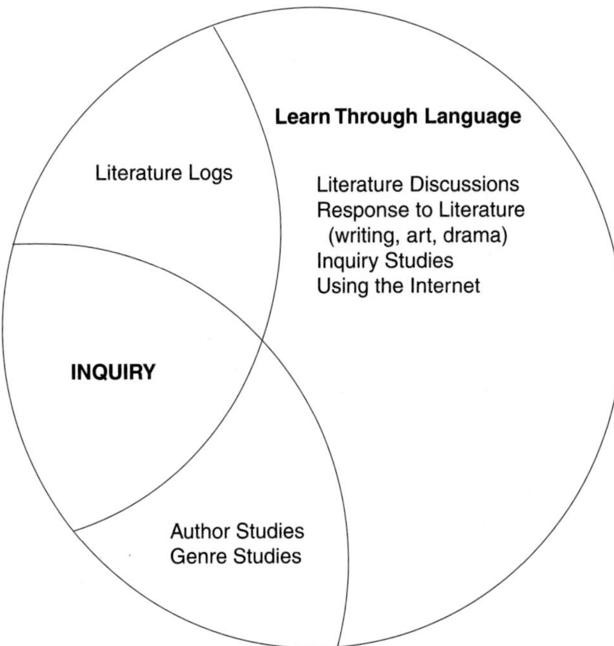

Source: Adapted from Short, K.G. (1999). The Search for "Balance" in a Literature-Rich Curriculum. *Theory into Practice, 38*(3), 130–137.

Literature Discussions. Literature discussions afford students the opportunity to compare their feelings and interpretations of material they have read to those of their classmates. Such discussions also provide opportunities for discussing strategies that have been used to read materials successfully. For example, students can share how they determined the theme, identified the problem and the solution, or remembered important details. Literal recall questions are not usually helpful in assessing reading abilities, but if students can share how they remembered the details, this strategy can help other students learn how to remember details for the instances when it would be important to do so. Literature discussions are so important to the growth of these students as readers that they should be scheduled as often as possible, but certainly two or three times weekly.

Hill, Noe, and King (2003) recommend a record sheet, a grid of rectangles that fit a 1½" × 2" Post-It Note below each child's name. The names are permanently on the sheets. As the teacher observes the discussions, she writes quick anecdotal records and scores the discussion participation on a rubric from 1 to 4. These ratings would indicate whether a child was engaged or paying no attention, the depth and quality of his contributions, and so on. The highest rating would indicate a deep understanding of the text and real effort to sustain a discussion. Students getting the highest rating would have done something extra to make their contribution valuable to the group, such as looking up a word in the dictionary or finding a bit of background information that would help illuminate the topic.

Response to Literature. The many possible responses to literature include drama and art. Since documentaries of the life of many heroes or heroines have been produced, one drama activity would be to compare the facts as presented in a dramatic or documentary piece with those of print material. Such activities will help students recognize the reasons for choosing to include or omit certain kinds of material and the necessity for creating some dramatic tension in either a biography or a documentary. Students can make dramatic presentations about the hero or heroine they have selected for study. A student or small group of students can produce an I-movie that illuminates the life of a hero or heroine. As in reader's theater, this activity will require students to make judgments about the content, the

Middle grade students can have lively and productive literature discussions.

language used for presentation to an audience, and the style of the presentation. PowerPoint offers another avenue for sharing either information or responses to reading. As in an I-movie, students need to make thoughtful choices in creating an interesting presentation.

Art. Art as a response mode to literature is often underused (Roser, 2001). Art is an important response to literature because it offers students who need to express their knowledge and understanding through art a chance to be successful. Options include creating posters, collages, portraits, puppets, costumes, and stage sets that share information with the viewer about a given person.

A triptych is another option for art in response to literature. A triptych is a presentation on a trifold board. A triptych about a hero or heroine would have a picture of the person and perhaps pictures of important events related to the person on the middle section. Each side panel could contain other information, such as a bibliography of the person's writing, a time line of important events in his or her life, a set of facts about the person, a news article about the person, an interview with the person, sources for additional research about the person, and any other information that would be interesting to the reader/viewer. Artistic decisions about the information to be included, the style, and the format would require knowing the character well and choosing the best representations for illuminating that person's life.

The same kinds of information about an individual can be presented on a cube. Given a cube pattern, students can easily make a cube with the dimensions they select. Each face of the cube (six faces) will display some information about the hero or heroine they have selected. The faces can be decorated to emphasize the content if the student chooses to do so. The cubes can be displayed by hanging them from the ceiling (if allowed in your school).

Drawing is another response to reading that can be useful in middle school. Students can produce poster-sized drawings about their hero or heroine and then include labels and explanations to complete the poster. Students should not be required to draw, but for some students, drawing is an avenue for expression that is important. If you think of the game Pictionary, then you can see how drawing a picture of a vocabulary word or a new concept would be helpful especially for second language learners.

Using the Internet. The Internet offers new reading challenges to middle school students in comprehending the incredible amount of information to be found on the Internet and in learning how to uncover the authors and the truth behind the sites posted on the net. For example, one negative site about Martin Luther King, Jr. can be traced back to group of white supremacists. Students need to learn to be wary of sites that fail to include an author's name or information about the sponsoring group or institution. Uncovering the truth about the sources and reliability of information on the web is a necessary reading skill that becomes more important every day.

A web site that is especially useful for a study of heroes and heroines is *My Hero* at *www.myhero.com.* This site offers biographical sketches of heroes from around the world and the opportunity to submit student work for inclusion on the site. This site also includes resources for teachers; one source is a list of links to stories especially suited to middle school students.

In the intersection between circle 2 and circle 3, author studies and genre studies are both listed. These studies would help students learn about language and learn through language at the same time.

Author Studies. As students read about the people they consider heroes or heroines, some will naturally read books by the same authors. Biographers such as Jean Fritz, Russell Freedman, Diane Stanley, and Milton Meltzer all have books about people who are heroes or heroines. On a class chart, students can list the books they are reading under the names of the authors. As two or three people read books by the same authors, they could form groups to discuss the work of that author. They would want to talk about style, format, and preferences of the author. They could make a list of the people about whom the author has written and speculate about the characteristics of people the author seems to find heroic. In addition, readers can compare the elements of this author's work to those of another author with whom they are familiar.

Genre Studies. A study of heroes and heroines will naturally focus on biographical writing. Students can learn to evaluate biography in terms of authentic material, adequate references, and the bias of the author. As students read biography and biographical sketches, they can learn to determine how material is selected to be included in a biography or a sketch. It is important that they recognize that not everything about a person can be recorded (nor should it be) and that authors must make decisions about what to include and what to leave out. Students can learn to check the facts in one account of a person's life with various other accounts, such as those in an encyclopedia, newspaper, magazine, or online entry to compare the details and information included in each.

Learn About Language

The third circle, Learn about Language, is reproduced in Figure 14.7. This circle includes guided reading, strategy lessons, mini-lessons/focus lessons, teacher/student conferences, writing engagements, strategy sharing discussions, word study, and literacy centers. The activities in this circle are critical as they are the basic instructional pieces offered by the teacher for the development of skills and strategies that will help students become ever more skillful readers and writers.

Figure 14.7
Learn About Language

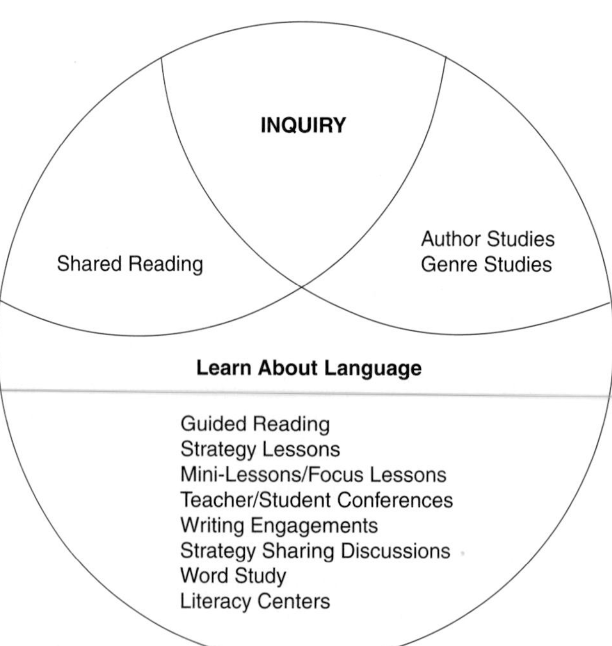

Source: Adapted from Short, K.G. (1999). The Search for "Balance" in a Literature-Rich Curriculum. *Theory into Practice, 38*(3), 130–137.

Guided Reading. In the past, schools often stopped reading instruction after grade six unless a student was having difficulty in reading or writing. The only reading instruction was offered by English teachers who assigned, discussed, and tested comprehension of various pieces of literature. Today, schools recognize that reading instruction can and should continue through grade eight or longer. Very few students in grade eight have learned so much about reading that they could not benefit from additional reading instruction. Guided reading, therefore, is an appropriate part of the reading curriculum.

Critical Literacy. For most students in middle school, guided reading lessons most often focus on writing style and comprehension. For these students, the focus is often critical reading in the sense of teaching students to look for the author's bias and word choice. For example, students might read a piece about a given person that presents a positive view of the person. As they read it, the teacher might ask them to stop and list all the loaded words the author used. Determine how those words are generally interpreted and how the cumulative effect of those words triggers a response in readers. Students might find elements of persuasive writing in a biographical sketch that is meant to convince the reader to feel positively about a person. Other strategies that might be discussed in guided reading would be how to determine the goals of the author in writing the piece and who would benefit if those views were accepted. Critical reading is extremely important in today's world, and guided reading experiences can help students recognize that not everything in print is accurate or true.

Critical literacy helps readers to look more deeply into the texts they are reading and to deal with issues of our society as they are portrayed in various texts. It would be important, for example, in reading about heroes or heroines to note the ratio of texts about women compared to texts about men. If a person is deemed a hero by one cultural group, does that make him or her a hero to all groups (Columbus and Cesar Chavez, for example)? What is the ratio of holidays celebrated for heroic white men compared to heroic women and heroic people of color? Other issues likely to arise in a study of heroes and heroines are racism, recognition of people of color, and the silencing of some groups. Such critical literacy activities will help meet the criteria for excellence in middle school programs outlined by Ciardi, Kantrov, & Goldsmith (2001). Specifically they recommend that language arts should link "to the real world and allows students to explore ideas that help them make sense of human experience" (p. 21).

Graphic Organizers. Guided reading is also useful for teaching students graphic organizers and how to use them to help clarify their own knowledge about a topic. Given a graphic organizer, a guided reading lesson might help students read through the text, fill in the organizer, and learn how to use it to help them summarize and remember important information. For example, a story pyramid might help students as they read about a hero or heroine and fill in the lines. Story pyramids can be used to outline story structure (Curriculum Review, 1997), to organize informational writing (Therriault, 2003), and to organize information about a person. Students can use the following structure to help them summarize the information about the person they have chosen to research:

Line 1: Name of person
Line 2: Two words describing the person
Line 3: Three words describing a trait of the person
Line 4: Four words describing actions of the person
Line 5: Five words describing contributions of the person
Line 6: Six words describing importance of the person
Line 7: Seven words describing a personal reflection on the person' life.

Questioning the Author. Another reading technique often used in guided reading is called *questioning the author* (recall the explanation of this strategy in Chapter 8). Beck, McKeown, Hamilton, and Kucan (1997) and Hoyt (2002) recommend that students be encouraged to ask questions of the author as they are reading. They could ask what the author intended to achieve by writing this text, who the author wanted to read this text, and so on. Helping students learn to apply this strategy is appropriate in guided reading.

However, some students may need to know how to decode various kinds of words. If so, that instruction can be done in guided reading.

Strategy Lessons. Strategy lessons for readers in this age group are often focused on summarizing, recognizing the motivation of characters, learning to skim and scan, and comparing and contrasting texts. The need for these lessons will be determined by the individual needs of the students in your classes, of course. There is no reason to teach a strategy if the student already understands and applies it appropriately.

Several strategy lessons would probably be appropriate while reading biographies and biographical sketches. For example, reading several biographies of the same person would enable students to compare and contrast the treatment of that person by different writers. Skimming a piece can be taught as a strategy for preparing oneself to read it. By skimming, readers can quickly determine how long a biography is, what are its physical characteristics (typeface, margins, etc.), and what seems to be its essence. Scanning would help students look for words or headings that might help them understand the piece better. When students can identify the headings and structure of the piece by scanning it for expected words and forms, they are better prepared to comprehend the material.

For some readers, strategy lessons need to focus on more basic skills such as thinking about the purpose for reading and thinking about how to adjust reading appropriately (close reading of details for material to be on a test but reading more quickly materials that are for personal enjoyment). When given the title for a piece, readers should be able to predict ideas likely to be included.

Mini-Lessons/Focus Lessons. The content of lessons offered at the beginning of both reading and writing workshops are determined by the demonstrated needs of the students and curriculum requirements. For example, if students are having difficulty with understanding how a biographical sketch is composed, then you might read several such sketches, discuss their format, and call attention to a specific feature such as interesting leads. Then ask students to examine the sketches they are writing to rethink their leads.

In reading workshop, you might select several different biographies written in different styles. For example, you might use a biography that is ordered chronologically and another told by explaining a major event in the person's life and then working backward to illuminate the person's growth or experiences that led to that event. Another style describes the person's life set against a background of the times in which they live, and still another offers a snapshot of one or more important events in the person's life. Over several days, you can read from these examples and discuss with students the organizational structure chosen by the author and possible reasons for selecting that style. As students read their own choices of material, they can begin to classify the work by organizational style and determine which styles are easier to read or which are more challenging.

Teacher/Student Conferences. Middle school students need an adult to demonstrate a personal interest in their work and progress. As they become less interested in sharing their thoughts and work with their parents, they need a close personal relationship with an adult. Therefore, the teacher/student conferences recommended for other age groups become even more critical to successful instruction in middle school. Student/teacher conferences in both reading and writing workshop can be scheduled by either students or teachers. Students may choose a conference when they are at a stage in their reading or writing they feel needs either some confirmation that they are doing well or some help in moving forward. Teachers need to keep good records of the conferences they have held, keep a record of the outcomes of every conference, and make sure they are conferencing with every student on a regular basis. Most teachers use a checklist to note the date of conferences and perhaps a line about the results of the conference. These brief records can be kept with other information in a monitoring notebook (as described in Chaper 3). Additional information from the conference can be kept in student folders or in a section of the portfolio being developed by the students.

Notes of these conferences should record the kind of material being read or written, instruction offered at the conference, and the student's response. A quick look at these notes will help the teacher plan the next instructional steps for the student and for the class.

Writing Engagements. As children choose their hero or heroine to study, they will be engaged in producing information to share with their peers in various ways. For example, they might write a script for a video or I-movie of the person's life, they might write a biographical sketch to be used in a class book of heroes or heroines, or they might write an encyclopedia entry for the person they have chosen to study. They might also learn to write a short biography of a person who is a hero to them in some way or to write an autobiography. Each of these genres has rules that should be discussed and writing styles that need to be demonstrated and modeled.

Moline (1996) suggests that teachers help children match the text to the purpose of their writing and help them think about what kind of visuals might be appropriate for the text they are presenting. For example, if students are presenting information about a person, they might include a photograph of the person, a time line of their life, photographs of inventions or something the person created, or illustrations of their homes. It is important for students to think through the best ways to present information both in print and visually.

Strategy Sharing Discussions. These discussions can be organized around the various types of reading and writing experiences taking place in the classroom. For example, if a small group is reading a biography of a selected hero, they might share with the class one or two strategies they have found to be especially helpful in comprehending the material. Others might share a strategy they have used for selecting pieces of information in summarizing a reading selection or for writing a sketch about their selected hero. Still others might share how they made a decision about what to present to the class about their hero. These sessions need to be scheduled on a regular basis. The teacher can arrange with a student or two to share a selected strategy and then lead a class discussion on the value of that strategy and how it applies in reading and writing outside school as well as for school projects.

One recommended strategy is what Hoyt (2002) calls VIP (Very Important Points). Students are given sticky notes that they cut or tear into narrow strips. As they read through a piece, they place a strip on the edge of the page next to an important point or where they are confused or have a question. If students do this in groups, they learn that some people mark the spots as they go although they may modify them as they read on. Others read all through the piece and then go back to select the points where they want to put the strips. Discussing how one decides to solve the problem can be useful to all learners.

An additional strategy might be discussing how one reads a newspaper. Hoyt (2002) suggests that newspaper readers must learn to shift their strategies to match the purpose of the reading, recognize the column structure of a newspaper, and use the photographs and captions to get more information. They must comprehend the shifts in language and style between articles, letters to the editor, classified ads, and advertisements. And they must use tables and graphs to get information and discuss points of view in an article.

Sharing strategies is an appropriate use for the focus lesson or mini-lesson in either reading or writing workshop. Helping students learn how to explain what they have done that helped them read more effectively is a good use of classroom time. Middle school students are more likely to believe a strategy works when they hear it from a peer.

Word Study. The study of words in the middle school years is much more than simply learning the definitions of words found in reading. For children who still need the instruction, word study may focus on prefixes and suffixes and the origin of words of interest. Other word study may be examining the figurative or symbolic use of words, the connotation of words as opposed to their dictionary definition, and the meaning of "loaded" words. Examples of figurative language can be found in *Paul Revere's Ride* (Longfellow, 2001), where the author describes the cemetery below the church as an "encampment" and the belfry of the church as "spectral." In his book on Harriet Tubman, Petry (1996) says freedom is not bought with dust.

Helping students understand the connotation of words is useful for comprehension and for writing. Checking the thesaurus for words that have similar meanings can help students begin to understand the shades of meaning between two similar words or the emotional feelings associated with words beyond their dictionary definitions. Petry (1996) uses *indomitable* to describe Harriet. What is the difference in using *indomitable* and *strong* in the description? Petry also states that "they trusted her implicitly, totally." Why would the author choose to use both those words together? Does implicitly differ from totally in meaning or in connotation?

Loaded words are those words that have a negative connotation and are often used to influence our perceptions of a person, cause, or language. An example of loaded words would be to describe Native Americans as *primitive, treacherous,* or *savages.* These words have a connotation that is usually quite negative. If they find loaded words in their reading, students can discuss why the author might have chosen to use the word and what they felt when they read it.

You may choose to engage in explicit word study for difficult vocabulary encountered in texts. Allen (2002) recommends that only words critical to understanding be taught before reading and that most words encountered during reading should be interpreted through context or structural analysis. As students encounter these words, they can be discussed, charted, and compared to other similar words. Students can draw pictures to help them remember the meanings and employ other techniques for explicit word study.

Many strategies for building vocabulary are effective with middle school readers. One strategy is to create word maps. These maps can be constructed for important words only; they are too time consuming for words that are not likely to be used again. A word map consists of short definitions of the word, what the word is like (synonyms), and examples of the word (Robb, 2003).

Another strategy would be to generate a list of words related to the topic (heroes). Once these words are generated, they can be grouped under labels that are appropriate for the topic. Grouping and labeling words will help children understand how words are related and how they are used in a particular topic (Robb, 2003).

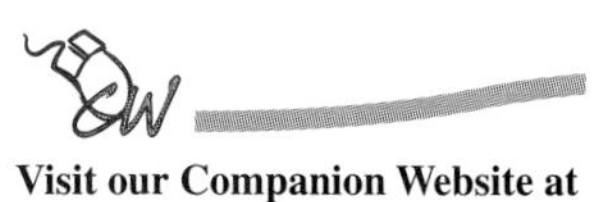

Visit our Companion Website at www.prenhall.com/harp to find links to some of the reading programs frequently used in middle school classrooms.

Literacy Centers. In the middle school classroom, most literacy center work will be done at the computer. Several published programs provide practice in literacy skills on the computer. Some of these programs are useful if the student needs the practice. Computer programs can help the teacher arrange for practice following individual instruction or for the student who needs particular skill practice the rest of the class does not. Computers can also help students with writing and presentation skills that go beyond skill practice or drill on a rule. The important thing about computers is that they should be used to enhance instruction, not to replace the teacher. No computer can make a judgment about the needs of a particular student. Even those programs that move a student to another lesson when a given lesson is mastered cannot know if the student actually needs the following lesson.

The final section of the graphic is the intersection between circle 3 and circle 1. Shared reading is in this intersection because it is a strategy for learning language and learning about language use. Shared reading at the middle school level is used to introduce a new genre of literature, to examine a style of writing that is new or unusual, or to help groups of students prepare a presentation to an audience. Examples of shared reading in a study of heroes and heroines would be reading a play about a hero, reading a heroic story that is written in verse such as the writings of Homer, or helping students read the script of a production they wish to present to the class. Although shared reading is still important as an instructional strategy, it is used less often in the middle grades than with younger children. It should not be overlooked as a strategy for helping students become more skillful readers.

HOW WILL I MODIFY INSTRUCTION FOR STRUGGLING READERS?

Sadly there are many struggling readers in middle school. Some of them lack basic skills, some are poorly motivated and read as little as possible, and some have specific needs for strategy instruction that will help them to be successful readers. The key to good instruction for these readers is careful observation and assessment of the skills and strategies they can use. Of course, the motivation to read is also critical. Without reading, students are not likely to become more skillful readers.

Unrau's (2004) summary of categories of adolescent readers in Figure 14.8 can help guide your choices of assessments and planning for instruction.

Selection of Texts

The selection of texts for reading allows for modifications in reading instruction. Cunningham and Allington (2003) and their colleagues support selecting texts students can read successfully. This can be done in a study of heroes by collecting stories from newspapers and magazines that are short and of appropriate reading levels for the students who need the most help. If mounted on construction paper, there is no stigma attached to reading these articles because all students are reading them.

Responses to Reading

Other adaptations can be made in the expected responses to reading. Kathleen Murphy, a teacher at a vocational school, has developed the following forms for use with struggling readers. The goal of these activities is to provide success for each student and make the curriculum accessible to all learners.

Figure 14.8
Categories of Adolescent Readers

1. *Non-Decoders or Weak Decoders:* Non-alphabetic readers who have not grasped the alphabetic principle that each speech sound has a graphic representation; very impaired reading comprehension and word recognition; little letter–sound or phonological knowledge; profound spelling difficulty.
2. *Compensatory Readers:* Grasp alphabetic principle; impaired word recognition and reading comprehension; limited orthographic and phonological knowledge; use sight-words and sentence context to compensate for lack of phonological knowledge; significant spelling difficulty.
3. *Slow Comprehenders or Non-Automatic Readers:* Accurate but non-automatic, effortful word recognition; naming-speech correlated with slowness in word recognition; lack of practice reading also contributes; use sentence context to help with word recognition; impaired reading comprehension; significant spelling difficulty.
4. *Delayed Readers:* Slow acquisition of automatic word recognition skills; few comprehension strategies, lack awareness of text organization; impaired reading comprehension; lag behind others of similar age; some difficulty with spelling; attribute problems with reading to ability ("stupid") rather than to lack of effort; thus, use fewer strategies; questions arise about cause of strategy deficits.
5. *Readers with Monitoring Difficulties:* Fail to monitor comprehension; experience "illusions of knowing"; root of monitoring difficulty may lie in one or more of the following areas (Hacker, 1998):
   - Lack linguistic or topic knowledge to detect dissonance,
   - Have linguistic and topic knowledge but lack monitoring strategies,
   - Have knowledge and strategies but lack conditional knowledge about when and where to apply them,
   - Comprehension and/or monitoring demand too much of readers' memory and other resources, and
   - Lack motivation to engage in monitoring.
6. *Readers with Control Difficulties:* Fail to execute control over perceived breakdowns in reading process; root of control difficulty may lie in one or more of the following areas (Hacker, 1998):
   - Lack knowledge needed to control problems monitored,
   - Have knowledge needed to control problems but lack strategies to apply their knowledge,
   - Have strategies for application but lack conditional knowledge about when and where to apply them,
   - Comprehension and/or control demand too much of readers' memory and other resources, and
   - Lack motivation to engage control resources.
7. *Readers Lacking Specific Topic Knowledge:* Decode but trouble making meaning because of weak topic knowledge in particular domain, including vocabulary, specifically in relation to subject of current reading; these readers may attain proficiency in some topic domains.
8. *Sub-Optimal Readers:* No problems with word recognition; limited repertoire of basic comprehension strategies; few higher-level language skills/strategies, such as knowledge of different genre, syntax sophistication, grammar mastery; adequate spelling skills.
9. *Disengaged or Inactive Readers:* Have adequate to advanced knowledge base, skills, and strategies but lack motivation or sufficient degree of connection with schooling to read; don't make time in their schedules for reading; may also be seen as disaffiliated or misidentified readers.
10. *English Learners:* Includes students in "immersion" programs, English as a Second Language programs; Bilingual programs; programs using specially designed academic instruction in English techniques.
11. *Advanced, Highly Proficient Readers:* Connects to knowledge base, monitors comprehension, categorizes information while they read, uses metacognitive abilities.

Source: *Content Area Reading and Writing: Fostering Literacies in Middle and High School Cultures.* by Unrau, Norman, © Reprinted by permission of Pearson Education, Inc., Upper Saddle River, NJ.

Activity 1

1. Select a daily hero from the given list (this list might be generated by the students or it might be generated by students with some teacher input).
2. Preview the vocabulary and read the selection. (Selected vocabulary words are defined on the back of the paper.)
3. Complete an assignment answer sheet on the selection.
4. Participate in a class discussion about your hero.

Daily Hero Assignment Sheet

1. Name of hero in today's selection ______________________________
2. Reason you think this person was chosen for the "heroes" series:
   ____
   ____
3. Using your Adjective Selection Sheet as a guide, list three characteristics that you think describe this hero.
   a. ______________________________
   b. ______________________________
   c. ______________________________
4. List three achievements of this hero:
   a. ______________________________
   b. ______________________________
   c. ______________________________

An additional assignment is to create a poster that answers the question "What is a hero?"

Activity 2

Who are some famous inspiring people?

Spend time thinking about this question. Inspiring people are like vitamins for our spirit.

Then with the help of your classmates, create a list of famous, inspiring people and their accomplishments in the chart that follows.

Famous Hero	***Accomplishment***
______________	______________
______________	______________
______________	______________
______________	______________
______________	______________
______________	______________
______________	______________

Activity 3

INSPIRATION

Inside these shapes, write the name of some favorite inspiring people (famous or personal) and write why you find them inspiring. (Six geometric shapes are arranged roughly in two columns on the page where students are requested to write. At the bottom of the page it says:) Now pick your favorite personal hero from the people you have listed. You will be asked to write a report about this individual.

Activity 4

Acts of heroism are not always performed by strangers or celebrities; often they are performed by family members or friends. Using the graphic organizer that follows and the adjective sheet to organize your thoughts, write a well-developed, four-paragraph essay that describes your personal hero.

My Hero

Graphic Organizer

Paragraph One

Topic Sentence

Definition of a Hero

Kind of Hero

Paragraph Two

Description of My Hero

Physical

Character Traits/Heroic Traits

Paragraph Three: Act of Heroism/Good Deeds

Where

When

How

Why

Paragraph Four

Its Impact on Me/Others

Conclusion: "In conclusion . . . "

Source: From Kathleen Murphy, Language Arts Teacher, Greater Lowell Technical High School.

Activity 5 is to complete the essay using the information from Activity 4. For this part of the assignment, students are given four pages, each marked with the paragraph number and the information on the graphic organizer. Students can begin without facing that dreaded blank page. A page of transitional words and phrases is provided to be kept in students' writing folder and used with other writing assignments. An assessment rubric is also provided to help students evaluate their own work before submitting it.

As you can see from these activities, the point is to provide as much scaffolding and support as needed to help students successfully complete the study of heroes and meet the curriculum goals. As students become more confident and skilled, the supports are withdrawn until they can write an essay without being told what the content of each paragraph must be and they will have more choice in their writing. Even with the supports provided by Murphy's activities, there is as much choice as possible about the content of the writing. Her goal is to help students become writers who know they can succeed at writing and who feel confident that their ideas are worth writing about.

Instruction of Struggling Readers

Certainly not all struggling readers need the same instruction. It is critical with readers who are having difficulty that you assess carefully what they can do and what they want to do. Blanket generalizations that struggling readers need phonemic awareness, phonics instruction, or any other instruction are useless. Some readers have had years of phonics instruction; to give them more would only frustrate them further. Some probably did not have effective phonics instruction, and perhaps a few carefully chosen lessons on letter/sound relationships might help them see how to use such knowledge as a reader. But you must always remember that there is no one answer for all readers who are having difficulty.

The other area of critical importance with struggling readers is to find what they are interested in and what purpose they see in learning literacy skills. Students who have no motivation to learn to read and can see no personal reason to engage in literacy activities will not respond to phonics lessons or any other kind of lessons until you have helped them find some personal reason to learn to read and write. You may have to give up your ideas about what middle school readers *should* be reading and find something they *will* read and enjoy. Horror novels, comic books, car repair manuals, fashion magazines, and anything else that sparks some interest (and does not cross the line of being indecent) should be considered as possible instructional material.

What Supports Will I Need to Offer My English Language Learners?

Schools across the country treat second language learners, those students whose first language is not English, in many different ways.

1. Some are enrolled in bilingual programs until they are proficient enough in English to move to a mainstream classroom.
2. Some are provided extra language help through special teachers who teach English as a second language, usually in small groups or one on one with a tutor.
3. Some are placed in content classrooms with teachers especially trained in sheltered English instruction.
4. Some have none of these options, but are placed in regular classes with teachers with no special training.

We know it takes time for a student to become proficient in a second language. Some reach what Cummins (1984) describes as *basic interpersonal communication skills* or the ability to use conversational English in a relatively short time, perhaps in a year or two if they are in an English-speaking environment. However, the English required for academic success (what Cummins calls *cognitive academic language proficiency*) takes many years to master. Cummins has estimated that it takes five to seven years to learn a language well enough to compete with native speakers in a content class such as history or science.

What the Law Requires for English Language Learners

Federal law based on the 1974 court case *Lau v. Nichols* states that school districts are obligated to provide educational services to students with limited English proficiency. The law requires that the schools take "appropriate action," but does not specify what methods or programs are to be used. Generally, appropriate action has been guided by the principles specified in another federal case (*Casteneda v. Pickard,* 1981). These principles require sound theory (some expert must view the theory as appropriate for making instructional decisions) and the provision of adequate support (the school is obligated to provide resources, procedures, and personnel to implement the program). In addition, the program must achieve results; students must become able to participate in instructional programs without a disadvantage. Schools interpret these laws and principles in many ways; therefore, approaches to teaching English language learners vary from state to state and from district to district. Recently some states have voted to restrict programs for English language learners to programs that provide English immersion or sheltered English and have dismantled their bilingual programs. There is no evidence that either English immersion or sheltered English meet the federal criteria for effective programs.

Structured English Immersion and Sheltered English Instruction

These terms are often used interchangeably, and both refer to programs where academic content goals and English language learning goals are considered in planning instruction and where teachers have training in how to modify instruction to meet the needs of students who are not yet proficient in English. Some principles of good sheltered English instruction are:

- Individual student language ability determines language objectives.
- Instruction provides the content of the core curriculum for that grade.
- Students are taught strategies for building content knowledge, English proficiency, and problem solving.
- Content is organized around important topics.
- The rate of teacher's speech is slower and may be accompanied by pictures or illustrations to clarify meaning.
- Drama and gestures are used to help clarify meaning.
- Visual aids such as maps, drawings, graphs, and pictures are used to help clarify content. Wood and Tinajero (2002) studied the use of a strategy called the *picture word inductive model.* In this model students study a picture selected by the teacher, identify what they see in the picture, and use the words generated to build word lists, study patterns in words, and develop titles and paragraphs about the picture.
- Film, videotapes, and bulletin boards are used to support learning.
- Various grouping formats are used to help students master content and language, including pairs, small groups, and skill building groups.
- Assessment is not limited to tests; portfolios, self-evaluation, diagnostic procedures, and performance-based evaluations are also employed.

Many of the strategies and techniques that mark sheltered English instruction are simply good instruction for all students.

For example, explaining to students what they are going to learn and then reviewing what they have learned at the end of the class, engaging students in meaningful activities,

Sheltered English instruction is facilitated by cooperative learning groups.

providing timely feedback, linking new learning to past learning are all strategies that benefit second language learners, but they also benefit all learners. Some strategies that are especially important to second language learners include paying attention to wait time (second language learners may have to translate the question, compose the answer, and then translate the answer before replying), presenting key vocabulary terms before reading assignments, clarifying meaning in the student's first language whenever possible, providing extra materials such as films, photos, and so on, and building on student background experiences. (Echevarria & Graves, 2003).

Possible Adaptations for a Study of Heroes for Second Language Learners

1. Choose the vocabulary you want to teach. For example, in this study of heroes and heroines, you might want to emphasize *courage, bravery, contribution, incomprehensible, incentive, disheveled,* and *preoccupation.* You would plan to use these words several times in various contexts and to act out some of them because they are not concrete words.
2. Choose any language structures you want to emphasize during this study. You might want to work on alliteration in poetry or narrative structure in poetry. When you have decided what structures your students need to learn, then you will find models of these structures in literature, use them in your own speech, write them on the chalkboard or overhead transparency, and place examples on a chart or bulletin board.
3. Encourage students to find stories about heroes or heroines in their own culture. Make sure they can post these stories, share them with their peers, and compare them to heroes and heroines of other cultures.
4. Provide video or computer programs that will help clarify the meaning of the content and the importance of the content for life outside school. For heroes and heroines, this might mean searching the archives of the local news station for stories about heroes and how they helped their communities.
5. Make sure second language learners are treated as knowledgeable students. They may lack language skills in English, but they do not lack intelligence or the ability to learn.

6. Require that some assignments be completed with partners and some in small groups. Students could compare the characteristics of the heroes or heroines they have selected in pairs and make a Venn diagram of the comparison.
7. Provide written and oral directions. Seeing the words in print is often helpful for students learning a language.
8. Be sure these students get to tell about and write about their own personal heroes and heroines. If they need to tell their stories in their native language first, they can do so. Then with help from you or another student, they can tell some parts in English.
9. Teach students how to take notes by modeling note taking from an article in a book and an article on the computer.
10. Help second language students learn to monitor their reading comprehension. You may need to do guided reading lessons that focus on monitoring comprehension. Sometimes students can pronounce every word of a selection correctly but do not understand it at all.

THINKING AS A TEACHER

1. Think carefully about how you feel personally about students who attend American schools and who do not speak English. Determine what you can do to increase your knowledge about these students and programs that are available for them.
2. Many of the struggling readers found in middle school are boys who do not like to read. What materials would you collect for your classroom that you think middle school boys would like to read? Can you find these materials at different levels of difficulty?
3. Some reading programs include a study of American heroes as one of the topics for instruction. Do you think there is an advantage to limiting the study of heroes to American heroes, or would you argue for a broader view of heroes?

FIELD-BASED ACTIVITIES

1. Examine the contents of a reading series for middle grade classes. Do you think the topics suggested would be of interest to middle school readers? Interview two or three middle school students to determine what topics they would like to learn about in school and compare those to the topics in the reader.
2. Create a lesson plan for a reader based on material that is high interest, low difficulty. How could you present this material so that the reader did not feel stigmatized or different from his or her peers?
3. Examine some of the computer reading programs available for struggling middle school readers. Plan how you would incorporate one of these programs into your reading program or explain why you do not believe the material fits your philosophy of teaching reading.

REFERENCES

Allen, J. (2002). *On the same page.* Portland, ME: Stenhouse.

Beck, I. L., McKeown, M. G., Hamilton, R. L., & Kucan, L. (1997). *Questioning the author: An approach for enhancing student engagement with text.* Newark, DE: International Reading Association.

Brown, V. L., Hammill, D. D., & Wiederholt, J. L. (1995). *Test of reading comprehension: Examiner's manual* (3rd ed.). Austin, TX: Pro-ed.

Center for Early Adolescence. (1987). *School environments for young adolescents: What parents should look for.* Retrieved from National Parent Information Network at *www.nipn/org/library/pre1998/n00286.html*

Ciardi, M. R., Kantrov, I., & Goldsmith, L. T. (2001). *Guiding curriculum decisions for middle-grades language arts.* Portsmouth, NH: Heinemann.

Cummins, J. (1994). Primary language instruction and the education of language minority students. In *Schooling and language minority students: A theoretical framework* (2nd ed.). Los Angeles: California State University, National Evaluation, Dissemination and Assessment Center.

Cunningham, P. M., & Allington, R. L. (2003). *Classrooms that work: They can all read and write.* Boston: Allyn and Bacon.

Curriculum Review. (1997). Outline stories with pyramid power, Vol. 37(4). author.

Echevarria, J., & Graves, A. (2003). *Sheltered content instruction: Teaching English-language learners with diverse abilities.* Boston: Allyn and Bacon.

Finders, M. J., & Hynds, S. (2003). *Literacy lessons: Teaching and learning with middle school students.* Columbus, OH: Merrill.

Goleman, D. (1995). *Emotional intelligence.* New York: Bantam.

Hacker, D. J. (1998). Self-regulated comprehension during normal reading. In D. J. Hacker, J. Dunlosky, & A. C. Graesser (Eds.) *Metacognition in educational theory and practice* (pp. 165–191). Mahwah, NJ: Erlbaum.

Hammill, D. D., & Larsen, S. C. (1996). *Test of written language examiner's manual.* Austin, TX: Pro-ed.

Hill, B. C., Noe, K. L. S., & King, J. A. (2003). *Literature circles in middle school: One teacher's journey.* Norwood, MA: Christopher-Gordon.

Hoyt, L. (2002). *Make it real: Strategies for success with informational texts.* Portsmouth, NH: Heinemann.

Moline, S. (1996). *I see what you mean: Children at work with visual information.* York, ME: Stenhouse.

Pate, P. E., Homestead, E., & McGinnis, K. (1995). Student and teacher co-created integrated curriculum. In Y. Siu-Runyan & C. V. Faircloth (Eds.), *Beyond separate subjects: Integrative learning at the middle level.* (pp. 117–126) Norwood, MA: Christoper-Gordon.

Robb, L. (2003). *Teaching reading in social studies, science, and math.* New York: Scholastic.

Roser, N. (2001). A place for everything and literature in its place. *The New Advocate, 14,* 211–221.

Stern, R., & Rosenzweig, D. (1999). Hormone-driven kids: A call for social and emotional learning the middle school years. *Voices from the Middle, 7,* 3–8.

Unrau, N. (2004). *Content area reading and writing: Fostering literacies in middle and high school cultures.* Columbus, OH: Merrill.

Therriault, T. (2003). Using the expository pyramid to stimulate informational writing. In L. Hoyt, M. Mooney, & B. Parkes (Eds.), *Exploring informational texts: From theory to practice.* Portsmouth, NH: Heinemann.

Wood, K. D., & Tinajero, J. (2002). Using pictures to teach content to second language learners. *Middle School Journal, 33,* 47–51.

Children's Books

Anderson, L. H. (2001). *Speak.* New York: Puffin.

Anonymous. (1998). *Go ask Alice.* New York: Simon & Schuster.

Bierhorst, J. (1971). *In the trail of the wind: American Indian poems and ritual orations.* New York: Farrar, Straus, & Giroux.

Bruchac, J. (2000). *Sacajawea.* San Diego, CA: Silver Whistle.

Delacre, L. (2000). *Salsa stories.* New York: Scholastic.

Ewing, L. (1998). *Drive-by.* New York: Harper Trophy.

Hoose, P. M. (2001). *We were there, too: Young people in U. S. history.* New York: Farrar, Straus, & Giroux.

Longfellow, H. W. (2001). *The midnight ride of Paul Revere.* Illus by Bing. New York: Handprint Books.

Meyers, W. D. (1990). *Scorpions.* New York: Harper Trophy.

Nelson, M. (2001). *Carver: A life in poems.* Asheville, NC: Front Street.

Partridge, E. (2002). *This land was made for you and me: The life and songs of Woody Guthrie.* New York: Viking.

Pelzer, D. J., & Pelzer, D. (1995). *A child called "It."* Deerfield Beach, FL: Health Communications.

Pelzer, D. J., & Pelzer, D. (1997). *The lost boy.* Deerfield Beach, FL: Health Communications.

Petry, A. (1996). *Harriet Tubman: Conductor on the Underground Railroad.* New York: Harper Trophy.

Stanley, J. (2000). *Hurry freedom: African Americans in gold rush California.* New York: Crown Publishers.

Talbott, H. (2000). *Forging freedom: A true story of heroism during the Holocaust.* New York: Putnam.

Taylor, M. D. (2001). *The land.* New York: Penguin Putnam.

PART

4 ONGOING PROFESSIONAL GROWTH

Now that you are nearly to the end of your study of this text, let's visit one last time the reading process questions to which you have responded twice. This time compare the depth and breadth of your current answers to the answer you gave at the beginning of Part Three. Celebrate how much you have learned!

READING PROCESS QUESTIONS

- How do I understand the reading process?
- How do I get children to understand the reading process?
- How do I teach children to monitor their use of the reading process?
- How do I discern that children are monitoring their use of the reading process?

The course in which you are currently enrolled and your study of this text are only the beginning of your journey toward becoming a truly informed reading teacher. To provide increasingly polished, professional instruction, you will need to attend carefully to your own professional growth. To that end, we conclude this text with a chapter on professional growth, Becoming an Even More Informed Reading Teacher. It is unusual to find a chapter of this kind in a reading text, but we include it here because of our deep conviction that your continuing professional development will be the basis for your growth as a teacher.

Our late friend, Jan Duncan, a New Zealander who spent countless hours delivering in-service education to American and New Zealand teachers, said, "There are only two kinds of teachers in the world. They are either green and growing or ripe and rotting." We want you to remain, throughout your career, "green and growing."

Chapter 15

Becoming an Even More Informed Reading Teacher

LOOKING AT THE RESEARCH

Recent research on school change and teacher development suggests seven conditions that are vital to teacher learning in the workplace:

1. Teachers engage in self-study of their own practice. This condition grounds the work of teacher improvement.
2. Schools contain within them both collegial structures and personal support for reflection and for study of the knowledge base on teaching.
3. The knowledge base on teaching is construed as areas of performance, repertoires, and matching, not "effective behaviors."
4. The risk taking and vulnerability conducive to teacher growth and learning are successfully managed.
5. There is systematic and varied access to two kinds of professional knowledge: one's own personal practical knowledge and that of one's colleagues and the public domain research-based knowledge on teaching.
6. Professional knowledge and data about student needs should inform teachers' choices regarding the content and process of their own learning.
7. Leaders act in congruence with the previous six conditions and explicitly support them.

Source: J. Saphier & R. Gower. (1997). *The skillful teacher: Building your teaching skills* (p. 563). Acton, MA: Research for Better Teaching.

Focus Questions

- How do I become an even more informed reading teacher?
- What should I know about professional organizations that support the teaching and learning of reading?
- What should I know about professional conferences?
- What Internet resources are available to help me stay informed?

REAL TEACHERS, REAL PRACTICE

Meet Julie Taylor, *a fifth-grade teacher*

One can spend a lifetime teaching and never be aware of the wider world around them. Such was my career until 1994. I had been teaching 24 years by that point, working with groups of Young Astronauts, student council, and our school cheerleaders. I was busy trying to balance being a deacon for my church, racing after two active daughters, being a firefighter's wife, raising and showing Appaloosa horses, and teaching school.

One day my principal called me into her office to tell me that she had placed my name in for the Presidential Award for Elementary Science. "When you get the paper work, I want you to fill it out!" she declared. I had absolutely no idea what a Presidential Award was or what was involved in the application. I was honored that she even thought I should be considered for such an award. Time came and went. I filled out the application and then forgot all about it. I completed the process out of respect for my principal, but I was positive that I didn't belong in any such group. I taught children, attended a few conferences, got my own daughters and classroom children involved in the world around them, and had designed a few activities to enhance the curriculum for my students, but as far as I was concerned, I taught. That's all. To my amazement I was notified that I was a finalist for the state of California. It made me sit up and think. What was going on here? My principal's decision to place my name in for this award was about to change my life completely.

What has happened because I was encouraged to reach outward from my class, to try for things beyond my borders? Here are a few things that happened during this adventure that started in 1994. When I became a finalist, the world outside my local community learned that I existed. I discovered that people who influence a larger educational community look for people who are willing to become part of this wider world.

One person who had an influence over the change that was happening in my life was a fellow finalist who presented on a national level. As we became friends, she first encouraged me to help with workshops and then eventually to share my own ideas. At these conferences I learned about other doors of opportunity. The first was NASA Educator Workshops. After filling out another application, I was selected to participate in a two-week class at the Jet Propulsion Laboratory in Pasadena, Calif. Other doors began to open. I met scientists and engineers who were willing to interact with my class and were interested in what I had to say. I also became friends with the educator administrator who encouraged me to become involved with the Council for Elementary Science International. First I was an awardee and served on its board, and now I am the council secretary.

I also learned about the Space Telescope Science Institute's Amazing Space Summer Program. Since 1998 I have helped the program design two web sites (Galaxies Galore and Planet Impact) and have spent two summers working on science activities to go with current missions. Because of my connections with the Jet Propulsion Laboratory, I have become a Solar System Educator and have worked on several projects for the lab. This last year I become California's Presidential Awardee for Elementary Science, and I applied for and received my National Board Certification. New doors continue to open because of the connections I made after that first award and my principal's faith in me.

What does all this mean to new teachers? Teach and teach well. Become involved with your students, develop activities to help them learn, and learn yourself by taking classes, reading, and going to conferences. Be the very best that you can be and never accept second best from yourself or your students. And then when your principal, fellow teacher, or friend puts your name in for something new, be brave and fill out the application. When an opportunity arises for presenting at a local or national conference, designing a web site, or writing material to influence education, you need to jump at the chance because you will grow from the experience.

There is another realm of teaching beyond your classroom where your influence reaches farther than your school. You need to be aware of it whether you decide to help build it or if you are just learning from it. Your personal growth transfers to the abilities of your students and their development. There is a world beyond your classroom. Discover it!

HOW DO I BECOME AN EVEN MORE INFORMED READING TEACHER?

The course on the teaching of reading in which you studied this text is only the beginning of your journey toward becoming an informed reading teacher. Each interaction you have with a child, each day you teach, each conversation you have with a colleague, each interaction you have with a parent will move you toward deeper understandings. Attending to the conditions for teacher development described by Saphier and Gower (1997) will guide your on-the-job learning, known as in-service education.

Self-Study of Your Own Practice

Carefully observing your students' progress and reflecting on your practice with them is one of the best ways to begin self-study. The sequence of events are: assessing what your learners know and what they need to learn next, planning instruction, delivering instruction, assessing and evaluating student learning, and reflecting carefully and thoughtfully on the process, based on informed observation of your students at each step along the way. You may decide either to keep a journal or to assemble a portfolio.

Journaling as Reflection. Buy a blank book and begin writing your reflections on your teaching there. You might decide to write a daily entry, though the multiple pressures of teaching may dictate that you can only do this writing on a weekly basis. The following questions may guide your writing:

What went really well with your teaching?
What would you change if you could do it over again?
What did you learn about your learners?
What did you learn about yourself?
What did you learn about teaching?

Even if you don't have time to write your reflections in a journal, try to think through your answers to these questions on a frequent basis.

Portfolios. Throughout the year, select items to include in your teaching portfolio. Portfolios have been proven to be an effective method to encourage teachers to evaluate their abilities and enhance their skills (Campbell, Cignetti, Melenyzer, Nettles, & Wyman, 1997). Your portfolio might contain written documentation of your planning, curriculum, organization and presentation methods, interactions with students and parents, assessment methods and data, classroom management approaches, and student work samples. If you are working with emergent readers, you might include running records, developmental reading checklists, developmental writing checklists, samples of children's writing, and summaries of anecdotal records.

If you are working with developing and fluent readers in grades 3–5, you might include many of the items listed previously. Additional items might be samples of work produced by children as parts of themes or integrated units, records of genres children have read and written, and documentation of children's progress in meeting the challenges of content-area reading, including research using print and electronic media. The list would be similar if you are working with older children.

Studying the Knowledge Base

You should attend to two aspects of the knowledge base on teaching and learning. The first is your own personal, practical knowledge and that of your colleagues; the second is the public domain, research-based knowledge on teaching (Saphier & Gower, 1997). You may set the goal of becoming comfortable operating within each of these knowledge bases.

Your Personal Knowledge and That of Your Colleagues. You can expand your personal knowledge base and share in the knowledge of your colleagues in several helpful ways, including book discussion groups, mentoring partners, and peer observations.

Book Discussion Groups. Professional book discussion groups are chaired by a colleague who volunteers to give leadership to this activity. A date and time are announced for the first meeting of the group, and when those wishing to join come together, they select a title to read. The person organizing the group may have selected three or four titles from which the group chooses, or the choice may be wide open. The group decides on a meeting schedule and how much will be read before each meeting. If the group is small enough, the decision might be made to have some discussions via e-mail.

Mentoring Partners. Some schools have formalized the process of assigning a mentor to new teachers. In other settings informal mentoring partnerships develop as new teach-

Figure 15.1
Collaborative Professional Development

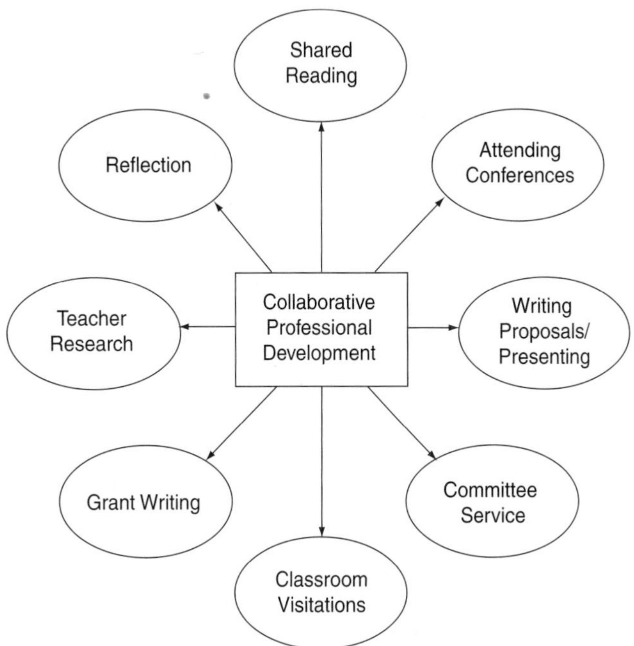

Source: M. P. Correia & J. M. McHenry. (2002). *The Mentor Handbook: Practical Suggestions for Collaborative Reflection and Analysis* (p. 65). Norwood, MA: Christopher-Gordon Publishers, Inc. Reprinted with permission.

ers seek advice from more experienced professionals. A mentor is an experienced professional who is willing to serve as a coach, guide, and/or model for less experienced teachers (Correia & McHenry, 2002). Figure 15.1 illustrates some of the forms of collaborative professional development you and your mentor might choose.

- Shared reading implies that you and your mentor agree on a professional journal (more on these later) that you both enjoy reading. Plan a regular meeting time when the two of you can come together to discuss your readings. You may identify certain articles to read within a journal, or you may select other journals, research articles, or books. Keep a record of your readings to include in your portfolio.
- Attending conferences is a wonderful way to keep up with what is new in the field. Both the International Reading Association and the National Council of Teachers of English (more on these later) sponsor conferences focused on literacy at the local, state, national, and international levels.
- Writing proposals/presenting is another good way to stretch your knowledge and skills. When you attend a conference, pick up a proposal form for the next conference. You and your mentor may decide on some aspect of your teaching that the two of you could present at a conference. Send in the proposal form. You may be pleasantly surprised when you are invited to present!
- Committee service is something you and your mentor can decide to do together. Check with your principal or district curriculum coordinators to learn about committees. Volunteers are always needed and welcome. This is an excellent way to get to know professionals beyond the walls of your school.

Teachers improve in the art and craft of teaching through peer feedback.

- Grant writing may be a way for you and your mentor to fund a special project you wish to do together. Check web sites for professional organizations and their journals for requests for grant proposals.
- Teacher research implies asking questions about your practice, collecting data on that practice, and drawing conclusions and implications for future work.
- Classroom visitations are helpful when novice teachers observe master teachers. Some school districts build visitation days into their schedules so that new teachers may observe others.
- Reflecting on your classroom visitations and your own teaching will provide you with insights that will promote your growth as a teacher. Some teachers keep their reflections in journals so they may revisit them over time.

Peer Observations. Peer observations can be done between you and your mentor or between you and another trusted teacher working at the same grade level. The challenge here is to find a time when you can leave your classroom to observe another teacher. A goal of grant writing might be to get the funds to hire substitute teachers to release classroom teachers for observations. Another key is having solid plans about what to observe and what data to collect during the observation.

The Central Dauphin School District in Harrisburg, Pennsylvania, has developed a Reading Lesson Observation Framework (RLOF) you and your peer observer may wish to use. The RLOF is displayed in Figure 15.2.

Development of the framework began with the staff agreeing upon goals for the literacy program and then developing shared understandings of effective literacy practices. Once effective practices were agreed upon, teams of teachers were engaged in creating the classroom observation framework consistent with these practices (Henk, Moore, Marinak, & Tomasetti, 2000). You and your peer observer may wish to try out the framework as it is presented and then modify it as you gain experience using it.

Figure 15.2
Reading Lesson Observation Framework

THE READING LESSON OBSERVATION FRAMEWORK

Teacher ______________________ Observer ______________________

School Year ____________ Date of Observation ____________ Observation # ________

Observation occurred: Before reading ________ During reading ________ After reading ________

Component I. Classroom Climate	**O**	**C**	**R**	**N**
A. Many different types of authentic reading materials such as magazines, newspapers, novels, and nonfiction works are displayed and are available for children to read independently.	☐	☐	☐	☐
B. The classroom has a reading area such as a corner or classroom library where children are encouraged to go to read for enjoyment.	☐	☐	☐	☐
C. An area is available for small-group reading instruction.	☐	☐	☐	☐
D. Active participation and social interaction are integral parts of reading instruction in this classroom.	☐	☐	☐	☐
E. The classroom environment indicates that reading and writing are valued and actively promoted (e.g., purposeful writing is displayed, journals are maintained, Word Walls are used, book talks and read-alouds by teacher occur regularly).	☐	☐	☐	☐
F.	☐	☐	☐	☐
G.	☐	☐	☐	☐

Component II. Pre-reading Phase	**O**	**C**	**R**	**N**
A. During the pre-reading discussion, the teacher asked the children to preview the text by having them read the title of the selection, look at the illustrations, and then discuss the possible contents of the text.	☐	☐	☐	☐
B. Children were encouraged to activate their background knowledge through the use of K-W-L charts, webs, anticipation guides, etc.	☐	☐	☐	☐
C. By generating a discussion about the topic before reading the selection, the teacher created an interest in the reading.	☐	☐	☐	☐
D. The teacher introduced and discussed the new vocabulary words in a meaningful context, focusing on those new words that were central to the understanding of the story.	☐	☐	☐	☐
E. The children were encouraged to state or write predictions related to the topic of the reading selection.	☐	☐	☐	☐
F. Before reading occurred, the teacher helped the children identify the type of material that was to be read to determine what their purpose should be for reading it.	☐	☐	☐	☐
G. The objective for the reading lesson was clearly identified for the children, along with how the objective related to previous lessons.	☐	☐	☐	☐
H. The teacher continually assessed children's prereading discussion and made appropriate adjustments.	☐	☐	☐	☐
I.	☐	☐	☐	☐
J.	☐	☐	☐	☐

(Continued)

Source: Figure from Henk, William A., Moore, Jesse C., Marinak, Barbara Ann, & Tomassetti, Barry W. (2000, February) A reading lesson observation framework for elementary teachers, principals, and literacy supervisors. *The Reading Teacher, 53*(5), 358–359.

Figure 15.2
Reading Lesson Observation Framework *Continued*

THE READING LESSON OBSERVATION FRAMEWORK				
Component III. Guided Reading Phase	**O**	**C**	**R**	**N**
A. At appropriate points during the reading of the selection, the children were asked to evaluate their initial predictions.	☐	☐	☐	☐
B. The children were asked to identify or read aloud portions of text that confirmed or disproved predictions they had made about the selection.	☐	☐	☐	☐
C. The comprehension discussion focused on the purposes that were established for reading the selection.	☐	☐	☐	☐
D. An appropriate mix of factual and higher-level thinking questions were incorporated into the comprehension discussion.	☐	☐	☐	☐
E. During the reading lesson, the teacher modeled fluent reading and then encouraged the children to read fluently and with expression.	☐	☐	☐	☐
F. The teacher encouraged the children to adjust their reading rate to fit the material.	☐	☐	☐	☐
G. The teacher monitored the children and gave proper assistance and feedback while they read or completed practice activities.	☐	☐	☐	☐
H. The teacher modeled and encouraged the use of new vocabulary during the discussion.	☐	☐	☐	☐
I. The children were encouraged to use a variety of word study strategies (e.g., words within words, context, syllabication) to decipher the meaning of unknown words as appropriate.	☐	☐	☐	☐
J. The children were encouraged to use appropriate comprehension monitoring and fix-up strategies during reading (e.g., paraphrasing, rereading, using context, asking for help).	☐	☐	☐	☐
K. The teacher reminded the children to make use of their knowledge of text structure (e.g., fictional story grammar, nonfiction text structures).	☐	☐	☐	☐
L. The teacher periodically assessed the children's ability to monitor meaning.	☐	☐	☐	☐
M.	☐	☐	☐	☐
N.	☐	☐	☐	☐
Component IV. Post-reading Phase	**O**	**C**	**R**	**N**
A. During the post-reading discussion, the children were asked to read aloud sections of the text that substantiated answers to questions and confirmed or disproved predictions they had made about the selection.	☐	☐	☐	☐
B. The teacher asked the children to retell the material they had read, concentrating on major events or concepts.	☐	☐	☐	☐
C. The children were asked to explain their opinion and critical judgments.	☐	☐	☐	☐
D. The teacher had the children provide a written response to the reading (e.g., written retelling, written summarization, written evaluation).	☐	☐	☐	☐
E. Children were encouraged to use new vocabulary in written responses. Examples and modeling were provided by the teacher.	☐	☐	☐	☐
F. Writing was used as a natural extension of reading tasks.	☐	☐	☐	☐
G. The teacher continually monitored children's comprehension and provided appropriate feedback.	☐	☐	☐	☐
H.	☐	☐	☐	☐
I.	☐	☐	☐	☐

Figure 15.2
Continued

THE READING LESSON OBSERVATION FRAMEWORK

Component V. Skill and Strategy Instruction	**O**	**C**	**R**	**N**
A. The teacher provided a clear explanation about the structure of the skill or strategy to be learned and described when and how it could be used.	☐	☐	☐	☐
B. The teacher modeled the use of skill or strategy so children were able to see how it would be used in an appropriate situation.	☐	☐	☐	☐
C. Any direct teaching of a phonemic element was immediately followed by children using the skill in a meaningful context.	☐	☐	☐	☐
D. Explicit skill and strategy instruction was provided and applied in the context of the reading selection.	☐	☐	☐	☐
E. The children were encouraged to use before, during, and after reading strategies as appropriate.	☐	☐	☐	☐
F. Reading skill and strategy instruction moved children toward independent use through scaffolding.	☐	☐	☐	☐
G.	☐	☐	☐	☐
H.	☐	☐	☐	☐

Component VI. Materials and Tasks of the Lesson	**O**	**C**	**R**	**N**
A. The selections used for the reading lesson were appropriate for children of this ability and grade level.	☐	☐	☐	☐
B. The reading materials represented authentic types of texts.	☐	☐	☐	☐
C. Reading materials and tasks reflected a sensitivity to the diverse learning needs of the children.	☐	☐	☐	☐
D. The amount and type of independent work was appropriate for the level of the children and instructional goals it was designed to achieve.	☐	☐	☐	☐
E. Independent work often contained open-ended questions that encouraged children to enhance and extend their understanding of the selection.	☐	☐	☐	☐
F. The literacy tasks the children were asked to perform during the lesson were meaningful and relevant.	☐	☐	☐	☐
G. The children engaged in various modes of reading during the lesson (e.g., silent, oral, guided, shared).	☐	☐	☐	☐
H. The teacher provided opportunities for the children to read for enjoyment.	☐	☐	☐	☐
I. Children were encouraged to respond personally or creatively to the reading material.	☐	☐	☐	☐
J. A balance existed in the reading lesson between teacher-initiated and student-initiated activities.	☐	☐	☐	☐
K. Reading materials and tasks were organized around themes when appropriate.	☐	☐	☐	☐
L.	☐	☐	☐	☐
M.	☐	☐	☐	☐

Figure 15.2
Reading Lesson Observation Framework *Continued*

THE READING LESSON OBSERVATION FRAMEWORK

Component VII. Teacher Practices	**O**	**C**	**R**	**N**
A. The teacher focused on reading as a meaningful process.	☐	☐	☐	☐
B. The instructional techniques used by the teacher and the ways they were executed reflected an awareness of recommended practices.	☐	☐	☐	☐
C. Children were grouped appropriately and flexibly.	☐	☐	☐	☐
D. The teacher's management of the reading lesson provided for active student engagement.	☐	☐	☐	☐
E. The pace and flow of the various phases of the reading lesson represented an effective use of time.	☐	☐	☐	☐
F. The teacher's instruction was sensitive to the diversity of children's experiences and their social, cultural, ethnic, and linguistic needs.	☐	☐	☐	☐
G. The teacher actively promoted the integration of the language arts in this lesson.	☐	☐	☐	☐
H. The teacher encouraged the children to take informed risks and promoted safe failure.	☐	☐	☐	☐
I. The teacher's conferences with children were timely, focused, and positive in nature.	☐	☐	☐	☐
J. Authentic assessment practices were used in this lesson.	☐	☐	☐	☐
K. The teacher's planned goals, actual instruction, and assessment practices were aligned.	☐	☐	☐	☐
L.	☐	☐	☐	☐
M.	☐	☐	☐	☐

Key to Checklist

O = Observed	This component was observed and was judged to be of *satisfactory* quality.
C = Commendation	This component was observed and was judged to be of *very high* quality.
R = Recommendation	This component either was not observed or was judged to be of *unsatisfactory* quality.
N = Not applicable	This component was *not observed* because it was not appropriate for the lesson.

The Public Domain Research-Based Knowledge on Teaching. There are many useful ways to access this knowledge base. You can access a great deal of information through two particularly helpful web sites, the Center for the Improvement of Early Reading Achievement (CIERA) and Ask ERIC.

To visit the CIERA web site, go to our Companion Website for a link.

Center for the Improvement of Early Reading Achievement (CIERA). The CIERA home page provides links to a variety of technical reports on current topics in reading education and to an extensive library of previously published work, recent news, and presentations. The search engine on this site works easily and effectively. CIERA is housed at the University of Michigan School of Education.

To visit the Ask ERIC web site, go to our Companion Website for a link.

Ask ERIC. ERIC is a clearinghouse on information and technology housed at Syracuse University. A visit to the Ask ERIC web site provides access to thousands of journal articles and ERIC digest articles across a dozen topic areas in education, such as teaching, general education, specific populations, and educational technology. When you get to the Ask ERIC home page, choose from the following links: About Ask ERIC, Search ERIC Database, Ask an ERIC Expert, Question Archive, Lesson Plans, Mailing Lists, and Ask ERIC Update Newsletter.

Another invaluable source of information on the ever deepening and widening knowledge base is the array of journals published by professional organizations.

WHAT SHOULD I KNOW ABOUT PROFESSIONAL ORGANIZATIONS THAT SUPPORT THE TEACHING AND LEARNING OF READING?

Two professional organizations are dedicated to teaching and learning in the language arts. One is the International Reading Association (IRA), and the other is the National Council of Teachers of English (NCTE). You will discover a rich array of products, services, and publications available from both organizations.

International Reading Association (IRA)

Classroom teachers, reading specialists, consultants, administrators, supervisors, researchers, psychologists, librarians, college professors, media specialists, literacy volunteers, students, and parents make up the membership of the IRA. Today, the association has more than 90,000 members. Worldwide, through IRA Councils and Affiliates, more than 350,000 individuals and institutions are involved in 100 countries.

The IRA serves members at local, state, provincial, national, and international levels through more than 1,250 councils, 42 national affiliates, and 39 special interest groups. These special interest groups provide a forum for sharing information about specific areas of interest and as a source for your professional growth. Examples include Balanced Reading Instruction, Children's Literature and Reading, Content Area Reading, and Disabled Reader. For a complete listing of all special interest groups, go to *www.reading.org/dir/sig*.

The IRA publishes 6 journals and approximately 25 new books, videotapes, and brochures each year. You may find some of the journals helpful in keeping up with the latest changes in the field of reading education.

The Reading Teacher (RT). RT is a journal focused on the literacy education of children to the age of 12. It is published eight times per year. *The Reading Teacher* provides consideration of teaching practices, research, and trends in literacy education. Articles are published in the journal only after critical review and acceptance by an editorial board. This process is known as *peer review. RT* also sponsors an unmoderated listserv called RTEACHER. The listserv assists a diverse population, now numbering more than 1,000 educators, interested in issues of literacy in the elementary classroom. You must have an e-mail account to participate. For additional information go to *www.reading.org/publications/rt/rt_listserv*.

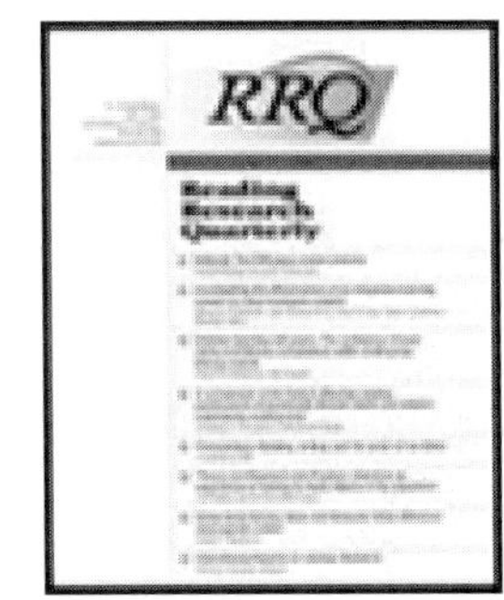

Reading Research Quarterly (RRQ). *Reading Research Quarterly* is a professional research journal focusing on scholarship and questions of literacy among learners of all ages. There is also an online version of *RRQ,* and RRQ Online Supplements offer online-only material that complements the content of the print journal.

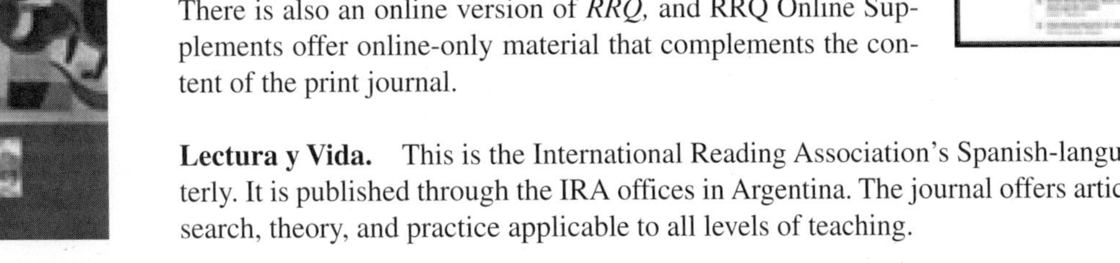

Lectura y Vida. This is the International Reading Association's Spanish-language quarterly. It is published through the IRA offices in Argentina. The journal offers articles on research, theory, and practice applicable to all levels of teaching.

Journal of Adolescent & Adult Literacy (JAAL). This is the only journal published exclusively for teachers of adolescents and adults. The journal offers suggestions for teaching techniques, reviews of student and teacher resources, and tips for integrating media into your instruction.

Reading Online. *reading online* is a journal of K-12 practice and research found only in an online format. Each issue features articles and book reviews, a "from the editors" section, international perspectives on practice and research from literacy leaders worldwide, discussions of media literacy, critical literacy and visual literacy, and an opportunity to join in conversations in online communities. For more information about *reading online,* go to *www.readingonline.org.*

Thinking Classroom. This quarterly journal is also published in Russian as *Peremena,* which means "change." *Thinking Classroom* serves as an international forum of exchange among teachers, teacher educators, and others interested in promoting democratic teaching practices. The journal features articles that foster learner-centered teaching strategies, including critical and creative thinking, active and cooperative learning, and problem solving.

In addition to the journals described previously, the IRA publishes a bimonthly newspaper, *Reading Today.* The newspaper publishes news and features about trends and issues that influence literacy education. The newspaper also reports information about association activities, publications, and meetings.

Source: This information on the IRA and IRA journals was adapted from *www.reading.org/publications/* and "We Teach the World to Read: Report to the Global Community," available at *www.reading.org*. Used with permission.

LOOKING AT THE RESEARCH

What the research says about excellent reading teachers

The IRA Board of Directors adopted a position statement on the nature of excellent reading teachers in January 2000 (IRA, 2000). The position statement provides a research-based description of the distinguishing qualities of excellent classroom reading teachers:

1. They understand reading and writing development and believe all children can learn to read and write.
2. They continually assess children's individual progress and relate reading instruction to children's previous experience.
3. They know a variety of ways to teach reading, when to use each method, and how to combine the methods into an effective instructional program.
4. They offer a variety of materials and texts for children to read.
5. They use flexible grouping strategies to tailor instruction to individual students.
6. They are good reading "coaches" (that is, they provide help strategically).

Compare this list with the things you have learned in this text. To what extent are you prepared to be an excellent reading teacher? What will be your next learning goal?

National Council of Teachers of English (NCTE)

NCTE is devoted to improving the teaching and learning of English and the English language arts at all levels of education. NCTE has 75,000 members and subscribers in the United States and other countries. Individual members are teachers and supervisors of English programs in elementary, middle, and secondary schools; faculty in college and university English departments; teacher educators; local and state agency English specialists; and professionals in related fields. Individuals belong to any of four broad sections of membership: elementary, middle, secondary, or college.

NCTE sponsors major interest groups called *conferences* and informal special interest groups called *assemblies.* Four conferences serve teachers of college writing and rhetoric, teacher educators in higher education and in-service posts, teachers with interests in whole language, and English department chairs. Assemblies ranging over a wide variety of topics meet at NCTE conventions.

NCTE commissions monitor and report on trends and issues in the teaching of language, composition, literature, reading, media, and curriculum.

There are about 125 NCTE affiliates, one in each state and in five of the Canadian provinces. In addition, many states have local NCTE affiliates. To find your local affiliate, go to *www.ncte.org/affiliates.*

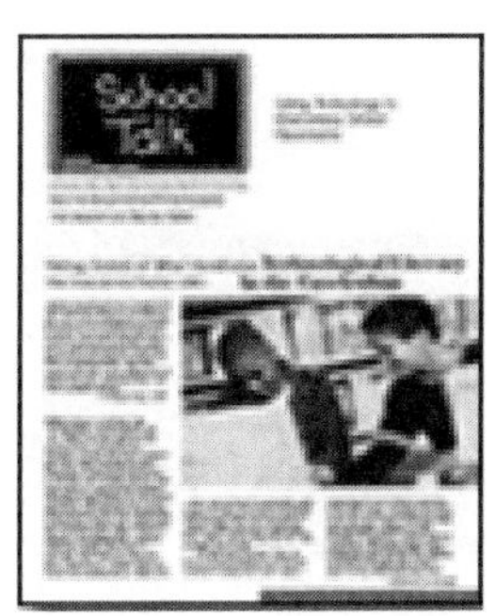

NCTE publishes a wide array of professional journals ranging in interest from elementary school through college teaching of English. Here we review five journals of particular interest to teachers in elementary and middle schools.

Language Arts. This peer-reviewed journal is for elementary and middle school teachers and teacher educators. It covers all aspects of language arts learning and teaching, primarily concerned with children in prekindergarten through the eighth grade. Issues discuss both theory and classroom practice, highlight current research, and review children's and young adolescent literature. The journal is published bimonthly, September, November, January, March, May, and July.

School Talk. This six-page newsletter is intended to help classroom teachers bridge the gap between the ideal and the real worlds of teaching. Each issue focuses on one particular topic and deals with questions teachers are asking. Teachers choose the topics for each newsletter.

Voices from the Middle. This journal devotes each issue to one topic or concept related to literacy and learning at the middle school level. Each issue includes teachers' descriptions of classroom practices, middle school students' reviews of adolescent literature, a technology column, and reviews of professional resources for teachers. Connections between theory and practice are explored in issues published in September, December, March, and May.

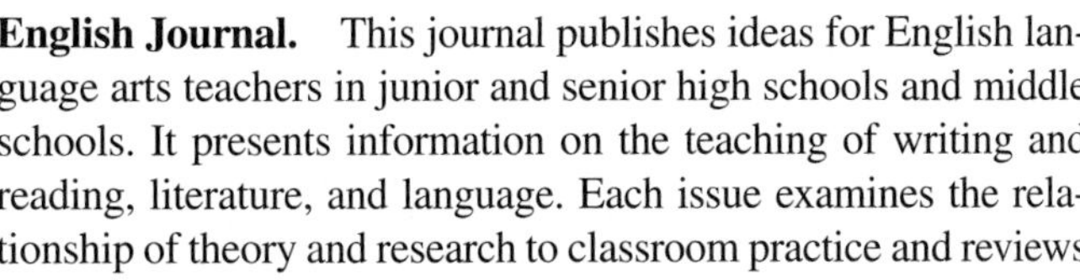

English Journal. This journal publishes ideas for English language arts teachers in junior and senior high schools and middle schools. It presents information on the teaching of writing and reading, literature, and language. Each issue examines the relationship of theory and research to classroom practice and reviews

current materials of interest to English teachers, including books and electronic media. The journal is published bimonthly, September, November, January, March, May, and July.

Classroom Notes Plus. This is a quarterly collection of practical teaching ideas contributed by middle school and junior and senior high school English teachers across the country. Features include in-depth writing activities in "Focus on Writing" and practical suggestions for teaching literature in "Focus on Literature." It is published August, October, January and April.

Source: Information on NCTE and NCTE journals was adapted from *www.ncte.org* and *www.ncte.org/journals/*. Used with permission.

Other Professional Organizations with Links to Literacy

While IRA and NCTE are the two largest professional organizations with a primary interest in literacy, other groups offer support for teachers on literacy issues. They are the National Reading Conference, the National Association for the Education of Young Children, Teachers of English to Speakers of Other Languages, and the Association for Childhood Education International.

National Reading Conference (NRC). This professional organization is made up of members particularly interested in literacy research and dialogue around literacy and related topics. Their purpose is to support the professional development of emerging and established scholars and to advocate research-informed improvements in education. You can learn more about NRC at *http://nrc.Oakland.edu/information/missionstatement.asp*.

National Association for the Education of Young Children (NAEYC). NAEYC's purpose is "leading and consolidating the efforts of individuals and groups working to achieve healthy development and constructive education for all young children." This organization represents the largest number of early childhood educators in the United States with over 100,000 members and a national network of nearly 450 local, state, and regional affiliates. For more information about NAEYC visit *www.naeyc.org*.

Teachers of English to Speakers of Other Languages (TESOL). The mission of TESOL is to ensure excellence in English language teaching to speakers of other languages. The association is global, with approximately 14,000 members. For more information about TESOL, visit *www.tesol.org*.

Association for Childhood Education International (ACEI). The mission of ACEI is to "promote and support in the global community the optimal education and development of children, from birth through early adolescence, and to influence the professional growth of educators and the efforts of others who are committed to the needs of children in a changing society." As a nongovernmental organization, ACEI has consultative status with the United Nations Economic and Social Council and the United Nations Children's Fund. For more information on ACEI, visit *www.udel.edu/bateman/acei/*.

WHAT SHOULD I KNOW ABOUT PROFESSIONAL CONFERENCES?

Many professional organizations seek to lend support to you and your teaching across the curriculum. Some examples include the National Council of Teachers of Mathematics (*www.nctm.org*), National Council for the Social Studies (*www.ncss.org*), National Science

Teachers hone their skills and learn new techniques by attending conferences.

Teachers Association (*www.nsta.org*), and the Association for Supervision and Curriculum Development (*www.ascd.org*). You may want to become familiar with each of these professional organizations and others by visiting their web sites. Each of them sponsors national conferences. Here we will draw examples from the conferences sponsored by IRA and NCTE and their affiliates. These are the conferences most directly related to literacy teaching and learning.

Conferences on Many Levels

The International Reading Association and the National Council of Teachers of English sponsor conferences that range in size from fairly small local conferences to larger state conferences, to yet larger regional conferences and large national conferences.

Local Conferences. Both IRA and NCTE sponsor conferences by local affiliates. These local affiliates usually serve teachers in a few adjacent counties, so the local conferences will draw teachers from your school system and nearby schools. There are typically a few hundred attendees. One of the greatest advantages of participating in local conferences is that you will be able to network with teachers from your system and those closest to yours. Local conferences usually invite speakers from the nearby area rather than bringing in speakers from great distances. This means you will be able to hear from speakers who may share some of the same challenges, interests, and dilemmas you and your colleagues face. Another advantage is that registration and travel costs are usually quite reasonable. If you join a local affiliate, you could become active in planning and producing local conferences.

State Conferences. The state affiliates of both NCTE and IRA sponsor statewide conferences. These are usually annual and draw up to a thousand or more attendees (of course some larger states have much larger conferences). State conferences usually invite well-known speakers from within the state as well as from across the country. These conferences typically extend over two or three days, so you have many opportunities to hear speakers, participate in round-table discussions, and view exhibits. The exhibits are usually presented by publishers who produce school materials such as basal readers, children's trade books, and professional books for teachers. One of the advantages of a state conference is the chance to look at the exhibits. Participation in a state conference will be more costly than a local conference because of higher registration fees, travel, and food and lodging costs.

Regional Conferences. Regional conferences are to state conferences as state conferences are to local conferences. By participating in an IRA or NCTE sponsored regional conference, you will be able to network not only with professionals from your state, but from nearby states within your region. This means there will be a larger program than at state conferences, with well-known teachers, researchers, and authors from across the country.

National Conventions. IRA and NCTE national conventions are held annually in large North American cities. It is usually exciting just to visit the host city. The national conventions are wonderful professional experiences because of their size and the number and caliber of the speakers. It is enlightening to be able to choose from such rich program selections that permit you to hear from teachers, researchers, authors, and policy makers from throughout the country. IRA national conventions usually attract 16,000 or more attendees and offer more than 2,000 speakers. NCTE national conventions are smaller with approximately 6,000 attendees.

The national conventions offer the greatest variety of program activities. Day-long institutes focus on a broad topic, such as "Exploring Informational Texts Through Guided Reading and Writing." Within these institutes are several small sessions that offer opportunities to hear from practicing teachers and researchers and to participate in round-table discussions. In symposia of two or more hours, several speakers deliver short addresses on a common topic and then talk with each other and the audience. Other hour long sessions permit you to hear one or two short presentations on a topic. Finally, there are poster sessions. Poster sessions present research, demonstrate classroom or administrative practice, and teacher preservice and in-service innovations. They are called poster sessions because the presenters make a poster display you can visit before the presentation to look at artifacts, and then you return later for an informal presentation and discussion.

One of the most interesting features of a national convention is the exhibit hall. The IRA Annual Convention has between 300 and 400 exhibitors. You can spend hours strolling and examining the exhibits. You will note that the exhibits represent a wide range of philosophical points of view, and not all of them agree with what you hear from speakers or your own philosophical stance. We hope you will be able to attend some national conventions as well as conventions at each of the levels we have described.

Go to the Weblinks in Chapter 15 at our Companion Website at www.prenhall.com/harp for links to the IRA and NCTE where you can learn about the schedule for national conferences for the next several years.

WHAT INTERNET RESOURCES ARE AVAILABLE TO HELP ME STAY INFORMED?

Throughout this text you have had invitations to visit our Companion Website for links to other sites, and we have suggested yet many other sites along the way. Here we draw your attention to some effective sites we have not mentioned before.

American School Directory

The American School Directory (ASD) has as its mission to provide an Internet home page location for every school in the United States. You can have your school's home page placed on the ASD server, and you can access other schools' pages from all across the country. This can be an exciting way to find out what other schools are doing. When you locate a school's information page, you are told the school's name and address as well as contact information, including the principal's name, the office phone, fax, e-mail address, and web address. School information includes the number of students, homerooms, grades, computer platform, and other helpful information. There is a yearly subscription fee of $36 or a one-month fee of $9.99. Contact American School Directory at *www.asd.com*.

You learned about the Reading Teacher listserv and the new teacher listserv previously. You may find two other listserv addresses helpful.

Topica

This is a comprehensive site for mailing lists with a search engine. If you type "elementary teacher" into the search inquiry you will find a wide array of listserv groups you may wish to join to share teaching ideas. To contact Topica, use *www.liszt.com*

International Federation of Library Associations and Institutions

This site contains information about many list directories. You may find it useful as another avenue to tap into listserv discussions that will provide you with immediate teaching ideas and professional growth. Contact *www.ifla.org/I/training/listserv/lists.htm*

Kathy Schrock's Guide for Educators

This web site is a categorized list of sites you will find useful in both planning instruction and for professional growth. It is part of Discovery School, and it is indexed for easy use. The home page has the following major headings: subject access, search tools, teacher helpers, and Schrockguide stuff. When you click on the Literature/Language Arts subject access link, you will hotlink to a site with 75 literature and language arts links. Among them are: Children's Picture Book Database, a keyword-searchable database of more than 4,000 picture books; Database of Award-Winning Children's Literature, a site that allows you to create a tailored reading list for a student or an entire class; and Reading Corner, access to author pages, award-winners lists, and book reviews for students in grades 2–10. To reach Kathy Schrock's Guide for Educators (Schrock, 1995), go to *www.school.discovery.com/schrockguide/*.

The possibilities for further growth as a teacher are much greater than just those described in this chapter. It is highly likely that, as technology develops, the opportunities for professional growth will expand in ways we cannot conceive today. It is an exciting time to be a teacher.

THINKING AS A TEACHER

1. You have enjoyed using some Internet resources to get lesson plan ideas, to learn about books for a theme you are doing, and to find out how other schools are treating that theme. The teacher next door to you asserts that the Internet is an unreliable source of teaching ideas because "just anyone" can post unreliable information there. How will you respond?
2. You and some of your colleagues are interested in beginning a book discussion group. What would you suggest as a process for selecting books and organizing and

managing the group. Think specifically about these challenges. Also, consider your justifications for your decisions and recommendations.

3. You like the idea of having a mentoring partner, but you need to think deeply about the qualities this person should display and your feelings about the partnership. What qualities would you expect in this partner, and under what conditions would you be comfortable with such a partnership?

FIELD-BASED ACTIVITIES

1. Use one of the Internet sites presented in this chapter to find and join a listserv. Engage with the list on at least three occasions, making contributions to the discussions. Write a reflection on your experience. What did you like about the experience? What challenges and discomforts, if any, did you encounter? What role do you see listserv Internet resources playing in your future as a teacher?
2. Use the Reading Lesson Observation Framework (Figure 15.2) to observe another teacher conducting a reading lesson, or invite another persons to use it as they observe you. Have a discussion with this person about both of your reactions to the instrument. Think about what changes you might want to make in the framework, and think about how it could be helpful to you in the future.
3. Visit the IRA or NCTE web site to learn about affiliates in your area. Contact the affiliate to learn about future conferences. Make every effort to attend a local conference. Write a reflection on the experience.

REFERENCES

Campbell, D. M., Cignetti, P. B., Melenyzer, B. J., Nettles, D. H., & Wyman, R. M. (1997). *How to develop a professional portfolio: A manual for teachers.* Boston: Allyn and Bacon.

Correia, M. P., & McHenry, J. M. (2002). *The mentor's handbook: Practical suggestions for collaborative reflection and analysis.* Norwood, MA: Christopher-Gordon.

Henk, W. A., Moore, J. C., Marinak, B. A., & Tomasetti, B. W. (2000). A reading lesson observation framework for elementary teachers, principals, and literacy supervisors. *The Reading Teacher, 53,* 358–369.

Saphier, J., & Gower, R. (1997). *The skillful teacher: Building your teaching skills.* Acton, MA: Research for Better Teaching.

Schrock, K. (1995, June). *Kathy Schrock's guide for educators.* Retrieved from *http://discoveryschool.com/schrockguide/*

MOTIVATION TO READ PROFILE

SCORING DIRECTIONS: MRP READING SURVEY

The survey has 20 items based on a 4-point scale. The highest total score possible is 80 points. On some items the response options are ordered least positive to most positive (see item 2 below), with the least positive response option having a value of 1 point and the most positive option having a point value of 4. On other items, however, the response options are reversed (see item 1 below). In those cases it will be necessary to *recode* the response options. Items where recording is required are starred on the scoring sheet.

EXAMPLE: Here is how Maria completed items 1 and 2 on the Reading Survey.

1. My friends think I am _____.
   - ☐ a very good reader
   - ■ a good reader
   - ☐ an OK reader
   - ☐ a poor reader
2. Reading a book is something I like to do.
   - ☐ Never
   - ☐ Not very often
   - ☐ Sometimes
   - ■ Often

To score item 1 it is first necessary to recode the response options so that

a poor reader equals 1 point,
an OK reader equals 2 points,
a good reader equals 3 points, and
a very good reader equals 4 points.

Since Maria answered that she is *a good reader* the point value for that item, 3, is entered on the first line of the Self-Concept column on the scoring sheet. See below.

The response options for item 2 are ordered least positive (1 point) to most positive (4 points), so scoring item 2 is easy. Simply enter the point value associated with Maria's response. Because Maria selected the fourth option, a 4 is entered for item 2 under the Value of Reading column on the scoring sheet. See below.

Scoring sheet

Self-Concept as a Reader	Value of Reading
*recode 1. 3	2. 4

To calculate the Self-Concept raw score and Value raw score, add all student responses in the respective column. The Full Survey raw score is obtained by combining the column raw scores. To convert the raw scores to percentage scores, divide student raw scores by the total possible score (40 for each subscale, 80 for the full survey).

MRP READING SURVEY SCORING SHEET

Student name ____________________

Grade ____________________ Teacher ____________________

Administration date ____________________

Recoding scale

1 = 4

2 = 3

3 = 2

4 = 1

Self-Concept as a Reader		Value of Reading	
*recode	1. _____		2. _____
	3. _____	*recode	4. _____
*recode	5. _____		6. _____
*recode	7. _____	*recode	8. _____
	9. _____	*recode	10. _____
*recode	11. _____		12. _____
	13. _____		14. _____
*recode	15. _____		16. _____
	17. _____	*recode	18. _____
	19. _____	*recode	20. _____

SC raw score: _____ /40 **V raw score:** _____ /40

Full survey raw score (Self-Concept & Value): _____ /80

Percentage scores

Percentage scores	Self-Concept	☐
	Value	☐
	Full Survey	☐

Comments: ____________________

____

____

MOTIVATION TO READ PROFILE

Reading survey

Name ______________________________ Date ______________________________

Sample 1: I am in __________.

- ☐ Second grade
- ☐ Third grade
- ☐ Fourth grade
- ☐ Fifth grade
- ☐ Sixth grade

Sample 2: I am a __________.

- ☐ boy
- ☐ girl

1. My friends think I am __________.

- ☐ a very good reader
- ☐ a good reader
- ☐ an OK reader
- ☐ a poor reader

2. Reading a book is something I like to do.

- ☐ Never
- ☐ Not very often
- ☐ Sometimes
- ☐ Often

3. I read __________.

- ☐ not as well as my friends
- ☐ about the same as my friends
- ☐ a little better than my friends
- ☐ a lot better than my friends

4. My best friends think reading is __________.

- ☐ really fun
- ☐ fun
- ☐ OK to do
- ☐ no fun at all

5. When I come to a word I don't know, I can __________.

- ☐ almost always figure it out
- ☐ sometimes figure it out
- ☐ almost never figure it out
- ☐ never figure it out

6. I tell my friends about good books I read.

- ☐ I never do this.
- ☐ I almost never do this.
- ☐ I do this some of the time.
- ☐ I do this a lot.

7. When I am reading by myself. I understand ___________.
- ☐ almost everything I read
- ☐ some of what I read
- ☐ almost none of what I read
- ☐ none of what I read

8. People who read a lot are ___________.
- ☐ very interesting
- ☐ interesting
- ☐ not very interesting
- ☐ boring

9. I am ___________.
- ☐ a poor reader
- ☐ an OK reader
- ☐ a good reader
- ☐ a very good reader

10. I think libraries are ___________.
- ☐ a great place to spend time
- ☐ an interesting place to spend time
- ☐ an OK place to spend time
- ☐ a boring place to spend time

11. I worry about what other kids think about my reading ___________.
- ☐ every day
- ☐ almost every day
- ☐ once in a while
- ☐ never

12. Knowing how to read well is ___________.
- ☐ not very important
- ☐ sort of important
- ☐ important
- ☐ very important

13. When my teacher asks me a question about what I have read, I ___________.
- ☐ can never think of an answer
- ☐ have trouble thinking of an answer
- ☐ sometimes think of an answer
- ☐ always think of an answer

14. I think reading is ___________.
- ☐ a boring way to spend time
- ☐ an OK way to spend time
- ☐ an interesting way to spend time
- ☐ a great way to spend time

15. Reading is ___________.
- ☐ very easy for me
- ☐ kind of easy for me
- ☐ kind of hard for me
- ☐ very hard for me

16. When I grow up I will spend ___________.

☐ none of my time reading
☐ very little of my time reading
☐ some of my time reading
☐ a lot of my time reading

17. When I am in a group talking about stories, I ___________.

☐ almost never talk about my ideas
☐ sometimes talk about my ideas
☐ almost always talk about my ideas
☐ always talk about my ideas

18. I would like for my teacher to read books out loud to the class ___________.

☐ every day
☐ almost every day
☐ once in a while
☐ never

19. When I read out loud I am a ___________.

☐ poor reader
☐ OK reader
☐ good reader
☐ very good reader

20. When someone gives me a book for a present, I feel ___________.

☐ very happy
☐ sort of happy
☐ sort of unhappy
☐ unhappy

TEACHER DIRECTIONS: MRP CONVERSATIONAL INTERVIEW

1. Duplicate the Conversational Interview so that you have a form for each child.
2. Choose in advance the section(s) or specific questions you want to ask from the Conversational Interview. Reviewing the information on students' Reading Surveys may provide information about additional questions that could be added to the interview.
3. Familiarize yourself with the basic questions provided in the interview prior to the interview session in order to establish a more conversational setting.
4. Select a quiet corner of the room and a calm period of the day for the interview.
5. Allow ample time for conducting the Conversational Interview.
6. Follow up on interesting comments and responses to gain a fuller understanding of students' reading experiences.
7. Record students' responses in as much detail as possible. If time and resources permit, you may want to audiotape answers to A1 and B1 to be transcribed after the interview for more in-depth analysis.
8. Enjoy this special time with each student!

MOTIVATION TO READ PROFILE

Conversational Interview

Name ______________________________ Date ______________________________

A. EMPHASIS: NARRATIVE TEXT

Suggested prompt (designed to engage student in a natural conversation): I have been reading a good book. . . I was talking with a friend about it last night. I enjoy talking about good stories and books that I've been reading. Today I'd like to hear. . . about what you have been reading.

1. Tell me about the most interesting story or book you have read this week (or even last week). Take a few minutes to think about it. (Wait time.) Now, tell me about the book or story.

Probes: What else can you tell me? Is there anything else? ______________________________

____

____

____

____

____

____

2. How did you know or find out about this story? ______________________________

____

____

☐ assigned ☐ in school
☐ chosen ☐ out of school

3. Why was this story interesting to you? ______________________________

____

____

____

B. EMPHASIS: INFORMATIONAL TEXT

Suggested prompt (designed to engage student in a natural conversation): Often we read to find out about something or to learn about something. We read for information. For example, I remember a student of mine. . . who read a lot of books about/to find out as much as he/she could about. . . Now, I'd like to hear about some of the informational reading you have been doing.

1. Think about something important that you learned recently, not from your teacher and not from television, but from a book or some other reading material. What did you read about? (Wait time.) Tell me about what you learned.

Probes: What else could you tell me? Is there anything else? ______________________________

____

____

____

____

2. How did you know or find out about this book/article? ______________________________

☐ assigned ☐ in school
☐ chosen ☐ out of school

3. Why was this book (or article) important to you? ______________________________

C. EMPHASIS: GENERAL READING

1. Did you read anything at home yesterday? __________ What? ______________________________

2. Do you have any books at school (in your desk/storage area/locker/book bag) today that you are reading? Tell me about them.

3. Tell me about your favorite author.

4. What do you think you have to learn to be a better reader?

5. Do you know about any books right now that you'd like to read? Tell me about them.

6. How did you find out about these books?

7. What are some things that get you really excited about reading books?

   Tell me about…

8. Who gets you really interested and excited about reading books?

____

____

Tell me more about what they do. ____

____

____

____

Source: Figures from Gambrall, Linda B., Palmer, Barbara Martin, Codling, Rose Marie, & Mazzoni, Susan Anders. (1996, April). Assessing motivation to read. *The Reading Teacher, 49*(7), 518–533.

THE READER SELF-PERCEPTION SCALE

THE READER SELF-PERCEPTION SCALE

Listed below are statements about reading. Please read each statement carefully. Then circle the letters that show how much you agree or disagree with the statement. Use the following:

SA = Strongly Agree
A = Agree
U = Undecided
D = Disagree
SD = Strongly Disagree

Example: **I think pizza with pepperoni is the best.** SA A U D SD

If you are *really positive*, that pepperoni pizza is best, circle SA (Strongly Agree).
If you *think* that is good but maybe not great, circle A (Agree).
If you *can't decide* whether or not it is best, circle U (Undecided).
If you *think* that pepperoni pizza is not all that good, circle D (Disagree).
If you are *really positive* that pepperoni pizza is not very good, circle SD (Strongly Disagree).

	1.	I think I am a good reader.	SA	A	U	D	SD
[SF]	2.	I can tell that my teacher likes to listen to me read.	SA	A	U	D	SD
[SF]	3.	My teacher thinks that my reading is fine.	SA	A	U	D	SD
[OC]	4.	I read faster than other kids.	SA	A	U	D	SD
[PS]	5.	I like to read aloud.	SA	A	U	D	SD
[OC]	6.	When I read, I can figure out words better than other kids.	SA	A	U	D	SD
[SF]	7.	My classmates like to listen to me read.	SA	A	U	D	SD
[PS]	8.	I feel good inside when I read.	SA	A	U	D	SD
[SF]	9.	My classmates think that I read pretty well.	SA	A	U	D	SD
[PR]	10.	When I read, I don't have to try as hard as I used to.	SA	A	U	D	SD
[OC]	11.	I seem to know more words than other kids when I read.	SA	A	U	D	SD
[SF]	12.	People in my family think I am a good reader.	SA	A	U	D	SD
[PR]	13.	I am getting better at reading.	SA	A	U	D	SD
[OC]	14.	I understand what I read as well as other kids do.	SA	A	U	D	SD
[PR]	15.	When I read, I need less help than I used to.	SA	A	U	D	SD
[PS]	16.	Reading makes me feel happy inside.	SA	A	U	D	SD
[SF]	17.	My teacher thinks I am a good reader.	SA	A	U	D	SD
[PR]	18.	Reading is easier for me than it used to be.	SA	A	U	D	SD
[PR]	19.	I read faster than I could before.	SA	A	U	D	SD

[OC]	20. I read better than other kids in my class.	SA	A	U	D	SD
[PS]	21. I feel calm when I read.	SA	A	U	D	SD
[OC]	22. I read more than other kids.	SA	A	U	D	SD
[PR]	23. I understand what I read better than I could before.	SA	A	U	D	SD
[PR]	24. I can figure out words better than I could before.	SA	A	U	D	SD
[PS]	25. I feel comfortable when I read.	SA	A	U	D	SD
[PS]	26. I think reading is relaxing.	SA	A	U	D	SD
[PR]	27. I read better now than I could before.	SA	A	U	D	SD
[PR]	28. When I read, I recognize more words than I used to.	SA	A	U	D	SD
[PS]	29. Reading makes me feel good.	SA	A	U	D	SD
[SF]	30. Other kids think I'm a good reader.	SA	A	U	D	SD
[SF]	31. People in my family think I read pretty well.	SA	A	U	D	SD
[PS]	32. I enjoy reading.	SA	A	U	D	SD
[SF]	33. People in my family like to listen to me read.	SA	A	U	D	SD

DIRECTIONS FOR ADMINISTRATION, SCORING, AND INTERPRETATION

The Reader Self-Perception Scale (RSPS) is intended to provide an assessment of how children feel about themselves as readers. The scale consists of 33 items that assess self-perceptions along four dimensions of self-efficacy (Progress, Observational Comparison, Social Feedback, and Physiological States). Children are asked to indicate how strongly they agree or disagree with each statement on a 5-point scale (5 = Strongly Agree, 1 = Strongly Disagree). The information gained from this scale can be used to devise ways to enhance children's self-esteem in reading and, ideally, to increase their motivation to read. The following directions explain specifically what you are to do.

Administration

For the results to be of any use, the children must: (a) understand exactly what they are to do, (b) have sufficient time to complete all items, and (c) respond honestly and thoughtfully. Briefly explain to the children that they are being asked to complete a questionnaire about reading. Emphasize that this is not a *test* and that there are no *right* answers. Tell them that they should be as honest as possible because their responses will be confidential. Ask the children to fill in their names, grade levels, and classrooms as appropriate. Read the directions aloud and work through the example with the students as a group. Discuss the response options and make sure that all children understand the rating scale before moving on. It is important that children know that they may raise their hands to ask questions about any words or ideas they do not understand.

The children should then read each item and circle their response for the item. They should work at their own pace. Remind the children that they should be sure to respond to all items. When all items are completed, the children should stop, put their pencils down, and wait for further instructions. Care should be taken that children who work more slowly are not disturbed by children who have already finished.

Scoring

To score the RSPS, enter the following point values for each response on the RSPS scoring sheet (Strongly Agree = 5, Agree = 4, Undecided = 3, Disagree = 2, Strongly Disagree = 1) for each item number under the appropriate scale. Sum each column to obtain a raw score for each of the four specific scales.

Interpretation

Each scale is interpreted in relation to its total possible score. For example, because the RSPS uses a 5-point scale and the Progress scale consists of 9 items, the highest total score for Progress is 45 ($9 \times 5 = 45$). Therefore, a score that would fall approximately in the middle of the range (22–23) would indicate a child's somewhat indifferent perception of her or himself as a reader with respect to Progress. Note that each scale has a different possible total raw score (Progress = 45, Observational Comparison = 30, Social Feedback = 45, and Physiological States = 40) and should be interpreted accordingly.

As a further aid to interpretation, Table 2 presents the descriptive statistics by grade level for each scale. The raw score of a group or individual can be compared to that of the pilot study group at each grade level.

Table 2
Descriptive statistics by scale and grade level

		Progress			Observational Comparison			Social Feedback			Physiological States		
Grade level	*n*	Mean	SD	SE	Mean	SD	SE	Mean	SD	SE	Mean	SD	SE
4	506	39.6	4.8	.21	20.7	4.7	.21	33.2	5.3	.24	31.8	5.9	.26
5	571	39.5	5.2	.22	21.0	4.8	.20	32.7	5.4	.22	31.0	6.4	.27
6	402	39.0	5.1	.25	21.3	4.6	.23	32.0	5.5	.27	30.5	6.2	.31
Total	1,479	39.4	5.0	.13	20.9	4.7	.12	32.7	5.4	.14	31.2	6.2	.16

Note: Total possible raw scores are Progress (45), Observational Comparison (30), Social Feedback (45), and Physiological States (40).

THE READER SELF-PERCEPTION SCALE SCORING SHEET

Student name ______________________________

Teacher ______________________________

Grade ____________________ Date ____________________

Scoring key: 5 = Strongly Agree (SA)
4 = Agree (A)
3 = Undecided (U)
2 = Disagree (D)
1 = Strongly Disagree (SD)

		Scales		
General Perception	Progress	Observational Comparison	Social Feedback	Physiological States
1. _____	10. _____	4. _____	2. _____	5. _____
	13. _____	6. _____	3. _____	8. _____
	15. _____	11. _____	7. _____	16. _____
	18. _____	14. _____	9. _____	21. _____
	19. _____	20. _____	12. _____	25. _____
	23. _____	22. _____	17. _____	26. _____
	24. _____		30. _____	29. _____
	27. _____		31. _____	32. _____
	28. _____		33. _____	
Raw score	_____ of 45	_____ of 30	_____ of 45	_____ of 40
Score interpretation				
High	44+	26+	38+	37+
Average	39	21	33	31
Low	34	16	27	25

Appendices A and B from Henk, William A., & Melnick, Steven A. (March 1995) The reader self-perception scale (RSPS): A new tool for measuring how children feel about themselves as readers. *The Reading Teacher, 48*(6), 470–482.

APPENDIX C

FORTY-FIVE PHONIC GENERALIZATIONS

	Percentage of Utility		
Generalization (*example*)	Primary (Clymer, 1963)	Grades 1–6 (Bailey, 1967)	Grades 4–6 (Emans, 1967)
1. When there are two vowels side by side, the long sound of the first vowel is heard and the second vowel is usually silent. (*leader*)	45	34	18
2. When a vowel is in the middle of a one-syllable word, the vowel is short. (*bed*)	62	71	73
3. If the only vowel letter is at the end of a word, the letter usually stands for a long sound. (*go*)	100	100	100
4. When there are two vowels, one of which is final *e*, the first vowel is long and the *e* is silent. (*cradle*)	63	57	63
5. The *r* gives the preceding vowel a sound that is neither long nor short. (*part*)	78	86	82
6. The first vowel is usually long and the second silent in the digraphs *ai*, *ea*, *oa*, and *ui*. (*claim*, *bean*, *roam*, *suit*)	66	60	58
ai		71	
ea		56	
oa		95	
ee		87	
ui		10	
7. In the phonogram *ie*, the *i* is silent and the *e* is long. (*grieve*)	17	31	23
8. Words having double *e* usually have the long *e* sound. (*meet*)	98	87	100
9. When words end with silent *e*, the preceding *a* or *i* is long. (*amaze*)	60	50	48
10. In *ay*, the *y* is silent and gives its *a* long sound. (*spray*)	78	88	100
11. When the letter *i* is followed by the letters *gh*, the *i* usually stands for its long sound and the *gh* is silent. (*light*)	71	71	100
12. When *a* follows *w* in a word, it usually has the sound *a* as in *was*. (*wand*)	32	22	28
13. When *e* is followed by *w*, the vowel sound is the same as represented by *oo*. (*shrewd*)	35	40	14
14. The two letters *ow* make the long *o* sound. (*row*)	59	55	50

15. *W* is sometimes a vowel and follows the vowel digraph rule. (*arrow*)	40	33	31
16. When *y* is the final letter in a word, it usually has a vowel sound. (*lady*)	84	89	98
17. When *y* is used as a vowel in words, it sometimes has the sound of long *i*. (*ally*)	15	11	4
18. The letter *a* has the same sound (*o*) when followed by *l*, *w*, and *u*. (*raw*)	48	34	24
19. When *a* is followed by *r* and final *e*, we expect to hear the sound heard in *care*. (*flare*)	90	96	100
20. When *c* and *h* are next to each other, they make only one sound. (*charge*)	100	100	100
21. *Ch* is usually pronounced as it is in *kitchen*, *catch*, and *chair*.	95	87	67
22. When *c* is followed by *e* or *i*, the sound of *s* is likely to be heard. (*glance*)	96	92	90
23. When the letter *c* is followed by *o* or *a*, the sound of *k* is likely to be heard. (*canal*)	100	100	100
24. The letter *g* is often sounded similar to the *j* in *jump* when it precedes the letter *i* or *e*. (*gem*)	100	100	100
25. When *ght* is seen in a word, *gh* is silent. (*tight*)	100	100	100
26. When the word begins with *kn*, the *k* is silent. (*knit*)	100	100	100
27. When a word begins with *wr*, the *w* is silent. (*wrap*)	100	100	100
28. When two of the same consonants are side by side, only one is heard. (*dollar*)	100	100	100
29. When a word ends in *ck*, it has the same last sound as in *look*. (*neck*)	100	100	100
30. In most two-syllable words, the first syllable is accented. (*bottom*)	85	81	75
31. If *a*, *in*, *re*, *ex*, *de*, or *be* is the first syllable in a word, it is usually unaccented. (*reply*)	87	84	83
32. In most two-syllable words that end in a consonant followed by *y*, the first syllable is accented and the last is unaccented. (*highly*)	96	97	100
33. One vowel letter in an accented syllable has a short sound. (*banish*)	61	65	64
34. When *y* or *ey* is seen in the last syllable that is not accented, the long sound or *e* is heard. (*turkey*)	0	0	1
35. When *ture* is the final syllable in a word, it is unaccented. (*future*)	100	100	100
36. When *tion* is the final syllable in a word, it is unaccented. (*nation*)	100	100	100
37. In many two- and three-syllable words, the final *e* lengthens the vowel in the last syllable. (*costume*)	46	46	42

38. If the first vowel sound in a word is followed by two consonants, the first syllable usually ends with the first of the two consonants. (*dinner*)	72	78	80
39. If the first vowel sound in a word is followed by a single consonant, that consonant usually begins the second syllable. (*china*)	57	48	37
40. If the last syllable of a word ends in *le*, the consonant preceding the *le* usually begins the last syllable. (*gable*)	97	93	78
41. When the first vowel element in a word is followed by *the*, *ch*, or *sh*, these symbols are not broken when the word is divided into syllables and may go with either the first or second syllable. (*fashion*)	100	100	100
42. In a word of more than one syllable, the letter *v* usually goes with the preceding vowel to form a syllable. (*travel*)	73	65	40
43. When a word has only one vowel letter, the vowel sound is likely to be short. (*crib*)	57	69	70
44. When there is one *e* in a word that ends in a consonant, the *e* usually has a short sound. (*held*)	75	92	83
45. When the last syllable is the sound *r*, it is unaccented. (*ever*)	95	79	96

Source: B. Harp & J. A. Brewer. (1996). *Reading and Writing: Teaching for the Connections*. Fort Worth, TX: Harcourt Brace College Publishers.

APPENDIX D

THE YOPP-SINGER TEST OF PHONEME SEGMENTATION

Student's name ______________________ Date ______________________

Score (number correct) ______________________

Directions: Today we're going to play a word game. I'm going to say a word and I want you to break the word apart. You are going to tell me each sound in the word in order. For example, if I say "old," you should say /o/-/l/-/d/." (*Administrator: Be sure to say the sounds, not the letters, in the word.*) Let's try a few together.

Practice items: (*Assist the child in segmenting these items as necessary.*) ride, go, man

Test items: (*Circle those items that the student correctly segments; incorrect responses may be recorded on the blank line following the item.*)

1. dog ______________________
2. keep ______________________
3. fine ______________________
4. no ______________________
5. she ______________________
6. wave ______________________
7. grew ______________________
8. that ______________________
9. red ______________________
10. me ______________________
11. sat ______________________
12. lay ______________________
13. race ______________________
14. zoo ______________________
15. three ______________________
16. job ______________________
17. in ______________________
18. ice ______________________
19. at ______________________
20. top ______________________
21. by ______________________
22. do ______________________

 The author acknowledges the contribution of the late Harry Singer to the development of this test.

Source: Figure from Yopp, Hallie, Kay. (1995, September). A test for assessing phonemic awareness in young children. *The Reading Teacher, 49*(1), 20–29.

METACOMPREHENSION STRATEGY INDEX

STRATEGIES MEASURED BY THE MSI

Predicting and Verifying

Predicting the content of a story promotes active comprehension by giving readers a purpose for reading (i.e., to verify predictions). Evaluating predictions and generating new ones as necessary enhances the constructive nature of the reading process.

Item nos. 1, 4, 13, 15, 16, 18, 23

Previewing

Previewing the text facilitates comprehension by activating background knowledge and providing information for making predictions.

Item nos. 2, 3

Purpose Setting

Reading with a purpose promotes active, strategic reading.

Item nos. 5, 7, 21

Self Questioning

Generating questions to be answered promotes active comprehension by giving readers a purpose for reading (i.e., to answer the questions).

Item nos. 6, 14, 17

Drawing from Background Knowledge

Activating and incorporating information from background knowledge contributes to comprehension by helping readers make inferences and generate predictions.

Item nos. 8, 9, 10, 19, 24, 25

Summarizing and Applying Fix-up Strategies

Summarizing the content at various points in the story serves as a form of comprehension monitoring. Rereading or suspending judgment and reading on when comprehension breaks down represents strategic reading.

Item nos. 11, 12, 20, 22

METACOMPREHENSION STRATEGY INDEX

DIRECTIONS: Think about what kinds of things you can do to help you understand a story better before, during, and after you read it. Read each of the lists of four statements and decide which one of them would help *you* the most. *There are no right answers.* It is just what *you* think would help the most. Circle the letter of the statement you choose.

I. In each set of four, choose the one statement which tells a good thing to do to help you understand a story better *before* you read it.

1. Before I begin reading, it's a good idea to:
   a. See how many pages are in the story.
   b. Look up all of the big words in the dictionary.
   <u>c.</u> Make some guesses about what I think will happen in the story.
   d. Think about what has happened so far in the story.

2. Before I begin reading, it's a good idea to:
   <u>a.</u> Look at the pictures to see what the story is about.
   b. Decide how long it will take me to read the story.
   c. Sound out the words I don't know.
   d. Check to see if the story is making sense.

3. Before I begin reading, it's a good idea to:
   a. Ask someone to read the story to me.
   <u>b.</u> Read the title to see what the story is about.
   c. Check to see if most of the words have long or short vowels in them.
   d. Check to see if the pictures are in order and make sense.

4. Before I begin reading, it's a good idea to:
   a. Check to see that no pages are missing.
   b. Make a list of the words I'm not sure about.
   <u>c.</u> Use the title and pictures to help me make guesses about what will happen in the story.
   d. Read the last sentence so I will know how the story ends.

5. Before I begin reading, it's a good idea to:
   <u>a.</u> Decide on why I am going to read the story.
   b. Use the difficult words to help me make guesses about what will happen in the story.
   c. Reread some parts to see if I can figure out what is happening if things aren't making sense.
   d. Ask for help with the difficult words.

6. Before I begin reading, it's a good idea to:
   a. Retell all of the main points that have happened so far.
   <u>b.</u> Ask myself questions that I would like to have answered in the story.
   c. Think about the meanings of the words which have more than one meaning.
   d. Look through the story to find all of the words with three or more syllables.

7. Before I begin reading, it's a good idea to:
   a. Check to see if I have read this story before.
   <u>b.</u> Use my questions and guesses as a reason for reading the story.
   c. Make sure I can pronounce all of the words before I start.
   d. Think of a better title for the story.

8. Before I begin reading, it's a good idea to:
   <u>a.</u> Think of what I already know about the things I see in the pictures.
   b. See how many pages are in the story.
   c. Choose the best part of the story to read again.
   d. Read the story aloud to someone.

9. Before I begin reading, it's a good idea to:
   a. Practice reading the story aloud.
   b. Retell all of the main points to make sure I can remember the story.
   <u>c.</u> Think of what the people in the story might be like.
   d. Decide if I have enough time to read the story.

10. Before I begin reading, it's a good idea to:
   a. Check to see if I am understanding the story so far.
   b. Check to see if the words have more than one meaning.
   <u>c.</u> Think about where the story might be taking place.
   d. List all of the important details.

*Underlined responses indicate metacomprehension strategy awareness.

II. In each set of four, choose the one statement that tells a good thing to do to help you understand a story better *while* you are reading it.

11. While I'm reading, it's a good idea to:
    a. Read the story very slowly so that I will not miss any important parts.
    b. Read the title to see what the story is about.
    c. Check to see if the pictures have anything missing.
    d. Check to see if the story is making sense by seeing if I can tell what's happened so far.

12. While I'm reading, it's a good idea to:
    a. Stop to retell the main points to see if I am understanding what has happened so far.
    b. Read the story quickly so that I can find out what happened.
    c. Read only the beginning and the end of the story to find out what it is about.
    d. Skip the parts that are too difficult for me.

13. While I'm reading, it's a good idea to:
    a. Look all of the big words up in the dictionary.
    b. Put the book away and find another one if things aren't making sense.
    c. Keep thinking about the title and the pictures to help me decide what is going to happen next.
    d. Keep track of how many pages I have left to read.

14. While I'm reading, it's a good idea to:
    a. Keep track of how long it is taking me to read the story.
    b. Check to see if I can answer any of the questions I asked before I started reading.
    c. Read the title to see what the story is going to be about.
    d. Add the missing details to the pictures.

15. While I'm reading, it's a good idea to:
    a. Have someone read the story aloud to me.
    b. Keep track of how many pages I have read.
    c. List the story's main character.
    d. Check to see if my guesses are right or wrong.

16. While I'm reading, it's a good idea to:
    a. Check to see that the characters are real.
    b. Make a lot of guesses about what is going to happen next.
    c. Not look at the pictures because they might confuse me.
    d. Read the story aloud to someone.

17. While I'm reading, it's a good idea to:
    a. Try to answer the questions I asked myself.
    b. Try not to confuse what I already know with what I'm reading about.
    c. Read the story silently.
    d. Check to see if I am saying the new vocabulary words correctly.

18. While I'm reading, it's a good idea to:
    a. Try to see if my guesses are going to be right or wrong.
    b. Reread to be sure I haven't missed any of the words.
    c. Decide on why I am reading the story.
    d. List what happened first, second, third, and so on.

19. While I'm reading, it's a good idea to:
    a. See if I can recognize the new vocabulary words.
    b. Be careful not to skip any parts of the story.
    c. Check to see how many of the words I already know.
    d. Keep thinking of what I already know about the things and ideas in the story to help me decide what is going to happen.

20. While I'm reading, it's a good idea to:
    a. Reread some parts or read ahead to see if I can figure out what is happening if things aren't making sense.
    b. Take my time reading so that I can be sure I understand what is happening.
    c. Change the ending so that it makes sense.
    d. Check to see if there are enough pictures to help make the story ideas clear.

III. In each set of four, choose the one statement which tells a good thing to do to help you understand a story better *after* you have read it.

21. After I've read a story it's a good idea to:
    a. Count how many pages I read with no mistakes.
    b. Check to see if there were enough pictures to go with the story to make it interesting.
    c. Check to see if I met my purpose for reading the story.
    d. Underline the causes and effects.

*Underlined responses indicate metacomprehension strategy awareness.

22. After I've read a story it's a good idea to:
    a. Underline the main idea.
    b. Retell the main points of the whole story so that I can check to see if I understood it.
    c. Read the story again to be sure I said all of the words right.
    d. Practice reading the story aloud.

23. After I've read a story, it's a good idea to:
    a. Read the title and look over the story to see what it is about.
    b. Check to see if I skipped any of the vocabulary words.
    c. Think about what made me make good or bad predictions.
    d. Make a guess about what will happen next in the story.

24. After I've read a story, it's a good idea to:
    a. Look up all of the big words in the dictionary.
    b. Read the best parts aloud.
    c. Have someone read the story aloud to me.
    d. Think about how the story was like things I already knew about before I started reading.

25. After I've read a story it's a good idea to:
    a. Think about how I would have acted if I were the main character in the story.
    b. Practice reading the story silently for practice of good reading.
    c. Look over the story title and pictures to see what will happen.
    d. Make a list of the things I understood the most.

---

*Underlined responses indicate metacomprehension strategy awareness.

Source: From Schmitt, Maribeth Cassidy. (1990, March) A questionnaire to measure children's awareness of strategic reading processes. *The Reading Teacher, 43*(7), 454–461.

LITERATURE CIRCLE INDIVIDUAL EVALUATION

Literature Circle Individual Evaluation

Scale 1 = never 2 = sometimes 3 = usually 4 = always

I, ______________________________

	Student	Teacher
Reading		
1. Kept up with reading	1.	1.
2. Used reading time wisely & didn't disturb others	2.	2.
3. Returned books on time (1 = no; 2 = yes)	3.	3.
4. Had book at school each day	4.	4.
Goals for next time: ______________________________		
Group Discussion		
1. Participated (voluntary or only when asked)	1.	1.
2. Contributed quality comments & conversation	2.	2.
3. Asked legitimate questions	3.	3.
4. Listened to others in group and responded to them	4.	4.
5. Made predictions & connections to other things in the book and connections to real life situations, when appropriate	5.	5.
6. Behaved appropriately in group	6.	6.
Goals for next time: ______________________________		
Responses		
1. Kept up with entries and other assignments	1.	1.
2. Wrote quality responses to literature & not just retell or summary	2.	2.
3. Made connections to what was happening to characters & to out-of-book situations	3.	3.
Goals for next time: ______________________________		
TOTALS	_____	_____

The overall grade I think I deserve for this Lit Study is _____ because:

____

____

Signature ______________________________ Date ______________________________

Adapted by Janice Holt, April Bryson, Kathleen Burda, & Kirsten Morgan from Dr. Barbara H. Bell, Director, Reading Center, Western Carolina University, 138 Killian Building, Cullowhee, NC, 28723.

INDEX

Aarnoutse, C., 222, 251
Adams, M. J., 38, 65, 181, 295, 308
Adoff, A., 348
Aesthetic listening, 355
Aesthetic stance to text, 285–286
Afflerbach, P., 254, 291
Agee, J., 220
Alexander, J., 405, 432
Alexander, L., 410, 432
Alexander, S., 351
Algier, A., 302, 308
Algozzine, B., 302, 308
Allen, J., 452, 460
Allen, L., 223, 250
Allen, R. V., 48, 65
Allington, R. L., 58, 65, 111, 112, 126, 146, 160, 167, 181, 205, 299, 305, 307, 308, 350, 371, 405, 432, 453, 460
Al-masi, J., 208
Alphabet books, selection of, 349
Alternative or augmentative communication devices (AAC), 133
Alverman, D., 31
Alvermann, D. E., 278, 289
Ambrosio, A. L., 338, 339
American School Directory (ASD), 480–481
Analytical Reading Inventory, 80, 82, 84
Analytic phonics, 38, 166, 169
Anderson, L. H., 443, 461
Anderson, R., 222, 250
Anderson, R. C., 160, 181, 211, 213, 250, 278, 289, 369, 371
Anderson, T. H., 276, 286, 289
Anderson, V., 200, 207
Anecdotal records, use of, 89–90, 104
Anglin, J. M., 211, 250
An Observation Survey of Early Literacy Achievement, 382
Applebee, A. M., 44, 65, 311
Applebee, A. N., 338
Archambault, J., 357
Armbruster, B. B., 276, 286, 289
Art centers, 395
Ask ERIC, 474
Assessment and evaluation
- *Analytical Reading Inventory,* 80, 82, 84
- anecdotal records, use of, 89–90, 104
- assessment defined, 71
- checklists, developmental, 90, 91–92, 93, 104
- *Comprehensive Test of Phonological Processing,* 89
- connections between author and reader (CAR), 80
- criterion-referenced tests, 94–95
- *Degrees of Reading Power,* 89
- Developmental Reading Assessment (DRA), 87–88, 104
- DIBELS, 89
- evaluates and substantiates (EAS), 80
- evaluation defined, 71
- functional reading levels, 80, 82, 84
- *Gates-MacGinite Reading Test,* 89, 95
- graded word lists, using, 77
- *Gray Oral Reading Test,* 89
- high-stakes testing, 99, 100
- informal reading inventories (IRIs), 77, 104
- instructional goals, establishing, 82
- interviewing children about their perceptions of reading, 73–75, 104
- interviewing children about their perceptions of writing, 76–77, 104
- *Motivation to Read Profile (MTRP),* 75–76, 104
- narrative passage, introducing, 77
- norm-referenced tests, 94–95
- *Peabody Picture Vocabulary Test,* 89
- portfolios, use of, 101–103
- principles of, 72–73
- puts information together (PIT), 80
- reader, text relationship (RTR), 80
- *Reader Self-Perception Scale,* 76, 104
- Reading First grants, influence of, 88–89
- retelling, 80, 81
- retells in fact (RIF), 80
- rubrics, use of, 90, 92, 93–94
- running records, use of, 82–84, 85–87, 104
- scoring, 80–81
- standardized testing, use of, 94–98, 104
- standards, understanding, 99, 100
- *Stanford Diagnostic Reading Test, Fourth Edition,* 89, 96
- student profile summary, 83
- student's reading and teacher's coding, 80
- teacher record data, 78–79
- *Writer Self-Perception Scale,* 77, 104

Association for Childhood Education International (ACEI), 478
Associations of Service Providers Implementing IDEA Reforms in Education Partnership (ASPIIRE), 120
Attention deficit/hyperactivity disorder, students with, 137–138, 139
Atwell, N., 326, 329, 338
Au, K. H., 262, 290
Audiotapes for reading along, using, 298
Auditory discrimination, role of, 164
Ault, M. J., 382, 400
Authentic assessment, 58
Authentic writing experiences, 320
Author/illustrator studies, using, 364–365, 447–448
Automaticity, 157, 294
Avoke, S., 115, 118, 146
Aylesworth, J., 357

Babbitt, N., 347
Background knowledge, activating, 263–265
Baechtold, S., 302, 308
Bailey, M. H., 157, 181
Baker, K., 144, 146
Baker, S., 129, 146
Barkley, R.A., 146
Barnes, M., 99, 105
Barnhart, C. L., 65
Barr, R., 152, 181
Barrett, J., 220
Bartlett, B. J., 269, 290
Bartoletti, S. C., 356
Barton, A., 65
Base, G., 349
Basic interpersonal communication skills, 457
Baumann, J. F., 59, 65, 275, 290
Baumgart, A., 190, 207
Baylor, B., 333, 339
Bean, T. W., 207
Bear, D. R., 20, 30, 181
Beatty, A. S., 305, 308

Beaver, J., 87, 105, 290
Beck, I. L., 283, 290, 449, 460
Begay, S., 351
Bell, A., 420, 432
Beneduce, A. K., 421, 432
Bereiter, C., 275, 290, 314, 339
Berglund, R. L., 229, 250
Bergman, J. L., 208
Berk, L., 6, 7–8, 30
Berko Gleason, J., 131, 146
Berry, J., 229, 250
Betts, E. A., 65
Biber, D., 27, 30
Biddle, W. B., 278, 289
Bierhorst, J., 443, 461
Bindman, M., 164, 182
Bird, M., 275, 290
Blachowicz, C., 218, 248, 249, 250
Block, C. C., 205, 208
Bloom, B., 279, 280, 290
Bloomfield, L., 65
Bloom's Taxonomy, 279, 280
Blum, I. H., 296, 308
Bluth, G. J., 269, 290
Bober, N. S., 357
Bodino, S., 325, 339
Bond, G. L., 34, 65, 167, 181
Book discussion groups, 468
Booth, R. C., 138, 146
Boothby, P. R., 278, 289
Bormuth, J. R., 284, 290
Bottomley, D. M., 77, 105, 411, 432
Bottom-up view of reading, 38
Bowman, H., 185, 207
Boyle, O. F., 144, 146
Bradley, L., 168, 171, 181
Brandt, D. M., 269, 290
Bransford, J. D., 188, 207
Brewer, J., 27, 31
Brewer, J. A., 424–426
Bridge, C. A., 43, 65
Brock, C. H., 368
Brown, A. L., 256, 290
Brown, E., 213, 250
Brown, F., 115, 118, 146
Brown, R., 200, 207, 208
Brown, V. L., 135, 146, 460
Browsing boxes, 260, 296
Bruchac, J., 461
Bruck, M., 295, 308
Bryan, J., 191, 207
Bryant, B., 147, 164, 168, 171, 307
Bryant, B. R., 183, 309
Bryant, P., 182
Bryant, P. E., 181, 182
Buchan, A., 325, 339
Buddy reading, use of, 201, 298–299
Bunting, E., 368
Burke, C. L., 16, 31, 187, 188, 207
Burleigh, R., 421, 432
Burns, M. S., 177, 182
Burris, N. A., 20, 31
Burrows, A. T., 66
Butterfield, D., 354, 371
Button, K., 336, 339
Byer, J., 339

Caldwell, J., 410, 432
Calhoun, E., 33, 65
Calkins, L. M., 315, 320, 328, 339
Cambourne, B., 28, 29, 30, 394, 400
Cambourne's Conditions for Literacy Learning, 39
Campbell, D. M., 468, 482
Campbell, J. R., 305, 308
Carle, E., 286, 291, 400
Carlisle, J. F., 146
Carpenter, R. D., 100, 106
Casteneda v. Pickard, 458
Categories of readers, 454
Censorship considerations, 353
Center for the Improvement of Early Reading Achievement (CIERA), 474
Chall, J. S., 18, 19, 30, 43, 65
Chall's stages of reading development, 18–19
Chapman, S., 256, 291
Cheek, E., 90, 92, 94, 106, 280, 291
Chomsky, C., 11, 24, 30, 222, 250, 314, 339
Chomsky, N., 31
Choral reading, using, 300, 301–302, 388–389, 420
Chunking words and syllables, 170
Ciardi, M. R., 449, 460
Cignetti, P. B., 468, 482
Clark, B. A., 140, 141, 146, 213
Clark, E. V., 156, 181, 250
Clark, K., 205, 208, 369
Clarke, D., 99, 105
CLASP model, 125
Classroom Notes Plus, 478
Clay, M. M., 15, 20, 26, 31, 82, 106, 173, 181, 193, 194, 207, 305, 308, 314, 339, 382, 383, 400
Cleary, B., 220, 356
Clicking and clunking, 204
Clifton, L., 302, 309
Cline-Ransome, L., 357
Cloze procedure, 284
Clymer, T., 157, 181
Coding, R. M., 368
Codling, R. M., 75, 106, 410, 432
Coefficient of correlation, 98
Coffman, G. A., 338, 339
Cognitive academic language proficiency, 457
Cognitive apprenticeship approach, 37
Coles, G., 167, 181
Collaborative strategic reading (CSR), 202–205
Collett, M. J., 302, 308
Compound words, 236–237
Comprehension, reading
  aesthetic stance to text, 285–286
  background knowledge, activating, 263–265
  Bloom's Taxonomy, 279, 280
  browsing boxes, 260
  checklist, comprehension, 281, 288
  cloze procedure, 284
  cooperative learning-cooperative support, 272–274
  defining, 255–256
  dramatic roles, 268–269
  efferent response to text, 286–287
  Experience-Text-Relationship Approach (ETR), 262
  exploring text structures, 266–271
  expository text structures, 269–270
  Facts, Questions, Responses (FQR), 283–284
  Frederick Davis's Analysis of Comprehension, 279
  graphic and semantic organizers, using, 276–278
  guiding reading, using, 256–261, 287
  jackdaws, 265
  Judith Irwin's Comprehension Processes, 279
  leveled books, 259–260
  monitoring, comprehension, 274–275
  narrative text structures, 266
  prediction making, using, 270–271
  processing after reading, 254
  processing before reading, 253
  processing during reading, 253–254
  question answering, role of, 278–280

Question-Answer-Relationships (QAR), 282
question generating, importance of, 281–284
Questioning the Author (QtA), 283
reasons for reading text, determining, 266
Reciprocal Questioning (ReQuest), 282–283
retellings, 280
shared reading, 259
simplified drawings, use of, 266–267
story cubes, 266
story maps, 266, 267
structuralism, 268
structured opposites, 269
summarization skills, teaching, 286
Comprehensive Receptive and Expressive Vocabulary Test (CREVT), 233
Comprehensive Test of Phonological Processing, 89
Computer center, 395
Concentration, 163
Conference checklist, reading, 55
Conferences, attending, 478–480
Conferences, writing, 329, 331–332
Connections between author and reader (CAR), 80
Construct validity, 97
Content validity, 97
Context cues, using, 239, 241, 246
Continuum checklist, 323–324
Cook, V., 11, 31
Cooperative learning-cooperative support, 272–274
Cooperative learning roles, 205
Core book experiences, using, 366
Corliss, J. C., 351, 371
Correa, V. I., 113, 147
Correia, M. P., 469, 482
Council for Exceptional Children (CEC), 120
Cowley, J., 380, 400
Creech, S., 356
Cress, C., 171, 182
Criterion-referenced tests, 94–95
Critical literacy, 449
Crummel, S. S., 351
Cueing systems, 154–157
Cullinan, B. E., 346, 359, 368, 371
Cummins, J., 457, 460
Cunningham, J. W., 164, 182
Cunningham, P. M., 58, 65, 164, 181, 182, 350, 371, 453, 460
Curriculum graphic, 428
Curtis, C.P., 356

Dahl, K. L., 343, 368, 371
Dale, E., 213, 250
Daniels, H., 364, 371
Davis, F. B., 217, 250, 279, 290
Davis, Z. T., 271, 290
Day, J. P., 405, 432
Dean, M., 339
DeBettencourt, L. U., 123, 146
Decodable text, 39
Decoding skills, development of
analytic phonics lesson, 166, 169
assessment of student progress, 178
auditory discrimination, role of, 164
automaticity, skill, 157
chunking words and syllables, 170
concentration, 163
cueing systems, 154–157
discussion, using, 171
Ehri's developmental phases, 158
Ekwall/Shanker Reading Inventory, 166
Elkonin boxes, using, 165
explicit phonics instruction, providing, 180
flip books, using, 170
games, using, 162–163
graphophonic cueing system, 154, 155–156, 166–173
guided practice, using, 171
independent reading, using, 180
lists of words, using, 175
magnetic sheets and letters, using, 170
making discoveries about words, 171
modified cloze, using a, 174
onset and rime instruction, 168, 169–170
parental involvement, 179
phonemes, 154
phonological awareness, role of, 164–165
pocket charts, using, 162
principles, teaching, 159–160
purpose of, 154
rearranging sentence strips, 173–174
scattegories, 163
semantic cueing system, 154, 156
semantic cues, using, 174–175
sentence strips, using, 160–161
sight vocabulary development, 157–158, 160–164
skills lessons, components of, 175–177
small group, focused instruction, 172–173
small group reading, using, 174, 175, 179–180
sorting picture cards and sound cards, 170
spelling, use of, 171
student engagement, fostering, 179
syntactic cueing system, 156–157, 173–174
synthetic phonics lesson, 166, 168
Test of Phonological Awareness (TOPA), 165
think-alouds, using, 174, 175
usage of, 158–159
visual discrimination, role of, 164
word advocacy, 175
word analysis, 171
word banks, using, 161–162
word deletion activities, 173
Wordo, 162
word walls, using, 161
writing for sounds, 170
Yopp-Singer Test of Phoneme Segmentation, 165
Deford, D. E., 371
Degrees of Reading Power, 89
DeGross, M., 220
Delacre, L., 443, 461
Delayed language development, 6–7
Demonstrations, using, 202
Demonstration writing, 337
Deshler, D., 127, 146, 147
Developmental Reading Assessment (DRA), 87–88, 104
Dewsbury, A., 20, 21, 31
DIBELS, 89
DiCamillo, K., 208
Dickinson, D. K., 25, 31
Dickson, S. V., 266, 290
Dictionaries and reference texts, using, 233, 235–236
Difficulty of text, assessing the, 365–366
Direct instruction model, 37
Dishner, E. K., 302, 309
Diversity in the classroom, 397–399
Dolch Basic Sight Word List, 233
Dole, J. A., 222, 250
Donant, L., 196, 207
Donnelly, K., 171, 182
Douville, P., 302, 308

Dowhower, S. L., 188, 207, 296, 308
Dramatic roles, 268–269
Drawing, use of, 336
Dreeben, R., 152, 181
Drop Everything and Read (DEAR), 297
Duffield, J. A., 416, 417, 432
Duffy, G. G., 34, 65
Duffy-Hester, A. M., 42, 66, 160, 182
Duke, N. K., 196, 207, 266, 280, 288, 290, 349, 371
Dunn, L. M., 215, 250
Durkin, D., 290
Durrell, D. D., 170, 182
Dykstra, R., 34, 59, 65, 167, 181

Easton, S., 420, 432
Echevarria, J., 459, 460
Eckhoff, B., 371
Eckoff, B., 314, 339
Edwards, C., 376, 400
Edwards, L., 320, 339
Efferent listening, 355
Efferent response to text, 286–287
Ehri, L. C., 157, 158, 171, 182
Ehri's developmental phases, 158
Ekwall, E. E., 182
Ekwall/Shanker Reading Inventory, 166
El-Dinary, P. B., 208
Eldredge, J. L., 354, 371
Elkonin, D. B., 182
Elkonin boxes, using, 165
Eller, G., 213, 250
Elliott, R. N., 125, 147
Ellis, N., 166
Emans, R., 157, 182
Emberley, R., 430, 432
English is a second language, students for whom, 142–145
English Journal, 477–478
English Language Learners (ELL), 142, 457–458
Evaluates and substantiates (EAS), 80
Evans, E. D., 190, 202, 208
Ewing, L., 443, 461
Experience-Text-Relationship Approach (ETR), 262
Explicit instruction approach, 37
Explicit phonics instruction, providing, 180
Exploring text structures, 266–271
Expository text structures, 269–270
Extensive reading, importance of, 224

Facts, Questions, Responses (FQR), 283–284
Fairbanks, M. M., 228, 251
Falwell, C., 220
Families and Advocates Partnership for Education (FAPE), 120
Farest, C., 368
Farmer, L., 339
Farr, R., 103, 106
Fennacy, J., 298, 308
Fergerson, P., 336, 339
Ferriero, E., 20, 31
Fiction, selection of, 346–348
Fielding, L., 160, 181, 190, 208, 222, 250
Fielding, L. G., 369, 371
Figurative language, 232
Figures of speech, 232
Finders, M. J., 444, 461
First Steps Oral Language Development Continuum, 223
Fisher, D., 73, 106, 248, 249
Fisher, P. J., 218, 250
Fitzgerald, J., 57, 65, 333, 339
Flashlight readers, 289
Fleet, J., 190, 202, 208
Fleishman, P., 302, 309, 388, 400
Fleishman, S., 356
Fleming, D., 219, 381, 400
Flesch, R., 65
Fletcher, J. M., 166, 182
Fletcher, R., 332, 339
Flip books, using, 170
Flood, J., 73, 106, 159, 182, 318, 326, 339
Florian, D., 388, 400
Fluency, development of reading
  automaticity, 294
  choral reading, 300, 301–302
  juncture, 294
  pitch, 294
  previewing a text, 299–300
  prosody, 294, 299
  reader's theater, 300, 301
  reading rates, 304–306
  repeated readings, role of, 296–299
  sight vocabulary, development of, 295–296
  songs, incorporating activities using, 302–304
  stress, 294
Focus lessons, planning, 326–327, 393, 450
Foertsch, M. A., 44, 65

Folk literature, introducing, 413, 414, 423, 426–427, 429–430
Foorman, B. R., 166, 182
Formal assessment, 438
Forman, G., 376, 400
Form class words, 215–216
Fountas, I. C., 197, 207, 259, 290, 308, 336, 339, 397, 400
Four Blocks Program, 58–59
Fox, B. J., 170, 182
Fox, M., 333, 339
Francis, D. J., 166, 182
Frantantoni, D. M., 295, 308
Frasier, D., 220
Frayer, D. A., 223, 250
Frayer Method, 224, 228
Frederick, W. D., 223, 250
Frederick Davis's Analysis of Comprehension, 279
French, F., 432
French, M. P., 229, 250
Freppon, P. A., 343, 368, 371
Frith, U., 166, 182
Frost, J., 164, 182
Fry, E., 233, 250
Fry's New Instant Word List, 233, 234
Fuchs, L. S., 129, 146
Fullan, M., 33, 65
Functional reading levels, 80, 82, 84
Funk, C. E., 220

Galda, L., 346, 359, 368, 371
Gambrell, L. B., 75, 106, 354, 367, 368, 371, 410, 432
Games and puzzles, using, 162–163, 217–218
Gandini, L., 376, 400
Garcia, G. E., 36, 37–38, 65
Gardner, E. F., 106, 147
Garland, S., 285, 291
Garner, R., 190, 207
Gaskins, I. W., 171, 182, 208
Gates-MacGinite Reading Test, 89, 95
Gatheral, M., 266, 290
General interest inventory, using a, 22
Genres, word, 232
Genre studies, using, 359–361, 448
George, J. C., 356
Gerstein, M., 220
Gersten, R., 129, 146
Giard, M., 202, 203, 207, 299, 308
Gibbons, G., 357
Gifted and talented students, 138–142

Gilbert, L., 362
Gilhool, M., 339
Glasman, L. D., 229
Glazer, S. M., 13, 31
Goatley,V. J., 364, 368
Goldilocks Strategy, 365–366
Goldsmith, L. T., 449, 460
Goleman, D., 435, 461
Goodchild, F., 190, 202, 208
Goodman, K. S., 53, 65
Goodman, Y., 63, 65, 90, 106
Goodman, Y. M., 16, 31, 187, 188, 207
Goswami, U. C., 168, 182
Goudvis, A., 194, 195, 197, 199, 207, 283, 290
Gough, P. B., 305, 308
Gower, R., 465, 467, 468, 482
Graded word lists, using, 77
Grade equivalent scores, 97
Grades 6-8 reading program, developing a
  art as a response to literature, 447
  author studies, using, 447–448
  categories of readers, 454
  challenges of, 435–436
  classroom environment, 436
  critical literacy, 449
  English Language Learners, techniques for, 457–458
  focus lessons, using, 450
  formal assessment, 438
  genre studies, using, 448
  graphic organizers, 449
  independent reading, using, 443
  informal assessment, 438
  instructional materials, 437
  interest inventory, 438, 439–440
  Internet, using the, 447
  learning about language, 448–453
  learning language, 442–445
  learning through language, 445–448
  literacy centers, 453
  literature logs, using, 444–445
  planning inquiry, 441–442
  questioning the author, 449–450
  reader's theater, using, 443
  reading alouds, using, 443
  schedule, 436–437
  self-evaluation, 438
  Sheltered English Instruction, 458–460
  songs, chants, and rhymes, using, 444
  storytelling, using, 444
  strategy lessons, 450
  strategy sharing discussions, 451–452
  Structured English Immersion, 458–460
  struggling readers, techniques for, 453, 455–457
  teacher/student conferences, 450–451
  word study, using, 452
  writing engagements, using, 451
Grades 3 through 5 reading program, developing
  arrangement, classroom, 405–408
  assessment techniques, 410–412
  children, importance of understanding the, 404
  choral reading and chants, using, 420
  curriculum graphic, 428
  daily schedule, developing the, 408
  folk literature, introducing, 413, 414, 423, 426–427, 429–430
  guided reading, using, 428–429
  independent reading, using, 419
  Kamishibai, 426
  language patterns, using, 421
  learning about literature, 427–428
  learning language, 419–420
  learning through language, 422–427
  literature logs, using, 421–422
  management and record keeping, 431
  read-alouds, using, 419
  reader's theater, using, 421
  research skills, learning, 413–418
  social studies connections, 423
  storytelling, using, 420–421
  strategy lessons, 429–430
  teaching materials, 409
  topics for inquiry, 412–413
  transformation stories, 430
  unmotivated readers, 404–405
  work areas, managing the, 408–409
  zig-zag book, making a, 424–426
Graphemes, 38
Graphic and semantic organizers, using, 229, 276–278, 449
Graphophonic cueing system, 154, 155–156, 166–173
Graves, A., 459, 461
Graves, D., 315, 339
Graves, D. H., 320, 339
Graves, M. F., 211, 214, 217, 222, 223, 250, 251
Gray Oral Reading Test, Fourth Edition (GORT-4), 118
Gray Oral Reading Test (GORT), 89
Greaney, V., 222, 250, 369
Green, G. M., 214, 250
Greenburg, D., 333, 339
Greenfield, E., 357
Gregg, S., 146
Gregory, K. M., 301, 309
Griffin, P., 177, 182
Grossen, B., 39, 40, 65
Guice, S., 69, 106
Guided practice, using, 171
Guided reading, using, 256–261, 287, 392, 428–429
Guided writing, 337
Gussetti, B. J., 343, 372
Guthrie, J., 3, 31
Gywnne, F., 214, 220, 251

Haberman, M., 33, 65
Hacker, D. J., 461
Hague, M., 261, 291
Haley, D., 43, 65
Hall, K., *185,* 207
Halliday, M. A. K., 6, 31, 270, 290, 411, 432
Hamilton, R. L., 283, 290, 449, 460
Hammill, D. D., 135, 146, 233, 251, 315, 339, 411, 432, 440, 460, 461
Hancock, S., 320, 339
Hanf, M. B., 276, 290
Hanna, J., 327, 340
Harness, C., 195
Harp, B., 27, 31, 55, 75, 76, 77, 90, 93, 97, 106, 165, 182, 194, 223, 225, 226, 227, 250, 270, 290, 331, 339, 360, 424–426
Harris, A. J., 305, 306, 308
Harris, T. L., 71, 154, 156, 182, 232, 236, 238, 250
Harris, V. J., 351
Harris, W. B., 125, 147
Hartman, B., 430, 432
Harvey, S., 194, 195, 197, 199, 207, 283, 290
Hayes, B., 229
Heald-Taylor, G., 302, 308
Hegarty, M., 222, 250
Heimlich, J. E., 229, 250
Heller, R., 220, 357
Hemmeter, M. L., 382, 400
Henk, W. A., 76, 77, 105, 106, 411, 432, 470–474, 482
Henkes, K., 355
Hepworth, C., 220
Herman, P. A., 213, 250

Hesse, K., 347
Heward, W. L., 117, 135, 146
Hiebert, E. H., 311, 339
High-frequency words, teaching, 232–233
High quality strategy instruction, 190
High-stakes testing, 99, 100
Highwater, J., 357
Hill, B. C., 322, 323, 324, 339, 446, 461
His Input Hypothesis (HIH), 222
Hodges, R. E., 71, 154, 156, 182, 232, 236, 238, 250
Hoffman, J., 164, 182
Hoffman, J. V., 33, 34, 44, 65, 368
Hollowell, E. M., 138, 146
Homestead, E., 441, 461
Homographs, 231
Homophones, 231
Hoose, P. M., 443, 461
Hopkins, L. B., 250, 348, 357
Howard, M. R., 12, 31
Howe, F. C., 404, 432
Hoyt, L., 443, 449, 451, 452, 461
Hubbell, P., 357
Hughes, C. A., 127, 146, 147
Hulit, L. M., 12, 31
Hulme, C., 168, 182
Hutchins, P., 356, 383, 400
Hynds, S., 444, 461

IDEA Local Implementation by Local Administrators Partnership (ILIAD), 118
Illustration in children's books, role of, 351, 352
Imlach, R. H., 305, 308
Independent reading, 180, 222–223, 349–350, 369, 370, 388, 419, 443
Individualized Education Program (IEP), 117, 119–120, 121–123
Individuals with Disabilities Act (IDEA), understanding, 114–120, 124
Individual words, teaching, 224, 228–232
Informal assessment, 438
Informal reading inventories (IRIs), 77, 104
Information/reference books, selection of, 348–349
Inquiry studies, using, 390–391
Instructional experiences, planning, 28, 30
Instructional goals, establishing, 82
Instructional materials, 437
Integrated anthology approach, 44–45
Interactive teaming, 113
Interactive writing, 336
Interest inventory, 438, 439–440
International Federation of Library Associations and Institutions, 481
International Reading Association (IRA), 475–476
Internet, using the, 391, 447
Interrelationships of words, understanding, 215
Intervention assistance team (IAT), referrals to the, 113–114
Interviewing children about their perceptions of reading, 73–75, 104
Interviewing children about their perceptions of writing, 76–77, 104
Invernizzi, M., 20, 30, 181
I-R-E, 364
Irwin, J. W., 279, 280, 290
Irwin, P. A., 290
Isolated skill emphasis, 58
Ivey, G., 59, 65

Jackdaws, 265
Jalongo, M. J., 352
Jepsen, M., 366
Jipson, J., 351
Johnson, D., 229, 250
Johnson, M., 336, 339
Johnson, M. K., 188, 207
Johnston, F., 20, 30, 181
Johnston, P., 205
Johnston, P. H., 69, 106, 207, 405, 432
Jones, K., 325, 339
Jones, L. A., 275, 290
Journal of Adolescent & Adult Literacy (JAAL), 476
Journal writing, 334–335
Joyce, B., 33, 65
Judith Irwin's Comprehension Processes, 279
Juel, C., 151, 159, 164, 182, 399, 400
Juncture, 294

Kahn, L. H., 303, 309
Kalman, M., 349
Kameenui, E. J., 266, 290, 370
Kamishibai, 426
Kanner, L., 118, 147
Kantrov, I., 449, 460
Karlsen, B., 106, 147
Kathy Schrock's Guide for Educators, 481
Kauffman, G., 303, 309
Kays, J., 371
Kear, D. J., 338, 339
Keats, E. J., 260, 291
Keats, E. Z., 356
Keene, E. L., 197, 207
Kellogg, S., 421, 432
Kerley, B., 351
Kettmann, J., 204
Keyword method, 229
Kidwatching, 63–64, 112–113
Kiefer, B. Z., 301, 308
Kimmel, E. A., 421, 432
King, J. A., 446, 461
King, S., 325, 333, 339
Kintsch, W., 290
Kirk, S. A., 125, 147
Klausmeier, H. J., 223, 250
Klinger, J., 202, 207
Klinger, J. K., 202, 203, 204, 207
Knowledge basis, expanding your, 468–470
Knowlton, J., 349
Koskinen, P. S., 296, 308
Kowalinski, B. J., 343, 371
Krashen, S., 55, 65, 167, 222, 250, 393, 400
Krashen, S. D., 182, 409, 432
Kress, G., 335, 339
K through grade 2 reading program, developing a
- arrangement of the room, 376–377
- art centers, 395
- assessment strategies, 382–384
- choral reading, use of, 388–389
- computer center, 395
- daily schedule, developing the, 378–381
- diversity in the classroom, and, 397–399
- elements of a quality program, 384–396
- environment, role of the classroom, 376
- evaluating the classroom environment, 381–382
- focus lessons, using, 393
- guided reading, using, 392
- independent reading, 388
- inquiry studies, using, 390–391
- Internet, using the, 391
- learning about language, 391–393
- learning centers, using, 378, 379
- learning language, 388–389
- learning through language, 389–391
- lesson plan for shared reading, 381

listening centers, 395
literacy centers, 393–396
literature discussions, using, 389–390
literature logs, using, 390
management techniques, 396–397
overhead projector, using the, 396
pocket charts, using, 396
read-alouds, use of, 388
read around the room, 396
reader's theater, use of, 388
shared reading, using, 391–392
strategy lessons, using, 392–393
strategy-sharing discussions, 393
student conferences, 393
teaching materials, 382
themes, importance of selecting, 385–387
word study, 380
writing center, 395
Kucan, L., 283, 290, 449, 460
Kuhn, M. R., 293, 294, 308
KWLS chart, 386–387
K-W-L strategy, 191

LaBerge, D., 157, 182
Langer, J. A., 44, 65
Language Arts, 477
Language development
caregiver support for learning language, 9
characteristics of, 5–6
definition of, 5
delayed language development, 6–7
environment, fostering the proper learning, 8–9
learning, 6
limitations of learning, 12–13
milestones, developmental, 7–8
morphemes, 10
morphology, 10
phonemes, 10
phonology, 10
pragmatics, 12
preschool through third grade goals, 13
reading and writing, role on, 13–14
semantics, 11–12
supports for, 8–9
syntax, 10–11
Language Experience Approach (LEA), 48–52
Language patterns, using, 421
Lapp, D., 73, 106, 159, 182, 318, 326, 339
Larsen, S. C., 315, 339, 411, 432, 440, 461
Lau v. Nichols, 458
Lavoie, R. D., 128, 131, 147
Layden, J., 357
Learner-directed discovery, 57–58
Learning, 6
Learning centers, using, 378, 379
Learning disabilities, accommodations for students with, 125–131
Learning Strategies curriculum, 127
Least restrictive environment (LRE), 115, 117
Lectura y Vida, 475
Legislative implications, 34
Leinart, A., 305, 308
Lenz, B. K., 127, 147
Leslie, L., 410, 432
Lester, J., 356
Leu, D. J., 426, 427, 432
Leveled books, 259–260
Levin, J., 229
Levin, J. R., 229, 250
Levin, K., 229, 250
Levin, M. E., 229
Levine, G. C., 419, 432
Levstik, L. S., 301, 308
Lewis, A. C., 102, 106
Lewis, J. P., 348, 357
Lewis, M. J., 368
Lexile Framework for Reading (LFR), 260
Liberman, I. Y., 127, 147
Library, creating a classroom, 296
Limitations of learning, 12–13
Limited English proficient (LEP), 142
Listening centers, 395
Lists of words, using, 175
Literacy centers, 393–396, 453
Literature-based approach, 52–54
Literature Circle Individual Evaluation, 505
Literature discussions, using, 389–390
Literature in the classroom
alphabet books, selection of, 349
author/illustrator studies, using, 364–365
biography, selection of, 348
censorship considerations, 353
combining organizational patterns, 366
core book experiences, using, 366
fiction, selection of, 346–348
genre studies, using, 359–361
illustration in children's books, role of, 351, 352
impact on growth in literacy, 367–370
independent reading, literature in, 369, 370
independent reading, selections for, 349–350
information/reference books, selection of, 348–349
multicultural literature, selection of, 351, 352
poetry, selection of, 348
reading aloud programs, 354–359
reading program, literature in the, 367–368
review guides, using, 353
study groups, using literature, 362–364
writing program, literature in the, 368–369
Literature logs, using, 390, 421–422, 444–445
Literature study groups, 222
Longfellow, H. W., 452, 461
Lourie, P., 208
Lowry, L., 347
Lundberg, I., 164, 182
Lyon, G. E., 214

MacGillivray, L., 333, 340
MacGinitie, R. K., 106
MacGinitie, W. H., 106
Mackert, J., 320, 339
Magnetic sheets and letters, using, 170
Malkovych, I., 380, 400
Manning, B. H., 263, 290
Manning, D., 298, 308
Manzo, A. V., 282, 290
Marcellino, F., 421, 432
Marchisan, M. L., 320, 339
Marinak, B. A., 470–474, 482
Marsh, J., 335, 339
Martin, B., 357
Martin, J. B., 351
Martin, R., 421, 429, 432, 433
Martinez, M., 300, 308, 359
Mason, J. M., 262, 290
Massoni, S. A., 432
Mastropieri, M. A., 128, 129, 135, 136, 139, 142, 147, 305, 308
Mathews, J., 138, 147
Maxwell, K. L., 382, 400
Mayer, M., 419, 433
Mazzoni, S. A., 75, 106, 410
McCabe, A., 25, 31
McCarrier, A., 336, 339
McCarthey, S. J., 44, 65

McConaghy, J., 314, 339
McCormick, C., 229, 250
McCully, E. A., 285, 291
McFalls, E. L., 216, 251
McGill-Franzen, A., 126, 146, 160, 181
McGinley, W., 26, 31
McGinnis, K., 441, 461
McGivern, J. E., 229, 250
McGowan, T. or McGowarn, 343, 371
McHenry, J. M., 469, 482
McIntire, J., 115, 118, 146
McIntyre, E., 343
McKenna, M. C., 338, 339
McKeown, M. G., 283, 290, 449, 460
McKinley, R., 419, 433
McLaughlin, T. F., 222, 250
McLeskey, J., 126, 147
McMackin, M., 328, 339
McMahon, S. L., 364
McNeil, J., 196, 207
McQuillan, J., 55, 65, 167, 182
Meisels, S. J., 88, 106
Meister, C., 256, 291
Melenyzer, B. J., 468, 482
Melnick, S. A., 76, 77, 105, 106, 411, 432
Mental retardation, students with, 134–137
Mentoring partners, 468–470
Merriam, E., 232
Mesmer, H. A. E., 40, 65
Metacomprehension Strategy Index (MSI), 206, 501–504
Metaphors, 232
Meyer, B. J. F., 269, 290
Meyer, L. A., 354
Meyers, W. D., 443, 461
Milestones
  developmental, 7–8
  historical, 61–63
Millard, E., 335, 339
Miller, G., 229, 250
Miller, S. S., 288, 400
Minden-Cupp, C., 151, 182
Miscue analysis, 202
Mitchell, J. N., 280, 290
Modified cloze, using a, 174
Moe, A. J., 77–79, 81, 83, 84
Moline, S., 451, 461
Monitoring, comprehension, 274–275
Montesorri, M., 376, 400
Mooney, M. E., 259, 290, 316, 339, 400
Moore, B. H., 367
Moore, I., 380, 400
Moore, J. C., 470–474, 482
Moore, L., 400
Moorman, M., 350
Morphemes, 10
Morphology, 10
Morrow, L. M., 52, 66, 205, 208, 296, 308, 343, 354, 367, 371, 372
Morsink, C. V., 113, 147
Moss, G., 404, 432
Motherese, 9
Motivation to Read Profile (MRP), 410, 483–490
Motivation to Read Profile (MTRP), 75–76, 104
Mullis, I. V. S., 44, 65
Multicultural literature, selection of, 351, 352
Multiple meanings, understanding words with, 213–214
Murphy, J., 195
Murray, B. A., 167, 183
Musgrove, M., 349
Myers, J., 185, 207

Nagy, W., 211, 213, 214, 215, 216, 250
Nagy, W. E., 250
Narrative passage, introducing, 77
Narrative text structures, 266
Nathan, R. G., 20, 31
Nathenson-Meija, S., 89, 106
Nation, K., 168, 182
National Association for the Education of Young Children (NAEYC), 478
National Council of Teachers of English (NCTE), 477–478
National Reading Conference (NRC), 478
Naylor, P. R., 347
Nelson, J., 41, 66
Nelson, K. M., 325, 339
Nelson, M., 443, 461
Nettles, D. H., 468, 482
Newkirk, T., 314, 339
Newton, J., 380, 400
No Child Left Behind Act (NCLB), 111
Noe, K. L. S., 446, 461
Nondiscriminatory multifactored evaluation (MRE), 116–117
Nordwall, M. B., 229
Normal curve equivalent scores, 97
Norm-referenced tests, 94–95
Norton, D. E., 351
Novick, R., 165, 182
Nunes, T., 164, 182
Oda, L. K., 367
Odean, K., 405, 432
Ogle, D., 191, 208, 386, 400
O'Hara, C., 171, 182
O'Hare, A., 339
Ohlhausen, M., 366
O'Neill, L. T., 301, 309
Onset and rime instruction, 168, 169–170
Onyefulu, I., 349
O'Reilly, J., 405, 432
Organizations, professional, 475–478
Origins of affixes and roots, 240–241, 242–246
Osborne, M. P., 430, 433
Ostertag, J., 276, 286, 289
Overhead projector, using the, 396

Padak, N., 162, 163, 182, 265, 291, 298, 309
Pagnucco, J., 19, 31
Paley, N., 351
Palinscar, A.S., 256, 290
Palmer, B., 75, 106, 371
Palmer, B. M., 368, 410, 432
Pappas, C. C., 213, 250, 301, 308, 314, 339
Paradis, E. E., 368
Parental involvement, 179
Paris, A. H., 100, 106
Paris, S. G., 100, 106, 311
Park, L. S., 285, 291
Parker, E. M., 296, 308
Parker, N. W., 357
Parrish, P., 232
Partridge, E., 444, 461
PASS variables, 136, 140
Pate, P. E., 441, 461
Paterson, K., 289, 290, 333, 339, 356, 430, 433
Payne, B. D., 263, 290
Peabody Picture Vocabulary Test, 89
Peabody Picture Vocabulary Test-III, 215
Pearson, D., 205, 208, 213
Pearson, P. D., 36, 37–38, 65, 190, 196, 207, 208, 266, 276, 281, 288, 290, 311, 339, 369
Peer conferences, 333
Peer observations, 470
Pelzer, D., 443, 461
Pelzer, D. J., 443, 461
Pennington, C., 367, 371
Percentile scores, 97

Peregoy, S. F., 144, 146
Petersen, O. P., 164, 182
Petry, A., 452, 461
Phonemes, 10, 38, 154
Phonic generalizations, 495–497
Phonics-based approached, 38–43
Phonological awareness, role of, 164–165
Phonology, 10
Piker, R. A., 88, 106
Pikulski, J. J., 305, 308
Pinker, S., 5, 31
Pinkney, A. D., 357
Pinnell, G. S., 197, 207, 259, 290, 297, 305, 308, 336, 339, 400, 412, 432
Pitch, 294
Pittleman, S., 229, 250
Pittleman, S. D., 250
Pocket charts, using, 162, 396
Poetry, selection of, 348
Polacco, P., 351
Policymaker Partnership (PMP), 120
Popham, W. J., 99, 106
Portfolios, use of, 101–103
Potter, D. C., 126, 146
Pragmatics, 12
Prediction making, using, 192, 270–271
Prefixes, 237–238
Prelutsky, J., 348, 357
Pressley, M., 57, 66, 190, 200, 202, 205, 207, 208, 254, 285, 290, 291, 295, 309, 343, 372
Previewing a text, 299–300
Pringle, L., 284, 291, 357
Processing after reading, 254
Processing before reading, 253
Processing during reading, 253–254
Professional development
  American School Directory (ASD), 480–481
  Ask ERIC, 474
  Association for Childhood Education International (ACEI), 478
  book discussion groups, 468
  Center for the Improvement of Early Reading Achievement (CIERA), 474
  Classroom Notes Plus, 478
  conferences, attending, 478–480
  English Journal, 477–478
  International Federation of Library Associations and Institutions, 481
  International Reading Association (IRA), 475–476
  Journal of Adolescent & Adult Literacy (JAAL), 476
  Kathy Schrock's Guide for Educators, 481
  knowledge basis, expanding your, 468–470
  Language Arts, 477
  Lectura y Vida, 475
  mentoring partners, 468–470
  National Association for the Education of Young Children (NAEYC), 478
  National Council of Teachers of English (NCTE), 477–478
  National Reading Conference (NRC), 478
  organizations, professional, 475–478
  peer observations, 470
  public domain research-based knowledge, using, 474
  Reading Online, 476
  Reading Research Quarterly (RRQ), 475
  Reading Teacher (RT), 475
  Reading Today, 476
  resources, 480–481
  School Talk, 477
  self-study, using, 467–468
  Teachers of English to Speakers of Other Languages (TESOL), 478
  Thinking Classroom, 476
  Topica, 481
  Voices from the Middle, 477
Proficiency testing, 322, 325
Prosody, 294, 299
Proudfoot, L., 128, 147
Public domain research-based knowledge, using, 474
Pullman, P., 421, 433
Purcell-Gates, V., 172, 182, 343
Puts information together (PIT), 80

Qualitative Reading Inventory III, 410
Question answering, role of, 278–280
Question-Answer-Relationships (QAR), 282
Question generating, importance of, 281–284
Questioning the Author (QtA), 283
Questioning the Author (QtA), 449–450
Questions aimed at strategy use, 197, 199

Raphael, T. E., 282, 291, 368
Rasinski, T., 162, 163, 182, 265, 291, 296, 298, 305, 309
Ray, K. W., 331, 332, 339
Read-alouds, using, 354–359, 388, 419, 443
Read around the room, 396
Readence, J. E., 302, 309
Reader, text relationship (RTR), 80
Reader Self-Perception Scale, 491–494
Reader Self-Perception Scale, 76, 104
Reader's theater, using, 300, 301, 388, 421, 443
Reading development
  Chall's stages of reading development, 18–19
  cycle of reading development, 17–19
  definitions of, 15–16
  process of, 16–17
Reading First grants, influence of, 88–89
Reading instruction, approaches to
  authentic assessment, 58
  balanced approach, 56–59
  bottom-up view of reading, 38
  cognitive apprenticeship approach, 37
  comparison of models, 37
  conference checklist, reading, 55
  developing your teaching philosophy, 60
  direct instruction model, 37
  explicit instruction approach, 37
  Four Blocks Program, 58–59
  integrated anthology approach, 44–45
  isolated skill emphasis, 58
  kidwatching, 63–64
  Language Experience Approach (LEA), 48–52
  learner-directed discovery, 57–58
  legislative implications, 34
  literature-based approach, 52–54
  milestones, historical, 61–63
  phonics-based approach, 38–43
  planner, sample, 46–47
  sight-based approaches, 43–44
  standardized norm-referenced assessment, 58
  systematic instruction, 40–41
  teacher-directed explicit instruction, 57–58
  top-down view of reading, 38
  traditional basal reading programs, 44–45
  whole language approach, 37, 54–55
  Wilson Reading System, 41–42
Reading Lesson Observation Framework (RLOF), 470, 471–474

Reading Online, 476
Reading rates, 304–306
Reading Research Quarterly (RRQ), 475
Reading strategies
buddy reading, use of, 201
collaborative strategic reading (CSR), 202–205
cooperative learning roles, 205
demonstrations, using, 202
high quality strategy instruction, 190
K-W-L strategy, 191
miscue analysis, 202
prediction making, 192
questions aimed at strategy use, 197, 199
and the reading process, 187–188
strategic reading, 188–190
strategy use with fiction and nonfiction, 197, 198
Students Achieving Independent Learning (SAIL), 200
teaching after-reading strategies, 196–197
teaching before reading strategies, 190–191
teaching during-reading strategies, 192–196
transactional strategy instruction (TSI), 199, 200
verbal prompts to teach strategy use, using, 197
visual reminders, 200
Reading Teacher (RT), 475
Reading Today, 476
Rearranging sentence strips, 173–174
Reasons for reading text, determining, 266
Reciprocal Questioning (ReQuest), 282–283
Recursive model, 315–317
Reinking, D., 247, 250
Repeated readings, role of, 296–299
Research skills, learning, 413–418
Resources, 480–481
Retellings, 80, 81, 280
Retells in fact (RIF), 80
Reutzel, D. R., 367
Review guides, using, 353
Revising groups, 223
Revision process, 333
Rhodes, L. K., 89, 106
Richards, M., 299, 309
Richardson, V., 311
Rich oral language, using, 221
Rickards, D., 10o6, 90, 92, 94, 280, 291
Rickman, S. S., 247, 250
Riddles, jokes, and puns, using, 219
Rinaldi, L., 222, 250
Ring, E., 388, 400
Robb, L., 452, 461
Root words, 238–239
Rose, T. L., 300, 309
Rosen, A. M., 325, 339
Rosen, M., 220
Rosenblatt, L. M., 15, 16, 31, 285, 291, 355
Rosenfeld, S. J., 124, 147
Rosenshine, B., 256, 291
Rosenzweig, D., 435, 461
Roser, N., 447, 461
Roser, N. L., 285, 291, 300, 308, 359, 368
Ross, B. D., 368
Routman, R., 164, 182
Rowe, D. W., 333, 340
Rubrics, using, 90, 92, 93–94, 321
Running records, use of, 82–84, 85–87, 104
Ryden, H., 388, 400
Rylant, C., 356

Salvia, J., 114, 147
Samuels, J., 196
Samuels, S., 157, 182
Samuels, S. J., 208, 309
San Souci, R. D., 429, 433
Saphier, J., 465, 467, 468, 482
Scarborough, H. S., 164, 182
Scardamalia, M., 314, 339
Schatschneider, C., 166, 182
Schedule, 436–437
Scheer, J., 220
Scheu, J. A., 262, 290
Schmitt, M. C., 208
Schon, D., 33, 66
School interest inventory, using a, 227
School Talk, 477
Schrock, K., 481, 482
Schroeder, A., 347
Schuder, T., 200, 207
Schumaker, J. B., 127, 146, 147
Schumm, J. S., 203, 207
Schuster, J. W., 382, 400
Schwanenflugel, P. J., 216, 251
Scieska, J., 356
Scieszka, J., 430, 433
Scoring, 80–81
Scott, C. M., 27, 31, 213, 215, 216
Scott, J. A., 250
SCREAM variables, 129, 133
Scruggs, T. E., 128, 129, 135, 136, 139, 142, 147, 305, 308
Section 504 of the Rehabilitation Act of 1973, 120, 123–125
Seifert-Kessell, N., 275, 2909
Self-evaluation, 324, 438
Self-study, using, 467–468
Sells, D., 222, 250
Semantic cues, using, 154, 156, 174–175
Semantic feature analysis, 229
Semantic maps, using, 229, 276–278
Semantics, 11–12
Sendak, M., 351
Sentence strips, using, 160–161
Servis, J., 418, 432
Shanahan, T., 314, 339
Shanker, J. L., 182
Shankweiler, D., 127, 147
Shared reading, 259, 391–392
Sharing time, 333–334
Sheltered English Instruction, 144, 458–460
Shields, C. D., 347
Short, K. G., 303, 309, 384, 389, 390, 392, 400, 406, 419, 422, 428, 441, 442, 445, 448
Shriberg, L., 229, 250
Sidelnick, M. A., 335, 339
Siegel, B., 328, 339
Sight-based approaches, 43–44
Sight vocabulary, development of, 157–158, 160–164, 295–296
Similes, 232
Simmons, D. C., 266, 290
Simons, J., 423, 433
Simons, S., 423, 433
Simont, M., 356
Simplified drawings, use of, 266–267
Sindelar, P. T., 300, 309
Sipay, E. R., 305, 306, 308
Sis, P., 356
Skills lessons, components of, 175–177
Slater, W. H., 211, 222, 251
Sloan, C., 222, 250
Small group, focused instruction, 172–173
Small group reading, using, 174, 175, 179–180
Smith, C., 369
Smith, F., 53, 66, 167, 182, 256, 291

Smith, J. A., 309
Smith, J. K., 343, 372
Smith, L., 356
Smith, M., 343, 372
Sneve, V. D. H., 357
Snow, C. E., 177, 182, 213, 251
Soderman, A. K., 301, 309
Songs, incorporating activities using, 302–304, 444
Sorting picture cards and sound cards, 170
Soto, G., 430, 433
Sowell, J., 237, 238, 239, 251
Spandel, V., 337, 339
Spear, L., 420, 433
Special needs education
- alternative or augmentative communication devices (AAC), 133
- Associations of Service Providers Implementing IDEA Reforms in Education Partnership (ASPIIRE), 120
- attention deficit/hyperactivity disorder, students with, 137–138, 139
- CLASP model, 125
- continuum of educational services, 115–116
- Council for Exceptional Children (CEC), 120
- distribution of disability, 109
- English is a second language, students for whom, 142–145
- environmental adaptation considerations, 134
- evaluation of, 118
- Families and Advocates Partnership for Education (FAPE), 120
- gifted and talented students, 138–142
- goals, consideration of learning, 112
- IDEA Local Implementation by Local Administrators Partnership (ILIAD), 118
- identifying a child for special education, 116
- implementation process, 118
- Individualized Education Program (IEP), 117, 119–120, 121–123
- Individuals with Disabilities Act (IDEA), understanding, 114–120, 124
- interactive teaming, 113
- intervention assistance team (IAT), referrals to the, 113–114
- kidwatcher, framework for being a mindful, 112–113
- learning disabilities, accommodations for students with, 125–131
- Learning Strategies curriculum, 127
- least restrictive e environment (LRE), 115, 117
- mental retardation, students with, 134–137
- modifications, planning instructional, 112–113
- No Child Left Behind Act (NCLB), 111
- nondiscriminatory multifactored evaluation (MRE), 116–117
- PASS variables, 136, 140
- Policymaker Partnership (PMP), 120
- processes and procedures, learning, 113
- SCREAM variables, 129, 133
- Section 504 of the Rehabilitation Act of 1973, 120, 123–125
- "specific learning disability," definition of, 126
- speech or language impairments, accommodations for, 131–134
- staff resources, learning about, 113
- teacher, role of the, 111–112

Speech or language impairments, accommodations for, 131–134
Spelling, use of, 171
Spiegel, D. L., 57, 58, 66
Spier, P., 208
Spinelli, J., 421, 433
Spiro, R. J., 27, 31
Sprague, K., 25, 31
Stages of, 213
Stahl, K. A. D., 42, 66, 160, 182
Stahl, S., 19, 31, 213, 251
Stahl, S. A., 36, 42, 66, 159, 160, 167, 182, 183, 216, 228, 251, 293, 294, 308
Standardized norm-referenced assessment, 58
Standardized testing, use of, 94–98, 104
Stanford Diagnostic Reading Test, Fourth Edition (SDRT-4), 89, 96, 127
Stanine scores, 97
Stanley, D., 357
Stanley, J., 356, 443, 461
Stanovich, K. E., 157, 164, 183
Status of the class report, 329, 330
Stauffer, R. G., 66
Steenwyk, F. L., 207
Steig, W., 351, 430, 433
Stephens, M., 99, 105
Stern, R., 435, 461
Stevens, J., 351
Stewart, R. A., 368
Stewig, J. W., 420, 433
Stoplight readers, 289
Story cubes, 266
Story maps, 266, 267
Storytelling, using, 420–421, 444
Strategic reading, 188–190
Strategy lessons, 392–393, 429–430, 450
Strategy-sharing discussions, 393, 451–452
Strategy use with fiction and nonfiction, 197, 198
Straub, M., 296, 308
Strecker, S., 300, 308
Stress, 294
Strickland, D., 325, 339
Strickland, D. S., 52, 66
Structuralism, 268
Structured English Immersion, 458–460
Structured opposites, 269
Structured overviews, 229, 276
Structure words, 215–216
Struggling readers, techniques for, 453, 455–457
Student conferences, 393
Student engagement, fostering, 179
Student profile summary, 83
Students Achieving Independent Learning (SAIL), 200
Student's reading and teacher's coding, 80
Study groups, using literature, 362–364
Suffixes, 238
Sulzby, E., 13, 31
Summarization skills, teaching, 286
Super, Quiet, Uninterrupted Independent Reading Time (SQUIRT), 297
Supports for, 8–9
Sustained Silent Reading (SSR), 297
Svoboda, M. L., 335, 339
Syntactic cueing system, 156–157, 173–174
Syntax, 10–11
Synthetic phonics, 38, 166, 168
Systematic instruction, 40–41

Taback, S., 351
Taberski, S., 382, 400
Take-home book bags, 298
Talbott, H., 443, 461
Tan, A., 31

Taylor, B., 205, 208
Taylor, B. M., 166, 178, 183, 311, 369
Taylor, D., 183
Taylor, M. D., 443, 461
Taylor, V. M., 27, 31
Teacher-directed explicit instruction, 57–58
Teacher modeling, 319–320
Teacher record data, 78–79
Teachers of English to Speakers of Other Languages (TESOL), 478
Teacher/student conferences, 450–451
Teaching after-reading strategies, 196–197
Teaching before reading strategies, 190–191
Teaching during-reading strategies, 192–196
Teale, W. J., 31
Teberosky, A., 20, 31
Temple, C., 268, 269, 291
Temple, C. A., 20, 31
Temple, F., 20, 31
Templeton, S., 20, 30, 181
Tennant, N., 296, 308
Test of Phonological Awareness (TOPA), 165
Test of Reading Comprehension, 440
Test of Reading Comprehension, Third Edition (TORC-3), 135
Test of Written Language-3, 315, *411,* 438, 440
Thaler, M., 251
Themes, importance of selecting, 385–387
Therriault, T., 461
Think-alouds, using, 174, 175, 275
Thinking Classroom, 476
Thomas, C. C., 113, 147
Thomason, T., 332, 340
Tierney, R. J., 26, 31, 302, 309
Time for writing, providing sufficient, 320
Tinajero, J., 458, 461
Tolhurst, M., 430, 433
Tomasetti, B. W., 470–474, 482
Tomesen, M., 222, 251
Toms-Bronowski, S., 229
Top-down view of reading, 38
Topica, 481
Torgensen, J. K., 183
Tracy, E., 369
Traditional basal reading programs, 44–45
Trait writing schemes, 337
Transactional strategy instruction (TSI), 199, 200
Transformation stories, 430
Trathen, W., 222, 250
Turner, M., 350

Uninterrupted Sustained Silent Reading (USSR), 297
Unmotivated readers, 404–405
Unrau, N., 453, 454, 461
Unsworth, L., 269, 270, 291

Vancil, S., 213, 251
Van Dijk, T. A., 290
Van Meter, P., 200, 207
Vardell, S., 301, 309
Vaughn, S., 202, 203, 204, 207, 320, 327, 328, 329, 340
Veatch, J., 53, 66
Venn diagrams, 196, 229, 230
Verbal prompts to teach strategy use, using, 197
Viorst, J., 349
Visovatti, K., 200, 201, 208
Visual discrimination, role of, 164
Visual reminders, 200
Vocabulary, development of
- as an incremental process, 213
- books, using, 219–220
- complexity of, 213
- compound words, 236–237
- context cues, using, 239, 241, 246
- dictionaries and reference texts, using, 233, 235–236
- evaluating a vocabulary program, 249
- extensive reading, importance of, 224
- figurative language, 232
- figures of speech, 232
- form class words, 215–216
- Frayer Method, 224, 228
- games and puzzles, using, 217–218
- general interest inventory, using a, 22
- genres, word, 232
- graphic organizers, using, 229
- high-frequency words, teaching, 232–233
- His Input Hypothesis (HIH), 222
- homographs, 231
- homophones, 231
- independent reading, using, 222–223
- individual words, teaching, 224, 228–232
- interrelationships of words, understanding, 215
- keyword method, 229
- literature study groups, 222
- metaphors, 232
- multiple meanings, understanding words with, 213–214
- origins of affixes and roots, 240–241, 242–246
- prefixes, 237–238
- reading and writing interest inventory, using a, 226
- revising groups, 223
- rich oral language, using, 221
- riddles, jokes, and puns, using, 219
- root words, 238–239
- school interest inventory, using a, 227
- semantic feature analysis, 229
- semantic maps, using, 229
- similes, 232
- stages of, 213
- structured overviews, 229
- structure words, 215–216
- suffixes, 238
- Venn diagrams, using, 229, 230
- word of the day, using a, 221, 222
- word parts, using, 236–237
- word play, using, 217–220
- word walls, using, 230

Voices from the Middle, 477
Voltz, D. L., 125, 147
Vozar, D., 430, 433
Vygotsky, L., 364

Waber, B., 282, 291
Waldron, N., 126, 147
Wall, M. E., 126, 147
Wallace, G., 233, 251
Wallach, G., 27, 31
Wallner, J., 258, 291
Walpole, S., 205, 208, 369
Walsh, R., 320, 339
Walter, V. A., 432
Wardrop, J. L., 354
Watson, D. J., 16, 31, 187, 188, 207
Watts-Taffe, S. M., 217, 223, 250
Weaver, B. M., 259, 291
Weaver, C., 167, 183, 201
Weber, L., 369
Wells, G., 222, 251
Wells, R., 356
Wharton-McDonald, R., 205, 208
White, E. B., 15, 179, 422, 433

White, T. G., 211, 222, 237, 238, 239, 251
Whole language approach, 37, 54–55
Wiederholt, J. L., 135, 146, 307, 309, 460
Wiederholt, L., 147
Wilder, D., 65
Williams, J. P., 129, 146, 200, 208
Wilson, B. A., 66, 160, 222
Wilson, P., 181, 250
Wilson, P. T., 369, 371
Wilson Reading System, 41–42
Winer, Y., 348
Winograd, P. N., 43, 65
Wisniewski, D., 351
Wixson, K. K., 305
Wolfe, V. E. or Wolff, 357
Wood, A., 219
Wood, D. K., 461
Wood, K. D., 458
Wood-Garnett, S., 115, 118, 146
Woods, M. L., 77–79, 81, 83, 84, 106
Word advocacy, 175
Word analysis, 171
Word banks, using, 161–162
Word deletion activities, 173
Word of the day, using a, 221, 222
Word parts, using, 236–237
Word play, using, 217–220
Word study, 380, 452
Word walls, using, 161, 230
Work areas, managing the, 408–409
Worthy, J., 350
Wright, J. R., 357
Writer Self-Perception Scale, 77, 104, *411*
Writer's workshop, 325–326
Writing
  Clay's stages in developing writing, 20
  conventional stage, 24, 26
  linear repetitive stage, 21, 22
  phonemic stage, 22, 23
  proficient stage, 24, 25
  random letter stage, 22, 23
  scribbling stage, 21
  spelling, stages of development, 20–21
  stages of development, 20
  transitional stage, 24, 25
Writing center, 395
Writing engagements, using, 451
Writing for sounds, 170
Writing process
  assessment, 322–325
  authentic writing experiences, 320
  classroom environment, role of the, 320
  conferences, writing, 329, 331–332
  connection to reading, 313–314
  continuum checklist, 323–324
  demonstration writing, 337
  drawing, use of, 336
  focus lessons, planning, 326–327
  goals for writing, 321–322
  guided writing, 337
  interactive writing, 336
  journal writing, 334–335
  peer conferences, 333
  proficiency testing, 322, 325
  recursive model, 315–317
  revision process, 333
  role of, 314–315
  rubric, writing, 321
  self-evaluation, 324
  sharing time, 333–334
  status of the class report, 329, 330
  teacher modeling, 319–320
  time for writing, providing sufficient, 320
  tools of, 321
  topics, selecting, 327–328, 329
  trait writing schemes, 337
  writer's workshop, 325–326
Wyman, R. M., 468, 482

Yaden, D. B., Jr., 333, 340
Yanagihara, A., 237, 238, 239, 251
Yolen, J., 232, 327, 340, 351, 369, 430, 433
Yopp, H., 164, 165, 182
Yopp, H. K., 183, 400
Yopp-Singer Test of Phoneme Segmentation, 165, *382,* 499
Yorinks, A., 433
Young, E., 351
Young, T. A., 301, 309
Youngquist, C. V., 430, 433
Ysseldyke, J. E., 114, 147

Zajchowski, R., 190, 202, 208
Zaragoza, N., 320, 327, 328, 329, 340
Zelinsky, P., 351
Zig-zag book, making a, 424–426
Zimmermann, S., 197, 207
Zoehfeld, K. W., 388, 400